ENCYCLOPEDIA OF
NATIVE AMERICAN
TRIBES

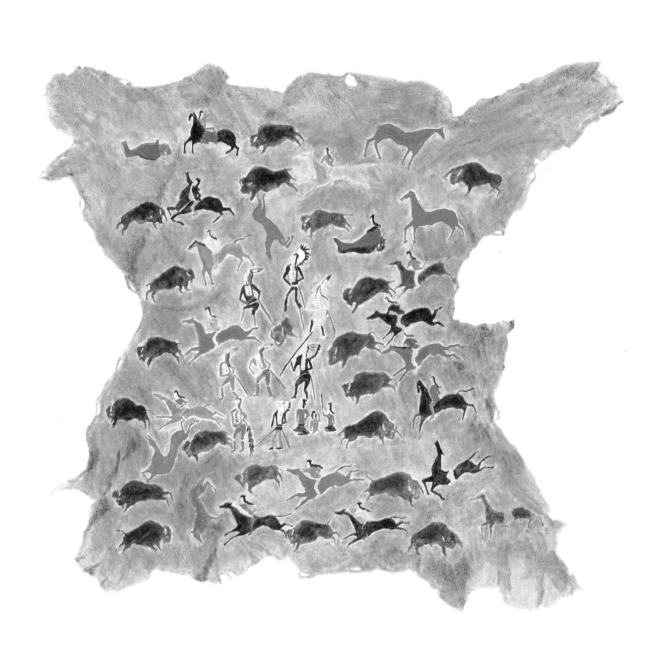

ENCYCLOPEDIA OF NATIVE AMERICAN TRIBES

Carl Waldman

Illustrations by Molly Braun

Facts On File Publications
New York, New York • Oxford, England

Encyclopedia of Native American Tribes

Library of Congress Cataloging-in-Publication Data

Waldman, Carl.
    Encyclopedia of native American tribes.

    Bibliography: p.
    Includes index.
    Summary: An alphabetical encyclopedia covering the
history, culture, and present status of more than 150
Indian tribes of the United States, Canada, and Mexico.
    1. Indians of North America—Dictionaries, Juvenile.
[1. Indians of North America—Dictionaries] I. Braun,
Molly, ill. II. Title.
E76.2.W35 1987   970.004′97′00321   86-29066
ISBN 0-8160-1421-3

Text Design: Debbie Glasserman

Printed in Hong Kong

10 9 8 7 6 5 4 3

For Chloe and Devin

Contents

Author's Note

There are two general ways to relate the history of the Americas. One is from the viewpoint of the many different peoples who came to the Western Hemisphere from elsewhere to form new nations. The other is from the viewpoint of the first Americans, the people who were already here. They are the American Indians, or Native Americans.

In schools in the United States and Canada, relatively little is taught about Native Americans. Students spend a great deal of time memorizing the names of United States presidents, for example, but little time learning the names of tribes. Often, more is taught about cultures in other parts of the world than about Indian cultures. Students are more likely to know about the pyramids of Egypt than the pyramids of the Americas.

Yet Native American history is central to the history of the Americas. It goes back at least 50,000 years, while the history of other peoples in the Americas goes back only 500 years (or, taking into consideration the Vikings, 1,000 years). Moreover, for many stages in the historical development of the United States and other nations in the Americas, there are corresponding stories of disruption and migrations of Indian peoples.

This book tells part of the story of Native North Americans. It discusses their exciting and poignant history, along with their rich and wondrous culture. It lists alphabetically a representative sampling of Indian tribes, as well as some general cultural categories of Native Americans. Because of the great number of tribes and their differing histories and cultures, Indian studies are especially complex. For this reason, the following section explains how to use this book.

I would like to thank all the people who helped with this project: my wife, who drew the illustrations and contributed many ideas to the text; our shared families, both adults and children, who showed such enthusiasm and support; all our other friends, who participated directly or indirectly; the academicians and librarians who generously provided us with help; and the wonderful people at Facts On File. A special thanks also to the Anderson family of Fort Totten, North Dakota, and Matthew and Dolores Montour of Kahnawake, Quebec, for their friendship.

How to Use This Book

This book is called *Encyclopedia of Native American Tribes*. But what does the word *tribe* mean? The answer is not a simple one. *Tribe* is used in many different ways to indicate varying kinds of social organization. In some cases, it refers to a group of local bands or villages with common ancestry, culture, and language. In other cases, it refers to groups of peoples spread over a wider area but united politically in what is called a confederacy. In still other cases, the word *tribe* refers to just one village.

Furthermore, scholars do not always agree on how to classify a particular people. Some may define a group of people as a distinct tribe while others consider the same people a subtribe or band of a larger tribe.

In addition to the word *band*, there are other terms that scholars sometimes use interchangeably with *tribe* for Indians in different parts of North America. The term *chiefdom* is sometimes used for Southeast Indians, and *tribelet* for California Indians. In Mexico and Central America, some Indians lived in cities and are said to have organized into *city-states* or *civilizations*. Many contemporary Indians prefer the term *nation* rather than *tribe* because it implies the concept of political sovereignty, indicating that their people have goals and rights like other nations. And one more confusing use of terms: In the study of prehistoric Indians, the term *culture* is used for a group of people rather than the term *tribe*.

Because this book is an encyclopedia, it lists different Indian peoples alphabetically. Most of the names that head the various sections are considered names of tribes. But there are other headings that are more general cultural names ("Prehistoric Indians"; "Cliff Dwellers and Desert Farmers"; and "Mound Builders"). Other headings apply to entire civilizations ("Aztec"; "Maya"; "Olmec"; and "Toltec"). Still others apply to entire language families ("Algonquian"; "Athapascan"; and "Iroquois").

There is another category of heading in this book: culture areas. A culture area is a geographic region where the various Indian peoples had lifeways in common. The system of culture areas has been devised by scholars to make Indian studies easier. That way, students can get an overall sense of both cultural similarities and distinctions. One can see, for example, that the tribes on the Great Plains lived differently from the tribes of the Great Basin. The culture area entries in this book are accompanied by maps that show general tribal locations.

Throughout the text, cross-references lead the reader to different levels of organization. For example, within each culture area entry, there are cross-references to all the tribes of that culture area listed in this book. And, under each tribe, its culture area is cited, so that by turning to the culture area entry the reader can get an overview of the entire geographic region and all its peoples. Also, under each tribe, other tribes are cited that have a special relationship historically or culturally with the given tribe. Serious students should follow the cross-references to wherever they lead for a better understanding of the complicated information.

Some other points: (1) Certain tribes have alternate spellings for their names, or completely different names. Many of these are given in the text. The pronunciations of the primary names are given. These are the pronunciations in use today and not necessarily the historical pronunciations. (2) There are many unfamiliar terms used in Indian studies: for cultural, political, and geographic concepts; for natural phenomena; and for various objects. A glossary at the end of the book defines some of the more difficult and important terms. (3) The illustrations in this book convey a great deal about Indians. Most are drawings of ancient objects; those drawn from objects made by 20th-century Indians are identified as such. Some of the objects shown are reconstructions, since no originals have been found or photographed. The scenes, of course, give a hypothetical view of Indian life. Some are based on early or contemporary photographs. (4) This book has space enough to cover only a selection of tribes. Hundreds more are not listed; South American tribes are not covered at all. Deciding which tribes to include was a difficult and sometimes arbitrary process. Those tribes selected are especially important historically or especially good representatives of a way of life. Some tribes without their own entries are mentioned in the culture area entries. Others are mentioned along with related tribes. The index will help you find where different tribes are mentioned in the text. The bibliography will help you further pursue Indian studies.

The following chart identifies how different Indian peoples are organized in this book. The chart does not include a further level of subdivision, generally known as the *bands*. Bands are discussed, when especially important, under tribal entries.

The Indian Culture Areas, showing one system of categorizing Indian peoples by culture and geography

Culture Areas, Language Families, and Tribes of Native American Peoples Listed in This Book

ARCTIC CULTURE AREA
    Eskimaleut Language Family
        Aleut
        Eskimo (Inuit)

CALIFORNIA CULTURE AREA
    Algonquian Language Family
        Yurok

    Athapascan Language Family
        Hoopa

    Hokan Language Family
        Chumash
        Pomo
        Yahi

    Penutian Language Family
        Maidu
        Miwok
        Patwin
        Wintun
        Yokuts

    Uto-Aztecan Language Family
        Mission Indians

GREAT BASIN CULTURE AREA
    Uto-Aztecan Language Family
        Bannock
        Paiute
        Shoshone
        Ute

NORTHEAST CULTURE AREA
    Algonquian Language Family
        Abnaki
        Algonkin
        Chippewa (Ojibway)
        Delaware
        Fox
        Illinois
        Kickapoo

        Mahican
        Malecite
        Massachuset
        Menominee
        Miami
        Micmac
        Mohegan
        Montauk-Shinnecock
        Narraganset
        Nipmuc
        Ottawa
        Passamaquoddy
        Pennacook
        Penobscot
        Pequot
        Potawatomi
        Powhatan
        Sac
        Shawnee
        Wampanoag
        Wappinger

    Iroquoian Language Family
        Cayuga
        Huron-Wyandot
        Mohawk
        Oneida
        Onondaga
        Seneca
        Susquehannock
        Tuscarora

    Siouan Language Family
        Winnebago

NORTHWEST COAST CULTURE AREA
    Nadene Language Family
        Haida
        Tlingit

    Penutian Language Family
        Chinook (probably Penutian)
        Tsimshian

Wakashan Language Family
Kwakiutl
Makah
Nootka

PLAINS (or GREAT PLAINS) CULTURE AREA

Algonquian Language Family
Arapaho
Blackfoot
Cheyenne
Gros Ventre
Plains Cree (see Cree under Northeast
Culture Area)
Plains Ojibway (see Chippewa under
Northeast Culture Area)

Athapascan Language Family
Kiowa-Apache (see Apache under
Southwest Culture area)
Sarcee

Caddoan Language Family
Arikara
Pawnee
Wichita

Kiowa-Tanoan Language Family
Kiowa

Siouan Language Family
Assiniboine
Crow
Hidatsa
Iowa
Kaw
Mandan
Missouri
Omaha
Osage
Oto
Ponca
Quapaw
Sioux

Tonkawan Language Isolate
Tonkawa

Uto-Aztecan Language Family
Comanche

PLATEAU CULTURE AREA

Kutenai Language Isolate
Kootenai

Penutian Language Family
Cayuse
Klamath
Modoc

Nez Perce
Palouse
Umatilla
Wallawalla
Yakima

Salishan Language Family
Coeur d'Alene
Flathead
Kalispel
Spokane

SOUTHEAST CULTURE AREA

Algonquian Language Family
Lumbee (mixed languages)

Caddoan Language Family
Caddo

Chitimacha Language Isolate
Chitimacha

Iroquoian Language Family
Cherokee

Muskogean Language Family
Alabama
Apalachee
Calusa (probably Muskogean)
Chickasaw
Choctaw
Coushatta
Creek
Seminole
Yamasee

Natchez Language Isolate
Natchez

Siouan Language Family
Catawba
Yuchi

Timucuan Language Isolate
Timucua

Tunican Language Isolate
Tunica
Yazoo

SOUTHWEST CULTURE AREA

Athapascan Language Family
Apache
Navajo

Kiowa-Tanoan Language Family
Pueblo Indians

Penutian Language Family
Zuni

Uto-Aztecan Family
Hopi
Papago
Pima
Yaqui

Yuman Language Family
Havasupai
Hualapai
Mojave
Yavapai
Yuma

SUBARCTIC CULTURE

Beothukan Language Isolate
Beothuk

Algonquian Language Family
Cree
Metis (part French and Scottish)

Montagnais
Naskapi

Athapascan Language Family
Carrier
Chipewyan
Kutchin

OTHER CATEGORIES INCLUDED IN THIS BOOK
Prehistoric Indians
Cliff Dwellers and Desert Farmers
Mound Builders

Mesoamerican Civilizations
Aztec
Maya
Olmec
Toltec

Caribbean Tribes
Arawak

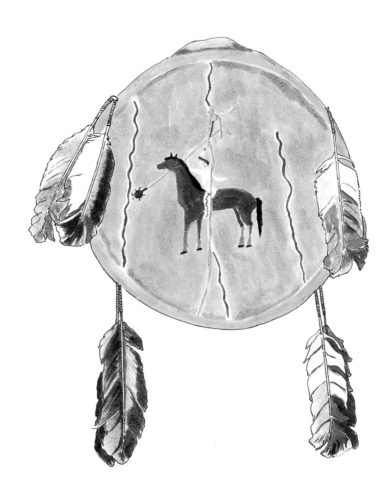

Alphabetical List of Tribes and Peoples

Abnaki

Abnaki, or Abenaki (both pronounced *ab-NAH-kee*) originally Wabanaki, means "those living at the sunrise," or "easterners." The Indians with this name lived mostly in territory that became the state of Maine, the easternmost of all the states.

The Abnakis were really a confederacy of many Algonquian tribes or bands (see "Algonquian"). The Passamaquoddies and Penobscots of Maine were two of the most important members of the Abnaki Confederacy (see "Passamaquoddy" and "Penobscot"). Other sometime members of the once-great Abnaki Confederacy were the Micmacs and Malecites of Canada and the Pennacooks of Vermont (see "Micmac"; "Malecite"; and "Pennacook").

The Abnaki way of life resembled that of other Woodland Algonquians of the Northeast, combining some farming with hunting, fishing, and gathering (see "Northeast Indians" and "Algonquian"). However, the Abnakis were less dependent on agriculture than were Algonquians living further south; because the ground where the Abnakis lived was stony and the growing season short.

Furthermore, unlike most other New England Algonquians, the Abnakis built cone-shaped wigwams rather than dome-shaped wigwams. They used birchbark and elm-bark mats over sapling frames to shape these woodland-style tents. Like the Great Plains tepees (see "Plains Indians"), these tents had holes in the top to let out the smoke from cooking fires. The bark mats could be rolled up and carried to other sites if the Indians wanted to move their village, perhaps to set out on a long hunting or warring expedition, or travel to the ocean to collect shellfish. In the winter, the Abnakis lined the interior walls of the wigwam with bear or deer furs for insulation. They also built walls of upright logs around their villages for protection called palisades.

During the French and Indian Wars, the French and their Indian allies fought against the English and their Indian supporters. These various conflicts for control of North America lasted almost a hundred years—from 1689 to 1763—and included King William's War (1689-1697), Queen Anne's War (1702-1713), King George's War (1744-1748), and the French and Indian War (1754-1763). The Abnakis were staunch allies of the French. They were especially active during the King William's and Queen Anne's wars and launched many raids against British settlements in New England. Sometimes historians refer to these battles as the Abnaki Wars.

The Abnakis first became involved in the fighting through their friendship with a Frenchman, Jean Vincent de l'Abadie, Baron de St. Castin. St. Castin established a fur trading post at the site where Castine, Maine, now stands. His marriage to the daughter of a sachem sealed his friendship with the fierce Abnakis. When British troops raided and plundered his trading post and home in 1688, the Abnakis sought revenge against English settlers.

Over the following years, the British colonists dreaded the onslaught of Abnaki warriors, who swept out of the northern woods in a rampage of killing, burning, and looting. No settlement was safe from

Abnaki conical wigwam with elm-bark covering

their vengeance: Saco in Maine; Dover and Salmon Falls in New Hampshire; Haverhill and Deerfield in Massachusetts. Many other villages were also attacked.

In 1724, the Abnaki stronghold known as Norridgewock finally fell into British hands. Many of the Indian warriors and their families withdrew to Quebec, where they made new homes among their French allies. Descendants of these brave people still live in Canada, where they go by the Abnaki name. Their Passamaquoddy and Penobscot relatives now have reservation lands in Maine. There is also a community of Abnakis in the Swanton-Highgate-St. Albans area of Northern Vermont. They are applying for federal recognition as a tribe.

There is a famous saying by an Abnaki named Bedagi (Big Thunder) that sums up the special relationship Abnakis and all Native Americans had with the spirit world and nature: "The Great Spirit is our father, but the Earth is our mother."

Alabama

The Alabamas' name (also spelled *Alibamu*) has been passed to the state. The name, pronounced like that of the state, probably means "plant (or weed) gatherers." The Alabamas had the same ancestors as the Creeks and were part of the powerful Creek Confederacy, with which they shared the Muskogean language and a similar way of life; both tribes are considered part of the Southeast Culture Area. They were also closely related to the neighboring Choctaws (see "Southeast Indians"; "Creek"; and "Choctaw").

For most of their history, the Alabamas lived along the upper course of the Alabama River in what is now the center of the state bearing their name. However, when the Spanish expedition led by Hernando de Soto encountered them in 1540, the Alabamas might have lived farther to the north. This first contact with the Spanish was not friendly. De Soto and his men, who sought gold and empire in North America, treated the Indians with arrogance and cruelty. They cared little about native peoples and wildlife.

The Alabamas eventually became allies of the French, who founded Mobile on Mobile Bay in 1710 and then, three years later, built Fort Toulouse in Alabama country. When France lost its holdings in North America in 1763 to England, after the French and Indian War, many Alabamas left their homeland. Some joined the Seminoles in Florida. Others resettled north of New Orleans on the banks of the Mississippi River, and later moved to western Louisiana. The majority of this same band eventually moved to Texas, where they were later granted state reservation lands along with the Coushatta Indians (see "Coushatta").

Those who stayed behind in Alabama fought on the side of the Creeks and against the whites in the Creek War of 1813-14. In the 1830s, long after the defeat of the Creeks, both Creeks and Alabamas were resettled in the Indian Territory. The only Alabamas remaining today as a tribal unit are those who share the reservation with the Coushattas in Polk County, Texas.

Aleut

Almost 100 in number, the Aleutian Islands extend westward about 1,200 miles into the Pacific Ocean from the tip of the Alaska Peninsula. They are really a partly submerged continuation of the Aleutian Range, a volcanic mountain chain. The climate of the islands is cold and damp, with thick fog. Few trees grow in the rocky soil, only bushes, grasses, and marsh plants called sedge.

These rugged, barren islands were the homeland of the Aleuts. Their name, pronounced *a-LOOT* or *AL-ee-oot*, may have been either a native word meaning "island" or a Russian word meaning "bald rock." The name *Alaska* was taken from an Aleut phrase, *alaeksu* or *alaschka*, meaning "mainland."

The Aleut dialect resembles the languages of the numerous Eskimo (Inuit) bands, which shows the close relationship between the two peoples. But the Aleut dialect is different enough for scholars to consider the Aleuts a distinct group. The language family is called Eskimaleut (see "Eskimo").

Some scholars do not use the word *Indian* for Aleuts and Eskimos, but apply the phrases *native peoples, indigenous peoples,* or *Native Americans*. This is because, in terms of their ancestry, both the Aleuts and the Eskimos are more closely related to Siberian peoples in Russia than to the other Native American peoples in this book. The Aleuts and Eskimos came to the Americas much later than the other tribes, from about

Aleut baidarka (skin-covered boat)

3000 B.C. to 1000 B.C., and they came by boat and not over the Bering Strait land bridge (see "Prehistoric Indians").

Two main groups of Aleuts established permanent villages on the Aleutian coasts: the Unalaska, closer to the mainland; and the Atka, farther west.

Both the Aleuts' culture and their language are related to those of the Eskimos. Scholars classify the two peoples in the Arctic Culture Area (see "Arctic Peoples"). But, because of their location, the Aleuts also had cultural traits similar to the Indians in the Northwest Coast Culture Area (see "Northwest Coast Indians"). The Aleuts traded both objects and ideas with these neighbors.

The Aleuts based their economy on the sea. They hunted the mammals of the ocean, such as sea otters, seals, sea lions, walruses, and whales. They also fished, especially for salmon and shellfish; hunted birds; and gathered roots and berries.

The Aleuts lived in *barabaras*, large communal houses with roof beams made from driftwood or whale bones and walls made from chunks of sod. The smokehole or a separate passageway served as a door. The houses were heated and lighted with stone oil lamps.

Aleut kayaks, or *baidarkas*, were made like Eskimo kayaks, with oiled walrus or seal skins stretched over light wood frames. They were short, with the bow curved upward and the stern squared off. Sometimes the bows were shaped like a bird's open beak. Usually there were two cockpits—one in back for the paddler and one in front for the harpooner. The harpooner used a throwing board (like an atlatl) for extra leverage in flinging the harpoon. The harpooner also used a stabbing spear on the prey.

Aleut clothing was efficient for rain and cold. It came in double layers and was made mostly from gut—especially seal intestines—as well as from hide. The parkas had hoods. Hunters wore wooden helmets with long visors that were decorated with ivory and sea lion whiskers. The Aleuts added intricate decorations to their clothing by using hair bristles and animal skin dyed different colors.

Aleuts also crafted elegant baskets, as did the Northwest Coast Indians, using rye grass growing on the beaches. The stems of the grass were split with the fingernails to make threads, and some of the threads were dyed in order to make baskets with intricate woven designs.

Another cultural trait Aleuts had in common with Northwest Coast Indians was their type of social organization. The Aleuts were more concerned with rank and wealth than the Eskimos were. The *toyons*, or village chiefs, and the nobles under them, demonstrated their importance through their possessions, such as tooth shells or amber. Under the chiefs and nobles were commoners and slaves. Unlike the Northwest Coast Indians, Aleuts did not have potlatches, which were elaborate feasts with the exchanging of gifts.

In the case of the Aleuts, it was the Russian traders and trappers who forever altered their way of life. Vitus Bering was a Danish navigator in the service of Russia's czar, Peter the Great. In 1741, he carried out his famous voyage of exploration, sailing from eastern Russia to the Bering Sea, Aleutian Islands, and Gulf of Alaska.

Bering's reports of plentiful sea mammals in the region soon brought the sailing ships of the *promyshlenniki* (the Russian word for fur traders and trappers). They had previously worked their way across Siberia, trapping animals for their pelts. Now they had a whole new domain to exploit. They came first to the Aleutians, which was especially rich in sea otters. And they took advantage of the Aleuts to make their fortunes in fur.

The traders would sail to a native village; take hostages by force; pass out traps to the Aleut men; then demand furs in exchange for the women and children. The women and children also were forced to work, cleaning the furs the men brought in.

The *promyshlenniki* worked eastward along the Aleutian chain. When the Atka Aleuts failed to deliver furs or made any effort to rebel, the traders taught them a lesson, executing some of them or destroying a village. The first organized resistance came from the Unalaska Aleuts on the Fox group of islands. In 1761, they wiped out a party of traders. The next year, they managed to destroy a fleet of five ships. The Russians responded in 1766 with an armada of war ships, armed with cannon and manned by European mercenaries. They bombarded many of the Aleut villages, destroying the houses and killing those inside.

Aleut resistance against the Russians was only sporadic after that. The *promyshlenniki* established their first permanent post in North America at Three Saints on Kodiak Island in 1784.

Russian officials and businessmen began regulating and restricting the behavior of the traders more and more. As a result, the Aleuts received better treatment. Supposedly the Aleuts and Eskimos were to get paid for their work. But the traders consistently cheated them by charging them fees for food, protection and other kinds of made-up expenses. In 1799, the czar granted the charter of the Russian American Company, creating a huge monopoly that competed in the 1800s with the Hudson's Bay Company for the world fur market.

Those Aleuts who had survived the violence of the past years and the diseases carried by the white man were essential to this huge fur operation. They were, after all, some of the best sea-mammal hunters in the world. Another people, the Tlingits, would take up the mantle of resistance against the Russians (see "Tlingit").

Russian missionaries would further change the culture of the Aleuts. In 1824, the Russian Orthodox priest Veniaminoff began his work among the Indians. The Aleuts came to trust him and converted to his religion because he fought for their rights.

In 1867, Russia sold the territory of Alaska to the United States, and the native peoples came under American control.

The majority of Aleuts now live on the mainland, in protected native villages. Many Aleuts work as fishermen or labor in fish canneries. Most live in frame houses. Some still practice the Russian Orthodox religion. Some are artists, making traditional crafts.

Algonkin

Indian tribal names can be confusing. Alternate names or different spellings of the same name are often used. Sometimes the Indians themselves use different names for their tribes than those given by whites. Or tribes may be known by names given to them by another tribe. Moreover, early historians may have applied names inconsistently. There were often French versions from French-speaking historians, explorers or traders, as well as English versions. In the case of the southern and southwestern Indians who lived in territories where the Spanish settled in North America, there were sometimes varying Spanish names as well.

The use of the name *Algonquian* or *Algonquin* or *Algonkin* is an example of possible confusion. Different writers use different spellings. To add to the mix-up, the name is sometimes used to discuss one small Canadian tribe, the people who originally held the name. But at other times it is used to denote many different tribes who spoke a common language but who were spread all over the Northeast and other areas as well. One might see the phrase *Algonquian proper* to distinguish the original tribe from other Algonquian-speaking peoples. Another way is to use the *Algonkin* spelling for the original tribe and to use the *Algonquian* spelling for the whole language family of tribes (see "Algonquian").

And so we come to the Algonkins (pronounced *al-GON-kin*). In addition to being the first bearers of the now widespread name, the Algonkins are important historically as early allies and trading partners of the French. Samuel de Champlain was a French explorer and fur trader. He came to North America in 1603 and helped establish New France in what is now the eastern part of Canada. He had extensive contact with the Algonkins. He was the first white man to lead expeditions along the Ottawa River, which now forms part of the border between Quebec and Ontario. (The Ottawa River is named after another Indian tribe; see "Ottawa.") But the river flowed through Algonkin territory, too. The Algonkins also lived along the Ottawa River's northern tributaries.

Samuel de Champlain and his men alienated the powerful Iroquois to the south by attacking some of their people. So the Iroquois tribes became allies of the enemies of the French in North America—first the Dutch and then the English (see "Iroquois"). The Iroquois made raids into the north against the French and their Indian allies and drove the Algonkins and other tribes from their homelands. Some Algonkins joined other Algonquian tribes, such as the Ottawas. Others eventually returned to their original territory, where their descendants live today in various Canadian Indian bands.

In their heyday, the Algonkins lived like other northern Algonquians—little farming and much hunting, fishing, and gathering. They left their villages to track game when necessary for survival. Their houses were usually cone-shaped like tepees rather than dome-shaped like New England wigwams. They also built rectangular houses. In the summer, they traveled in birchbark canoes; in the winter, they used snowshoes and toboggans.

Algonkin religion and legend resembled those of other Algonquian peoples of the northern forest. The Algonkins believed that objects had special powers. For example, for one Algonkin man, the most important religious possession or totem was a hair that he claimed he had pulled from the mustache of Manitou, the all-powerful spirit. He kept the hair wrapped in duck down, which was placed in a leather pouch beautifully decorated with porcupine quills, which was placed in another pouch, which was placed in still a third pouch. This Algonkin brave claimed that Manitou's mustache hair had saved the brave from drowning and from sickness and had led him to moose when he was hunting.

Like Native Americans all over the continent, the Algonkins loved to dance. In their Feast of the Dead, Algonkins entertained visiting tribes with a dance depicting warfare. In one such dance, a warrior would chase another with a warclub, but would lose the

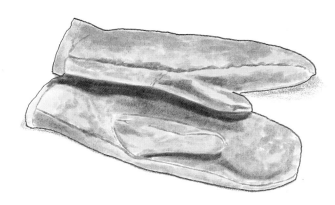

Algonkin deerskin mittens (modern)

advantage and almost be killed by the enemy. But, by weaving and bobbing, all in time to the beat of the drum, he would eventually manage to outmaneuver his opponent and win the day.

There are currently nine Algonkin bands with reserve lands in Quebec, and one band in Ontario. Many practice traditional crafts.

Algonquian

There were many different Indian languages, perhaps more than 2,000 in all of the Americas, with about 300 in North America. The Algonquian (pronounced *al-GON-kwee-in*) language is really a language family made up of many different dialects, or regional variations. That is to say, there were many different Indian tribes who spoke different Algonquian dialects. Algonquian dialects had vocabulary, grammar, and pronunciation in common. But they still had many differences. In fact, Indians speaking one Algonquian dialect might not understand Indians speaking another, and they might have to use sign language to help them communicate.

We can learn much about the early histories of tribes by studying their languages. We can discover, for example, that two tribes might have been one group in earlier times and then divided before Europeans came to the Americas. Yet, in studying Indian culture, geography is usually more important than language. Even if tribes spoke similar languages, they would have different ways of life if they lived in different environments—Plains people would live differently than

Woodland people, for instance, whether they spoke the same language or not.

Nevertheless, in some cases, when tribes of the same language family lived in the same environment, it is convenient to study them as one group. The family of tribes known as Algonquians is such a group. Most Algonquian tribes lived in the Northeast Woodlands and they had much in common (see "Northeast Indians"). However, there were many differences from tribe to tribe, too. That is why Algonquian tribes are listed in this book by their individual names. In this section we'll take a look at what the various Algonquian tribes had in common.

Sometimes the Algonquians are divided into more specific groups: (1) New England Algonquians, such as Abnaki, Massachuset, Mohegan, Narraganset, Nipmuc, Passamaquoddy, Pennacook, Penobscot, Pequot, and Wampanoag; (2) Hudson River Algonquians, such as Mahican and Wappinger; (3) Middle-Atlantic Algonquians, such as Delaware and Montauk; (4) Southern Algonquians, such as Powhatan; (5) Great Lakes Algonquians, such as

Chippewa, Menominee, Ottawa, and Potawatomi; (6) Prairie Algonquians, such as Illinois, Miami, and Shawnee; (7) Combined Great Lakes/Prairie Algonquians, such as Fox, Kickapoo, and Sac; (8) Canadian Woodland Algonquians, such as Algonkin, Malecite, and Micmac; and (9) Canadian Subarctic Algonquians, such as Cree, Montagnais, and Naskapi (and some Chippewa bands).

These are not all the Algonquian tribes that ever existed. There were others living in the East, such as the Niantics of New England and the Nanticokes of Delaware Bay. There were also Algonquians who migrated far west to the Great Plains, such as the Arapaho, Blackfoot, Cheyenne, and Gros Ventre tribes (see entries for those tribes). But these are usually considered Plains Indians (see "Plains Indians"). And there were Algonquians on the Pacific Coast, such as the Yuroks, but they are considered California Indians (see "Yurok" and "California Indians"). It is the eastern tribes that historians generally refer to when they use the name Algonquian. These are the Algonquians that played such an important part in American and Canadian early history, from colonial times until about 1830.

Since so many Algonquians lived along the Atlantic seaboard, they were among the earliest contacts of the European explorers and settlers, such as the Jamestown colonists, the Pilgrims, and the founders of Quebec and Montreal. From the Algonquian language have come such familiar English words as *hickory*, *hominy*, *moccasin*, *moose*, *papoose*, *powwow*, *sachem*, *squash*, *squaw*, *succotash*, *tomahawk*, *totem*, *wigwam*, and *woodchuck*.

Many Algonquians were scattered or pushed westward soon after the arrival of whites in the colonial years. The Algonquians of the Great Lakes region lasted longer in their original homelands, but, by the early 1800s, most of them were also relocated. Many of these tribes ended up in Oklahoma.

In general, the Algonquians were friendly with the French and often fought as their allies against the British and their allies, the Iroquois (see "Iroquois"). Then, in later years, many Algonquians fought the Americans. To learn each tribe's exciting and sometimes tragic history, and its special place in the history of the United States and Canada, look up the entries for the individual tribes previously listed.

To better understand the Algonquians as a group, here we will discuss some of their cultural traits under the following categories: social organization and political systems; food; shelter; transportation; clothing; tools and weapons; and religion, rituals, and legends. Some of these same subjects will also be discussed under the individual tribal names.

Social Structure

Concerning their intertribal organization, the Algonquians commonly formed confederacies, such as the Abnaki Confederacy, the Wappinger Confederacy, and the Powhatan Confederacy. These alliances were not as structured as the Iroquois League, which had an intricate system of laws governing tribal interaction (see "Iroquois"). Rather, the Algonquian confederacies were usually a loose network of villages and bands who traded together and who helped one another in times of war. These confederacies usually had a grand sachem with greater authority than regular sachems. Sometimes the lesser sachems in charge of a particular village or band were known as sagamores. In some instances, the grand sachem served as little more than a mediator between the sagamores during intertribal councils. In other cases, however, as with the Powhatans of Virginia, the grand sachem was more like a king, with absolute power over life and death.

But not all Algonquian tribes were part of a confederacy with a grand sachem. In the Great Lakes area, it was more common to have two chiefs for each tribe, the peace chief and the war chief. The first was usually a hereditary position, passed on from father to son. The second was chosen for his military prowess in times of war. Some tribes also had a third leader, the ceremonial leader. He was the tribe's shaman, or medicine man, and was in charge of religious rituals.

For the Algonquian tribes of northern Canada, the band was the most important political unit. These peoples moved around so much in small hunting groups that they had little social organization other than the extended family—parents, brothers and sisters, cousins, in-laws, and so on. Many of these bands met with one another once a year for a communal celebration, and then their various leaders met as equals.

Among all the Algonquians, the family played an important part in society. Many tribes were organized into clans, which are clusters of related families traced back to a common ancestor. Tribes that traced descent through the female line are called matrilineal by scholars. Those that traced back through a male line are called patrilineal. Clans usually had favorite animals as symbols and names to distinguish them from one another. These are called totems. The animal totems were thought of as spiritual guardians or supernatural ancestors.

Tribes often organized their clans into two different groups, called moieties, meaning "halves." These moieties would be responsible for different duties and chores. They would also oppose each other in sporting events. Clans, totems, and moieties were common to Indians all over North America, not just to Algonquians.

Food

Most of the year, in spring, summer and fall, the Algonquians lived in villages, usually located along rivers, where they grew crops. Corn was the staple food for the farming tribes; beans and squash also provided nourishment. In the wintertime, Algonquians left the villages in small bands to track game. For some of the Algonquian tribes of Canada, the soil was too rocky to break up with wood, bone, or antler digging sticks. They had to depend on hunting, fishing, and gathering wild plants for all their food. These northern peoples covered greater distances than their kinsmen to the south. The Algonquians did not raise domestic animals for meat or wool as modern farmers do; but they did have trained dogs who helped them hunt.

Algonquians hunted whatever game they could, large or small. All the Algonquians hunted deer, rabbit, squirrel, beaver, and various birds, such as turkey, partridge, duck, and goose. Algonquians in the northern woods also hunted moose, elk, and bear. Some lived far enough north to track caribou herds, too. And some Algonquian tribes living near the prairies of the Mississippi River Valley hunted buffalo.

Before whites brought the horse to North America, the Native Americans had to do all their hunting on foot. In addition to spears, arrows, and clubs, they used traps, snares, and deadfalls, which are devices that drop heavy objects on the prey. And they sometimes used disguises, such as animal skins; and calls, such as a birchbark instrument to lure moose; and fire, to drive herds into an ambush.

Algonquians also fished the rivers, streams, lakes, and ponds in their territory. They used harpoons, hooks, nets, traps, and weirs (fence-like enclosures placed in the water). Algonquians living along the Atlantic Coast depended on shellfish for part of their warm-weather diet. A common method of preserving both fish and meat was hanging it over a fire and letting smoke penetrate it for a long time. Fish and meat smoked this way could be kept through the winter or taken on long journeys.

All the Algonquians ate wild plants: berries, nuts, roots, stalks, and leaves. Algonquians living in maple country collected the sap from the trees in early spring and boiled it down into maple syrup and sugar. Some tribes living along the Great Lakes gathered the grain of a tall grass plant known as wild rice.

Many of the foods of the Algonquians were unknown to Europeans before they came to North America. From the Algonquians, whites first learned to eat corn, pumpkin, maple sugar, wild rice, cranberries, blueberries, lobster, clams, and oysters.

Houses

Algonquians lived in many different types of houses, but the dwelling most often associated with Algonquians is the wigwam. The typical wigwam frame consisted of small trees bent and tied together in a dome shape and covered with strips of birchbark that were sewn together. But some Algonquians did not

Algonquian wigwam

round off the framework; rather, they propped the saplings together to form a cone resembling a small tepee. And, if birchbark wasn't available, they might use another bark, such as elm, to make the coverings. Or they might weave some other plant matter, such as cattail reeds, into mats that also served to keep out rain, snow, and wind. Or they might use animal skins as the Plains Indians did on their tents (see "Plains Indians"). Or they would use combinations of all these things. The men usually built the framework, then the women added the coverings.

Swamp grass and animal furs made good insulation for the wigwams. Branches covered with hides served as floors and beds. All the different-shaped Algonquian dwellings had holes in their roofs to let smoke out.

Some Algonquians also constructed large rectangular buildings similar to the Iroquoian longhouses (see "Iroquois"). These might serve as places where the tribal council met. Or a family might choose to use one of these roomy and airy structures as their home. On the trail, of course, the smaller, portable structures with removable coverings were more practical. Algonquian villages often had walls, or palisades, of upright logs surrounding them for protection.

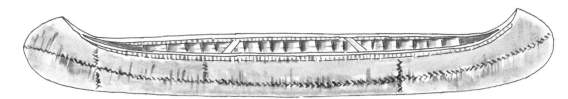

Algonquian (Chippewa) birchbark canoe

Like some other Indian peoples, the Algonquians had special buildings for sweating. These sweathouses were often dome-shaped like a wigwam. Water would be poured over hot rocks to make steam for the purpose of purifying the body and spirit. Following the steam bath would usually be a dip in a cold stream, lake, or snowbank.

Transportation

The Algonquians have a special place in Native American history because of their birchbark canoes (other Indian peoples in western Canada also used birchbark canoes). These remarkably light, swift, and graceful craft are probably, along with the Plains tepee, warbonnet, and peace pipe, the most well-known of all Indian objects. Using the network of rivers and lakes, Algonquians could travel throughout their territory to hunt, fish, trade, and make war. They could use more than one waterway by portaging, or carrying, their light canoes overland from one body of water to another. And, on the trail, the canoes could be used as makeshift lean-tos to provide shelter from the elements.

These canoes were made in a variety of sizes, materials, and styles: with a low bow and stern, offering little wind resistance, for calm waters; or with high ends, which could slice through large waves, for rough waters (such as the Great Lakes). They differed in size: A small river canoe could be paddled by one or two persons; whereas large lake canoes could be handled by eight or ten persons, four or five to a side. Cedar, which could be split easily and evenly, was normally used for the framework. Then the bark of the paper birch would be peeled off the tree in large sheets. The paper birch had few imperfections on its surface. Moreover, birchbark did not shrink or stretch. The pieces of bark would be sewn together with spruce roots and shaped around the cedar frame. Then the resins of spruce trees would be spread on the seams to waterproof them. Maple was the wood of choice for the thwarts, the braces that extended from side to side and held the gunwales, or sides, together. Maple was also used to make paddles.

When birchbark was not available, the Algonquians sometimes used the heavier elm bark or spruce bark on their boats, or even moosehide. Or they hollowed out the trunk of a single tree to make a dugout canoe. Large dugouts proved more durable in the waters of the open sea for those Algonquians along the Atlantic Coast who went on whaling expeditions.

In wintertime, Subarctic Algonquians used toboggans. These didn't have runners like the sleds used by the Eskimos. Rather, the platform for people or possessions rested directly on the snow. The platform was made of smooth planks curved upward at the front end. The Northern Algonquians also used snowshoes to travel in deep snow. Spruce, birch, or willow was usually used to make the snowshoes' oval-shaped frame, with rawhide webbing strung in between.

Clothing

Buckskin was the Algonquian's favorite material for making clothing, especially the hide of the white-tailed deer. Moose, elk, and caribou, also of the deer family, provided some tribes with materials for their garments. The hides were cured to make soft leather. Men wore shirts, breechcloths, leggings, and moccasins. Women wore either skirts and blouses or dresses, plus moccasins. Algonquian clothing often had short fringes hanging from the seams and edges. Both men and women wore fur robes for extra warmth in the winter. They also wore belts and sashes of cured leather or woven plant material.

Both men and women liked to decorate their clothing with quillwork. The quills of the porcupine would be soaked and softened in water and then dyed with vegetable coloring. Paint, feathers, and shells were also used to add color and designs to clothing. Shell and stone jewelry served as decorations, too. So did moosehair embroidery. After whites came, the Indians began using glass beads in place of quills and shells.

Women often wore their hair in braids and decorated it with a small cap or a band of shells. Men usually went bareheaded in order to show off their hair. They wore their hair in a variety of styles, depending on individual taste. Hair for Algonquians, as for other Indians, was a symbol of selfhood and strength.

Other Arts and Crafts

In our discussion of food, shelter, transportation, and clothing, we have already gotten a sense of the wide range of Algonquian technology. The Algonquians, like other Native Americans, ingeniously used the materials at hand to shape tools, weapons, and ceremonial objects. They used wood and bark, other plant materials, stone, clay, hide, bone, antler, shells, quills, and feathers in making their objects. Some Algonquians around the Great Lakes even used copper located there to make metal objects. After whites came, the Indians adapted their crafts to new materials, using metals, glass beads, and strips of cloth in original ways.

The Algonquian use of a variety of materials to make a variety of containers shows the extent of their ingenuity. Some Algonquians favored birchbark for their containers. Some of these birchbark containers, like the mocuck, were watertight, their seams smeared with pitch, and were used for carrying and storing

Algonquian birchbark mocuck (modern)

water. Others were used as bowls, dishes, and trays, or for winnowing (separating chaff from grain) wild rice.

Algonquians also carved their containers out of wood. The burls or knots of birch, elm, and maple, or some other hardwood, were charred in a fire to soften for scraping with stone or bone tools. Wood was also used to make the mortars and pestles needed for grinding corn.

Wood splints and sweet grass were used in basketry, the wood splints to make plaited baskets and the sweet grass to make coiled baskets.

Pottery was also used to make containers for cooking, carrying, and storing. Algonquians did not develop techniques in ceramics as much as Indians of the Southeast and Southwest did. The Algonquians had one main practical design. They made elongated clay pots for cooking with rounded or pointed bottoms and a neck at the top. They shaped the clay into pots without a potter's wheel, then smoothed the outside with a cord-wrapped paddle before firing. The pots were unpainted, but had geometric designs from tapping, pressing, or scratching objects into the clay either before or after firing.

The Algonquians applied this same sort of ingenuity to the making of weapons for hunting and warfare. They used wood, stone, bone, and, after the whites began to trade with them, metal, to make deadly spears, clubs, and bows and arrows. Some among them also used wood for armor and shields.

Both the eastern Algonquians and their neighbors the Iroquois used wampum for ceremonial purposes.

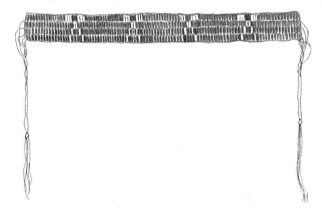

Algonquian wampum

They made wampum from seashells, especially of the quahog clam, grinding the raw material into purple and white beads, then stringing the beads on a belt. They used wampum belts as tribal records and to commemorate special events, such as a peace treaty or a festival. They also exchanged wampum belts as gifts or as trade goods. In later years, after whites came to North America, the Indians used European glass beads to make wampum. Dutch and English settlers also began manufacturing wampum from glass beads in order to trade with the Indians. In this way, wampum became a form of money.

An item common to the western Algonquians was the peace pipe. *Peace pipe* is really not the best name for these pipes, because they were used for other types of ceremonies, too, such as councils of war. The word *calumet*, a French word referring to the long stems of the pipes, is a better word. Another name is *sacred pipe*.

It was the Indians of the Great Lakes and the nearby prairies who originally used ceremonial pipes. In later years, the practice spread onto the Great Plains. A pipe was usually a tribe's most valued object. A pipe might also serve as a passport through hostile territory. Sometimes white explorers carried them to show their good intentions.

The bowl of the pipe was carved from pipestone. This kind of stone is also called catlinite after 19th-century frontier painter George Catlin, who lived among the Indians. The red, pink, or gray stone is

Algonquian sacred pipe

found in Great Lakes country. It can be carved with a knife when first quarried, but then it turns hard after it is exposed to the air. The pipestems were made from light wood or reeds and were often carved with intricate designs. The pipes were usually decorated with feathers. White feathers meant peace; red feathers meant war. Quillwork or beadwork might be wrapped around the stem.

The Algonquians grew tobacco to smoke in their pipes. They also smoked a concoction called *kinnikinnik*, or "mixture," which consisted of dried plant matter, such as willow bark, mixed with tobacco leaves.

Religion

Indians in general were a reverent people. We have already discussed how the Algonquians used animal totems to identify clans and how they used wampum and sacred pipes in rituals. We have also mentioned their shamans, or medicine men, who led tribal members in religious activity.

Yet there is so much more to the study of Algonquian religion that it is a difficult subject to summarize in just a few paragraphs. The Algonquians believed that a Great Spirit pervaded all existence. This spirit was called Gitche Manitou, or simply Manitou. But the Manitou had many manifestations. That is, the Great Spirit was found in all things—animals, plants, water, rocks, and other natural phenomena, such as the sun, moon, weather, or sickness. Lesser individual

manifestations of the Great Spirit can also be called manitous or may have other names, such as Thunderbird, Bringer of Rain.

Shamans were supposed to be able to control these spirits, found in all living and nonliving things. Some tribes also had secret medicine societies, like the Midewiwin Society of the Great Lakes, in which all the members could come in contact with the spirit world.

In addition to the general belief in Manitou, Algonquian tribes had different mythologies and legends, with various supernatural beings. Some of these beings were heroes or guardian spirits, such as Manibozho (or Manabush), the Great Hare, who, according to Algonquian legend, remade the world after bad spirits destroyed it with a flood. Others were demons, such as the Windigos of the northern forests who supposedly ate people.

Although different Algonquian tribes had different rituals and festivals, they all celebrated with singing, drumming, and dancing. Some rituals had to do with hunting; others, such as the Green Corn Festival, related to farming; others concerned peacemaking or warfare; others were to cure illness; still others were for rites of passage, such as a boy passing to manhood.

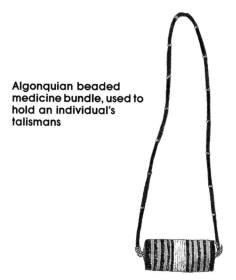

Algonquian beaded medicine bundle, used to hold an individual's talismans

As a rite of passage into adulthood, both boys and girls were sent into the woods to fast and pray for a vision. If the child were fortunate, a spirit, usually in the form of an animal, would come to promise protection and to give the child his or her own special identity.

As we can see, there is much to learn about the many eastern tribes who spoke the Algonquian language. To get a fuller sense of Algonquian culture and history, read the entries for all the tribes listed at the beginning of this entry.

Apache

On hearing the name *Apache* (pronounced *uh-PATCH-ee*), most people think first of the chief Geronimo, along with the warlike nature of the tribe. Throughout most of their history, the Apaches raided other tribes for food and booty. The Zunis, who feared them, gave them the name *Apachu*, meaning "enemy" (see "Zuni"). But there was of course much more to Apache culture than warfare. Like all Indian peoples, the Apaches had a well-defined society and a complex mythology that are as fascinating to learn about as their wars.

The Apaches lived in the part of North America referred to as the Southwest Culture Area (see "Southwest Indians"). The numerous Apache bands roamed far and wide in this region—territory that now includes much of New Mexico and Arizona, as well as northern Mexico, western Texas, southeastern Colorado, western Oklahoma, and southern Kansas.

The various Apache peoples migrated to the Southwest later than other Indians. Long before Europeans reached North America, Athapascan-speaking bands broke off from other Athapascans in western Canada and migrated southward, probably as early as A.D. 850, and became known as the Apaches. Other Athapascans who followed in later years became known as the Navajos (see "Athapascan" and "Navajo").

The Apaches can be organized by dialects into the following groups, each made up of various bands: San Carlos, Aravaipa, White Mountain, Northern Tonto, Southern Tonto, and Cibecue in Arizona; Chiricahua and Mimbreno in Arizona and New Mexico; Mescalero in New Mexico and Mexico; Lipan in Texas and Mexico; Jicarilla in New Mexico and Colorado; and Kiowa-Apache in Oklahoma. Members of these different groups intermarried or were placed together on reservations by whites later in their history, altering the various subdivisions. For example, the San Carlos and White Mountain groups, sometimes together called the Western Apaches, came to include members from other more easterly groups, such as the Chiricahuas and Mimbrenos. (In the case of the Apaches, it is important to try to keep the band names straight rather than lumping them all together, because, in the Apache Wars, different bands fought different battles.)

Lifeways

The Apaches were primarily nomadic hunters and gatherers, seeking whatever game, especially deer and rabbits, and whatever wild plant foods, especially cactus and mesquite seeds, found within their territory. (The Mescalero band was named after a kind of cactus important in the Apache diet, mescal.) When they could not find enough food to eat in their rugged lands, much of which was desert country, Apaches raided the farming villages of the Pueblo peoples, as well as, in later years, Spanish, Mexican and Anglo-American settlements (see "Pueblo Indians").

The various Apache groups adopted lifeways from other Indians with whom they came into contact. For instance, some of the Western Apaches, living close to the Indians of the Rio Grande pueblos, took up farming. The Jicarilla Apaches borrowed cultural traits from the Plains Indians. On acquiring horses in the late 1600s through raids on the Spanish and on Pueblo Indians, mounted Jicarillas often rode in pursuit of the great buffalo herds (see "Plains Indians"). The Kiowa-Apaches lived close to the Kiowa Indians, a Plains tribe, and their culture was closer to that of the Kiowa than to their own Apache kinsmen (see "Kiowa"). Similarly, the Lipans shared some traits with Mexican tribes to their south, such as raising dogs to eat.

The most common type of dwelling for most of the Apache bands was the wickiup, a domed or cone-

Apache wickiup

shaped hut with a pole framework covered with brush, grass, or reed mats. Wickiups frequently had central fire pits and a smoke hole. The Jicarillas and Kiowa-Apaches used hide tepees.

The Apaches originally wore deerskin clothing. They never grew or wove cotton as many Southwest peoples did, nor did they become sheepherders as their Navajo relatives did, preferring to eat the sheep instead. But Apaches acquired cotton and wool clothing through trade or raids.

Apaches made little pottery. Yet they were master basketmakers, crafting coiled baskets of many shapes and sizes and with intricate designs. After the coming of whites, the Apaches became known for an instrument called the Apache fiddle. The painted sound box was crafted from a yucca stalk and held a single string

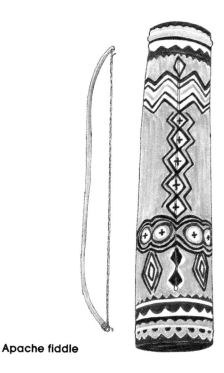

Apache fiddle

of sinew attached to a tuning peg. The instrument was played with a bow made of wood and sinew.

Apache bands had a loose social and political organization. Each band, which was made up of extended families, had a headman who was chosen informally for his leadership abilities and military prowess. But other warriors could launch raids on their own without the headman's permission.

Shamans presided over religious rituals. The Apaches believed in many supernatural beings. They considered Ussen (also spelled *Yusn*), the Giver of Life, the most powerful of the supernatural beings. The Gans, or Mountain Spirits, were especially important in Apache ceremonies. Men dressed up in elaborate costumes to impersonate the Gans in dances, wearing kilts, black masks, tall wooden-slat headdresses, and body paint. They carried wooden swords.

Apache Wars

The Apaches' earliest contacts with whites were friendly. The Spanish explorer Francisco de Coronado called Apaches he encountered in 1540 the Querechos. Yet, by the late 1500s, Apache bands were sweeping southward in raids on Spanish settlements. During the 1600s, the Spanish established a line of presidios (forts) across northern Mexico to try to protect their settlements from Apache attacks. Yet the Apaches continued their lightning-swift raids, disappearing into the wilderness before the soldiers could rally an effective defense. The Spanish also tried to convert the Apaches to Christianity and have them move into missions, but with little success. However, the Apaches did not try to drive the Spanish completely from their territory as the Pueblo Indians did in their successful rebellion of 1680. Instead, the Apaches preferred to raid the Spanish settlers for plunder, especially horses and cattle. The Apaches kept up their raids against the Spanish throughout the 1700s and into the 1800s. Only the Comanche Indians, who advanced into Apache territory from the east about 1740, proved a match for the fierce Apaches.

In 1821, Mexico and New Mexico became independent from Spain. But the new government in Mexico City did no better than the old one had in stopping the relentless Apache attacks along Mexico's northern frontier. During this period, the Apaches also proved hostile to early Anglo-American traders and trappers who traveled through or near their territory.

In 1848, with the Treaty of Guadalupe Hidalgo following the Mexican War, Mexico lost its northern holdings to the United States. Soon American troops began arriving in Apache country in great numbers. At this same time, with the discovery of gold in California, the number of all Anglo-Americans traveling westward dramatically increased. Although the United States government now claimed their land, the Apaches considered the travelers as trespassers. The United States had defeated Mexico, the Apache leaders reasoned, but since Mexico had never defeated the Apaches, their lands still rightfully belonged to them.

During the 1850s, the Apaches still preyed mostly on ranchers in Mexico. Major hostilities with the Americans did not occur until the 1860s. The first significant outbreak involved the Chiricahua Apaches. Their headman at the time was named Cochise. A lieutenant in the U.S. Army named George Bascom wrongly accused Cochise's band of kidnapping children and stealing cattle, and Bascom took some of Cochise's people as hostages. In retaliation,

Cochise and his warriors began laying ambushes along Apache Pass on the Butterfield Southern Route (or the Southern Overland Trail) that ran through the Southwest from El Paso to Los Angeles.

Before long, the Mimbreno Apaches, led by Cochise's father-in-law, Mangas Colorado, joined the resistance. U.S. troops managed to drive the insurgents into Mexico for a while, but then abandoned the region to head east to fight in the American Civil War. California volunteers under General James Carleton rode in to man the posts in Chiricahua country, but the Chiricahuas and Mimbrenos proved unconquerable to the new troops as well. The Apaches lost one of their most important leaders, however. Mangas Colorado was captured in 1862 through trickery and was later killed by angry guards.

Meanwhile, to the east, the Mescalero Apaches carried out raids on travelers near the El Paso end of the Butterfield Southern Route. General Carleton appointed the former fur trader, scout, Indian agent, and Union soldier Christopher "Kit" Carson as his leader in the field against the Mescaleros. Through relentless pursuit, Carson and his men wore down the Mescaleros and finally forced them to surrender. Then the soldiers relocated the Mescaleros at Bosque Redondo in the barren flatlands of the Pecos River Valley near Fort Sumner. After this phase of the Apache Wars, Carson turned his attention to the Navajos, who were also relocated to Bosque Redondo (see "Navajo").

In 1871, settlers from Tucson marched on Camp Grant and massacred over 100 innocent Aravaipa Apaches—most of them women and children—under Chief Eskiminzin. This incident convinced President Ulysses S. Grant that there was a need for a reservation system to separate Apaches from white settlers.

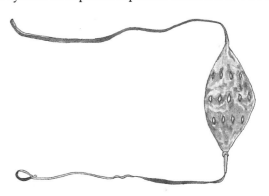

Apache sling for rock-throwing

After extensive negotiations, the formerly hostile Cochise of the Chiricahuas signed a peace treaty, and from that time until his death in 1874, he helped keep peace along Apache Pass.

Another important episode occurred in 1872-73, when General George Crook led the successful Tonto Basin Campaign against the Apache militants from various western bands and against their Yavapai allies (see "Yavapai").

The final two episodes in the Apache Wars had much in common. Both involved warriors from earlier fighting. Victorio, a Mimbreno Apache, had fought alongside Mangas Colorado. Geronimo, a Chiricahua, had fought under Cochise. Both Victorio and Geronimo began uprisings on the San Carlos Reservation in Arizona. In both rebellions, the insurgents escaped from the reservation and hid out in the rugged country in much of the Southwest as well as in Mexico. Both rebellions forced the army to put many men in the field for long campaigns.

The first of the two conflicts, Victorio's Rebellion, lasted from 1877 to 1880. After numerous skirmishes with both American and Mexican armies, he was final-

An Apache warrior of the Apache Wars

ly defeated by a Mexican force at the Battle of Tres Castillos. His death in that battle brought the Mimbreno resistance to a virtual end.

Some of the survivors of Victorio's Rebellion joined Geronimo's Rebellion of 1881-86. This was the last sustained Indian uprising in the United States, and it generated a great deal of interest in all the American newspapers.

The Apaches, who had been wanderers throughout their history, had a hard time adapting to the confining reservation life. Geronimo spent some time on the Mescalero reservation at Ojo Caliente in New Mexico. Then he joined his people, the Chiricahuas, at the San Carlos Reservation in Arizona. At that time in history, Indians on reservations were not permitted to leave. But Geronimo and his followers managed to escape three times.

The first breakout resulted from the death of the White Mountain medicine man named Nakaidoklini, who preached a new religion to Apaches that claimed that dead warriors would return to drive the whites from Apache territory. Soldiers out of Fort Apache, Arizona, tried to arrest Nakaidoklini for his teachings, but, when fighting broke out at Cibecue Creek in August, 1881, they killed him instead. The Chiricahuas and other bands revolted, fled the San Carlos reservation, and began a new series of raids. After a prolonged campaign led by General George Crook and after many negotiations, Geronimo and his men agreed to return peacefully to San Carlos in 1884.

The second breakout resulted from the reservation ban on a ceremonial alcoholic drink of the Apaches called *tiswin*. Again, the Apaches resented interference in their religion by white officials. Crook's soldiers tracked the Apaches to Canyon de los Embudos in the rugged highlands of Mexico; after negotiations, Geronimo and his men surrendered a second time, in 1886. Yet, on the return trip to San Carlos, Geronimo and some of his followers escaped.

Because of this incident, General Crook was relieved of his command. It was General Nelson Miles's turn to try to tame the fierce Apaches once and for all. Miles put 5,000 men in the field to do so. They rode all over the Southwest, on both sides of the Mexican border, in pursuit of the Indian guerillas, who seemed to always stay one step ahead of them.

Hunger and weariness finally brought in Geronimo and his followers for the last time. They surrendered at Skeleton Canyon in 1886, not far from Apache Pass, where the Apache Wars had started 25 years before.

Geronimo and the other braves were put in chains and sent by train to Fort Pickens in Pensacola, Florida. They were also imprisoned for a time at Mount Vernon Barracks in Alabama. In the terrible conditions of these

jails, about a quarter of the Indians died from tuberculosis. Finally, the surviving Apaches were allowed to return to the west. However, because the citizens of Arizona opposed the return of the Chiricahuas to San Carlos, Geronimo and his followers were taken instead to Fort Sill on the Comanche and Kiowa Reservation in the Indian Territory. By that time, Geronimo was already a legend all over the United States. People came from far away just to get a glimpse of him and to take his picture. White officials never let Geronimo return to see his homeland. He was still a prisoner of war when he died many years later, in 1909. The other Chiricahuas were permitted to return home in 1914.

The San Carlos Reservation still exists. It is located in Gila and Graham counties of Arizona. Apaches also live on other reservations in Arizona: on the Camp Verde Reservation, which they share with the Yavapais, in Yavapai County; on the Fort McDowell Reservation, which they share with Mojaves and Yavapais, in Maricopa County; and on the Fort Apache Reservation in Apache, Gila, and Navajo Counties. In New Mexico, there is the Jicarilla Reservation in Rio Arriba and Sandoval counties; and the Mescalero Reservation in Otero County. The Fort Sill Apaches have their business committee headquarters in Apache, Oklahoma. These Apaches are sometimes referred to as Chief Geronimo's Band of Apaches.

Apache pottery ashtray (modern)

Today, Apaches support themselves through a number of tribal enterprises, including stock raising, sawmills, stores, gas stations, oil and gas leases, and tourist facilities. Individual tribal members also farm and hire themselves out as laborers to earn a living. Some Apaches supplement their income by making traditional arts and crafts, in particular, baskets, cradleboards, and beadwork.

Apalachee

The Apalachee Indians' (pronounced *ap-uh-LATCH-ee*) homeland was situated in what is now northwest Florida, near the capital of the state, Tallahassee. The nearby bay on the Gulf of Mexico is named after the tribe: Apalachee Bay.

The tribe is now extinct. The Apalachees were once known as great farmers and great warriors. They had at least 20 villages of many pole-frame houses with palmetto-thatched roofs. Sometimes the Indians packed the walls of their houses with mud, a technique called wattle and daub. They also built mounds with temples on top for religious ceremonies. The tribe is classified as part of the Southeast Culture Area (see "Southeast Indians").

To the north of the Apalachees lived the Creeks (see "Creek"). Both peoples spoke dialects of the Muskogean language family, but they were enemies. The Apalachees, although they were not as numerous as the Creeks, successfully managed to hold their own against the larger tribe.

In 1528, the Apalachees attacked and drove off an early Spanish expedition led by the explorer Panfilo de Narvaez. But Hernando de Soto and his men lived among the tribe in the winter of 1539-40 during the first part of De Soto's ambitious expedition in the Southeast. During this time, some of the more militant Apalachees resented the presence of the conquistadors and quarreled with them.

By 1633, Spanish missionaries had a foothold among the Apalachees. By the 1640s, the Spanish had built seven churches and had converted eight of the principal Apalachee chiefs to Catholicism. In 1647, the Apalachees, angry because they were forced to work on the Spanish fort at St. Augustine, briefly rebelled against the Spanish. But the Spanish soldiers, with superior weapons, quickly put down the uprising. Then in 1656, some Apalachees joined the Timucuas in their revolt (see "Timucua"). However, the faction in the tribe who wanted the Spanish as allies, valuing European trade goods and the protection against other Indians, prevented further violence in the ensuing years.

Nevertheless, as allies of the Spanish, the Apalachees suffered attacks from other colonists. Spain sided with France during its colonial struggles with England, and in 1703-04, Carolina militiamen and Creek warriors under Colonel James Moore moved against the Apalachees. The force destroyed many villages and killed many inhabitants, and they took some Apalachee captives back to South Carolina. Some of these Apalachees later joined with the Yamasees in the Yamasee War of 1715 (see "Yamasee").

During the remainder of the 1700s, the Apalachees migrated often. Some joined their former enemies, the Creeks. Others moved to new villages among the Spanish. After 1763, at the end of the French and Indian War, when Spain lost Florida to England, many Apalachees moved to Louisiana. The Spanish regained control of Florida in 1783 after the American Revolution, holding it until 1819. By that time, however, their Apalachee allies had already dispersed. The small bands that remained intermarried with other Indian peoples, as well as with blacks and whites, and gradually lost their tribal identity.

Arapaho

The name *Arapaho*, pronounced *uh-RAP-uh-ho*, has a beautiful ring to it. It is easy to say in the English language, but it still sounds like an Indian word. Where did this name come from? The etymology, or derivation, of Indian tribal names is fascinating. The exact source of the name is not always known. The Arapahos originally called themselves *Inuna-ina*, meaning "our people." Some tribes also called the Arapahos "dog-eaters" in their various languages. The name *Arapaho*, which has become the official name of the tribe, probably comes from the Pawnee word *tirapihu*, meaning "trader." It is also close to the Kiowa name for the tribe: *Ahyato*.

The Arapahos were an Algonquian people, one of the few western tribes to speak a dialect of this language (see "Algonquian"). It is thought that they once lived in the Red River region of what is now Minnesota and North Dakota, one people with other Algonquians called the Gros Ventres (see "Gros Ventre"). Other Algonquian tribes who eventually settled in the West, the Blackfeet and the Cheyennes, might also have been relatives of the Arapahos (see "Blackfoot" and "Cheyenne").

The Arapahos and the Gros Ventres are believed to have migrated westward to the headwaters of the Missouri River sometime in the 1700s, possibly as far west as territory now in Montana. At some point, the Gros Ventres and Arapahos separated. The Gros Ventres migrated to the north to what is now northern Montana and southern Saskatchewan. The Arapahos headed south.

At some point in the 1800s, the tribe again divided into the Northern Arapahos and the Southern Arapahos. The northern branch of the tribe settled in the vicinity of the North Platte River in what is now Wyoming. The southern group settled along the Arkansas River in what is now Colorado. The two groups stayed in close contact with each other, however.

Lifeways

By the 1800s, the Arapahos had evolved into a typical tribe of the Great Plains Culture Area. They were master horsemen, using their horses to hunt buffalo and to carry out raids on other Indians and on white

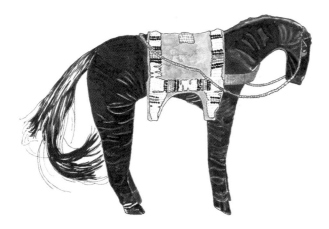

Arapaho leather and bead toy horse

settlers. They lived in buffalo-skin tents called tepees. They changed their campsites often, following the migrations of buffalo herds (see "Plains Indians").

Three customs shared by many of the tribes that migrated onto the Plains are military societies, medicine bundles, and the Sun Dance.

The military societies of the Plains Indians were clubs built around the act of warfare. The different societies had different initiation rites, different pre-battle and post-battle ceremonies, different songs and dances, and different costumes. In the case of

Arapaho drumstick with head of green-painted hide and quillwork eagles on both sides

Arapahos, the eight secret societies were age-graded. That is to say, boys of a certain age joined one society, then graduated into others. Other tribes with age-graded military societies were the Gros Ventres, Blackfeet, Mandans, and Hidatsas. Some tribes with non-graded military societies, often with membership determined by invitation only, were the Cheyennes, Sioux, Crows, Assiniboines, and Omahas (see entries for those tribes).

Medicine bundles were containers of various shapes and sizes with objects inside thought to have magical powers. Some were owned by individual Indians, and the owner might have seen the objects in a dream or vision during his Vision Quest, the ceremony that marked his passage into adulthood. Those medicine bundles belonging to the medicine men were used in healing ceremonies. Each secret society had its own medicine bundles. Other medicine bundles belonged to the whole tribe. The most important medicine bundle for the Cheyennes contained many objects, including a hat made from the hide of a buffalo, plus four arrows, two for warfare and two for hunting. The Sioux treasured a pipe supposedly given to the tribe by a white buffalo calf. The most sacred object of the Arapahos was the flat pipe. This was a long tobacco pipe with a stem about the length of a man's arm. It was wrapped in a bundle, to be opened and smoked only on very special occasions and with elaborate rituals. Another sacred relic of the tribe kept in a bundle was a wheel or hoop.

The Arapahos, like most Indian peoples, were very religious. Many of their everyday acts had symbolic meaning. For instance, when Arapaho women crafted some of their beautiful beadwork on clothing, bags, or tepees, or when they painted designs with vegetable coloring, they depicted tribal legends or spiritual beings.

The most important ceremony for the Arapahos was the Sun Dance, which they used to ask for the renewal of nature and future tribal prosperity. This event took place once a year, when berries were ripening. The Lodgemaker directed the construction of an enclosure of poles and greenery, and a sacred tree trunk was erected at the center. A rawhide doll was usually tied to the top of the sacred tree. The various societies performed complex rituals around the tree, many of them involving medicine bundles, and gazed toward the sun. The Sun Dance was a test of endurance for Arapaho participants. They went without food or sleep for days. But the Arapaho version of the ritual did not involve extreme self-torture. In some Plains tribes, the braves, attached to the sacred tree by ropes and wooden skewers in their chests, danced backward until their flesh actually ripped.

Wars for the Great Plains

The Arapahos, like many of the Plains Indians, were great warriors. The Arapahos made war at one time or another with the Shoshones, Utes, Pawnees, Crows, Sioux, Comanches, and Kiowas (see entries for those tribes). By 1840, the Arapahos had made peace with the Sioux, Comanches, and Kiowas. Other 19th-century allies of the Arapahos were the Southern Cheyennes.

The Arapahos played a major role in the wars with whites for the Great Plains. The Northern Arapahos, along with the Northern Cheyennes, fought alongside the Sioux in most of their wars for the northern Plains. The Southern Arapahos fought along with the Southern Cheyennes in the wars for the central Plains. And the Southern Arapahos also fought as allies of the Comanches and Kiowas in some of their conflicts for the southern Plains. (To get an overall picture of the Plains wars, see the entries under "Sioux," "Cheyenne," and "Comanche.")

Two of the most famous Indian leaders in the Plains wars were Black Bear of the Northern Arapahos and Little Raven of the Southern Arapahos. At the start of the War for the Bozeman Trail, described in detail under the entry "Sioux," it was Black Bear's band that suffered the only major defeat at the hands of the whites, in 1865. Little Raven, famous for his grasp of legal issues and his oratorical abilities, proved a wily match for any negotiator the federal government could come up with.

By the Medicine Lodge Treaty of 1867, in which Little Raven served as a spokesman for his people, the Southern Arapahos were placed on a reservation in the Indian Territory along with the Southern Cheyennes. The Northern Arapahos resisted placement on a reservation longer than their southern

Arapaho painted hide shield

kinsmen. By the Fort Laramie Treaty of 1868, they were supposed to settle on the Pine Ridge Reservation in South Dakota with the Sioux, but they wanted their own hunting grounds. Then in 1876, they were supposed to settle in the Indian Territory with their southern kinsmen, but they insisted on staying in Wyoming. Finally, in 1878, the federal government pressured the Northern Shoshones, traditional enemies of the Arapahos, into accepting them on their Wind River Reservation (see "Shoshone").

As a very religious people who had lost their homeland and their traditional way of life, the Arapahos, especially those on the Wind River Reservation, became very involved with the Ghost Dance Religion that spread among the Plains tribes in the late 1880s. The man who founded the religion, Wovoka, was a member of the Paiute tribe. The brief uprising that resulted from the religion occurred among the Sioux. As a result, the Ghost Dance Religion is discussed in detail under the entries "Paiute" and "Sioux." But most of the Ghost Dance songs recorded by historians are from the Arapaho tribe. Here is an example:

Hey, my children, here is another pipe!
Now, I am going to holler on this earth.
Everything is in motion!

Many descendants of the Southern Arapahos still live in Oklahoma and earn a living through farming. Many descendants of the Northern Arapahos still live on the Wind River Reservation in Wyoming and earn a living by raising cattle.

Arawak

This book for the most part discusses Indians in the continental United States and Canada. Of course, there were and there still are many other Indian peoples throughout the Americas, each group with its own fascinating culture and history. One example is the people known as the Arawaks (pronounced *AH-ruh-wock* or *AH-ruh-wak*) who lived south of the North American mainland on the islands of the Caribbean. The Arawaks are important to the history of the rest of the Americas because of their contacts with Christopher Columbus.

The Arawaks lived in the West Indies, the archipelago, or chain of islands, stretching from the southern tip of Florida to the northern tip of South America. The West Indies, also called the Antilles, are now subdivided roughly north to south into: (1) the Bahama Islands; (2) the Greater Antilles, including Cuba, Jamaica, Haiti-Dominican Republic, and Puerto Rico; and (3) the Lesser Antilles, including the Leeward Islands, the Windward Islands, Barbados, and Trinidad-Tobago. These islands in the Caribbean Sea are called the West Indies because Christopher Columbus, the first European to explore them, was seeking a route to India at the time. He thought he had landed in the East Indies. And, of course, this is the same reason that he referred to the native peoples he encountered as "Indians," a name that has stuck with them through subsequent history.

Christopher Columbus is known as the "discoverer" of the Americas. However, since there were already millions of people living in the Western Hemisphere, the term is not really accurate. Moreover, it now is thought that the Vikings reached the Americas much earlier than Columbus did (see "Beothuk" and "Micmac"). Yet Christopher Columbus brought the Americas to the attention of the rest of the world and started the wave of European exploration and settlement of the "New World," thus changing the course of history for Europeans and Indians alike. In that sense, he "discovered" America. Columbus never reached North America proper, but other European explorers soon did.

On his initial trip across the Atlantic Ocean from Spain, Columbus first landed on a small island in the Bahama Group. The exact location of the first landfall has never been proven. Until recently, it was thought that Columbus first reached Watling Island (now San Salvador). Now some scholars believe that he and his men first touched soil on Samana Cay, 65 miles southeast of Watling Island. After a stopover of a few days, Columbus and his men sailed farther west, sighting Cuba and landing on Hispaniola (now Haiti and the Dominican Republic). He established a colony of men among the Arawaks of Hispaniola before returning to Spain. He later led three more expeditions to the Caribbean Sea, among the islands and along the coastline of Central and South America. Island-dwelling Arawaks, however, were the only Indians with whom he had extensive contacts.

The Arawaks lived on many different islands. They also had relatives—people of the same language family—living in Central and South America. Before whites came to the Americas, the Arawaks had migrated northward from South America onto the Caribbean islands. These Arawaks on the islands called themselves the Taino.

The West Indies have a tropical climate, warm all year with abundant rain. The Arawaks were farmers, as well as hunter-gatherers. Their most important crops were manioc, corn, potatoes, sweet potatoes, beans, peanuts, peppers, cotton, and tobacco. The manioc plant was grown for its roots, which were ground into a pulp to make a kind of bread (nowadays manioc is used to make tapioca pudding). The juice from grinding the roots was used as the stock for soup. The Arawaks also collected edible wild plants to supplement their diet.

The Arawaks hunted a variety of animals and birds. The main source of meat was the small furry mammal called the hutia. Hunters used clubs as well as spears, bows and arrows, and blowguns. Using torches and trained dogs, they also drove hutias into corrals. In addition to dogs, the Arawaks kept parrots as pets.

The Arawaks fished from dugout canoes, using spears, nets, and hooks and lines. They had an ingenious method of catching the large sea turtles. The Arawaks trained remoras, a kind of fish with sticky patches on their heads, to swim under turtles and attach their heads to them. Using a line attached to the remoras, the Indians then pulled the giant turtles to the surface.

The Arawaks needed little clothing in the mild Caribbean climate. Men and children usually went naked. Women wore aprons made from grass, leaves, or cotton. Both men and women wore necklaces, bracelets, earrings, and nose pendants, made from shell, bone, stone, or clay. They also twisted cotton into jewelry. Chiefs and nobles wore ornaments of gold and copper, hammered and beautifully shaped.

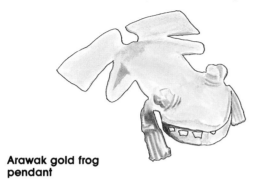

Arawak gold frog pendant

At ceremonies, Arawaks wore wooden or shell masks with feathers in their hair. They also painted their bodies, usually red or white.

The chiefs lived in rectangular houses with slanted roofs forming a peak. The houses of the common people had circular walls with cone-shaped roofs. Both types of houses were made from the stems of palm trees and cane plants. Palm leaves were sometimes used as thatch for roofs. The Arawaks slept in hammocks made from twisted cotton.

Each Arawak village had a chief, and he was very powerful, a supreme ruler who made decisions in times of both peace and war. The position was hereditary. The next-in-line to the chief was his oldest sister's oldest son. A class of nobility, made up of the chief's relatives, served as his counselors.

In general, the Arawaks were a peaceful people. They took up arms to defend themselves only when necessary, as when attacked by the fierce and cannibalistic Carib Indians. The Caribs, in fact, advancing northward from the South American mainland, had driven the Arawaks off most of the islands of the Lesser Antilles in the years before Columbus's arrival.

There were many trade contacts between the Carribbean Indians and the South and Central American Indians. The Arawaks also traded with North American peoples of the Florida coast (see "Timucua" and "Calusa"). Many Indians of the entire region had seaworthy dugouts of varying shapes and sizes. With the exchange of food, crafts, and raw materials, other cultural traits were passed. That is why, for instance, many of the people living in or around the Caribbean Sea and the Gulf of Mexico, such as the Arawaks, Aztecs, and Natchez (see "Aztec" and "Natchez"), had rigidly structured societies with supreme rulers and distinct social

classes, unlike the more democratic societies of other Indians to the north.

The meeting between Columbus's men and the Arawaks was momentous in more ways than one. Not only did it lead to the European exploration and settlement of the Americas, it also led to the diffusion of various cultural traits all over the world. For example, this was the first time Europeans had seen or heard of the tobacco plant. In fact, the word *tobacco* comes from the Spanish word *tabaco* which is derived from the Arawak word for "cigar." Moreover, the Europeans had never thought to use hammocks before encountering the Arawaks. Afterward, they started using these comfortable beds on their ships. This was also the first time the Europeans saw most of the plants cultivated by the Arawaks. Some of these, such as corn and potatoes, would eventually become food staples all over the world.

The peaceful Arawaks treated the Spanish well, sharing their food and knowledge with them. They also helped rescue some of Columbus's men during a shipwreck off Hispaniola. But the Spanish treated the Indians with arrogance. Columbus forced some Arawaks from Watling Island to accompany him on the rest of his first journey. When the colonists left behind by Columbus on Hispaniola treated the Indians cruelly, forcing them to help look for gold, the normally peaceful Arawaks rose up in rebellion, killing all the outsiders.

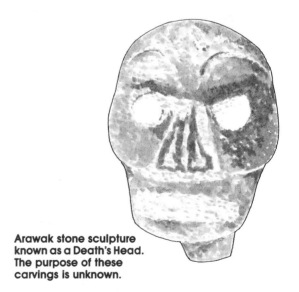

Arawak stone sculpture known as a Death's Head. The purpose of these carvings is unknown.

On his second voyage, Columbus established another colony on the coast of Hispaniola. The Spanish now treated the Indians with total contempt, forcing them to work for the Europeans. Columbus also ordered the Arawaks to bring the colonists gold on a regular basis.

This pattern of cruelty continued in Spanish and Indian relations. Columbus eventually lost favor with the King and Queen of Spain and never realized many of his ambitions. When he died in Europe, he was a forgotten man. But the Spanish who followed him to the Americas further exploited the Indians, forcing them to work in mines and on farms. They also made the native peoples give up their traditional religions to practice Catholicism. The Spanish pushed on into Mexico, Florida, and other parts of the Americas to expand their empire (see "Aztec").

As for the Indians of the Caribbean Islands, they gradually died out. Many were struck down by European diseases. Others died from starvation because the Spanish overworked them and underfed them. Some even committed suicide out of despair over the loss of their freedom. Mothers sometimes killed their newborn sons rather than see them grow up as slaves. Those who remained when the Spanish began treating the Indians better lost their Indian identity through intermarriage with the colonists.

Today, no pure Arawaks—the Indians who were first called Indians—live in the West Indies. The only surviving people of Arawakan lineage are descended from South American ancestors. They live along the Amazon River in Brazil.

Arctic Peoples

The region known as the Arctic Culture Area extends more than 5,000 miles, all the way from the Aleutian Islands in Alaska to Labrador in Canada. Although most of it lies in northern Alaska and northern Canada, the culture area also includes territory in Siberia (part of the USSR) to the west, as well as in Greenland (part of the kingdom of Denmark) to the east. The Arctic Culture Area touches upon three oceans—the Pacific, the Arctic, and the Atlantic.

The climate of the Arctic is fierce. Winters are long and bitterly cold, with few hours of sunlight. In the northernmost latitudes of the Arctic, beyond the

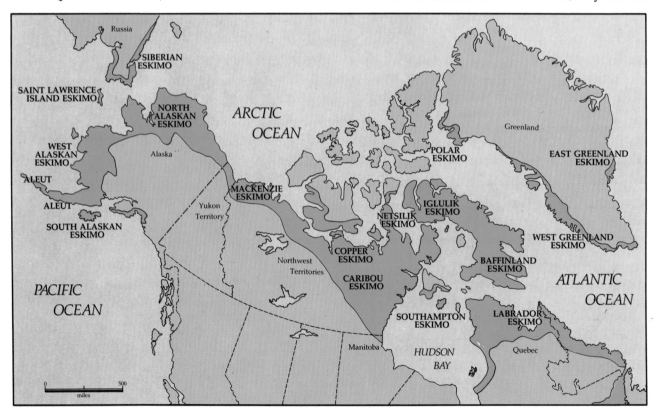

The Arctic Culture Area, showing the approximate locations of Eskimo and Aleut bands—circa 1500, before displacement by whites (with modern boundaries)

Arctic Circle, the sun never rises above the horizon for part of the winter, resulting in the phenomenon known as midnight sun. Likewise, for part of the summer, the sun never sets below the horizon.

During the long winter, the land is covered by ice. The subsoil never thaws, remaining frozen all year round in a state known as permafrost. When the surface ice thaws during the short summer, the water does not drain, but forms numerous lakes and ponds along with mud and rising fog.

The Arctic Ocean freezes over in the winter, then breaks up into drift ice during the summer thaw. The cold Arctic has little precipitation. It is actually a frozen desert. Arctic blizzards are not characterized by huge amounts of snowfall. Rather, gale-force winds stir up what surface snow already exists, forming snowdrifts.

The Arctic's land environment is called tundra. Because of the cold climate and permafrost, the tundra is treeless. Little vegetation grows other than mosses, lichens, and stunted shrubs. Most of the tundra consists of rolling plains. In the western part, there are some mountains, the northern reaches of the Rockies.

Wildlife in the Arctic includes sea mammals, such as whales, walruses, seals, and sea lions; saltwater and freshwater fish; seagulls and other birds; polar bears; and caribou. These along with other game that appear in certain locations on the tundra in summertime, such as rabbits, rodents, and owls, provided subsistence for Arctic peoples, who of course could not practice farm-ing on the cold and barren tundra. Arctic peoples migrated when necessary to obtain food.

The inhabitants of the Arctic came later to North America than did other native peoples. They came from Siberia in boats, starting about 3000 B.C., whereas the other native peoples traveled over the Bering Strait land bridge. The Arctic peoples are generally shorter and broader than other Native North Americans, with rounder faces, lighter skin, and epicanthic eye folds, the small fold of skin covering the inner corner of the eyes that is typical of Asian peoples. As a result, Arctic peoples are not generally referred to as *Indians*. One sees instead phrases such as *native peoples* and *Arctic peoples*.

There were two distinct groups of Arctic peoples: Eskimo and Aleut. Many contemporary Eskimos prefer to be called by their native name, *Inuit*, which means "the people," rather than *Eskimo*, which was originally applied to them by Algonquian Indians and which means "eaters of raw meat."

The Eskimos and Aleuts shared many cultural traits. But there were differences, too. For instance, Aleuts did not construct snow houses (igloos), as many Eskimo peoples did.

The various subdivisions of the Eskimos and Aleuts, along with their respective cultures and histories, are discussed in detail under the entries "Eskimo (Inuit)" and "Aleut."

Arikara

The Arikaras are sometimes called the Arikarees, or simply the Rees. Their name (pronounced *uh-RICK-uh-ruh*) is thought to mean "horns," in reference to the ancient custom of wearing two upright bones in their hair. The Arikaras settled farther north than all the other Caddoan-speaking tribes, splitting off from the Pawnees (see "Pawnee"). They lived along the banks of the upper Missouri River in what is now North Dakota near the South Dakota border. They lived to the south of two Siouan-speaking tribes, the Hidatsas and Mandans, with whom they have been associated throughout their history (see "Hidatsa" and "Mandan").

The Arikaras, like the Hidatsas and Mandans, were villagers and farmers. It is thought that it was they who originally brought agricultural skills to other tribes of the upper Missouri River. Unlike their Caddoan kinsmen to the south, the Arikaras did not live in grass huts. Rather, they built earthlodges on bluffs overlooking the river. They planted fields nearby.

The Arikaras hunted buffalo to supplement their diet. After they gained horses in the 1700s, they ranged even farther from their villages in pursuit of the great herds. During their hunting trips, they lived in tepees. They had hunting grounds in what is now eastern Montana as well as in the Dakotas. The Arikaras are considered part of the Great Plains Culture Area (see "Plains Indians"). But they were not as nomadic as other Plains tribes (see "Prairie Indians").

The Arikaras shared many customs with the Mandans, a tribe more thoroughly documented than either the Arikaras or the Hidatsas. Customs of all three tribes were passed from one to another.

Sometimes customs were even bought and sold. For example, one tribe would trade horses, tools, and ornaments for the right to use a certain dance. One dance of the Arikaras that spread to the other tribes was known as the Hot Dance. For the occasion, tribal members would build a large fire, place a kettle of meat cooking in water over it, and spread hot coals on the ground. Young braves, naked and barefoot, with feet and hands painted red, would dance on the coals to prove their courage. Then the braves would dip their hands in the scalding water, grab the meat, and eat it.

An Arikara Indian in meditation

Because of their location on the Missouri River, the villages of the Arikaras, like those of the Mandans and Hidatsas, became important centers of commerce. Other Plains peoples often traveled to the villages to trade buffalo meat and robes, as well as horses, for farm products. French and English traders also stopped regularly at the river villages to exchange guns and other European trade goods for furs.

After the Louisiana Purchase by the United States in 1803, the federal government sponsored the Lewis and Clark Expedition up the Missouri River to explore the new American holdings. Meriwether Lewis and William Clark encountered the Arikaras on the Missouri between the Grand and Cannonball rivers and wrote about them in their journals.

In 1823, after Arikara warriors had attacked an American trading party and killed 13 people, most of the Arikaras, fearing revenge by the whites, hid out for two years with the Pawnees in what is now Nebraska. On returning to the upper Missouri, the Arikaras settled farther north. By 1851, they had villages as far north as the mouth of the Heart River. Disease, brought to them by white traders, greatly reduced their numbers over the years. They suffered through the great smallpox epidemic of 1837 which practically wiped out the neighboring Mandans.

In 1862, the Arikaras moved to Fort Berthold, North Dakota. The federal government established a permanent reservation there for the Arikaras, Hidatsas, and Mandans in 1871, which the tribes still share today. The Three Affiliated Tribes have a museum at New Town which gives visitors a fascinating glimpse of upper-Missouri Indian history and culture.

Assiniboine

The Assiniboines spoke a Siouan dialect. Their name, pronounced *uh-SIN-uh-boin*, is from the Algonquian language and means "those who cook with stones." This refers to stone-boiling, the practice of heating stones directly in a fire then placing them in water to make it boil for cooking. British explorers and traders also used the name Stoney for the tribe.

The Assiniboines were once part of the Yanktonai Sioux, living as one people with them in the Lake Superior region of what is now northern Minnesota and southwestern Ontario (see "Sioux"). The Assiniboines split off from the Sioux probably in the 1600s. They migrated westward onto the northern

Plains, first settling west of Lake Winnipeg in what is now the province of Manitoba. Some bands later moved farther west to the banks of the Assiniboin and Saskatchewan rivers in what is now Saskatchewan. (The southern part of Saskatchewan was once known as Assiniboia.) The Assiniboines also lived at times in territory that is now Montana and North Dakota.

By the time whites encountered them, the Assiniboines did not live in permanent villages. Rather, they were nomadic hunter-gatherers, moving their tepees when necessary to find more food. After they acquired horses through trade with other Indians, they ranged over greater expanses in search of buffalo and wild plant foods. Some of the more northerly bands pursued moose, bear, beaver, and porcupine in the northern evergreen forests bordering the Plains. The Assiniboines sometimes traded their meat and pelts with farming tribes for agricultural products. After white traders entered their domain, the Assiniboines also bartered their furs with both the French and English in exchange for guns and other European trade goods.

Because of their typical Plains way of life, the Assiniboines are classified as part of the Great Plains Culture Area (see "Plains Indians"). Like other tribes who became Plains hunters, the Assiniboines gave up making pottery, which was too heavy and fragile on the trail. The Assiniboines instead began boiling their water in buffalo-hide bags. The Sun-god and Thunder-god were the most important manifestations of the Great Spirit for the Assiniboines. Like many Plains tribes, they participated in the Sun Dance. They also took guidance from personal visions, a practice known as the Vision Quest.

For part of their history, the Assiniboines were allied with the Plains Crees against the Blackfeet and the Sioux. In a well-known incident, traditional tribal enemies became lifelong friends. In 1857, a group of Sioux warriors attacked a party of Assiniboines. Among the Sioux was Sitting Bull, who would later become one of the most famous of Indian leaders in the wars against the whites for the Plains. There was an 11-year-old boy among the Assiniboines named Jumping Bull. The young boy did not flee from the attacking Sioux but fought valiantly with his child-sized bow. When Sioux warriors threatened to kill Jumping Bull, Sitting Bull ran in front of the youth and proclaimed, "This boy is too brave to die! I take him as

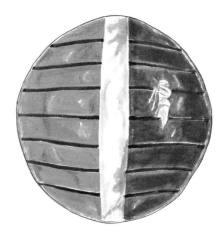

Assiniboine shield with attached medicine bundle

my brother." Sitting Bull and Jumping Bull were great friends from that time on, like brothers. Jumping Bull died along with Sitting Bull in 1890, trying to defend him (see "Sioux").

Some Assiniboines worked as scouts for the whites. In 1885, Assiniboine scouts helped the Canadian North West Field Force track down renegade Crees who were participating in the Second Riel Rebellion (see "Cree" and "Metis").

In the 1870s, different bands of Assiniboines were settled on reservations on different sides of the border in both the United States and Canada. In Montana, the Assiniboines now share the Fort Belknap Reservation with the Gros Ventres, and the Fort Peck Reservation with the Sioux. In Saskatchewan, the Assiniboines share one piece of land with the Sioux, and another with the Crees and Ojibways (Chippewas). A third band of Assiniboines holds the rights to two other tracts in Saskatchewan.

Athapascan

The name *Athapascan*, pronounced *ath-uh-PAS-kun* and sometimes spelled *Athabascan*, refers to a family of Indian languages. Athapascan was one of the most widespread language families in North America. Many different tribes spoke Athapascan dialects in territory now comprising parts of Alaska, Arizona, California, New Mexico, Oregon, Texas, western Canada, and northern Mexico.

Nevertheless, as is the case with the Algonquian language family, Athapascan is commonly used to refer to a group of people as if it were a tribal name. And, just as the name *Algonquian* is usually used to

group together eastern Algonquians to the exclusion of western Algonquians (see "Algonquian"), *Athapascan* is used to group together northern Athapascans as separate from the southern Athapascans.

The southern Athapascans broke off from the other Athapascans and migrated southward before Europeans came to North America, probably in the 9th and 11th centuries. They came to be known as Apaches and Navajos and played an important part in the history of the American Southwest (see "Apache"; "Navajo"; and "Southwest Indians").

Other Athapascans dispersed from the original group in the north and ended up in the midst of peoples speaking different languages. For example, the Sarcees lived among northern Plains people and are usually grouped in the Great Plains Culture Area (see "Sarcee" and "Plains Indians"). The Hoopas migrated down the Pacific Coast and settled in California (see "Hoopa" and "California Indians"). And the Clatskanies settled in Oregon and are classified in the Northwest Coast Culture Area (see "Northwest Indians").

The northern Athapascans, the Indians to whom the name is usually applied, are categorized as part of the Subarctic Culture Area (see "Subarctic Indians"). Subarctic refers to the territory of the taiga, or the great Northern Forest of mainly spruce and fir trees, stretching all the way across North America. It lies to the south of the tundra of the Arctic Culture Area (see "Arctic Peoples"). The Athapascans lived in the western part of the Subarctic.

The Subarctic Athapascans did not make up unified tribes. Rather, they lived and traveled for the most part in small bands of families or extended families, including in-laws. Yet, by studying the various locations, languages, and lifeways of the various bands, scholars have been able to group the Athapascans into tribes. Because of limitations of space, most of the distinct Athapascan groups do not have separate entries in this book, although each deserves further in-depth study.

The northern Athapascans were nomadic hunter-gatherers who did not farm. For many of them, the caribou was a staple food and source of materials for clothing, dwellings, and babiche (leather thongs used as bindings). The quest for food in the cold northern environment was all-consuming. Many of the Athapascans lived in portable skin tents, smaller versions of the Plains tepees. Many domesticated dogs and depended on them for hunting and hauling. Many of them used snowshoes and toboggans in the winter. Many were important to French and British fur trading in the late 1700s and early 1800s.

But there were many cultural distinctions and exceptions among the various tribes. The northern Athapascans can be further broken down into three general groups:

Canadian Rocky Athapascans: These tribes lived in or near the northern part of the Rocky Mountains. They include the Carrier (at the headwaters of the Fraser River); Chilcotin (Chilcotin River); Kaska or Nahani (Liard and Nahani rivers); Sekani (Finlay, Parsnip, and upper Peace rivers); Mountain (mountains west of Mackenzie River); Tagish (Tagish and Marsh lakes); Tahltan (upper Stikine River); Tsetsaut (Iskut and White rivers); and Tutchone (Pelly and Stewart rivers).

Lake Athapascans: These tribes lived near the Great Slave and Great Bear lakes. They include Beaver (Peace River); Chipewyan (between Great Slave Lake and Churchill River); Dogrib (between Great Slave and Great Bear lakes); Hare (northwest of Great Bear Lake along lower Mackenzie River); Slave (between Mackenzie River and Great Slave Lake); and Yellowknife (between Coppermine River and Great Slave Lake).

Alaskan Athapascans: These tribes lived in territory now in Alaska, plus neighboring parts of Canada. They include Ahtena (Copper River); Han (upper Yukon River); Ingalik (Anvik and Kuskokwim rivers); Koyukon (Yukon River); Kutchin (Yukon River to Mackenzie River); Nabesna (Nabesna and Chisana rivers); Tanaina (Cook Inlet); and Tanana (Tanana River).

In this book, the culture and history of three northern Athapascan tribes, one from each group, are discussed in detail: Carrier, Chipewyan, and Kutchin (see "Carrier"; "Chipewyan"; and "Kutchin").

Aztec

The Aztecs (pronounced *AZ-tec*), unlike most Native American peoples discussed in this book, call up images of great cities, tall pyramids, golden objects, feathered priests, and human sacrifices. The culture of the Aztecs is often compared to that of ancient Rome, as the Mayas' is to ancient Greece. Like the Romans, the Aztecs were a warlike people who founded a great empire and who drew on knowledge from other peoples to further their civilization.

The Aztecs were influenced especially by the Toltecs before them and by the Mayas. These various peoples owed much to the Olmecs, the founders of the first great Mesoamerican civilization. Mesoamerica is the name given by scholars to an Indian culture area in parts of Mexico and elsewhere in Central America where Native American society was centralized and highly organized (see "Olmec"; "Toltec"; and "Maya").

The Olmecs reached their cultural peak in what is called the Preclassic period in Mesoamerica, from about 1000 B.C. to A.D. 300. The Mayas flourished during the so-called Classic period, from about A.D. 300 to 900. The Postclassic period is defined as from A.D. 900 to 1500. The Toltecs were dominant from about 900 to about 1200. Then the Aztecs were at their height from about 1200 to the time of the Spanish arrival in their homeland, about 1500.

Like the Toltecs, the Aztecs were originally one of the Chichimec tribes, living as nomadic hunters. Known as Mexicas, they spoke the Nahuatl dialect of the Uto-Aztecan language family. They migrated into the Valley of Mexico from the highlands to the north, arriving in that region about 1168.

At the time of the Mexicas' arrival, the Toltec Empire was in a state of decay. The Mexicas competed with a number of other peoples for territory. Their warriors, armed with powerful bows and long arrows—weapons passed to Mesoamerica from Indians to the north—found work as mercenaries in the armies of local cities. Finally, in 1325, they founded two villages of their own on swampy islets in Lake Texcoco—Tenochtitlan and Tlatelolco.

The Aztec Empire

Eventually the inhabitants of Tenochtitlan, who called themselves Tenochas, conquered Tlatelolco. Tenochtitlan rapidly expanded. The Tenochas actually created new land to farm and build on by anchoring wicker baskets to Lake Texcoco's shallow bottom and piling silt and plant matter on top of them, thus making *chinampas*, artificial islands.

The Tenochas formed an alliance with a people called the Alcohuas against other peoples of central Mexico. They took a new name too. They began to call themselves Aztec after Aztlan, their legendary homeland.

In the following years, Tenochtitlan grew on top of the *chinampas* to a city of thousands of stone buildings, interconnected by many canals, with about 300,000 inhabitants. This ancient city is the site of present-day Mexico City, one of the largest cities in the world.

The Aztecs launched many military campaigns against surrounding peoples, from the Gulf of Mexico to the Pacific Ocean. Aztec armies were well organized and well armed. They used bows and arrows, darts and dart throwers, clubs, maces, and swords with blades of volcanic glass. Thick, quilted cotton was used to make shields as well as armor. Through conquest, the Aztec Empire came to comprise five million people.

The Aztecs conquered their neighbors for economic purposes. They imposed taxes on their subjects, taking raw materials from them (such as gold; silver; copper; jade, turquoise; obsidian, or black volcanic glass; and pearls) as well as food products (such as corn; beans; squash; tomatoes; potatoes; chili peppers; mangoes; papayas; avocadoes; and cacao, or chocolate). They also demanded cotton for clothing and for armor, and domesticated animals, such as dogs and turkeys, for meat.

Religion

Through warfare the Aztecs obtained captives for human sacrifice. In their religion, the letting of human blood was believed to appease the gods. There were many different deities to which to offer sacrifice. An important god for the Aztecs was Quetzalcoatl, the Great Plumed Serpent, who was central to the religions of the earlier Mesoamerican civilizations as

Aztec sacrificial knife

well. But Quetzalcoatl was a benign figure who, according to tradition, showed mercy. It was the war god Huitzilopochtli who demanded the most blood. Priests sacrificed thousands of prisoners to Huitzilopochtli in the temples at the top of the massive stone pyramids. Earlier Mesoamerican civilizations practiced human sacrifice, but the Aztecs carried out their bloody rituals on the largest scale.

Social Structure

In Aztec society, the priests had a great deal of influence. They shared the power with noblemen who each ruled a sector of the city. An emperor, or Chief of Men, was the most powerful ruler of all. The noblemen selected him from among the royalty. After the emperor, noblemen, and priests, the next most influential social classes were the war chiefs—Eagle Knights and Jaguar Knights—and the wealthy merchants. Beneath them were common soldiers, craftsmen, and farmers. Still lower on the social scale were a group of unskilled laborers who owned no land. And below them were the slaves.

Clothing

Aztec clothing revealed social status. The Chief of Men wore tunics of coyote fur, white duck feathers and feathers from other birds, and dyed cotton. He also wore gold, silver, and jade jewelry, including a nose ornament made from turquoise. He was the only person in Aztec society who could wear turquoise jewelry or turquoise-colored clothing. The noblemen also wore brightly colored cloaks, plus a variety of jewelry, including necklaces, earrings, armbands, and nose

Aztec rhythm instrument made from a human bone

and lip ornaments. The merchants wore white cotton cloaks, sometimes decorated with designs. Eagle Knights wore feathered outfits and helmets in the shape of eagle heads. Jaguar Knights dressed in jaguar skins, including the heads of the animals. Common soldiers wore breechcloths and knee-length shirts. They shaved their heads except for a scalplock in back, but they were allowed to grow their hair long and wear decorated tunics if they had taken prisoners in battle. For footwear, soldiers and the higher social classes had sandals made of leather or woven from plant matter. Workers and farmers went barefoot. Nor were they permitted to dress so colorfully. These men wore only breechcloths of woven plant leaves, and the women wore plain white shirts and ankle-length skirts.

Houses

Likewise, the types of houses Aztecs lived in were determined by social class. The Chief of Men and the wealthiest noblemen had two-story, multi-roomed palaces, with stone walls and log and plaster roofs. Less wealthy noblemen and merchants had one-story houses. Some of the rich planted gardens on the flat roofs. Commoners lived in small huts, made from clay bricks or from pole frames and plant stems packed with clay, usually with only one room.

Food

Much of the modern Mexican diet, including tortillas and tamales, came from the Aztecs. Corn and beans provided the basic Aztec diet, as they still do in that part of the world. The Aztec upper classes had a much more varied diet, with other foods such as meat, fruits, tomatoes, chili peppers, and a beverage made from chocolate, vanilla, and honey. The Aztecs also made beer and wine from different plants. Alcoholic beverages were used in rituals and in medication and prophecy, but public intoxication was frowned upon. In some instances, for both nobles and commoners, drunken behavior in public was punished by death.

Writing

The Aztecs carried on the Mesoamerican tradition of a form of writing called hieroglyphics. Most hieroglyphics were pictures of the objects they represented, but some represented sounds. The Aztecs used their writing to record history, geography, religion, poetry, public events, and calendars. But the Aztecs did not develop writing to the same degree as the Mayas.

The Coming of the Spanish

When the Spanish reached the mainland of the Americas, after having explored the Caribbean islands (see "Arawak"), the Aztec Empire was still intact. The Spanish explored the Panama region in Central America and the Yucatan Peninsula in the early 1500s. During these expeditions, they heard of the powerful Aztec Empire to the north, with a great city of towering pyramids, filled with gold and other riches, rising out of Lake Texcoco. In 1519, Hernando Cortes landed with about 400 soldiers and marched toward the city of Tenochtitlan.

With this small army of men, Cortes managed to conquer the huge armies of the Aztecs. How did he accomplish this remarkable feat? There were various reasons. First of all, he managed to gain as allies other Mesoamerican peoples who wanted to be free of Aztec rule—peoples such as the Totonacs, Tlaxcalans, and Cholulans (from the ancient city of Cholula, site of the largest structure in the Americas, the Great Pyramid, 180 feet high and covering 25 acres). In order to accomplish these alliances, Cortes played various factions against one another. He also had the help of a talented Mayan woman, originally a slave, named Malinal, called Lady Marina by the Spanish, who served as a translator and arbitrator among the different peoples. Moreover, the conquistadors were armed with guns, which frightened the Indians. Nor had the Indians ever seen horses.

Still another factor played an important part in the Spanish conquest of the Aztecs. Aztec legends told of the return of the god Quetzalcoatl. The Aztecs thought that the white-skinned Cortes might be this god. The Aztec emperor Moctezuma was indecisive in his actions when faced with this possibility. He lost his life during the period of political maneuvering, at the hands of either the Spanish or some Aztecs who resented his indecisiveness. By the time the Aztecs mounted a sizable defense against the invaders, the Spanish had thousands of Indian allies. The Spanish conquest, after fierce fighting in the streets of Tenochtitlan, was complete by 1521.

The Spanish worked to eradicate all traces of Aztec civilization. They destroyed temples and pyramids; they melted down sculptured objects into basic metals to be shipped back to Spain; they burned Aztec books. They also forced the Aztecs to work for them as slaves. New Spain (Mexico) became the base from which the Spanish sent conquistadors northward to explore what is now the American Southwest and California.

Some Spanish eventually intermarried with Aztec survivors. As a result, there is some Aztec blood in modern-day Mexicans. The Aztec language, Nahuatl, has also survived among some of the peasants living in the small villages surrounding Mexico City.

Bannock

The Bannocks (pronounced *BAN-uck*) are considered an offshoot of the Paiute tribe. Both peoples spoke a dialect of the Uto-Aztecan family, as did the Utes and Shoshones. All these tribes are classified by scholars as being in the Great Basin Culture Area and have at times been referred to as Digger Indians because they foraged and dug for anything edible—wild plants, rodents, reptiles, insects—in their harsh mountain and desert environment (see "Great Basin Indians"; "Paiute"; "Ute"; and "Shoshone"). They also had a staple food in common with the tribes to their north, on the Columbia Plateau—the roots of the camas plant (see "Plateau Indians").

The nomadic Bannocks occupied territory that has since become southeastern Idaho and western Wyoming. After they acquired horses in the early 1700s, they ranged over a wider area into parts of Colorado, Utah, Montana, and Oregon. Their way of life came to resemble that of the Plains Indians, including buffalo-hunting and the use of tepees (see "Plains Indians").

A Mountain Man by the name of Jim Bridger opened up trade relations with the Bannocks in 1829. Yet in the following years, Bannock warriors preyed on migrants and miners traveling through their territory on the Oregon Trail. In 1869, after the Civil War, when more federal troops could be sent west to build new forts and to pacify the Indians, the government established the Fort Hall Reservation for the Bannocks and Northern Shoshones.

Bannock parents with child

The Bannocks resisted reservation life. Their food rations on the reservation were meager, and the Indians continued to wander over a wide expanse of territory in search of the foods they had hunted and gathered for generations. As more and more whites settled in the region, they disrupted these traditional food staples of the Bannocks. White hunters were killing the buffalo wholesale on the Plains to the east. And hogs belonging to white ranchers were destroying the camas plants near Fort Boise, Idaho. The Bannocks, along with their neighbors, the Northern Paiutes, revolted.

The Bannock War occurred in 1878. A Bannock warrior wounded two whites, who reported the incident to the army. Meanwhile, about 200 Bannock and Northern Paiute warriors gathered under a Bannock chief named Buffalo Horn. This war party clashed with a volunteer patrol in June. When Buffalo Horn was killed, the Indians headed westward into Oregon to regroup at Steens Mountain with Paiutes from the Malheur Reservation. Two Paiutes became the new leaders: a chief named Egan and a medicine man named Oytes.

Regular army troops rode out of Fort Boise in pursuit. They were under the command of General Oliver O. Howard, who had tracked down the Nez Perces during their uprising the year before (see "Nez Perce"). The soldiers caught up with the Indians at Birch Creek on July 8 and dislodged them from steep bluffs. Warriors under Chief Egan tried to hide out on the Umatilla Reservation. The Umatillas sided with the whites, however. They killed Egan and led soldiers to his men. Oytes managed to elude capture until August, but eventually turned himself in. A party of

Bannocks escaped eastward to Wyoming, but they were captured in September.

After the short-lived Bannock War, the Malheur Reservation was closed. The Paiutes were settled among the Yakimas on their reservation in the state of Washington. The Bannocks were held prisoners at military posts for a time but were finally permitted to return to their reservation in Idaho.

That same year, 1878, another Indian war broke out in Idaho. This was the Sheepeater War. The Sheepeaters were Bannocks and Shoshones who had migrated northward into the Salmon River Mountains of central Idaho and hunted mountain sheep as their main food. They too began raiding settlers who were crowding their homeland. There were not many of them, perhaps only 50, but they proved a stubborn and wily enemy for the army in the rugged highlands. They routed one army patrol and eluded another. But the army wore them down with continuous tracking, and the Sheepeaters surrendered in October. They were placed on the Fort Hall Reservation with their Bannock and Shoshone kinsmen.

The Native Americans presently on the Fort Hall Reservation hold many traditional festivals every year, including a week-long celebration in August, several Sun Dances, and an all-Indian rodeo.

Beothuk

The ancient Beothuk language has some word roots in common with the Algonquian language. As a result, the Beothuks (pronounced *BAY-uh-thuk*) were originally classified as Algonquians. But the two languages differ in vocabulary to such a degree that now the Beothuk language is classified alone as Beothukan, and the Beothuks are considered a distinct people with different ancestors from the Algonquians (see "Algonquian").

That makes the Beothuks, along with the Eskimos, the only native people along the Atlantic Coast of Canada and the northeastern United States who did not speak an Algonquian dialect (see "Subarctic Indians" and "Northeast Indians"). Perhaps one reason the Beothuks were a distinct group with their own language was that they lived on an island—the large island of Newfoundland.

Because of their location at the northeastern corner of North America, the Beothuks had early contacts with many explorers. It is theorized that either the Beothuks or the Micmacs were the Indians the Vikings supposedly encountered in the year 1000 (see

"Micmac"). In their writings, the Vikings called the natives *Skraelings*. It is certain that John Cabot, sailing in the pay of England, encountered the Beothuks in 1497; Giovanni da Verrazano, sailing in the pay of France, met up with them in 1523; and Jacques Cartier, also sailing for France, made contact with them in 1534.

After these early contacts, the Beothuks associated with many more Europeans because fishermen, especially the French, frequented their shores. A problem arose between the two peoples when the Beothuks stole from the fishermen. In Beothuk culture, ownership of possessions was not so important, and petty thievery was allowed. The French, however, became irritated by the loss of equipment and turned on the Indians. Not only did they use their own guns in attacks on the unfortunate Beothuks, but they also armed the Micmacs and placed a bounty on Beothuk scalps.

By the early 1700s, the Beothuks were practically extinct. Those who survived did so by hiding out among other Indians, mostly the Naskapis. A century later,

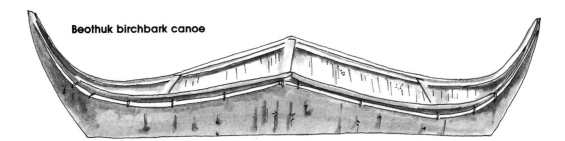

Beothuk birchbark canoe

the Beothic Society for the Civilization of the Native Savages combed the island for Beothuk descendants but did not find any. The last Beothuk on record, Nancy Shawanahdit, a captive at St. Johns, Newfoundland, died in 1829.

The Beothuks were different from other Indians in that they lived a lifestyle similar to both Algonquians and Eskimos. Like the Algonquians, they slept in birchbark wigwams and cooked in birchbark containers. They also made birchbark canoes, but with an original design. The gunwales, or sides, curved up not just at the ends, but also in the middle, like two sets of crescent moons. In the winter, the Beothuks lived like Subarctic Algonquians, staying in the inland forests and hunting land mammals. In the summer, however, they traveled to the ocean to hunt sea mammals, using Eskimo-style weapons and methods.

The Beothuks had other cultural traits unlike those of either the Algonquians or the Eskimos. For example, in caves and rock shelters where the Beothuks buried their dead long ago, archaeologists have found uniquely carved bone ornaments.

The Beothuks had a custom in which they painted their bodies and clothing with red ocher, a mineral found in the soil. They probably did this for practical as well as religious reasons, because the substance helped keep insects away. It is theorized that Native Americans were first called "redskins" because of this practice, and not because of the color of their skin, as is commonly believed.

Blackfoot

The powerful Blackfoot Confederacy controlled a huge expanse of the northeastern Plains, from the North Saskatchewan River in what is now Alberta all the way to the upper Missouri River in Montana, flanked on the west by the Rocky Mountains. Members of the Blackfoot Confederacy included the Blackfoot band, the Blood band, and the Piegan band, plus the Gros Ventres and Sarcees. The first three bands appear in books together as the Blackfeet because they all dyed their moccasins black. These three tribes were related, Algonquian-speaking peoples, separated by geography: the Blackfoot proper, or *Siksika*, lived the farthest north; then the Bloods, or *Kainah*, so named because they painted their bodies with red clay; then the Piegans, or *Pikuni*, meaning "poorly dressed," to the south. The Gros Ventres lived to the northwest of the three Blackfoot bands; and the Sarcees lived to their southeast (see "Gros Ventre" and "Sarcee").

The Blackfeet probably migrated to their homeland from the northeast, after separating from other Algon-quians. They adapted to the nomadic life on the open grasslands, with buffalo meat as their staple food. They hunted other game, including deer, elk, and mountain sheep, but little fowl or fish. They also gathered wild plants, such as berries and chokecherries. But they called buffalo their "real food." They moved their camps of hide tepees to new hunting grounds when necessary, but in the cold

Blackfoot parfleche (rawhide storage bag)

Blackfoot couple with horse and travois

northern winters, the Blackfeet generally stayed in one place. They grew only one crop, tobacco. About 1740, the tribe obtained horses and guns. They rapidly became accomplished horsemen and marksmen. The Blackfeet are placed by scholars in the Great Plains Culture Area (see "Plains Indians").

The Blackfeet were known for their beautiful craftwork—tepees, riding equipment, clothes, tools, and weapons. They had unique warbonnets, the feathers of which stood straight up. They practiced the

Blackfoot headdress with upright feathers

Sun Dance, as did other Plains tribes, but women participated in the Blackfeet version. The women also had a powerful society known as *Motokik*. It was thought that their blessing of a child would give that child good fortune his whole life. The Vision Quest, another Plains custom, was critical in the passage from childhood to adulthood. Blackfoot men were organized into warrior societies based on age, called the *Ikunuhkats*, or All Comrades.

The Blackfeet were enemies of the Crows and Sioux on the Plains; and the Shoshones, Flatheads, and Kootenais in the mountain country to their west. Blackfeet war parties would ride hundreds of miles on raids. A boy going on his first war party was given a silly or derogatory name. But after he had stolen his first horse, or killed an enemy, he was given a name of which he could be proud.

The Blackfeet preyed on American explorers, traders, miners, and settlers who traveled the Oregon

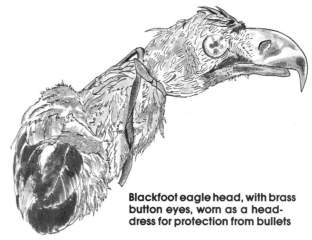

Blackfoot eagle head, with brass button eyes, worn as a headdress for protection from bullets

and Bozeman trails. Their hostility toward whites started when one of their braves was killed in a horse-stealing raid on the Lewis and Clark Expedition in 1804. The Blackfoot name, probably more than any other, aroused fear in the Mountain Men. In 1867, the Blackfeet killed the man after whom the Bozeman Trail, the cutoff from the Oregon Trail, is named—John Bozeman. The Blackfeet were on better terms with the British than with the Americans. Canadian traders encouraged Blackfoot warriors to kill American traders to stop their northward advance.

Because they were so warlike, the Blackfeet slowed down the opening of both the Canadian West and the American West. Smallpox epidemics in 1836, 1845, 1857, and 1869-70, along with the decline of the buffalo herds, did more to weaken the Blackfoot Confederacy than Canadian or U.S. armies did. One incident, however, proved especially costly to the Blackfeet. In 1870, U.S. soldiers under the command of Colonel E. M. Baker, who were tracking several braves for killing a white settler, attacked the Blackfoot winter camp of chiefs Heavy Runner and Red Horn on the Marias River in Montana. They killed 173 men, women, and children and took 140 more Blackfeet prisoner.

The Blackfeet signed treaties with the United States in 1855 and Canada in 1877. They ceded much of their land in the 1870s and were settled on reservations on both sides of the U.S.-Canadian border in the 1880s. The parcels they managed to keep were part of their ancestral homeland.

Blackfoot toy drum (modern)

The Blackfeet now hold a reservation in Montana. This group is made up mostly of South Piegans. Three bands—the North Blackfoot, Blood, and North Piegan—have rights to lands in Alberta. The Montana tribal headquarters is located in the town of Browning, the gateway to the beautiful Glacier National Park. The Museum of the Plains Indian is also located at Browning.

A quote by a dying Blackfoot brave by the name of Crowfoot in 1890 beautifully expresses the Native American attitude toward nature: "What is life? It is the flash of a firefly in the night. It is the breath of a buffalo in the winter time. It is the little shadow which runs across the grass and loses itself on the sunset."

Caddo

The Caddos were really many different tribes that lived in territory stretching from the Red River Valley, in what is now Louisiana, to the Brazos River Valley in Texas, including parts of Arkansas. They included tribes of the Natchitoches Confederacy in Louisiana; tribes of the Hasinai Confederacy in Texas; and tribes of the Caddodacho Confederacy in Texas and Arkansas, the group that gave the Caddos their name (pronounced CAD-o). There were other tribes of the same Caddoan language family who migrated farther to the north (see "Arikara"; "Pawnee"; and "Wichita").

The Caddos are usually included as part of the Southeast Culture Area (see "Southeast Indians"). They were primarily villagers and farmers. They had a class system in their social organization, like other Southeast tribes. They lived in conical houses, about

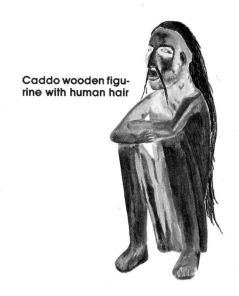

Caddo wooden figurine with human hair

15 feet high and 20 to 50 feet in diameter, framed with poles and usually covered with grass thatch. The smoke from cooking fires did not exit through smoke holes, but seeped out directly through the thatch. The Caddos also built temples in which they kept sacred fires burning. Their boats for travel on the various rivers in their territory were dugouts, carved from single logs.

Since the Caddos lived on the edge of the Plains, they also possessed some cultural traits of their northern kinsmen in the Great Plains Culture Area, such as hunting buffalo (see "Plains Indians"). After they acquired horses from the Spanish, the Caddos roamed over a wider area in search of the large herds.

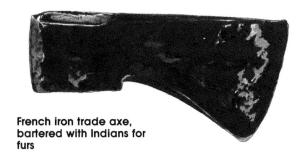

French iron trade axe, bartered with Indians for furs

The Caddos had early contacts with the Spanish. Some tribesmen met up with Hernando de Soto's expedition in 1541 soon after the conquistadors crossed the Mississippi. After Rene Cavalier de la Salle claimed the Mississippi Valley for France in 1682, the Caddos established a lasting trade relationship with French fur traders.

Caddos and Wichitas, called Taovayas by the French, acted as middlemen for the *coureurs de bois* (see "Metis"). The Indians grew crops to barter with other tribes for animal pelts which they then traded with the French. The Taovayas and backwoods fur traders conducted most of their business from villages on the Red River—San Bernardo and San Teodoro (called the Twin Villages), and Natchitoches—which became centers of commerce. The Taovayas prospered during the mid-1700s. Although the French lost their claim to the Louisiana Territory in 1763 after the French and Indian War, the Taovayas remained active for some years to come. But Spanish restrictions on their trade eventually ended their prosperity.

The French regained the Louisiana Territory from Spain in 1801, but sold it to the United States in 1803. Soon afterward, the Louisiana Caddos ceded their lands and moved to Texas. Texas became a republic in 1835 and part of the United States in 1845. In 1859, the federal government settled the Caddos on a reservation along the Washita River in the Indian Territory in what is now Caddo County, Oklahoma, near Anadarko (named after one of the Caddoan tribes). The Wichitas, who were granted the reservation with the Caddos, lived in Kansas during the Civil War before joining their kinsmen.

During the Plains Indian wars after 1865, the Caddos provided scouts for the U.S. Army. One of their chiefs, Guadalupe, considered the wars more a struggle between farmers and raiders than a war between whites and Indians. Since he was a farmer, he encouraged his warriors to assist whites against the nomadic Plains tribes.

With the General Allotment Act of 1887, much of the Caddo-Wichita reservation in Oklahoma was divided among tribal members. The Caddo tribe now jointly holds certain trust lands in the state with the Wichita and Delaware tribes (see "Delaware").

California Indians

The phrase *California Indians* refers to people of many different tribes within the California Culture Area. The California Culture Area corresponds roughly to the state of California as it exists today. But it also includes the Lower California Peninsula, which is part of Mexico.

In the eastern part of this geographical region, the Sierra Nevada, a tall and rugged mountain range, provides a natural barrier. Therefore, some of the tribes that once lived in territory that is now mapped as the eastern part of the state of California are categorized in the Great Basin and Southwest culture areas. And to the north, some of the tribes who lived on both sides of the California-Oregon border are included in the Northwest Coast and Plateau culture areas. Looking at the maps of the various culture areas helps the student understand just how the native peoples were grouped culturally and how their territory corresponds to modern-day states.

In addition to the Sierra Nevada, the smaller Coast Range runs north-south within the California Culture Area. Between the two mountain ranges, in the heart of the culture area, is the Great California Valley, formed by the San Joaquin and Sacramento rivers and

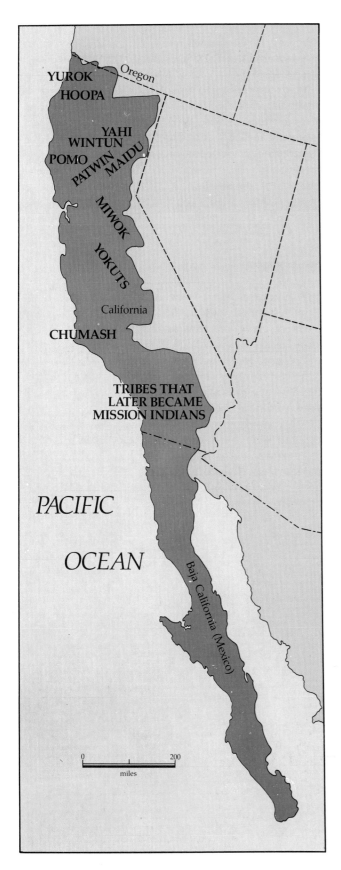

The California Culture Area, showing the approximate locations of Indian tribes listed in this book—circa 1500, before displacement by whites (with modern boundaries)

their tributaries. The Coast Range extends all the way into Mexico.

The amount of rainfall in the California Culture Area varies dramatically from north to south. The northern uplands receive the greatest amount of precipitation, mostly in winter. As a result, there are many tall forests in northern California. The south of the culture area is much drier. Near the California-Arizona border is the Mojave Desert. In Mexico, most of the coastal lowlands, especially along the Gulf of California, are also desert country.

Yet, generally speaking, for native peoples the entire region was a bountiful environment, offering up many wild plant foods and game. California Indians prospered and grew to high population levels as hunter-gatherers without a need for farming. The only cultivated crop found in the culture area was tobacco.

There were many different California peoples, speaking many different languages. Scholars have identified at least 100 distinct dialects spoken in the culture area. The main language families were Hokan, Penutian, and Uto-Aztecan. Among the Hokan-speaking tribes were the following: Achomawi, Atsugewi, Chimariko, Chumash, Esselen, Karok, Pomo, Shasta, Salinan, Yana-Yahi, and various Mexican tribes. Among the Penutian tribes were the following: Costanoan, Maidu, Miwok, Patwin, Wintun, and Yokuts. Among the Uto-Aztecan tribes were the following: Cahuilla, Serrano, Tubatulabal, and others who came to be known as Mission Indians. There were other language families in the California Culture Area as well: the Algonquian language family, spoken by the Yurok tribe; the Athapascan, spoken by the Hoopa and Tolowa; and the Yukian, spoken by the Wappo and Yuki.

There is not space enough in this book to have separate entries for all the California tribes. The above list is not even complete. The lifeways of California Indians as a whole will be summarized here. But to learn more about the lifeways of California Indians, plus their history, be sure to see the tribal entries "Hoopa" and "Yurok," for the northern tribes; "Maidu," "Miwok," "Patwin," "Wintun," "Yahi," and "Yokuts," for the central tribes; and "Chumash" and "Mission Indians," for the southern tribes.

Food

The dietary staple of California Indians was the acorn, the fruit of the oak tree. The Indians collected them in the fall. They removed the kernels from the shells, placed them in the sun to dry out, pounded them into a flour, then poured hot water over the flour repeatedly to remove the bitter-tasting tannic acid. Then the Indians boiled the acorn meal into a soup or mush, or baked it into a bread. California peoples ate many other wild plant foods, including berries, nuts, seeds, greens, roots, bulbs, and tubers. They made cakes out of sun-dried berries, roots, and seeds.

California Indians also ate insects. They picked grubs and caterpillars off plants. They boiled the caterpillars with salt, considering them a delicacy. They drove grasshoppers into pits, then roasted them. And they collected honeydew as another delicacy, rolling it into pellets. Insects called aphids suck the juices of plants and secrete sweet-tasting honeydew.

To catch deer, California Indians journeyed into the hill country to hunt with bows and arrows. They also herded them into corrals. Rabbits were much more common throughout the culture area. The Indians used snares and other kinds of traps to catch them as well as bows and arrows and clubs. Waterfowl also provided meat. Ducks, geese, swans, and other birds migrating from the north in the autumn descended upon the marshes. The Indians shot at them from blinds with bows and arrows or bagged them from boats with nets. California Indians had many different methods of fishing, including hooks and lines, spears, nets, and weirs. Lakes, rivers, and the sea offered their catch. Along the seashore and in tidal basins, the Indians also gathered clams, oysters, mussels, abalones, and scallops. And they caught seals and sea otters.

Houses

California Indians lived in many different kinds of houses. The most typical house throughout the culture area was cone-shaped, about eight feet in diameter at the base. It was constructed from poles covered with brush, grass, reeds, or mats of tule (a kind of bulrush). Other kinds of dwellings included domed earth-covered pit houses and lean-tos of bark slabs. In the northern part of the culture area, some Indians built wood plank houses more typical of the Northwest Coast Indians. Most of the California houses served as single-family dwellings, but some were communal or ceremonial. Others served as sweathouses.

Clothing

Clothing in much of the region was minimal because of the warm climate. Men often went completely naked or wore simple animal-skin or bark breechcloths. Women always wore at least fringed aprons in the front and back, made from animal skins or shredded willow bark. After the coming of the whites, cotton came to replace bark in many instances. Headwear included basket hats, iris fiber hairnets, feather headbands, and feather crowns. Some California Indians went barefoot; others wore ankle-high leather moccasins or sandals made from the yucca plant. In cold weather, robes and blankets of rabbit skin, sea-otter fur, or feathers were draped over the shoulders. Shell jewelry was widespread, as was the practice of tattooing.

Transportation

With regard to transportation, California Indians usually traveled by foot. But they also had different kinds of craft for transporting supplies by water. Some, such as the Yuroks, made simple dugouts, carved from redwood logs. Rafts were more common in the culture area. These were made from logs or from tule. The tule rafts are known as balsas. The tule reeds were tied together into watertight bundles. The bundles would become waterlogged after repeated use, but would dry out in the sun. One tribe, the Chumashes, made boats out of pine planks lashed together with fiber cordage and caulked with asphalt. These were the only plank boats made by Native Americans.

One type of California dwelling, tule (cattail) over a framework of poles

Arts and Crafts

California Indians are famous for their basketry. They used baskets for cooking, placing heated stones in them to boil water (stone-boiling), as well as for carrying, storing, winnowing, and other purposes. There were six to eight different kinds of baskets alone for processing acorns. Basketwork was also used to make hats, mats, traps, and baby carriers. The Pomos decorated their baskets with feathers.

Other California household items included wooden and ceramic bowls, soapstone (steatite) vessels, antler and shell spoons, tule mats, and wooden headrests. Ceremonial objects included stone and clay pipes; rattles made from gourds, rawhide, turtle-shell, deer hooves, and cocoons; plus various other instruments, including drums, flutes, whistles, bull-roarers, and stick-clappers. Strings of disk-shaped dentalium shells were used as a medium of exchange. Trading was widespread among California peoples.

Religion

For California Indians, as for the vast majority of Native Americans, religion played a central and daily role in their lives. Some tribes had single shamans; others had secret societies made up of several members, such as the Kuksu cult of the Patwins, Wintuns, Maidus, and other tribes of the central California region. Initiation rites were important to most California peoples, especially rites involving passage from childhood into adulthood. Death rites were also important. Many California Indians, especially in the central and southern region, cremated their dead. As with all Native Americans, music and dancing played an important part in ceremonies. Some peoples used a tea made from parts of the poisonous jimsonweed plant to induce visions.

Social Structure

Concerning social and political organization, the California peoples were not made up of true tribes, but rather interrelated villages. The term *tribelet* is often applied to California Indians in reference to the relationship between the permanent central village and temporary satellite villages. A single chief, a fatherly figure, presided over each tribelet. Most clans, groups of related families within the tribelet, were traced through the father's line. California Indians did not have war chiefs, as did other Indians, nor systems of bestowing war honors. Warfare was usually carried out for the purpose of revenge rather than for acquiring food, slaves, or possessions.

Recreation

California Indians enjoyed many kinds of games. One favorite was hoop-and-pole, in which a pole was thrown or slid at a rolling hoop. Another game involved catching a ring on a stick or throwing the ring at a pin, as in quoits. Ball games were also popular, including a variety of both lacrosse and soccer. Shinny, in which participants used curved sticks to throw blocks of wood, was also widespread. Indoor games included dice and other counting games involving betting. Cat's cradle, in which a string looped on one person's hands in the shape of a cradle is transferred to another person, was a favorite hand game.

As this book shows time and again, it is difficult to generalize about Indian tribes even in a region where the peoples had as many cultural traits in common as they did in the California Culture Area. In order to grasp the subtleties and distinctions among California Indians and what happened to them after the whites came, be sure to see the entries for various tribes listed earlier in this section.

Calusa

The Calusas—pirates, cannibals, master builders and carvers. Or were they? Were they Muskogeans from the north, or some unknown people, perhaps even migrants from the Caribbean or South America? The mysteries surrounding this tribe are intriguing, veiled in the shrouds of history. In this case, archaeologists, anthropologists, and linguists are the detectives.

The Calusas (pronounced *cuh-LOO-suh*) lived along the Gulf Coast of the Florida peninsula from present-day Tampa Bay southward to the Florida Keys. One mystery surrounding these people is their origin. It is thought that they were a Muskogean-speaking people related linguistically to other Muskogeans of the Southeast Culture Area, but this connection is not known for certain (see "Southeast Indians"). Since the

Calusas had cultural traits in common with native peoples across the Gulf of Mexico, such as the use of blowguns for hunting and fighting and the use of poison for fishing, it has even been theorized that they perhaps arrived long ago in Florida from the sea. In any case, it is known that the Calusas had seaworthy dugout canoes and communicated with the Arawaks of the Caribbean (see "Arawak").

The Calusas perhaps had another trait typical of Indian peoples to their south—human sacrifice, along with cannibalism. Some North American tribes practiced cannibalism, but it was usually for ritualistic purposes, such as eating an enemy's heart to gain his strength. Eating human flesh for survival, as some South American tribes did, was rare. The exact extent of the Calusa cannibalism is a mystery, however. Early explorers sometimes exaggerated in their writings about Indians.

The Calusas have also been referred to as pirates. By the time the Spanish had contact with them in the 1500s, the Calusas already had quantities of gold and silver. Some Calusas might have been pirates who raided Spanish galleons on treasure runs from Mexico

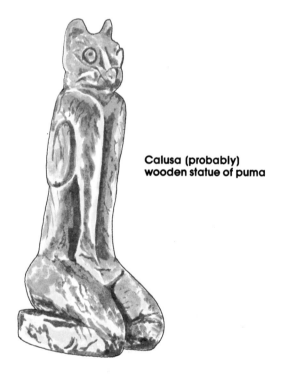

Calusa (probably) wooden statue of puma

to Spain. Others might have attacked shipwrecked crews. In any case, it is known for certain that the Calusas were beachcombers who gathered up the cargos of ships destroyed in the tricky waters off their coast.

One other tantalizing mystery surrounds the Calusas. Were they the Indians of Key Marco? In 1884,

an archaeologist by the name of Frank Hamilton Cushing found on this small island the remains of a highly developed culture, including man-made seawalls, jetties, and drainage basins; shell, bone, and tooth tools; and exquisitely carved wooden masks and wooden animal figures with movable parts. These complex structures and beautifully crafted objects may have been the work of early Calusas. But the connection will probably never be proved beyond a doubt because real estate development of what is now called Marco Island is hindering future archaeological excavation.

Nevertheless, much is known about the Calusas from the writings of early Spanish explorers as well as from those of later Anglo-American military men and settlers. Other tribes have also passed on information about the Calusas through their own oral traditions.

It is known that Juan Ponce de Leon, the man who claimed Florida for Spain and gave that part of North America its name (*Florida* is the Spanish word for "flowers"), visited the Calusa Indians in 1513; Diego Miruelo made contact with them in 1516; and Hernandes de Cordoba did in 1517. Ponce de Leon again landed among them in 1521 with intentions of founding a settlement. But he offended his hosts, who attacked him and his men, fatally wounded him with an arrow, and forced the Spanish back to Cuba. A Spaniard by the name of Hernando de Escalante Fontaneda was shipwrecked onto Calusa shores and was held captive from 1551 to 1569. His stay among the Indians proved valuable to future anthropologists and historians because he wrote about his experience.

The Spanish tried again to establish a mission among the Calusas about this same period, but they abandoned the post before very long and never converted the Indians to Catholicism. However, because of their trade relations with the Spanish, the Calusas were later subject to attacks by the British and their Indian allies. By 1745, many Calusas, along with Apalachees and Timucuas, had been taken to the Carolinas as slaves (see "Apalachee" and "Timucua"). Other Calusas emigrated to the West Indies to escape the raids.

Descendants of those Calusas who stayed behind later fought alongside the Seminoles in the Second Seminole War of 1835-42 (see "Seminole"). In 1839, a band of Calusas, calling themselves Muspas after a village name, attacked the camp of Colonel William Harney, killing 18 of his men. What happened to the Calusa Indians after this period is not known. Perhaps remaining tribal members traveled west with the Seminoles or disappeared into the Everglades with them. Perhaps survivors followed their ancestors to Cuba. Their ultimate fate is a mystery, like so much else about this tribe.

Carrier

The name of this tribe, translated into English from the dialect of a neighboring tribe, is from the word *carry* and refers to a custom in which a widow had to carry the charred bones of her dead husband in a basket for three years. The French name for Carrier is *Porteur*, with the same meaning. The Carriers preferred to use their various band names, or starting in the 1900s, the shared name *Takulli*, meaning "people who go upon the water."

The Carriers lived in the southwestern corner of the area called the Subarctic Culture Area (see "Subarctic Indians"). Their homeland included the headwaters of the Fraser River as well as the territory around Babine and Stuart lakes. This rugged terrain lies between the Coast Mountains and the Rocky Mountains in British Columbia. Other Athapascan tribes living near them in the foothills of the Rocky Mountains with similar ways of life were the Chilcotin, Han, Kaska (Nahani), Mountain, Sekani, Tagish, Tahltan, Tsetsaut, and Tutchone.

The Carriers, like other Subarctic tribes, were hunter-gatherers who did not farm at all. They hunted the caribou and other game in the forests; they fished the lakes and rivers; they foraged for roots and berries. They wore leather clothing—robe, leggings, and moccasins, with a cap and mittens for cold weather.

Carrier moccasins (modern)

But the Carriers are an interesting cultural mix because they had elements in their society similar to those of tribes west of them along the Pacific Coast as well as some elements similar to tribes south of them along the Columbia River (see "Northwest Coast Indians" and "Plateau Indians"). For example, like Northwest Coast peoples, the Carriers lived in villages much of the year; they had social classes of nobles, commoners, and slaves; tribal members could improve their social position through the potlatch, the custom of giving possessions away; warriors wore armor made from slats of wood; and they prized Chilkat blankets that they received in trade from coastal peoples (see "Tlingit").

Like the Plateau Indians, the Carriers depended on fish as their primary food staple, pursuing salmon during the summer runs up the rivers. They also built pit houses like the Plateau peoples for winter use. Nor were their summer houses the typical conical skin tents of the Subarctic, but rather open shelters with spruce-bark roofs and no walls. Another way the Carriers were unusual for Subarctic people: They did not use snowshoes or toboggans.

The Carriers, being an inland western people, avoided early contacts with whites. Alexander Mackenzie, the Scotch explorer and fur trader who worked for the North West Company out of Montreal, visited the Carriers in 1793 during his epic journey all the way across North America. Simon Fraser, another Canadian explorer for the North West Company, established trading posts in Carrier territory in 1805-06. And in 1843, a Catholic missionary, Father Demers, began work among the Carriers. Many miners came to Carrier country, starting in the late 1850s. The building of the Canadian Pacific transcontinental railroad, completed in 1885, brought more white settlers to the Carrier homeland. Contacts with whites brought epidemics to the Carriers and eroded their traditional way of life.

The Carriers have gradually rebuilt their lives. They work in a variety of fields, including farming and railroad work. Some tribal members earn a living through hunting and trapping as their ancestors did. There are currently 15 Carrier bands in British Columbia, each owning a number of tracts of land.

Catawba

The Catawbas made their original homeland in territory that now is the border region between North and South Carolina. Scholars consider them part of the Southeast Culture Area. For a long time, scholars were unable to place the Catawba's unusual dialect in any language family. Now it is thought that the Catawba tongue is Siouan. There were many other Siouan peoples in the Southeast, especially in the Carolinas and Virginia, but few exist as tribes today. The Waccamaws of South Carolina, like the Catawbas, still have communities there (see "Southeast Indians").

The Catawbas, like most of the tribes of the Southeast, were village dwellers who depended heavily on agriculture for food. They usually located their villages in river valleys, especially along the Catawba River. Their name, pronounced *cuh-TAW-buh*, means "people of the river." Nauvasa was one of the six main early villages. The Catawbas lived in pole-frame, bark-covered houses. They also constructed temples of worship, as did other Southeast tribes. They supplemented their diet with fish and game from river and forest.

The Catawbas were once a very numerous and powerful tribe. They were traditional enemies of the Cherokees. Catawba war parties traveled great distances to raid other Indians, sometimes even all the way across the Appalachian Mountains to the Ohio Valley.

The Spanish were the first whites to have contact with the Catawbas, in the latter part of the 1500s. The English explored, settled, and developed the region in the late 1600s and early 1700s. The Catawbas wanted British trade goods, so when war broke out between the colonists and the Tuscaroras in 1711-13, the Catawbas aided the colonists (see "Tuscarora"). Nevertheless, in the Yamasee War of 1715 some

Catawba pottery

Catawba war parties joined the Yamasees in attacks on British settlements, rebelling against unfair trade practices, forced labor, and slave raids on Indians (see "Yamasee").

After this brief period of unrest, the Catawbas maintained peace with the colonists. But the Indians suffered for their friendship with the colonists in two ways. First, European diseases took their toll on them. Two outbreaks of the dreaded smallpox, in 1738 and 1758, reduced the tribe by more than half. Second, the tribe also suffered from attacks by other Indians who were not always on friendly terms with the colonists, such as the Shawnees and the Iroquois (see "Shawnee" and "Iroquois"). The Catawbas sided with the rebels in the American Revolution against the British.

The Catawbas lived on both sides of the North and South Carolina border. Up until 1762, they lived mainly in North Carolina. From 1762 on, they lived mostly in South Carolina, where they came to hold reservation lands. Their relationship with the federal government as a unified tribe ended in 1962 during the Termination period (see "Menominee"). At that time, the tribe distributed its remaining lands to individuals, many of whom still hold the same tracts. Other Catawbas have moved out West, some joining the Choctaws in Oklahoma (see "Choctaw").

Cayuga

The Cayugas (pronounced *ki-YOO-guh*) were one of the five original tribes in the Iroquois League. They had a great deal in common with other tribes in this important confederacy. As a result, their shared culture and history is discussed in this book along with the other tribes under "Iroquois." The Cayugas were a distinct group with their own villages, leaders, and traditions. But be sure to see the "Iroquois" entry too, plus the entry under "Northeast Indians."

The Cayugas lived in the Finger Lakes country of New York State, especially along the longest of the lakes (38 miles), which is named after them, Cayuga

Lake. Sandwiched between the Senecas to the west and the Onondagas to the east, the Cayugas controlled the smallest expanse of territory of all the tribes in the League. They had at least 13 important villages. Since many of these villages were near wetlands, the Cayugas were known as the People of the Marsh. The Cayugas sent 10 sachems, or chiefs, as tribal representatives to the League's Great Council. The Cayuga totem, or symbol, at the annual gathering was the Great Pipe.

Cayuga headdress. (Different Iroquois tribes used varying numbers of feathers.)

In 1774, the year before the American Revolution, Iroquois living on the Ohio and Scioto rivers in Pennsylvania, known as the Mingo band, joined the Shawnee's fight against the British in Lord Dunmore's War (see "Shawnee"). The Mingo chief, Logan, was a Cayuga.

Yet, during the American Revolution, when the various Iroquois tribes chose sides, most Cayugas sided with the British, along with the Mohawks, Onondagas, and Senecas, against the American rebels. After American victory in the war, many Cayugas migrated to Ontario, Canada, where they were granted lands along with the Mohawks and other Iroquois who had sided with the British. Their shared reserve at Oshweken on the Grand River is called the Six Nations Reserve. Other Cayugas settled with the Senecas in western New York (see "Mohawk" and "Seneca").

Although the Cayugas have no remaining tribal lands in New York State, they still exist there in spirit, so-to-speak, as part of the state's rich history. As the Cayuga Peter Wilson (Wa-o-wo-wa-no-onk) communicated to the New York Historical Society in 1847:

"That land of Ganono-o—or 'Empire State' as you love to call it—was once laced by our trails from Albany to Buffalo—trails that we had trod for centuries—trails worn so deep by the feet of the Iroquois that they became your own roads of travel . . . . Your roads still traverse those same lines of communication and bind one part of the Longhouse to another. The land of Ganono-o, the Empire State, then is our monument! We shall not long occupy much room in living. The single tree of the thousands which sheltered our forefathers—one old elm under which the representatives of the tribes were wont to meet—will cover us all. But we would have our bodies twined in death among its roots, on the very soil on whence it grew . . . . In your last war with England, your red brother—your elder brother—still came up to help you as of old on the Canada frontier. Have we, the first holders of this prosperous region, no longer a share in your history? Glad were your fathers to sit down upon the threshold of the Longhouse, rich did they then hold themselves in getting the mere sweeping from its door. Had our forefathers spurned you from it when the French were thundering at the opposite side to get a passage through and drive you into the sea, whatever has been the fate of other Indians, the Iroquois might still have been a nation, and I, instead of pleading here for the privilege of living within your borders—I—I might have had a country!"

Today, Cayugas return to New York along with other Canadian Iroquois to participate in festivals, such as the annual Six Nations Festival held on Labor Day Weekend at Cobleskill.

An Iroquois boy at the Six Nations Festival in Cobleskill, New York

Cayuse

The name of the Cayuse Indians, pronounced *ki-YOOS*, has come to mean "pony" in the English language. The original meaning of their name is unknown. But since the Cayuse were such proficient horsebreeders and horse-dealers, their name has taken on the general meaning of a small, domesticated Indian horse.

The Cayuses lived in what today is northeast Oregon and southeast Washington State. They made their homes along tributaries of the Columbia River, such as the Grande Ronde, Umatilla, and Wallawalla rivers. They are considered part of the Plateau Culture Area (see "Plateau Indians"). They spoke a dialect of the Penutian language. They lived in oblong lodges as well as in cone-shaped tents, each type of structure covered with woven-reed mats or buffalo hides. The family made up the most important social unit, with several families organized into bands with chiefs. Salmon, deer, small game, roots, and berries were the Cayuses' main food sources.

The Cayuses were famous as traders, exchanging buffalo robes and reed mats with the coastal Indians for shells and other items. Horses, brought to North America by the Spanish, reached them in the early 1700s, and became their most important product for trade with other Indians. In later years, once the fur trade with whites was underway, the Cayuses traded buffalo robes and other animal pelts for guns, tools, and blankets.

The Cayuses were involved in the first war between Indians and whites in the Columbia Plateau region. This was the Cayuse War of 1847-50. In 1836, about 30 years after the Lewis and Clark Expedition had opened this part of North America to white settlement, Marcus Whitman founded among the Cayuses a Presbyterian mission known as Waiilatpu. His wife, Narcissa Whitman, came with him from the East. She and Eliza Spalding, the wife of Henry Spalding, another missionary to the region, were the first white women to cross North America.

Even though they worked among the Cayuses for 10 years, the Whitmans never developed a strong rapport with the Indians. They were intolerant of Indian culture and beliefs and fanatically demanded total conversion to Presbyterian ways. Moreover, when more and more white emigrants began arriving in Oregon Country, the Whitmans turned their attention to them and became rich from trade and land sales, keeping

A Cayuse Indian with pony and dog

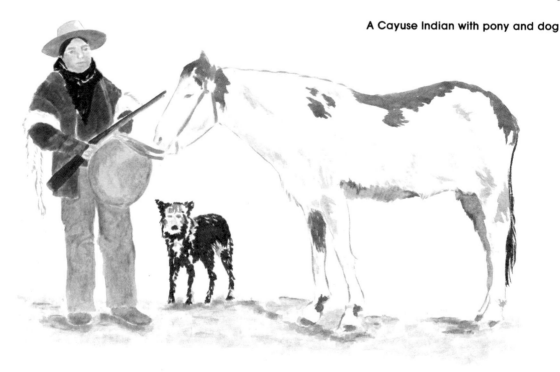

the money for themselves and not sharing it with the Indians who worked alongside them.

The particular incident that sparked the Cayuse War was an outbreak of measles. Cayuse children enrolled at the mission school came down with the disease and started an epidemic among the Indians. Cayuse leaders blamed the missionaries. Chief Tilokaikt and one of his braves named Tomahas came to the mission for medicine. Before leaving, however, the Indians took out their wrath on Marcus Whitman and killed him with tomahawk blows. Soon afterward, other Cayuses raided the mission, killing 11 other whites, including Narcissa Whitman.

Oregon Country organized a volunteer army under a clergyman by the name of Cornelius Gilliam. When the militiamen attacked an encampment of innocent Cayuses, killing as many as 30, other Indians, including warriors from the Palouse tribe, joined the Cayuse cause. Gilliam's continuing campaign enraged other Indians and threatened to unite even more Plateau tribes in a general uprising. But then Gilliam was killed by his own gun in an accident, and his troops gave up the campaign.

Tilokaikt and Tomahas hid out for two more years. Growing tired of the fugitive life and hoping for mercy from white courts, they turned themselves in. But white jurors convicted them of murder and the judge sentenced them to hang. Before their execution, the two braves rejected Presbyterian rites and asked for Catholic ones instead.

The Cayuse War hastened the pace of change in Oregon Country. The federal government established new military posts in the region and organized a territorial government. Furthermore, many tribes of the Columbia Plateau now distrusted whites. Other wars eventually occurred. The Cayuses fought in two of them: the Yakima War of 1855-59 and the Bannock War of 1878 (see "Yakima" and "Bannock"). Some Cayuses also settled among the Nez Perces and fought alongside them in their uprising of 1877 (see "Nez Perce").

Most Cayuses were settled with the Umatillas and the Wallawallas on the Umatilla Reservation, established in 1853 (see "Umatilla" and "Wallawalla"). Their descendants live there today, with a tribal headquarters in Pendleton, Oregon.

Cherokee

The Trail of Tears occupies a special place in Native American history. Many tribes have similar incidents from their history, as this book shows. Yet this event involving the Cherokees has come to symbolize the land cessions and relocations of all Indian peoples, just as Wounded Knee, involving the Sioux, has come to represent the numerous massacres of Indian innocents (see "Sioux").

Yet before we further discuss the Trail of Tears, we'll take a look at the Cherokee (pronounced CHAIR-uh-key) language and culture and other important events in their history.

When Europeans first arrived in North America, the Cherokees occupied a large expanse of territory in the Southeast. Their homeland included mountains and valleys in the southern part of the Appalachian chain. The Cherokees had villages in the Great Smoky Mountains of western North Carolina and the Blue Ridge of western Virginia, as well as in the Great Valley of eastern Tennessee. They also lived in the Appalachian high country of South Carolina and Georgia, and as far south as northern Alabama.

In Indian studies, this region of North America is classified within the Southeast Culture Area (see "Southeast Indians"). The Cherokees spoke dialects of the Iroquoian language, the southernmost people to do so. Their ancestral relatives, the Iroquois, lived in the Northeast Culture Area (see "Iroquois").

The Cherokee name for themselves in Iroquoian was Ani-yun-wiya, meaning "real people." The name Cherokee was probably given to them by the neighboring Creeks—tciloki in its original form, meaning "people of the different speech."

Lifeways

The Cherokees placed their villages along rivers and streams, where they farmed the rich black soil. Their crops included corn, beans, squash, pumpkins, sunflowers, and tobacco. They grew three different kinds of corn, or maize—one to roast, one to boil, and a third to grind into flour for cornbread. The Cherokees also took advantage of the wild plant foods in their homeland, including edible roots, crab apples, berries, persimmons, cherries, grapes, hickory nuts, walnuts, and chestnuts.

The rivers and streams also provided food for the Cherokees. They used spears, traps, and hooks and

Cherokee cane-stalk blowgun plus darts

lines to catch different kinds of fish. Another method included poisoning an area of water to bring the unconscious fish to the surface.

The Cherokees were also skilled hunters. They hunted large animals, such as deer and bear, with bows and arrows. To get close to the deer, they wore entire deerskins, antlers and all, and used deer calls to lure the animals to them. The Cherokees hunted smaller game, such as raccoons, rabbits, squirrels, and turkeys, with blowguns made from the hollowed-out stems of cane plants. Through these long tubes, the hunters blew small wood-and-feather darts with deadly accuracy from as far away as 60 feet.

The products of the hunt were also used for clothing. In warm weather, Cherokee men dressed in buckskin breechcloths and women in buckskin skirts. In cold weather, men wore buckskin shirts, leggings, and moccasins; women wore buckskin capes. Other capes, made from turkey and eagle feathers along with strips of bark, were used by Cherokee headmen for ceremonial purposes. Their leaders also wore feather headdresses on special occasions.

Ceremonies took place inside circular and domed council houses or domed seven-sided temples. The temples were usually located on top of flat-topped mounds in the central village plaza, a custom inherited from the earlier Temple Mound Builders of the Southeast (see "Mound Builders").

Cherokee families, like other people of the Southeast, usually had two houses—a large summer home and a smaller winter home. The summer houses, rectangular in shape with peaked roofs, had pole frameworks, cane and clay walls, and bark or thatch roofs. The winter houses, which doubled as sweathouses, were placed over a pit with a cone-shaped roof of poles and earth. Cherokee villages were usually surrounded with walls of vertical logs or palisades, for protection from hostile tribes.

The Cherokees practiced a variety of crafts, including plaited basketwork and stamped pottery. They also carved, out of wood and gourds, *Booger* masks, representing evil spirits. And they shaped stone pipes into animal figures, attached to wooden stems.

Cherokee Booger mask. The term *booger,* **from which** *bogeyman* **comes, is African in origin, taken by the Cherokees from the native language of black slaves.**

Cherokee river cane basket

Among the many Cherokee agricultural, hunting, and healing rituals, the most important was the Green Corn Ceremony. This annual celebration, shared by other tribes of the Southeast, took place at the time of the ripening of the last corn crop (see "Creek").

Another important event for the Cherokees, shared with other Southeast peoples, was the game of lacrosse. This game was played between clans from the same villages as well as between clans from different villages (see "Choctaw"). Chunkey, or *chenco*, a game played by throwing sticks at rolling stones, was also popular.

With regard to political and social organization, the many Cherokee villages, about 100, were allied in a loose confederacy. Within each village, there were two chiefs. The White Chief, also called the Most Beloved Man, helped the villagers make decisions concerning farming, lawmaking, and disputes between individuals, families, or clans. He also played an important part in religious ceremonies along with the Cherokee shamans. The Red Chief gave advice concerning warfare. One such decision was choosing who would be the War Woman, an honored woman chosen to accompany braves on their war parties. The War Woman did not fight, but helped feed the men, offered them council, and decided which prisoners would live or die. The Red Chief also was in charge of the lacrosse games, which the Cherokees called the "little war."

From First Contact Through the Colonial Years

Early explorers to encounter the Cherokees were impressed by their highly advanced culture. Hernando de Soto, the Spanish explorer who traveled throughout much of the Southeast, was the first European to come into contact with the Cherokees, when he arrived in their territory from the south in 1540. In later years, occasional French traders worked their way into Cherokee lands from the north. But the most frequent Cherokee-white contacts were with English traders from the east. The traders began appearing regularly after England permanently settled Virginia, starting with the Jamestown colony of 1607 and then, before long, the Carolina colonies.

In the French and Indian Wars, lasting from 1689 to 1763, the Cherokees generally sided with the English against the French, providing warriors for certain engagements. In these conflicts, they sometimes found themselves fighting side by side with other Indian tribes who had been their traditional enemies, such as the Iroquois.

In 1760, however, the Cherokees revolted against their English allies in the Cherokee War. The precipitating incident involved a dispute over wild horses in what is now West Virginia. A group of Cherokees on their journey home from the Ohio River, where they had helped the English take Fort Duquesne, captured some wild horses. Some Virginia frontiersmen claimed the horses as their own and attacked the Cherokees, killing 12. Then they sold the horses and collected bounties on the Cherokee scalps, which they claimed they had taken from Indians allied to the French.

On learning of this incident, various Cherokee bands, led by Chief Oconostota, began a series of raids on white settlements. The Cherokees also managed to capture Fort Loudon in the Great Valley of the Appalachians. The war lasted two years, before the British troops defeated the Cherokees by burning their villages and crops. Even then, the insurgents continued to fight from their mountain hideouts for a period of time. Eventually, war-weary and half-starving, the Cherokees surrendered. In the peace pact, the Cherokees were forced to give up a large portion of their eastern lands lying closest to British settlements.

In spite of the Cherokee War, the Cherokees supported the English against the rebels in the American Revolution of 1775-83. Most of their support consisted of sporadic attacks on outlying American settlements. In retaliation, North Carolina militiamen invaded the Cherokees' territory and again destroyed villages and demanded land cessions.

During the colonial years, the Cherokees also suffered from a number of epidemics. The worst outbreaks—from the dreaded smallpox that killed so many native peoples—occurred in 1738 and 1750.

Tribal Transformation

Still, despite these various setbacks, the Cherokees rebuilt their lives. They learned from the settlers around them, adopting new methods of farming and business. They now were faithful allies of the Americans, even fighting with them under Andrew Jackson in the Creek War of 1813. A Cherokee chief named Junaluska personally saved Jackson's life from a tomahawk-swinging Creek warrior at the Battle of Horseshoe Bend. In 1820, the Cherokees established among themselves a republican form of government, similar to that of the United States. In 1827, they founded the Cherokee Nation under a constitution with an elected principal chief, a senate, and a house of representatives.

Much of the progress among the Cherokees resulted from the work of a man named Sequoyah, also known as George Gist. In 1809, he began working on a written version of the Cherokee language so that his people could have a written constitution, official records, books, and newspapers like the whites around them. Over a 12-year period, he devised a written system that reduced the Cherokee language to 85 characters representing all the different sounds. Sequoyah is the only person in history to singlehandedly invent an entire alphabet (or a syllabary, because the characters represent syllables). In 1821, he finished his vast project. In 1827, the Cherokees wrote down their constitution. And in 1828, the first Cherokee newspaper, the *Cherokee Phoenix*, was published in their language.

The Trail of Tears

Yet, despite the new Cherokee way of life, the settlers wanted the Indians' lands. The discovery of gold near Dahlonega, Georgia, helped influence white officials to call for the relocation of the Cherokees, along with other eastern Indians. In 1830, President Andrew Jackson signed the Indian Removal Act to relocate the eastern tribes to an Indian Territory west of the Mississippi River.

Despite the fact that the principal chief of the Cherokees, the great orator John Ross, passionately argued and won the Cherokee case before the Supreme Court of the United States; despite the fact that Junaluska, who had saved Jackson's life, personally pleaded with the president for his people's land; despite the fact that such great Americans as Daniel Webster, Henry Clay, and Davy Crockett supported the Cherokee claims; still, President Jackson ordered the Indians' removal. And so began the Trail of Tears.

The state of Georgia began forcing the Cherokees to sell their lands for next to nothing. Cherokee homes and possessions were plundered. Whites destroyed the printing press of the *Cherokee Phoenix* because it published articles opposing Indian removal. Soldiers began rounding up Cherokee families and taking them to internment camps in preparation for the journey westward. With little food and unsanitary conditions at these hastily built stockades, many Cherokees died. In the meantime, some Cherokees escaped to the mountains of North Carolina, where they successfully hid out from the troops.

The first forced trek westward began in the spring of 1838 and lasted into the summer. On the 800-mile trip, the Cherokees suffered because of the intense heat. The second mass exodus took place in the fall and winter of 1838-39 during the rainy season; the wagons bogged down in the mud, and then there were freezing temperatures and snow. On both journeys, many Indians died from disease and inadequate food and blankets. The soldiers drove their prisoners on at a cruel pace, not even allowing them to properly bury their dead. Nor did they protect the Cherokees from attacks by bandits.

During the period of confinement, plus the two separate trips, about 4,000 Cherokees died, almost a quarter of their total. More Cherokees died after arrival in the Indian Territory because of epidemics and continuing shortages of food. During the 1830s, other Southeast tribes endured similar experiences, including the Chickasaws, Choctaws, Creeks, and Seminoles (see entries for those tribes). This was a shameful time in American history.

The Indian Territory

Nor was the injustice enacted upon the Cherokees and other tribes of the Indian Territory over. The Indian Territory was supposed to be a permanent homeland for various tribes. Originally, the promised region stretched from the state boundaries of Arkansas, Missouri, and Iowa to the 100th meridian, about 300 miles at the widest point. Nonetheless, with increasing white settlement west of the Mississippi in the mid-1800s, the Indian Territory was reduced again and again.

In 1854, by an act of Congress, the northern part of the Indian Territory became the territories of Kansas and Nebraska, which later became states. Then, starting in 1866 after the Civil War, tribes living in those regions were resettled on lands to the south, supposedly reserved for the Southeast tribes, now known as the Five Civilized Tribes.

During the 1880s, the Boomers arrived—white home-seekers squatting on Indian reservations. Various white interests—railroad and bank executives, plus other developers—lobbied Congress for the opening of more Indian lands to white settlement.

Assimilation and Allotment

In 1887, Congress passed the General Allotment Act (or the Dawes Severalty Act). Under this law, certain Indian reservations held by tribes were to be divided and allotted to heads of Indian families. Some politicians believed that the law would help Indians by motivating individuals to develop the land. They also believed it would bring about the assimilation of Indians into the mainstream American culture. But others were just interested in obtaining Indian lands, since it was much easier to take advantage of individuals than of whole tribes. Many of the same people advocated stamping out Indian culture and religion and sending Indian children to white-run boarding schools. This period in United States Indian policy is called the Assimilation and Allotment period.

Cherokee Eagle Dancers

By 1889, two million acres had been bought from the Indians, usually at ridiculously low prices, and thrown open to white settlement. The Oklahoma Land Run took place that year, with settlers lining up at a starting point to race for choice pieces. Those who cheated and entered the lands open for settlement were called "sooners." In 1890, Oklahoma Territory was formed from these lands.

Cherokee and Choctaw leaders refused allotment and took their case to federal courts, as John Ross had done years before. In reaction, Congress passed the Curtis Act of 1898, which dissolved their tribal governments and extended land allotment policy to them against their wishes. Piece by piece, the Indian lands were taken. Oklahoma, all of which had once been Indian land, became a state in 1907.

During this period, in 1924, the federal government passed the Citizenship Act, conferring citizenship on Native Americans. Two states—Arizona and New Mexico—delayed giving Indians voting rights until much later.

Restoration and Reorganization

In 1934, with the Indian Reorganization Act (or the Wheeler-Howard Act), the policies of Assimilation and Allotment ended. This was the start of the Tribal

Restoration and Reorganization period, sponsored by President Franklin D. Roosevelt and his Commissioner of Indian Affairs, John Collier. The Cherokees and other native peoples all over North America began to rediscover their cultural heritage, which the assimilationists had tried to take away, and to reorganize their tribal leadership into vital and effective governing bodies.

Yet, unfortunately, those tribes who underwent allotment never regained the lands given to whites. Remaining Indian lands in Oklahoma are not called reservations, as most tribally held pieces are in other states. In Oklahoma, they are called Indian trust areas. Some are tribally owned and some are allotted to families or individuals. Yet, by an act of Congress in 1936, the lands are protected as reservations from outside speculators.

Termination and Urbanization

The federal government went through other phases in its policy toward Indians. In the 1950s, some politicians sought to end the special protective relationship between the government and Indian tribes (see "Menominee"). Indians in Oklahoma and elsewhere were encouraged to move to cities in order to join the economic mainstream.

Self-Determination

Termination as a policy failed. The Cherokees and other tribes knew that their best hope for a good life in modern times was tribal unity and cultural renewal as called for in the earlier policy of Restoration and Reorganization. Since the 1960s, the federal Indian policy has been one of tribal self-determination, which means Indian self-government and strong tribal identity.

Cherokee tribal headquarters in the West is located in Tahlequah, Oklahoma. Some of the western Cherokees have made money from oil and other minerals found on their lands. There is a pageant for tourists every summer with dancers, musicians, and actors. The pageant is called *The Trail of Tears*. A famous American humorist by the name of Will Rogers was a Western Cherokee. He gained a wide audience in the 1920s and 1930s through radio, movies, books, and newspapers. He was called the "cowboy philosopher."

There are still Cherokees in the East too, in North Carolina. Descendants of those who hid out in the mountains during the relocation period still live there. They presently hold rights to the picturesque Cherokee Reservation in the Great Smoky Mountains in the western part of the state. There, the Cherokees have a factory where they make crafts sold in stores all over North America, as well as a lumber business, and motels and shops for tourists. The Cherokees lease some of these businesses to whites. At the reservation in North Carolina, visitors can watch the annual pageant of the eastern Cherokees called *Unto These Hills*. Participants perform many dances, including the stunning Eagle Dance, passed down through the centuries among many generations of Cherokees. The dancers, wearing colorful costumes, move in swooping circular patterns, like birds in flight. The feathered eagle wands they wave are symbols of peace.

Cheyenne

The Cheyennes called themselves *Tsistsistas*, meaning "beautiful people." The name *Cheyenne*, pronounced *shy-ANN*, was originally the Sioux name for the tribe. It means "red talkers" or "people of a different speech." To Sioux ears, the Cheyenne language sounded foreign because the Sioux spoke Siouan dialects and the Cheyennes spoke Algonquian ones.

Migrations

The Cheyennes originally lived close to other Algonquian-speaking peoples of the Great Lakes region in territory that is now Minnesota (see "Algonquian"). They lived in permanent villages and practiced farming in addition to hunting and gathering. The general location and time period is confirmed in the historical records of the French explorer Rene Robert Cavelier de la Salle. In 1680, a group of Cheyennes came to visit la Salle's fort in Illinois, the first time whites came into contact with members of the tribe.

At some point soon after this date, the Cheyennes crossed the Minnesota River and migrated westward into what is now North and South Dakota. They were probably pushed westward by hostile bands of Sioux and Chippewas (see "Sioux" and "Chippewa"). The

Cheyennes settled along the Missouri River, still living as villagers and farmers.

Sometime in the late 1700s, the Cheyennes gained use of the horse. During that period, their way of life became that of nomadic buffalo hunters on the grasslands of the Great Plains. As their legend tells it, they "lost the corn," meaning they stopped planting crops. They also gave up making pottery because it broke too easily on the trail. And the Cheyennes began

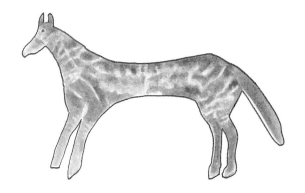

Cheyenne rawhide horse effigy

living in temporary skin tepees instead of permanent earthlodges. However, at least some Cheyenne bands still lived along the Missouri River in 1805, when Lewis and Clark made their expedition up the Missouri.

Sometime in the early 1800s, the Cheyennes pushed westward along the Cheyenne River, a branch of the Missouri, into the Black Hills. During this period, another Algonquian people originally from east of the Missouri, known as the Sutaio tribe, merged with the Cheyennes and became one of the 10 bands of their camp circle.

The Sioux pushed the Cheyennes farther south to the vicinity of the North Platte River in what is now eastern Wyoming and western Nebraska. The Cheyennes in turn pushed the Kiowas southward (see "Kiowa").

About 1832, the Cheyennes separated into two groups. One group stayed along the headwaters of the Platte River. They became known to whites as the Northern Cheyennes. In time, they became allies of their former enemies, the Sioux. The other group migrated farther south to the upper Arkansas River in what is now eastern Colorado and western Kansas. They became known as the Southern Cheyennes. In their new location, the Southern Cheyennes made war against the Kiowas and Comanches (see "Comanche"). But then in 1840, they formed a loose alliance with these two tribes against their enemies, the Crows, Pawnees, Shoshones, Utes, and Apaches.

During this period too, the Northern Cheyennes became close allies of the Northern Arapahos, who lived near them in Wyoming. Likewise, the Southern Cheyennes became allies of the Southern Arapahos in Colorado (see "Arapaho"). These various tribes—the Cheyennes, Arapahos, Sioux, Comanches, and Kiowas—were the most important players in the Native Americans' struggle against whites for the Great Plains. We shall look at the Cheyenne role in these conflicts in a moment. But first we'll take a look at some cultural traits of the Cheyennes.

Lifeways

The Cheyennes are classified as part of the Great Plains Culture Area. We have seen how it was fairly late in their history that the Cheyennes began using horses, living in tepees, and depending on buffalo as their primary source of food. Once they migrated onto the Great Plains, they adopted other typical Plains customs too, such as the ceremony of the Sun Dance, which the Cheyennes called the New Life Lodge. Plains Indian lifeways are summarized under the entry "Plains Indians," but here we'll look at some of these lifeways in order to try to see something of what it was like to be a Cheyenne.

The Cheyennes were organized into the Council of Forty-Four. Each of the 44 peace chiefs represented a band and was the headman of an extended family. The responsibilities of the chiefs included such matters as settling disputes and deciding on when to move camp. The ideal traits for these chiefs, and by extension all Cheyennes, were wisdom, calmness, kindliness, fairness, selflessness, generosity, energy, and bravery. The chiefs were concerned with the well-being of the tribe as a whole and also with the well-being of individuals. They readily made sacrifices to help others improve their life.

The Council of Forty-Four also made decisions concerning tribal war policy and alliances with other tribes. But they involved themselves little in specific raids or military strategy. These decisions were left to the military societies. The chiefs on the Council of Forty-Four had in all likelihood once been members of the soldier societies themselves. But after joining the Council, they resigned from their military positions.

The military societies consisted of warriors from different bands. The warriors carried out raids together and fought side by side. But the societies were not just like outfits in a modern army. They were also clubs. Members met to review military campaigns in addition to discussing plans for future ones. Each society had its own rituals, sacred objects, symbols, and articles of clothing. In the case of the Cheyennes, the military societies were not grouped by age. Some tribes, such as the Arapahos, had societies based on age, with members graduating upward to different societies as the members got older.

Different Cheyenne societies were the Dog, Fox, Elk (or Hoof Rattle), Shield, Bowstring (or Contrary), Wolf, and Northern Crazy Dogs. The last two came later in Cheyenne history than the other original five. The most famous of all of these was the *Hotamitanio*, or the Dog Soldiers, who played an important part in the wars against the United States for the Great Plains.

In Cheyenne social organization, the most important unit was the family, then the band, then the tribe as a whole. The Cheyennes had many rules governing behavior inside and outside these groups. For

Cheyenne backrest of willow rods, lashed together with sinew, and supported by a wood tripod

example, Cheyenne women were famous for their chastity. They were desired as wives only if they behaved properly before they were married.

Because of the taboo on relationships before marriage, courting was very complicated and prolonged. Sometimes it took a young man as long as four years to court his bride-to-be. He sometimes waited for hours day after day along a path she traveled daily—from her family's tepee to the stream where she went for water or the stand of trees where she went for firewood—hoping to have a word with her. He sometimes tugged on her robe as she walked by to get her attention, or whistled to her, or called out to her. If she did not like him, she would never talk to him. But if she liked him, she eventually stopped to make small

talk, but never about love. That came later after many meetings, when they finally met outside her tepee. Before the two could join in marriage, however, both families had to be consulted. And the man's family had to offer gifts to the woman's family to prove their good intentions.

The most important ceremonies of the Cheyennes were the Arrow Renewal, the New Life Lodge, and the Animal Dance. The Arrow Renewal concerned the four Sacred Arrows of the tribe that were supposedly passed to the tribe by its legendary ancestral hero, Sweet Medicine. Sweet Medicine supposedly made a pilgrimage early in Cheyenne history to the Sacred Mountains near the Black Hills where Maiyun, the Great Spirit, gave him four arrows—two for hunting and two for war. The Cheyennes kept the Sacred Arrows in a medicine bundle with other tribal objects, including a hat made from the hide of a female buffalo. The objects symbolized the collective existence of the tribe. After much planning, the 10 Cheyenne bands camped together once a year or every several years to renew the arrows. They placed their tepees in a circle. At the circle's center stood three special lodges—the Sacred Arrow Lodge, the Sacred Arrow Keeper's Lodge, and the Offering Lodge. During a four-day period, the male participants performed a series of rituals to renew the Sacred Arrows and by doing so renew the tribe.

The New Life Lodge, or Sun Dance, was also a renewal ceremony, performed yearly to make the world over again. Many Plains tribes practiced the Sun Dance with varying rituals. But for all the tribes it was an eight-day ceremony, involving the building of a special lodge with a sacred pole in the center, rituals performed by medicine men, dancing before the pole, and self-torture. This last was usually carried out with ropes stretching from the center pole to skewers in the chests of braves. When the braves danced or leaned backward, the skewers tore at their flesh, finally ripping through it. This self-torture aspect of the ceremony led to the banning of the Sun Dance by the federal government in 1910.

The Animal Dance was a hunting ceremony supposedly taught to Sweet Medicine at the Sacred Mountain to help Cheyenne hunters provide enough food for their people. This five-day ceremony was usually held every year as long as there was an individual to organize the event. The first four days were given over to preparations, such as painting a wolfskin to be worn by the pledger and the building of a corral. Women helped in preparations for this event, unlike in the Arrow Renewal and Sun Dance. On the fifth day, the fun began for everyone. Men dressed up as animals. Members of the Bowstring Society pretended to hunt them and herd them into the corral. During the dance, these warriors did everything backwards. There was much clowning around, to the delight of all the spectators. Because of their silly backwards behavior, the Bowstring Society was also called the Contrary Society. And the Animal Dance was also known as the Crazy Dance.

Wars For the Great Plains

Most of the Cheyennes—as we have seen, a religious, thoughtful, and fun-loving people—wanted peace with the whites. They signed a treaty with the federal government in 1825. Soon afterward, Bent's Fort was built on the upper Arkansas River. The Southern Cheyennes settled nearby to trade with the whites. Then in 1851, the Cheyennes participated in the first of two treaties signed at Fort Laramie in Wyoming, the purpose of which was to assure safe passage for white settlers along the Oregon Trail from Missouri to Oregon.

Yet white settlers violated the terms of the treaties. Prospectors entered the Cheyennes' domain along the Smoky Hill Trail to the Rocky Mountains, and some of the Southern Cheyennes attacked the travelers. As a result, cavalrymen rode in to punish them in 1857, resulting in the Battle of Solomon Fork in western Kansas, where the cavalry used a saber charge to force the warriors to retreat.

The next year brought the start of the Pike's Peak Gold Rush, also known as the Colorado Gold Rush. More miners and settlers came to Colorado to stay. In the following years, Colorado officials, especially Governor John Evans, sought to open up Cheyenne and Arapaho hunting grounds to white development. But the two tribes refused to sell their lands and move to reservations. The Governor decided to force the issue through war. He ordered volunteer state militiamen into the field under the Indian-hating territorial military commander, Colonel John Chivington.

In the spring of 1864, Chivington launched a campaign of violence against the Cheyennes and Arapahos, his troops attacking any and all Indians, plundering their possessions and burning their villages. Indians went on the warpath, raiding outlying settlements. This period of conflict is referred to as the Cheyenne-Arapaho War (or the Colorado War) of 1864-65.

With continued attacks, the soldiers pressured the Indians into holding negotiations at Camp Weld outside Denver. At this meeting, the Indians were led to believe that if they camped nearby and reported to army posts, they would be declaring peace and would be safe from attack. Black Kettle led his band of about

A Cheyenne brave

600 Southern Cheyennes, plus some Southern Arapahos, to Sand Creek near Fort Lyon. He informed the garrison of his people's peaceful intentions.

Shortly afterward, Chivington rode into the fort with the Third Cavalry. The post commander told him that Black Kettle's band had surrendered. Chivington ignored him. He believed in the policy of extermination of Indians, with no prisoners taken.

Sand Creek rates as one of the most cruel massacres in Indian history. It is not as famous as the incident involving the Sioux at Wounded Knee. But it is just as horrible, with even more people dying. It is also important historically because it began the most intense period of warfare on the Plains after the Civil War. Wounded Knee ended those wars.

In the early morning of November 29, 1864, Chivington's men, many of them drunk, took up positions around the Indian camp. Black Kettle raised both a white flag of truce and an American flag over his tepee. Chivington ordered the attack anyway. His men opened up with cannon and rifles. A few warriors, including Black Kettle, managed to take cover behind the high bank of Sand Creek and fight back briefly before escaping. When the shooting stopped, 200 Cheyennes were dead, more than half of them women and children.

Chivington was later denounced in a congressional investigation and forced to resign. Yet it was too late to prevent further warfare. The Indians who escaped the massacre spread word of it to other tribes. The incident confirmed the worst fears of tribal leaders about the behavior of the outsiders who had permanently invaded their homeland.

Cheyenne painted shield, taken by Custer on the Washita River in 1868

In the years after the Civil War, the army launched two campaigns against the Plains Indians—the Bozeman Campaign on the northern Plains and the Hancock Campaign on the southern Plains. In the War for the Bozeman Trail of 1866-68, some Northern Cheyennes under Dull Knife fought with Red Cloud's Sioux. To the south, after an unproductive parley with the Southern Cheyenne chiefs Tall Bull and White Horse, General Winfield Scott Hancock ordered troops to round up Cheyenne rebels. One of his leaders in the field was a young cavalry officer named George Armstrong Custer (who would later gain fame in one of the greatest Indian victories in American his-

tory, at Little Bighorn). The war parties stayed one step ahead of the soldiers and continued their attacks on wagon trains, stagecoaches, mail stations, and railroad work sites.

The failure of the army in both the Bozeman and Hancock campaigns, plus the earlier massacre at Sand Creek, caused white officials to try to seek peace with the powerful Plains tribes. In the Fort Laramie Treaty of 1868, the Sioux were granted a reservation on the northern Plains. In the Medicine Lodge Treaty of 1867, the Southern Cheyennes and Southern Arapahos received lands in the Indian Territory, as did the Comanches and Kiowas.

Again whites violated the terms of the treaties, settling on Indian lands, and warriors continued their raids. The Dog Soldiers of the Cheyennes attacked settlements along the Sabine and Solomon rivers. General Philip Sheridan was given the new command. The first major conflict involving his troops was the Battle of Beecher Island in 1868, which ended in a stand-off. Lieutenant Frederick Beecher and a much-revered Dog Soldier named Roman Nose lost their lives in this battle, along with several others on both sides.

The following winter, Sheridan launched a three-pronged attack, with three converging columns out of forts in Colorado, Kansas, and New Mexico against Cheyennes, Arapahos, Comanches, and Kiowas. The Sheridan Campaign broke the resistance of most Southern Cheyenne bands.

The first critical battle was along the Washita River in the Indian Territory in November of 1868. A column under Custer attacked Black Kettle's band. Even after Sand Creek, Black Kettle had never gone to war. He had led this group into the Indian Territory to avoid the fighting in Kansas and Colorado. But Custer, desperate for a victory, like Chivington four years before, attacked anyway. The Indians managed only a brief counterattack. Black Kettle and about 100 others died in this tragic repeat of history.

The army kept up its pressure. In March 1869, Southern Cheyenne bands under Little Robe and Medicine Arrows surrendered. Then soon after, the Dog Soldiers under Tall Bull were cut off by troops as they headed northward to join their northern relatives. Tall Bull and about 50 others died in the Battle of Summit Springs in Colorado.

Pockets of Southern Cheyenne resistance remained, however. Some Cheyenne warriors fought with the Comanches and Kiowas in the Red River War of 1874-75. Others reached the Northern Cheyennes and with them joined the War for the Black Hills of 1876-77, fighting at Little Bighorn in 1876 and getting their revenge on Custer by killing him and all his men. But the same year in Nebraska, a force under Colonel Wesley Merritt intercepted and defeated a force of about 1,000 Cheyennes at War Bonnet Creek before they could join up with Sitting Bull and Crazy Horse of the Sioux. Then troops under Ranald Mackenzie routed Northern Cheyennes under Dull Knife in the battle named after that famous Northern Cheyenne leader.

Cheyenne resistance had ended. Dull Knife's band was placed in the Indian Territory among the Southern Cheyennes. Spurred by scarce food rations, an outbreak of malaria, and a longing for their homeland in Wyoming and Montana, Dull Knife led his warriors on an epic flight northward in September 1877. Crossing lands now developed by whites—with ranches, farms, roads, and railroads—the approximately 300 Cheyennes avoided a pursuing force of 13,000 for six weeks before they were finally caught. Many Cheyennes died in the bloody roundup, including Dull Knife's daughter. Dull Knife and others surrendered on the Sioux Reservation at Pine Ridge in South Dakota. But other Cheyennes made it to the Tongue River in Montana. In 1884, after further negotiations, the Northern Cheyennes were finally granted reservation lands in Montana.

Most Northern Cheyennes still live on the Northern Cheyenne Reservation. The tribal headquarters is located at Lame Deer, Montana. The Southern Cheyennes currently share federal trust lands with the Southern Arapahos in Oklahoma. Their tribal headquarters is located at Concho. Farming and the leasing of mineral rights play an important part in the economies of both groups.

Chickasaw

The heart of the Chickasaw (pronounced *CHICK-uh-saw*) ancestral homeland was located in northern Mississippi, with some additional territory in what is now western Tennessee, western Kentucky, and eastern Arkansas. The Chickasaws were closely related in language and culture to the Choctaws of southern Mississippi (see "Choctaw"). Both peoples spoke the Muskogean language and had cultural ties to the Creeks living to the east in Alabama and Georgia (see "Creek").

In terms of political organization, the Chickasaws were somewhere between the Creeks and the Choctaws; not as rigidly structured as the Creeks, but not as informal as the Choctaws. None of these people had the elaborate social structure of the Natchez, who also lived along the lower Mississippi River (see "Natchez"). The Chickasaws and these other tribes are all considered part of the Southeast Culture Area (see "Southeast Indians").

The land once inhabited by Chickasaws is a fertile floodplain formed by soil deposited when the Mississippi overflows its banks. The wild vegetation along the river is generally thick and low. Some trees, such as the bald cypress tree, grow in the lowland swamps of Mississippi and Louisiana. Drier parts of the floodplain have tall hardwood trees, such as oak, ash, and hickory. The black, moist soil of the floodplain makes for excellent farming. The forests provide shelter for all sorts of wildlife, such as white-tailed deer and black bear. The Mississippi River and its several tributaries offer many kinds of fish, such as the huge Mississippi catfish, sometimes weighing as much as 200 pounds.

The Chickasaws liked to locate their villages on patches of high ground, safe from flooding. They placed them near stands of hardwood trees, in order to have a source of wood for building houses and dugouts. They also sought fertile soil for planting corn, beans, squash, sunflowers, and melons. Chickasaw houses had the typical pole-frame construction of the Southeast with a variety of materials used as coverings—grass thatch, cane thatch, bark, or hide.

The Chickasaws, like other Indian peoples, practiced what some scholars have called the "law of hospitality." An English trader named James Adair, who lived among many tribes of the Southeast, including the Chickasaws, for almost 40 years in the 1700s, wrote, "They are so hospitable, kind-hearted, and free, that they would share with those of their own tribe the last part of their own provisions, even to a single ear of corn; and to others, if they called when they were eating; for they have no stated meal time. An open, generous temper is a standing virtue among them; to be narrow-hearted, especially to those in want, or to any of their own family, is accounted a great crime, and to reflect scandal on the rest of the tribe. Such wretched misers they brand with bad characters."

The Spanish had early contacts with the Chickasaws. Hernando de Soto led his expedition into their territory in 1541. True to the "law of hospitality," the Chickasaws let the outsiders live among them. But De Soto tried to force the tribal chiefs into providing 200 bearers to carry his supplies. He also had his men execute two Chickasaws for stealing pigs and cut off the hands of a third. The proud Chickasaws were indignant at this treatment. They launched an attack on the conquistadors from three different directions, inflicting much damage before disappearing into the wilderness.

In the later colonial period, the Chickasaws became allies of the English. They were among the few tribes of the lower Mississippi not to join with the French in the French and Indian Wars, and the Chickasaw support of the English created a balance of power in the region. English traders from the Carolinas, such as James Adair, helped keep this alliance with the Chickasaws intact.

The Chickasaws provided a constant threat to French travelers on the Mississippi River between New Orleans and Canada. The French ordered the Chickasaws to expel British traders. They also demanded the expulsion of Natchez refugees who had fled to Chickasaw villages after the Natchez Revolt of 1729. And the French armed their allies, the Choctaws, against the Chickasaws. But the Chickasaws refused to yield. They carried out raids against both the French and Choctaws. They even managed to halt all traffic on the Mississippi for a time. The French organized many armies against the Chickasaws—in 1736, 1741, and 1752—but they were all unsuccessful in vanquishing the fierce tribe. The Chickasaws remained unconquered right up until 1763 and the ultimate English victory in the last of the French and Indian Wars.

In the American Revolution of 1775-83, the Chickasaws did not wholeheartedly throw their support behind either the British or the Americans. Some warriors fought for each side. Others decided not to fight at all. When the Shawnee chief Tecumseh tried to organize a united Indian stand against the United States in 1809-11, the Chickasaws again withheld total commitment (see "Shawnee").

White settlement increased rapidly in the early 1800s. During the 1820s, many Chickasaws migrated west of the Mississippi by their own choice. But the majority wanted to stay in their ancestors' homeland. In 1830, President Andrew Jackson signed the Indian Removal Act to relocate eastern Indians west of the Mississippi in a specified territory away from white settlements. The Chickasaw removal occurred mostly after 1837. This tribe did not suffer as much during the actual journey as the other relocated tribes—the Cherokees, Choctaws, Creeks, and Seminoles—who later, with the Chickasaws, became known as the Five Civilized Tribes (see each by name). But many Chickasaws died of cholera and food poisoning after their arrival in the Indian Territory.

Within the Indian Territory (which became the state of Oklahoma in 1907), the Chickasaws have had political ties with the other Five Civilized Tribes from the 1830s until today. Like all Native Americans, they have experienced many different approaches by the federal government to the Indian issue: Allotment and Assimilation; Tribal Restoration and Reorganization; Termination and Urbanization; and Self-Determination (see "Cherokee"). The Chickasaws have blended elements from both their traditional culture and non-Indian society to rebuild their lives in their new homeland.

Chinook

People living east of the Rocky Mountains in both the United States and Canada at times feel warm, dry Chinook winds blowing from the west. In the Swiss Alps and elsewhere, winds of this kind are called *foehn* winds. The Chinook name, pronounced *shi-NOOK*, was originally applied to moist sea breezes blowing from the coast in Oregon and Washington. There, early settlers referred to the winds by that name because they came from the general direction of Chinook, or Tsinuk, Indian villages.

The Chinooks lived at the mouth of the Columbia River where it opens up into the Pacific Ocean, mostly

on the north side in territory now part of the state of Washington. On the south side of the Columbia River, in Oregon, and farther inland in both states, there were other tribes who spoke similar Chinookan dialects, probably of the Penutian language family. Some of the other Chinookan-speaking tribes are the following: Cathlamet, Cathlapotle, Chilluckittequaw, Clackamus, Clatsop, Clowwewalla, Multomah, Wasco, and Wishram. Some scholars divide them into the Lower and Upper Chinooks depending on their location on the river, near the mouth (Lower) or more inland (Upper). Their location also determines in what culture group they are placed, either the Northwest Coast Culture Area or the Plateau Culture Area (see "Northwest Coast Indians" and "Plateau Indians").

One way to think of the Chinooks proper and all the other Chinookan-speaking tribes along the Columbia River is as the Indians who provided the link between Northwest Coast tribes and Plateau tribes. The Columbia River was a main trading thoroughfare between coastal and inland peoples, and the Chinooks met with Plateau tribes regularly at the Dalles, an area of rapids up the river. With the trading of food and objects, ideas and customs were also exchanged.

The Chinooks, like their Northwest Coast neighbors, constructed rectangular houses of cedar planks, but they placed them partly underground over pits, an architectural style more common to the plateau. They also built temporary mat shelters when on the trail, again similar to those of the Plateau peoples. The Chinooks carved large dugout boats, as did their coastal neighbors, but they did not make large totem poles. The Chinooks were known instead for their horn carvings, made from the horns of bighorn sheep and other animals. They practiced the potlatch, a system of exchanging gifts, as did all Northwest Coast peoples, but they did not have the many secret societies common to the area. The Chinooks depended on salmon as a food staple, as did both Northwest Coast and Plateau tribes. But they were less dependent on sea mammals as a food source than were their coastal neighbors.

As with the Plateau Indians along the upper Columbia, the river was the primary domain of the Chinooks. They even charged other Indians tolls to paddle through their territory.

Of all the tribes of the southern Northwest Coast, the Chinooks were the most famous traders. Like the Tlingits to the north, they acted as middlemen among many different tribes (see "Tlingit"). They used tooth shells as a form of money and dealt in dried fish, fish oil, seal oil, furs, dugouts, cedar boards, cedar bark, mountain sheep horns, jadeite, copper, baskets, other goods, and even slaves. In fact, the Chinooks developed a special trade language that was a mixture of local languages, to carry out their bartering.

The Chinooks continued to work as middlemen after whites reached the area. Early European explorers reached the Oregon coast as early as the 1500s.

Chinook bowl made from the horn of a bighorn sheep

It wasn't until the late 1700s, however, that the area came to be developed for trade, especially after 1792 when Robert Gray and William Broughton explored the Columbia River. Thereafter, both British and American trading ships anchored near Chinook territory seeking to exchange European trade goods for pelts. Lewis and Clark, traveling overland rather than by sea, reached Chinook country in 1805. Soon after, in 1811, John Jacob Astor, the owner of the American Fur Company and the Pacific Fur Company, founded a trading post called Astoria near the Chinook lands. Before long Chinook Jargon, as it came to be called (or the Oregon Trade Language), had incorporated English and French words as well as Indian ones and came to be known throughout the entire Northwest, from Alaska to California. An example of a word in Chinook Jargon is *hootchenoo* for homemade liquor, from which our slang word "hootch" is derived.

The traditional way of life of the Chinooks began to change in the 1830s, when a Methodist minister named Jason Lee established a mission among Chinookan-speaking tribes of the Willamette Valley. Lee encouraged white development of the rich farmland, and, by the 1840s, settlers were arriving in great numbers. By 1859, Oregon had achieved statehood, and Washington became a state in 1889. The Chinooks eventually settled among the Chehalis Indians, a Salishan-speaking tribe, for whom a reservation had been established near present-day Oakville, Washington, in 1864.

Chinook paddle

Chipewyan

Chipewyan bands once ranged over much of western Canada between Great Slave Lake and the Churchill River. What was once Chipewyan homeland now falls within the southeastern part of the Northwest Territories and the northern parts of Alberta, Saskatchewan, and Manitoba provinces. The Chipewyans also controlled a wedge of land on the west shore of Hudson Bay, between the Eskimos to the north and the Crees to the south (see "Eskimo" and "Cree").

The Chipewyan name (pronounced *chip-uh-WHY-an*), given to them by the Crees, means "pointed skins," because of their shirts, which were pointed at the bottom. The name of a band of Chipewyans, the *Athabascas*, has come to be used for all Indian peoples of the *Athabascan* (also spelled *Athapascan*) language family. The Chipewyans were the largest of the Athapascan tribes who lived in Canada and Alaska. Their lifeways are typical of their neighbors in the vicinity of Great Slave and Great Bear lakes, such as the Beavers, Dogribs, Hares, Slaves, and Yellowknives, all of whom are classified as part of the Subarctic Culture Area (see "Athapascan" and "Subarctic Indians"). The Subarctic tribes were organized into small bands of extended families, all of them nomadic hunter-gatherers.

The Chipewyans lived along the northern edge of the Subarctic where the Northern Forest, or taiga, gives way to the Barren Grounds, or tundra. Winters were long and bitterly cold; summers were all too short and plagued with blackflies and mosquitoes. The Chipewyans, frequently on the move in search of food, lived in portable skin tents similar to the tepees of the Plains Indians. They made a framework of poles by setting them in a circle and leaning them against one another and tying them at the top. Then they covered the framework with caribou hides sewn together. They left a hole at the top for smoke to escape, and they placed spruce boughs and caribou skins at the base to form a floor.

Life for the Chipewyan bands revolved around the seasonal migrations of the caribou herds. In the spring, many bands gathered at the edge of the forested taiga to intercept the animals as they migrated northward onto the treeless tundra. In the fall, the Chipewyans returned to hunt the caribou on the animals' southern migration. The hunters used a variety of tricks to catch the animals. They drove them into corrals made of brush where they could kill them in great numbers. Or they snared animals with ropes strung between two trees. Or they attacked the caribou from canoes—made from either birchbark or spruce bark—as the animals swam across a river or lake. Another trick was to bang antlers together to make a caribou bull think two other bulls were fighting over a female. When the animal came to investigate, the Chipewyans' favorite weapon was a birch bow with stone-tipped or bone-tipped arrows, but spears were also used for the kill.

The Chipewyans used every part of the caribou. They boiled fresh meat in birchbark or caribou-skin containers, by adding heated stones. They ate the head and the stomach with all its contents. Some of the meat was made into pemmican—dried and pounded meat mixed with fat—which was packed into the animal's intestines (like sausage) to be carried on the trail. The hide of the caribou was cured to make tents, clothing, and babiche (leather thongs that were used to lace snowshoes, make nets, and for many other applications). Finally, the bones and antlers of the caribou were used to make tools.

The Chipewyans hunted other animals, too, such as moose, musk-ox, buffalo, deer, bear, beaver, and waterfowl. In the winter, they stalked game on snowshoes and used toboggans to haul their catch. They also fished the many lakes and rivers in their territory, going after freshwater fish such as trout, bass, pike, and whitefish. They used many different techniques in fishing, including nets, hooks, barbed arrows, and spears. The Chipewyans also built weirs, wooden or stone pens, to trap fish. They fished from canoes too. The fish they did not eat immediately, they smoked or sun-dried to preserve.

The Chipewyans had few plants in their diet. But they did use some of the tundra plants for nourishment. Moss, they made into a soup. And lichens, they

Chipewyan toboggan

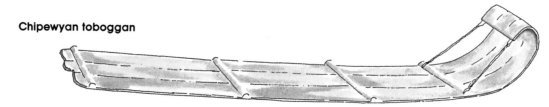

Chipewyan birchbark canoe

ate in their fermented state in the caribou's stomach.

In addition to their leatherwork, woodwork, stonework, and bonework, the Chipewyans also worked in metal. They found copper nuggets in the soil along the Coppermine River and used annealing techniques—alternate heating and hammering—to work the material into the desired shape. They made knives, axes, awls, drills, ice chisels, scrapers, arrowheads, spearheads, and other tools from copper. They also traded the raw material to other tribes for food, shells, and other products.

The women did much of the hard work within the Chipewyan bands—making fires, preparing food, curing leather, and many other chores. They also did much of the hauling, carrying supplies on their backs as well as pulling toboggans. In fact, women ranked at least as low if not lower in Chipewyan society than among any other Native American peoples, and they were at the mercy of their husbands. When the food ran out, the women were the first to go hungry.

Dogs were very important to the Chipewyans. The dog held a special place in Chipewyan mythology. In their creation myth, it was a dog that fathered the human race. The Indians fed their dogs well whenever possible. But when faced with starvation in the worst of the winter months, they would eat their dogs to survive. When desperate enough, the Chipewyans would also eat their own dead to survive, although cannibalism was considered a terrible deed and used only as a last resort. Normally, the Chipewyans left their dead exposed, to be devoured by scavenging birds and animals.

The Chipewyans played an important role in the white exploration of western Canada. The fur companies had early contacts with them. The Hudson's Bay Company founded the trading post of Churchill on Hudson Bay in 1717, establishing an early trade relationship with the Chipewyans. Samuel Hearne, who explored the Churchill, Coppermine, and Slave rivers all the way to the Arctic Ocean for the Hudson's Bay Company from 1768 to 1776, had a Chipewyan guide named Matonabbee. Alexander Mackenzie, an explorer for the North West Company and the first white man to cross the entire North American continent, from 1789 to 1793, also had the help of Chipewyans. His base of activity was Fort Chipewyan, founded on Lake Athabasca in 1788 in the heart of the tribe's territory.

The arrival of the fur traders and the establishment of trading posts in their territory changed the life of the Chipewyans. For one thing, French traders armed the neighboring Crees with guns. The Crees, who had been longtime enemies of the Chipewyans, were then able to take over some Chipewyan land. The traders also brought disease to the Chipewyans. A smallpox epidemic ravaged the Chipewyan bands in 1781, killing the majority of their people.

The first missionary to the Chipewyans was the Catholic Father Henri Faraud in 1858 at Fort Resolution. He wrote an abridged version of the New Testament in the Chipewyan dialect.

The tribe signed a series of treaties with the Canadian government in 1876, 1877, 1899, and 1906 in exchange for reserve lands, supplies, and annual payments. A number of Chipewyan bands presently hold five reserves in Alberta, six in Saskatchewan, two in Manitoba, and two in the Northwest Territories. Many of their members still hunt as a way of life.

Chippewa (Ojibway)

The Chippewas (pronounced *CHIP-uh-wah*) are also known as the Ojibways (pronounced *o-jib-WAY*). The former name is commonly used in the United States and the latter in Canada. Both names, different versions of an Algonquian phrase, refer to a puckered seam in the Chippewas' style of moccasins. The Algonquian-speaking Chippewas also called themselves *Anishinabe*, meaning "first men" (see "Algonquian").

The Chippewas were one of the largest and most powerful tribes in North America. They inhabited the country of the western Great Lakes, especially around

Lake Superior. When they migrated to the region, before the arrival of whites, the Chippewas were supposedly one people with the Ottawas and Potawatomis. The three tribes remained allies through much of their history. They called themselves the Council of Three Tribes.

Lifeways

Like other Algonquians of the Northeast and the eastern Subarctic, the Chippewas were a Woodland people. Southern bands can be classified in the Northeast Culture Area and northern bands in the Subarctic Culture Area (see "Northeast Indians" and "Subarctic Indians"). Or they can all be referred to as Great Lakes Algonquians.

Although they sometimes moved their villages from one region to another if wildlife became scarce, the Chippewas generally remained in one place. They used birchbark for their wigwams, canoes, and containers. They usually dressed in buckskin. They were

Chippewa cone-shaped birchbark wigwam

farmers who grew corn, beans, pumpkins, and squash in small patches. They were also hunter-gatherers who sought the mammals, fish, shellfish, fowl, and wild edible plants of the forest, lakes and rivers.

A staple food of the Chippewas was wild rice. This plant, found along the edges of lakes, streams, and swamps, is not really a kind of rice but rather a tall grass with an edible seed that resembles rice. The Chippewas harvested it in the summer months. While the men hunted ducks and geese from their sleek and swift birchbark canoes, the women, also in canoes, drifted beside the clumps of the lush plants and collected the valuable seeds in the bottoms of the boats.

Chippewa Midewiwin water drum. The water inside adds resonance.

Like certain other Indian peoples of the Great Lakes and the prairies flanking the Mississippi River, the Chippewas participated in the secret and magical Midewiwin Society, also sometimes called the Grand Medicine Society. In early times, entry into this club (or sodality) was very difficult to achieve. A man or woman normally had to have a special visitation by a spirit in a dream to even be considered for membership. A secret meeting to initiate those accepted was held only once a year in a specially constructed elongated lodge. One member recorded the events of the meeting on bark scrolls, using a bone implement for carving and red paints for coloring. The members might sing, "We are now to receive you into the Midewiwin, our Mide brother." And the initiate might reply, "I have the medicine in my heart and I am strong as a bear."

Members in the Midewiwin Society wore Mide, or medicine bags, made from mink, weasel, rattlesnake, hawk, or owl skins, or from wildcat or bear paws around their necks. The Chippewas believed that all living and non-living things, had spirits that could be tamed to help the sick or to harm one's enemies. And, like other Algonquians, the Chippewas believed in one all-pervasive spirit from which all lesser spirits drew their power—the Manitou. Nowadays, the Midewiwin Society makes use of elements from other religions such as Christianity and is no longer so difficult to join.

History and Wars

The Chippewas were early and consistent allies of the French. Because they were trusted friends and trading partners, they were among the first Indians to receive French firearms. With these guns, they drove the Sioux westward onto the Great Plains, and the Sacs, Foxes, and Kickapoos southward from what today is northern Wisconsin (see entries for those tribes). Some of these fights were naval battles, with warriors fighting from canoes. The Chippewas even managed to repel the powerful Iroquois, invading from the east (see "Iroquois").

During the late 1600s and early 1700s, various Chippewa bands came to dominate parts of Wisconsin, Minnesota, Michigan, North Dakota, and southern Ontario, their empire stretching from Lake Huron to the Missouri River. Important bands of Chippewas were the Missisaugas and the Salteaux. Other Chippewas adopted the Plains Indian lifestyle in the southern part of Manitoba and came to be known as the Plains Ojibway (see "Plains Indians").

In the mid-1700s, the Chippewas fought the British in the French and Indian Wars (see "Abnaki" and "Iroquois") and in Pontiac's Rebellion (see "Ottawa").

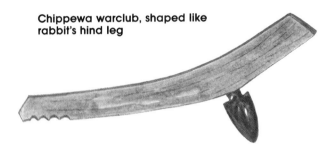

Chippewa warclub, shaped like rabbit's hind leg

Then in 1769, the Chippewas joined forces with the Ottawas, Potawatomis, Sacs, Foxes, and Kickapoos to defeat the Illinois Indians (see "Illinois").

In the American Revolution, the Chippewas became allies of the British against the American rebels. Then they fought the Americans again in the Indian wars for the Old Northwest, including Little Turtle's War, Tecumseh's Rebellion, and in the War of 1812 (see "Miami" and "Shawnee"). In 1815, when the British surrendered, the Chippewas were forced to cede much of their land to the expanding United States.

Modern-Day Activism

The fighting spirit has carried over to modern-day Chippewas. In 1968, three Chippewas—Dennis Banks, George Mitchell, and Clyde Bellecourt—founded AIM, the American Indian Movement, in Minneapolis, Minnesota. Many of its original members were urban Indians who had left the reservations to work in the cities. Of course, not all Native Americans live on reservations or on tribal trust lands. In fact, it is estimated by the United States

Census Bureau that 64 percent of all Native Americans live elsewhere. AIM is one of the most active and militant of all the Native American political groups fighting for Indian rights and improved social conditions on and off reservations.

Members of AIM participated in the 1969 takeover of Alcatraz Island in San Francisco, the 1972 occupation of the Federal Bureau of Indian Affairs in Washington, D.C., and the 1973 seizure of Wounded Knee in South Dakota, the site of the Wounded Knee Massacre of 1890 (see "Sioux"). Like many of the conflicts of past centuries, each of these events is a dramatic story of moves and countermoves—and sometimes violence—between Indians and federal agents. At the modern-day Wounded Knee incident, two Indians—Frank Clearwater and Buddy Lamont—were killed and a federal marshall was wounded. One result of these protests was to help call public attention to the violation of treaty rights by the federal and state governments and to the resulting poverty of the Native American.

Songs and Poems

In addition to being great warriors and freedom fighters, the Chippewas are famous for their sense of humor. They have always been an individualistic and self-contained people, repressing public displays of extreme emotion. But they have always known how to laugh heartily with one another, even in times of trouble. They have also always been a romantic

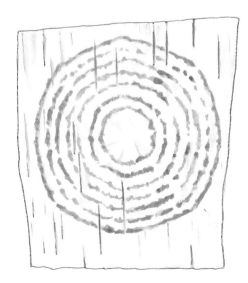

Chippewa birchbark transparency, made from a piece of inner bark, folded and bitten to form a design that shows clearly when held up to light

people. The following is the traditional love song of a Chippewa girl:

Oh, I am thinking
Oh, I am thinking
I have found my lover
Oh, I think it is so.

After she was married and had a baby, the same girl, now a woman, might sing the following cradle song:

Who is this? Who is this?
Giving light on the top of my lodge?
It is I, the little owl, coming,
It is I, the little owl, coming,
Down! Down!

The most famous of all Chippewa children is really a fictional character. Even his name is not really a Chippewa name but an Iroquois name—Hiawatha. Henry Wadsworth Longfellow wrote a poem in 1855 about this make-believe Chippewa youth living along

Chippewa container, made of porcupine quills, birchbark, and sweetgrass (modern)

the Great Lakes. It begins: "By the shores of Gitche Gumee, By the shining Big-Sea-Water . . ." The "Song of Hiawatha" is not an accurate depiction of Indian culture. Yet this fanciful tale evokes colorful images that can fuel the imagination.

Nowadays, the still-populous Chippewas live on reservations in Minnesota, Wisconsin, Michigan, North Dakota, Montana, Ontario, and Manitoba, as well as in cities in the Midwest and central Canada.

Chitimacha

The Chitimachas (pronounced *chid-uh-MA-shuh*) lived in what is now the lower part of the state of Louisiana, along the Mississippi Delta in the vicinity of Grand River, Grand Lake, and the lower course of Bayou La Teche. The Chitimacha language is unique, although it may be related to Tunican, spoken by neighboring tribes (see "Southeast Indians"; "Tunica"; and "Yazoo").

The Chitimachas lived in pole-frame houses with walls and roofs of palmetto thatch. Sometimes the walls were plastered over with mud, a technique called wattle and daub. Alligators, turtles, fish, and shellfish were abundant in their territory, along with other game. The men used blowguns in addition to bows and arrows to shoot small game, and they could send the small darts flying up to 60 feet. The Chitimachas grew sweet potatoes and melons in addition to corn, beans, and squash. For food storage, the women made patterned cane baskets with fitted tops.

In 1682, Rene Cavalier de la Salle claimed the Mississippi Valley for France, naming it Louisiana, after France's King Louis XIV. Then in 1699, Pierre le Moyne, Sieur d'Iberville, founded a settlement near present-day Biloxi. And in 1718, Iberville's brother, Sieur de Bienville, founded New Orleans. The Chitimachas therefore were under the French sphere of influence for most of the colonial period.

The relations between the two peoples were not always peaceful, however. After some of their people were enslaved by Indians who lived among the French in 1706, the Chitimachas killed a French missionary to the Natchez Indians, named St. Cosme, and his three companions. For the next 12 years, the Chitimachas and the French engaged in a series of raids and counter-raids. During that period, the majority of Indian slaves among the French colonists were from the Chitimacha tribe. Peace was made in 1718, when the Chitimachas agreed to settle at a site on the Mississippi River, near present-day Plaquemine.

By 1881, the only surviving Chitimachas lived at Charenton, Louisiana, where a small community exists today. The Chitimachas are still famous for their beautifully crafted baskets of narrow cane splints with black, red, and yellow designs.

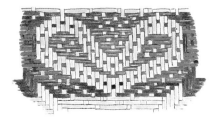

Detail of Chitimacha basket showing intricate weave and vegetable-dye colors

Choctaw

According to tribal legend, the Choctaws originated from *Nanih Waiya*, the Mother Mound, at a location near what is present-day Noxapater, Mississippi. This creation myth indicates that the Choctaws were descended from the earlier Temple Mound Builders of the Southeast (see "Mound Builders"). At the time of early European contacts with them, the Choctaws were one of the largest tribes of the Southeast, occupying territory in what is now southern and central Mississippi and with some groups in Alabama, Georgia, and Louisiana as well.

Lifeways

The Choctaws (pronounced *CHOK-taw*) were a Muskogean-speaking people, closely related in language and culture to other descendants of the Mound Builders—the Chickasaws, living to the north of them, and the Creeks, living to the northeast of them (see "Chickasaw" and "Creek"). Yet the Choctaws had a more democratic system of government than other Southeast tribes (see "Southeast Indians"). In this regard they were more like the Northeast tribes, who did not have autocratic rulers with absolute power.

The Choctaws, like most Southeast tribes, were primarily villagers. They used a variety of materials to build their dwellings—wood for the pole frames; grass or cane reeds for thatched roofs; clay and crushed shells for walls (or in some cases bark, hide, or woven mats). The Choctaws had both winter and summer houses. To keep the winter houses warm the Indians built fires, and to keep them moist they poured water over heated rocks. For additional warmth, they twisted turkey feathers into thread to weave blankets.

The Choctaws were highly skilled farmers. In fact, they were probably the best farmers in the entire Southeast, with large fields in the fertile bottom lands of the lower Mississippi River. Their main crops were corn, beans, squash, sunflowers, and melons. For the Choctaws, hunting, fishing, and the gathering of edible wild plants were secondary in importance to their frequent plantings and harvestings.

For transportation on hunting, fishing, and trading trips, the Choctaws carved dugout canoes. Choctaw traders developed a simple trade language that they could use in combination with sign language to communicate with other tribes.

Choctaw men let their hair grow long, unlike the males of most other Southeast tribes, who shaved their heads. The Chickasaws called them *Pansh Falaia*, meaning "long hairs." The Choctaws and Chickasaws both practiced head deformation, using a hinged piece of wood to apply pressure over a period of time to the foreheads of male infants. They believed that head-flattening made men more handsome.

The Choctaws, like many Indian peoples, were great players of lacrosse, sometimes called Indian stickball. The purpose of the game was to toss a leather ball between posts with rackets, or sticks with curved and webbed ends. Players weren't allowed to touch the ball with their hands or to use the sticks to fight. But just about everything else was fair play—tripping, bumping, stomping, and piling on top of one another. There were many injuries, even deaths, during lacrosse games. Sometimes great matches were held between villages with hundreds of participants. There would be pregame ceremonies with dancing and singing during the days preceding the big event. Villagers

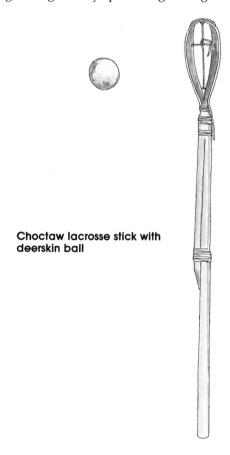

Choctaw lacrosse stick with deerskin ball

would place bets on their team, gambling many of their possessions. Medicine men would act as "coaches," but they would use incantations, rather than strategy, to get their team to score the 100 points that they needed to win. After the men played their marathon games, the women played their own rough version.

The Choctaws were a very musical and poetic people. The various villages competed with one another to write new songs that would be performed at festivals, but kept their new melodies and words secret until performance time. Someone from another village or tribe who spied on a musical practice was called a "song thief." The following is a hunting song, sung by a hunter to his wife:

Go and grind some corn, we will go camping.
Go and sew, we will go camping.
I passed on and you were sitting there crying.
You were lazy and your hoe is rusty.

The following is a verse from a song written by a Choctaw girl whose father and brothers were killed in a raid:

All men must surely die,
Though no one knows how soon.
Yet when the time shall come
The event may be joyful.

After a death, the Choctaws placed the deceased on a scaffold. There was a "cry-time" for family members, during which they went into retreat, fasted, covered their heads, and mourned. When the corpse had dried out in the open air, tribesmen, officially appointed as bone-pickers, scraped the flesh away with their extra-long fingernails. Then the bones would be buried.

Contacts With Whites

It was the Spanish who first came into contact with the Choctaws. Choctaw warriors harassed Hernando de Soto's expeditionary force when it entered their territory near the Mississippi River in 1540. The conquistadors possessed firearms, but the Indians proved a stubborn menace.

The Choctaws later became important allies of the French, who established themselves along the lower Mississippi Valley after Rene Cavalier de la Salle's expedition of 1682. Choctaw warriors helped to crush the Natchez Revolt of 1729 (see "Natchez"). The fact that the Choctaws generally sided with the French, and the Chickasaws with the English, created a balance of power in the region during the French and Indian Wars from 1689 to 1763.

After 1763, when the French were finally defeated, the English controlled the part of the Southeast that included the Choctaw homeland. Then, at the end of the American Revolution in 1783, when the British were defeated, the Spanish gained control of the Gulf of Mexico region as payment for helping the American rebels. In 1819, the United States gained Spanish holdings in the Southeast after General Andrew Jackson invaded Florida (see "Seminole").

The Choctaws generally sided with the Americans against the British. Choctaw warriors fought under American generals in the American Revolution, the War of 1812, and the Creek War of 1813-14. Moreover, it was a Choctaw chief named Pushmataha who was instrumental in keeping many Southeast bands from joining Tecumseh's Rebellion of 1809-11 (see "Shawnee"). The Choctaws gained a reputation as a peaceful tribe that had adopted many white customs. They came to be considered as one of the Five Civilized Tribes, along with the Cherokees, Creeks, Chickasaws, and Seminoles.

Relocation

Nevertheless, in spite of all their contributions to American causes and their acceptance of white ways of life, the Choctaws were mistreated in return. White settlers wanted their lands, and both state governments and the federal government sided with whites over Indians. In the Creek War, the Choctaws had fought under the man who later became President of the United States, Andrew Jackson. Even so, Jackson signed the Indian Removal Act of 1830, calling for the relocation of all eastern tribes to territory west of the Mississippi River. This was the start of the Trail of Tears, a phrase originally used to describe the Cherokee removal but which has come to stand for the forced march of all Five Civilized Tribes westward (see "Cherokee").

The Choctaws were the first tribe to be relocated. In 1830, a few among them, who did not represent the majority, were bribed into signing the Treaty of Dancing Rabbit Creek, which ceded to the whites all Choctaw lands in the state of Mississippi. Some Choctaws refused to depart and hid out in the back-woods of Mississippi and Louisiana. But the vast majority were herded westward by U.S. Army blue-coats. Conditions on the many forced marches from 1831 to 1834 were terrible. There were shortages of food, blankets, horses, and wagons. The soldiers turned their backs when bandits ambushed the migrants. Disease also struck down the exhausted travelers. About a quarter of the Choctaws died on the trip, and many more died after their arrival in the Indian Territory, from disease, starvation, and attacks by hostile western Indians.

The Choctaws persisted, reorganizing as a tribe and making the most of their new home. Pressures caused by white expansion did not cease, however. The General Allotment Act of 1887, designed to force the break-up of tribal landholdings for increased white development, and the Curtis Act of 1898 caused the eventual loss of much acreage among all the Five Civilized Tribes. What was supposed to exist permanently for native peoples as the Indian Territory became the state of Oklahoma in 1907. (Oklahoma is a Muskogean word, coined by the Choctaw Allen Wright to mean "Red People," and first applied to the western half of the Indian Territory in 1890.)

The western Choctaws presently hold trust lands near Durant, Oklahoma. Descendants of those who stayed in the East have a reservation near Pearl River, Mississippi.

Chumash

The Chumash Indians (pronounced *CHOO-mash*) of the Pacific Coast are the only native peoples in all of North America who built boats out of planks. Other Indians used planks to make houses but never applied this technology to boat making, instead either carving dugouts from single logs or fashioning boats by stretching bark or skin over a wooden frame.

Chumash craftsmen split logs of cedar with antler wedges and smoothed the lumber with shell and stone rubbing tools. Then they lashed the planks together with animal sinew or plant bindings, and caulked them with asphalt to form 25-foot double-bowed hulls. A crew of four paddlers could handle these boats in ocean waters.

The Chumash lived in the vicinity of present-day Santa Barbara in central California, on the mainland and on the three closest of the eight Channel Islands. It is thought that they used their boats for passage among the different Chumash villages, as well as for fishing and hunting sea mammals. The Chumash are sometimes referred to as the Santa Barbara Indians.

The Hokan-speaking Chumash are grouped by scholars in the California Culture Area. They shared many traits with neighboring peoples. They were politically organized by villages rather than by tribe; they hunted small game and fished; they prepared

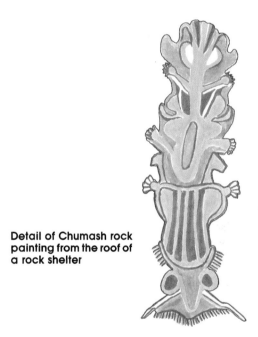

Detail of Chumash rock painting from the roof of a rock shelter

various foods from acorns; they lived in domed houses, covered with various plant materials; and they wore little clothing (see "California Indians").

Yet the Chumash culture was more maritime than that of their inland neighbors. For that matter, the Chumash depended on the sea for food more than did the Salinans and Costanoans to their north,

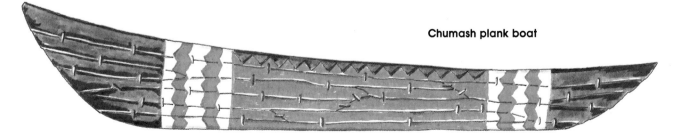

Chumash plank boat

between them and San Francisco Bay. The Santa Barbara Channel's kelp beds drew many different species of fish, which in turn drew many sea mammals. To honor the marine life so essential to their existence, the Chumash carved exquisite animal figures in soapstone.

The Chumash were supposedly the first California coastal Indians found by Spanish explorers, namely Juan Cabrillo and Bartolome Ferrelo, who reached the Santa Barbara Channel in 1542. For the next two centuries, the Spanish used the channel as a stopover for galleons making the Pacific crossing from Mexico to the Philippines, and the early impact on the Chumash was minimal. But then the Franciscan order of Catholic priests built the Santa Barbara Mission in

1786 and began converting the Indians to a new religion and a new agricultural way of life (see "Mission Indians").

In 1834, 13 years after Mexican independence from Spain, the Mexican government secularized the missions and released the Indians from their servitude. But, by that time, many native peoples had forgotten how to survive in the wilderness. Then, with the Anglo-American population increasing, especially after the California Gold Rush of 1849 and California statehood in 1850, the Indians suffered from further losses of land and culture, as well as from white violence and diseases. The Chumash were one of the California tribes driven to virtual extinction, with only a few tribal members remaining by the early 1900s.

Cliff Dwellers and Desert Farmers

Most of the tribes listed in this book existed when Europeans first reached the shores of the Americas, about 1500, or in the course of the following centuries, when whites explored inland. But what about the ancestors of these tribal Indians? How did they live?

Prehistoric Indians are discussed as a whole under another entry (see "Prehistoric Indians"). As seen in that section, Indian prehistory is usually divided into three periods, called Paleolithic, Archaic, and Formative. During the last of these three periods, the Formative, from about 1000 B.C. to A.D. 1500, Indian life north of Mexico reached a high degree of organization and artistic expression among farming peoples. Those east of the Mississippi River built mounds (see "Mound Builders"). Those west of the Mississippi, in the Southwest, were the cliff dwellers and the desert farmers.

The various cultures have names. The early Southwest cultures are known as the Mogollon, Hohokam, and Anasazi. There were other cultures in the Southwest during the Formative period, from 1000 B.C. to A.D. 1500, but the three mentioned here were the most organized and most widespread.

It was farming that shaped these three cultures and made them different from the hunting and gathering cultures of the same period. The cultivation of plants for food meant that people no longer had to constantly travel to find wild foods. This village life led to the further development of tools, arts, and crafts, especially basketry and pottery. The earliest evidence of agriculture north of Mexico comes from this region, Bat Cave, New Mexico, where archaeologists have

found several cobs of corn from a primitive cultivated species, dating back to about 3500 B.C. The Indians who planted this corn are considered Archaic Indians, part of a culture known as Cochise. Yet farming did not become common in the region until centuries later—about A.D. 100, during the Formative period.

Why did farming flourish in this rugged and arid part of North America? Scholars suggest two reasons for this phenomenon. First of all, the peoples of the Southwest were close to the Mesoamerican civilizations of what is now Mexico and Central America. It was in Mesoamerica that farming originated in the Americas and reached a high level of development (see "Olmec"); these skills could have been passed on to the peoples to the north. Second, since the Southwest had scarce game and few edible wild plants, farming was an appealing way to get food for the Indians who lived there.

Mogollon Culture

The name *Mogollon*, pronounced *mo-goi-YONE*, comes from the mountain range along the southern Arizona-New Mexico border, this cultural group's core area. The Indians of the Mogollon culture, probably direct descendants of the Indians of the earlier Cochise culture, are considered the first Southwest people to farm, build houses, and make pottery. Their culture thrived from about 300 B.C. to A.D. 1300.

The Mogollon Indians farmed the high valleys in the rugged mountains, cultivating corn, beans, squash, tobacco, and cotton. They prepared the soil with primitive digging sticks. They also gathered wild food plants and hunted the small game living in the high country. The adoption of the bow and arrow about A.D. 500 made hunting easier for them.

Farming enabled the Mogollon Indians to live at one location all year long. For their villages, they chose sites near mountain streams, or along ridges that were easy to defend from raiding peoples. They designed houses especially suitable to the extreme temperatures of the region—pit houses, with the ground providing natural insulation. The frameworks of these pit houses were made from logs which were covered with reeds, saplings, and mud. The largest of these structures served as social and ceremonial centers called kivas.

The earliest Mogollon pottery was brown. The Indians shaped it by rolling the clay into thin strips and then making coils in the shape of pots. They smoothed it over, then covered it with a slip (coat) of clay, and finally baked the pot in an oven. Late in their history, the Mogollon Indians painted their pottery with intricate designs. A subgroup of the Mogollon culture, the Mimbres culture, is famous for their lovely black-on-white pottery from about A.D. 900.

Mogollon pottery dish in black-on-white Mimbres style

Mogollon Indians also wove plant matter into baskets. They used their cultivated cotton or animal fur to make yarn for weaving clothing and blankets. Feathers were added as decoration. The Mogollon Indians also had many tools and ornamental objects made from wood, stone, bone, and shell.

Hohokam Culture

The name *Hohokam*, pronounced *ho-HO-kum*, means "vanished ones" in the Pima language. The core area of the Hohokam Indians was along the Gila and Salt river valleys in what is now southern Arizona. Their culture thrived from about 100 B.C. to A.D. 1500.

What once was the homeland of the Hohokam Indians is torrid desert country today, broken only by the slow-flowing rivers and rugged volcanic hills. In order to make use of the sandy soil, the Hohokam Indians developed a remarkable irrigation system. They dug wide, shallow canals as long as 10 miles, and they made dams using woven mats to redirect the water from the rivers to their fields of corn, beans, squash, tobacco, and cotton.

Because of their advanced farming techniques, the Hohokam Indians grew enough food to support a sizable population. The principle Hohokam village—Snaketown (near present-day Phoenix)—had about 100 pit houses. East of Snaketown was Point of Pines, another large settlement. The Hohokam houses resembled the Mogollon pit houses in construction but were larger and shallower. At Snaketown, archaeologists have also found the remains of two sunken ball-courts and some rubber balls.

The evidence of an ancient ball game indicates a connection between the Hohokam culture and Mesoamerican cultures (see "Maya"; "Toltec"; and "Aztec"). Other artifacts and customs also indicate influence from the south: coiled pottery colored red and pale yellow; colorful textiles; mirrors made by inlaying small pieces of shiny minerals in stone disks; copper bells; stone palettes incised with designs and probably used in rituals; earthen pyramids; and the keeping of macaws as house pets.

The Hohokam Indians are thought to be the first people in the world to practice etching, starting about A.D. 1000. They covered shells with acid-resistant pitch from trees, carved designs on the pitch, then soaked the shells in an acid solution made from fermented saguaro cactus fruit. When they removed the pitch coating, they had a design etched in the shell's surface.

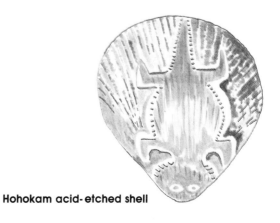

Hohokam acid-etched shell

Anasazi Culture

Over the same period—from about 100 B.C. to A.D. 1300—a third culture, known as Anasazi, thrived in the Southwest. The name *Anasazi*, pronounced *ah-nuh-SAH-zee*, means "ancient ones" in the Navajo language. The Anasazi core area was the Four Corners region, where present-day Colorado, Utah, Arizona, and New Mexico meet. The Four Corners region is a dry, rugged country of high mesas and deep canyons. The Anasazi culture was the most widespread of the three cultures described in this section and had considerable influence on the other two.

Anasazi development can be divided into distinct phases. The first of these is called the Basket Maker period, from about 100 B.C. to A.D. 750. During this phase, the Anasazi Indians mastered the technology of weaving containers and sandals from plant matter, such as straw, vines, and rushes. They also refined their skills in farming and pottery. Like the Mogollon and Hohokam Indians, the Anasazi Indians of the Basket Maker period lived in pit houses.

The second Anasazi phase is known as the Pueblo period. After A.D. 750, the Anasazi Indians developed a new kind of architecture. They kept the underground dwellings as kivas, or social and ceremonial structures. But they also built aboveground structures called pueblos. Using either stone and adobe mortar, or adobe bricks, plus roofs of logs covered with sticks, grass, and mud, the Indians at first made single-room dwellings. Then they began grouping the rooms together and on top of one another, interconnecting the different levels with ladders. The later Pueblo Indians built similar terraced, apartment-like dwellings out of adobe (see "Pueblo Indians").

The Anasazi Indians usually built their pueblos on top of mesas. Pueblo Bonito at Chaco Canyon in what is now New Mexico—first occupied about A.D.

Remains of an Anasazi yucca fiber sandal

900—is an example of an Anasazi mesa-top village. The Indians built the pueblo in the shape of a huge semicircle, with five stories and 800 rooms.

After A.D. 1000, the Anasazi Indians evacuated most of their mesa-top villages. From that time on, until about 1300, they built their great pueblos on cliff ledges, which offered better protection against invaders. That is why the Anasazi Indians are often

Montezuma National Monument in Arizona, a cliff dwelling of the Sinagua culture (about A.D. 1100), an offshoot of Anasazi culture

referred to as cliff dwellers. Examples of sizable villages built in recesses of canyon walls are Cliff Place at Mesa Verde in Colorado, and Mummy Cave at Canyon de Chelly in Arizona.

During this Pueblo phase of Anasazi culture, sometimes referred to as their Golden Age, the Anasazi Indians used irrigation to increase their farm yields and to support large village populations. In addition to being skilled builders and farmers, they were master craftsmen, designing elaborately painted pottery, brightly colored cotton-and-feather clothing, exquisite turquoise jewelry, and intricate mosaic designs.

During the Anasazi Golden Age, their culture influenced other Indians of the region. For example, starting about 1200, the Mogollon culture came to include many Anasazi cultural traits and lost its distinct identity.

But what happened to the great Hohokam and Anasazi centers of civilization? Why did the Indians of the region abandon their cliff dwellings, starting about 1300, and move to smaller settlements? It is not known for certain. Scientists do know that, during the late 1200s, a prolonged drought struck the entire Southwest. With no rain whatsoever, the Indians had to leave their villages and farmlands and track game in small hunting bands. Another contributing factor might have been invasions by other nomadic Indian peoples, such as the Athapascans who arrived from the north (see "Apache" and "Navajo"). Or perhaps the various pueblos began fighting among themselves for food. The depletion of the wood supply might have been an additional reason to move.

Even though the great villages died out, the ancient Southwest peoples passed on much of their knowledge to later generations. Most of the Indians of the region remained farmers, and many continued to live in pueblos. They also sustained their high level of craftsmanship. It is thought that the Mogollon Indians were some of the ancestors of the present-day Zuni Indians; the Hohokam Indians, the ancestors of the present-day Pimas and Papagos; and the Anasazi Indians, the ancestors of the Hopis and other Pueblo Indians (see "Zuni"; "Pima"; "Papago"; "Hopi"; and "Pueblo Indians").

As any tour book of the region will show, there are many different archaeological sites to visit in the American Southwest. Visitors can stand in the wondrous ruins of the great Indian cultures. And, with a little imagination, one can sense the hustle-and-bustle, the coming-and-going, the talk, the laughter, and the hard work of the ancient Native Americans. It is a powerful experience.

Coeur D'Alene

Coeur d'Alene (pronounced *kur-duh-LANE*) is a French name, meaning "heart of awl" or "pointed heart." The phrase was probably first used by a chief as an insult to a trader who then mistook it for the tribe's name. The tribe's own name for itself is Skitswish, the meaning of which is unknown.

The Coeur d'Alenes occupied territory that has since become northern Idaho and western Washington State, especially along the Spokane River and Coeur d'Alene River and around Coeur d'Alene Lake. They spoke a dialect of the Salishan language family, as did many of their neighboring tribes, such as the Flatheads, Kalispels, and Spokanes (see entries for those tribes). They are considered part of the Plateau Culture Area (see "Plateau Indians"). They depended heavily on salmon fishing and the gathering of wild plant foods in addition to the hunting of small game. They lived in cone-shaped dwellings placed over pits and built out of poles covered with bark or woven mats.

The Coeur d'Alenes, like other Interior Salishan tribes, had extensive contacts with whites only after the Lewis and Clark Expedition in the early 1800s. They were generally peaceful toward whites and bartered their furs with them for guns, ammunition, and other trade goods. In the 1850s, however, because of white treaty violations, the Coeur d'Alenes joined in an uprising against settlers. The Coeur d'Alene War of 1858 grew out of the Yakima War of 1855-56 (see "Yakima"). Other tribes participating in this second rebellion included the Palouses, Paiutes, and Spokanes (see entries for those tribes).

In May 1858, a combined force of about 1,000 Coeur d'Alenes, Spokanes, and Palouses attacked and routed a column of 164 federal troops under Major Edward Steptoe at Pine Creek in the western part of Washington Territory. Next, about 600 troops under Colonel George Wright rode into the field to engage the rebels. In the first week of September, the two forces met at Spokane Plain and Four Lakes. The Indians, who were not as well armed as the whites, suffered heavy losses.

Afterward, Wright's force rounded up Indian dissidents, including Qualchin, one of the Yakima warriors who had started the Yakima War three years earlier with an attack on white miners. Qualchin was tried, sentenced to death, and hanged. Kamiakin, his uncle, the Yakima chief who organized the alliance of tribes, escaped to Canada, but he returned in 1861 and lived out his life on the Spokane Reservation. He died in 1877, the same year that the next outbreak of violence occurred in the region, this one among the Nez Perce tribe (see "Nez Perce").

Most of the surviving Coeur d'Alenes settled on a reservation in Idaho after their war. Their descendants still live there today, with tribal headquarters in the town of Plummer, Idaho.

Comanche

The meaning of the name *Comanche* (pronounced *cuh-MAN-chee*) is not known, but it is thought to be a Spanish adaptation of an Indian word. Whatever the meaning of their name, the Comanches fostered great respect among other peoples who came in contact with them throughout history because of their rugged individualism and their prowess in battle. The Comanches have been called the "Lords of the Southern Plains." The phrase shows that they were lordlike in their ways, that is to say, powerful and proud.

Lifeways

The Comanches spoke a dialect of the Uto-Aztecan language family. Their language was close to that of the Shoshone Indians (see "Shoshone"). It is thought that sometime during the 1600s the Comanches separated from the Shoshones in territory that is now Wyoming and migrated south along the eastern face of the Rocky Mountains. Sometime in the late 1600s, they gained use of the horse, which was not native to North America but was brought here by the Spanish. By 1719, the Comanches were in Kansas. During the 1700s and 1800s, as horse-mounted hunters and raiders, the Comanches roamed through territory that now includes Texas, eastern New Mexico, western Oklahoma, southwestern Kansas, southeastern Colorado, and northern Mexico. Even the fierce Apaches, whose territory in New Mexico they first invaded about 1740, could not contain the Comanches.

Because of their wide range, the Comanches helped spread horses through trade to more northern Plains peoples. Through much of their history, they raided white settlements and other tribes to steal horses.

Comanche horse whip

They also tracked wild mustangs. The Comanches became skilled horse breeders and trainers and maintained huge herds, more than any other tribe.

Both boys and girls were given their first mounts when they were only four or five years old. Boys worked hard to become skillful riders, then, as teenagers and young men, they used these skills in warfare. A Comanche rider, galloping at full speed, could lean over to use his horse as a shield while he shot arrows from under its neck. He could also rescue a fallen friend by pulling him up onto his horse while in motion. The Comanches' horses were so well-trained, in fact, that they responded to spoken and touch commands. Girls also became accomplished riders. When they grew up, they went antelope hunting with the men.

As was the case with other tribes of the Great Plains Culture Area, horses enabled the Comanches to travel great distances in pursuit of the buffalo herds, which the Plains Indians relied on for food, clothing, bedding, and shelter. The Comanches lived in temporary villages of buffalo-hide tepees year-round, so they would be ready to follow the buffalo migrations when necessary (see "Plains Indians").

Wars for the Southern Plains

It is estimated that, in proportion to their numbers, the Comanches killed more whites than any other tribe. The Spanish were the first Europeans to try to contend with the Comanches, but without much success. Comanche riders rode hundreds of miles to launch surprise attacks on Spanish settlements for horses, slaves, and other booty. In fact, the Comanche presence helped prevent the Spanish from extensively developing the Texas region. During the 1700s, the Spanish managed to establish and maintain only a few missions there, such as the one at San Antonio in 1718.

About 1790, the Comanches allied themselves with the Kiowas, another southern Plains tribe, who had settled directly to the north of them (see "Kiowa"). About 1840, they also united in a loose confederacy with the Southern Cheyennes and Southern Arapahos, who also lived to their north (see "Arapaho" and "Cheyenne").

In 1821, Mexico achieved independence from Spain, and part of the territory falling under Mexican rule was Texas. In the following years, more and more Mexican-American and Anglo-American settlers arrived in Texas. Many died at the hands of the Comanches. The

Comanche metal-tipped arrow

Comanches also attacked travelers heading to New Mexico from Missouri on the Santa Fe Trail. The Comanches even attacked soldiers who dared to enter their region. For example, in 1829, a Comanche war party attacked an army wagon train that had been sent out under Major Bennett Riley to explore the Santa Fe Trail.

In 1835, the Texas Revolution against Mexican rule erupted. The next year, the famous battle of the Alamo occurred. It was during this revolution that the Texas Rangers were organized. Their principal function during the 10 years of the Texas Republic, and after the annexation of Texas by the United States in 1845, was to protect settlers from attacks by hostile Indians, in particular the Comanches.

During the 1830s, the Comanches had the upper hand, defeating the Texas Rangers in several battles. In the Council House Affair of 1838, the Rangers tried to seize a delegation of Comanches who had come to San Antonio for negotiations concerning the release of white captives. A fight broke out and 35 Comanches were killed. Then other warriors under Chief Buffalo Hump took their revenge in raids on white settlements as far south as the Gulf of Mexico.

During the 1840s, the Rangers fared somewhat better in their encounters with the Comanches because now they had a strict disciplinarian in charge, named John Coffee Hays, as well as new guns, Walker Colt six-shooters. The Battle of Bandera Pass in 1841 proved a stand-off. Yet, all in all, the Comanches lost few men in battle. White diseases, especially a cholera epidemic in 1849-50, carried to the Comanches by travelers heading westward during the California Gold Rush, exacted a much heavier toll on their people.

From 1849 to 1852, after Texas had become part of the United States, federal troops moved in to build a chain of seven forts from the Red River to the Rio Grande to help police the frontier. Also, in 1853, officials in Kansas negotiated the Fort Atkinson Treaty with southern Plains tribes to protect the Santa Fe Trail. Yet many Comanche bands kept up their raids.

In 1854, the federal government placed some Comanches and Kiowas on one of two reservations on the Brazos River. The Indians, however, did not take to this lifestyle forced upon them. In 1859, the Brazos River reservations were abandoned.

A new offensive was launched in 1858 by both Texas Rangers and army regulars, who engaged the Comanches north of the Red River in the Indian Territory and in Kansas. The Texas Rangers fought the Comanches in the Battle of Antelope Hills. Then the army's Wichita Expedition fought the Battle of Rush Springs against Buffalo Hump's band and next the Battle of Crooked Creek. Despite some losses in these battles, the powerful Comanches and Kiowas would continue their resistance to white settlement on the southern Plains for almost 20 more years.

During the Civil War years, from 1861 to 1865, when federal troops went east to fight against the South, the Comanches took advantage of the situation to step up their campaign of raiding. The Confederates even supplied the Comanches with guns, trying to encourage their support against Union soldiers. The only offensive against the Comanches during this period was by troops under Colonel Christopher "Kit" Carson, who had previously fought Apaches and Navajos in New Mexico (see "Apache" and "Navajo"). In 1864, Carson's men fought the Comanches at the first Battle of Adobe Walls on the Staked Plain of the Texas Panhandle, driving off the Indians with howitzer cannon and burning their winter supply of food.

During the years after the Civil War, the army launched new campaigns to pacify the southern Plains. One of these was the Sheridan Campaign. Most of the action was against Southern Cheyennes and Southern Arapahos, but General Philip Henry Sheridan's southern column fought Comanches and Kiowas at the Battle of Soldier Spring on Christmas Day in 1868. The soldiers drove the Indians away, burned their tepees, and destroyed their food supplies. By the Medicine Lodge Treaty of 1867, a new reservation had been established for the Comanches and Kiowas in the southern part of the Indian Territory between the Washita and Red rivers. But both tribes refused to be confined on reservations. They had been nomadic hunters and raiders for generations and did not want to give up their traditional way of life.

Yet time was running out for them. The 1870s saw the last uprising of the Comanches and Kiowas. It also saw the end of the great buffalo herds. During this last period of bitter fighting, a great Comanche chief would become famous. His name was Quanah Parker.

Quanah Parker was a mixed-blood whose white mother, Cynthia Parker, had been kidnapped in 1836 as a nine-year-old by Caddo Indians, who then traded her to the Comanches (see "Caddo"). As a teenager, she had become the wife of the Comanche chief Peta Nocona of the Nocona band. She had become a dedicated Comanche, preferring the Indian way of life to that of her blood relatives.

The son of Cynthia and Peta, called Quanah, also grew up favoring the Comanche way of life. As a young boy, the mixed-blood youth proved himself by his horsemanship, bravery, and leadership. He also came to hate whites with a passion when he lost his family. First, his father died from a wound inflicted by whites. Then his mother was captured by soldiers and returned to the white world. She died soon afterward, supposedly of a broken heart at separating from the people of her choice. Next, Quanah's brother died of a white disease. On his own now, Quanah joined the powerful Kwahadie band of Comanches who lived in the Texas Panhandle. In 1867, only 15 years old, he became one of their chiefs.

The final phase of the combined Comanche and Kiowa wars began in 1871 with Kiowa attacks on travelers along the Butterfield Southern Route (or Southern Overland Trail) leading from St. Louis through the Southwest to California. In retaliation, General William Tecumseh Sherman sent the Fourth Cavalry under Colonel Ranald Mackenzie into Kiowa and Comanche country. After riding through the reservation, they invaded the Staked Plain of the Texas Panhandle.

It was here the army first became aware of Quanah Parker. The fearless young leader personally led two charges against the cavalry. In the first, the warriors rode right through the army camp at Rock Station, stampeding and capturing many of their horses. In the second, he and his warriors attacked and routed a scouting party. The teenage brave fought with a fury, personally killing and scalping a soldier.

Although military expeditions against the Comanches and Kiowas had so far been unsuccessful, another activity by whites threatened the Indian way of life. Before 1870, white hunters had killed buffalo only during the winter when their furs were long. But then a new tanning process was developed that enabled furriers to make shorthair hides workable as well, meaning year-round hunting. Furthermore, by the 1870s, white hunters were armed with new kinds of guns, high-powered telescopic rifles effective at a range of 600 yards. The animals, essential to the Plains Indian economy, were now being slaughtered by whites at a furious pace.

When the hunters entered the Staked Plain and set up camp at the abandoned trading post of Adobe Walls, where Comanches and Kiowas had fought Kit Carson's men a decade before, Quanah Parker called a council of war. He even had his warriors hold a Sun Dance, which was not a traditional Comanche custom, so that Cheyennes and Arapahos from the neighboring reservation would come. Preparations were made for an attack.

In June 1874, Quanah Parker led his sizable force against the buffalo hunters at Adobe Walls. This was the start of the Red River War of 1874-75, sometimes also called the Buffalo War. Despite their overwhelming numbers, the Indians were repelled by the repeater rifles of the buffalo hunters.

In the following months, the Comanches and Kiowas, with some Cheyennes and Arapahos, carried out numerous raids on white settlements. But then General Sheridan launched a massive offensive with troops out of Texas, Kansas, and New Mexico. He had the experienced Indian fighters Colonel Ranald Mackenzie and Colonel Nelson Miles in the field, and they kept up pressure on the militant bands, finally dealing a crushing blow to the Indians in September at their stronghold in Palo Duro Canyon. The soldiers managed to kill most of the Indians' horses and destroy most of their tepees.

With relentless pursuit by the soldiers, the Indian fighters, weary and half-starved, began trickling in to the army posts to surrender. The last of the Kiowa militants held out until February 1875. Quanah Parker and his Comanche warriors turned themselves in the following June.

The Peyote Road

Quanah Parker's influence on Indian history was not over, however. He quickly adapted to the reservation life. He taught himself the ways of the whites, such as the laws governing the leasing of lands and right-of-way, and he made deals with white investors for the benefit of the Comanches.

Moreover, Quanah Parker played a major role in spreading a new religion to Indians of many tribes. This religion involved the use of the peyote cactus, which grows in northern Mexico, especially along the Rio Grande Valley. The Indians cut off the rounded top of the plant, dried it, and made it into a "peyote button." When eaten raw or brewed into a tea, the buttons created a heightening of the senses, a feeling of well-being, and visions. Earlier Comanches had probably helped spread the use of peyote northward when they brought back knowledge of the plant and its properties after raids in Mexico.

Quanah Parker discovered what is known as the Peyote Road, or the use of peyote for religious purposes, sometime after 1890, following the collapse of the Ghost Dance Religion (see "Paiute" and "Sioux"). His work and that of other peyotists, such as Big Moon of the Kiowas, led to the spread of peyote use among Indians of the Plains, Southwest, Prairies, and Great Lakes and the eventual founding of a

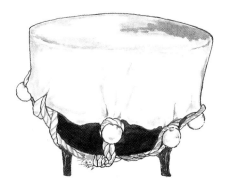

Comanche drum for peyote ceremonies

church. Quanah Parker died in 1911, revered by Indians of many tribes. In 1918, the Native American Church was chartered. This organized religion incorporated certain Christian beliefs and practices with the sacramental use of peyote. Oklahoma Territory tried to ban the use of peyote in 1899 as did some states in later years, but after 1934 and the new policy of Tribal Restoration and Reorganization, no more official attempts were made to ban the religion. By the 1930s, about half the Indian population in the United States belonged to the church. Today, the Native American Church still plays a central role in Indian religion and the fight for Indian rights.

The present-day headquarters of the Comanche tribe is in Lawton, Oklahoma, where the tribe and individual tribal members have lands with their long-time allies the Kiowas and with the Apaches of Oklahoma. Many of the present-day Comanches support themselves through farming and through the leasing of mineral rights.

Coushatta

The Coushattas (pronounced *coo-SHAH-tuh*), or Koasatis, lived in what is now the state of Alabama, especially where the Coosa and Tallapoosa rivers merge to form the Alabama River. They were a Muskogean-speaking people and were closely related to the Creek tribe in history, language, and culture. The Coushattas lived near another Muskogean people, the Alabamas. Both Coushattas and Alabamas were part of the Creek Confederacy. The Coushattas, village farmers, are classified, along with these other tribes, in the Southeast Culture Area (see "Creek"; "Alabama"; and "Southeast Indians").

It is thought that the Coushattas had contact with the Spanish expedition of 1539-43 led by Hernando de Soto, and, after De Soto's death, led by Moscoso de Alvaro. Other Spanish explorers passed through their territory in the 1500s and 1600s.

In the 1700s, after Rene Robert Cavelier de la Salle's 1682 voyage of exploration along the lower Mississippi River, the French became established in the region, founding the settlement of Mobile on the Gulf of Mexico in 1710. They became allies and trading partners with many of the Muskogean tribes of the region. Meanwhile, the English were pushing inland from the Atlantic Coast and developing relations with the Creeks living to the east of the Coushattas.

When the French were forced to give up their holdings in the Southeast in 1763 after they lost the French and Indian War against the British, most of the Coushattas dispersed. Some moved to Louisiana. Others joined the Seminoles in Florida. Others went to Texas.

Those that stayed in Alabama threw their lot in with the Creeks and were relocated west of the Mississippi to the Indian Territory (now Oklahoma) at the time of the Trail of Tears in the 1830s; their descendants still live there today (see "Cherokee"). Descendants of those Coushattas who moved to Louisiana presently have a non-reservation community near the town of Kinder, as well as a recently purchased 15-acre reservation. Those in Texas were granted reservation lands in Polk County along with the Alabamas.

Coushatta alligator basket

Cree

When French traders, seeking valuable furs, and French missionaries, spreading the Catholic faith, first learned of the existence of the Crees, these Indians were widespread. Bands of Crees (pronounced the way it is spelled) hunted in territories extending all the way from the Ottawa River in the present-day province of Quebec to the Saskatchewan River of western Canada. The Crees belonged to the Algonquan language family (see "Algonquian").

The Crees were Subarctic peoples, meaning that they lived in a part of North America where winters were long and summers were short and the seasons dictated the rhythm of life (see "Subarctic Indians"). Lakes, rivers, and forests of spruce and fir trees were plentiful. Snowshoes and birchbark canoes were the main methods of transportation. The bark of the birch tree was also used to cover dwellings, small cone-shaped tents. Mammals, fowl, fish, and edible wild plants were the main source of food, since farming was so difficult in the cold climate and the rocky topsoil.

Different groups of Crees in different parts of the continent took on names based on their surroundings. There were the Swampy Cree of the wet north country near Hudson Bay, and the Western Wood Cree of the forests north of Lake Winnipeg. Those who headed southward onto the Great Plains and began to hunt buffalo in addition to moose, caribou, deer, and elk came to be called the Plains Cree. Some of these Crees, who wandered the northeastern Plains, began using true tepees of hide like other Plains Indians rather than the bark-covered tents common to their woodland relatives (see "Plains Indians"). Other important Cree groupings were the Tete de Boule Cree and the Mistassini Cree in what is now Quebec, both of whom can be called the Eastern Wood Cree. With their wide range, the Cree Indians are historically one of the most important tribes of Canada.

The Fur Trade

In early Canadian history, the Crees are associated with the fur trade. The Crees trapped the animals of the northern forests, especially the beaver; then they exchanged the animal pelts for French trade goods, such as tools, cloth, beads, and, most valued of all,

guns. With firearms, the Crees could hunt more efficiently. They could also gain the upper hand over other Indians who did not yet possess firearms, such as their traditional enemies to the west, the Athapascans (see "Athapascan").

Many of the French fur traders admired the lifestyle of the Crees so much that they chose to live and raise families among them. The French traders and canoemen who worked for fur companies were called *voyageurs* (the French word for "traveler") because they traveled through the network of rivers and lakes in search of furs. Their offspring—the Cree-French mixed-bloods, or *Metis*—carried on this tradition (see "Metis"). The unlicensed backwoods traders, who did not work for fur companies, were called *coureurs de bois* or "runners of the woods." Like the *voyageurs*, some of them were mixed-bloods.

Both the *voyageurs* and the *coureurs de bois* were a rugged breed. They usually dressed in buckskin

Cree knife for skinning animals

shirts, breechcloths, and leggings, like full-blooded Crees, and they knew Indian survival techniques. Yet they also practiced European customs such as the Catholic religion. Those who wanted to prove their courage might even undergo the Cree custom of tattooing. This was a painful process in which needles were run under the skin, followed by leather threads dipped in water and pigment.

The most far-reaching fur companies in the 1700s and 1800s were the Hudson's Bay Company, formed in 1670, and the North West Company, formed in 1779. These were English-run companies, not French-run. (For more about the French fur trade in the 1600s, see "Huron.") Fur-trading posts came to dot the wilderness all across Canada, places where Indians, whites, and mixed-bloods would all come together to barter their goods. The two big trading companies

Cree powderhorn with copper ornamentation and leather pouches, from the fur-trading period

western wilderness; and the North West Field Force, an army sent from the East to put down the uprising. In an Indian council at Duck Lake in 1884, Big Bear said, "I have been trying to seize the promises the whites made to me; I have been grasping but I cannot find them. What they have promised me straight away, I have not yet seen the half of it."

Poundmaker and 200 warriors attacked Battleford in March 1885, and Big Bear plus the same number of warriors took the settlement at Frog Lake the following April. Government troops pursued the two renegade bands. They caught up with Poundmaker's warriors at Cut Knife Creek in April, but the Indians counterattacked, then escaped. Big Bear's men outflanked their enemy at Frenchmen's Butte in May and again at Loon Lake in June. Neither Cree chief was captured in the field. But, because the Metis had given up the fight, the Cree leaders also eventually turned themselves in and were imprisoned for two years. Both Poundmaker and Big Bear died shortly after their release from prison, broken and bitter men.

Cree pipe bag of caribou hide with quillwork (modern)

united in 1821 under the name of Hudson's Bay Company. The Hudson's Bay Company helped bring about the exploration of Canada and at one time it claimed much of the Canadian West and Northwest as its own property.

The Indians and mixed-bloods were the most skilled scouts and made it possible for the white traders to find their way through the wilderness. Many of the later fur traders were Scotsmen rather than French, and they too mixed with the Cree Indians. As a result, some of the Metis were Cree-Scotch. Like the Cree-French, the Cree-Scotch knew how to live off the land Indian-style, but this group practiced Protestantism, not Catholicism.

The Second Riel Rebellion

The Crees were involved in one of the few Canadian Indian wars, which occurred in Saskatchewan late in the 1800s when the Canadian Pacific Railway was being built. Along with the railroad came more and more white settlers who wanted Indian lands. The western Crees joined up with their Metis relatives in the Second Riel Rebellion to protect their land rights.

The chiefs Poundmaker and Big Bear led warriors against two different forces: the North West Mounted Police (also known as the Mounties), who patroled the

Although Cree numbers have decreased because of many epidemics from white diseases over the years and a continuing low birthrate, the Cree Indians are still widespread in Canada, having reserve lands in Alberta, Saskatchewan, Manitoba, Ontario, and Quebec. The Crees also share a reservation with the Chippewas in Montana (see "Chippewa").

The Crees still have to fight for their land rights. They recently lost a huge chunk of territory along James Bay when their lands were flooded in the building of a huge hydroelectric plant. Cree lands in the west are also threatened; along Lubicon Lake in Alberta, drilling by oil companies has created a serious pollution problem.

Creek

Early English traders gave these Indians their name because they built most of their villages on woodland rivers and creeks. In reality, the Creeks were not just one group but consisted of many different bands with many names. The various Indians that the English referred to as Creeks had villages throughout much of the Southeast. This territory now includes most of Georgia and Alabama, as well as small parts of northern Florida, eastern Louisiana, and southern Tennessee. The majority of Creek villages were situated along the banks of the Coosa, Tallapoosa, Flint, Ocmulgee, and Chattahoochee rivers. In historic times, many of these villages were united under a loose organization called the Creek Confederacy.

The native name for the most powerful band of Creeks was the Muskogees. From Muskogee comes the name of one of the important language families: Muskogean. Other important tribes who also spoke dialects of the Muskogean language family were the Alabamas, Coushattas, Chickasaws, Choctaws, and Seminoles (see entries for those tribes). Of these tribes, the Alabamas and Coushattas were part of the Creek Confederacy along with the Muskogees and many other Creek bands.

Lifeways

The Creeks, along with the other tribes mentioned, are part of the Southeast Culture Area, and all of them shared many cultural traits (see "Southeast Indians"). Since the Creeks were the most widespread and powerful of all these tribes, they are cited in many books as representing the typical Southeast Indian way of life. It is thought that the Creeks were descendants of the Temple Mound Builders who lived in the Southeast in prehistoric times (see "Mound Builders").

We have already seen how the Creeks lived along the rivers and streams coursing through the piney woods of their extensive territory. The villages were the main political unit. Each had a chief called a *mico*. He was not an absolute ruler as in other Southeast tribes, such as the Natchez and Timucuas (see "Natchez" and "Timucua"). His functions were more like those of a modern-day mayor. A council of elders, the Beloved Men, helped him make decisions, and a town crier announced the decisions to the other villagers.

The villages were organized into Red towns and White towns. In the Red towns lived the warriors who launched raids far and wide for purposes of honor and revenge. Red Creeks held ceremonies such as war dances. In the White towns lived the peacemakers who kept track of alliances and gave sanctuary to refugees. White Creeks held ceremonies such as the signing of treaties.

Each village had a town square at its center with earthen banks where spectators could sit. The square was used for ceremonies and games. Each village also had a circular town house with clay walls and a cone-shaped bark roof about 25 feet high. This was the ceremonial lodge; and it was also used to shelter the old and the homeless. Other houses were grouped in clusters of four small rectangular, pole-framed structures with bark-covered, gabled (slanted and peaked) roofs. One of these clusters had tiers of benches and served as a meeting place for the Beloved Men.

Creek house

The other clusters of houses served as homes for individual families. Each family had a winter house, a summer house, a granary, and a warehouse. The winter house and summer house were built with closed mud-packed walls for insulation from the cold and heat. The summer house also doubled as a guesthouse. The granary was half-open, and the warehouse was open on all four sides like a Seminole chickee.

The Creeks were farmers first and hunter-gatherers second. They grew corn, beans, squash, pumpkins, melons, and sweet potatoes. Each family planted and tended its own garden. But everyone helped with a communal field and contributed to communal stores that were used to feed warriors, the poor, and guests.

The major form of social organization beyond the family was the clan, each of which had an animal name. In the case of the Creeks, as with many other agricultural tribes, one's ancestral identification and clan membership was determined by the mother and not the father. One was not permitted to marry someone in one's own clan.

The Green Corn Ceremony was the most important of the many Creek ceremonies. It is also called the Busk, from the Creek word *boskita*, meaning "to fast." Other tribes of the Southeast also practiced this renewal ritual, which took place near the end of the summer when the last corn crop ripened and which was four to eight days long.

In preparation for the ritual, men made repairs to the communal buildings; and women cleaned their houses and cooking utensils, even burning some possessions, then extinguished their hearth fires. The most important villagers, including chiefs and shamans plus elders and warriors, all fasted. They then gathered for a feast, where they ate corn and had the lighting of the Sacred Fire. They also drank the Black Drink, a ceremonial tea made from a poisonous shrub called *Ilex vomitoria*, tobacco, and other herbs. The Black Drink induced vomiting and supposedly purified the body. Some participants danced the Green Corn Dance.

Then all the other villagers joined in the ceremony. They took coals from the Sacred Fire to rekindle the hearth fires and they cooked food for an even bigger feast, this time of deer meat. Games, such as lacrosse and archery contests, were held. There was more dancing. Everyone closed the ceremony with a communal bath in the river for purification. At the end, the entire village was ready for a fresh start of the New Year. All past wrongdoings were forgiven, except murder.

The Early Colonial Years

The first European to make contact with the Creeks was the Spanish explorer Hernando de Soto, who passed through part of their territory in 1540. He was much impressed by them. In his journals, he wrote about their tall physique and their proud bearing, as well as their colorful dress. Because of their central location in the Southeast—between English, Spanish, and French settlements—the Creeks played an important role in colonial affairs in later years.

For most of the colonial period, the Creeks were allies of the British. Early British traders cultivated a relationship with them by giving them European tools and other goods. In the late 1600s and early 1700s, Creek warriors joined Carolina militiamen in attacks on Indians who had been missionized by the Spanish, such as the Apalachees and Timucuas (see "Apalachee" and "Timucua").

Creek warriors also launched attacks on the Choctaws, who were allies of the French (see "Choctaw"). They also battled the Cherokees regularly (see "Cherokee").

Some Creek bands joined the victorious British forces in the French and Indian War of 1754-63. Some bands later joined the losing British troops against the rebels in the American Revolution of 1775-83. Yet many village leaders hedged in choosing sides in these conflicts in order to play the white powers against each other to the Indians' own advantage.

The Creek War

In the early 1800s, Tecumseh traveled south to seek allies for his rebellion against the United States (see "Shawnee"). Again, many Creek leaders hedged. But during the years immediately following Tecumseh's Rebellion of 1809-11, many Creeks joined forces in their own uprising. This was called the Creek War of 1813-14.

The Red Stick faction of Creeks wanted war with the whites; the White Stick faction wanted peace. Two mixed-bloods, Peter McQueen and William Weatherford, led the Red Sticks; Big Warrior, a full-blooded Creek, led the White Sticks.

The first incident concerned another full-blooded Creek by the name of Little Warrior, who had led a band of Creeks against the Americans in the War of 1812. On the trip back from Canada after the engagement, his men killed some settlers along the Ohio River. The White Stick faction arrested and executed him for his deeds. Soon afterward, Peter McQueen led a force of Red Sticks to Pensacola on the Gulf of Mexico, where the Spanish gave them guns. This group then raided a party of settlers on Burnt Corn Creek in July 1813.

The most famous incident of the Creek War occurred the following month. William Weatherford, also known as Red Eagle, led a force of about 1,000 Red Sticks against Fort Mims on the Alabama River. Black slaves reported to the commanding officer of the garrison, Major Daniel Beasley, that Indians were crawling toward the fort in the high grass. Yet Beasley failed to order the outer gates closed. Sure enough, the attack came. Beasley himself was killed in the first onslaught.

The settlers took cover behind the inner walls and held the warriors at bay for several hours. Eventually, flame-tipped arrows enabled the Indians to break through the defenses. Once inside Fort Mims, they killed about 400 settlers. Only 36 whites escaped. But the Red Sticks freed the black slaves.

Federal and state troops were mobilized to put down the uprising. General Andrew Jackson, whom the Indians called "Sharp Knife," was given the command. Davy Crockett was one of his soldiers. There were many more battles. In November 1813, soldiers drew the Red Sticks into a trap at Tallasahatchee, then relieved the White Stick village of Talladega, which was under attack by a party of Red Sticks. In December, Red Eagle managed to escape troops closing in on his hometown of Econochaca by leaping off a bluff into a river while mounted on his horse. In January 1814, there were two indecisive battles at Emuckfaw and Enotachopco Creek.

The final battle took place at Horseshoe Bend in March 1814. There, Jackson's men moved into position around the Red Sticks' barricades, removed their canoes, and attacked. Fighting lasted all day until the Indians, with most of their warriors killed, retreated. Red Eagle survived, however, because he had departed before the attack to inspect other fortifications.

Red Eagle surrendered several days later. He walked into Jackson's camp and announced, "I am Bill Weatherford." To punish the Creeks, Jackson forced them to sign the Treaty of Horseshoe Bend, which took away 23 million acres of land—from both the militant Red Sticks and the peaceful White Sticks.

Relocation

In 1830, Andrew Jackson, who was now President of the United States, signed the Indian Removal Act, beginning a period of relocation of eastern tribes to the Indian Territory west of the Mississippi River. Thus the Creeks lost their remaining ancestral lands to whites. Many lost their lives too. During their forced march in 1836 and soon after their arrival, about 3,500 of the 15,000 who were forced to leave the Southeast died from exposure, hunger, disease, and bandit attacks. This was a tragic and cruel time in American history. That is why the Cherokees called their journey the Trail of Tears, a phrase now applied to the removal of the Creeks, Chickasaws, Choctaws, and Seminoles as well. After their relocation, these tribes came to be called the Five Civilized Tribes by whites because they adopted many of the customs of the white settlers around them.

Eventually, much of the Indian Territory was also taken from the tribal members. This new homeland was supposed to have been permanent for the tribes placed there. Yet, after many reductions in its size, it became the state of Oklahoma in 1907. This event took place six years after a Creek by the name of Chitto Harjo (Crazy Snake) led a rebellion against the allotment, or the breaking up of tribal holdings to give them to individuals, which made it easier for unscrupulous whites to take over the lands. In the Snake Uprising, as newspapers called it, the rebels harassed whites and destroyed their property until overwhelming government forces rode in to arrest them.

The following is a song by a Creek woman:

I have no more land
I am driven away from home
Driven up the red waters
Let us all go
Let us all go die together.

The Creeks have rebounded from the loss of their lands and traditional way of life. Early in the 20th century, tribal members recognized the need for education and began learning the skills necessary to cope in the culture that had displaced their own. As a result, many Creeks have succeeded in a variety of well-paying fields, such as medicine and law.

In addition to the scattered pockets of Creeks in the Southeast, there are three main groups in Oklahoma—the Creek Nation, the Kialegee Creeks, and the Thlopthlocco Creeks. Some Alabama-Coushattas are joined with them in the present-day Creek Confederacy, which has its seat of government at Okmulgee in eastern Oklahoma.

Crow

The Crows called themselves the *Absaroka*, Siouan for "bird people." Their name among whites became that of the well-known bird. Early in their history, they split off from the Hidatsas of the upper Missouri in what is now North Dakota because of a dispute over buffalo (see "Hidatsa"). The Crows then migrated farther upriver, to the Yellowstone River at the foot of the Rocky Mountains. This territory is presently in southern Montana and northern Wyoming.

The Crows who settled north of the Yellowstone toward the Musselshell River became known as the Mountain Crow because of the high terrain. Those who ranged to the south along the valleys of the Big Horn, Powder, and Wind rivers came to be called the River Crow.

Lifeways

Both groups of Crows gave up the village life of their Hidatsa kinsmen. They stopped farming for food, growing only tobacco crops from now on; they no longer constructed earthlodges; and they ceased making pottery. The Crows chose the life of the Plains instead: They lived in hide tepees in camps which they moved often, following the herds of buffalo and other game. They also ate wild plant foods. The horse, when they acquired it in the 1700s, revolutionized hunting and warfare, allowing them to travel faster and farther than before (see "Plains Indians").

The Crows, like many Plains tribes, participated in the Sun Dance and the Vision Quest (the ritualistic use of visions for rites of passage). They also had their own special societies, such as the Crow Tobacco Society, with rituals surrounding their one crop.

A Crow warrior

Crow rattle used in Tobacco Society ceremony

The Crows had elaborate rules governing the behavior of adults toward children. For example, fathers sponsored feasts where they made speeches about their children's future success. Fathers also spent a lot of time teaching their sons survival skills, such as archery, and lavishing praise on them whenever they showed improvement. On returning from his first war party, a boy would be surrounded by singing and dancing relatives. One of these relatives, usually a cousin, would be the "joking relative" who offered ridicule in a friendly way if the boy's behavior called for it. In the meantime, mothers would give great care to their daughters' upbringing, preparing them in the mothering and domestic skills essential to the survival of the tribe, such as preparing food and making clothing.

The Crows were also famous for their striking appearance: fine features and muscular build; long black hair, sometimes made to reach all the way to the ground with the help of added interwoven strands; and elegantly crafted clothes, blankets, pouches, saddles, and bridles. Some traders called the Crows the Long-haired Indians. George Catlin, the frontier painter who lived among many different Plains peoples in the 1830s, painted many stunning portraits of the Crows.

The Crows were longtime enemies of the other powerful tribes on the northern Plains—the Sioux and the Blackfeet—fighting for horses, hunting grounds, and fame (see "Sioux" and "Blackfoot"). To achieve glory in battles, the weapon of choice was the coup stick, which the Indians used to only touch their enemies and prove bravery.

Crow bow

Wars

The Crows, like many other Plains tribes, launched raids for horses against other tribes and against white traders. In 1821, Mountain Men held a fur-trading rendezvous along the Arkansas River with Cheyenne, Arapaho, Comanche, and Kiowa Indians. A party of Crows camped within striking distance. Every night, no matter how many guards were posted, Crow warriors would sneak into the camp and silently make their way to the log pens where the horses were kept. Fighting would sometimes break out and men would be killed on both sides. But, more often than not, the Crows would be too fast for the traders, escaping with the choice mounts.

In the wars for the West, the Crows earned a reputation as allies of the U.S. Army. They served as scouts and fought alongside the bluecoats, especially during the 1870s against the Sioux and the Nez Perces. Chief Plenty Coups encouraged his warriors to side with the army because, as he expressed it, "When the war is over, the soldier-chiefs will not forget that the Absarokas came to their aid."

With the arrival of more and more miners and settlers in Indian country, the building of forts and railroads, and the depletion of the buffalo herds, the rugged but free-spirited life of the Crows ended. Despite their assistance to the whites in making the Plains safe for settlement, the Crows were treated no differently than the resisting tribes. By 1888, the Crows had been forced into ceding most of their land to whites and had been settled on a reservation. The territory they were allowed to keep was part of their ancestral homeland.

The Crows were also given a place of honor in a historic national ceremony. In 1921, after World War I, the now-aged Crow chief Plenty Coups was the Indian chosen to represent all other Indians at the dedication of the Tomb of the Unknown Soldier in Washington, D.C. To close the national ceremony, Plenty Coups placed his warbonnet and coup stick on the grave.

The Custer Battleground National Monument is located on the Crow Reservation in Montana. The tribe holds annual reenactments of the Battle of the Little Bighorn, in which Lieutenant Colonel George Armstrong Custer and his men were wiped out by Sioux and Cheyenne warriors. The tribe also sponsors the annual Crow Fair and Rodeo and an annual Sun Dance.

Delaware (Lenni Lenape)

The name *Delaware*, given by whites, is really not the best name for this tribe. *Delaware* comes from the name of the river where many of these Indians originally lived. But the river itself was named after Lord De La Warr, the second governor of Virginia, who also had the state of Delaware named in his honor. The tribe's own name is *Lenni Lenape*, or "true men."

There were three major divisions of the Delaware Indians: Munsee (Wolf), Unami (Turtle), and Unalactigo (Turkey). These groups all had further subdivisions with other names. Other Algonquians called the Delawares "Grandfather," because they considered the Delawares' territory the original homeland of all Algonquians. The Delawares lived much like other eastern Algonquians (see "Northeast Indians" and "Algonquians"). They placed their villages on river meadows. Each village was surrounded by sovereign hunting territories and fields of corn, beans, and squash. Their houses were domed wigwams or Iroquois-like longhouses (see "Iroquois").

Migrations

The Delawares are a good example of Indians who were forced to cede their lands and migrate time and again on account of the increasing number of white settlers. At one time, different bands of these people held territories in New York, New Jersey, Pennsylvania, and Delaware.

First it was the Dutch who entered the Delawares' homelands, in the 1600s from the Hudson River. The Algonquian-speaking Indians called them *swanneken*. The Dutch were interested in fur trade with the Indians. To the south, traders from Sweden lived in Delaware Indian country along Delaware Bay, starting in 1638. During this early period, many Delawares moved inland and settled along the Susquehanna River.

Then after 1664, when England took control of the entire region, it was the British who entered the Delawares' domain. Settlers, hungry for more and more land, pushed farther and farther westward. By the mid-1700s, Delawares were beginning to settle along the Ohio River in Ohio, then in Indiana. They thought the whites would never settle as far west as Ohio.

But the whites kept coming: next the Americans, who pushed into the Old Northwest around the Great Lakes. In the late 1700s, some Delawares moved to Missouri for a while, and then to Texas. By 1835, many from this group had resettled in Kansas in the northern part of the original Indian Territory. In 1867, when whites broke their promises and began to settle west of the Mississippi River in great numbers, most of the Delawares relocated in the southern part of the Indian Territory, which is now the state of Oklahoma (see "Cherokee"). In the meantime, other Delawares had chosen to live in Canada.

Delaware centerpost for use in a longhouse

Early Relations With Colonists

In the course of this long and complicated story of migration, in which the Delawares lived in at least 10 different states and signed 45 different treaties with the whites, the tribe made its mark on American history. They were involved in many key events.

One famous early incident is the selling of Manhattan Island, now the central borough of New York City. First, the Canarsee band from Brooklyn tried to sell the island to the Dutch. But it was really the Manhattan band who controlled this territory. In 1626, they made the deal with Peter Minuit for 60 guilders' (24 dollars) worth of trade goods—that is, beads, trinkets, and tools.

Some scholars believe that the Manhattan Indians were really part of the Wappinger Confederacy and should be classified as Wappingers rather than as Delawares (see "Wappinger"). In any case, the Delawares and Wappingers both spoke the Algonquian language and were closely related. The Delawares generally lived west of the Hudson River and the Wappingers east of it.

The Manhattan Indians did not really believe that they were selling the land forever. To them no one "owned" land; it belonged to all people. Rather, they thought they were selling the right to use the land,

more like a lease. Delawares have a saying about the sale of Manhattan: "The great white man wanted only a little, little land, on which to raise greens for his soup, just as much as a bullock's hide would cover. Here we first might have observed his deceitful spirit."

Another important historical event involving the Delawares was the treaty of friendship they signed with William Penn, the Quaker founder of Pennsylvania, in 1682. This was the first treaty Indians ever signed with whites. Of all the early colonial leaders, William Penn was the most fair in his dealings with Indians, protecting their rights to land as well as their freedom of religion. A famous Delaware chief at these meetings was Tamanend. Because he was such a wise leader and so clever in his dealings with whites, in 1786 his name was taken, in the form of Tammany, as the name of a political club important in New York history.

Penn's example and the respect whites held for Tamanend did not prevent other whites from massacring a band of Moravian Christian Delawares at Gnaddenhutten, Pennsylvania, in 1782, because of a stolen plate.

The Delawares are also famous as the first tribe to sign a treaty with the United States government—at Fort Pitt in 1778 during the American Revolution.

Wars Involving the Delawares

The Delawares fought in many wars. Some of their warriors first rebelled against the Dutch in 1641, when settlers' livestock destroyed some cornfields of the Raritan Indians, a band of Delawares living on Staten

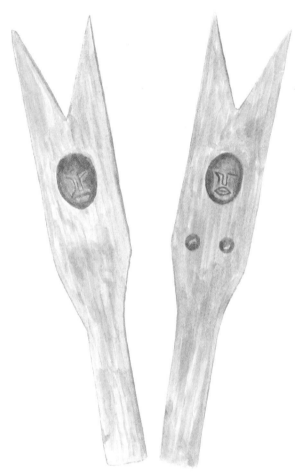

Delaware drumsticks

Island at the mouth of the Hudson River. Willem Kieft was governor-general of New Netherland at the time. A cruel man, he placed a bounty on Raritan heads and scalps, making it profitable for Dutch settlers to kill local Indians.

Then an incident called the Pavonia Massacre occurred in 1643, when Dutch soldiers tortured and murdered a band of Wappingers who sought protection among the Dutch from the Mohawk Indians (see "Wappinger"). After the incident, all the Algonquians of the region, Delawares and Wappingers alike, wanted revenge against the Dutch in their midst and raided many outlying settlements. However, by attacking and burning Indian villages, Kieft's armies crushed the uprising in a year.

The Delawares along with the Wappingers also battled the Dutch under Peter Stuyvesant, the next governor-general, in the so-called Peach Wars, starting in 1655, when an Indian woman was killed by a white farmer for picking peaches from his orchard. After warriors took revenge against the farmer, Stuyvesant not only raided Delaware and Wappinger villages and burned their homes and crops, but also took children hostages, threatening to kill them, so that their fathers would not fight.

In later conflicts, the Western Delawares sided with the French in the French and Indian Wars of 1689-1763 (see "Abnaki" and "Iroquois"). They again fought the British in Pontiac's Rebellion of 1763-64 (see "Ottawa").

A medicine man named Delaware Prophet played an important role in Pontiac's Rebellion. In 1762, he began preaching to the Indians of the Old Northwest, urging them to make peace among themselves, to give up alcohol, and to live pure lives according to traditional Indian ways. The message of this Delaware Indian helped inspire and unite the tribes who fought together against the British under Pontiac. Some Western Delawares later sided with the British in the American Revolution of 1775-83 (see "Iroquois"). They also supported the Miamis and other Indians of the Old Northwest in Little Turtle's War of 1790-94 (see "Miami") and Tecumseh's Rebellion of 1809-11 (see "Shawnee").

Walum Olum

There is a traditional history of the Delawares in the form of pictographs (picture writing) engraved on wood, called the *Walum Olum*, or "Red Score," which speaks of the tribe's legends and early migrations. As the *Walum Olum* says, "Long ago the fathers of the Lenape were in the land of spruce pines . . . A great land and a wide land was the east land. A land without snakes, a rich land, a pleasant land."

The powerful Delawares, or Lenni Lenape, the "Grandfather" of the Algonquians, once roamed the forests of much of the Northeast, hunting deer and other game; they grew corn in their fields; they sang songs around their village campfires; they whispered of love within their domed wigwams and prayed to the Great Spirit, Manitou. Now their life has changed. Today, the Delawares have little land left—some in Oklahoma, some in Wisconsin, and some in Ontario. (Those Lenni Lenapes in Wisconsin and Ontario go by the name of Munsees and Moravians.) Even without their once vast territory, they still are a proud, productive, and poetic people.

Eskimo (Inuit)

The name *Eskimo* (pronounced *ES-kuh-mo*) means "eaters of raw meat" in the Algonquian language. When the Algonquians called their northern neighbors by this name, they meant it as an insult. The name *Eskimo* began to be used by whites, however, and has lasted until modern times. Many of the modern-day people to whom it is applied prefer the name *Inuit* (pronounced *IN-yoo-it*), which means "people" in their own language.

The Eskimo language family is called Eskimaleut, and the dialects of the different Eskimo bands are closely related. Moreover, the dialects of the Aleut people from the same language family are close to the Eskimo tongues, indicating an ancestral link between the two peoples (see "Aleut").

The Eskimos and Aleuts are generally considered a separate group from other Native Americans. They are usually shorter and broader than Indians, with rounder faces and lighter skin. They look much more like Asians than Indians do. This is because their ancestors arrived in North America from Siberia from about 3000 to 1000 B.C., whereas the ancestors of the

Indians arrived much earlier by foot over the Bering Strait land bridge (see "Prehistoric Indians").

There are still Eskimos in Siberia; they are now citizens of the Soviet Union. There are also Eskimos as far east as Greenland, now citizens of Denmark. We will touch upon these peoples and their ancestors in our discussion of Eskimo lifeways and history. But this section applies for the most part to the Eskimos located in what is now United States and Canadian territory, including the state of Alaska, the Northwest Territories, and the provinces of Quebec and Newfoundland.

Before the Europeans settled in America, there were three groups of Eskimos: (1) the Alaskan Eskimos (including North Alaskan Eskimo, West Alaskan Eskimo, South Alaskan Eskimo, and Saint Lawrence Island Eskimo, plus the Mackenzie Eskimo in Canada and the Siberian Eskimo in Russia); (2) the Central Eskimo (including Iglulik Eskimo, Netsilik Eskimo, Copper Eskimo, Caribou Eskimo, Baffinland Eskimo, Southampton Eskimo, and Labrador Eskimo); and (3) the Greenland Eskimo (including the East Greenland

An Eskimo navigating Arctic waters in a kayak

Eskimo, West Greenland Eskimo, and Polar Eskimo). These general groups can be further divided into various bands and villages, much too numerous to list here.

All these groups had lifeways and language in common. But there were differences among the various groups too. For example, we'll see that not all Eskimos lived in igloos.

The homeland of all the Eskimos, as well as the Aleuts, is called the Arctic Culture Area (see "Arctic Peoples"). The Arctic is a land of snow and ice. So far north that trees are unable to grow there, it consists of plains called tundra, where only mosses, lichens, scrub brushes, and a few kinds of flowering plants can live. Winters are long and cold, with only a few hours of daylight each day. Summers are short. The ground never completely thaws, a condition called permafrost. Although there is less precipitation in the cold Arctic climate than there is farther south, the snow that does fall is whipped up by frigid winds into intense blizzards and huge drifts.

Most Eskimo peoples lived along the sea—the Arctic Ocean, Pacific Ocean, Atlantic Ocean, or Hudson Bay. Some of these northern waters freeze over in winter, then break up into ice floes during the short summer thaw.

Food

The Eskimos adapted remarkably well to the harsh Arctic environment. They had to become highly skilled and resourceful hunters and fishermen to survive where there was so little edible vegetation. They migrated often in quest of whatever game was available. Sea mammals provided a reliable source of food for most Eskimos, and materials for Eskimo clothing, bags, tools, and weapons, plus oil for lighting and cooking. The Eskimos called them *puiji*, meaning "those who show their noses," because the mammals surfaced to breathe, unlike fish.

Of all the sea mammals, the seal was the most important to the Eskimo economy. In the summer, the Central Eskimos hunted them with harpoons from their kayaks—light and maneuverable boats made by stretching seal or walrus hides over driftwood frames. Or, crawling on their bellies over ice floes, Eskimo hunters snuck up on the seals and harpooned or netted them. In the winter, however, when the Arctic Ocean froze over, Eskimo hunters had another way of capturing the creatures. The hunter's dog, a husky, would help him find one of the seals' breathing holes in the ice. Then the hunter would place a feather on the tiny patch of exposed water and wait until a seal returned. When the feather moved, the harpoonist would strike. To pull the heavy animal up onto the ice, the hunter would usually have to enlarge the hole. Some Eskimo hunters had a system of netting seals through the holes in the ice.

Eskimos also hunted walruses and sea lions who swam around the ice floes during the summer or lay on top of them to bask in the sun. The tusks of the walrus provided ivory for tools, ornaments, and ceremonial objects. In the winter, however, these mammals left the ice-covered Arctic Ocean to head south for warmer waters, where they could still surface to breathe.

Some Eskimos also pursued whales. Along the Arctic Coast, they used their kayaks to frighten small species of whales close to or onto the shore. Along the Alaskan coast, hunters went after larger whales in another kind of boat, called an *umiak*, similar to a kayak but open and much bigger, up to 40 feet long. Like the Makah whalers (see "Makah"), the Alaskan Eskimos used harpoons attached to inflated buoys to wear down the animals before closing in with spears for the kill.

Most Eskimos also depended on land mammals, especially the caribou, for meat and materials. When these animals made their summer migration to the coast to graze on the tundra and to escape the inland swarms of black flies and mosquitoes, Eskimo hunters used a variety of techniques to get close enough to kill them with either bows and arrows or spears. Hunters snuck up on individual animals on foot or in kayaks; they hid in snow pits near where the caribous were known to travel; or they drove herds into corrals or into the water. The Central Eskimo band known as the Caribou Eskimos were an inland people who did not hunt sea mammals but followed the caribou herds on their migrations.

Other game for Eskimo hunters in different parts of the Arctic included polar bears, musk oxen, mountain

Eskimo umiak

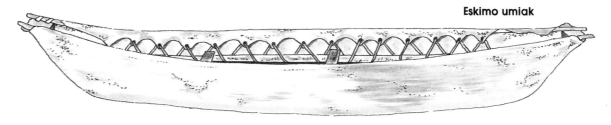

sheep, wolves, wolverines, and smaller mammals as well, such as foxes, hares, marmots, squirrels, and wildfowl. In addition to spears and bows and arrows, the Eskimos used bolas, weighted ropes thrown at game to entangle the animal. They also used blinds to hide from game as well as a variety of snares and traps. Still another method of hunting wolves and other meat-eating animals was to conceal dried and folded whalebones in pieces of fat; when the bait was swallowed, the fat would melt, and the bones would straighten to full size and slowly kill the animal.

Similarly, the Eskimos had many ingenious techniques for fishing. They fished from kayaks; they fished through holes in the ice; and they fished in shallow waters where they built enclosures, called weirs, out of stones. They used hooks and lines, lures, harpoons, and leisters. (The Eskimo-style leister is a spear with three bone prongs—one for penetrating and two for grasping the catch.)

Transportation

For transportation, in addition to the kayak and umiak, the Eskimos had a kind of sled called a *komatik*. To make their sleds, Eskimo craftsmen lashed together wooden frames with strips of rawhide and attached either slats of wood or a large piece of rawhide to form a raised platform. They shaped the runners out of wood or bone and covered them with a coating of ice to reduce friction. Sometimes they also put hide on the runners with a coating of frozen mud and moss.

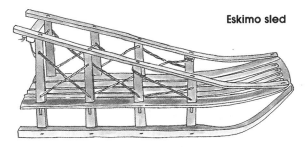

Eskimo sled

Teams of the famous northern husky dogs pulled the sleds. Hunters traveling on ice floes sometimes pulled their own sleds, with upside-down kayaks on top. Then when they reached the water between the drift ice, they could turn the sleds over and use the kayaks without detaching them. Some Eskimos used snowshoes, as did the Subarctic peoples to their south. Others used crampons, spikes attached to their boots, for walking on the ice, as well as test staffs, resembling ski poles, to judge the thickness and strength of the ice. The Eskimos and other Native North Americans did not have skis, however.

Houses

Eskimos lived in all kinds of dwellings—igloos; hide tents; and huts. The igloo, or snow house, is the most recognizable type of Eskimo dwelling. Nevertheless, this type of house was used only by the Central Eskimos and only in the winter.

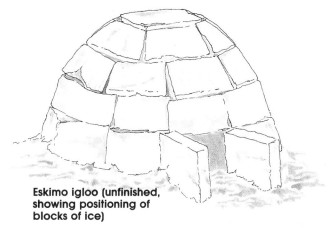

Eskimo igloo (unfinished, showing positioning of blocks of ice)

To build an igloo, the Eskimo craftsman looked for an area of snow of the same consistency—preferably a layer that fell in a single storm, then hardened into ice all at once. He then drew a circle 9 to 15 feet wide that served as the floor plan. Then he cut the large blocks of ice—about 24 inches long, 20 inches wide, and 4 inches thick—from within the circle and started the first row of blocks along the circle's outline. Every row he added spiraled upward and leaned inward slightly, so that each one was smaller than the one before it. When he added the single top block, he had a nearly perfect dome. In the meantime, his wife covered the outer walls with soft snow. A hole in the dome provided ventilation and a block of clear ice served as a window. Igloos normally had a second, smaller domed porch for storage and a covered passageway as an entrance. Sometimes a third, sizable dome was joined to the two so that an Eskimo family could have a separate bedroom and living room. A platform of ice covered with furs served as a bed. The igloos were warm—sometimes even too warm—when oil was burned in stone lamps for lighting and cooking.

In the summer, the Central Eskimos used tents made from driftwood poles and caribou-hide coverings. But Eskimos in Alaska and Greenland had more permanent houses made from either stones and sod or logs and sod, depending on what materials were available. These were sometimes built in a dome shape, like igloos, but more often they were rectangular. Whale ribs were also used in construction. And the intestines of sea mammals were stretched over the windows.

Clothing

Eskimo clothing was as ingenious as other aspects of Eskimo life. It offered protection from the cold but was comfortable to wear even for arduous tasks. The basic clothes, in a variety of materials and styles, were parkas, pants, mittens, stockings, and boots. The favored materials were seal and caribou skin. Sealskin was water-resistant, so it was good for summer, when the rains came and when hunters went to sea. Caribou skin was better suited for winter since it was warmer and lighter in weight. Other animal skins were used as well in different parts of the Arctic: hides of dog, bird, squirrel, marmot, fox, wolf, wolverine, and polar bear. Sea mammal intestines were sometimes sewn together in place of hides. The parkas were tailored to fit the contours of the body and fit snugly at the waist, neck, and wrists to keep cold air out. They were worn with the fur facing the body. Moreover, many of the winter parkas had two layers for added insulation—the sleeveless inner one with the fur facing in, and the outer one with the fur facing out. The parkas had hoods. The Eskimos used as many as four layers of caribou fur on their feet. They also insulated their mukluks (boots) and their mittens with down and moss.

The Eskimos decorated their clothing with designs and borders of different colored furs, leather fringes, embroidery, and ivory buttons. Some Eskimos, mostly women, wore jewelry, such as ear pendants, nose rings, and labrets (lip-plugs or chin-plugs, placed in slits cut in the flesh, and made of ivory, shell, wood, or sandstone). Tattoos were also common.

Recreation

So far we have discussed subsistence, transportation, shelter, and clothing, the practical side of Eskimo life. But there was much more to the Eskimo existence. For instance, the Eskimos loved to play games. A favorite outdoor sport was kickball, played with a soft leather ball stuffed with caribou hair. This was played much like modern-day soccer, but without goals. A player and his team simply tried to keep control of the ball longer than the other side. Men, women, and children played this game. The Eskimos also enjoyed gymnastics. A favorite indoor game was *nugluktag*, in which players tried to poke sticks through a twirling spool that dangled from above.

Another way to pass the cold and long winter days was by telling stories. To illustrate their tales, the storytellers used story knives—usually made of ivory with etched designs—to draw scenes in the snow.

Religion

The Eskimos also carved beautiful objects out of various materials—especially wood, bone, and ivory, with fur and feathers added—for their religious rituals. At ceremonial dances, men wore face masks while women wore tiny finger masks. The masks represented the spirits of animals and the forces in nature. The carving and the ceremonies themselves were directed by Eskimo shamans.

Eskimo mask representing the Soul of the Salmon

One such ceremony, performed by Alaskan Eskimos, was the Bladder Dance. This event lasted for days inside the large *kashim*, the men's ceremonial lodge. The Eskimos thought that the animals' souls resided in their bladders. They danced to music and performed rituals with inflated bladders of sea mammals, then returned them to the sea.

Social Structure

The extended family was the Eskimos' most important unit of social and political organization. Villages were loosely knit without headmen and lasted only as long as the food supply allowed. Yet to allow for friends and allies in the difficult Arctic environment, the Eskimos had special kinds of partnerships with non-family members. The men had "sharing partners," with whom they shared their food catch. They also had "song partners," with whom they performed religious rituals. Their friendship was so great that "song partners" sometimes even shared their wives. Men and women had "name partners," people of the same name with whom they exchanged gifts.

The Eskimos were a peaceful people, but they would fight vigorously if attacked by other Eskimo bands, which was very rare, or by Indian tribes, which was more common. Some Eskimos wore ivory armor that was stitched together with rawhide. Within Eskimo bands, an act of murder created blood feuds that might last for generations despite their forgiving nature in other matters.

Contacts with Whites

Because of their locations in the remote northern wilderness, the Eskimos had few early contacts with whites. The Eskimos of Greenland, however, were the first native peoples of the western hemisphere to encounter Europeans. In this case, their contacts were with the Vikings, who first arrived on Greenland in about A.D. 984 under the famous Norseman called Eric the Red. Eskimos in Labrador might also have had contacts with Vikings who reached North America from 986 to 1010 (see "Beothuk" and "Micmac").

The English explorer Martin Frobisher, who sought the Northwest Passage—a nonexistent water route through North America to the Far East—is the next European on record to have had contacts with Eskimos (both Greenland and Central Eskimos) during his three trips from 1576 to 1578. Frobisher kidnapped an Eskimo and took him back to England.

Other explorers from various European nations visited the Arctic regions from the east, still in search of the Northwest Passage, from the late 1500s into the 1800s. Europeans came in contact with Alaskan Eskimos from the west starting in 1741 with Vitus Bering's exploration for Russia. After that, the presence of the Russian fur traders in Alaska had a much greater impact on the Aleuts, however. In the late 1700s, Samuel Hearne, exploring for the Hudson's Bay Company, reached the Central Eskimos by land. Some of the Central tribes had no contacts with whites, however, until the expeditions of Vilhjalmur Stefansson and Diamond Jenness in the early 1900s. In the meantime, starting in 1721, the Danes settled Greenland and had extensive contacts with Greenland Eskimos. And during the 1800s, there were many missionaries, especially Moravians, among the Labrador Eskimos. Also, after 1848, commercial whaling ships began working Alaskan and Arctic waters.

It was during the early 1800s that many Eskimos began using white trade goods, such as guns, knives, kettles, and cloth, which altered their traditional cul-

ture. Alcohol and European diseases also had a great impact on the Eskimos.

In the late 1800s, two developments led to further, rapid change among the Eskimos. In 1867, the United States purchased Alaska from Russia and began developing it economically. Around this same time, the Hudson's Bay Company of Canada established many posts in the Arctic for the development of the fur business.

Eskimos Today

By the 1920s, few Eskimos retained their traditional way of life. Many still hunted and fished part of the year, however, as many Eskimos do nowadays. Of course, Eskimos now have rifles and shotguns instead of harpoons, spears, and bows and arrows; power-driven canvas canoes instead of kayaks; snowmobiles instead of dog-sleds; frame houses instead of igloos, hide tents, and wood, stone, and sod huts; electricity, kerosene, or oil as fuel instead of animal fat; factory-made wool, cotton, and synthetic clothes instead of handmade sealskin and caribou ones; and so on.

Nevertheless, since the 1950s, there has been a renaissance in Eskimo art, with traditional techniques, materials, and themes, as well as new ones. Eskimo sculptures, drawings, and prints are valued the world over by art collectors.

Two other developments are helping to improve the quality of Eskimo life in the modern world. In 1971, the Alaska Native Claims Settlement Act protected United States Eskimo lands and granted the bands funds for economic growth. The numerous Eskimo villages are now organized into six native corporations, some of which are united with either Aleuts or Athapascans. Hunting and fishing are still central to the Alaskan Eskimo economy.

The other important development: In Canada, the Eskimos (or Inuits, as they are now officially called by the Canadian government) might have their own territory one day, called Nunavut. It would be carved out of the eastern and northern parts of the present Northwest Territories. Frobisher Bay would be its capital. The idea has been approved in a territorial vote and has the endorsement of the national government. Many details have to be worked out before Nunavut becomes a reality, but it is an exciting prospect. Various Native American leaders throughout history have dreamed of a native territory, state, or province, and the dream might finally come true. North Americans of other backgrounds would of course be permitted to live in Nunavut, but the Inuits would be the majority political force.

Flathead

The Flathead Indians are also known as the Salish Indians. The latter name can be confusing, however, since this tribe was just one of many different tribes in the American Northwest who spoke the Salishan language. As a result, the Flathead name is generally used.

But this name is also misleading. Some other Salishan-speaking tribes to the west along the Northwest Coast practiced a custom known as head-flattening. This was a gradual process of deforming the head by tying a padded board to the forehead, usually starting in infancy. Their heads took on a tapered, pointed look. The Indians with the deformed heads thought that people with normal heads looked funny, and they called them "flatheads." However, French fur trappers also started using this name for the Interior Salish instead of the Coast Salish. The name has stuck until modern times.

The Flatheads lived mainly in territory that became the state of Montana. But they ranged into northern Idaho as well. Much of their homeland was mountainous, part of the Rocky Mountain chain. The Flatheads are categorized in the Plateau Culture Area (see "Plateau Indians"). Like the tribes to their west, they depended on fishing in the tributaries of the Columbia River that coursed through their lands, as well as on hunting. Early in their history, the Flatheads, like other Interior Salishan tribes, built longhouses over pits, using pole frames and vegetable coverings, such as cedar bark or woven mats of Indian hemp. In later years, they lived mainly in conical tents, the poles of which were placed around the edges of an excavated pit, and then covered with grass or bark, and finally earth.

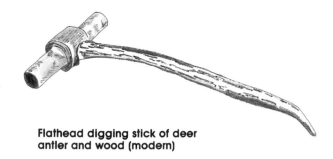

Flathead digging stick of deer antler and wood (modern)

After they acquired horses in the early 1700s, the Flatheads adopted cultural traits similar to those of the Plains tribes to their east, and the Flatheads ventured onto the northern Plains to hunt buffalo (see "Plains Indians"). They continued to use vegetable coverings for their dwellings, however, rather than the typical buffalo-skin coverings of the Plains.

The Blackfeet were traditional enemies of the Flatheads and kept them from expanding their territory eastward. The two tribes were in a deadly cycle of raid and retaliation when Lewis and Clark first had contact with them in 1806. It was a Jesuit missionary by the name of Father Pierre Jean de Smet who finally established peace between the two peoples. He lived among the Flatheads and other tribes from 1840 to 1846.

The Flatheads signed a treaty in 1855 in which they gave up to the whites the majority of their lands in Montana and Idaho except for two pieces. In 1872, they lost one of these. The Flatheads now live on a single tract south of Flathead Lake near Dixon, Montana, which they share with the Kootenai tribe. The Indians of the Flathead Reservation hold an annual four-day-long powwow the first week of July.

Fox

The Fox Indians lived in the region of the western Great Lakes. Like most other Algonquians, the Foxes are generally classified as a Woodland people (see "Northeast Indians" and "Algonquian"), because they usually located their villages along river valleys where

the soil was rich enough for forests and for crops. In early writings, the Foxes are often called *Mesquakie*, their own name, meaning "red earth people," after the reddish color of the soil in their homeland. Their better-known name, after the animal, was probably originally the symbol of a particular clan within the tribe and mistakenly applied to the whole tribe by whites.

Fox courting flute

The Foxes are also sometimes classified as Prairie Algonquians, because they lived near the prairies of the Mississippi Valley, with its tall, coarse grasses and few trees and its herds of buffalo (see "Prairie Indians").

Being seminomadic, the Foxes could take advantage of both forests and prairies. During the summer, they lived in villages of bark-covered houses and raised corn, beans, squash, pumpkins, and tobacco; during the winter they tracked herds of game and lived in portable wigwams.

The Foxes and other tribes of the western Great Lakes region are also sometimes grouped together as the People of the Calumet because they used calumets, or sacred pipes, in their ceremonies. The Indians placed tobacco, or *kinnikinnik*, a mixture of tobacco and willow bark, in the pipe bowls carved from pipestone (catlinite); then they inhaled the burning matter through long wooden or reed stems.

The Foxes had three kinds of leader: the peace chief, the war chief, and the ceremonial leader. The first position was the only one that was hereditary, passed on from father to son. The peace chief kept peace within the tribe and was in charge at councils when village matters were discussed. On these occasions, the calumets were decorated with white feathers and were truly "peace pipes," the popular name for the long Indian pipes.

A war chief was chosen for each military campaign by other braves on the basis of fighting skills and visions. He would be in charge at councils when matters of war were discussed. On these occasions, the calumets would be decorated with red feathers.

The ceremonial leader, or shaman, instructed others in religious rituals. These ceremonies had many purposes, such as making game plentiful, or helping crops grow, or curing the sick. On these occasions, participants would also smoke the sacred pipe.

Historically, the Foxes are most closely associated with Wisconsin. The territory where they first had contact with whites in the 1600s—along the Fox River bearing their name—is now part of that state. But the Foxes might have earlier lived east of Lake Michigan in what is now the state of Michigan.

The Foxes were the only sizable Algonquian tribe to make war on the French during the early part of the French and Indian Wars, especially in the 1720s and 1730s (see "Abnaki" and "Iroquois"). Most of the other Algonquians sided with the French against the English. The Foxes followed a different path, however, because they were traditional enemies of the Chippewas, who maintained close ties with the French. The Foxes demanded tolls in the form of trade goods from any outsiders who passed along the Fox River, which angered the French. The French and Chippewas launched a campaign against the Foxes and drove them down the Wisconsin River to new homelands.

It was during this period, in 1734, that the Foxes joined in an alliance with the Sacs, one that has lasted to present times. In 1769, the two tribes plus others defeated the Illinois, and some Foxes moved farther south into what has become the state of Illinois (see "Illinois"). In 1780, Foxes also formed a temporary alliance with the Sioux to attack the Chippewas at St. Croix Falls, but in this conflict they were defeated.

Fox skirt (made in modern times using antique ribbon applique)

After the American Revolution and the birth of the United States, Fox history closely follows that of their permanent allies, the Sacs (see "Sac"). The Foxes were active in Little Turtle's War of 1790-94 (see "Miami") and Tecumseh's Rebellion of 1809-11 (see "Shawnee"). Fox warriors also fought alongside the Sacs under the Sac chief Black Hawk in the famous Black Hawk War of 1832, the final Indian war for the Old Northwest. Today, the two tribes share reservations and trust lands in Iowa, Kansas, and Oklahoma.

Great Basin Indians

The phrase *Great Basin* refers to an immense desert basin in the western part of North America. It has the shape of a bowl: a central depression surrounded by highlands. To the east stand the Rocky Mountains; to the west, the Sierra Nevada; to the north, the Columbia Plateau; and to the south, the Colorado Plateau. The Great Basin Culture Area, where Indians shared a similar way of life, includes territory now comprising practically all of Nevada and Utah; parts of Idaho, Oregon, Wyoming, Colorado, and California; and small parts of Arizona and New Mexico.

The Great Basin is a region of interior drainage. That is to say, rivers and streams drain from the flanking higher ground and flow into the central depression, disappearing into "sinks" in the sandy soil. The mountains block the rain and snow blowing in from the ocean. Few rain clouds ever reach the Basin, resulting in little precipitation and high evaporation. In past ages, the Basin contained many large lakes. The largest lake remaining in the region is the Great Salt Lake in what is now Utah. Because of the geological formation of the region, the Basin has many alkaline flats—soil with mineral salts from bodies of water that have since evaporated. Only occasional low and long rocky uplands break up the long stretches of barren desert.

Death Valley is part of the Great Basin Culture Area. This depression in the desert is the lowest point in all the Americas—280 feet below sea level. It also has some of the most extreme temperatures, as high as 140 degrees Fahrenheit.

Because of the dryness of the Great Basin, little vegetation grows there. The dominant flora on the desert floor are low grasses and sagebrush, a plant that sends its roots far down into the earth for moisture. The hills of the Basin have some trees that are adapted to dryness, such as juniper and piñon trees. Also because of the dryness, there is little game in the Great Basin. The most common large mammal is the antelope, which grazes on grass and brush and which can go a long time without water. Mountain goats subsist in the rocky highlands. Jackrabbits live in the desert, as do rodents, including field mice, kangaroo rats, muskrats, gophers, and ground squirrels. Certain birds and reptiles, particularly snakes and lizards, are also suited to desert life, as are insects, such as the grasshopper.

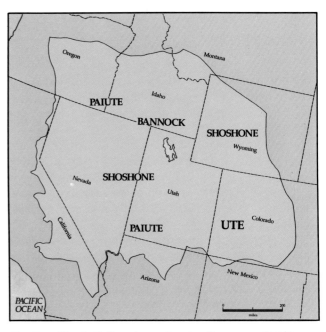

The Great Basin Culture Area, showing the approximate locations of Indian tribes listed in this book—circa 1500, before displacement by whites (with modern boundaries)

All these creatures provided food for the Great Basin Indians. The Indians also foraged and dug for edible wild plants—roots, berries, seeds, and nuts. With a few exceptions, Basin inhabitants practiced no agriculture in the extreme environment. Because of their foraging practices, the hunter-gatherers of the region are sometimes referred to collectively as Digger Indians.

Having such meager food supplies, Great Basin Indians traveled for the most part in small bands of extended families. Most lived in small, simple cone-shaped structures, made of pole frames covered with brush or reeds.

There are four major tribal groups considered part of the Great Basin: Paiute, Ute, Shoshone, and Bannock (see entries for those tribes). All four tribes, plus smaller tribal offshoots, spoke dialects of the Uto-Aztecan language family. The only exception was the Washo tribe in the western part of the culture area, which is not listed separately in this book. The Washos spoke a Hokan dialect.

Gros Ventre (Atsina)

Gros Ventre means "big belly" in French. It is pronounced *grow-VAHN-truh*. Early French fur traders on the northern Plains gave this name to two different tribes, the Atsinas and the Hidatsas, because of the hand motions used to designate both tribes in the sign language of the Plains Indians. In this sign language, invented by the Indians so that they could communicate with each other despite their many different spoken languages, each tribe had a particular hand sign. In the case of the Atsinas, the sign was a sweeping pass in front of the abdomen with both hands to show that they were big eaters. In the case of the Hidatsas, an early sign was a similar gesture in front of the abdomen, to indicate their custom of tattooing parallel stripes across the chest. Therefore, to the French the Atsinas were the Gros Ventres of the Plains, and the Hidatsas were the Gros Ventres of the River. Yet, in modern usage, only the Atsinas have come to be known as the Gros Ventres. The Hidatsas are now generally referred to by their Indian name rather than by their French one (see "Hidatsa").

The Gros Ventres, or Atsinas, lived for most of their history on the Milk River branch of the Missouri River in country that is now northern Montana. They also ranged into southern Saskatchewan as far north as the Saskatchewan River. Similarities in their languages indicate that the Gros Ventres split off from the Arapahos, another Algonquian-speaking people (see "Arapaho"). For much of their history, the Gros Ventres were part of the Blackfoot Confederacy; the Blackfeet, another Algonquian people, lived to their west (see "Blackfoot").

On acquiring horses and guns, the Gros Ventres became a typical Plains tribe. They depended on buffalo more than any other game for sustenance and lived in camps of tepees. They also conducted raids for horses on other tribes (see "Plains Indians").

In the mid-1800s, the Gros Ventres joined the Crows in a fight with their former Blackfoot allies (see "Crow"). They suffered a major defeat in 1867. Disease brought to the northern Plains by white traders also killed many of their people.

In the 1880s, the surviving Gros Ventres were placed on the Fort Belknap Reservation in northern Montana, where their descendants live today. They share the reservation with the Assiniboine tribe (see "Assiniboine").

Gros Ventre pouch

The elders among the Gros Ventres are currently working to preserve the tribe's traditional culture for future generations. Some of them are preparing a dictionary of the Gros Ventre language. It is not easy to translate Indian words into English. For example, the Gros Ventre language has a single word that means "to eat fat while eating meat."

Haida

Native Americans made all kinds of boats. The most famous Indian craft is the birchbark canoe, used on rivers and lakes. Yet some tribes who lived along the ocean made seaworthy boats. The most skilled maritime boatbuilders were the Haidas.

The Northwest Coast Culture Area was an area of master woodcarvers (see "Northwest Coast Indians"). This was the part of North America where giant totem poles, objects that have become a famous symbol for all Indian peoples, were crafted, along with elaborate

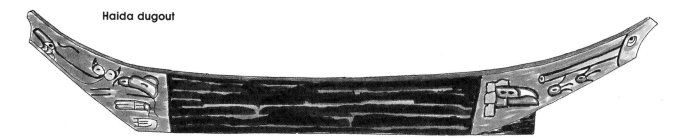

Haida dugout

ceremonial masks, chests, headdresses, and other objects. Of the many skilled woodworkers along this heavily populated strip of coastal land, stretching from northern California to southern Alaska, the Haida craftsmen were perhaps the best. Their boats were especially prized by other tribes. Individuals of other tribes showed off their wealth by trading for a Haida dugout and displaying it at ceremonies, such as weddings.

The Haidas lived on the Queen Charlotte Islands off present-day British Columbia. In the early 1700s, a group of Haidas migrated northward to the southern part of Prince of Wales Island, now part of Alaska, where they used the name *Kaigini*. The Haidas, whose name means "people" (pronounced *HI-duh*), belonged to the Nadene language family, distant relatives of the Tlingits to their north and perhaps of the Athapascans to the east (see "Tlingit" and "Athapascan").

Since the Haidas lived on an island whose streams were too small for salmon, they depended more on fish such as halibut and cod. The candlefish provided oil for cooking and lamps. The Haidas also hunted sea

Haida fishhook

mammals, such as seals, sea lions, and sea otters. Unlike the Nootkas and Makah peoples to the south, however, the Haidas did not pursue whales (see "Nootka" and "Makah"). The forests in the interior of the Queen Charlotte Islands had little game, but the Haidas did hunt black bears.

Haida men constructed some of the largest gabled houses (houses with slanted roofs) in the Pacific Northwest, some of them 60 feet by 100 feet. The houses were made from cedar planks, and their openings faced the sea, with one or more totem poles in the front. Haida women wove twine baskets. Haida clothing was made from woven cedar bark or from the pelts of otters and other animals.

Haida women tattooed their faces and bodies, and the backs of their hands, with family symbols. Haida society was divided into two clans, the Bear Clan and the Raven Clan. The Haidas practiced the potlatch, the ritualistic giving of gifts to guests. Shamans, or medicine men, were organized into secret societies and held great power through their supposed contact with the Ocean Beings. The medicine men used "soul-catchers," which were carved bone tubes, supposedly to capture the wandering souls of sick people and return them to their bodies. The dead were placed in carved grave-houses overlooking the ocean, and only the shamans could visit these open coffins.

The favorite wood of the Haidas for making their famous dugouts was the giant redwood, although cedar was also used. A tall, straight tree would be felled and floated to the worksite. The log would be split along its center with wooden wedges. Then the remaining round side of one of the logs would be further split to partly flatten it. The wood would be charred with a torch to make it easier to scrape with a stone adz (later, the Haidas used metal tools, which they acquired from whites). Both the inside and outside of the hull would be scraped, chiseled, and rubbed smooth, until the sides of the boat would be two fingers thick at the bottom, one inch at the top. The cockpit would be widened by putting water inside and adding hot rocks; by burning fires near the outside to further heat the wood; and by forcing the sides outward with oversize wooden braces. The bow and stern pieces, the former longer than the latter, would be carved separately and attached with either cedar pegs or

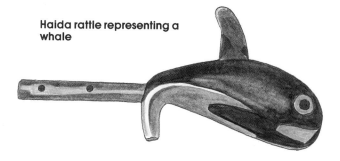

Haida rattle representing a whale

spruce lashings. Strips of cedar would also be added to the tops of the sides. The hull would be sanded with stone and polished with sharkskin to prevent friction in the water. The bow and stern would be decorated with carvings, inlays, and paintings of totemic designs. The resulting boat could be as much as 60 feet long and seven feet wide at the center and could hold about 60 warriors or the same weight in cargo. At first the Indians propelled their boats with paddles, but sails were added after contact with Europeans.

Haida paddle

Spanish, Russian, British, and French ships that sailed off the Pacific coast starting in the mid to late 1700s must have been surprised at the sight of these elegant craft manned by proud warriors. After the first trips of exploration, the fur traders came and established trading posts, and Hudson's Bay blankets bought from whites became the main gift at Indian potlatches. Soon after came the missions, both Episcopal and Methodist. Disease, liquor, and alien religions all contributed to the gradual decline of the Haida people and their traditional culture.

Haida whistle

Today few Haidas remain. There are only two communities left in Canada—Masset and Skidegate. Work in fishing and canning provides income for some band members. Others generate income through their rediscovered traditional artwork. A community of Haidas lives at Hydaburg on the southern end of Prince of Wales Island in Alaska. This group has joined in a corporation with the Tlingits, called the Sealaska Corporation. Both Haidas and Tlingits have a reputation as being among the best Alaskan fishermen.

Havasupai

The Havasupais lived along a branch of the Colorado River. The tribe's ancestral homeland, from about A.D. 1100, was Cataract Canyon, part of the Grand Canyon complex. This territory, now part of northwestern Arizona, contains some of the most spectacular landforms in all of North America—amazing high-walled canyons with colorful layers of sandstone; deep, dark caves; and steep waterfalls.

The Havasupais might be an offshoot of the Hualapai tribe. Both peoples, along with the Yavapais, were Upland Yumans, and lived north of the River Yuman tribes such as the Mojaves and Yumas (see entries for those tribes). Scholars categorize all these tribes as part of the Southwest Culture Area (see "Southwest Indians").

Although the Havasupais lived in dry country, it was the Colorado River that defined their way of life and came to be associated with them. Havasupai, pronounced *hah-vah-SOO-pie*, means "people of the blue-green water." The Colorado River, which provided sustenance for many native peoples, created in

Cataract Canyon a fertile strip of land unlike any other in that arid and rocky region.

The Havasupais learned to irrigate their fields with water from the river and till the soil with planting sticks. They grew corn, beans, squash, melons, sunflowers, and tobacco. The Havasupais were thus able to live most of the year in permanent villages. They lived in two different kinds of dwellings: pole-framed houses, circular or rectangular in shape and covered with brush and earth; as well as rock shelters, either naturally formed or dug by hand in canyon walls. The Havasupais also built small domed lodges that doubled as sweathouses and clubhouses. In their agricultural lifestyle, the Havasupais resembled the Hopis to the east more than they did their Yuman kinsmen to the south (see "Hopi"). The Havasupais often traded with the Hopis, exchanging deerskins, salt, and red mineral paint for agricultural foods, pottery, and cloth.

After the autumn harvest, the Havasupais left their villages for the winter. They climbed the canyon walls to the top of the plateau, where they lived in temporary camps in the midst of plentiful game. Individual hunters, carrying bows and arrows, stalked mountain lions and other wildcats, deer and antelope, and mountain sheep. Men, women, and children also participated in communal hunting drives. By stomping and beating the ground, tribal members forced rabbits into the open, where they could be clubbed. The Havasupais also gathered piñon nuts, the edible seed from a small pine tree, on the canyon rims.

The Havasupais wore more clothing than most other Yumans, mostly buckskin. They painted and tattooed their faces. They made both baskets and pottery for use as containers and cooking vessels.

The main unit of social organization for the Havasupais was the family. The tribe as a whole was loosely structured under six hereditary chiefs. Their religion was dominated by shamans, priest-magicians, but with few organized rituals other than the use of prayer sticks and dances for a particular purpose, such as to ask for rain. Tribal members participated in at least three ceremonies a year, with music, dancing, and speechmaking.

The Havasupais were peaceful; not one of their leaders was a war chief. Their seclusion behind canyon walls enabled them to avoid attacks by more warlike neighbors. The only Spanish explorer thought to have visited them was Father Francisco Garces, in 1776. The tribe managed to avoid further contact with outsiders well into the 1800s.

The Havasupais still live along the Colorado River, now on a reservation originally established in 1880, near Supai, Arizona. In 1975, with the signing of the Grand Canyon National Park Enlargement Act, the Havasupais regained a portion of their ancestral homeland along the Grand Canyon's South Rim. Because of their location, 3,000 feet below the rim of the Grand Canyon, the Havasupais earn a decent income from tourism. The Havasupai Tourist Enterprise provides facilities, guides, and mules for tourists.

Hidatsa

The Hidatsas (pronounced *he-DOT-suh*) lived along the upper Missouri River in what is now North Dakota. They are also known as the Minitaris. In early colonial history, they were called the Gros Ventres of the River by French traders, but the name Gros Ventre is more commonly applied to another tribe, the Atsinas (see "Gros Ventre").

The Hidatsas spoke a dialect of the Siouan language. They were close relatives of another Siouan-speaking people who settled to their west in what is now Montana, the Crows (see "Crow"). According to tribal tradition, the Hidatsas once lived near Devil's Lake, also in what is now North Dakota, but were pushed southwestward by the Sioux (see "Sioux"). The Hidatsas settled along the Missouri River and came to be associated with the tribes whose villages flanked their own—the Mandans and Arikaras (see "Mandan" and "Arikara").

All three peoples—the Hidatsas, Mandans, and Arikaras—were primarily village farmers. They lived in earthlodges on bluffs overlooking the Missouri River. They made pottery, unlike the more nomadic Plains Indians who used less fragile hide bags for cooking and storing food. The Hidatsas acquired some of their meat through trade with other tribes, exchanging corn for buffalo and deer meat and hides.

The Hidatsas shared many rituals with the Mandans. One custom the two tribes had in common was the Corn Dance Feast of the Women. They believed that the Old Woman Who Never Dies sent waterfowl to them in the spring as a symbol of the seeds the Indians planted. The geese represented

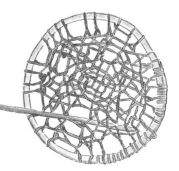

Hidatsa hoop-and-pole game, the object being to toss the pole through the moving hoop

corn; the ducks, beans; and the swans, gourds. To repay the Old Woman, the elderly women of the tribe would hang dried meat on poles as a sacrifice to her, then perform a dance to her. During the ceremony, young women of the tribe would feed the dancing women meat and receive grains of corn to eat in return. Some of the consecrated grain from the ceremony would be mixed with the tribe's planting seeds. The sacrificed meat would be left on the poles until harvest time.

The Hidatsas hunted as well as farmed. They organized an annual buffalo hunt. Like the Mandans, the Hidatsas had a White Buffalo Society for women only. Women would dance in ceremonies to lure the buffalo to the hunters. After the Hidatsas acquired horses from other tribes through trade, they tracked buffalo herds farther from their villages, onto territory that is now South Dakota and Montana. The Hidatsas also shared customs, such as the Sun Dance, with their more nomadic Siouan relatives. They are usually classified as part of the Great Plains Culture Area, but they are also referred to as Prairie people (see "Plains Indians" and "Prairie Indians").

Early French and English traders plying the muddy waters of the Missouri River in their flatboats and pirogues (boats resembling canoes) made regular stops at Hidatsa villages to barter their trade goods—guns, liquor, tools, cloth, glass beads—for furs. Early explorers traveling the Missouri, such as the United States' first great exploration of the American West, the Lewis and Clark Expedition of 1803-06, also lived among the Hidatsas.

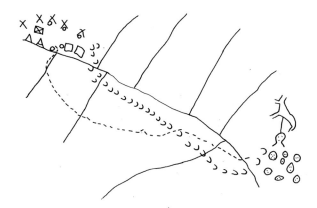

A copy of a map, drawn by the Hidatsa Indian Little Wolf, about 1880. It shows the route he took along the Missouri River in a successful raid for horses on a Sioux encampment. The circles represent Hidatsa lodges, with dots showing the number of poles supporting each roof. The crosses represent Sioux tepees. Combined circles and crosses represent dwellings belonging to intermarried Hidatsas and Sioux. Squares represent dwellings of whites. The square with a cross represents the house of a white man and Sioux woman. Lean Wolf's original path is shown in footprints and his return with the stolen horses in hoofprints.

After the smallpox epidemic of 1837, which decimated the tribes of the upper Missouri, Hidatsa survivors regrouped into a single village. In 1845, the tribe moved this village to the vicinity of Fort Berthold, North Dakota. In 1871, by executive order of the federal government, a reservation was established for the Hidatsas, to be shared with the Mandans and Arikaras.

The Three Affiliated Tribes still share this reservation today, where they run a tourism complex.

Hoopa (Hupa)

The Hoopas, or Hupas, lived along the Trinity River in territory now part of northern California. Their villages were located especially on an eight-mile stretch, known as the Hoopa Valley, where the Trinity River flows northwestward from the Coast Range, merging with the Klamath River flowing out of Oregon. To the north of the Hoopas, along the Klamath River, lived two tribes with whom the Hoopas are closely related culturally, the Karoks and Yuroks (see "Yurok"). In fact, the name *Hoopa* (pronounced *HOOP-uh*) is taken from the Yurok name for the valley where the Hoopas lived.

All three tribes shared lifeways with the other tribes of the California Culture Area: hunting, fishing, and gathering; the making of bread and other foods from acorns; and finely twined basketry for storage, cooking, hats, and cradles (see "California Indians"). The three tribes also shared cultural traits with peoples of the Northwest Coast Culture Area directly north of them: They made cedar-planked houses, with pole-and-beam construction, as well as dugout canoes. And, in their social organization, the Hoopas defined status by material possessions (see "Northwest Coast Indians"). Moreover, if there were a dispute or a crime between individuals, differences could be settled by a fine. A mediator would negotiate the amount between the opposing parties.

The Hoopas, Karoks, and Yuroks all practiced annual World Renewal ceremonies. The season they

Hoopa purse made from an elk's antler, the incised design rubbed with pigment

were held and their length varied from group to group. For all three peoples, however, the event involved two parts: First, a shaman, or medicine man, who had purified himself with special rites, would lead his assistants to different locations where he performed secret rites to renew nature; then dancers performed for all the villagers. Sometimes tribesmen would provide the dancers with their costumes in order to show off their wealth and their standing in the tribe.

The participants, whose numbers increased throughout the ceremonies, performed two main dances: the White Deerskin Dance and the Jumping Dance. In the former, the dancers wore animal-skin aprons, tooth-shell necklaces, and feather headdresses. They carried poles draped with deer hides, the heads of which were decorated with the red-feathered scalps of woodpeckers. Rare white deerskins were thought to cast the greatest powers of renewal and provided the dancer and his sponsor with much prestige. In the latter ritual, the Jumping Dance, the dancers wore woodpecker scalps, fashioned into headdresses, on their own heads, and carried tubular wands woven out of plant materials.

Interestingly, although all three peoples had so much in common in terms of culture, their languages differed. Different tribes in a given region typically spoke different dialects, but usually from the same language family. In this case, the Hoopas spoke a dialect of the Athapascan language family; the Karoks, a dialect of the Hokan family; and the Yuroks, a dialect of the Algonquian family. This language discrepancy among neighboring tribes demonstrates the fact that geography plays a more important role in determining a tribe's culture than language does.

Because of the isolated location of the Hoopa Valley in California's highlands, the Hoopas had few historical contacts with whites. The Spanish and the

A Hoopa Indian using a fire-drill (based on a cigarette silk, distributed with cigarettes as souvenirs in the early 1900s)

Russians never colonized their domain. Occasional fur traders and trappers followed the Trinity River from the Klamath but never established permanent posts. Some Anglo-Americans and Chinese mined the river with pans during the California Gold Rush of 1849, but there were not enough gold strikes to cause prospectors to overrun Hoopa territory. More and more settlers arrived in the region after California statehood (1850), but the Hoopas managed to hold on to their ancestral homeland. In 1876, the federal government made Hoopa Valley a reservation.

Hoopas live in Hoopa Valley today, with members from other area tribes. They farm, raise livestock, cut lumber, and are generally self-sufficient. They still practice traditional customs, such as hunting, fishing, acorn-gathering, basketmaking, beadwork, and the White Deerskin and Jumping dances. Because the Hoopas live where their people have always lived and because they retain many of the ancient ways, they have a sense of continuity with their ancestors and a sense of tribal vitality.

Hopi

Hopi legend tells how their tribal ancestors climbed up through three cave worlds along with all the animals. They were helped by two Spirit Masters who were brothers. After time spent in each chamber of the underworld, the people and animals finally emerged from the Grand Canyon into a fourth world, which was the earth. But darkness blanketed all the land. And the land was wet. The people met with different animals to try to bring light to the world. Spider spun a ball of pure white silk to make the moon. The people bleached a deerskin and shaped it into a shield, which became the sun. Coyote opened a jar he had found in one of the cave worlds. Sparks flew out of it, turned his face black, then flew into the sky and became stars. Then Vulture flapped his wings and made the water flow away, forming dry land. The Spirit Masters helped the water flow by forming grooves in the earth, which became the valleys. Different clans then formed with various animal names and traveled to many different locations before finally settling in their permanent homes.

This is one of many different Indian creation myths. Although mythology, the story contains many elements relating to the history and culture of the Hopis. For example, as the legend indicates, Hopi ancestors migrated from various locations to form the tribe. They settled near the Grand Canyon. They lived in arid desert country, depending on natural springs to water their crops. Both guardian spirits and animals played an important part in their elaborate religion. Underground chambers, called kivas, were considered as the doorway to the underworld and were used for ceremonies. The legend also shows how the Hopis

were a cooperative and peaceful people, willing to work with others to make their life better.

In fact, the Hopi name, pronounced *HO-pee*, is a shortening of their word *Hopituh*, meaning "peaceful ones." These people were formerly called the Moki (or Moqui) Indians, probably a name given to them by another tribe.

The Hopis were the westernmost of the Pueblo peoples, classified with them in the Southwest Culture Area (see "Pueblo Indians" and "Southwest Indians"). They were the only Pueblo Indians to speak a dialect of the Uto-Aztecan language family. Yet, like the other Pueblo Indians, they were probably descended from Anasazi peoples, earlier inhabitants of the Southwest (see "Cliff Dwellers and Desert Farmers").

The Hopis occupied different village sites on what they called the First Mesa, Second Mesa, and Third Mesa, all part of a still-larger rocky formation called Black Mesa. These various tablelands, overlooking dry valleys, were carved by erosion out of the enormous Colorado Plateau situated between the Colorado River and the Rio Grande. The Hopi homeland has since become part of northeastern Arizona.

The Hopis are famous for their religious, intellectual, and peaceful natures. They called their approach to life the Hopi Way. The Hopi Way refers to every aspect of existence, including religious beliefs, the relationship to nature, behavior toward other people, craftsmanship, and survival. In the Hopi world view, these various elements were seen as a whole. Indians in general practiced holism, as this type of philosophy is sometimes called. To further understand the Hopi Way, however, we have to divide

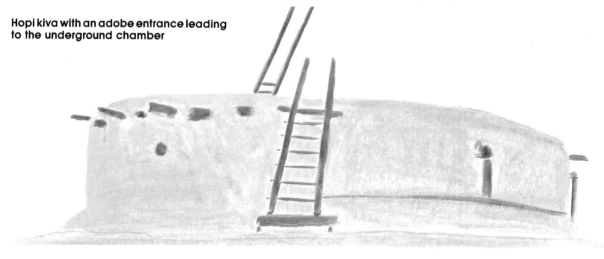

Hopi kiva with an adobe entrance leading to the underground chamber

their culture by such categories as shelter, food, crafts, political and social organization, and rituals.

Pueblos

Hopis built the walls of their pueblos with stones set in mud, then plastered the surface with more mud. Trees were rare in Hopiland, so the Indians traveled far to find pine and juniper trees for beams. The men provided the building materials, but the women shaped them into houses. They stretched the beams from one wall to another, forming a flat roof, which was filled in with poles, branches, leaves, and grass, then packed with plaster. The walls had no doors or windows. The Hopis entered through an opening in the roof, climbing down a notched log. Just as in an apartment building, the walls of one dwelling were connected to the walls of others. When a family wanted another room, they might have to build upward. Pueblos were sometimes four or five stories high.

The Hopis usually dug kivas, underground rooms with stone walls, in the village plazas. Hopi men used them for chapels as well as for clubhouses. In most kivas, a *sipapu*, a stone-lined hole in the floor, represented the entrance to the cave world from where the Hopi ancestors supposedly came. Women were not permitted in the kivas unless the men invited them for a special purpose, such as taking part in a council. Yet the women owned the houses.

Food

The Hopis were primarily farmers who supplemented their diet with some hunting and gathering. The men farmed and hunted; the women collected wild plant foods and did all the cooking. The women also owned the crops. Considering how hot and dry the climate was in their homeland, it's remarkable what good farmers the Hopis were. The men studied all the patches of soil for miles around their pueblos, looking for areas of moisture. They usually planted their crops in the sandy soil at the base of the mesas, where they could catch runoff from the tablelands after the rare rainstorms. They also looked for underground springs. They had to protect their plants from sandstorms by building windbreaks out of branches and brush. They grew corn, beans, squash, cotton, and tobacco. Corn by far was the most important food for the Hopis. They had more than 50 ways to prepare it, including a thin bread called *piki*. The Hopis also kept flocks of tame turkeys, which helped provide meat, since deer, antelope, rabbits, and other game were scarce in Hopiland.

Arts and Crafts

The Hopis ate out of clay bowls made by the women and decorated with geometric designs. The women also wove beautiful baskets out of plant matter. Hopi men wove cotton to make blankets and clothing. Women dyed the threads with orange, yellow, red, green, and black dyes made from plants. The Hopis

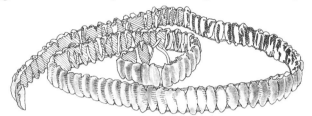

Hopi sash made from cocoons

also used leather for moccasins and rabbit-skins for robes. Unmarried Hopi girls had a hairdo unique to their tribe protruding from both sides in the shape of a squash blossom.

A Hopi woman with the squash-blossom hairdo, a symbol of maturity and readiness for marriage

Social Structure

Most Indian tribes had chiefs as well as medicine men, or shamans. In the case of the Hopis, the shamans were the chiefs. Different clans, groups of related families, such as the Snake, Badger, and Antelope clans, also helped direct religious events and helped make village decisions.

Religion

The Hopis conducted religious ceremonies all year long. The purpose of most of these rituals was to affect the weather and bring enough rain to ensure bountiful harvests. Kachinas played a major role in the Hopi religion. These guardian spirits, recreated in masks and dolls by the tribesmen, were also important in the religion of the Zunis, another Pueblo people on the Colorado Plateau (see "Zuni").

The Hopis believed that the kachinas were supernatural beings dwelling in their own world high up in the mountains to the west. Every year, at the winter solstice, the shortest day of the year, the kachinas supposedly traveled to the world of humans, where they entered the peoples' bodies and stayed in residence until the summer solstice, the longest day of the year. Hopi men impersonated the kachinas with elaborate painted masks of wood, feathers, and other materials.

The masked kachina dancers performed at many festivals, such as the 16-day summer festival called the Niman Kachina. At these ceremonies, they performed many different kinds of raindance. One of these was the famous snake dance, performed last of all. The kachinas danced with live snakes wrapped around their necks and arms, and even in their mouths. At the end of the dance, they threw the snakes on a design made with corn meal. Then they released the snakes outside the pueblo, and the kachina dancers were sent off at the same time to bring cloudbursts of rain.

Scare-kachinas had faces with long teeth and bulging eyes. Hopi men wore scare-kachina masks to frighten children who had been bad.

Children could learn the names of the different kachinas, and what they stood for, through the dolls their fathers and grandfathers carved for them. These are known as kachina dolls, but a better description would be statues or god-figures. They are not for play, but to be treasured, studied, worshiped, and passed on to one's own children.

The fear caused by the scare-kachinas, as well as great love and attention from their parents, helped the Hopi children grow up to be friendly and sharing. This

Hopi kachina doll

was the Hopi Way: to be in balance with both nature and other people. If a child or adult acted with cruelty, he was shunned by others until he changed. But the Hopi Way also taught forgiveness.

Contacts with Whites

The fact that the *Hopituh*, the "peaceful ones," went to war with the Spanish shows what an impact the outsiders had on them. The first explorers to reach them were two of Francisco de Coronado's men, Pedro de Tobar and Juan de Padilla, in 1540. Hopis let these two Franciscan priests and their soldiers stay with them for several days. The Spanish first learned of the existence of the Grand Canyon at this time.

Another Spanish explorer, Antonio de Espejo, visited the Hopis in 1583. Then Juan de Onate followed with many more men in 1598. He made the Hopis swear allegiance to the Spanish crown. The first missionaries settled in Hopiland in 1629 with more to follow.

Because of the Spanish soldiers, the Hopis were forced to tolerate the new religion among them. But they continued to practice their traditional beliefs. When the Spanish tried to eliminate all kachina worship once and for all, the normally peaceful Hopis rebelled. They joined the Rio Grande pueblos in the Pueblo Rebellion of 1680 and destroyed the missions in their midst. At that period in their history, the Hopis established new pueblos that were easier to defend. The Spanish reconquered the Rio Grande pueblos, starting in 1689, but they did not push as far as the Hopi pueblos to the west. The Hopis remained free to practice their own religion. Some Tewa Indians from the Rio Grande pueblos fled to Hopiland at this time to start a new life.

Hopis Today

None of the current Hopi pueblos are on the exact sites of the pueblos of the early 1500s. The names of present-day villages on the Hopi Reservation are as follows: Walpi, Sichomovi, Hano on First Mesa; Shungopovi, Mishongnovi, and Shipaulovi on Second Mesa; and Oraibi, Kiakochomovi, Hotevilla, Bakabi, Moenkopi on Third Mesa. Modern pueblos have doorways and glass windows as well as other present-day conveniences, in some cases electricity. But the Hopi homes have much in common with those of their ancestors.

In fact, of all the Indian tribes in North America, the Hopis probably live closest to their traditional way. Many Hopis still farm their traditional crops, along with wheat. They have also learned to raise sheep. Many continue to produce traditional craftwork: pottery, basketry, weaving, and kachina dolls. The Hopis are also famed for their silverwork, a craft learned later in the mid-1800s, from the Navajos who had learned it from the Mexicans. The Hopis are especially known for belt buckles, bracelets, and boxes with silver cutouts overlaid on a dark background of copper, oxidized silver, or a kind of coal called jet.

Many Hopis still shape their lives around their ancient religion. Many still perform the old dances, some with kachina masks and some without. Certain of these colorful and complex dances are open to the public. The dances are a form of prayer for the Hopis, who use the rituals to ask the gods for rain, food, and the well-being of the human race.

Not all Hopis live the traditional way, however. The Hopis are a good example of a people with an inner conflict. Many tribes have disagreements between those who want to preserve or rediscover the old ways and those who want to join mainstream American culture. In the case of the Hopis, the split has led to a very difficult situation.

The Hopi Tribal Council, originally appointed by the U.S. Bureau of Indian Affairs, wants control of lands that were signed over to the Hopis in the late 1800s. But the Navajos now live on these lands. Navajo territory, in fact, has come to surround the Hopi Reservation. The Hopi Tribal Council has been working with white lawyers and energy companies to reclaim the land, especially in the vicinity of Big Mountain. They all want to make money by mining coal, oil, and uranium found there. These forces influenced Arizona politicians to work for the passage of an act of Congress in 1974, calling for the removal of the Navajos. The Navajo Tribal Council, like the Hopi Tribal Council, has ties with mining companies.

But the Hopi traditionalists do not want the Navajos pushed off these lands. They long ago made peace with the Navajos who used to raid the Hopis for food, and the Hopis taught the Navajos how to farm and herd sheep. They are friends and neighbors of one another and relatives by marriage. The Hopi traditionalists do not want the Navajos to suffer another removal, to be forced to undergo an experience like the Long Walk of 1864. The federal government has even threatened to use force to relocate the Navajos, many of whom are elderly and who have lived for their whole lives where they are now. The Hopi traditionalists consider the lands in question to belong to the Navajos as much as to them. They also want the Navajos to stay so the land will not be mined and will stay the way it is. In any case, it is the Hopi Way to share.

The story of this tribal conflict, the story of Big Mountain, is powerfully told in the movie *Broken Rainbow*, which won the Academy Award for best documentary picture in 1985, making many Americans aware of the Hopi-Navajo situation. Big Mountain is a reminder that many Indian issues have yet to be resolved. It is a reminder that the patterns of history are being repeated, with Indians still suffering great hardship in the name of progress. It shows that the Indians' story does not just belong in the history books.

Hualapai (Walapai)

The name of this tribe is pronounced *WAH-lah-pie* and is sometimes spelled *Walapai*. The name means "pine tree people," after a kind of small pine—the piñon—growing in the Hualapai homeland.

The Hualapais, or the Pais as they are sometimes called, along with their kinsmen the Havasupais and Yavapais, are often described as Upland Yumans to distinguish them from the River Yumans living to their south, such as the Mojaves and Yumas (see entries for those tribes). These various Yuman-speaking peoples lived along the Colorado River in territory now part of western Arizona and southeastern California. All the Yumans are classified by scholars as part of the Southwest Culture Area (see "Southwest Indians").

The Hualapais occupied the middle course of the Colorado River in northwestern Arizona between the Mojave and Havasupai Indians' territory. Most of their mountainous homeland, unlike that of their neighbors, was not farmable. As a result, other than occasional farming, the tribe depended on wild plant foods, such as piñon nuts, as well as various animals, such as deer, antelope, and rabbits, plus some fish. They often had to wander far from the river in small bands to find enough to eat. They lived in domed huts of poles, brush, thatch, and earth, as well as more temporary brush wickiups similar to those of the Apaches who lived southeast of them (see "Apache").

Hualapais crafted simple clothing out of buckskin or bark. Men usually wore shorts and breechcloths; women wore skirts or aprons. In cold weather both men and women used blankets made from rabbit skins and wraparound robes.

The Hualapai religion centered on an unseen world of gods and demons. Hualapai medicine men supposedly took their power from dreams. Through a combination of singing, shaking a gourd rattle, pretending to suck out disease through a tube, and applying various herbs, they tried to cure the sick.

The Spanish, exploring out of Mexico, reached the Hualapai homeland in the 1500s—probably Hernando de Alarcon in 1540 and definitely Marcos Farfan de los Godos in 1598. Then in 1776, Francisco Garces made contact with the tribe. But the Spanish and subsequently the Mexicans never fully developed Hualapai country as they did other parts of the Southwest and California.

The pace of change quickened for the Hualapais after the Mexican Cession of their territory to the United States in 1848. With growing numbers of Anglo-Americans entering their domain and a number of treaty violations by whites, the Hualapais reacted with occasional violence. By 1870, the principal chief at the time, Schrum, negotiated a lasting peace with the United States and was granted a permanent reservation for his people.

The Hualapai Reservation is located near Peach Springs, Arizona, not far from the Grand Canyon. The tribe makes some income through the sale of baskets, but the main livelihood is raising animals. Some tribal members also hunt and farm. The tribe as a whole leases out some lands for mining and lumbering.

Huron (Wyandot)

The Huron Indians are important to both United States and Canadian history. The name *Huron* was given to them by the French, and means something close to "rough" or "boorish." Their name for themselves was *Wendat, Guyandot,* or *Wyandot,* probably meaning "islanders" or "peninsula dwellers." The Huron name (pronounced *HYUR-on*) is generally used when referring to early Canadian history. The Wyandot name (pronounced *WHY-un-dot*) is usually applied to descendants of the tribe who moved to the United States.

The Hurons were an Iroquoian-speaking people with typically Iroquoian customs. Nevertheless, they are rarely referred to as Iroquois, a name applied to the six tribes of the Iroquois League (see "Iroquois"). The Hurons originally lived north of these other tribes in the Lake Simcoe region of Ontario lying between Georgian Bay (part of Lake Huron) and Lake Ontario (see "Northeast Indians"). In historical accounts, the Huron homeland is sometimes called Huronia.

Lifeways

The Hurons were divided into various clans, living in different parts of Huronia. These were the Rock Clan, the Cord Clan, the Bear Clan, the Deer Clan, and the One House Lodge.

Like their Iroquois neighbors, the Hurons built elm-bark longhouses within walled villages. They liked to locate their villages on high ground near a navigable river and a clear spring. They cultivated the same crops as the Iroquois, mainly corn, beans, squash, and sunflowers for food, and tobacco for smoking. They supplemented their diet by hunting, fishing, and gathering wild plant foods.

Huron pottery pipe

The Hurons sometimes drove deer into the rivers or into fenced-in areas, then used bows and arrows to kill them. They often snared beaver with nets. They also snared bears in traps, then fed and fattened them over a period of one or two years before eating them.

The Hurons fished the bay, lakes, and rivers. Unlike the Iroquois, the Hurons had birchbark canoes similar to those of the Algonquian tribes. They used bone hooks and bone harpoons. They also used huge nets—some 400 yards long—woven from plants called nettles and held in place by stone weights and wood floats. Every fall, they traveled to the islands of Georgian Bay to fish, especially for whitefish. A Preacher to the Fish cast spells to draw the fish to the nets. The Hurons also made annual expeditions to the north to gather ripe blueberries.

The Hurons kept fires burning constantly in fire-pits for cooking or warmth. One of their many ritualistic dances was the Dance of Fire. The dancers carried smoldering coals or heated stones in their mouths; they also plunged their arms into boiling water. This was thought to invoke a spirit, or *Oki*, to cure the sick.

When the soil in one area became depleted, or the game became scarce, or wood for building, heating, and cooking ran out, the Hurons moved their villages to new sites.

European-made tomahawk for trade with Indians

Hurons wore deerskin shirts, breechcloths, leggings, skirts, and moccasins, plus fur cloaks for extra warmth. They often decorated articles of clothing with fringed edges, painted designs, and strips of fur. Sometimes they painted their faces black, red, green, or violet with vegetable and mineral dyes mixed with sunflower oil or bear fat.

The Hurons were very affectionate toward their children, praising them for good behavior but rarely scolding them for bad behavior. Mothers carried their babies in wooden cradleboards, cushioned with moss or cattail down. When babies were old enough to eat solid food, Huron mothers would make digestion easier for them by partially chewing the food first.

Children had to start learning adult skills when they were young. Boys learned how to shoot with bows and arrows and how to throw harpoons, plus other skills of hunting, fishing, and warfare. Girls learned how to plant crops, store food, cook, sew, make pottery, and weave baskets and nets.

When a Huron died, the village held a feast for relatives and friends. The corpse, wrapped in furs, was placed on top of a litter inside the village. Mourning went on for days. After a period of time, villagers

carried the litter to a cemetery, where they built a small cabin over the body. They placed food, oil, and tools inside the cabin to help the dead person on his journey to the spirit world. Presents were also given to the relatives to comfort them.

Every 10 years or so, the Hurons held the Feast of the Dead. At this celebration, families brought remains of their dead relatives from the cemetery back to the village, scraped the bones clean of any dried flesh, and rewrapped them in furs. The villagers also feasted, told stories about the dead, gave presents to children, and held sporting events.

The Fur Trade

The Hurons are famous as early trading partners of the French. Samuel de Champlain, who founded New France in the early 1600s, established a lasting trade relationship with them. Jesuit missionaries also settled among the Hurons. Quebec City on the St. Lawrence River was originally a Huron village called Stadacona. Montreal, farther south on the St. Lawrence, was the Huron village of Hochelaga. The Hurons traded their furs to the French for European goods. But their most important role in the fur trade was as middlemen between the French traders and other Indian tribes.

From the years 1616 to 1649, the Hurons were the central tribe in a great trade empire resulting from the European demand for beaver pelts to make hats and coats. The Hurons had a regular river and portage route over hundreds of miles, plus a fixed yearly schedule. At specific places and times, they traded their own agricultural products to other tribes in exchange for pelts; carried the furs to the French in Quebec City and Montreal, where they bartered them for European goods; then returned to the tribes with these goods to trade for more pelts. The Hurons dealt with many different tribes all over the Northeast: fellow Iroquoians, known as the Tobaccos and Neutrals (living between Lake Erie, Lake Ontario, and Lake Huron); Algonquians, such as Ottawas, Algonkins, and Nipissings (living north of Lake Huron); and Siouan-speaking tribes, such as Winnebagos (living west of Lake Michigan). Of these tribes, the Ottawas, Algonkins, and Winnebagos have their own entries in this book.

What a colorful time in Canadian history! Imagine the Hurons, dressed in buckskin and standing on a riverbank, haggling with Indians of another tribe and language over how much grain to be traded for beaver pelts. Imagine the Hurons in their flotilla of birchbark canoes, now piled high with furs, paddling along the rapid, winding northern rivers. Imagine the Hurons carrying the boats and furs along a portage route through an evergreen forest to another river. Then imagine the rugged French fur traders, many of them also in buckskin, coming to the edge of their fortified settlements to greet the arriving Hurons. Imagine the meetings and bickering over prices that followed between these two peoples from different continents. And then imagine the Hurons on their way back to Indian country, their canoes now laden with such products as glass beads, fancy cloth, bright paints, sharp metal knives and hatchets, and shiny kettles. Also imagine the eagerness of the other tribes to get their hands on these goods, and finally the excitement of the Hurons in returning home after the long trek.

But the days of the Great Huron Trade Circle came to a close with Iroquois invasions from the south in 1648-49. The tribes of the Iroquois League and the Hurons had been enemies for a long time. The Iroquois had also become enemies of the French after several hostile encounters with Champlain and his men and had become allies and trading partners with the Dutch, who supplied them with firearms. When beaver became hard to find in their own country, the Iroquois looked to Huron country in the northern woods for a fresh supply so they could keep up their trade.

The well-armed and well-organized Iroquois launched many raids into Huron territory. The Hurons burned their own villages as they scattered in retreat through the countryside. The Iroquois captured Jesuit missionaries who stayed behind, burning some at the stake. In the following years, the powerful Iroquois also attacked other tribes in the area, disrupting French fur trade and settlement.

A small group of Hurons managed to find safety among the French and were granted reserve lands at Lorette near Quebec City, where their descendants now live. Other Hurons settled among other tribes for a time, such as the Tobaccos, but eventually began a series of migrations in the 1600s and 1700s to territory that became the states of Michigan, Wisconsin, Illinois, and Ohio. These bands of Hurons came to be known as Wyandots.

The Wyandots fought the British in Pontiac's Rebellion of 1763 (see "Ottawa"). Yet they sided with the British in both the American Revolution and the War of 1812 (see "Iroquois" and "Shawnee"). By 1842, the Wyandots had sold off all their lands east of the Mississippi River and moved to the part of the Indian Territory that became Wyandotte County, Kansas. In 1867, however, the Wyandots were relocated in the northeastern part of the new Indian Territory, which later became the state of Oklahoma (see "Cherokee"). Their descendants still live there today. Thus, like many Indian tribes, the Huron-Wyandots presently have members in both the United States and Canada.

Illinois

The Illinois are notable for four reasons: One, they are good examples of the so-called Prairie Algonquians. Two, they were important early allies of the French. Three, they were a tribe who were practically wiped out by fellow Indians. And four, their name is used for a river and a state.

First, their culture: The Illinois are classified as part of the extensive Northeast Culture Area, running from the Mississippi River to the Atlantic Coast and peopled mostly with Algonquians (see "Northeast Indians" and "Algonquian"). The Illinois lived in the western reaches of this area. Their extensive territory was situated to the south of the Great Lakes and to the east of the Mississippi River.

The Illinois can be called either Woodland Algonquians or Prairie Algonquians. They had villages in the wooded river valleys where there was a good supply of fresh drinking water and shelter from the wind and sun. And, in the forests, they found abundant materials for making things: plenty of wood and bark for shaping houses, boats, tools, and weapons; and for fuel to keep warm in the bitter winters. Birch trees did not grow that far south, so the Illinois did not have that pliable bark for coverings. They used elm bark instead. And they made dugout canoes from butternut trees. There was also plenty of wildlife in the forests and rivers; and, along the banks, there was rich soil for growing corn.

Illinois (Kaskaskia) wooden effigy bowl in the shape of a beaver

But the Illinois also ventured out onto the windswept prairies along the wide Mississippi Valley (see "Prairie Indians"). On the prairies, they could hunt the herds of buffalo that grazed in the tall grass. Before the whites came to North America and brought horses with them, the Indians had to hunt on foot. These early buffalo hunters had the most success when they worked in groups. A proven method was to surround a herd with a ring of fire, then, while the animals were trapped, pick them off with bows and arrows. To kill even one of these huge hoofed mammals meant a good supply of meat for one's family, plus a large shaggy fur for robes and blankets. Women went along on the hunts to pack in the meat and dry it, and to tan the hides; children also helped with these chores. There were also numerous elk on the prairies. The elk, of all the members of the deer family, was second in size only to the moose and was a valuable catch.

When Europeans first arrived in their territory, the Illinois lived in what has since become the state of Illinois, as well as in southern Wisconsin. Some bands also lived to the west of the Mississippi River in Iowa and Missouri. But the center of their homeland was in Illinois along the river that also bears the people's name. The most important bands were the Cahokia, Kaskaskia, Michigamea, Moingwena, Peoria, and Tamaroa.

The French were the first Europeans in Illinois country. In the 1670s, the Jesuit priests Louis Jolliet and Jacques Marquette had contacts with the Illinois. Father Claude Jean Allouez lived among them for several years. Henri Tonti, the lieutenant of Rene Robert de la Salle, won the Illinois over to the French cause in 1680. La Salle himself visited them in 1682. The Illinois were important to the French because they controlled a stretch of the Mississippi River, the trading lane to Louisiana.

Also during the 1680s, the Illinois suffered attacks from the Iroquois, who invaded from the east. But the failure of the Iroquois to take the Illinois's Fort St. Louis on the Illinois River marked the end of the Iroquois League's westward expansion (see "Iroquois").

In the following century, however, the Illinois were defeated by an alliance of other tribes. The Illinois had been enemies of the Great Lakes Algonquians on and off for many years, as well as enemies of the Sioux. Yet, as allies of the French against the British in the struggle for colonial North America (the French and Indian Wars, from 1689 to 1763), they maintained an uneasy truce with these other tribes, who also backed the French. Some Illinois warriors even fought under the Ottawa leader Pontiac in his rebellion against the British in 1763 (see "Ottawa"). Yet, when an Illinois Indian, supposedly in the pay of the British, killed Pontiac in 1769, many tribes united against the Illinois. These allies were the Ottawas, Chippewas, Potawatomis, Sacs, Foxes, and Kickapoos (see entries for those tribes).

Their attacks against the Illinois were relentless, and the Illinois did not have the numbers to resist them. With the Illinois's defeat, many other Indians migrated south onto their lands. Supposedly, by the end of this conflict, the population of the Illinois tribe had fallen from 1,800 to 150. The few survivors took refuge at the French settlement of Kaskaskia, where the Kaskaskia River meets the Mississippi in Illinois.

Then in 1833, with increased numbers of American settlers in the region, this group of Illinois—the Kaskaskia and Peoria bands—sold off their land and moved west of the Mississippi River to Kansas. There they joined the Miami bands—the Wea and the Piankashaw—in the northeast corner of the Indian Territory, which later became the state of Oklahoma. Illinois descendants still live there today.

The name Illinois is a French adaptation of the tribe's word for "people." It was taken for the name of a river, and then for the name of a territory—the Illinois Territory—which, in 1818, became a state. Although few Illinois Indians remain in their original homeland, the name of the state is a monument to their once-commanding presence and their proud heritage.

Iowa

The Iowas, or Ioways, usually pronounced the second way, lived for most of recorded history in territory now part of the state bearing their name. The name is derived from the Siouan word *ayuhwa*, meaning "sleepy ones." Yet, according to tribal legend, the Iowas migrated to the prairies between the Mississippi and Missouri rivers from the Great Lakes region, where they were once a united people with other Siouan-speaking tribes, the Winnebagos, Otos, and Missouris (see entries for those tribes). Supposedly, a group separated from the Winnebagos and followed the buffalo to the mouth of the Iowa River, where it feeds the Mississippi. This group further divided, and the band that continued farther westward later became the Otos and Missouris. The band that stayed closer to the Mississippi River became the Iowas.

It is not known for certain whether these locations and this sequence of events are historically accurate. But language similarities indicate that all four tribes—Iowas, Winnebagos, Otos and Missouris—were once related. Furthermore, the Iowas did retain some customs of the Woodland tribes in the East, such as farming and living in villages. Sometimes the Iowas are referred to as Prairie Indians because they lived in permanent wood-frame houses and hunted buffalo in the tall-grass prairies of the Mississippi and Missouri river valleys (see "Prairie Indians"). When the Iowas began using horses and ranged farther, they became more like the tribes of the western Plains (see "Plains Indians").

Because of pressure from other tribes and from white settlers, the Iowas moved their villages many times within the region now comprising the state of Iowa, as well as into territory now a part of other states. In 1700, they lived in what is now southwestern Minnesota, near the Red Pipestone Quarry where In-

dians collected catlinite to make pipes and other carvings. Some Iowas lived in Nebraska for a while before returning to lands in Iowa. In the early 1800s, some bands established villages near the Platte River in Missouri, where Lewis and Clark encountered them during the two explorers' famous survey of the American West.

In the 1820s and 1830s, with white settlement increasing, the Iowas signed a series of treaties ceding to the United States claims to lands in Iowa, Missouri, and Minnesota. In 1836, they were assigned a reservation on land that was later subdivided between the states of Kansas and Nebraska. In 1854 and again in 1861, this tract was reduced in size. Iowas still hold the remainder of this reservation in Brown County, Kansas, and Richardson County, Nebraska. Other Iowas were relocated to the Indian Territory in 1883. This second group now has a federal trust area in Lincoln, Payne, and Logan counties of central Oklahoma.

Iroquois

The Iroquois (pronounced *IR-uh-kwoy*) were the most widespread Indians of upstate New York and the Lake Ontario region of Canada. Like their Algonquian neighbors, they are frequently represented in books and movies about colonial America, usually wearing loincloths and carrying warclubs. They are often depicted with what has come to be known as the Mohawk hairstyle, a single strip of hair down the middle of the head, or with a scalplock, a single long lock of hair.

Iroquoian is a language, and many different Indian tribes of eastern North America spoke versions, or dialects, of this same basic language. The Hurons and Susquehannocks are two other Iroquoian-speaking tribes listed in this book. But when we speak of the Iroquois Indians we are referring specifically to the Cayugas, Mohawks, Oneidas, Onondagas, Senecas, and Tuscaroras—the Six Nations.

It has been a mystery among scholars how Iroquoian-speaking peoples came to inhabit the woodland territory in the midst of the many Algonquian-speaking tribes there (see "Northeast Indians" and "Algonquian"). Did the Iroquois come from the north up along the St. Lawrence River? Did they come from west of the Mississippi? Or from the south? Or were they indigenous to their homelands in New

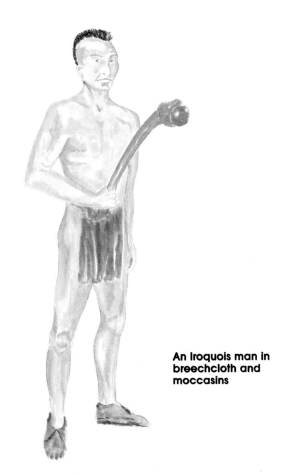

An Iroquois man in breechcloth and moccasins

York, descendants from an earlier Woodland culture, such as the Owasco culture found in various archaeological sites? This last theory, although still unproven, is now the most widely believed.

The Iroquois League

As for the Iroquois after the arrival of whites, much is known from both historical writings and archaeological studies. The Iroquois were famous statesmen. Iroquois tribes were organized into the Iroquois League, also known as the Iroquois Confederacy. At first, about 1570, the Iroquois formed the League of Five Nations—that is, Mohawks, Oneidas, Onondagas, Cayugas, and Senecas.

Two men brought the five tribes together to found the League: Deganawida, the Peacemaker, a Huron prophet from the north who had had a vision of the tribes united under the sheltering branches of a Tree of Great Peace; and Hiawatha, a Mohawk medicine man, who paddled through Iroquois country preaching the message of unity and carrying a wampum belt that symbolized the Great Law of Peace. Over a century later, in the early 1700s, when the Tuscaroras migrated to New York from North Carolina, the Iroquois became the League of Six Nations.

The Founding Fathers of the United States who shaped the new democratic government after the American Revolution—people like George Washington, Thomas Jefferson, and Benjamin Franklin—used the Iroquois League as a model for the new democracy. The various states were like the different Iroquois tribes; the senators and congressmen were like the 50 Iroquois sachems, or chiefs, chosen as representatives or spokesmen; the president and his cabinet were like the honorary Pine Tree Sachems; and Washington, D.C., was like Onondaga, the main village of the Onondaga tribe, where the Great Council Fire burned continually and the Great Council was held every year.

Lifeways

The Iroquois were great builders. They made clearings in the woods, usually near streams or rivers, and surrounded them with palisades, tall walls made from sharpened logs stuck upright in the earth. They lived in longhouses made of elm bark. These structures, from 50 to 100 feet long, were communal; that is, more than one family shared the space. The longhouses, sometimes crowded with as many as 20 families, plus their dogs, were noisy and smelly. And because the Iroquois used only holes in the roof to let smoke from the fires escape, their homes were smoky.

The Iroquois used the longhouse as a symbol for their League. They thought of their League as one big longhouse extending across New York State, with the Mohawks guarding the Eastern Door and the Senecas guarding the Western Door. Today, the Iroquois, in addition to their individual tribal names, call themselves *Haudenosaunee*, or People of the Longhouse.

The Iroquois were great hunters. Like the Algonquians, they are often referred to as Woodland Indians

Iroquois elm-bark longhouse

and were skilled in chasing and trapping the animals of the northern forests. They used their catch for both food and clothing. They made deerskin shirts, skirts, leggings, breechcloths, and moccasins. They made robes and mittens from beaver and bear furs. They used feathers and porcupine quills for decoration.

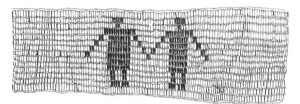

Detail of an Iroquois wampum belt

They also used quills to make belts of wampum which served as public records for treaties, and, after the whites arrived, as a form of money. The Iroquois considered animals their kindred spirits and took animal names to identify clans (groups of families descended from a common ancestor); for example, the Beaver Clan, the Deer Clan, the Wolf Clan, the Bear Clan, the Turtle Clan, the Hawk Clan, the Heron Clan, the Snipe Clan, and the Eel Clan.

The Iroquois were also great farmers, using stone, bone, antler, and wooden implements to work the soil. Their three most important crops—corn, beans, and squash—were the Three Sisters in their religion. Iroquois women had a lot of power in Iroquois society and owned the crops. The family name was passed on through them (this is called a matrilineal society), and Iroquois leaders, the sachems, were chosen by women. Three of the Iroquois' important festivals related to the growing of corn: the Corn-Planting Festival, the Green-Corn Festival, and the Corn-Gathering Festival. Two of the other festivals involved wild plant foods: the Maple-Sugar Festival and the Strawberry Festival. The other most important festival was the New-Year Festival, at the first new moon of the new year.

The Iroquois also had a great knowledge of herbal medicines. In healing ceremonies, their medicine men, or shamans, wore special masks that were supposed to be magical. These masks were called False Faces and were carved from a living tree. Wearing these sometimes fierce and sometimes comical faces, the shamans danced, waved turtle-shell rattles, and sprinkled tobacco. They invoked the good spirits to drive away the evil spirits that made people sick. The Iroquois believed that the most powerful spirit of all was *Orenda*, the Great Spirit and the Creator, from whom all other spirits were derived.

The Iroquois were great athletes too, masters of the game of lacrosse. The Iroquois version was much rougher than modern lacrosse, and many of the participants suffered injuries. Warriors from different villages competed and spectators placed bets on them.

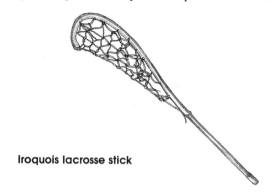

Iroquois lacrosse stick

Another favorite Iroquois sport was snowsnake, in which a player would see how far he could slide a javelin along a trench dug in the snow.

The Iroquois were great travelers. They traveled to hunt and to make war. They covered their canoes with

Iroquois toy elm-bark canoe

elm or spruce bark. These boats were sturdy, but not as fast or nimble as the birchbark canoes made by their Algonquian neighbors. But Iroquois canoes possessed other advantages. Because of the thick, rough bark, they could be used as ladders to scale enemy walls or as shields to block enemy arrows.

Wars Involving the Iroquois

The Iroquois were great warriors. Iroquois boys began developing military skills when young, practicing with knives, warclubs, and bows and arrows. By the time they were teenagers, they were ready for their first raids against hostile bands of other Indians or against intruding whites. Through military exploits they could gain respect in their society. A man who gained great prestige in this way might become a war chief.

Although women and children captured in raids were sometimes adopted by Iroquois tribes, male prisoners were usually forced to run the gauntlet. The prisoners had to move between two lines of men, women, and children, who lashed out at them with sticks or thorny branches. Those who made it all the way to the end might be accepted into the tribe. Those who did not might be given to the widows of Iroquois warriors, who would avenge the death of their husbands by torturing the prisoners. Still other captives might be cooked and eaten so that their strength could be absorbed by the Iroquois warriors. In order to extend their influence, the Iroquois also followed the practice of adopting whole tribes as allies. The name Iroquois means "real adders" or "poisonous snakes." (The adder is a kind of snake.) This name was the French version of the name given to the Iroquois by the Algonquians because the Iroquois were so fierce in battle.

During the 1600s, the tribes of the Iroquois League expanded their territories in every direction, helping one another when necessary. Their main purpose for invading the territory of other Indian peoples was to find a new source of furs. Their trading partners—first the Dutch, then the English—wanted especially the pelts of beavers. At the time, beaver hats were popular in Europe. Iroquois tribes held the advantage over other Indians on the battlefield because they were united in a confederacy and because they obtained firearms from the Europeans. Guns, which made loud explosions and which could kill a man at a great distance, seemed like magic to Indians who had never seen them before. Indians also traded with whites to get tomahawks with metal heads.

In the mid-1600s, the Iroquois decimated the Huron Indians to the north as well as smaller Iroquoian-speaking tribes, such as the Tobaccos, Neutrals, and Eries. They also attacked another Iroquoian people, the Susquehannocks. They made war on the Algonquian tribes of the Northeast, too, including the Algonkins, Ottawas, Illinois, Miamis, Potawatomis, Delawares, Mahicans, and Wappingers. The Iroquois eventually controlled a huge expanse of territory, east to west from the Hudson River to the Illinois River, and, north to south, from the Ottawa River to the Tennessee River.

The Iroquois were so powerful, in fact, that they stopped the French from expanding southward from Canada. Iroquoia, the huge wedge of Iroquois homeland across upstate New York, served as a barrier to European travel and development. The French were the allies and trading partners of various Algonquian tribes. The British with their Iroquois allies suffered occasional setbacks but were the eventual victors in the French and Indian Wars from 1689 to 1763. This long struggle was marked by: (1) King William's War, 1689-97; (2) Queen Anne's War, 1702-13; (3) King George's War, 1744-48; and (4) the French and Indian

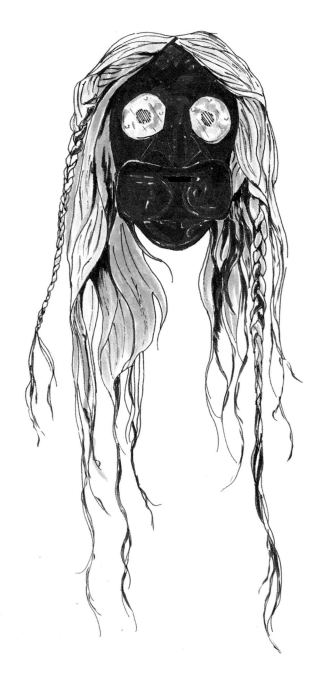

Iroquois False Face carved from a living tree

War, 1754-63. The Iroquois fought on their own against the French, mounting raids northward into Canada. They also fought alongside the British. Either way, the British were happy to have such skilled fighters as allies. If it weren't for the Iroquois contribution in these wars, French might nowadays be the main language in North America, and this book might be printed in that language.

One colonial officer who greatly appreciated the Iroquois was New York's renowned trader and politician, Sir William Johnson. He lived in Mohawk country along the Mohawk River, which branches off from the Hudson River. Johnson married a Mohawk woman named Molly Brant. With Mohawk warriors under Chief Hendrick, William Johnson defeated the French at Lake George in 1755, one of the critical British victories in the last of the French and Indian Wars.

Iroquois warriors participated in other wars after the French were defeated. Some Senecas joined Pontiac to fight the British in his Rebellion of 1763 (see "Ottawa"). Some other Iroquois, usually referred to as Mingos, under the Cayuga chief Logan, joined the Shawnees in Lord Dunmore's War of 1774 (see "Shawnee"). The Iroquois fought their former allies, the British, in these conflicts because English-speaking settlers were taking Indian lands.

In the American Revolution from 1775 to 1783, however, most Iroquois again sided with the British, this time against the American rebels. The Iroquois thought that the Americans offered the greater threat to Indian lands. During this period, the Mohawk Thayendanegea, or Joseph Brant, Molly Brant's brother, rose to prominence as a great leader. William Johnson had treated Joseph Brant like a son and had provided for his education. Joseph Brant had grown up as a close friend to John Johnson and Guy Johnson, Sir William's son and nephew. The Mohawk, who drew on both his Indian and white experience, became an eloquent speaker in several different languages as well as a master tactician in warfare.

After having visited England with Guy Johnson to meet King George III, Joseph Brant traveled among all the Iroquois tribes to encourage their support for the British. His people, the Mohawks, agreed with him, as did Senecas, Onondagas, and Cayugas. Chiefs Cornplanter and Red Jacket, both Senecas, were other important leaders in the fight. But the Oneidas and Tuscaroras sided with the Americans, causing the first major split in the Iroquois League in 200 years. Samuel Kirkland, a Protestant missionary living among the Oneidas, counteracted the influence of the Johnson family and won that tribe over to the American side.

The tribes who sided with the British launched many raids on American settlements near their territory. In one of the most famous incidents, Joseph Brant and his warriors, plus Walter Butler and his Tory troops, raided the Cherry Valley settlement, west of Albany, on November 11, 1778. Although the fort held, those settlers who did not make it from the outlying settlements or fields to the stockade in time were killed or taken prisoner—32 dead and 40 captured.

Because of the Iroquois threat on the New York frontier, the American commander-in-chief, General George Washington, who would later become the first president of the United States, sent an invading army into Iroquoia in 1779 under generals John Sullivan and James Clinton. The Sullivan-Clinton Campaign defeated the mighty Iroquois, not so much through direct warfare but by burning their houses and destroying crops. The Iroquois called Washington "Town Destroyer."

This was the end of the Iroquois stronghold in upstate New York. In the years following the Revolution and the birth of the United States, the Iroquois had to give up most of their vast land holdings. Some tribes were granted small tracts of state reservation lands. Other Iroquois, like Joseph Brant, moved to Canada.

The Iroquois Today

Contemporary Iroquois live mainly on seven reservations in New York and five in Ontario and Quebec. Others live in large cities of the Northeast, such as New York, Buffalo, Albany, and Toronto. Relatives of the Iroquois live in Wisconsin and Oklahoma. The Iroquois are still united. They meet frequently at festivals, where they sell their traditional and modern art—beautiful paintings; stone, wood, bone, and antler sculptures; baskets, leather goods; featherwork; beadwork; and lacrosse sticks. They stage colorful pageants with traditional songs and dances.

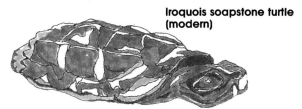

Iroquois soapstone turtle (modern)

It is mostly Iroquois who are the world-renowned high-steel construction workers. They have remarkable balance and work on the tallest skyscrapers in the world, bravely climbing atop towering piles of steel girders. The Iroquois are also among the most politically active Indians in the Northeast, writing influential newsletters about modern Native American causes.

The six tribes of the Iroquois League had much in common: political unity through their confederacy, similar histories, and similar lifeways. That is why it is convenient to discuss them as one people. But, as contemporary Native Americans will point out, although the ties among the various Iroquois tribes are strong, each tribe has its own unique identity. Therefore, to accurately depict the Iroquois tribes, more information is provided in this book under the tribal name of each one (see "Cayuga"; "Mohawk"; "Oneida"; "Onondaga"; "Seneca"; and "Tuscarora").

Kalispel (Pend d'Oreille)

The Kalispels are also known as the *Pend d'Oreille*. The first name, pronounced *KAL-uh-spell*, means "camas" in the tribe's Salishan dialect, after the wild plant which many Indians of the American Northwest dug up for food. The second name, pronounced *pon-duh-RAY*, is French for "earrings" because when French traders first met these Indians, many of them wore shells dangling from their ears.

The Kalispels occupied territory that is now northern Idaho, northwest Montana, and northeast Washington State. A lake at the heart of their homeland bears their French name with an alternate spelling, Pend Oreille, as does a river flowing west of the lake. The Kalispels also lived along the Clark Fork to the east of the lake. The Bitterroot Range, part of the Rocky Mountain chain, rises up in what was once Kalispel country.

The Kalispels depended heavily on fishing in the waterways that were part of the Columbia River network winding along the Columbia Plateau all the way to the Pacific Ocean. They supplemented their diet by hunting small game and gathering wild plant foods. They lived in cone-shaped dwellings constructed over pits. First they dug circular holes. Then they set poles around the edges of the holes, their tops lean-

ing against one another. They covered the framework with branches, then grass or cedar bark, and finally earth. The Kalispels, like other Interior Salishan tribes, are considered part of the Plateau Culture Area (see "Plateau Indians").

Lewis and Clark encountered the Kalispels in 1805. The North West Company established trading posts on Pend Oreille Lake and Clark Fork in 1809. In later years, the American Fur Company, founded by John Jacob Astor, also developed the fur trade with the Kalispels. A Jesuit priest by the name of Father Pierre Jean de Smet established a mission among them in 1844 and ensured the continuing tradition of friendly relations between the Kalispels and whites. He also worked among the Flatheads, another Salishan-speaking tribe in the region (see "Flathead").

In 1855, the Kalispels signed a treaty with the United States in which they ceded most of their lands. The federal government settled them on a reservation, where their descendants still live. The Kalispel Reservation is located in Pend Oreille County near Usk, Washington. Some Kalispels also share the Colville Reservation in Washington and the Flathead Reservation in Montana with other tribes.

Kaw (Kansa)

The Kaws are also known as the Kansa Indians, a longer version of the same word. Their name, pronounced the way it is spelled, means "people of the south wind." They were a Siouan-speaking people, close relatives of the Osages, and also related to the Omahas, Poncas, and Quapaws (see entries for those tribes). It is thought that these tribes lived as one people along the Ohio Valley in early times, then migrated west of the Mississippi onto the prairies before white explorers reached their domain. The Kaws, or Kansas, settled along the river that bears their name, the Kansas River, which is a tributary of the Missouri River. Their name has also been given to the state comprising what was once their homeland.

Kaw territory stretched north of Kansas into southern Nebraska as well.

The Kaws are classified as part of the Great Plains Culture Area because they hunted buffalo, as did other Plains tribes (see "Plains Indians"). Yet the Kaws were originally Prairie villagers who farmed as well as hunted (see "Prairie Indians"). After they obtained horses in the early 1700s from other tribes, the Kaws adopted even more cultural traits of the nomadic Plains tribes, ranging over a wider area to hunt.

The Kaws occupied territory in the center of North America. Many travelers passed through their homeland: the Spanish from the southeast; the French from the northeast; and the English, and later the

Americans, from the east. In the early 1800s, an old Indian trail, running from the Missouri River to New Mexico through the heart of Kaw territory, assumed importance as a trade and migration route for white settlers: the Santa Fe Trail. All its travelers—traders, migrants, soldiers—were able to recognize the Kaws by their distinct hairstyle. Tribal members plucked or shaved their entire head, except for a single lock at the back.

From 1820 to 1846, the Kaws gave up to the whites most of their lands in Kansas and Nebraska. William Clark, formerly of the Lewis and Clark Expedition of 1803-06, which had come into contact with the Kaws and other Missouri River tribes, negotiated many of these treaties with them. The Kaws' territory was originally the northern part of the Indian Territory. In order to make room for the tribes that the whites relocated from east of the Mississippi, government officials forced local tribes to occupy smaller pieces of land. In 1846, the Kaws were assigned a reservation at Council Grove on the Neosho River.

Yet white settlers overran these lands. In 1852, by an Act of Congress, the northern part of the Indian Terri-tory became the territories of Kansas and Nebraska. In 1861, Kansas became a state. In 1862, the Homestead Act opened up Indian lands in both territories to white homesteaders. In 1867, Nebraska became a state. In 1873, the Kaws were granted a new reservation near their kinsmen, the Osages, in the diminished Indian Territory, which came to be the state of Oklahoma. In 1887, tribal lands were allotted to individual tribal members. The tribe as a whole still holds a small trust area in Osage County, Oklahoma, not far from the Kansas border.

A Kaw Indian served as vice president from 1929 to 1933, under President Herbert Hoover. His name was Charles Curtis. He was a successful jockey when young, then became a lawyer. He ran for Congress and was elected in 1892. He served 14 years in the House of Representatives and 20 in the Senate before being chosen by Hoover as his running mate on the Republican ticket. During his career, he helped pass legislation helpful to Indians, including the Citizenship Act of 1924 which gave the right of United States citizenship to Native Americans.

Kickapoo

The name *Kickapoo*, in its original Indian form, *Kiwegapaw*, before whites adapted it to their language, means, "he moves about, standing now here, now there." The name (pronounced *KICK-a-poo*) is appropriate because throughout history the Kickapoos have lived in many different places.

The Kickapoos were originally a Great Lakes Algonquian people, closely related to the Sacs and Foxes (see "Algonquian"). When white missionaries and traders first had contact with them, all three tribes lived in what is now Wisconsin. The French Jesuit priest Claude Jean Allouez claimed that, in the late 1600s, the Kickapoos lived between the Wisconsin and Fox rivers. Yet all three tribes might have once lived on the other side of Lake Michigan, in what is now part of the state of Michigan. But ancient locations and migration routes are uncertain. Only oral tribal legends (and, in the case of the Kickapoos, carved wooden prayer sticks) remain from which to glean such information. The later explorers' written records are also unreliable.

In any case, the Kickapoos did not stay in Wisconsin. About a century after Allouez's visit, in 1769, they joined up with many of the neighboring tribes—Sac, Fox, Chippewa, Ojibway, Ottawa, and Potawatomi—to defeat the Illinois Indians to the south and divide their territory (see "Illinois"). This happened several years after the Kickapoos joined Pontiac in his rebellion (see "Ottawa"). The Kickapoos then

Kickapoo prayer stick with carved symbols representing prayers, myths, and historical events

migrated to the Illinois River in what is now the state of Illinois. The tribe eventually split in two. Some headed a little farther south to the Sangamon River. This western group, the Prairie band, hunted buffalo. Other Kickapoos headed east toward the Vermilion branch of the Wabash River, now part of the border between Illinois and Indiana. The Vermilion band hunted the animals of the forest. Because of this split, Kickapoos can be referred to as both Prairie Algonquians and Woodland Algonquians (see "Prairie Indians" and "Northeast Indians").

The Kickapoos lived in this part of the Old Northwest into the 1800s, when white settlers began arriving in increasing numbers. The Kickapoos made several stands against them, in Little Turtle's War and Tecumseh's Rebellion (see "Miami" and "Shawnee"). However, these conflicts only delayed white settlement. By 1819, the Kickapoos were being harassed by settlers and land agents working for the federal government, and some of their chiefs signed away all their lands in Illinois.

Two Kickapoo leaders, Mecina and Kennekuk, and their followers held out longer than other bands. Their efforts are sometimes called the Kickapoo Resistance. Mecina's men used sabotage to destroy or steal white property. Kennekuk (or Kanakuk), who was a medicine man as well as a chief, used nonviolent techniques, or passive resistance, to stall government officials for years. He came up with one excuse after another for not relocating: There was no food, his people were sick, he had seen evil omens. But finally, after more troops had entered the region because of the Black Hawk War of 1832 (see "Sac"), he and his followers also departed for Missouri.

Missouri proved only a temporary home. The Kickapoos pushed westward across the Missouri River into Kansas, which at that time was the northern part of the Indian Territory (see "Cherokee"). Some Kickapoos settled there permanently, and their descendants hold the rights to a reservation in the northeastern part of the state.

But other Kickapoos moved on in search of a new homeland. They tried Texas first, then crossed the Rio Grande into Mexico. This branch of the tribe came to be known as the Mexican Kickapoos. The Mexican Kickapoos staged an uprising during and after the American Civil War. When two different groups of Kickapoo migrants from Kansas traveled through Texas on their way to join their southern relatives, they were attacked—at Little Concho River in 1862 by a Confederate battalion, and at Dove Creek in 1865 by the Texas Rangers.

The Mexican Kickapoos retaliated with attacks on Texas border settlements. In 1873, after the end of the Civil War, the federal government sent in Colonel Ranald Mackenzie and his Fourth Cavalry, veteran Indian fighters from a campaign against the Comanches (see "Comanche"). Although they were not supposed to cross the border into Mexico, the government troops did and destroyed the main Kickapoo village at Nacimiento on the Remolino River. They also led women and children hostages back to the Indian Territory. During negotiations, many of the Mexican Kickapoos agreed to resettle in the Indian Territory to be with their loved ones. Their descendants still live there, in what is now the state of Oklahoma. There are still Kickapoos in Mexico too.

The various groups of modern-day Kickapoos—those in Kansas, Oklahoma, and Mexico—still have traditional beliefs, crafts, and artwork in common. All are the proud possessors of the rich Kickapoo heritage.

Kiowa

The migrations of the Plains Indians are especially intriguing. Most of the people of the Great Plains came late to the region, some of them even after Europeans arrived in North America. And then they continued to move around a great deal as nomadic buffalo hunters. To sort out all this movement, scholars have tribal legends, plus early historical accounts of explorers, missionaries, and military men, to help them.

The Kiowas migrated often. Scholars have pieced together much information about their migrations from the 1600s on, but earlier migrations are only guesswork, based on language relationships and customs.

The name *Kiowa*, pronounced *KI-uh-wuh*, comes from the word *Kaigwu*, meaning "main people" in the Kiowa language. It was once thought that the Kiowa language was unique to North America, with a distant connection with the Uto-Aztecan languages of the Bannocks, Comanches, Papagos, Paiutes, Pimas, Shoshones, Utes, and Mexican tribes (see entries for those tribes). Now it is theorized that the Kiowa language is closely related to the Tanoan dialects of the Rio Grande Pueblo Indians (see "Pueblo Indians").

Interestingly, despite this language connection with Indians of the Southwest, the first known homeland of the Kiowas, during the 1600s, was far to the north in what is now western Montana. Then, about 1700, the Kiowas migrated eastward across the Rocky Mountains to the Yellowstone River region in what is now eastern Montana. Then, soon afterward, the Crow Indians gave the Kiowas permission to move to the Black Hills of what is now eastern Wyoming and western South Dakota (see "Crow").

A Kiowa woman with child

While at this location, the Kiowas probably first acquired use of the horse through trade with the upper Missouri tribes, the Mandans, Hidatsas, and Arikaras (see entries for those tribes). With increased mobility, the Kiowas became a typical Plains tribe, following the huge buffalo herds and living in tepees. They also began to practice the Sun Dance, keep medicine bundles, and to organize into military societies, also typical of people of the Great Plains Culture Area (see "Plains Indians"). One of the most renowned of all the Plains warrior societies was the Kiowas' Principal Dogs (also called the Ten Bravest). This was an exclusive society, limited to 10 braves who had proven their courage time and again. The leader of the Principal Dogs wore a long sash reaching from his shoulders to the ground. When the Kiowas were engaged in battle,

he would dismount from his horse, fasten the sash to the earth with a spear, and fight from that spot or shout encouragement to the other warriors. Even if surrounded by enemy warriors or struck by enemy arrows, he could not leave the spot until another Principal Dog removed the spear.

Two unique cultural traits of the Kiowas, in addition to their language, suggest a possible ancient connection with Indians far from the Great Plains to the south in Mexico. The Kiowas worshipped a stone image they called the *taimay* and drew tribal records in the form of a pictographic calendar. Both these customs are more typical of Mesoamerican peoples such as the Aztecs than of Plains people (see "Aztec").

Toward the end of the 1700s, the Kiowas migrated again, pushed back from the Black Hills by the Sioux and Cheyennes (see "Sioux" and "Cheyenne"). Lewis and Clark, the famous explorers, reported in 1805 that the Kiowas lived along the North Platte River of what is now Nebraska. Yet, soon afterward, the Kiowas settled south of the Arkansas River in territory that is now southern Kansas and northern Oklahoma. The tribe eventually established its council fire on the Cimarron River.

To the south of the Kiowas lived the Comanche Indians. The Comanches at first proved hostile to the newcomers. About 1790, however, the two tribes formed an alliance which has lasted until modern times (see "Comanche"). An Apache band settled near the Kiowas and came to be closely associated with them, their leaders part of the Kiowa camp circle. They became known as the Kiowa-Apaches (see "Apache").

The Kiowa Wars

The Kiowas were among the most tenacious fighters among all the North American Indians. They launched raids, for horses and other booty, on many other Indian peoples—the Caddos, Navajos, Utes, and Apache bands other than the Kiowa-Apaches (see entries for those tribes). They also fought the Arapahos, Cheyennes, and Osages until reaching peace accords with these tribes in the 1830s (see those tribes). They also proved a much-feared menace to Spaniards, Mexicans, and Anglo-Americans traveling the Santa Fe Trail and the Butterfield Southern Route (Southern Overland Trail). They raided settlements far and wide, even in Mexico.

The Kiowa Wars of the 1800s closely parallel the Comanche Wars. In most engagements, Comanches, Kiowas, and Kiowa-Apaches fought side by side. Most of these conflicts are described in this book under the "Comanche" entry. Yet certain Kiowa leaders should be mentioned here because they were among

Kiowa ceremonial lance

the most important individuals in the history of the American West.

From the 1830s until the 1860s, Little Mountain was the principal Kiowa chief. It was his hand that recorded the tribal history with pictographs on buffalo hide. When the hide wore out, the entire chronicle was recreated on a new hide. And, in later years, when the buffalo herds had been slaughtered, Little Mountain's nephew used heavy manila paper to redraw 60 years of Kiowa history.

By the 1870s and the final phase of the Comanche-Kiowa Wars, the Kiowas had a number of chiefs whose names fill the history books. Sitting Bear (Satank) was the elderly leader of the *Koitsenko*, the Principal Dogs, or Ten Bravest, the Kiowas' most elite warrior society. White Bear (Satanta) led a faction of Kiowas who wanted war with the whites; he led many raids into Texas. Kicking Bird was the leader of the peace faction who wanted to make peace with whites. When Little Mountain died in 1866, Lone Wolf was chosen as the principal chief; he was a compromise choice instead of White Bear or Kicking Bird. Yet Lone Wolf came to support White Bear and the militants. Big Tree was the youngest of the Kiowa war chiefs in the Kiowa wars of the 1860s and 1870s. Sky Walker (Mamanti) was a medicine man who was supposed to have prophetic powers.

Old Sitting Bear died in 1871. Held as a prisoner by whites, he preferred to die fighting for his freedom, with a knife against army carbines. Kicking Bird died mysteriously in 1875 right after the Red River War—probably from poison given to him by members of the militant faction who resented his friendship with whites. Sky Walker died a prisoner at Fort Marion in Florida in 1875, supposedly right after learning about the death of Kicking Bird. Tribal legend has it that the medicine man willed himself to die because he had used his magical powers to kill his fellow Kiowa, Kicking Bird. White Bear died in 1878, while in a prison at Huntsville, Texas. Depressed at his fate, he jumped headfirst from the second-story balcony of a prison hospital. Lone Wolf had contracted malaria at Fort Marion in Florida and died in 1879, within a year

after he was finally permitted to return to his homeland. Big Tree, the young warrior, outlasted the others. In 1875, he was released from the Fort Sill prison in the Indian Territory and in later years became a Sunday school teacher for the Rainy Mountain Baptist Church.

Many of these Kiowa leaders, including White Bear and Kicking Bird, along with other famous Indian leaders, including the Comanche Quanah Parker and the Apache Geronimo, are buried in a graveyard at Fort Sill. Since there are so many Indian fighters there, this cemetery is known as the Indian Arlington after Arlington National Cemetery in Washington, D.C., where American soldiers are buried.

Kiowa pin of silver and turquoise, representing the Peyote Spirit Messenger Bird (modern)

Kiowas Today

Modern-day Kiowas are still allied with Comanches and the Apaches of Oklahoma (descendants of both Kiowa-Apaches and Geronimo's band). Most of the Kiowa lands, now protected as a federal trust area, are in Caddo County, Oklahoma, with tribal headquarters at Carnegie. Tribal members earn a living mainly through farming, raising livestock, and leasing oil rights to their lands.

A group of Kiowa artists have played an important part in the recent flowering of American Indian art. Some of their works are on display at the Southern Plains Indian Museum and Craft Center at Anadarko, Oklahoma. Another Kiowa, N. Scott Momaday, a professor of comparative literature, won the 1969 Pulitzer prize for his novel *House Made of Dawn*. Another book of his is *The Way to Rainy Mountain*.

Klamath

The Klamaths (pronounced *KLAM-uth*) called themselves *maklaks*, meaning "people" or "community." They occupied territory which has since become part of Oregon, near the Oregon-California border. These Indians lived especially in the vicinity of Upper Klamath Lake and the Klamath River.

The Klamaths, because of their dependence on fishing in inland waterways, are usually categorized in the Plateau Culture Area (see "Plateau Indians"). The Klamaths also depended heavily on small game and wild plant foods, especially roots and wokas, or water lily seeds.

Like many other Plateau tribes, the Klamaths spoke a Penutian dialect. Their language resembled that of their immediate neighbors, the Modocs, another southern Oregon and northern California tribe grouped with the Plateau Indians (see "Modoc").

The Klamaths were a warlike tribe. Kit Carson, the famous Mountain Man and scout, and later Indian agent and brigadier general, called the Klamath arrows the truest and most beautiful he had ever seen. Supposedly, Klamath bowmen could shoot these arrows right through a horse. Their warriors carried out many raids on the Northern California tribes, taking captives to keep as slaves or to sell to other tribes. Nevertheless, the Klamaths were friendly toward whites. The Canadian Peter Skene Ogden, who explored for the Hudson's Bay Company, first established trade relations with them in 1829.

The Klamaths signed a treaty with whites in 1864. They were settled on the Klamath Reservation in Oregon northeast of Upper Klamath Lake. They also agreed to give up the practice of slavery, an issue over which, at that very time, the North and the South were fighting the Civil War.

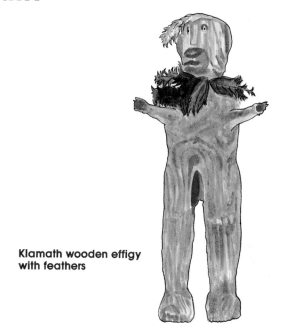

Klamath wooden effigy with feathers

The Klamaths later played an indirect part in the Modoc War of 1872-73. Because of tensions between the two tribes when the Modocs were forced to settle on the Klamath Reservation, a band of Modocs headed south and began a chain of events leading up to the most violent Indian war in California history (see "Modoc").

In 1954, the special relationship between the Klamaths and the federal government ended. The tribe's assets were liquidated and passed out to individual tribal members. The experience proved to be a difficult one for the Klamaths, who lost control of some of their lands and had to struggle to reestablish their tribal identity. Termination, as this policy of ending the special relationship between the federal government and Native American tribes is called, was phased out in the 1960s (see "Menominee").

Kootenai

There are different spellings of this tribal name—*Kootenai*, *Kootenay*, and *Kutenai*—all pronounced *KOOT-uh-nay*. The first spelling is generally used in the United States; the second in Canada; and the third in many historical accounts.

The Kootenais lived in territory that is now northwestern Montana, northern Idaho, northeastern Washington State, and southeastern British Columbia. The tribe depended heavily on the waterways in their homeland for food, including Kootenay

Kootenai birchbark canoe in the "sturgeon-nose" style

Lake, Kootenai River, and the upper course of the Columbia River. They used spears, basket traps, and wicker weirs (enclosures) to catch fish. They had both bark canoes and dugouts. They lived in cone-shaped dwellings, with pole frames and rush-mat coverings. They also made watertight baskets from split roots. The Kootenais are classified in the Plateau Culture Area (see 'Plateau Indians").

The Kootenais acquired horses through trade with other Indians in the 1700s, and adopted many of the customs of Plains tribes, venturing east of the Rocky Mountains on seasonal buffalo hunts during which they lived in buffalo-skin tepees (see "Plains Indians").

The Kootenais' language was different from those of all the other Plateau Indians. The other tribes of the region spoke dialects of either the Penutian or the Salishan language families. However, the Kootenai dialect seems to be related to the Algonquian language family. There were Algonquian-speaking peoples living near the Kootenais—the Blackfoot tribe. The warlike Blackfeet were traditional enemies of the Kootenais and kept them from expanding their territory eastward (see "Blackfoot").

The Kootenais were friendly toward whites. The Canadian explorer David Thompson, who established trade relations with many Indian tribes for the North West Company, entered their domain in the early 1800s. This fur trading company, whose headquarters were in Montreal, built a trading post called Kootenai House in 1807. When the western international boundary between the United States and Canada was defined once and for all in 1846, the territory of the tribe was divided. Today, some Kootenais live on the Kootenai Reservation in Idaho; others live on the Flathead Reservation in Montana (see "Flathead"); still others live on tracts of land in British Columbia.

Kutchin

The homeland of the Kutchins stretched many miles, from the Yukon River to the Mackenzie. Their territory included parts of what is now Alaska, as well as most of Canada's Yukon Territory and Northwest Territories.

The Kutchins consisted of nine major bands: Dihai, Kutcha, Natsit, Tennuth, Tranjik, and Vunta in Alaska; and Nakotcho, Takkuth, and Tatlit in Canada. The general name *Kutchin*, pronounced *kuch-IN*, means "people." The various band names refer to locations. After whites made contact with the Kutchins, five of these bands came to use the French name for the tribe, *Loucheux*, meaning "squinty-eyed."

The Kutchins belonged to the language family called Athapascan (see "Athapascan"). The majority of Athapascans lived in the taiga of the northern latitudes, a land of scrubby evergreen forest, plus numerous lakes, rivers, and swamps. This environment is also referred to as the Subarctic because it lies south of the Arctic tundra. Indians of this region are said to be of the Subarctic Culture Area (see "Subarctic Indians").

In their lifeways, the Kutchins are typical of a number of tribes not listed in this book, including the Ahtena, Han, Ingalik, Koyukon, Nabesna, Tanaina, and Tanana. Most of these peoples had extensive contacts with Eskimos and were influenced by them (see "Eskimo").

Food

The Kutchins generally spent the summer fishing and the winter hunting. For fishing gear they had dipnets, baskets, hooks, and harpoons. The harpoons resembled those of the Eskimos. Their hunting bows were also similar to the Eskimo style, formed by three pieces of wood joined together and backed with twisted sinew (animal tendons). The Kutchins also used snares of bàbiche (rawhide strips) to trap animals, as well as corrals to capture caribou. Moose and mountain sheep were also much sought after because their large size provided a great deal of food. Dogs were used to stalk game and keep it at bay. Waterfowl that migrated through the Kutchin domain were hunted in great numbers.

Houses

The Kutchins built unique dwellings. Dried, curved poles were placed upright in the ground and met at the top. Caribou hides were then sewn together and placed over the pole framework. A smokehole was left at the top. Fir boughs were placed on the floor. And snow was piled and banked around the walls for insulation. The Kutchins also erected food caches, covered platforms high up on poles, to keep food safe from animals.

Kutchin caribou-skin dwelling

Transportation

The Kutchins used Eskimo-type sleds, rather than the more common Subarctic toboggans. They also used snowshoes, which were long and narrow, sometimes six feet long. The Kutchins' birchbark canoes had a shape similar to Eskimo umiaks, with flat bottoms and nearly straight sides.

Clothing

Kutchin clothing also showed some Eskimo influences. Caribou was the dominant material. There were mittens and hoods for the bitter cold. Shirts had long, pointed tails in the front and back, like Eskimo shirts, to add protection from the cold. Kutchin shirts, however, for both men and women, had long fringes decorated with seeds or with beads of tooth shells, plus bead or porcupine-quill embroidery. Women sometimes enlarged their shirts in the rear to make room for carrying a baby against their naked back, as Eskimo women did, but the Kutchins more commonly used cradleboards instead. Leggings for men and women formed one piece with the moccasins, providing protection from cold and wetness. Headbands and bright feathers provided decoration, as did necklaces and nose-pendants made from shells. Compared

to other northern Athapascans, the Kutchins were exceptionally colorful in their dress. They also painted their faces with the minerals red ochre and black lead, or tattooed their faces.

Social Structure

The Kutchin bands were loosely knit. Their chiefs were chosen for their wisdom and bravery, but they had little authority beyond their own families, other than to settle disputes and lead war parties. Sometimes men without any relatives attached themselves to a family as servants. Otherwise, the women did most of the hard work around camp and most of the hauling. The men saved their energy for hunting, fishing, and warfare. When food became scarce, the Kutchins sometimes killed their female children to prevent overpopulation. The old and sick sometimes requested to be strangled to spare their families the task of providing for them.

Religion and Ritual

The Kutchins, like many other Indians, believed in supernatural beings that haunted certain locations. They also thought that spirits lived in plants, animals, and natural phenomena such as the weather. Before important communal hunts, men fasted and burned pieces of caribou fat on a fire as a form of sacrifice to their moon-god.

In Kutchin mythology, an important legend tells how one of the Kutchin ancestors as a small boy invented the tricks of the hunt—the corral for caribou and the snare for other game. As a reward for his inventions, he asked for the fattest caribou in the world. When the gods refused, he fled in anger to the moon. If one looks closely, one can see the boy on the moon, carrying a skin bag of caribou fat.

The Kutchins were horrified at the thought of burial in the ground. Instead, unlike most Indian peoples, they cremated their dead, along with the person's possessions. The ashes were hung in trees or on poles, painted and draped with streamers. When a chief died, his body was placed in a coffin on a platform for a year before being burned. At the funeral feasts, Kutchins sang and danced and gave gifts in honor of the deceased.

Recreation

The Kutchins played many kinds of games, including gambling games, guessing games, and games of strength and skill with or without weapons. Chiefs sometimes organized wrestling matches to settle minor disputes between families.

The Kutchins had a reputation for great hospitality when outsiders visited them. They were known to entertain guests for several weeks on end.

Contacts with Whites

The Kutchins came into contact with whites when Alexander Mackenzie entered their territory in 1789 during his voyage of exploration along the river now named after him. Most of the Kutchins' subsequent encounters with whites in the early and mid-1800s were through the Hudson's Bay Company, especially after the original Hudson's Bay Company and the North West Company merged in 1821. Fur traders established Fort Good Hope on the Mackenzie River in 1847. Starting in 1862, the Catholic missionary Father Emile Petitot worked among northern Athapascan peoples, including the Kutchins, and wrote papers about their language and culture. That same year, the Episcopal missionary W. W. Kirby came to the region to preach to the Kutchins and to study their language. Many other missionaries followed.

It was the Klondike Gold Rush that changed the life of the Kutchins and other northern Athapascans more than any other event. In 1896, the discovery of gold deposits in the Klondike caused a rush of prospectors to the area in that year and the next. As with other gold rushes in North America—the California of 1848-49, the Colorado of 1858-59, and the Black Hills of 1874—the Klondike Gold Rush led to much hardship among native peoples. The miners ignored the rights of Indians, taking their land and carrying out acts of violence against them.

There are currently eight Kutchin (or Loucheux) bands in Canada with reserve tracts of land. There are also Athapascan villages in Alaska organized into native corporations, some of them united with Eskimos. The Indians have a blend of traditional and modern ways of life. Many still hunt and fish as their ancestors did. Yet snowmobiles, televisions, and other modern tools and conveniences have changed their way of life.

Kwakiutl

The Kwakiutls, or Kwagiutls (both pronounced *KWAH-kee-oo-tel*), occupied the northern corner of Vancouver Island in the Pacific Ocean, as well as smaller islands and a large portion of the adjacent mainland, including its many bays and inlets. This territory now lies in western British Columbia, Canada. The name of this tribe probably means "beach at the north side of the river," perhaps referring to the Nimkish River.

The Kwakiutls spoke a dialect of the Wakashan language family. Their neighbors on Vancouver Island to the south of them, the Nootkas, also spoke a Wakashan dialect, as did the Makahs, farther south on Cape Flattery in Washington State (see "Nootka" and "Makah"). Other tribes of the Northwest Coast Culture Area not listed separately in this book, such as the Bella Bellas, Haislas, and Heiltsuks, spoke related languages (see "Northwest Coast Indians").

The Kwakiutls had a typical Pacific Northwest culture. They fished and hunted in the ocean and in rivers, especially for salmon, seals, and sea lions; they hunted in the tall forests, especially for elk and deer; they foraged for sea grass, shellfish, roots, and berries. They traded extensively with neighboring tribes. They carved beautiful functional and ceremonial objects out of wood. They had an elaborately structured society and religion and practiced the potlatch. There were certain aspects to Kwakiutl lifeways that were unique to their tribe, however.

The Kwakiutl potlatch was the most extravagant of all versions of this ritualistic gift-giving. The Kwakiutls developed a system in which a recipient of a gift had to repay twice as much in the next potlatch. In other words, if he were given 50 goat's-hair blankets or sea otter furs, he had to repay the giver with 100 of the same item during the next ceremony. Or an arbitrator

Kwakiutl wooden spoon

could decide that a certain number of cedar chests or copper plates had the proper value. Or perhaps a number of slaves would be given or even killed with a ceremonial club called a "slave killer" as a symbolic gift. In order to repay a debt, a man might be forced to give away all his possessions. The potlatch could therefore be used to humiliate and ruin enemies as well as to honor friends.

The Kwakiutls, along with the Haidas, were considered the most skilled woodcarvers of the Northwest Coast (see "Haida"). They built large wooden houses, as long as 60 feet. They made large seaworthy dugouts out of red cedar wood. They carved tall totem poles. They made wooden hats.

Kwakiutl painted wooden mask of Spirit of Sea with a killer whale on top

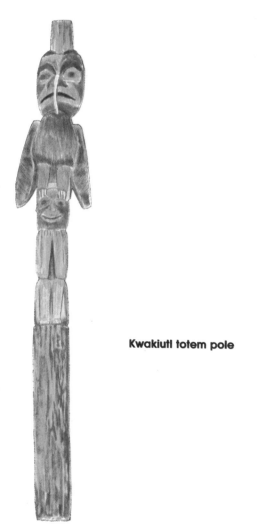

Kwakiutl totem pole

The most famous of all the Kwakiutl woodcarvings were their masks. These were beautifully shaped and painted objects, with feathers and hair added. The masks, which were worn in special ceremonies and used as props for storytelling, depicted various spirits in Kwakiutl mythology. Yet no two masks were exactly alike even when representing the same spirit. Some masks even had removable parts, such as different mouths, that were changed during the course of a story.

Some of these masks were used in the Hamatsa, or Cannibal Dance. The Kwakiutls, like other Northwest Coast Indians, had secret societies with exclusive membership. The most powerful club was the Shamans' Society, and their most influential members were the Hamatsas. During a Hamatsa dance, one member acted out the Cannibal Spirit, who was like the Devil. Other members represented his army of creatures, most of them birdlike. There was the Crooked Beak of Heaven, who supposedly devoured human flesh; the Raven, who devoured human eyes; the Hoxhok, who had a taste for human brains; and the Grizzly Bear, who used his massive paws to tear humans apart (he was usually portrayed by a member of the Bear Society). The Hamatsas did not really practice cannibalism. In fact, the ceremony showed the evil in eating fellow humans and helped discourage the practice. But the Hamatsas sometimes ended the ceremony with the ritualistic eating of dog meat. Then they held a potlatch to further display their power and wealth.

Membership in the Hamatsa Society and the Bear Society was highly sought after and difficult to achieve. A candidate had to fast for several days in the woods until he acted hysterically, as if possessed by a cannibal spirit. Wearing hemlock boughs on his head and wrists, he would be lured into the Hamatsa lodge by a woman. Then he would dance a frenzied dance while the Hamatsas sang:

Now I am about to eat,
My face is ghastly pale.
I am about to eat
What was given me by Cannibal
At the North End of the World.

Russian, British, and American trading ships sailed along Kwakiutl territory in the 1700s. Yet these Indians did not have numerous contacts with whites until the establishment of the settlement of Victoria on Vancouver Island in 1843. White diseases, alcohol, and missionaries all contributed to the change in the Kwakiutl way of life. A Canadian law of 1884 abolishing the potlatch ceremony also altered Kwakiutl culture.

There are currently 10 Kwakiutl bands in British Columbia with a number of reserves. Many band members earn a living in the salmon industry, either in fishing or in canning.

In the 1950s, a Kwakiutl made his mark on both Indian and Canadian history through his work concern-

A Kwakiutl woman, the daughter of a chief

ing totem poles. His Indian name was Naka'penkim; his English name, Mungo Martin. A hereditary chief who was also a master carver, Martin called public attention to the fact that many totem poles had been destroyed by over-zealous missionaries and that others were rotting in the humid weather of the Pacific Northwest. His efforts began a period of conservation on the remaining artworks.

Lumbee

Throughout American history, from colonial times to the present, one of the largest concentrations of Native Americans in the United States has been located in Robeson County and the surrounding counties of North Carolina. Yet, despite a rich and proud Indian heritage, these people have received little attention in books written about Indians.

One reason for this unique situation is that these people are of mixed ancestry, with both white and black blood in addition to Indian. Some have blue eyes. All have English names. Also, the exact Indian ancestry of these people has never been established.

It is possible that the Lumbees have ancestors from tribes of all three major Indian language families of the region, including Algonquians, Iroquoians, and Siouans. More likely, the majority of Lumbees are descended from the Algonquian-speaking Indians who lived along Cape Hatteras in North Carolina. If this is the case, then the Lumbees can also count

among their probable ancestors the lost Roanoke colonists.

Sir Walter Raleigh was a famous English soldier and explorer who in the late 1500s sponsored two attempts at establishing colonies in North America on Roanoke Island. These were the first British colonies in the New World. Both attempts failed, however. The later Jamestown colony of 1607 became the first permanent English colony in North America (see "Powhatan").

Raleigh's first Roanoke colony, from 1585 to 1586, led by his cousin Richard Grenville, failed when the colonists could not find enough to eat. The second settlement of 1587, led by John White, fared somewhat better, the colonists coping with the rugged conditions during the first months. However, the colony's governor, John White, returned to England that same year for supplies. He took with him many paintings of Indians, in particular of the Algonquian-speaking Secotans, neighbors of the Hatteras Indians. He also

Dugout canoe of the Cape Hatteras Indians, thought to be the ancestors of the Lumbees

took with him potatoes, which were unknown in Europe at the time.

When John White finally managed to return to Roanoke Island three years later, the colonists had disappeared. To this day, it is not certain what became of them. The only clue White found was the word "Croatan" carved on the stockade post. Some scholars have taken this to mean that the vanished settlers joined the Indians who lived on Croatan Sound, probably the Hatteras Indians who in later years showed signs of white ancestry.

Whatever their exact lineage, the Lumbees have been proud to call themselves Indians. For much of their history, they have sought tribal recognition, trying to change the attitude of those who referred to them in general terms, such as "people of the color." In 1885, the North Carolina General Assembly gave them the name "Croatan Indians" which lasted only temporarily. In 1911, the North Carolina legislature assigned to them the unwieldy name "Robeson County Indians." In 1913, the legislature used the name "Cherokee Indians of Robeson County," which was historically inaccurate. But then in 1953, the General Assembly accepted a name the Indians themselves had chosen—the Lumbees (pronounced *LUM-bee*)—after the Lumber River running through their territory. And, in 1956, the federal government followed suit, giving them official recognition as the Lumbee Indians.

The Lumbees' ancestors would have been proud of their determination. One of their people from earlier times helped inspire their courage and tenacity. His name was Henry Berry Lowry. Before the Civil War, the Lumbees were ill-treated by many southern whites who were prejudiced against all people of non-white ancestry. Lumbees did not have the right to vote or go to school. During the Civil War years, they were forced to work on Confederate fortifications under terrible conditions—with minimal sleep, prolonged exposure to the elements, and little food. Some Lumbees hid out to avoid this forced labor; others managed to escape.

The Home Guard troops tracked them down, terrorizing the entire Lumbee community in the process. In 1864, Henry Berry Lowry, a teenager at the time, began a campaign of resistance against this cruel treatment. He led a band of young men in raids on rich plantations and distributed the stolen food to poor Indians, blacks, and whites alike, like an Indian Robin Hood.

The Home Guard came after Lowry and his fighters, but the Indians escaped into the swamplands they knew so well. Lowry's men kept up their resistance even after the Civil War, now eluding federal troops. Lowry was tricked into capture on three occasions but managed to escape each time. He became a mythical figure among the Lumbees, some of whom claimed he could not be killed by bullets. Lowry also stood up to the Ku Klux Klan, the racist group who preached white supremacy, protecting his people from the Klan's violence.

In 1871, 18 militiamen ambushed Lowry from a bank of the Lumber River as he paddled by in a canoe. He jumped into the water and, rather than trying to escape, he used the boat as a shield as he returned fire with his rifle. Slowly advancing toward the militiamen, he single-handedly routed them. Yet, the following year, Lowry disappeared. His death was never proven and, as late as the 1930s, some among the Lumbees claimed he was still alive.

Lowry seemed to be present in spirit almost a century after his disappearance. In 1958, about 3,000 Lumbees, angered by the racism of Ku Klux Klansmen against both Indians and blacks, marched on a rally held by the group and drove them out of Robeson County once and for all.

The town of Pembroke, North Carolina, is presently a center of Lumbee activity. There are many Native Americans among its culturally diverse population. Lumbees have held such political offices as mayor, chief of police, and city councilman. Pembroke College was originally founded as a school for Lumbees but now has students of all backgrounds.

Mahican

Mahican, Mohegan, and Mohican are probably the three most-confused Indian names. All three are variations of the Algonquian word for "wolf." Yet the three names apply not to one tribe but two different ones—the Mahicans and the Mohegans. And both these tribes are sometimes referred to as Mohicans.

A lot of the confusion started when James Fenimore Cooper wrote the book *The Last of the Mohicans* in 1826.

This is a work of fiction, one novel in a series of five, telling the story of Natty Bumppo the frontiersman, nicknamed Leatherstocking. Bumppo's best friend is the "Mohican" brave Chingachgook. In the *Leatherstocking Tales*, Cooper wrote about both Iroquois and Algonquian Indians, drawing some facts from history, but making up the central stories. For Cooper "Mohican" was an alternate spelling of *Mohegan*. But he himself might not have known the difference between the Mohegans and the Mahicans, since he was writing after many of the Algonquian tribes had dispersed. And then, to make things more confusing, some other people began using the "Mohican" spelling to mean *Mahican.*

In fact, historical records show that Mahicans and Mohegans are two different sub-groups of Algonquian peoples. The Mahicans lived along the northern end of the Hudson Valley, mainly in New York, but also in Vermont and Massachusetts and even the northwest corner of Connecticut. Many Algonquian bands and villages near the Hudson River were united into the so-called Mahican Confederacy.

On the other hand, the Mohegans lived in Connecticut and were an offshoot of the Pequot tribe (see "Mohegan" and "Pequot"). In a way, the Mahicans and Mohegans are probably related, however. Mohegan legend has it that in the distant past, before the white man came and recorded history in writing, the Mohegans migrated from a group of Algonquians to the west—probably the Mahicans—which would mean that the Mahicans and the Mohegans are descendants of the same distant ancestors.

The Mahicans (pronounced *muh-HEE-cun*) were Woodland Indians, with lifeways typical of other Algonquian peoples (see "Northeast Indians" and "Algonquian"). Their capital and largest village at the time white explorers became aware of them in the 1600s was Schodac, near present-day Albany, but their territory stretched to Lake Champlain. They were enemies of the Iroquois tribes, especially the Mohawks immediately to their west who often invaded their villages (see "Iroquois"). The Mahicans traded with Algonquian allies to their east and south. They were masters of spears and clubs, bows and arrows, nets and traps. They depended on hunting and fishing; gathering wild plants, especially maple syrup; as well as growing corn, beans, and squash. The Mahicans built long bark lodges as well as domed wigwams that they covered with birchbark, elm bark, or mats woven from plant materials. They had light birchbark canoes.

They used porcupine quills to decorate their clothing and containers. They believed that Manitou, the Great Spirit, lived in all things.

After the Europeans came, Mahican life changed drastically. They traded with the whites for iron tools, which made life easier, but the whites' liquor made life harder, and the whites' diseases took away life. Moreover, Europeans aggravated traditional Indian rivalries by supplying some tribes with firearms to use against others. The *swanneken* (the Indian word for the Dutch) provided the Mohawks with guns in order to gain dominance over the Mahicans in their Hudson River territory, the primary trade route for Dutch boats.

In 1664, the same year that the British took control of the region from the Dutch, the Mohawks drove the Mahicans away from Schodac to lands farther to the east. The Mahican Confederacy moved the council fire to Westenhuck, among the Housatonic Band of Mahicans. But whites were settling in the Housatonic Valley of Massachusetts. The settlers called the village Stockbridge and in 1736 established a Calvinist (Protestant) mission there for the Mahicans. The various Mahican bands came to be known as the Stockbridge Indians. In the meantime, other Mahicans moved to Pennsylvania and Indiana and merged with other Indian tribes, especially their Algonquian kinsmen the Delawares (see "Delaware").

The Stockbridge band of Mahicans moved several more times in the 1700s and 1800s. In 1756, they founded a new settlement among the Oneidas of New York. In 1788, white officials forced many Algonquians of the region, including some Mahican bands, to settle in New York, not far from Stockbridge, Massachusetts. This group became known as the Brotherton Indians. Then in 1822, both the Stockbridges and the Brothertons were relocated to Wisconsin. There, in 1856, they were granted reservation lands along with the Munsee band of Delawares. They still hold this reservation today and use the Stockbridge name. Other Mahican descendants have chosen to live in Connecticut.

Maidu

The Maidus (pronounced *MY-doo*) lived along the eastern tributaries of the Sacramento River, including the Feather, American, and Bear rivers that flow from the Sierra Nevada. This territory lies in present-day northern California, not far from the Nevada border.

There were three main divisions of Maidus: the valley, foothill, and mountain groups. The valley group had the most villages or tribelets—permanent main hamlets with a number of temporary satellite hamlets. The Maidus, although not a particularly warlike tribe, regularly posted sentries on the hills surrounding their villages to protect themselves and their hunting grounds from outsiders.

The Maidus, who spoke the Penutian language, had many cultural traits in common with other central California Penutian tribes, such as the Miwoks, Yokuts, Patwins, and Wintuns (see entries for those tribes). They were all hunter-gatherers who depended on acorns and other wild plant foods, small game, and fish. They wore minimal clothing. Some Maidus lived in pole-framed, brush-covered shelters, as did other central California tribes, but some built earth-covered, domed pit houses, some as large as 40 feet in diameter. The openings in the roofs of these dwellings served as both a door and a smoke hole. The Maidus, like many of their neighbors, participated in the Kuksu Cult (see "Patwin"). And, typical of all California peoples, they crafted beautiful baskets. All the above-mentioned tribes are classified as part of the California Culture Area (see "California Indians").

The Maidus, like all Native North Americans, enjoyed many different games. Some of their favorite pastimes were hoop-and-pole, tossing games, dice games, and hand games. In a popular hand game, one player would switch marked and unmarked bones back and forth in his hands, then stop to let other players bet on which hand held which. Sometimes the participants would wager away all their possessions—shell-money, baskets, furs, tools, and weapons—over several days in a marathon game.

The Maidus and their neighbors maintained their traditional culture longer than the Southern California tribes and the coastal peoples despite Spanish attempts to move them into missions during the late 1700s and early 1800s. But the California Gold Rush of 1849 had a significant impact on the Maidus, drastically reducing tribal populations through violence and disease.

The few remaining Maidus now hold two small reservations—Berry Creek Rancheria and Enterprise Rancheria—in Butte County, California. They also share the Susanville Rancheria in Lassen County with other tribes.

Makah

The name of the Makahs, sometimes spelled Macaws (both pronounced *mah-KAW*), means "cape dwellers." They lived along Cape Flattery, territory now located in northwestern Washington. The Juan de Fuca Strait, merging with the Pacific Ocean, separates Cape Flattery from Vancouver Island and serves as the international boundary between the United States and Canada.

The Makahs spoke a dialect of the Wakashan language family, the southernmost people to do so. They are classified as part of the Northwest Coast Culture Area (see "Northwest Coast Indians").

The Makahs' culture was similar to that of other Indians living along the narrow strip of land between the Coast Mountains and the sea and stretching from northern California to southern Alaska. The Makahs ate food from the sea, especially salmon. They also ate deer, elk, and bear meat from the forests, plus wild greens, roots, and berries. They were master woodcarvers. They lived in villages of large, multi-family cedar-plank houses. They carved large oceangoing dugout canoes, totem poles, chests, and other wood products. They wore cedar-bark raincoats and hats. They wove blankets on a loom out of dog hair. They practiced the potlatch, the custom of giving away possessions to prove one's wealth. They were active traders. They also were among the foremost whalers

A Makah whaler, the harpooner. His harpoon has a razorsharp shell tip, with protruding bone spurs. It is attached by a line of sinew to a sealskin float.

in North America, respected for their precise skill by Indians and whites alike. Most of the Pacific Northwest people waited for beached whales. The Makahs, like the neighboring Nootkas on Vancouver Island, actively hunted them.

Makah whalers hunted with 18-foot-long wooden harpoons, tipped with sharp mussel-shell blades and protruding bone spurs. The spurs would keep the weapon hooked inside the whale once the blade penetrated the tough skin. The whalers used ropes of sinew (animal tendons) to tie the harpoon to a number of sealskin floats. When dragged, the floats would tire the whale out and then, after the animal died, keep it afloat.

The chief harpooner, an honored position in the tribe, stood in the front of the dugout, usually with six paddlers and a helmsman behind him. The harpooner sang to the whale during the pursuit, promising to sing and dance for the whale and give it gifts if it let itself be killed.

Whale-hunting was, of course, very dangerous. Whales might swim under a dugout and flip it. Or they might smash it with their enormous tails. It took many harpoons to kill one of the huge creatures—the initial harpoon with floats to weaken it, then others carried by spearsmen in other dugouts to finish it off.

The catch was towed back to the village, where it was butchered by the men and women. The chief harpooner was presented the choicest piece of blubber, taken from the animal's back. The villagers used every part of the whale. They ate both the meat and skin; they shaped the intestines into containers; they braided the tendons into rope; and they extracted oil from the blubber.

Much is known about early Makahs because of an archaeological find at Ozette at the tip of Cape Flattery. At least five centuries ago, a mudslide from a steep cliff buried this prehistoric seaside village. It was a great tragedy for the villagers, dooming them all, but the mud preserved skeletons, houses, and artifacts in nearly perfect condition for future generations to study. The artifacts found at the site include sculptures, harpoons, baskets, and various other household utensils.

Visitors can see these exciting archaeological discoveries at the Makah Tribal Museum at Neah Bay, Washington, on the Makah Reservation. This reservation, established in 1855, is the westernmost Indian-held land in the United States.

Malecite

The Malecites, or Maliseets, an Algonquian people, once located their wigwams along the St. John River in what is now New Brunswick, Canada, as well as in territory which is now the northeastern corner of Maine (see "Algonquian" and "Northeast Indians"). In some historical accounts, they are referred to as the Etchemin tribe.

The Malecites were once part of the Abnaki Confederacy and helped their French allies fight the British in the French and Indian Wars (see "Abnaki"). Malecites frequently intermarried with the French who settled among them.

Malecite culture resembled that of another Algonquian people of the Maritime Provinces, the Micmacs of Nova Scotia (see "Micmac"). It is thought that the name *Malecite*, pronounced *MAL-uh-seet*, comes from the Micmac word for "broken talkers." The Malecites were less dependent on hunting and fishing than their eastern neighbors, the Micmacs, and more dependent on farming, with large fields of corn.

Both the Malecites and Micmacs preferred their version of football, a kicking game, over lacrosse. Like Indians in many parts of the continent, they also liked to gamble, using pieces of stone, wood, and metal as dice; they threw the dice up in the air and caught them in a dish of wood or bark. Both the Malecites and

Malecite beaverskin hood, used as protection from cold and as a hunter's disguise

Micmacs wore caps to shield their heads from the cold winter winds, a rare custom among other Algonquians.

Present-day Malecites hold reserve lands in both New Brunswick and Quebec, in Canada. Some descendants, the Houlton Band of Maliseets, live in Maine.

Mandan

The Mandans (pronounced *MAN-dun*) were one of the earliest Plains tribes. By 1400, they had migrated westward from the Ohio River or Great Lakes country, breaking off from other Siouan-speaking peoples. They settled along the Missouri River, first near the mouth of the White River, territory now part of South Dakota; then, following the Missouri northward, they eventually settled near the mouth of the Heart River, now part of North Dakota. They lived in the latter location, near the Big Bend of the Missouri, when whites first made contact with them in the 1700s.

The Mandans lived in permanent villages and cultivated a variety of crops, including corn, beans, squash, sunflowers, and tobacco. Like their immediate neighbors along the Missouri—the Hidatsas

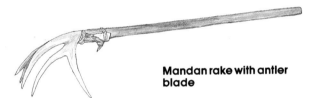

Mandan rake with antler blade

to the north and the Arikaras to the south—the Mandans are sometimes referred to as Prairie people (see "Arikara"; Hidatsa; and "Prairie Indians"). But since they ventured from their villages at least once a year to hunt buffalo on the open grasslands, the Mandans and other Missouri River tribes are usually considered part of the Great Plains Culture Area (see "Plains Indians"). On acquiring horses in the mid-1700s, the Mandans traveled even farther in search of the huge buffalo herds.

Houses

The Mandans built walls of upright logs—sturdy palisades—around their villages. Each village had anywhere from a dozen to more than a hundred earthlodges. They were usually grouped around a central plaza. Each round lodge held several families, with sometimes as many as 60 people, plus their dogs and in some cases even their horses. Each family had its own bed or beds next to the outer wall. A fireplace stood in the center, under a smokehole in the ceiling that was covered with a twig screen. The lodges were built around a pit one to four feet deep. They had

Mandan earthlodge

wooden frames, tied together with plant fibers, and were covered with layers of willow rods, then coarse grass, and then thick strips of sod overlapped like shingles. The lodges were so strong that many people could stand on the domed roofs at once. In fact, the Mandans often congregated on top of their houses to play games and to gossip, to do chores, or simply to doze in the sun. The roofs also served as places to store possessions.

Transportation

Some families stored their bullboats on top of their lodges. They also used the boats to cover the smokeholes when it rained. Bullboats were small, round, cup-shaped boats made from hide stretched over a wooden framework. In other parts of the world they are called *coracles*. The Mandans used them to cross rivers. The trick for the two paddlers was to keep the round boats from going in circles.

Mandan bullboat

The Mandans also used the bullboats to haul their meat and hides across the Missouri after buffalo hunts, bringing their catch as far as the water's edge on travois pulled by dogs, and later by horses. (A travois is a primitive sled made with poles in the shape of a V.)

Food

The buffalo hunt was an important event for the entire Mandan village. Scouts were posted on the grasslands to watch for a big herd. On spotting one, the scouts would report back to the village. Men, women, and children hurriedly made preparations, gathering up bows and arrows, food supplies, and tepees, which they placed on their travois.

Before acquiring horses that could run down the bison, the Mandans usually hunted together. First they built a trap out of two rows of piled stones or with a fence made of poles and brush. At one end, the trap had a wide opening. At the other, it narrowed, leading to the edge of a cliff or to an enclosure. Everyone except the Buffalo Caller hid behind the rockpiles or the fences with blankets in hand. The caller, who wore a buffalo skin on his back, crept on all fours near the grazing herd. He imitated the cry of a sick buffalo to lure the herd toward the mouth of the trap. When the herd was inside the rows of stones, the other hunters jumped up, shouted, and waved their blankets to make the animals stampede. If events went as planned, the frightened buffalo ran toward the narrow end of the trap and over the cliff or into the corral. Then, standing at a safe distance, the Indians killed the injured beasts with arrows.

After skinning their catch, the Mandans held a great feast on the spot, stuffing themselves with buffalo steak, liver, kidneys, and bone marrow. What they couldn't eat, they preserved by smoking. They packed up and took every part of the animal back to the village for future use—the meat for food; the hides for tepees, bullboats, shields, bindings, blankets, robes, and moccasins; and the bones and horns for spoons and cups to use with their pottery bowls.

The Mandans hunted other animals as well: deer, elk, antelope, bear, wolf, fox, beaver, rabbit, turtle, and various birds; in short, whatever hunters could track down in the wild. The Mandans also fished in the Missouri River. But their staples were their crops and buffalo meat.

Religion

Mandan ceremonies and societies reveal how important corn and buffalo were to their economy. Tribal members, usually women, performed corn dances, and the men's Bull Society performed buffalo dances. Secret medicine societies were especially active during the annual Okipa ceremony, held in the late spring or summer. Most of the ceremony centered around a sacred cedar post erected on the village plaza inside a small enclosure. The various rituals celebrated the creation of the Mandans and tried to ensure food supplies and bring about visions for youths passing into manhood. The ceremonies lasted four days. Unlike other Plains Indians, the Mandans did not practice the Sun Dance (see "Plains Indians"). But their Okipa ceremony was very similar. Youths fasted for days; had their chests, backs, and legs slashed; and were raised toward the roof of a ceremonial lodge on rawhide thongs and ropes. This torture proved their manhood and brought about trance-like states in which dreams seemed especially vivid and meaningful. This type of ritual is called a Vision Quest.

Medicine bundles were important in Mandan religious ceremonies, as they were in the rites of many Plains and Great Lakes tribes. These sacred objects served as portable shrines. Each one had its own special mythology. For example, the Lone Man medicine bundle, the post used in the Okipa ceremony, was supposedly given to the Mandans by the first human who triumphed over the hostile powers of nature. The Sacred Canoe medicine bundle was supposedly made from the planks on which tribal ancestors survived a great flood.

Games

Games played an important part in the upbringing of children. A good example is the sham battle in which boys were taught the art of war. All the boys in a village between the ages of seven and fifteen would be divided into two groups, each headed by an experienced warrior. The two warriors would coach their charges in battle techniques, then stage a mock fight outside the village. The boys shot at one another with small bows and blunt arrows. After the pretend battle, the boys returned to the village and engaged in a sham victory dance, using imitation scalps as props. During the dance, girls pretended that the boys were true heroes and acted out their great admiration for them.

Contact with Whites

The first whites to report the existence of the Mandans were a family of explorers—a father and three sons and a nephew—named Verendrye. Exploring out of Quebec and establishing fur trading posts along the way, they cut over to the Missouri River from the Assiniboine River and reached the Mandan villages in 1738.

The upper Missouri Indian villages had always been important trading centers for many native peoples. Nomadic Plains tribes bartered products of the hunt for the crops of farming tribes. Then in the mid-1700s, the Plains tribes began exchanging horses for farm products. The Mandans in turn bartered some of the horses to other tribes. In the meantime, French traders wanted pelts from the Indians and offered guns and European tools for them. As a result, the Mandans became middlemen, dealing in all sorts of products with various tribes and with Europeans.

Lewis and Clark wintered among the Mandans in 1804 and wrote about them extensively (see "Shoshone"). Other explorers followed, frontier painters among them. George Catlin, who traveled among different native peoples from 1830 to 1836, painted many famous portraits of Mandan braves and wrote about Mandan life. Another frontier painter, Karl Bodmer, a Swiss who traveled with the German Prince Maximilian zu Wied, also painted portraits and scenes of Mandans in 1833 and 1834. And Maximilian wrote about them in detailed journals.

Yet their friendly contacts with whites proved deadly for the Mandans. In 1837, they suffered a devastating epidemic of smallpox, which the whites had brought with them. It is estimated that of about 1,600 Mandans, all but 125 died that terrible year. The words of Four Bears, a Mandan chief dying of smallpox, have become famous and symbolic of the great misery endured by Indians from white diseases: "Four Bears never saw a white man hungry, but when he gave him to eat . . . and how have they repaid it! . . . I do not fear death . . . but to die with my face rotten, that even the wolves will shrink . . . at seeing me, and say to themselves, that is Four Bears, the friend of the whites."

In 1845, when the neighboring Hidatsa tribe moved to Fort Berthold, the surviving Mandans went with them. The Arikara tribe followed in 1862. In 1871, the federal government established a permanent reservation at that location for the three tribes. The Three Affiliated Tribes now run a tourism complex and museum.

Massachuset

The Massachuset Indians have been an extinct tribe since the 1600s, soon after the British settled on their shores. Yet a proud linguistic legacy remains, their beautiful Algonquian name (see "Algonquian" and "Northeast Indians"). The name was first given to the bay, and then to the colony which later became a state. What better name for a part of the United States so essential to its early history, where the Pilgrims settled and where the Revolution began? It is fitting that Native Americans are so honored, as they are with many place names, over 5,000 in New England alone. (The state is spelled with a double "t," the tribe usually with one.)

Nevertheless, the extinction of the Massachuset tribe is a sad comment on colonial and Indian relations and an unfortunate aspect of American history. The Massachusets tried to live peacefully with and provide help to the settlers, who were struggling to get a foothold near present-day Boston. But for their troubles, the Indians suffered from disease and violence, and lost their culture.

The Europeans brought with them diseases, especially smallpox, which ravaged Indian families from 1616 to 1620, and then again from 1633 to 1635.

During those years too, Protestant missionaries began work among the Massachusets. John Eliot came to Boston in 1631. He wanted to give Native Americans a new faith and a new life. He preached to them in their own language and, starting in the 1650s, established 17 villages in all—communities where the Indians lived more like Europeans and practiced the Puritan religion. The first and most famous of these was Natick (now a town near Boston). These converts

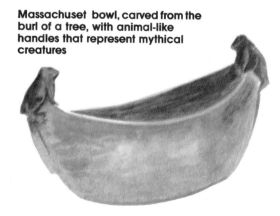

Massachuset bowl, carved from the burl of a tree, with animal-like handles that represent mythical creatures

from among the Massachuset bands, as well as from other Algonquian tribes, became known as Praying Indians.

Although Eliot's work helped give some of the Indian villagers a good life for a time and helped preserve for posterity the Massachuset language, it also stripped the Indians of their tribal identity. Some of the Indians gave up a way of life that had been passed from generation to generation for centuries. As a result, some became confused and depressed, caught between two worlds. Many turned to alcohol.

The Massachusets also suffered because of the revolt of other New England Algonquians in King Philip's War of 1675 (see "Wampanoag"). Because they had such close ties with the English, the Praying Indians were attacked by other Indians in the area. They were also attacked by settlers who hated and wanted revenge against all Indians.

Surviving Massachusets chose one way of life or the other, living either among the colonists or among other Algonquians. But so few continued to call themselves Massachusets that any remaining tribal identity faded beyond particular families. What would their six great sachems, who ruled the six main Massachuset bands at the time the settlers came—the chiefs Chickataubut, Nanepashemet, Manatahqua, Cato, Nahaton, and Cutshamequin—have said if they had known their way of life would soon disappear?

At least we have some record of their culture. We know that Massachuset lifeways resembled those of other New England Algonquians. And at least we still use the Massachuset name for what was once their homeland.

Maya

The Mayas (pronounced *MY-uh*) have long held a special meaning for students of Indian history because of their fascinating culture. Their intellect and artistry have led some people to compare the Mayan civilization with that of the ancient Greeks many thousands of miles away. Both the Mayas and the Greeks had great impact on other societies around them.

The Mayas lived in Mesoamerica, the name given by scholars to the Indian culture area including Mexico (except the northern part, which is included in the Southwest Culture Area); all of the present-day countries of Guatemala, Belize, and El Salvador; and parts of Honduras, Nicaragua, and Costa Rica. Mayan territory for the most part was situated in the Yucatan Peninsula of eastern Mexico and in Guatemala and Belize, with some population centers as well in western Honduras and El Salvador.

Lifeways

The Mayas were influenced by the Olmec culture before them. The Olmecs are sometimes called the "mother civilization" of Mesoamerica (see "Olmec" and "Prehistoric Indians"). But the Mayas carried the Olmecs' cultural traits to new heights of refinement.

The Mayan world, like that of the Olmecs, revolved around ceremonial and economic centers. More than 100 such Mayan centers are known. They are often referred to as city-states, because each population center had its own rulers.

The cities consisted of many stone structures, including pyramids with temples on top; shrines; platforms that served as astronomical observatories; monasteries; palaces; baths; vaulted tombs; ball-courts; paved roads; bridges; plazas; terraces; causeways; reservoirs; and aqueducts.

Each city-state had distinct social classes. There were the priests, the keepers of knowledge. There were also the Sun Children, in charge of commerce, taxation, justice, and other civic matters. There were craftsmen, including stoneworkers, jewelers, potters, clothiers, and others. In the countryside surrounding the central complex of buildings lived farmers, in one-room pole-and-thatch houses. They cut down and burned trees to make fields and used irrigation to water their crops.

In addition to their magnificent architecture, the Mayas are famous for their jade carvings and masks;

Mayan jade statuette

The Castillo, a Mayan pyramid temple at Chichén Itzá in the Yucatan, Mexico

ceramic figures of deities and real people, and other colored pottery; wood carvings, often mounted on buildings over doors; cotton and feather clothing; jade, pearl, alabaster, and shell jewelry; plus many other beautiful objects.

The Mayas are also known for their scientific knowledge. They developed intricate mathematical, astronomical, and calendrical systems. The Mayas' number system used bars, dots, and drawings of shells as symbols. Their writings about astronomy and their calendars were expressed in the form of hieroglyphics, with pictures representing events and units of time. But in addition to picture hieroglyphics, the Mayas had glyphs representing words and sounds.

These various types of hieroglyphic writing are now being deciphered by scholars. From them, we are learning more and more about the Mayas. Sometimes what we learn conflicts with past notions of the Mayas. For example, the Mayas have had a reputation as the most peaceful of the Mesoamerican civilizations. They definitely were not as warlike as the later Toltecs and Aztecs, who founded their empires through far-reaching military campaigns (see "Toltec" and "Aztec"). Yet it now appears that the Mayan city-states made war on one another, and that captives were sacrificed to their deities. Their ball games were especially violent, with captives playing for their lives and human heads sometimes used instead of the rubber balls. Also, Mayan aristocrats mutilated themselves to please their gods and to demonstrate their dedication to the commoners.

A great deal remains to be learned about Mayan history. Who and what brought about the change from villages into city-states? Were some or all of the city-states allied under one ruler? How extensive were Mayan relations, economic or otherwise, with other peoples (such as the inhabitants of the huge city of Teotihuacan to the west, which prospered at the same time as many of the Mayan city-states)? Why did Mayan civilization eventually decline?

History

What is known about Mayan history is organized as follows: The period when Mayan culture developed is called the Preclassic, which occurred in the centuries before A.D. 300, during the time of the Olmec civilization.

The period of Mayan dominance and highest culture is called the Classic period. The approximate dates assigned to this stage are A.D. 300 to 900. City-states such as Tikal and Palenque in what is now Guatemala prospered during the Classic period. Their inhabitants are sometimes called Lowland Mayas. Tikal alone had 3,000 structures, including six temple pyramids, located over one square mile. One structure there was a terraced, four-sided pyramid, 145 feet high, with a flight of steep stone steps leading to a three-room stone temple, topped by a roof comb (an ornamental stone carving). Another temple pyramid was 125 feet high.

The phase from about A.D. 900 to 1500 is known as the Postclassic period. During this time, Mayan culture thrived in the Guatemalan mountains to the south. The Mayas of such sites as Chama, Utatlan, and Kaminaljuya are called Highland Mayas. The Highland Mayas learned techniques of metallurgy, probably through trade with the Indians living to their south in Peru and Ecuador, and crafted beautiful objects out of gold, silver, tin, and zinc.

After about A.D. 1000, during the Postclassic period, still another strain of Mayan culture flourished, on the Yucatan Peninsula in what is now eastern Mexico. An invasion of Toltecs from the west spurred this new flowering of culture. The Toltecs interbred with the Mayas and adopted many of their cultural traits. City-states such as Chichen Itza, Tulum, and Mayapan reached their peak with many of the same traits as the Classic Lowland Mayas, such as elaborate stone architecture and carvings.

The exact chain of events leading to the decline of Postclassic Mayan civilization, as with the decline of

Classic Mayan civilization, is not known. Civil wars between different cities, or between farmers and the ruling classes, played a part, as did calamities, such as crop failure due to soil depletion or drought.

Indians in Mexico, Guatemala, and other Central American countries still speak Mayan dialects. Most of these descendants of the Mayan priests, scientists, Sun Children, and other members of ancient Mayan society, earn a meager living as peasant farmers. Some supplement their earnings through arts and crafts, making exquisite copies of ancient objects. In their midst, rising up from the jungle, stand the great stone ruins of their ancestors, monuments to a resplendent civilization.

Mayan doll (modern)

Menominee

Wild rice, also known as Indian rice, once had at least 60 different names in the many Indian dialects. One of the Algonquian versions, the Chippewa name for the plant, was *manomin* for "good berry." A variation of *manomin* became the name of a tribe of Algonquians who lived along the western Great Lakes and who harvested large quantities of wild rice—the Menominees, pronounced *muh-NOM-uh-nee* (see "Northeast Indians" and "Algonquian"). Explorers and historians have also referred to these Indians by the English translation—that is, "wild rice men," or Rice Indians.

The Menominees collected the wild rice (actually not rice at all but the seed of a kind of grass) from canoes in summertime. The women usually performed this task while the men used bows and arrows to hunt small game from other boats, or fished for sturgeon with hooks, spears, traps, and nets. First, the women would bend the tops of the tall aquatic grass over the canoe's sides. Then they would hit the heads with a paddle, knocking the seeds into the boat's bottom. The seeds could then be dried in the sun or by fire to open the hulls; next they were stamped on or pounded; and finally they were winnowed in a birchbark tray, in the wind, to separate the hulls from the grain. The grain was usually boiled and served with maple syrup or in a stew.

Consider what a plentiful and relatively easy food to gather and prepare! Indians who controlled lands

blessed with wild rice didn't have to depend on a crop of corn for food. The plant is sometimes found in the shallows of small lakes and ponds. But the marshes bordering the western Great Lakes are especially lush. No wonder the region's Algonquians, such as the Chippewas, Ottawas, and Potawatomis, plus the Siouan Winnebagos, vied with one another for this territory (see entries for those tribes). No wonder when there was peace among the tribes, it was an uneasy peace. A tribe which had wild rice also had a good trade commodity that could buy hard-to-get items, such as buffalo furs from the prairies to the west of the Great Lakes. No wonder wild rice captured the Indian imagination and pervaded Indian mythology.

When the first white explorer reached the region—the Frenchman Jean Nicolet in about 1634—the Menominees controlled the northwestern shore of Lake Michigan in what is now Michigan and Wisconsin. Because of wild rice, they stayed in one place more than other tribes of the region, having year-round villages with two kinds of structure. Their cold-weather houses were domed wigwams, framed with bent saplings and usually covered with mats of cattails and reeds rather than the more common birch or elm bark. Their much larger warm-weather houses were rectangular, with a peaked roof. The largest Menominee village stood at the mouth of the Menominee River where it empties into Green Bay, near the site of present-day Green Bay, Wisconsin.

Menominee arrow with knobbed tip

The Menominees were also known for their colorful clothing. Men generally wore deerskin shirts, breechcloths, leggings, and moccasins; women usually wore shirts of woven nettles, along with deerskin tunics, leggings, and moccasins. Both men and women decorated their clothing with painted designs, porcupine quills, and, after the white traders arrived, beadwork.

The Menominees also wore copper jewelry, pounded and shaped from the surface deposits of copper near their homelands. Menominee women were also famous for their woven pouches. They utilized plant fibers, especially those from basswood trees, plus buffalo hairs. They dyed, spun, and wove the materials into large, supple bags with intricate geometric designs. The bags served many purposes, such as carrying and storing food or protecting ceremonial objects. The women also wove durable nets of bark fiber for fishing.

Like other tribes of the region, the Menominees made frequent use of tobacco, smoking it in their long pipes, or calumets. Just about every important ritual—making peace, preparing for war, curing the sick, or initiating someone into the Midewiwin Society (see "Chippewa")—was accompanied by the smoking of tobacco. The Menominees thought that tobacco not only made a good ritualistic offering to Manitou, the Great Spirit, but that it also increased an individual's intelligence for problem-solving and decision-making.

The Menominees were generally on friendly terms with whites and avoided many of the wars that flared up in the Northeast in the 1700s and 1800s. Yet some Menominee warriors did fight against Americans in the American Revolution and the War of 1812. In 1854, the Menominees were pressured into giving up their lands except for a reservation on Wolf River in north-central Wisconsin.

Menominee warclub

Then in 1961, the tribe suffered the effects of Termination. The federal government has gone through many different stages in its policy toward In-

A Menominee boy, mounted on his horse, at the turn of the century

dians. One of these, starting in the 1950s, was Termination. The idea was to terminate the special relationship between the federal government and Indian tribes so that Native Americans could fit better into mainstream American culture. The Menominees were told by federal officials that they would be denied certain federal funds unless they agreed to Termination. The reservation became a county and the tribe became a corporation.

But the Menominees suffered a series of setbacks. They lacked enough money to get their lumber corporation going. Many individuals could not afford the new property taxes, which they had previously been exempt from. They were no longer protected from lumber companies who wanted to move in and take over the rich stands of timber. And, without federally sponsored programs in housing, education, and health, the tribe sank deeper and deeper into poverty.

Finally in 1973, after Termination was recognized as unfair and unnecessary, the federal government passed the Menominee Restoration Act to restore special trust status and to protect tribal lands and interests. But the tribe has never recovered economically from the loss of valuable land.

Metis

Metis means "mixed-blood" in French. When it is used with a lowercase *m*, the word refers to all peoples with mixed racial ancestry. When the word is used with a capital—*Metis*—it refers to a particular group of economically and politically unified people with a special place in Canadian history. It is pronounced *may-TEE*.

Most of the Metis were of French-Cree ancestry (see "Cree"). Some were Scotch-Cree. Some had a parent or grandparent from another Indian tribe. The reason there was such a large population of mixed-bloods in Canada was the fur trade. In the early stages of Canadian history, furs were the most important business. In Europe during the 1700s and part of the 1800s, beaver hats, as well as other fur fashions, were very popular, and men made fortunes by shipping furs back to Europe.

Lifeways

The rugged traders who traveled the wilderness in search of valuable furs associated with the Indians, their main suppliers of pelts. They lived not only like the Indians, but also among them, married them, and had children with them. In Canadian history, the men who paddled the trading canoes through the western wilderness for the big fur companies were called *voyageurs*, the French word for "travelers." Those who were independent and unlicensed traders were the *coureurs de bois*, or "runners of the woods." The mixed-blood children of both *voyageurs* and *coureurs de bois* were the Metis, many of whom eventually came to work the same jobs as their parents did.

By the 1800s, the Metis had developed a unique lifestyle with elements from both the white and Indian world. They spoke both French and Indian languages, the latter mostly Algonquian, the language of the Crees (see "Algonquian" and "Subarctic Indians"). Sometimes they practiced Catholic rites; at other times, Indian rituals. They farmed and lived in frame houses part of the year; they hunted and lived in tepees the rest. Moreover, they considered themselves a separate group with their own special interests and destiny. Out of their common hopes came the Metis wars, usually called the Riel Rebellions. The Second Riel Rebellion came to involve their Cree relatives as well.

The First Riel Rebellion

The First Riel Rebellion is also called the Red River War. It occurred in 1869, two years after the Canadian colonies became independent from England and united into a Confederation, with a centralized government at Ottawa. (England had taken control of Canada from the French in 1763.)

The Red River of the North runs from Lake Winnipeg in Canada to the Minnesota River in the

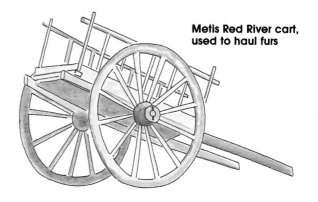

Metis Red River cart, used to haul furs

United States. It is not the same as the Red River of the South, in Texas. The Metis used to live along the Red River Valley in great numbers. Every year, these Red Riverites would lead their ox-drawn carts laden with furs along the valley all the way to St. Paul, Minnesota, to trade with the Americans. It is estimated that 2,000 different Metis caravans made this long trek in certain years. The Metis had had to fight for this right to cross the border to trade. A man named Louis Riel had led the Courthouse Rebellion of 1849, demonstrating at Winnipeg with a force of men for the release of a fellow Metis arrested by officials for smuggling goods across the border. In 1869, it was his son, also named Louis, who led the so-called First Riel Rebellion.

The reason for the revolt was not so much freedom of trade as land rights. After Confederation, more and more whites were streaming into the Red River region in search of homelands. In protest against white land-grabbing, Louis Riel, Jr., and the Metis took over Fort Garry at Winnipeg. They also formed the *Comite National des Metis* (National Committee of Metis) and issued a List of Rights, declaring themselves independent from the rest of Canada. Riel's right-hand man was Ambroise Lepine, a skilled hunter and tracker. The Metis were such good fighters that the central government decided to negotiate with them rather than fight. When the Metis agreed to peace, Ottawa passed the Manitoba Act, making the Red River area a province and guaranteeing most of the Metis' List of Rights.

The Second Riel Rebellion

Nevertheless, whites broke the terms of the treaty. Settlers kept coming onto Metis lands. Little by little, the Metis lost much of what they had been fighting for. Many of them decided to move westward to the Saskatchewan River to start a new life hunting the buffalo on the Great Plains. But the fight was not over. History would repeat itself. The central government was sponsoring the construction of the Canadian Pacific Railway linking the East and West coasts. In the 1880s, Protestant white settlers sought lands along the Saskatchewan River. Metis rights were again ignored.

Louis Riel was now at a mission school in Montana, teaching Indian children. The Metis thought him the man to lead another fight for Metis land rights and freedom of religion. They sent the renowned buffalo hunter, horseman, and sharpshooter, Gabriel Dumont, to fetch him. Riel agreed to return to Canada to lead the resistance, but only on the condition that the Metis try to avoid violence. Dumont, Riel's close friend and general, organized the Metis into an efficient force. Riel gave his approval for a campaign of sabotage—occupying government property, taking hostages, and cutting telegraph lines. The Metis also sent an ultimatum to the Northwest Mounted Police, or Mounties, at Fort Carlton, demanding the surrender of the post. The year was 1885; the Second Riel Rebellion had begun.

In spite of Riel's wish for a nonviolent campaign, the situation escalated. The Canadian government used the new railway to send troops, called the North West Field Force, from the East. Several battles resulted—at Duck Lake, Fish Creek, and Batoche. The Batoche battle in May of 1885 was the turning point. Earlier that day, Dumont and his men had knocked out of commission the *Northcote*, a riverboat converted by the North West Field Force into a gunboat. Dumont's men had damaged the boat by stringing a cable across the South Saskatchewan River to trap it, then firing on it. But at Batoche the Metis rebels were no match for the much more numerous government troops. After a three-day siege by their enemy, the Metis surrendered. Meanwhile, the Crees had been fighting their own battles (see "Cree"). After several more encounters and a period of hiding out in the wilderness, they too surrendered.

The last of the Riel Rebellions was over. This time, the government dealt harshly with the rebels. Louis Riel was sentenced to death. French Catholics wanted to spare him, but the British controlled the government. He probably could have saved his life by pleading insanity, but he refused to denounce his actions. The execution of Louis Riel was carried out on November 16, 1885, just nine days after the railroad was finished. Gabriel Dumont managed to escape to the United States and gained some notoriety in later years by appearing in Buffalo Bill Cody's Wild West Show. Metis power and culture were broken. Saskatchewan became an English-dominated province, as Manitoba had earlier.

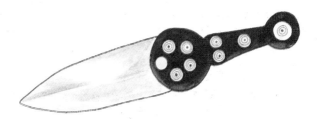

Metis knife with iron blade and black bone handle, inlaid with brass and white bone

There are still people who proudly consider themselves Metis, and there are Metis communities with their special cultural blend in both Canada and south of the border in Montana.

Miami

Miami is a common place name in the United States. But in different parts of the country it has different origins. In Florida, for example, it probably comes from *Mayaimi*, the name of a Creek Indian village. In Oregon, it comes from the Chinook Indian word *memie*, meaning "downstream." In the Midwest and Southwest, however, it comes from an Algonquian tribal name, probably meaning "people of the peninsula."

Lifeways

The tribe bearing this name, the Miamis, lived in southern Great Lakes country, especially the area south of Lake Michigan, which is now Indiana and western Ohio. They lived along timbered river valleys and shared many of the cultural traits of other Northeast Woodland Algonquians (see "Northeast Indians" and "Algonquian"). Without birch trees growing that far south, the Miamis used elm bark or mats of woven plant materials to cover their houses of various shapes. And they made dugout boats from single trees, usually butternuts.

The Miamis are sometimes called Prairie Algonquians because, like their neighbors to the west, the Illinois, they hunted buffalo on the open prairies (see "Prairie Indians" and "Illinois"). Native Americans did not have horses until after the whites came. Unlike the later Plains Indians, who chased the herds on their mounts (see "Plains Indians"), early Prairie hunters usually trapped the animals in a ring of fire, then picked them off with arrows. Most of the village, except the old and weak and a handful of warriors as guards, would go on the buffalo hunts. The women and children would help prepare the meat and hides for travel back to the river valley.

It is interesting that many of the cultural traits of the later Plains Indians evolved from the Prairie Indians. For example, the calumet, or peace pipe, originally evolved from the forest/prairie tribes. The stone used to make the bowls—pipestone, or catlinite—comes from the Great Lakes country. Blood red in color, it was carved and fitted onto a long reed, then decorated with feathers, white in times of peace, red during war. Therefore, so-called peace pipes were sometimes also war pipes.

Another custom that spread from the prairies was the Scalp Dance. After a battle, the warriors who had fought recounted their exploits by chanting and dancing while the calumet was passed around. In the dance, the brave might show how he tracked an enemy, struck him dead, and then scalped him. It was important that the warrior told the truth. If he fabricated an incident or even just exaggerated what had happened, the other braves would shout out the real events and disgrace him before all the village.

Little Turtle's War

The Miamis must have danced furiously on the night of November 2, 1791, after one of the greatest Indian victories in American history earlier that day—St. Clair's Defeat. This occurred in a war sometimes called the Miami War or Little Turtle's War of 1790-94.

Before this first of the wars for the Old Northwest between the young United States and various Indian tribes, the Miamis supported the French against the English and the Iroquois, in the French and Indian Wars from 1689 to 1763 (see "Iroquois"). They continued the fight against the English in Pontiac's Rebellion of 1763 (see "Ottawa"). In the American Revolution from 1775 to 1783, the Miamis supported their old enemies, the English, against the American rebels.

And then in the 1790s, with one of their own tribesmen, Little Turtle (Michikinikwa), as general-in-chief of all the warriors—including Chippewas, Ottawas, Potawatomis, Delawares, Shawnees, and Illinois—the Miamis fought the Americans again.

Little Turtle was one of the great military geniuses of all time. Although a great orator, he was not as famous a personality as other great Indian leaders of his age, like Pontiac, Joseph Brant, and Tecumseh (see "Ottawa"; "Mohawk"; and "Shawnee"). Yet he rates with the great generals from all over the world, and he helped develop many methods of guerilla warfare that modern armies now use, especially decoy techniques.

Little Turtle's War really started just after the American Revolution. With American victory in 1783, more and more settlers began arriving in the region and settling on Indian lands. The Indians responded with many raids. It is estimated that the Indians killed 1,500 settlers from 1783 to 1790. In 1790, President

George Washington ordered an army into the field under General Josiah Harmar to pacify the angry tribes. Militiamen from Pennsylvania, Virginia, and Kentucky made up the large force.

The army organized at Fort Washington (present-day Cincinnati, Ohio). In the fall, when they set out toward the many Indian villages located along the Maumee River that feeds Lake Erie, the militiamen were cocky. Many of these same men had helped defeat the British in the Revolution. They underestimated their enemy.

Little Turtle instructed his warriors from the allied tribes to pick off the invading army wherever possible. The warriors hid and used swift, small strikes to confuse the enemy. Little Turtle told them, after an ambush, even without any losses, to retreat farther into the wilderness. He also had them burn some of their own villages to make the retreat convincing. Then, when the soldiers were weary and far from a supply base, Little Turtle launched two big attacks and routed Harmar's army, inflicting more than 200 casualties.

Next it was General Arthur St. Clair's turn. In the fall of 1791, at President Washington's orders, St. Clair mustered an even bigger force at Fort Washington. And on the way toward the Maumee River, he built new bases for added security—Fort Hamilton and Fort Jefferson. But in the end he fared no better against Little Turtle. The Indian warriors surprised St. Clair and his men on the upper Wabash River, killing many, then retreated into the forest. The soldiers fell for the ploy and split up into groups. Those who chased the Indians were picked off. Then the Indians surrounded the remaining force and pressed the attack. After three brutal hours, when the count was taken, there were only a few Indian casualties. But St. Clair's force had 900 casualties—about 600 dead and 300 wounded. It was an enormous victory for the Indians.

However, the celebrating for the Indians, despite these two major victories, didn't last long. As history proved again and again, there were just too many whites for even the greatest Indian leaders to handle. Washington ordered a third army out, this one 3,000 strong under General "Mad" Anthony Wayne, a Revolutionary War hero. Wayne took two years to organize and train this force before sending it into battle against the Indians. His men built new, better-equipped forts—Fort Greenville and Fort Recovery. Little Turtle's warriors attacked Fort Recovery, but were repelled.

Little Turtle was a good judge of military matters. He recognized the inevitable. Wayne had built a huge, disciplined force. Whites would keep coming no matter how many armies the Indians defeated. Hoping to save Indian lives, Little Turtle counseled peace. But many of the still-angry warriors wanted war. They voted to have a new leader, Turkey Foot. It was their turn to be overconfident after the two earlier victories.

In 1794, Wayne's army advanced cautiously into Indian country. The Indians retreated. This time, without Little Turtle, they were disorganized, and "Mad" Anthony used the element of surprise to his advantage. And this time, in the Battle of Fallen Timbers, the Indians lost hundreds of men, including Turkey Foot, and the whites lost only a few.

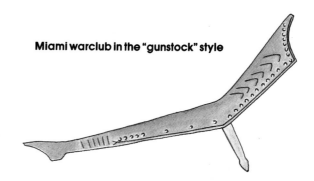

Miami warclub in the "gunstock" style

A year later, in August 1795, many of the chiefs of the allied tribes, including Little Turtle, signed the Treaty of Fort Greenville. The Indians ceded much of their territory to the whites—all of Ohio and most of Indiana. In exchange they were guaranteed other lands farther west, lands that they would, in time, have to fight for again. The next great Indian general would be Tecumseh (see "Shawnee").

Little Turtle never fought again. He became a celebrity among whites. He traveled a great deal and met many famous men. But he died of a disease he caught from whites—gout.

Most of the Miamis were pushed west of the Mississippi by 1840. They settled first in the part of the Indian Territory that became Kansas. When these lands were also taken, most Miamis went to the northeast corner of the shrunken Indian Territory that became Oklahoma, settling with the Illinois. Two of the important Miami groups used their band names: Wea and Piankashaw.

The Miamis' land in Oklahoma was broken up into pieces and allotted to individuals during the Allotment period, beginning in 1887 (see "Cherokee"), so the Miamis no longer have reservation lands or even trust lands as other Oklahoma Indians do. But, like other American citizens, they have some private property. And they have their proud cultural heritage and traditional crafts, plus their tales of great warriors such as Little Turtle.

Micmac

Micmac (pronounced *MICK-mack*) means "allies." These Algonquians of the Maritime Provinces in eastern Canada were once allies of other Algonquians to the south in the Abnaki Confederacy as well as allies of the French (see "Northeast Indians"; "Algonquian"; and "Abnaki"). They were enemies of other neighbors: the Eskimos and Beothuks to their north and the Malecites and Iroquois to their south (see entries for those tribes).

It is possible the Micmacs were the first Indians ever encountered by Europeans. Their wigwams dotted much of what was to become Nova Scotia and also Cape Breton, Prince Edward Island, and part of New Brunswick. It is theorized that Vikings who arrived along these shores of northeastern North America about A.D. 1000 had contact with Micmacs. Imagine Indians in buckskin with dark complexions and black scalplocks standing on a shore lined with spruce trees staring out at a Viking ship plying the northern waterways, pushed by wind filling a large, striped sail, or pulled by long wooden oars manned by fair-skinned and blond-haired Norsemen. And all almost 400 years before Columbus!

One can also imagine the Micmacs at a much later date, fleeing from the Italian explorers, John and Sebastian Cabot, who sailed under the British flag and who kidnapped three of their warriors; then, in 1534, befriending the French explorer, Jacques Cartier; and then, in 1603, befriending Samuel de Champlain. The Micmacs stayed faithful allies of the French after these early contacts, even serving as middlemen for them by gathering furs from other tribes, much as the Hurons did for the French in later years (see "Huron").

Another picture to call up is that of the Micmacs attacking the Beothuks (see "Beothuk"). Because the Beothuks, who lived in Newfoundland, had no sense of private ownership of property, they regularly stole from French fishermen who came to their shores. So in the 1700s, French officials put a bounty on Beothuk scalps, as Dutch and English officials also did with Indians who did not adjust to colonial laws. The French armed the Micmacs with deadly flintlocks. As a result, the Micmacs ravaged the Beothuks and virtually exterminated them.

Yet for modern people it is not just the big events of history that are interesting; it is also the daily life of

Micmac birchbark moose call

early North Americans. It is fascinating to study Indian life such as food, tools and weapons, arts and crafts, and religion.

The Micmacs, a Woodland people, lived and tracked game in small bands in the winter. These bands then gathered and camped together in the summer. The Micmacs hunted mainly moose, caribou, and porcupine in the winter with spears and arrows. They also used calls, such as birchbark moose callers, to attract game, and snares and deadfalls (traps that kill an animal by dropping a heavy weight on it) to trap game. In the spring and summer, the Micmacs fished the rivers with harpoons, hooks, and nets. They also collected shellfish along the ocean, and harpooned seals. They had spears with double-edged blades made from moose bone, plus stone points for their arrows. One method the Micmacs used to prepare their food was to suspend fish from a tree, letting it begin to decay before eating it.

The Micmacs were masters of quillwork, using porcupine quills dyed with vegetable colors to create intricate patterns on clothing and containers. The Micmacs also mastered the use of birchbark, constructing long, sleek canoes and conical wigwams. And they had a spiritual relationship with nature, seeing in every person, animal, plant, and rock a manifestation of Manitou, the Great Spirit.

Today, Micmacs have integrated into Canadian society. Many of them are farmers and many are Catholics. But some tribal members still practice traditional crafts on their reserves in Nova Scotia, New Brunswick, and Prince Edward Island. There are also Micmac descendants still living in the United States, in Maine.

Mission Indians

Mission Indians is a phrase applied to many different native peoples in North America who were converted by Christian missionaries and resettled on missions. Soon after the European discovery of North America, various churches sent their missionaries to the New World to seek converts. Then, at every stage of development thereafter, missionaries carried their work to the edge of the frontier.

Much of what we know about early Indians comes from the writings of missionaries. Some of the most famous North American explorers were missionaries, such as Isaac Jogues, who explored the eastern Great Lakes and New York's Lake George; Claude Jean Allouez, who explored the western Great Lakes; Louis Jolliet and Jacques Marquette, who reached the Mississippi River. These were all French Jesuit priests who explored Indian territory from bases in Quebec. Work by them and others like them among the Algonquians and Iroquoians during the middle to late 1600s brought about settlements of Mission Indians, such as the one found at Kahnawake (see "Mohawk").

French Jesuit priests, members of the Roman Catholic Society of Jesus, were the most active of all the missionaries in colonial times. But other Christian societies had an impact on Indian history as well, such as the Franciscans and Dominicans, who were also Catholic and who were mostly based in Mexico. Some of the Protestant denominations active in missionary work were the Puritans, the Society of Friends (the Quakers), Moravians, Presbyterians, Anglicans, Baptists, and Methodists. These missionaries advanced into Indian country mainly from the East Coast. Some of the better known mission settlements resulting from their efforts were Natick (see "Massachuset"); Stockbridge (see "Mahican"); Conestoga (see "Susquehannock"); Gnaddenhutten (see "Delaware"); and Metlakatla (see "Tsimshian").

Yet, although many different Indian groups are referred to as Mission Indians in history books, the name is most often applied to Indians in California. Many native peoples there, especially in the southern part, lost their tribal identities under the influence of Spanish missionaries.

The Spanish exploration of North America began at the Caribbean Sea. Christopher Columbus's voyage of exploration in 1492 led to many more expeditions in the 1500s (see "Arawak"). After they had explored and settled the West Indies in the Caribbean, the Spanish pushed on into Central and South America. The colony of New Spain (now Mexico) was founded in 1521 after the conquest of Tenochtitlan (Mexico City; see "Aztec"). Spain then gradually spread its dominion northward. In 1565, Pedro Menendez de Aviles founded St. Augustine in Florida, the first permanent European settlement in North America.

The territory that was to become the American Southwest was also soon developed by the Spanish. Explorers, the conquistadors, worked their way northward through Mexico. A military man and a priest often traveled together so that both state and church were represented. In 1598, Juan de Onate founded the settlement of San Juan de Yunque in New Mexico and Santa Fe in 1609 (see "Pueblo Indians"). In 1718, Martin de Alarcon founded San Antonio in Texas. By the mid-1700s, the Spanish were establishing missions, presidios (forts), and rancherias (ranches) in Baja California, which is now part of Mexico. The first Spanish settlement in the part of California that is now U.S. territory was San Diego, founded in 1769 by Gaspar de Portola and Junipero Serra.

Junipero Serra stayed on in California and founded many more missions along with other Franciscans—21 in the coastal region between San Diego and San Francisco. The Indians they missionized had been peaceful hunter-gatherers, living in tune with their plentiful environment (see "California Indians"). But soldiers at the missions' neighboring presidios rounded them up and forced them to live at the missions. The friars taught them to speak Spanish and to practice the Catholic religion. They also taught them how to tend fields, vineyards, and livestock, as well as how to make adobe and soap. Then they forced them to work—to build churches and to produce food. If the Indians refused or if they ran away and were caught, they received whippings as punishment.

The Spanish brought Indians of different tribes to each mission, mostly from groups living near the Pacific Coast. Before long, the Indians had lost their own language and religion as well as their tribal identity. Most thereafter came to be identified historically by the name of the mission. Thus the tribal names that have been passed down through history sound

Spanish: Cahuilla; Cupeno; Diegueno; Fernandeno; Gabrielino; Juaneno; Luiseno; Nicolena; Serrano. Most of these peoples originally spoke a dialect of the Uto-Aztecan language family before being forced to speak Spanish, except the Dieguenos who spoke Yuman. Other tribes of different language families and living farther north—Chumash, Salinan, Esselen, and Costanoan—were also missionized. The Chumashes, Salinans, and Esselens spoke Hokan; the Costanoans spoke the Penutian language (see "Chumash").

The missions robbed the Indians of their culture and broke their spirit. The Mexican government closed the missions in 1834, 13 years after Mexican independence from Spain. Mission Indians who had not already been killed by white diseases or poor working conditions, had a hard time coping without mission food. Their numbers continued to decline drastically. The United States took control of California after the Mexican Cession of 1848. The next year was the California Gold Rush, which further affected California's Indians, even those who had avoided mission life during the Spanish occupation (see "Miwok").

By the time the United States government finally began establishing reservation lands for the Mission Indians in the late 1800s, much of California had been settled by whites. The Indians received numerous small pieces, sometimes called rancherias. Today, there are many different bands of Mission Indians living on these parcels. Some are integrated into the American culture with jobs in industry and agriculture. Some have rediscovered the traditional ceremonies and crafts of their ancient ancestors.

Missouri

The Missouris, or Missourias, spoke the Siouan language. According to tribal legend, they once lived in the Great Lakes region as one people with the Iowas, Otos, and Winnebagos (see entries for those tribes). Yet, at some early point in their history, before whites reached the area, a group separated from the Winnebagos in search of larger herds of buffalo to the southwest. On reaching the mouth of the Iowa River, where it enters the Mississippi River, another separation occurred. One group, who became the Iowas, stayed in this region. Another group continued westward to the Missouri River, where the group again divided.

Legend has it that this last division happened because of a quarrel. The son of one chief supposedly seduced the daughter of another. The one chief led his people north up the Missouri River. His people came to be known as the Otos, or "lechers," because of his son's behavior. The group that stayed behind became the Missouris.

Their name later was taken as the name of the river. It probably originally meant "people with the dugout canoes." But it has come to be translated as "Big Muddy" after the river, which carries a lot of silt. The name was also adopted by whites as the name of the state.

When they lived farther to the east, the Missouris were Woodland Indians who farmed as well as hunted. They took their knowledge of woodworking and farming westward with them. They also continued to live in villages much of the time. Sometimes the Indians who once lived along the Mississippi River and its tributaries are called Prairie Indians because of the tall prairie grass there (see "Prairie Indians"). But the Missouris are usually considered a part of the Great Plains Culture Area (see "Plains Indians"). After the Spanish brought the horse to North America, the Prairie tribes began to wander over greater distances in search of buffalo and adopted cultural traits similar to those of the western Plains tribes.

In 1673, the French explorer Jacques Marquette visited Missouri villages on the Missouri River where it is joined by a tributary called the Grand River. The tribe lived in this part of what is now the state of Missouri for more than 100 years. In 1798, the Sacs and Foxes swept down from the northeast to defeat the Missouris. Survivors lived among the Otos, Osages, and Kaws for several years, then established some villages south of the Platte River in what is now a part of Nebraska. The Missouris lived here when the Lewis and Clark Expedition encountered them in 1805. Yet the Osages later attacked and once again dispersed the Missouris. In 1829, the Missouris joined the Otos, with whom they are still united as the Otoe-Missouria tribe (see "Oto").

Miwok

The Miwoks, or Me-Wuks (both pronounced *MEE-wock*) of central California can be divided into three main groups: Valley Miwoks, Coast Miwoks, and Lake Miwoks. The main group, the Valley Miwoks, lived on the western slope of the Sierra Nevada along the San Joaquin and Sacramento rivers and their tributaries. The Coast Miwoks lived to their west along the Pacific Coast north of San Francisco Bay. And the Lake Miwoks lived north of San Francisco Bay, near Clear Lake.

Miwok means "people" in the Penutian dialect of the tribe. The Miwoks are considered part of the California Culture Area (see "California Indians").

The lifeways of the three Miwok groups varied with the food sources available near their over 100 village sites. They gathered wild plant foods, especially acorns, hunted small game, and fished in rivers, ocean, and lakes. They built houses with frameworks of wooden poles covered with swamp plants, brush, grass, or palm fronds. They made beautiful coiled baskets with flared-out sides and black designs.

The Miwoks generally had peaceful relations with the Spanish but still managed to keep their independence from them. The Mexican government pretty much left the Miwoks alone after Mexico gained its independence from Spain in 1821 and took control of California. But life changed for the Miwoks in 1848. This was the year, by the Treaty of Guadalupe Hidalgo, that Mexico ceded California to the United States. It was also the year gold was discovered in the region, starting the California Gold Rush.

Whites came in great numbers to California over the next several years in search of the Mother Lode, the miners' name for a big strike of gold. The Indians suffered greatly. White diseases killed many of them. The presence of mining camps disrupted their hunting. And some whites, rough and lawless frontier types, shot Indians on sight. Most of the California Indians, unlike many other western tribes, were peaceful and endured this kind of treatment without retaliation.

The Valley Miwoks, and a powerful neighboring tribe, the Yokuts, fought back, however (see "Yokuts"). In 1850, warriors under Chief Tenaya began attacking prospecting parties and trading posts. The owner of the trading posts, James Savage, organized a state militia, called the Mariposa Battalion, which he led into the Sierra Nevada highlands after the Indians.

The two forces met in a number of indecisive skirmishes. With continuing white patrols, however, the Miwoks and Yokuts gave up their campaign of violence. That same year, 1850, California became the 31st state of the Union. As the white population continued to grow, the Indian population was quickly reduced by almost two-thirds.

In modern times, many Native Americans have come to California from other states, settling in urban areas. Moreover, there are many small reservations in California. These are often called rancherias, the Spanish word for "ranch." The Miwoks presently live on three of them: Jackson Rancheria, Sheep Ranch Rancheria, and Tuolomne Rancheria. In the 1980 census, California surpassed Oklahoma as the state with the largest Native American population. Arizona and New Mexico rank third and fourth respectively.

Modoc

Captain Jack, Curly Headed Doctor, Black Jim, Boston Charley, Scarfaced Charley, Schonchin Jim, and Hooker Jim are not typical-sounding Indian names. These were nicknames given to Indians by white settlers and military men in California and Oregon. The Indians of course had their own names while growing up. Yet some began using these nicknames themselves. And these are the names found in history books that discuss the Modoc War of 1872-73.

The Modocs (pronounced *MO-dock*) occupied territory along what is now the southern Oregon and northern California border, in the vicinity of Modoc Lake, Little Klamath Lake, Clear Lake, Goose Lake, Tule Lake, and Lost River. Their homeland was just south of that of the Klamath tribe, who spoke a similar dialect of the Penutian language family. Both the Modocs and Klamaths are thought of as tribes of the Plateau Culture Area, like their more northern Penutian kinsmen, with whom they often traded (see "Klamuth" and "Plateau Indians").

Plateau Indians were seminomadic, fishers, hunters, and gatherers. Their migrations revolved around the seasonal availability of food. Salmon runs were an important time of year. When these ocean fish swim upriver to lay their eggs, they make for an easy catch. So the houses of the migratory Plateau peoples included not only permanent, semi-underground earth lodges but also temporary mat-covered tents.

Although their culture was similar to that of Plateau peoples to their north, the Modocs are often discussed historically with California Indians living south of them because of their famous war. The Modoc War is one of the few Indian wars to occur within the boundaries of the state of California. Because California Indians generally tolerated mistreatment by whites without resorting to violence and because the federal government under the post-Civil War administration of President Ulysses Grant had a Peace Policy toward Indians, the nation was shocked by the Modoc uprising in 1872.

The Modoc War

The cause of the Modoc War dated back to 1864. At that time, the Modocs and Klamaths signed away most of their territory and retired to the Klamath Reservation in Oregon, northeast of Upper Klamath Lake. But the Modocs never felt content among the Klamaths. There was not enough food for both tribes. Many people became sick. Tensions mounted between the tribes over petty issues. The Modocs longed for a separate home. They asked for their own reservation across the California border, along the Lost River north of Tule Lake. The federal and California governments turned down the tribe's request.

A group of Indians under a young leader named Kintpuash, nicknamed Captain Jack by whites, took matters into their own hands. In 1870, they set out for their longed-for homeland and reestablished a village in the Lost Valley. For a time, officials ignored their move. But as white settlement in Northern California increased, so did complaints about the Modoc presence. The federal government ordered out troops.

In November 1872, Captain James Jackson set out from Fort Klamath with instructions to bring back the renegades. When Jackson announced his intentions to

A U.S. Army scout in the Modoc War

the Modocs, a fight broke out in the village. One Indian and one soldier died in the shooting. Captain Jack and his followers escaped to Tule Lake, then worked their way farther south to what the Indians called the "Land of Burnt Out Fires." This was a volcanic highland formed by hardened lava, a rugged and desolate place that made for natural fortifications. Meanwhile, a party of Modocs under Hooker Jim, who had been away from the village, eluded a posse of civilians trying to round them up. This group carried out several attacks on ranchers in the region, killing 15. Then they too fled to the lava beds.

Captain Jack had thought that perhaps peace negotiations were possible. On learning of Hooker Jim's actions, however, he knew that war was now inevitable. He was not surprised when California and Oregon regulars and volunteers under Lieutenant Colonel Frank Wheaton massed near the lava beds. The attack came in January 1873. While the bluecoat infantry advanced, the artillery fired rounds into the dense fog enveloping the "Land of Burnt Out Fires." But the shells fell closer to the advancing infantry than to the Indians. And the Modoc warriors, moving along lava trenches with sagebrush in their hair as camouflage, successfully counterattacked. The soldiers, suffering many casualties at the hands of Modoc sharpshooters, retreated.

The third phase of the war began. General Edward Canby, the military commander of the entire Northwest District, decided to personally lead the campaign. He built up a force of about 1,000 men. To his credit, he also set a peace plan in motion. With the help of Captain Jack's cousin Winema, who was married to a white man, he arranged for negotiations with the Indians. President Grant's peace commissioners, Alfred Meachem and Reverend Eleasar Thomas, represented the government along with General Canby.

Captain Jack thought that peace might still be possible. But he refused to turn over Hooker Jim and the militants who had killed the ranchers. A medicine man named Curly Headed Doctor convinced Captain Jack that if he killed the leaders of the army, the troops would be powerless to act. Captain Jack and his best friends among the warriors agreed to a plan of treachery. This was a grave mistake.

At a parley on April 11, Captain Jack drew a hidden revolver and shot and killed General Canby. Boston Charley killed Reverend Eleasar Thomas. Then the warriors escaped.

Now there would be no mercy for the Modocs. Any hope for their own reservation had ended. Some outraged whites even called for their complete extermination. The new commander in the field, Colonel Alvan Gillem, launched an attack that was again repulsed. The Modocs managed to sneak away to another lava formation farther south. A war party under Scarfaced Charley led an ambush on one army patrol in a hollow. Twenty-five soldiers, including all five officers, died in that one-sided fight.

Yet the Modoc rebellion was winding down. The Modocs lacked food and water and were arguing among themselves. A new commander, General Jeff Davis, organized a relentless pursuit of the now-scattered small bands. Hooker Jim turned himself in and, bargaining for his own life, betrayed Captain Jack, who had faithfully protected him. He led the troops to Captain Jack's hideout. Cornered in a cave, Captain Jack and his friends—Boston Charley, Black Jim, and Schonchin Jim—surrendered.

At the court-martial, Hooker Jim served as a witness against the others. Captain Jack and his friends were sentenced to hang. The execution took place on October 3, 1873. On the night after the hanging, grave robbers dug up Captain Jack's body, embalmed it, and displayed it in a carnival that toured eastern cities.

Surviving Modocs were sent to the Quapaw Reservation in the Indian Territory (see "Quapaw"). In 1909, 51 Modocs were allowed to return to the Klamath Reservation. Today, Modoc descendants live in both places.

Mohawk

Mohawk, pronounced *MO-hawk*, is a powerful-sounding name, strong and graceful. It brings to mind the bird of prey with a similar name. Yet the tribal name has nothing to do with the bird. It was an Algonquian name for their Mohawk neighbors; it means "eaters of men." The Algonquians used this name because these Iroquois sometimes practiced cannibalism in order to absorb the strength of their enemy (see "Algonquian" and "Northeast Indians").

The Mohawks thought of themselves rather as the People of the Place of Flint. They were the easternmost tribe of the Iroquois League. To all the Iroquois, the League was like a huge longhouse extending across upstate New York. That made the Mohawks the

Keepers of the Eastern Door. The Mohawks also used the symbol of the Shield for themselves at the League's Great Council held every year. The Mohawks sent nine sachems, or chiefs, to the meeting as their representatives.

(To learn more about the Iroquois Confederacy and Iroquois culture, see "Iroquois." This section has information primarily about one Iroquois tribe—the Mohawks.)

The Mohawks built most of their longhouses in villages along the northern valley of the river now named after them, the Mohawk River, which flows into the Hudson River. Mohawks could travel on it in their elm-bark canoes when they headed eastward to trade, hunt, or go to war.

Mohawk history in colonial times is similar to that of the other Iroquois tribes. The Mohawks were for the most part allies of the English and enemies of the French in the bitter struggle for North America.

Joseph Brant

The most famous Mohawk in American and Canadian history is Theyendanegea, better known by his English name, Joseph Brant. What makes Joseph Brant so intriguing and memorable is that he was so successful in both the Indian and white worlds. He was born in the Ohio Valley in 1742, while his Mohawk parents were on a hunting trip there. But he grew up in the Mohawk Valley of New York State.

An Englishman of Irish descent named William Johnson, a land speculator and trader, built Fort Johnson and later Johnson Hall in Mohawk territory. He was a good friend to the Iroquois and was always fair in his business dealings with them. He admired their character, participated in their ceremonies, and married a Mohawk woman by the name of Molly Brant. Her brother, Joseph Brant, played with William Johnson's son, John, and his nephew, Guy. Because of William Johnson's close relationship to the Indians, the king of England made him the superintendent of Indian affairs for the northern colonial region.

When fighting broke out between the English and French in the last of the French and Indian Wars, starting in 1754, William Johnson asked for the help of his Mohawk friends in an expedition to Lake George. Chief Hendrick led a Mohawk contingent. One of the Mohawk braves was Joseph Brant, a boy of only 13. Johnson and his British and Mohawk army won the Battle of Lake George in 1755. He received a knighthood from the king for his triumph. He later led an expedition against Fort Niagara on Lake Ontario. Again, many Mohawks, including the young Brant, fought with him.

William Johnson recognized Joseph Brant's exceptional talents. After the war, which ended in 1763, he sent the 19-year-old youth to Moor's Indian Charity School in Connecticut (which later was moved to New Hampshire and became Dartmouth College). Brant proved himself an excellent student, mastering spoken and written English.

Joseph Brant later acted as interpreter for Sir William Johnson. When Sir William died in 1774, Guy Johnson became the new superintendent of Indian affairs, and Brant became his interpreter and personal secretary. This was the period just before the outbreak of the American Revolution. When violence erupted in 1775 at Lexington, Massachusetts, with "the shot heard round the world," the Mohawks and other Iroquois tribes were pressured to choose sides—their traditional allies, the British, or the American rebels.

At this time, Joseph Brant traveled to England with Guy Johnson. He made quite an impression abroad as an Indian ambassador. He met many famous Englishmen, such as the writer James Boswell, and the painter George Romney, who painted the Mohawk's portrait. Brant also met King George III. Most people, when meeting kings, kneel and kiss their hands, but, as legend has it, not the proud Mohawk, who considered himself the king's equal. Instead, he grandiosely kissed the queen's hand.

When Joseph Brant returned to North America, he worked hard to win over all the Iroquois tribes to the English cause against the rebelling Americans. His natural leadership abilities and statesmanship now revealed themselves. His fellow Mohawks, plus the Senecas, Onondagas, and Cayugas, accepted his leadership. But not the Oneidas and Tuscaroras, who had many friends among the American settlers.

Joseph Brant, who had already demonstrated himself as a fighter, student, translator, secretary, ambassador, orator, and statesman, now proved himself as a general in the field. He led his warriors and Tory troops in many successful raids on settlements and forts in both New York and Pennsylvania.

One of the most famous battles took place in Cherry Valley, New York, on November 11, 1778. The small settlement was located about 50 miles west of Albany, near Otsego Lake. Joseph Brant and Ranger Captain Walter Butler led approximately 700 troops out of the southwest along an old winding Indian trail. They first attacked outlying settlements, picking off stranded settlers who could not make it back to the fort in time. Then they attacked the stockade, defended by the Seventh Massachusetts Regiment. The American troops repelled the Indian and Tory attack. Yet, by the end of the fighting, 32 settlers were dead. Forty more had been captured and led off to Fort Niagara. It is said that Brant personally saved the lives of many settlers, restraining his warriors from further attack. Time and again, he proved himself merciful in combat, urging his men to spare the innocent—not only women and children, but also men who didn't take up arms.

The Cherry Valley raid and others convinced General George Washington to send an invading army into Iroquois country. The Sullivan-Clinton Campaign, as it was called, after the generals in charge, succeeded in its goal of conquering the Iroquois by destroying their villages and crops. The Iroquois surrendered and in the coming years ceded vast holdings of land and retained only small state reservations. Most Mohawks left the United States for Canada. Joseph Brant and his followers were granted a parcel of land by the Canadian government at Oshweken on the Grand River in Ontario. There he helped found the town of Brantford. He also founded a Mohawk chapel and translated the Book of Common Prayer and Gospel of Mark into the Mohawk dialect. He died in 1807 of natural causes.

Iroquois descendants of all six tribes still live on the Six Nations Reserve at Oshweken, Ontario. They return to Mohawk country for various Indian festivals, such as the Labor Day Weekend festivals at Cobleskill and Hunter Mountain.

Kahnawake

Not all Mohawks followed this same order of migration, or this exact pattern of alliance. Some Mohawks had moved to Canada much earlier, as allies of the French. From 1667 to 1676, a group of Mohawks migrated from the Fonda, New York, region to La Prairie, a Jesuit mission, on the St. Lawrence River in Quebec. After having lived in several different locations in the area, they finally settled just south of Montreal at a site they called Kahnawake (English version:

Mohawk ash-splint and sweetgrass basket (modern)

Caughnawaga), after their original village in New York State.

The Kahnawake Mohawks practiced Catholicism, like the French. They also sometimes worked for the French as scouts and fur traders and sometimes fought with them as allies against the English. But they remained part of the Iroquois Confederacy and, at various times during the French and Indian Wars, supported the English, along with other Iroquois, against the French. They were a proud and independent people whom neither the French nor English could take for granted.

One famous Kahnawake Mohawk was Kateri Tekakwitha, called "Lily of the Mohawks." She was born and baptized a Christian in the Mohawk Valley but later moved to Kahnawake in Canada to escape persecution by non-Christian Indians. Her parents and brother died in a smallpox epidemic. She caught the disease too and her skin was severely scarred. But because of her great faith in Catholicism and her dedication to helping others, it is said that when she died at the age of 24 in 1680 a miracle occurred—her pockmarks disappeared. In 1943, the Roman Catholic Church declared Kateri "venerable." Then in 1980, the Church declared her "blessed," the second step toward sainthood.

It is mainly the Mohawks of the Kahnawake Reserve who have become the famous Iroquois high-steel workers of the 20th century. They are noted for their sense of balance, high up on tall buildings. Kahnawake construction workers travel all over Canada and the United States. A group of workers commute regularly between their Kahnawake relatives and their Brooklyn relatives to help build skyscrapers in New York City.

This tradition began in 1886 when the Mohawks proved themselves the most surefooted and fearless of all workers in the construction of a bridge across the St. Lawrence River. It was dangerous work, especially in the early years of high-steel construction, and appropriate for a people whose ancestors were such great warriors. A tragedy that occurred in the building of another bridge across the St. Lawrence in 1907 proved the degree of risk. The southern portion of the bridge collapsed, due to a faulty design, killing 33 ironworkers. Other Iroquois ironworkers came from their jobs all over North America for the memorial service.

Akwesasne

There are other Mohawk groups in both Canada and the United States besides those at Six Nations Reserve in Ontario and at Kahnawake in Quebec. There are also the Tyendinaga Mohawks on the north side of Lake Ontario in Canada; the Gibson Mohawks on Georgian Bay in Canada; and the Akwesasne Mohawks on the St. Lawrence River. The last group mentioned has a unique status. Their lands are found on both sides of the Canadian-U.S. border, so they are citizens of two countries. They are also known as the St. Regis Mohawks.

The Akwesasne (or St. Regis) Mohawks have been in the news a great deal in recent times. In 1968, tribal members staged a protest by blocking the St. Lawrence Seaway International Bridge. They claimed that the Canadian government was not honoring the Jay Treaty of 1794, guaranteeing them the right to travel unrestricted back and forth between Canada and the United States. Border officials changed their policy, making crossings easier for the Mohawks.

In 1974, some 200 Akwesasne Mohawks and others occupied New York State-held land at Eagle Bay on Moss Lake in the Adirondacks, claiming original title to it. They called this 612-acre parcel of land *Ganienkeh*. In 1977, after negotiations with the state, the Mohawk activists moved to Schuyler and Altona lakes in Clinton County.

The North American Indian Traveling College is based at Akwesasne on the St. Lawrence. From early spring to late autumn, teachers travel throughout Ontario and New York in vans, trucks, and campers for the purpose of educating other Native Americans (mostly Iroquois, Chippewas, and Crees) in their tribal

A Mohawk girl and her bike

histories and traditions. In winter months, teachers prepare lessons for the following school year.

Akwesasne Mohawks also publish an important Native American journal called *Akwesasne Notes*. In addition to covering Iroquois issues and traditions, this publication concerns itself with current and historical events of native peoples from all over North, Central, and South America.

Mohegan

The Mohegans (pronounced *mo-HEE-gun*) are a famous tribe among non-Indians because of the novel *The Last of the Mohicans* written by James Fenimore Cooper in 1826. The author chose to use an alternate spelling for the tribe, however, which has sometimes made for confusion with the Mahicans, whose name also is taken from the Algonquian word for "wolf" (see "Mahican"; "Algonquian"; and "Northeast Indians").

James Fenimore Cooper's family actually lived in Mohawk territory, in Cooperstown, New York, fairly close to Mahican land along the Hudson Valley (see "Mohawk"). And, long before whites came, the Mohegans might have migrated from this Mahican territory, as their legends describe. But it seems likely the author meant his "Mohicans" to be the Mohegans living much farther to the east because his character Chingachgook, an Algonquian chief and best friend of the hero Natty Bumppo, mentions a "Mohican land by

the sea." The reference fits with the Mohegans because they lived in Connecticut, along the Long Island Sound. Moreover, Cooper, who was writing about the French and Indian Wars of the 1700s, used the name Uncas for the son of Chingachgook. It seems he took this name from a real Mohegan chief of the 1600s.

The *Last of the Mohicans* and Cooper's other four novels in the *Leatherstocking Tales* all give the reader good atmosphere and detail about an exciting period in colonial times. But much of what he wrote came from his imagination and not from history. In the story, he made Chingachgook the "last of the Mohicans," but the Mohegans still exist as a tribe today.

As to the actual history of these Native Americans, the Mohegans had lifeways similar to other Algonquians in New England and Long Island (see "Algonquian"). Forests, oceans, bays, rivers, and lakes provided their food, their raw materials, and inspiration for their myths and legends. They lived in both domed wigwams and rectangular houses, usually covered with birchbark. They used framed birchbark canoes as well as dugouts made from a single tree.

The Mohegans were actually a subgroup of the Pequots (see "Pequot"). When white settlers arrived in their territory soon after the Pilgrims landed at Plymouth Rock in 1620, Sassacus ruled the Pequots. Their main village was on the Thames River in Connecticut. But a subordinate chief named Uncas rebelled and led a group to another village on the Thames. They became known as the Mohegans. When Sassacus was defeated by whites in the Pequot War of 1637, Uncas, who had befriended the whites, became chief of the remaining Pequots along with the Mohegans. As allies of the British against the French, Uncas's Mohegan band kept their power longer than their neighbors, the Wampanoags and Narragansets, who were defeated in King Philip's War of 1685 (see "Wampanoag" and "Narraganset").

But the British settlers eventually turned against the Mohegans too and took most of their land; they sold some Mohegans into slavery, as they did Pequots and Wampanoags. Other Mohegans died from European diseases.

As a result, there are not many Mohegans or Pequots left today. A small number of both peoples share two small reservations in Connecticut. They also maintain a museum together, displaying Indian art and artifacts. A land claim and lawsuit they filed against the state of Connecticut was vetoed in 1983 by

Mohegan wooden doll

President Reagan. The Mohegans and Pequots need funding for investments that would help them raise their standard of living, improve their health care, and maintain their tribal traditions. They have a will to survive as a unified people. If they do, America will be lucky to never see the last of the fascinating people known as the Mohegans.

Mojave

Mojave, or Mohave (both pronounced *mo-HAH-vee*), is taken from the native word *aha-makave*, meaning "beside the water." The Mojave Desert and Mojave River are named after these Indians.

The Mojaves spoke a dialect of the Yuman language family. They lived near other Yuman-speaking peoples along both sides of the Colorado River, the present border between the states of Arizona and California. The Mojaves are grouped together with other tribes in a category called the River Yumans (see "Yuma"). The Upland Yumans, such as the Havasupais, Hualapais, and Yavapais lived to the north of the Mojaves (see entries for those tribes). All the Yumans are considered part of the Southwest Culture Area, although they lived on the edge of the Great Basin and California culture areas (see "Southwest Indians").

The Mojave Desert is one of the most extreme environments in North America. Temperatures often

climb above 100 degrees Fahrenheit in the hot sun, then drop drastically at night. But the Mojaves coped with these extremes by settling along the bottomlands of the lower Colorado River. Every year, with the melting of snows in the mountains to the northeast, the lower Colorado floods and provides suitable conditions for farming. In this strip of silty soil cutting through the desert, the Mojaves planted corn, beans, pumpkins, melons, and, after they had received seeds brought from Europe by whites, wheat. The Mojaves also fished the Colorado River; hunted small desert game, especially rabbits; and gathered wild plant foods, such as piñon nuts (from a kind of pine tree) and mesquite beans.

The Mojaves lived in dwellings made of brush and earth. For the warm weather, they built flat-roofed, open-sided structures; for the cold periods, they made low, rectangular structures. Mojave clothing consisted of sandals and breechcloths for men, and sandals and aprons for women. In cold weather, both men and women wore rabbit-skin blankets and robes. Both men and women decorated their skin with tattoos and body paint.

The Mojaves were fierce fighters. A special society of warriors, called the *Kwanamis*, led the other men in battle. Mojave war parties were organized into three different fighting groups: archers, clubbers, and stickmen (or lancemen).

Mojave effigy jar

The Mojaves made war with certain neighboring peoples, such as the Pimas and Papagos (see "Pima" and "Papago"), but they traded with others. Mojave traders traveled all the way to the Gulf of California or to the Pacific Ocean to trade agricultural products with coastal tribes for shells and feathers. To cross the Colorado and other rivers, the Mojaves made rafts from bundles of reeds.

The Mojaves had early contacts with Spaniards, who entered their domain out of Mexico. Hernando de Alarcon may have encountered them as early as 1540 during his trip along the Gulf of California. Juan de Onate, who explored much of the Southwest, reached them in 1604. Francisco Garces visited them in 1775-76. Mojaves worked for Garces as scouts in his expedition to the Grand Canyon.

Despite Spanish attempts to move them to missions, the fierce and proud Mojaves kept their independence. The Spanish called them "wild Indians." When Anglo-Americans began entering their domain, the Mojaves often raided their caravans. Mojave warriors attacked the trapping expedition of the Mountain Man Jedediah Smith in 1827.

With the Mexican Cession of 1848, which granted most of the Southwest to the United States, and the discovery of gold in California that same year, more and more whites crossed through Mojave territory along the Southern Overland Trail. The Indians harassed many of the travelers. The establishment of Fort Yuma at the Yuma Crossing of the Colorado just south of Mojave territory decreased the number of raids.

Today, the Mojaves live on three different reservations: (1) the Colorado River Reservation (in Yuma County, Arizona; and San Bernardino and Riverside counties, California), which they share with the Chemehuevis, a River Yuman tribe not listed separately in this book; (2) the Fort Mojave Reservation (in Clark County, Nevada; San Bernardino County, California; and Mohave County, Arizona); and (3) the Fort McDowell Reservation (in Maricopa County, Arizona), which they share with Apaches and Yavapais (see "Apache" and "Yavapai").

Montagnais

The Montagnais of northeastern Canada had much in common with the Naskapis living even farther to the north (see "Naskapi"). The two peoples spoke nearly identical dialects of the Algonquian language family and had similar lifeways in the rugged Subarctic environment of Labrador and northern Quebec (see "Algonquian" and "Subarctic Indians"). The Montagnais were also close neighbors to the Mistassini Crees, but their dialect differed from that of this other Algonquian people (see "Cree").

Montagnais, pronounced *mon-tun-YAY*, means "mountaineers" in French. The Laurentian Mountains loom up in Montagnais territory, extending all the way

from James Bay to the Gulf of St. Lawrence. Samuel de Champlain, the explorer and founder of New France (now the eastern part of Canada), encountered the Montagnais at the mouth of the Saguenay River in 1603. The Montagnais stayed allied to the French during French rule in North America, trading furs with them and helping them fight the Iroquois and English to the south (see "Iroquois"). For one campaign southward, the Montagnais sent an army of 1,000 warriors along with the French.

The Montagnais did not try to farm their land of rocky soil and short growing season. Rather, they hunted and fished and gathered what wild plant foods they could. In order to eke out enough food in the harsh wilderness, they had to stay on the move.

The moose, common to the northern forests, was the Montagnais' chosen game in winter and early spring. Moose hunting necessitated long hours of tracking, usually on snowshoes. Because the animals weighed almost 1,000 pounds and had sharp horns and hoofs, they were difficult and dangerous to hunt with spears or arrows. However, Indians could use deep snow to their advantage; the heavy animal would sink into the snow while the hunters on snowshoes could stay on top. The safest way to kill a moose was to sneak up on one while it was feeding along a lake or river and drive it out into deep water. Then in canoes the hunters could overtake the animal and spear it from behind. The moose could not defend itself as well in water.

In the spring and summer, the Montagnais traveled to the rivers, using toboggans to help carry their possessions. There they speared salmon and eels. And sometimes they traveled all the way to the St. Lawrence River to harpoon seals. Occasionally on these trips the small nomadic bands would join up to form much larger groups. The mood after the long, isolated winter months was festive. However, spring and summer were the seasons when insects were abundant, especially black flies and mosquitoes. The Indians had to smear their bodies with seal oil to repel them.

Like most Algonquians, the Montagnais covered their cone-shaped wigwams with birchbark, a prized material in forests that had many more spruce and fir trees than birch trees. When the Montagnais could not find enough birchbark or elm bark, their second choice, they would do what their Naskapi friends and relatives to the north did—stretch animal hides over the wigwam frameworks. But the Montagnais would use moose hides, instead of the caribou hides the Naskapis used.

One custom of the Montagnais demonstrates just how hard their existence was in the Subarctic. When old people could no longer keep up on the constant

journeys in search of food, their families would not let them die of hunger and exposure. Instead, they would kill them as an act of mercy.

Many Algonquians of the eastern Subarctic, including the Montagnais, believed in the legend of the Windigos. (The Naskapis had a different name for these creatures—Atsan.) The Windigos were supposedly monsters, 20 to 30 feet high, who terrorized the northern forest. They had mouths with no lips but with long jagged teeth. They hissed when they breathed. They had claws for hands. They would eat animals if they had to, or other Windigos, but most of all they craved human flesh. Their mouths, eyes, and feet were steeped in blood. Every hunter lost in the woods, every child who disappeared, was thought to have been devoured by Windigos. Sometimes the Windigos took possession of human bodies and lived

Montagnais bone knife

inside them. These people with Windigo souls would start desiring human flesh and would become cannibals. The legend probably originated when humans resorted to cannibalism in the face of starvation. Having such fearful creatures as Windigos in Algonquian mythology served to discourage the practice in a land of little food and much hardship.

In spite of the extreme environment, the Montagnais survived year after year, century after century. Their numbers were stable until diseases brought to North America by whites caused their population to decline. Today, the remaining Montagnais live on reserves in northern Quebec, Canada. Most of them are still hunters and trappers, living a rugged existence and coping the same way their ancestors did.

Montauk-Shinnecock

Long Island, which extends eastward from New York City about 118 miles into the Atlantic Ocean, is the largest island in the United States, not counting islands in either Alaska or Hawaii. There were once many Algonquian bands living on Long Island, governed by as many as 13 chieftains (see "Algonquian"

and "Northeast Indians"). Many of these bands' names are familiar-sounding because they exist today as place names, such as Manhasset, Massapequa, Montauk, Patchogue, Poospatuck, and Shinnecock.

Some of the bands in the western part of Long Island, such as the Canarsees and Rockaways, spoke dialects similar to those spoken by the Algonquians on Manhattan Island. For that reason, these bands are generally classified among the Delaware or Wappinger Indians (see "Delaware" and "Wappinger"). But the bands in the central and eastern part of Long Island are classified in their own group. They were united in an alliance named after one of the most powerful bands, the Montauk Confederacy (pronounced MON-tawk).

The Montauks lived along the flat Atlantic Coast Plain that stretches southward from Long Island. As a result, their way of life was most similar to that of Algonquians living to the south, along the New Jersey, Delaware, and Virginia shoreline.

The Montauks planted their crops in the sandy lowlands. They speared fish and collected clams in the many bays and lagoons. They also hunted small mammals and gathered wild plant foods in the piney inland forests. Here too they could find the materials they needed for dugout canoes and wigwams.

Montauk-Shinnecock wigwam (unfinished, showing the sapling framework beneath a cattail covering)

The Montauks hunted whales on the open sea in their large dugouts. They also took advantage of "drift whales." The Montauks believed in a legendary figure named Moshup who stranded whales on beaches or in shallow waters in order to feed the people.

The Montauks also used the dugouts to cross the arm of the Atlantic Ocean that separates Long Island from Connecticut—the Long Island Sound. Here they could trade with other Algonquians, such as the Pequots and Narragansets who lived along the opposite shore (see "Pequot" and "Narraganset"). But contacts with the different groups were not always friendly. In the years just before white settlement, the Pequots attacked and conquered the Montauks. Then in later years, after the Pequots were defeated in the Pequot War, the Narragansets also made forays into Montauk territory.

The Montauks were generally on friendly terms with whites. Because of their location on the Atlantic, they had many early contacts with explorers from many European nations. They also traded with white settlers, first the Dutch in the early 1600s, then the English after 1664. The Long Island Indians were among the most productive manufacturers of wampum (sometimes called *sewan* or *siwan*), beads of polished shells strung together and used for ceremonial purposes, ornaments, and, especially after the whites came, money. In fact, Long Island was known to its native inhabitants as *Seawanhacky*, since it was such a good place to collect the seashells that were ground into the purple and white wampum beads. In later years, the Indians began using glass beads imported from Europe to make wampum. The European settlers also made wampum from glass beads to trade with the Indians for furs.

The population of the Indians on Long Island steadily declined after the arrival of whites. Part of the reason was intertribal warfare. In 1759, some of the Montauks took refuge from other Indians with the whites at Easthampton, Long Island. Others joined the Brotherton Indians up the Hudson River in 1788 (see "Mahican"). Still others lost their lives on whaling expeditions or in other maritime activities. One famous incident occurred in the winter of 1876, when Indians of the Shinnecock band, who were part of the rescue team trying to save the grounded English cargo ship *Circassian*, lost their lives in a violent storm. Yet, all in all, white diseases took the greatest toll on the Long Island Indians.

Since the 1700s, the small number of Montauk descendants have had to marry outside the tribe to keep up their numbers. As a result, many present-day Montauks are mixed-blooded, with white and black ancestry as well as Native American. The Montauks have the rights to two small reservations on Long Island. Like many of the reservations in the East, these are state reservations, not federal. Rights are guaranteed by the state of New York rather than by the federal government. The tribes holding these lands use the names Shinnecock and Poospatuck rather than the name Montauk.

The Shinnecocks (pronounced *SHIN-uh-cock*), who have 400 acres near Southampton, Long Island, sponsor a large annual powwow on Labor Day Weekend which draws Native American participants from all over North America. The *Shinnecock Indian Outpost* on the reservation sells Indian arts and crafts. The Shinnecocks also have a business enterprise, begun in 1984, called the Oyster Project. It is the first solar-assisted oyster hatchery ever developed.

Mound Builders

In the eastern part of North America, especially along the Ohio and Mississippi river valleys, there are thousands of mysterious mounds. It was realized long ago that these earthworks, many of them enormous and some in the shape of animals or people, were human-made. But it was not known who the makers were. Archaeologists of this century and the last have since provided the answers. It is now known that the Mound Builders were ancient Indians whose cultures lasted many centuries. The Mound Builders have been classified as three different cultural groups: Adena, Hopewell, and Mississippian.

The various Mound Builders lived during the phase of North American prehistory known as the Formative period, which followed the Paleolithic and Archaic periods (see "Prehistoric Indians"). The Formative period lasted from about 1000 B.C. until A.D. 1500 and was characterized by farming, house building, village life, pottery, weaving, plus other advances in technology. Along with the ancient cultures of the Southwest (see "Cliff Dwellers and Desert Farmers"), the Mound Builders had the most complex and organized way of life of all the Indians north of Mexico during this period. Some of their villages expanded into actual cities.

Adena Culture

The Adena culture lasted from approximately 1000 B.C. to A.D. 200. The name *Adena*, pronounced *uh-DEE-nuh*, comes from an estate near Chillicothe, Ohio, where a large mound stands. The Indians of the Adena culture also built mounds in territory that is now Kentucky, West Virginia, Indiana, Pennsylvania, and New York, primarily along the Ohio Valley.

Most of the Adena earthworks were burial mounds. Earthen hillocks were built up over burial pits or log-lined tombs. To make these imposing mounds in honor of their deceased leaders, the Indians dug up earth with sticks, bones, and shells, and carried it to the burial site in woven baskets or animal-skin bags. With each new burial, another layer of dirt was dumped on a mound, making it even higher.

The Adena Indians buried objects along with their leaders, just as the ancient Egyptians buried objects with their pharaohs under the great pyramids. At Adena sites, archaeologists have found beautifully crafted tools and ceremonial objects, including a wide range of stone, wood, bone, and copper tools; pottery; cloth woven from plant fibers; bone masks; stone pipes; stone tablets, often with bird designs; orna-

The Adena Pipe, made from catlinite

ments made from a mineral called mica; pearl beads; and stone and copper gorgets (worn over the throat).

In addition to burial mounds, the Adena Indians also constructed mounds with symbolic shapes. A famous example is the Great Serpent Mound near Peebles, Ohio. This earthwork is a rounded mound about four feet high, 15 to 20 feet across, and 1,330 feet long. When viewed from above, it has the shape of a snake, with head and jaws closing on another mound (probably representing an egg) and a coiled tail. Other Adena earthworks have geometric shapes, ridges of earth laid out in circles and usually surrounding the burial mounds.

The Adena Indians were primarily hunter-gatherers. They found enough game and wild plant foods in their homelands to be able to live in permanent villages of pole-framed houses covered with mud and thatch. Some Adena Indians might have grown sunflowers and pumpkins for food. Many of them eventually cultivated tobacco for smoking rituals.

It is not known for certain what became of the Adena Indians. Some of them might have been the ancestors of the Hopewell Indians whose culture came to displace them. Or perhaps the Hopewell Indians were outsiders who invaded Adena territory and killed off remaining Adena Indians.

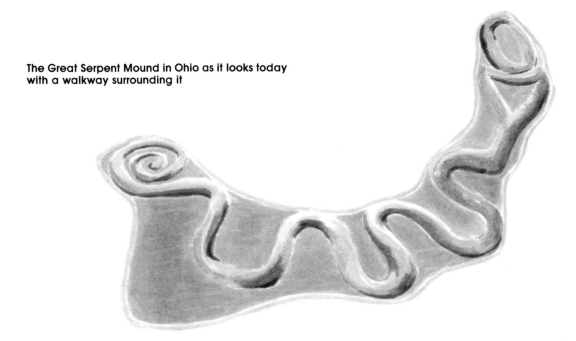

The Great Serpent Mound in Ohio as it looks today with a walkway surrounding it

Hopewell Culture

The Hopewell culture lasted from about 300 B.C. to A.D. 700. Like the Adena culture, it was centered along the Ohio Valley. Yet archaeologists have found Hopewell mounds and objects over a much wider area comprising the Illinois River Valley, the Mississippi River Valley, plus many other river valleys of the Midwest and East.

The Hopewell Indians established a wide trading network. At Hopewell sites, archaeologists have found objects made out of raw materials from distant locations, including obsidian (black volcanic glass) from as far away as the Rocky Mountains, copper from the Great Lakes, shells from the Atlantic Ocean, mica from the Appalachian Mountains, and alligator skulls and teeth from Florida. The Hopewell Indians were highly skilled craftsmen. They shaped raw materials into exquisite objects, such as stone pipes with human

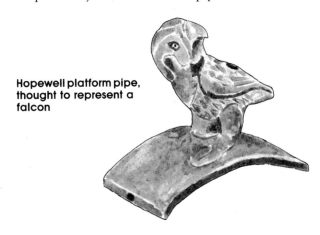

Hopewell platform pipe, thought to represent a falcon

and animal carvings; decorated pottery; ceramic figurines; obsidian spear points and knife blades; mica mirrors; shell drinking cups; pearl jewelry; gold and mica silhouettes (delicately carved in flat profiles); and copper headdresses and breast ornaments.

Like the Adena Indians, the Hopewell Indians placed these objects in tombs and under mounds. The Hopewell burial mounds were generally larger than Adena mounds. Many of them covered multiple burials and stood 30 to 40 feet high. Other Hopewell earthworks were mounds representing creatures. Still others served as walls, as much as 50 feet high and 200 feet wide at the base. These are often laid out in geometric shapes. At a Hopewell site in Newark, Ohio, over an area of four square miles, are found walls or enclosures in different shapes, including circles, parallel lines, a square, and an octagon.

The existence of these mounds indicates that the Hopewell Indians had a highly organized society. Villagers had to work in unison to build the giant earthworks, with their leaders and priests directing them. The trading expeditions required cooperation among the different villages.

The development of farming allowed villages to expand. Enough corn, beans, squash, and other crops could be cultivated to support growing populations. Hopewell villagers lived in domed structures, framed with poles and covered with sheets of bark, woven mats, or animal skins. The Hopewell dwellings were much like the wigwams of the later Algonquian people (see "Algonquian").

Perhaps the Hopewell Indians were direct ancestors of the later Indian tribes of eastern North America. Yet there is no proof of what happened to them and why their great culture fell into a state of decay. Changes in the climate, with prolonged periods of drought as well as crop failures, might have brought about the cultural decline. Warfare and epidemics could have also depleted their numbers and disrupted their way of life.

Mississippian Culture

The age of mound building was not over, however. Starting about A.D. 700, around the time of the demise of the Hopewell culture, a new culture evolved throughout much of eastern North America. It was centered along the Mississippi River and is therefore referred to as the Mississippian culture. Mississippian sites can be found from Florida to Oklahoma and as far north as Wisconsin. Mississippian Indians constructed mounds for a new purpose. They placed their places of worship on top of them. As a result, Mississippian Indians are also known as Temple Mound Builders.

One of the most exciting aspects in the study of prehistory is the question of contacts and influences between different cultures. Without hard evidence, such as an object from one culture found at the archaeological site of another, scholars have to guess about cultural connections, based on similarities in arts and crafts and other customs. A connection between the great Mesoamerican civilizations—the Olmecs, Mayas, Toltecs, and Aztecs (see those entries)—with early Indian cultures north of Mexico has long been theorized. For example, the Mississippian practice of placing temples on top of mounds is similar to the Mesoamerican practice of placing temples on top of stone pyramids. At various times in prehistory Indians most likely crossed the Gulf of Mexico in boats, perhaps even venturing up the Mississippi River to trade or to resettle.

A typical Mississippian mound had sloping sides and a flat top where the temple stood. Log steps ran up one side to a pole-and-thatch structure. Some of the mounds had terraced sides where other, smaller structures stood. These were homes of priests and nobles. The higher the rank of an individual, the higher he lived on the mound. The chieftain or king of a particular village often lived on top of his own mound. Other villagers—merchants, craftsmen, soldiers, hunters, farmers, and laborers—lived in pole-and-thatch huts surrounding the mounds. Some Mississippian dwellings were pit houses, with vertical logs extending from rectangular pits. Villagers conducted their business in the village's central open plaza.

The temple mounds could be enormous. For example, Monk's Mound at the Cahokia site in Illinois, covered 16 acres and stood 100 feet high. Archaeologists have guessed that it was built in 14 different stages, from about A.D. 900 to about 1150. Cahokia, once a great village—more properly called a city because it housed as many as 40,000 Indians—contained 85 mounds in all, both temple and burial mounds. In one burial mound, archaeologists have found remains of 110 young women, probably a sacrifice to the gods. The Indian city, covering about 4,000 acres near the Mississippi River where the Illinois River flows into it, had a central urban area and five suburbs.

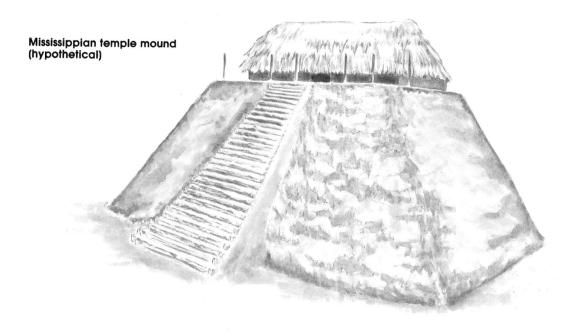

Mississippian temple mound (hypothetical)

Mississippian cedar mask with shell eyes and mouth

Cahokia was the largest Mississippian population center. Other large villages are known as Moundville in Alabama; Etowah and Ocmulgee in Georgia; Hiwassee Island in Tennessee; Spiro in Oklahoma; Belcher in Louisiana; Aztalan in Wisconsin; and Mount Royal in Florida. Many Temple Mound sites are state parks which welcome visitors. At some of them, there are ongoing archaeological excavations.

In order to support such large, centralized populations, Mississippian Indians had to practice farming on a large scale. They grew corn, beans, squash, pumpkins, and tobacco in the rich silt of riverbeds.

In addition to being master farmers, the Temple Mound Builders were skilled craftsmen, working in a variety of materials—clay, shells, marble, mica, a mineral called chert, copper, and feathers. They made highly refined tools, pottery, masks, gorgets, pipes, headdresses, and carvings.

Many of the ceremonial objects found at the Mississippian sites reveal symbols of death and human sacrifice—skulls, bones, buzzards, and weeping eyes. It is thought that the Temple Mound religion, called the Death Cult (or Buzzard Cult or Southern Cult), and its powerful priests served to unify the various villages. Trade between villages also helped to keep the peace.

Nevertheless, for some reason—warfare, overpopulation, drought, famine—the great Mississippian villages were abandoned. Cahokia ceased to be a thriving center about 1500. One theory has it that before European explorers reached the Temple Mound Indians, their diseases did. Coastal Indians might have unknowingly spread the European diseases inland through trade, starting deadly epidemics.

In any case, soon after about 1500, the custom of mound building stopped. Many eastern Indians, especially the tribes of the Southeast, continued to use the ancient mounds. Some of them, such as the Creeks, might have been direct descendants of the Temple Mound Builders (see "Creek"). Some tribes continued to practice many of the customs of the Mound Builders. The Natchez in particular had a society that scholars consider to be typical of their ancestors (see "Natchez").

Narraganset

The Narragansets, the "people of the point," lived in the part of the Northeast that is now Rhode Island, especially between the Providence and Pawcatuck rivers. They lived like other New England Algonquians (see "Algonquian" and "Northeast Indians"). They stayed most of the year in stockaded villages of dome-shaped wigwams. They combined farming with hunting, fishing, and gathering, making use of resources from forest, river, and ocean. Narragansett Bay is named after them (with an alternate spelling, both pronounced nah-ruh-GAN-sit).

The Narragansets played an important part in early colonial history and suffered many of the same consequences as the other tribes of the region. When the whites began settling the area in the early 1600s, the Narragansets had six main divisions, with six sagamores (subordinate chiefs) under one principal chief, or grand sachem. The Narragansets managed to avoid the first smallpox epidemic of 1616-20 that ravaged many of the native peoples after contacts with whites. But, in 1633, about 700 tribal members died in a second outbreak of the dreaded disease, which was carried from Europe by settlers.

The Narragansets were early allies of the English colonists, and some of their warriors fought against the Pequots in the Pequot War of 1636-37. In 1636, Canonicus, the grand sachem, sold tribal lands to Roger Williams, a renegade Puritan who broke away from the Massachusetts Bay Colony and founded Rhode Island Colony. Williams urged his fellow colonists to treat Indians humanely and to pay them fairly for their lands. In 1643, his dictionary of the Algonquian language was published, which helped further friendly relations with the Narragansets.

However, too many settlers ignored Roger Williams's advice and unfairly seized Indian lands. As a result, his friendship with the Narragansets was not enough to prevent them from joining the Wampanoags and Nipmucs in King Philip's War of 1675-76 against the colonists (see "Wampanoag"). Canonchet, a later grand sachem of the Narragansets, became the Indian chief King Philip's most important general in battle, with 3,500 braves under him.

It was the Narragansets who suffered the biggest defeat, which virtually ended the war—the Great Swamp Fight of December 1675. On a snowy day, a force of almost 1,000 Massachusetts, Connecticut, and Plymouth colonists, under Josiah Winslow, plus about 150 Mohegan warriors, attacked the Narraganset village near Kingston, Rhode Island. It was a bitter standoff for many hours, with the colonial militia unable to breach the Indian village's thick log walls that stood on high ground in the middle of a swamp. But the attackers finally broke through the rear entrance and drove the Narragansets out into the swamp by setting most of their 600 wigwams on fire.

The Narragansets lost more than 600 men, with 400 others captured and sold into slavery. Canonchet, the grand sachem, was brave to the end. When taken prisoner and sentenced to death, he said that, "It is well. I shall die before my heart is soft, before I have said anything unworthy of Canonchet."

When a Narraganset brave died, he was wrapped in skins or woven mats, along with his tools and weapons, so that he would be equipped for the journey to the God of Creation, who the Narragansets believed lived to their southwest.

After King Philip's War, some of the surviving Narragansets settled among Abnakis, Mahicans, and Niantics. Those who lived with the Niantics continued to use the Narraganset name. Some of their descendants joined the Brotherton Indians in 1788 (see "Mahican"). Other descendants still live in Rhode Island, near Charlestown.

In 1985, the state of Rhode Island returned to the Narraganset tribe two pieces of land of 900 acres each in the Charlestown area. The tribe had originally filed a claim in 1975 for land that had been taken away from them in 1880. At the time of the official transfer, the tribal secretary, Lawrence Ollivierre, expressed his feelings: "It's pretty difficult to be an Indian and not have your own land. It's like being a people without a country."

Naskapi

Because of language similarities, the Naskapis (pronounced *NAS-kuh-pee*) of Labrador are often grouped with the Montagnais tribe, their kinsmen to the south. But these two Algonquian peoples, although both well adapted to the Subarctic wilderness, had different ways of finding food. (See "Subarctic Indians"; "Algonquian"; and "Montagnais.")

Neither tribe farmed. In the winter months, the Montagnais depended primarily on the moose common to the forests of their own territory; the Naskapis, however, tracked the caribou herds that grazed on the grasses and lichens of the open plateau of the Labrador Peninsula, in present-day Canada. In their reliance on caribou, the Naskapis were like many of the western Subarctic peoples and certain Arctic Eskimos. Nomads, they followed the seasonal migration of the herds, using snowshoes and toboggans. The Naskapis used caribou hides rather than bark to cover their cone-shaped wigwams, and caribou thongs to bind their snowshoes.

Like the Montagnais, the Naskapis hunted small game such as the beaver, porcupine, otter, and a kind of bird called a grouse. They also fished the rivers that ran high with melted snow in the springtime, using stone, bone, and antler gear. Their favorite catch was trout. They used birchbark canoes to travel in the spring and summer, one way to find some relief from the abundant black flies and mosquitoes in their area.

Since they were so far north, where a layer of clothing could mean the difference between life and death in subzero weather, the Naskapis adopted certain Eskimo tricks of retaining body warmth. They often wore hoods attached to their snug caribou shirts, plus fur trousers and stockings rather than breechcloths and leggings. And, in the coldest months, they wore

Naskapi double-ended paint stick of caribou antler, used to make designs on leather

double layers of clothing with the fur facing their bodies on the inner layer and facing out on the outer layer.

The Naskapis had a special fondness for bright colors, perhaps because their environment was so harsh and bleak. They decorated their shirts with bright geometric patterns in red, yellow, or blue. They also liked to tattoo their bodies, as did their Cree neighbors. The Crees pushed a needle through their skin, then ran a wet thread dipped in charcoal through the hole. The Naskapis, however, made cuts on the surface, then used a piece of stone to rub the charcoal or soot into the skin. Both methods were painful and served as a test of courage as well as decoration (see "Cree").

The Naskapis also proved their bravery in warfare, usually against their traditional enemies, the Eskimos, who bordered their territory to the north (see "Eskimo"). But they were not as ferocious as the Montagnais, who adopted some of the Iroquois fighting techniques (see "Iroquois").

Murder was uncommon in Naskapi society, as was the case among most Indian peoples. A killing in self-defense would go unpunished. But in an unprovoked murder, the slain person's relatives could take revenge. If they failed to do so, a band chief might call a council of elders. If they decided the killing was not in self-defense, the guilty man would be told to walk away. Then warriors chosen by the chief as executioners would shoot the condemned man in the back. No one would even bury his corpse.

Although hunger was often a problem, the Naskapis abhorred cannibalism even if survival

Naskapi painted leather mask

depended on it. They believed in the existence of monsters called Atsan—evil creatures of the north country that kidnapped children and ate them, much like the Windigos in the legends of other Subarctic Algonquians.

For a long time after the arrival of whites—first the French, who became their allies and trading partners, and then the English—the Naskapis were able to maintain their traditional ways since they lived so far from most white settlements. But white diseases eventually depleted their numbers and devastated their culture. Remaining Naskapis hold reserve lands in northern Quebec. Many live by hunting, braving the fierce elements of the north country as their ancestors once did.

Natchez

When one envisions Native North Americans, one usually thinks about Plains Indians galloping after buffalo on horseback, or chiefs in eagle-feather warbonnets sitting in front of tepees and passing a peace pipe among them. Or one imagines Woodland Indians prowling through woods with tomahawks in hand, or paddling over rivers and lakes in birchbark canoes.

One rarely thinks about a king, called the Great Sun, with absolute powers over all his subjects. One rarely calls to mind an image of this monarch, with a crown of red-tasseled swan feathers, seated on a throne of goose feathers and furs, high on a mound above the rest of his village; or a temple located atop another

Natchez house

nearby mound, occupied by priests with shaved heads; or dwellings—four-sided and constructed of straw and sun-baked mud with arched thatch roofs—placed in precise rows around a central plaza; or members of the warrior class, tattooed from head to foot, strolling about, fanning themselves and watching commoners at their work.

These images remind one of Indian civilizations of Middle America (see "Olmec"; "Maya"; "Toltec"; and "Aztec"). In fact, it is thought that Mesoamerican cultures did influence the ancient Temple Mound culture of North America (see "Mound Builders"). And it is thought that certain among the Indians whom Europeans contacted as late as the early 1700s were the last remnants of the once widespread Temple Mound civilization. These were the Natchez Indians (pronounced *NATCH-is*). They lived along the lower Mississippi River in territory that is now part of the states of Mississippi and Louisiana. They spoke a language isolate (unlike other languages) referred to simply as Natchez. They are considered part of the Southeast Culture Area (see "Southeast Indians").

Social Structure

Other Southeast Indians shared some of the Natchez cultural traits. For example, the Creeks also had chiefs with great authority as well as an agriculture-based economy and organized village life. Yet, when whites arrived and began recording information about the native peoples, the Natchez had by far the most elaborate caste system. A caste system is a division of society into social classes, with strict rules governing behavior.

In addition to the king, known as the Great Sun, there was a royal family at the top of the pecking order. The king's mother, referred to as White Woman, lived on top of her own mound and served as the king's adviser. From among his brothers or uncles, called Little Suns, were chosen a war chief and a head priest. His sisters were called Women Suns and also had influence and power among all the other Natchez.

Below the Suns were the Nobles, an aristocratic class decided by heredity. Nobles had positions of rank in war parties and village functions. Below them were the Honored Men and Honored Women, who were lesser nobles. One could achieve this social status through deeds, such as bravery in warfare, or piety in religious matters.

Below the royalty and aristocracy was a class of commoners, called Stinkards (although not in their presence, because the name offended them). They performed all the menial tasks, such as farming and building mounds.

But there was a bizarre twist to this rigid social structure. All grades of royalty and nobility, even the Great Sun himself, could not marry among their own class. They had to marry Stinkards. Stinkards could marry among themselves and their children would naturally be Stinkards too. But, when a male from the upper classes had children, they were always a grade below him. For instance, children of male Suns and Stinkards were automatically nobles. The children of Nobles or Honored Men and Stinkards were automatically Stinkards.

On the other hand, the children of Women Suns and Stinkards were Suns; the children of female Nobles and Stinkards were Nobles; and the children of Honored Women were Honored People. In other words, although the men had the greater decision-making power in Natchez society, social rank was decided through the female line. And Stinkards had the opportunity to better their lives through marriage.

There was another strict rule governing the behavior of the nobility. When a Noble died, his or her Stinkard mate and servants would have to give up their lives to accompany the deceased to the next world.

This complex social system of the Natchez endured long after the arrival of Europeans in the Natchez homeland—first the Spanish in the 1500s (Hernando de Soto and his companions probably made contact in 1541-43); then the French in the 1600s (Rene Robert Cavelier de la Salle was the first to use the Natchez name in writings about his descent of the Mississippi in 1682). The caste system continued into the following century, when the French established a mission among the Natchez in 1706, and then, after 1713, a trading post and fort. Yet, in 1729, Natchez culture was disrupted because of a war with the French. Soon afterward, the tribe faded to extinction.

The Natchez Revolt

The cause of the Natchez Revolt was a land dispute. In order to keep the peace between Indians and whites and to encourage settlement by whites, the French had constructed Fort Rosalie overlooking the Mississippi River and the main Natchez village. The Natchez, many of whom were sympathetic to the French, accepted the fort and the garrison of French soldiers in their midst. Tattooed Serpent and Tattooed Arm, the brother and mother of the Great Sun, were especially devoted allies of the French. When Tattooed Serpent died, however, his brother began listening more to the tribe's anti-French faction.

Sieur Chepart, recently appointed the new governor of Louisiana, was oblivious to the factions within the tribe. Moreover, he was arrogant. He decided he wanted the site of the Natchez Great Village for his plantation and ordered immediate evacuation by the Indians. Rather than submit to this insult, the Great Sun, his priests, and his warriors plotted a rebellion.

At the time of the first autumn frost of 1729, Natchez war parties attacked Fort Rosalie and other French settlements along the Mississippi River, killing about 250 and capturing about 300 more. One of those captured was Sieur Chepart. The Natchez warrior-nobles wanted their revenge, but they did not want to soil their weapons with the blood of this French scoundrel. So they had a Stinkard club him to death.

The Yazoo Indians, a tribe living along the Mississippi north of the Natchez, joined them in the uprising and killed a missionary and French soldiers stationed in their territory (see "Yazoo"). But the Choctaws to the east, who had promised the Natchez support, sided with the French instead, as did the Tunicas to the north (see "Choctaw" and "Tunica").

The French sent two invading armies against the Natchez and succeeded in defeating and dispersing the tribe. Natchez captives were sold into slavery in the Caribbean. Other Natchez managed to hide out for a time and keep up their resistance, but without much effect. Some survivors settled with other tribes of the region and gradually lost their Natchez identity. And so the last traces of the fascinating Temple Mound culture came to an end along with the tribe known as the Natchez.

Navajo

Art and Religion

For the Navajos, as for all Indians, art and religion were intertwined. Art served a ceremonial purpose, as a way to relate to spiritual beings that the Navajos believed existed in both the natural and supernatural worlds. It was also a way to be closer to one's ancestors and a way to influence the spiritual beings to affect the weather or cure the sick. The Navajos had highly developed art and rituals for these purposes.

Detail of a Navajo sand painting

One Navajo art form was oral chants. The Navajos and most other Indians did not use the written word to record their legends. Rather, they recited their myths in songs and poetry, usually to musical accompaniment. In the case of the Navajos, the chants were especially long. For example, their *Mountain Chant* has 13 different episodes, containing 161 songs. These tell of the mythological origins of the Navajo peoples—creation myths, as they are called, or emergence myths. The *Night Chant* has 24 episodes with 324 songs. Navajo shamans, or medicine men, used these in healing ceremonies.

There were many more chants, passed on from one generation to the next through the spoken word without the help of writings. Fascinating creatures—many of them a combination of animals and people—come to life in these chants. Here is part of a creation myth called *Song of Coyote Who Stole the Fire*:

I am frivolous Coyote; I wander around.
I have seen the Black God's Fire; I wander around.
I stole his fire from him; I wander around.
I have it! I have it!
I am changing Coyote; I wander around.
I have seen the bumble-bee's fire; I wander around.
I stole his fire from him; I wander around.
I have it! I have it!

The coyote plays an important role in the mythology of tribes all over North America. Indians respected coyotes for their cunning and their ability to survive in forest, mountain, prairie, and desert country. In some Indian stories, the mythical culture hero Coyote helps people. But usually he is a trickster who plays practical jokes on people or a meddler who ruins people's plans. He is often regarded as greedy. Whether good or bad, however, Coyote is always clever.

Coyote was one of the Holy People in Navajo religion. Changing Woman, or the Earth Mother, was another. Unlike Coyote, she was always kind to the Navajos and gave their ancestors corn. Spider Woman, who taught the Navajos weaving, and Spider

A Navajo woman weaving a blanket on her loom

Man, who warned the Navajos of coming danger, could be mean like Coyote. The Hero Twins, who killed the monsters to make the world safe, could also turn nasty. There were many more Holy People among the Navajo gods. There were also the *chinde*, who the Navajos believed were malevolent ghosts of dead Navajos inhabiting the earth. Ghosts caused sickness and accidents, they thought. The Navajos also believed in witches. These were real Navajos who practiced black magic to harm others for revenge or for their own personal gain.

In addition to the mythology, poetry, songs, and music of their oral tradition, the Navajos developed an art form known as sand painting. Other Indians painted permanent designs on pottery, clothing, and tepees. Yet, in the Southwest, Indians created temporary drawings on the ground. The Navajos probably adopted this cultural trait from the Pueblo Indians, who might have learned it from the Yaqui tribe (see "Pueblo Indians" and "Yaqui").

The sand paintings were actually altars used in healing ceremonies. The animals and designs had symbolic meanings. The Indians created these intricate and colorful dry paintings by carefully trickling powders of minerals such as ocher, ground sandstone, gypsum, and charcoal into patterns on clean sand. At the end of the rituals, the paintings were destroyed. Participants took some of the powder away with them for its magical properties.

A distinction is usually made between arts and crafts. When an object has a practical purpose, it is usually thought of as a craft. Yet, with many Native Americans, their crafts were so highly developed that they can be thought of as true art. An example of this is Navajo weaving. The Navajos learned weaving from the Pueblo Indians. The Southwest Indians did not have domesticated sheep for wool until the Spanish introduced sheep, along with goats, to the region. Navajo women learned to spin the wool from sheep, dye the threads, and then weave them on a loom. The finished blankets and rugs had bright geometric designs, or in some cases pictures of animals. They are now treasured all over the world as wall-hangings.

Another Navajo craft considered a fine art is jewelry-making. Navajo men learned the art of silversmithing from the Mexicans in the mid-1900s and passed this skill on to Pueblo Indians. The Navajos became famous for their silverwork, especially necklaces, bracelets, and belt-buckles.

Navajo silver and turquoise bracelet (modern)

Location and Language

The Navajo artists we have been discussing lived (and still live) in territory that is now northern Arizona and New Mexico, plus a much smaller part of southern Utah and Colorado. The heart of their ancestral homeland was situated on the lower part of the Colorado Plateau between the San Juan and Little Colorado rivers. In Indian studies, this region is considered part of the Southwest Culture Area (see "Southwest Indians").

The Navajos, like the other Athapascan-speaking people in the region, the Apaches, came to the Southwest later than other Indians (see "Athapascan" and "Apaches"). From archaeological evidence, it is thought that the first Apache bands came about A.D. 825 and the Navajos came about 1025, long before the European nations sent their explorers to North America.

The name *Navajo*, or *Navaho* (both pronounced *NAH-vuh-ho*), is not Athapascan, however. It is a Pueblo Indian word, referring to an area of land in the Southwest. The Spanish started calling the Navajos by the name *Apaches de Navajo* to distinguish them from the Apaches, and this name has stuck through history. In their own language, the Navajos were the *Dine*, meaning "the people." They called their homeland *Dinetah*.

Food and Shelter

When the Navajos first came to the Southwest, they survived in the rugged, dry environment as nomadic bands of hunter-gatherers. Along with their kinsmen, the Apaches, they launched many raids on the agricultural Pueblo Indians for food, property, women, and slaves. Throughout most of their history, the Navajos were feared by Indian, Spanish, Mexican, and American inhabitants of the Southwest. Although they continued their raiding activity, the Navajos, through contacts with the Pueblo peoples, gradually adopted new cultural traits. From the other Indians, they learned farming, in addition to some of the skills already mentioned above, such as weaving and sand painting. They probably also learned how to make pottery, as well as new basketmaking techniques from the Pueblo peoples. As we have already discussed, the Navajos acquired sheep and goats from the Spanish. But they did not use up their supply for food, as the Apaches did. Instead, they raised them to increase their herds, which they kept for meat, milk, and wool. Livestock, especially sheepherding, soon became essential to Navajo economy. The Navajos first acquired horses at about the same time they acquired sheep and goats—the mid to late 1600s. Horses gave them greater mobility on their raids.

Navajo hogan (facing east)

The Navajos lived in shelters called hogans. These were generally cone-shaped, but later they were built with six or eight sides. Logs and poles were used for the framework, which was covered with bark and earth, and, in later years, with stone or adobe. The doorways of the hogans always faced east.

Warfare with Whites

The Spanish first became aware of the Navajos in the early 1600s. They sent missionaries to the tribe's homeland in the mid-1700s, but they had little success in converting the Navajos to Catholicism.

In the late 1700s and early 1800s, the Navajos became involved in a cycle of raids and counter-raids with the Spanish and Mexicans who rode northward for slaves, kidnapping Navajo children. In response, Navajos traveled south to prey on Mexican settlements, taking food, livestock, and slaves. The Navajos also made frequent attacks on early travelers of the Santa Fe Trail, the route connecting Missouri to New Mexico.

The Americans occupied New Mexico in 1846 during the Mexican War. Mexico did not formally cede the Southwest to the United States until the Treaty of Guadalupe Hidalgo two years later. Yet it was during the Mexican War that U.S. troops established American policy toward the Navajos. On taking control of the region, Colonel Stephen Kearny informed the Anglo-Americans and Mexican-Americans that they would henceforth be protected from Indian attacks. He did not inform the Indians, however, that they would be protected from Mexican slave raids.

During the winter of that same year, Colonel Alexander Doniphan led his Missouri volunteers into Navajo country to punish the Indians for stealing livestock. In their rugged highlands, the Navajos managed to avoid any major engagements. Most of the winter, they hid out in the deep and jagged Canyon de Chelly, their sacred stronghold. During this period, they learned that the Americans were dangerous new landlords. In 1846 and 1849, the Navajos signed treaties with the United States government, but they remained militant until the 1860s.

A point of contention between the Navajos and the soldiers during the 1850s was the grazing land at the mouth of Canyon Bonito near Fort Defiance. The soldiers wanted the pastureland for their horses. Yet the Navajos had led their horses there to graze for generations and continued to do so. The soldiers shot the Navajo horses. Then the Navajos raided army herds to make up for their losses.

The issue reached a climax in 1860 when the famous Navajo chief Manuelito and his ally Barboncito led warriors in an attack on the fort. The Indians nearly captured it but were driven back. Colonel Edward Canby led troops into the Chuska Mountains in pursuit of the warriors. Once again, the Indians disappeared in the craggy terrain, appearing only for sudden attacks on the army before vanishing again into the wilderness.

Another fight broke out in 1861, during the Civil War. The incident that sparked this fighting was a horse race at Fort Lyon between Navajo and army mounts. The Navajos claimed that a soldier had cheated by cutting one of their mount's reins. When the judges refused to hold the race again, the angry Indians rioted. The soldiers fired artillery into the Indian crowd, killing 10.

The troubles continued. By 1862, during the Civil War, Union troops had driven the Confederate troops out of New Mexico. They then turned their attention to the Indians, both the Apaches and Navajos. General James Carleton, the new commander of the Department of New Mexico, chose Colonel Christopher "Kit" Carson as his leader in the field. Carson, a former fur trader, scout, and Indian agent, knew Indians well. He moved first against the Mescalero Apaches. Then he began his campaign against the Navajos.

Rather than try to defeat the elusive Navajos in battle in their mesa and canyon country, Carson first began a scorched-earth offensive. During a six-month period in 1863, his men destroyed Navajo fields, orchards, and hogans, and confiscated their livestock. Then in January 1864, as a final blow against the Navajos, his troops advanced on Canyon de Chelly. They blocked the steep-walled canyon at both ends, then flushed out the pockets of resistance.

The will of the *Dine* had been broken. By March, about 6,000 half-starving Navajos had trickled into army posts, and, by the end of the year, another 2,000, making the Navajo surrender the largest in all the Indian wars. Manuelito and many of the remaining 4,000 Navajos surrendered in 1866. In the meantime, the army carried out its plan to relocate the Navajos, along with Apache prisoners, to the eastern part of New Mexico, at Bosque Redondo near Fort Sumner on the barren flats of the Pecos River Valley. About 200 Navajos died on the 300-mile trek eastward. The Navajos called this terrible time in their history the Long Walk.

The Navajos were miserable at Bosque Redondo, suffering from outbreaks of disease, shortages of supplies, infertile soil for planting, and quarrels with the Apaches. It is estimated that 2,000 Navajos died during their stay there. A delegation of chiefs, including Manuelito, traveled to Washington to plead their case for a return to their homeland. Finally, in 1868, the federal government granted the Navajos 3.5 million acres of reservation lands in the Chuska Mountains. The Navajos returned westward over the trail of the Long Walk and began rebuilding their lives.

Navajos Today

The Navajos are currently the largest tribe in North America and have the most reservation lands, now 16 million acres, including the Navajo Reservation, which is mostly in Arizona, with part in New Mexico and Utah; and the much smaller Canoncito and Ramah reservations in New Mexico. During World War II, Navajo marines became famous for the use of their native language as a combat communication code which the enemy was unable to decipher.

Because of mineral deposits on the extensive Navajo reservation lands, some tribal members have become wealthy in recent years. Peter Macdonald, Navajo tribal chairman as well as chairman of the intertribal organization known as the Council of Energy Resources Tribes, has been called the most powerful Indian in North America.

Yet not all the Navajos are wealthy, despite the oil, gas, coal, and uranium on their lands. Some prefer the traditional ways of life. With modern irrigation methods, some Navajos have been able to farm the previously infertile soil of their homelands. Others earn a modest living from raising sheep, goats, and cattle, herding their animals in the isolated areas of their reservation lands. Many practice traditional Navajo artwork, especially weaving and silverwork, to supplement their income. Some leave the reservation to seek work elsewhere, often as migrant agricultural workers.

It is the poor Navajos who will suffer from a federal law passed in 1974 called the Navajo-Hopi Land Settlement Act, which attempts to establish permanent boundaries. The Navajo Reservation surrounds the Hopi Reservation in Arizona (see "Hopi"), and the Navajos have come to live on lands that were reserved for the Hopis in the late 1800s. Yet most Hopis want their Navajo friends and neighbors, and in some cases their relatives by marriage, to be able to remain where they are. They do not want the land fenced any more than the Navajo sheepherders do. Nor do they want the land ravaged by strip-mining. They consider Big Mountain, situated at the center of the territory in question, a sacred site where peoples of both tribes

Detail of a Navajo blanket

have lived in harmony for years. They believe the mountain is the source of energy and healing for both tribes. The people who feel this way are the traditionalists among the Hopis and Navajos. Many still practice ancient art forms and ancient religious rituals.

Together, traditional Hopis and Navajos have formed a Navajo-Hopi Unity Council to work to repeal the law, which they view as unfair. They consider it the work of a few men on the Hopi Tribal Council and the Navajo Tribal Council, as well as executives of the mining companies, lawyers, and politicians. They claim that these forces created the issue of a land dispute between the two tribes for their own personal profit. About 4,000 Navajos will be relocated if the law is carried out. According to the powerful movie *Broken Rainbow*, which won the Oscar for best documentary film in 1985, taking the people from the land on which they have lived all their lives would be a modern version of the cruel Long Walk from Navajo history.

Nez Perce

"I will fight no more forever." These are among the most famous Indian words ever spoken. In 1877, at the time the Nez Perce Indian called Chief Joseph spoke them, many Indians of the West had come to the conclusion that continuing war with the much more numerous whites was hopeless and that their Indian way of life would never be the same.

Nez Perce is a French name, given to the tribe by fur traders, meaning "pierced noses." It can be pronounced the English way, *nes-PURSE*, or the French way, *nay-per-SAY*. Some members of the tribe did wear nose pendants, but not the majority. The Indians of this tribe called themselves *Nimipu*, meaning "the people." They were also called by the name *Sahaptin*, or *Shahaptin*, by nearby Salishian-speaking Indians, and by the name *Chopunnish* by Lewis and Clark. The name *Sahaptin* has come to identify the Nez Perce language, which was related to Penutian languages.

The Nez Perces lived in territory that is now central Idaho, southeastern Washington State, and northeastern Oregon. The heart of their homeland was in the vicinity of the Snake and Salmon rivers. These rivers merge with the Columbia River, which drains the high plateau country between the Rocky Mountains to the east and the Cascade Mountains to the west toward the Pacific Ocean. As a result, Indians of this region are often discussed in terms of the Plateau Culture Area (see "Plateau Indians").

Lifeways

The Nez Perces and other Plateau tribes did not farm but wandered the dry, rugged high country in search of a variety of foods, moving their village sites with the changing seasons. Important foods were fish, especially salmon, which swam upriver from the ocean to spawn and lay their eggs; mammals, especially elk, deer, mountain sheep, and rabbits; and wild plant foods, especially camas (lily) bulb and roots, and berries.

The Nez Perces were inventive in their fishing gear, using a number of techniques. They stood on the bank or on platforms they built and thrust at fish with long-handled spears. They also used nets, both hand-held nets on long poles and large weighted nets attached to floats. The Nez Perces also caught fish in small traps made from poles and brush, as well as in large enclosures called weirs. They normally did not fish with hooks and lines during the salmon spawning runs.

The Nez Perces had different houses for warm and cold weather. The warm-weather houses were easy to assemble and disassemble for moving from one place to another, such as to a streambed in late spring during the first salmon run. These temporary shelters consisted of poles in the shape of a ridged tent or a slanted lean-to, covered with mats of woven plant matter.

Earth-covered pit houses served as the Nez Perces' winter houses. A pole framework was made into a conical shape by erecting a large post in the center of a round pit and extending numerous other poles from its top to the edge of the pit. Then the roof poles were covered with mats of cedar bark, sagebrush, and other plants, as well as packed grass and earth. A Nez Perce village usually consisted of five or six of these dwellings.

Several families lived in each pit house. But the Nez Perces and other Plateau tribes were not organized into groups of families called clans, as many other Indian peoples were. They had shamans, or medicine men, but they did not have secret societies. Their chiefs were not as powerful as some other tribes' chiefs were. Their political, social, and religious organization was much looser than that of the Northwest Coast In-

A Nez Perce salmon fisherman on a river platform

dians, their neighbors west of the Cascade Mountains (see "Northwest Indians").

The Nez Perces did not make pottery. They did, however, weave exquisite baskets, which they used for cooking, by placing heated stones in them, and for gathering wild plants. They also wove soft bags of marsh plants with intricate designs.

To make their clothes, the Nez Perces used cedar bark, deerskin, and rabbit-skin. The women were famous for their handsome basket hats, which they wove out of dried leaves.

In the early 1700s, the Nez Perces acquired the horse through trade with other tribes. They rapidly became skilled horse-breeders and horse-trainers, as did other tribes of the region, such as the Cayuses and Palouses (see "Cayuse" and "Palouse"). Horses changed the life of the Nez Perces. Now they had more mobility and could range farther for food, even venturing onto the Plains east of the Rockies to hunt buffalo. Instead of

the small mat tents and lean-tos, they began using large hide tepees, like those of the Plains tribes, when on hunting and fishing trips (see "Plains Indians").

Early Contacts with Whites

White America was unaware of the Nez Perces until Meriwether Lewis and William Clark returned home in 1806 after their famous expedition, and later published their journals. The explorers reported how the friendly Nez Perces had provided them with food and shelter in the fall of 1805 and had even sent guides along to help them on part of their trip.

In the years following the Lewis and Clark Expedition, fur traders arrived in Nez Perce country: first the French Canadians, then the British Canadians, and then the Americans. Missionaries also soon began arriving. The Nez Perces proved reliable friends to these outsiders.

In 1855, at the Walla Walla Council, tribal leaders peacefully and readily agreed to the terms offered by whites. In exchange for some of their territory for white settlement, the various Nez Perce bands were guaranteed the rest of their lands, along with schools, money, livestock, and tools.

Yet the whites broke their promises. In the early 1860s, many miners came to Nez Perce country seeking gold. Some decided to build their homes on Indian lands. In 1863, white officials, supporting the settlers over the Indians, convinced some Nez Perce bands to sign an agreement giving up more lands. But other bands refused. A man named Old Joseph was the chief of a band living in the Wallowa Valley of northeastern Oregon. Missionaries had earlier converted him to Christianity, but on learning that the whites were trying to take his beloved homeland, he tore up his Bible.

Still, in spite of the threat to their lands, which were the center of their existence and the source of their well-being, the Nez Perces kept the peace. Nez Perces even bragged that in all their history, they had never killed a white man.

The Nez Perce War

This situation changed, however. Old Joseph died in 1871. Two of his sons, Joseph and Ollikut, became the leaders of the Wallowa band. In 1877, the band still lived in their ancestral valley. By this time, even more settlers wanted their valley for its good grazing land. White officials gave the band 30 days to relocate to the Nez Perce Reservation at Lapwai, Idaho Territory.

It was during this period that violence erupted. Young warriors attacked and killed a group of whites who had earlier mistreated Indians. The tradition of peace had ended. Joseph, who had always been a friend to whites, now gave his support to the rebels. He joined them at their hiding place at White Bird Canyon on the Salmon River in Idaho.

A detachment of cavalry was sent out to locate the Indians in June 1877. A party of six Nez Perces approached under a flag of truce to negotiate with the army. The soldiers, ignoring the white flag, fired at them. The Indians fired back, killing two soldiers. In the ensuing Battle of White Bird Creek, the Indians killed 34 whites and suffered no fatalities themselves.

Thus began the Nez Perce War. This Indian war, sometimes called the Flight of the Nez Perce, is one of the most remarkable stories of pursuit and escape in military history. The winding flight through the wilderness took the Indians 1,700 miles, through parts of three territories (soon to be states): Idaho, Wyoming, and Montana. The persistent Indians climbed

through mountains: the Bitterroot, Absaroka, and Bear Paw ranges in the Rocky Mountain chain. They descended canyons. They walked over many stretches of rocky and barren plains. They crossed many rivers: the Bitterroot, Yellowstone, Musselshell, and Missouri to name a few.

During this epic journey, the Indians were chased by three armies. They fought numerous battles: Clearwater Creek in Idaho in July; Big Hole Valley (Montana) in August; Camas Creek (Idaho) in August; Canyon Creek and Cow Island (Montana) in September; and Bear Paw (Montana) in October. The Nez Perces, until the final battle, consistently outsmarted, outflanked, and outfought the larger white forces.

There were other adventures as well. In one incident, the soldiers went to a lot of trouble to build a barricade blocking the Lolo Pass through the Bitterroot Mountains out of Idaho into Montana. However, the Indians managed to avoid a fight by leading their horses along the face of a cliff. Because the barricade served no purpose for the troops, they called it Fort Fizzle. In another incident, the Nez Perces entered the recently formed Yellowstone National Park in the northwest corner of Wyoming. The tourists were startled to see Indians marching through their midst. But the Nez Perces treated them well.

There were many fascinating personalities who played an important part in the conflict. In addition to Chief Joseph and his younger brother Ollikut, there were the Indians Looking Glass, Toohoolhoolzote, Red Echo, Five Wounds, Rainbow, and White Bird. There was also the mixed-blood Lean Elk, who was called Poker Joe by the whites. All of them played a part in the decision-making and military strategy. The Nez Perces made many of their decisions in council. But the wise Joseph became the most important leader because of his quiet strength and because he best understood the ways of the whites.

Leading the whites was a one-armed general named Oliver Howard. He was a humane man who had founded Howard University to provide an education for newly freed slaves. In the Nez Perce campaign, however, he found himself in pursuit of a group of formerly peaceful Indians who had originally wanted only their homeland and now wanted only their freedom in Canada. Many died along the way. With every additional mile of the long trek, the survivors were increasingly weary, hungry, and desperate for survival.

The Nez Perces never reached Canada. Their valiant march fell only 30 miles short. The troops overtook them once and for all at Snake Creek in the Bear Paw Mountains. It was at Bear Paw, after six days of fighting, that Chief Joseph gave his famous surrender speech: "Tell General Howard I know his heart. What he told me before, I have in my heart. I am tired of fighting. Our chiefs are killed. Looking Glass is dead. Toohoolhoolzote is dead. It is the young men who say yes or no. He who led the young men is dead [Ollikut]. It is cold and we have no blankets. The little children are freezing to death. My people, some of them, have run away to the hills, and have no blankets, no food. No one knows where they are—perhaps freezing to death. I want to have time to look for my children and see how many I can find. Maybe I shall find them among the dead. Hear me, my chiefs, I am tired. My heart is sick and sad. From where the sun now stands, I will fight no more forever."

Chief Joseph was never allowed to return to his ancestral Wallowa Valley. Officials sent him and others of his people to Kansas, then to the Indian Territory, and finally to the Colville Reservation in Washington State where he died in 1904. The reservation doctor reported that "Joseph died of a broken heart."

Today, there are descendants of the Nez Perces living on the Colville Reservation near Nespelem, Washington. Most Nez Perces live at the Nez Perce Reservation near Lapwai, Idaho. Many earn a living through leasing lands. Other Nez Perces, as is the case with all Indian tribes, have left the reservations to settle in cities, where work is easier to find.

Nipmuc

In the state of Massachusetts, the low coastal plains rise up to an inland plateau. The plateau is separated from even higher country to the west, the Berkshire Hills, by the Connecticut River. On this central plateau, covered with rich topsoil and dense woods, and coursed by swift-flowing rivers, once lived bands of Algonquians (see "Algonquian" and "Northeast Indians"). There were many different bands and villages, but they came to be known together as Nipmucs.

Their name, pronounced *NIP-muck*, is derived from the Algonquian word *nipmaug*, for "fresh water fishing place." The fact that they primarily used inland freshwater lakes and rivers for their fishing rather than the Atlantic Ocean marks their major difference from many other New England Algonquians who lived closer to the coast. In other ways—such as their hunting and farming methods, their tools, and their beliefs—they were much like their other Algonquian neighbors. The Nipmucs were noted in particular for their basketmaking, weaving, and leatherwork.

Historically, too, their story is linked to other area tribes. The Nipmucs were associated in early colonial years with the Massachuset tribe, and many of them also became Praying Indians (see "Massachuset"). But then in 1675, most of the Nipmuc braves joined the Wampanoags and Narragansets in King Philip's War (see "Wampanoag" and "Narraganset"). At the end of the war, many Nipmuc survivors joined Algonquian kinsmen, such as the Mahicans on the Hudson River (see "Mahican"). Others joined Algonquians in Canada.

The Nipmucs have one of the smallest reservations in the East, only 11.9 acres. It is called the Hassanamisco Reservation, after a village and tribal name. The Hassanamiscos once held the territory around what is now Grafton, Massachusetts. Before 1728, the reservation consisted of 8,000 acres. But most of the land was lost when tribal leaders were tricked into selling it for no payment at all. In 1848, the state set aside the tiny piece that now remains.

Nootka

Vancouver Island lies off the coast of the Pacific Northwest in Canadian waters, separated from the rest of the province of British Columbia by narrow straits. It is the largest island off western North America, approximately 285 miles long and 80 miles wide at its widest point. The island is made up of exposed parts of mountains in the Coast Range, their bases submerged in water. The tallest peak on the island, Golden Hinde Mountain, is 7,219 feet above sea level. Flat

lands extend inland for a distance from the shore on the eastern side of the island before the foothills begin. The more rugged and rocky western side is indented with fjords and inlets. There is more rainfall on the island than in any other place in North America. The island is forested with many lakes and streams.

The rugged western part of Vancouver Island was the homeland of the Nootka Indians. The name Nootka (pronounced *NOOT-kuh*), the meaning of which is unknown, was originally applied to a group of people on Nootka Sound. But it has since come to be used for more than 20 tribes of the Aht Confederacy. These tribes all spoke related dialects of the Wakashan language family.

The Nootkas are classified as part of the Northwest Coast Culture Area (see "Northwest Coast Indians"). Like other Indians of the Pacific Northwest, the Nootkas fished for salmon, halibut, and herring; hunted game in the forest; foraged for roots and berries; lived in long cedar-plank houses; and carved giant totem poles.

The Nootkas also shaped six different types of large dugout canoe. They made hats of woven fiber which have come to be called Nootka hats. They determined wealth by the number of possessions and practiced the custom of giving away possessions—known as the potlatch. The name comes from the Nootka word *patshatl* for "sharing." The principal gods of the Nootkas were the Sky-god, the Thunder-god, and the Wolf Spirits. All Nootka boys had to undergo an ordeal in which they were kidnapped for days by men dressed up as wolves, and taught Wolf songs and dances. Then they were rescued in a pretend battle and exorcised of the Wolf Spirits through more dancing.

The Nootkas, unlike most other Northwest Coast tribes, hunted the largest sea mammals—whales. Their whaling techniques resembled those of their kinsmen across the Juan de Fuca Strait, the Makahs (see "Makah"). Here is a part of a Nootka whaling song:

Whale, you must not run out to sea when I spear you.
Whale, if I spear you, I want my spear to strike your heart.
Harpoon, when I use you, I want you to go to the heart of the whale.

Because of their location along the Pacific Ocean, the Nootkas had early contacts with explorers. Juan de Fuca, exploring for Spain, was the first white to visit them, in 1592. Both Spain and England claimed Vancouver Island—Juan Perez for Spain in 1774 and Captain James Cook for England in 1778. Cook wrote extensively about the Indians. John Meares es-

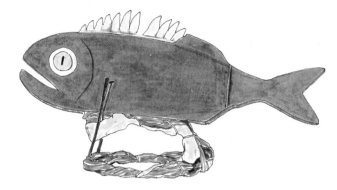

Nootka salmon headdress

tablished a British trading post on Nootka Sound in 1788. The Spanish seized this post the following year, leading to a dispute between the two countries. Spain signed the Nootka Convention in 1790, ceding the Pacific Northwest to England. Captain George Vancouver further explored Nootka country for England in 1792 and 1794, opening up the region to white settlement.

The Nootkas, who had always been great traders among Indian peoples, continued this tradition with the British and supplied them with furs. As a result, they were generally friendly toward whites. Nevertheless, when cheated by traders, they rose up against them. In 1803, Nootkas attacked and killed all except two people on board the *Boston*. Then in 1811, Nootkas seized another trading ship, the *Tonquin*. In this second incident, one of the ship's crew managed to reach the powder magazine and blow up the whole vessel and everyone on board, Indians and whites alike.

With the founding of the settlement of Victoria in 1843, which later became the capital of British Columbia, the pressures on the Nootkas increased. Missionaries tried to erase their culture, and white diseases killed many of them.

The Nootkas have since rebounded from a lowpoint in the early 1900s. There are currently 15 Nootka bands living on reserve lands in Canada. Many tribal members fish as their main source of income or operate salmon canneries. Some Nootkas have redis-covered traditional basketmaking skills.

Nootka dugout

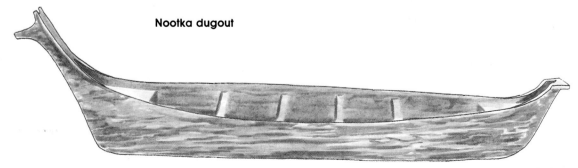

Northeast Indians

The Northeast Culture Area is one of many culture areas devised by scholars to group Indian tribes by their geography and lifeways. The type of geography, climate, and wildlife affected the way native peoples lived—what foods they ate, what materials they used for shelter and clothing, and how they viewed the world.

The Northeast Culture Area is defined as covering the following territory: east-to-west, from the Atlantic Ocean to the Mississippi River; north-to-south, from the Great Lakes to the Ohio Valley, including the Chesapeake Bay and Tidewater region. The following present-day states are included in this huge expanse of

land: Maine, Vermont, New Hampshire, Massachusetts, Rhode Island, Connecticut, New York, New Jersey, Pennsylvania, Delaware, Ohio, Indiana, Illinois, and Michigan; plus most of Maryland, West Virginia, Kentucky, and Wisconsin; and smaller parts of Virginia, North Carolina, Missouri, Iowa, and Minnesota. The following present-day provinces of Canada are also included in the Northeast Culture Area: Nova Scotia, New Brunswick, and Prince Edward Island, plus parts of Quebec and Ontario, as well as a tiny piece of Manitoba.

Most of this land is woodland. That is why the culture area is sometimes called the Northeast Woodland

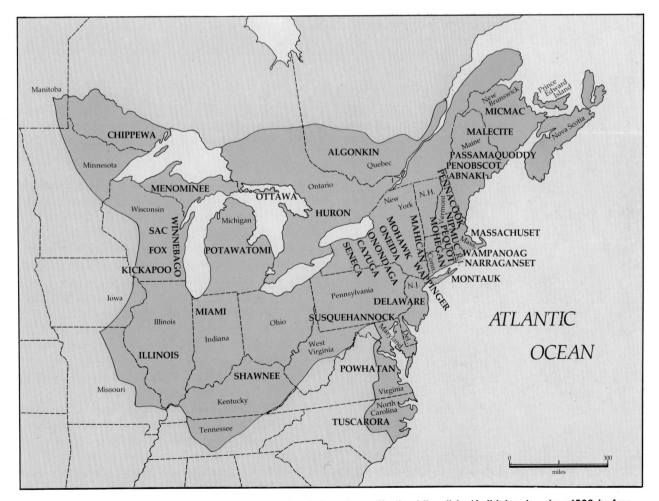

The Northeast Culture Area, showing the approximate locations of Indian tribes listed in this book—circa 1500, before displacement by whites (with modern boundaries)

Culture Area and the Indians of this region are sometimes called Woodland Indians. Yet since there were many other Indians living in the forests of North America—for example, in the Northern Forest of the Subarctic and in the Pacific Northwest—the term *woodland* can be confusing when used for just eastern Indians.

The forest is the one constant in the Northeast Culture Area. The terrain of the culture area is otherwise varied, including sea coasts, hills, mountains, lakes, and river valleys. The Appalachian Mountains run in a general north-south direction through the culture area. Enormous inland bodies of water—the five Great Lakes—are located in the north central region. Some of the big rivers flowing through the culture area are the St. Lawrence, Ottawa, Connecticut, Hudson, Delaware, Susquehanna, Allegheny, Ohio, Wabash and Illinois.

The forests of the Northeast provided a great natural resource for the native peoples: wood for houses, boats, tools, and fuel (plus bark for clothing, roofing, and bedding). Moreover, the forests were the home of abundant game that provided the Indians with meat for food, hides for clothing, and bones for tools. Of the many kinds of mammals living in the forests, deer were the most important resource to the Indians. The oceans, lakes, and rivers were a plentiful source of fish and shellfish.

In addition to being hunter-gatherers, Northeast Indians were also farmers. Many of their villages, where they had their cultivated fields, were permanent; but the Northeast Indians generally left the villages to hunt in certain seasons, living on the trail. Many Northeast Indians can be called "seminomadic."

The Indians of the Northeast Culture Area spoke dialects of two language families: Algonquian and Iroquoian. Algonquians and Iroquoians shared many cultural traits. Yet there were differences too. For example, most Algonquian peoples lived in wigwams, and most Iroquoian peoples lived in longhouses.

The various Algonquian tribes of the Northeast included in this book are listed under the entry "Algonquian" and the different Iroquoian tribes are listed under the entry "Iroquois." See those entries to learn more about the two language families in general, but also see the various entries under particular tribal names. Only one tribe of the Northeast Culture Area spoke a language other than Algonquian or Iroquoian: the Winnebagos, who spoke a dialect of the Siouan language family. They are discussed in a separate entry too.

Northwest Coast Indians

The Northwest Coast Culture Area is elongated, extending from north to south about 2,000 miles, but from east to west only about 150 miles at its widest. At its northern limits, it touches on territory that now is southern Alaska. At its southern limits, it touches on northern California. In between, it includes the western parts of British Columbia, Washington, and Oregon. A large part of the Northwest Coast Culture Area consists of islands, including Vancouver Island, the Queen Charlotte Islands, and the Alexander Archipelago, plus numerous smaller chains.

The many islands are actually the tips of submerged mountains, part of the Coast Range. These rugged mountains form a spine running north-south along the culture area. Many of the mountains come right down to the ocean, forming rocky cliffs. There are numerous inlets and sounds along the shoreline, as well as numerous straits between the islands. Farther inland, in Washington and Oregon, another mountain range, the Cascade Range, also runs north and south.

The climate of the Northwest Coast is surprisingly warm for the northern latitudes. That is because an ocean current, known as the Japanese Current, warms the ocean as well as winds blowing inland. But the westerly winds also carry abundant moisture. The mountains block the moisture, which turns to rainfall, as much as 100 inches or more a year, more than in any other part of North America. Abundant springs and streams run from the mountains to the ocean.

These climatic conditions led to the growth of vast forests. Giant evergreen trees, among the tallest in the world, cover most of the land, except mountain tops and rock faces too steep to have soil. The branches of tall trees form a dense canopy, blocking out sunlight. The forest floor is therefore dark and wet, with little undergrowth other than ferns and mosses.

Northwest Coast Indians usually lived right at the ocean's edge on narrow sand and gravel beaches. Mountains rose up to the east. The island chains to the west offered protection from stormy seas.

The Indians situated their houses facing the sea. They built them entirely of wood taken from the giant forests. Cedar was the wood of choice. The master architects of the Northwest Coast used giant timbers

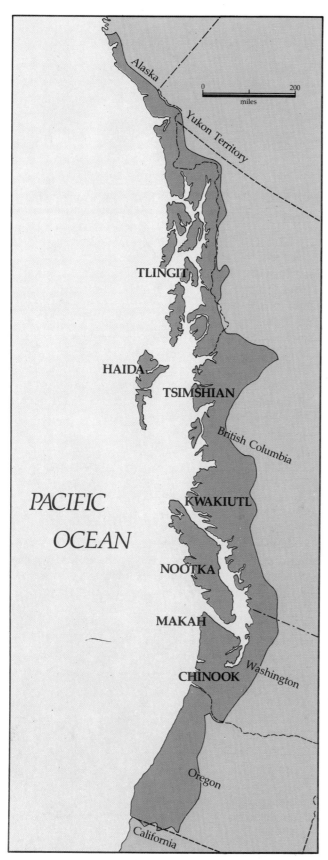

The Northwest Coast Culture Area, showing the approximate locations of Indian tribes listed in this book—circa 1500, before displacement by whites (with modern boundaries)

Northwest Coast Indian house with totem poles

for framing their rectangular houses. For their walls, they lashed hand-split planks to the framework, which ran either vertically or horizontally. They hung mats on the inside for additional insulation. The roofs were also plank-covered. Planks were used for flooring, sometimes on two different levels. There was usually a central firepit. Platforms ran along the walls for sleeping and storage. In size, the houses varied from about 20 by 30 feet, to 50 by 60 feet, to even 60 by 100 feet. The large houses provided shelter for several families.

Northwest Coast Indians often erected giant totem poles outside their houses. Powerful shamans and members of secret societies dictated the significance of the faces on the totem poles. The craftsmen also used wood from the forests to shape large, seaworthy dugouts and to carve chests, boxes, masks, and other

Northwest Coast (Coast Salish) shaman's wooden spirit helper

objects. They were among the premier Native American woodworkers. They also made exquisite baskets, textiles, and other goods. Villagers demonstrated their wealth and social status by the number of possessions they gave away in a custom unique to this culture area—the potlatch.

Since travel over the mountainous land was so difficult, Northwest Coast Indians moved about by sea.

They traveled up and down the coast for purposes of trade, slave-raiding, and hunting. The sea provided their primary game, sea mammals, including whales, seals, and sea lions. The sea also offered up plentiful fish, including salmon, halibut, herring, cod, and flounder. Northwest Coast Indians also fished the rivers when salmon left the ocean waters to lay their eggs. Their land game included deer, elk, bear, and mountain goat. The Indians in this part of North America had plenty of food and could support large populations in their seaside villages without farming.

There were many different tribes along the Northwest Coast, speaking many different languages. The language families, with their assorted dialects, were the following: Nadene, Wakashan, Penutian, Salishan, Chimakum, and Athapascan. These language groups were not neatly segregated geographically, but were interspersed. Sorting out and memorizing tribal locations is extremely difficult in the densely populated Northwest Coast Culture Area. Moreover, there are too many tribes for us to cover them all individually in this book.

Northwest Coast tribes of the Nadene language family included Eyak, Haida, and Tlingit (see "Haida"

Northwest Coast (Bella Coola) eagle mask

and "Tlingit"). Tribes of the Wakashan family included Bella Bella, Haisla, Heiltsuk, Kwakiutl, Makah, and Nootka (see "Kwakiutl"; Makah"; and "Nootka.") Tribes of the Penutian family included Alsea, Chinook, Clatsop, Coos, Kalapuya, Siuslaw, Takelma, and Tsimshian (see "Chinook" and "Tsimshian"). Tribes of the Salishan family included Bella Coola, Chehalis, Clallam, Comox, Cowichan, Cowlitz, Duwamish, Humptulips, Lumni, Quinault, Siletz, Skagit, Tillamook, and Twana. Tribes of the Athapascan family included Clatskanie and Tututni. There were many other tribes as well.

Olmec

The Olmecs (pronounced *OL-mec*) lived in Mesoamerica. The term *Mesoamerica* or *Middle America* refers to territory now known as Mexico and the northern part of Central America. In the centuries before whites reached the Americas, Mesoamerica was the most densely populated area of the Americas, with many different Indian peoples living there.

Scholars believe the Olmecs established the "mother civilization" of Mesoamerica. That is to say, their culture influenced other cultures that followed. From about 1500 B.C. to A.D. 300, Olmec culture dominated the region.

Sometimes the period when the Olmecs dominated Mesoamerica is referred to as the Preclassic period. Then came the Classic period, when the Mayas flourished. Then followed the Postclassic period, when the Toltecs and Aztecs flourished (see "Maya"; "Toltec"; and "Aztec"). In the study of Indians north of Mesoamerica, however, these three periods together are usually called the Formative period (see "Prehistoric Indians").

The Olmec homeland was situated mainly along the Gulf Coast to the east of present-day Mexico City. Yet

the Olmecs had extensive trade contacts all over Mesoamerica. On finding Olmec objects at sites far from the Gulf Coast, archaeologists are sometimes uncertain if the ancient inhabitants were actually Olmecs or were other Indians who obtained Olmec objects in trade.

The Olmecs were famous for giant heads carved from basalt, a type of volcanic rock. Some of these

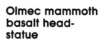
Olmec mammoth basalt head-statue

heads were as heavy as 20 tons, with helmet-like head-dresses. The Olmecs traveled far to obtain the basalt to make these mammoth sculptures. To transport the rock, they dragged it overland and floated it on rafts. The Olmecs also traveled great distances to get jade to make beautiful statues, the mineral magnetite to make mirrors, and an ore called serpentine to make pavement. Their statues, both large and small, were often representations of jaguars, which played an important part in Olmec religion. Another religious symbol frequently depicted, the Great Plumed Serpent (Quetzalcoatl), persisted as a deity among

Olmec jade Kunz Axe, depicting a man-jaguar

many other later peoples in Mesoamerica, indicating Olmec influence far and wide.

The Olmecs also influenced later Mesoamerican peoples with their system of social organization. Unlike most Indian tribes, Olmec society had classes of priests, merchants, and craftsmen. The priests had the most power. The social classes were fixed, meaning that members were born into them and could not change occupations.

The Olmec upper classes lived in finely built stone structures. The buildings, some of them temples on top of pyramids, were situated along paved streets. Aqueducts carried water to them. The Olmec population centers are not thought of as true cities, but rather as ceremonial and economic centers where religious rituals and trade were carried out. True cities with

giant populations, some of them on the very same sites, would evolve among later Mesoamerican peoples.

In the countryside, surrounding the Olmec centers of religious and economic activity, lived a population of farmers who supported the upper classes through agriculture. They practiced a method of farming called slash-and-burn in which they cut down trees and burned them to make fields. The main crop was corn.

Farming in Mesoamerica dates back as early as 7000 B.C. Cultivated beans, peppers, pumpkins, and gourds have been discovered in a dry cave. The earliest cultivated strain of corn ever found, also in Mesoamerica, dates back to 4000 B.C. These early Indians were perhaps the ancient ancestors of the Olmecs. It was farming that allowed the development of cities, because, with farming, a large number of people could live in a small area and still have plenty to eat.

Another Olmec cultural development passed to later Mesoamericans was a ball game that was played with a ball made from rubber on a paved court. The Olmecs were also the first Indians known to have number and calendar systems as well as hieroglyphic writing, with symbols representing words and ideas.

The most important Olmec population centers were San Lorenzo, dominant from 1200 to 900 B.C.; La Venta, dominant from 800 to 400 B.C.; and Tres Zapotes, dominant from about 100 B.C. to A.D. 300. La Venta was the location of the largest Olmec pyramid. At Copalillo, a recently excavated Olmec site to the west of these sites, have been found the oldest stone buildings in North America, dating back as far as 600 B.C.

It is not known why the Olmec culture declined. Invading tribes could have been responsible, or drought and failing crops, or disease. Because the Olmec culture has much in common with the later Mayan culture, some scholars have theorized that the Olmecs migrated eastward and became the direct ancestors of the Mayas. Whatever happened to them, the Olmecs, with their remarkable cultural developments and their great influence, changed the course of Indian history.

Omaha

The Omahas belonged to a group of Indians who spoke the Siouan language and who once lived along the Ohio River before migrating westward early in their history. In addition to the Omahas, these people became the various tribes known as Kaws, Osages,

Poncas, and Quapaws (see entries for those tribes). They settled at different locations on the eastern Plains. The Omahas and Poncas settled farther north than the other tribes of this group. These two tribes probably separated where the Niobrara River flows into the Missouri River. The Omahas eventually settled to the southeast of the mouth of the Niobrara River, downriver from the Poncas, in what is now northeast Nebraska.

The Omahas (pronounced *O-muh-haw*) are the tribe most closely associated with the state of Nebraska, where most tribal descendants live and whose largest city, Omaha, was named after them. But they occupied other territory as well. Before settling in Nebraska, the Omahas stayed for a time near the Pipestone Quarry, in what is now southern Minnesota, where Indians found catlinite (or pipestone), for carving into pipes. Bands of Omahas also had villages in South Dakota and Iowa in the course of their history. The Indians of course did not

Omaha mirror board with iron upholstery tacks and brass pins

think in terms of states. Rivers more than any other physical feature helped them delineate their homelands. The Omahas can be thought of as one of the many Missouri River tribes. Their name means "those going against the current."

Sometimes the tribes of the eastern Plains, who lived along the Mississippi and Missouri rivers, are referred to as Prairie people (see "Prairie Indians"). The Omahas were villagers and farmers. They lived in earthlodges most of the year and depended on their crops for food. They also fished the rivers in their territory. But they left their villages in search of buffalo,

deer, and smaller game. When the Spanish brought horses to North America and the horses spread to Indian peoples, the Omahas adopted many of the traits of the western Plains tribes, ranging over a wider area in search of the buffalo and living in hide tepees when on the trail. That is why the tribe is normally included as part of the Great Plains Culture Area (see "Plains Indians").

Here is an Omaha dance song about the buffalo hunt:

> One I have wounded, yonder, he moves,
> Yonder he moves, bleeding at the mouth.
> One I have wounded, yonder he moves,
> Yonder he moves, with staggering steps.
> One I have wounded, yonder he moves,
> Yonder he falls, yonder he falls.

The Omahas had a complex social structure with many rules governing behavior. They also had many tribal societies, or clubs. Some of these clubs were secret with exclusive membership. Others were open to everyone. The Thunder Society served as custodians of the tribe's most sacred relics, two pipes that had mallard duck heads attached to the stems. Another society, the Buffalo Dreamers, cared for the sick. Still another, the Bear Dreamers, used sleight-of-hand tricks in their rituals. One trick was swallowing long sticks.

The Omahas fought often with the Sioux Indians who lived to their north and west (see "Sioux"). Yet a smallpox epidemic in 1802, brought to the Omahas by white traders, had a greater impact on them than intertribal warfare, greatly reducing their population.

In 1854, at the time the original Indian Territory was reorganized, the Omahas ceded all their lands west of the Missouri River to the United States and were settled on a reservation in Nebraska. In 1865, the Omahas sold the northern part of the reservation to the federal government for the use of the Winnebago tribe (see "Winnebago").

The Omahas still practice some of their traditional rituals on their reservation. They also run the Omaha Tribal Farm, which raises livestock, and a recreation area, the Chief Big Elk Park.

Oneida

The Oneidas were one of the five original tribes of the Iroquois League. They controlled the wedge of territory in central New York between the Mohawk tribe to the east and the Onondaga tribe to the west, especially between Oneida Lake and the upper Mohawk River. Their culture and history are summarized along with the other tribes in the Iroquois Confederacy under "Iroquois" (see "Iroquois" and "Northeast Indians").

Yet, as is the case with all six tribes, the Oneidas are a distinct and important group and merit discussion on their own as well.

Their name, pronounced *o-NI-duh*, means "people of the boulder" or "stone people," referring to a large rock within their territory. At the League's annual Great Council in neighboring Onondaga territory, to which they sent nine sachems, or chiefs, as representatives of their tribe, the Oneidas' symbol was the Great Tree. At the Great Council the Oneida sachems also served as spokesmen for the Tuscaroras, the Iroquoian-speaking tribe from North Carolina that became the Sixth Nation of the Iroquois Confederacy in 1722.

The Oneidas were loyal to the League throughout the French and Indian Wars of 1689-1763, valuable allies of the British against the French and the Algonquian tribes. Yet, in the American Revolution of 1775-83, the Oneidas, along with the Tuscaroras, broke with the other League members and sided with the American rebels against the British. At first they tried to remain neutral during the conflict, not wanting to take up arms against fellow Iroquois or against Tory settlers near their homelands. But, by 1777, two years into the war, they took up arms.

It was a Presbyterian missionary by the name of Samuel Kirkland who won the Oneidas over to the American side. He had originally settled among the Oneidas in 1766 and preached to them and counseled them throughout this eventful period of American history. In 1793, Samuel Kirkland, with the help of Alexander Hamilton, founded the Hamilton Oneida Academy near Utica, New York, for the education of both white and Indian youths. Few Indians attended the school, and it became chartered as Hamilton College in 1812.

In the years after the Revolution, the Oneidas were persuaded to sell most of their New York lands and resettle westward. In 1838, a group of Oneidas purchased land in Wisconsin from the Menominees (see "Menominee"). Other Oneidas settled in Ontario, Canada, as part of the Six Nations Reserve at Oshweken on the Grand River. Still others settled on

Oneida soapstone
sculpture

another reserve in Ontario on the Thames River. Some stayed in New York with the Onondagas on their reservation lands near Syracuse. Others remained on their original homelands near Utica. This group still holds one parcel there which is not classified as an official state reservation.

The Oneidas currently have a land claim against the state of New York. They are asking for the return of 5.5 million acres of land unfairly taken from them in the late 1700s, or a payment based on the loss of those lands. In 1985, the courts upheld the Indians' lawsuit in a test case, but the entire claim will probably take years to resolve.

Onondaga

The Onondagas were the central tribe of the Iroquois League, the confederacy of tribes once extending across upstate New York. They located their villages especially in the vicinity of Onondaga Lake and Oswego River just to the south of Lake Ontario, not far from present-day Syracuse. As the central tribe, the Onondagas played the important role of Keepers of the Council Fire, the flame kept burning for two centuries—from about the 1570s to the 1770s. Their main village, Onondaga, was the meeting place of the Iroquois Great Council, held every year.

Since the Onondagas shared a culture and history with the other tribes of the Iroquois League, they are discussed together with those tribes (see "Iroquois"

and "Northeast Indians"). The section you are reading now has information particular to the Onondagas.

The name *Onondaga*, pronounced *au-nun-DAG-uh*, means "people of the hills," after the hilly land surrounding their villages. At the Great Council, the Onondagas also bore the epithet "Name-Bearer" because they had the responsibility of keeping the wampum belt that served as a record of the meeting and who was present. The Onondagas had the greatest number of sachems, or chiefs, as tribal representatives, 14 of the 50.

In Iroquois legend, an Onondaga chief known as Atotarhoh was the most stubborn about the formation of the League when the Mohawk called Hiawatha traveled from tribe to tribe preaching the message of Iroquois unity. Atotarhoh was so fierce and hostile to other tribes that he supposedly had serpents growing out of his head. All the people feared him. To pacify Atotarhoh and seal the alliance, Hiawatha combed the snakes from the chief's head. Atotarhoh had one condition, however, for the participation of the Onondagas: They must always serve as chairmen at the Great Council.

The Iroquois League split up during the American Revolution when the member tribes chose opposing sides. The Onondagas, along with the Mohawks, Senecas, and Cayugas, supported the British, whom they had supported in the earlier French and Indian Wars. The fact that the Oneidas and Tuscaroras sided with the American rebels meant that the Great Peace

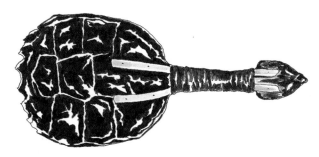

Onondaga turtle rattle

had ended and that unity was no more. The Onondagas let the Council Fire, which had burned continuously for 200 years, die out.

It took some time after the Revolution to heal the wounds among the opposing factions of the Iroquois League. Most Onondagas took refuge for a time in western New York; they were finally granted a reservation on part of their original homelands near Nedrow, New York. Other Onondagas settled in Canada as part of the Six Nation Reserve at Oshweken on the Grand River. The Iroquois tribes have since rediscovered their unity, and today the Onondagas again play a central role in the League. The Onondaga Reservation is the capital of the confederacy. The chief of the entire Iroquois Nation, the *Tadodaho*, is always of the Onondaga tribe. Only he can summon the Six Nation Council.

The Constitution of the Iroquois League reads as follows:

"The Onondagas lords shall open each council by expressing their gratitude to their cousin lords, and greeting them, and they shall make an address and offer thanks to the earth where men dwell, to the streams of water, the pool, the springs, the lakes, to the maize and the fruits, to the medicinal herbs and the trees, to the forest trees for their usefulness, to the animals that serve as food and who offer their pelts as clothing, to the great winds and the lesser winds, to the Thunderers, and the Sun, the mighty warrior, to the moon, to the messengers of the Great Spirit who dwells in the skies above, who gives all things useful to men, who is the source and the ruler of health and life. Then shall the Onondaga lords declare the council open."

The Onondaga Reservation came into the news in 1983, when a leader of AIM (the American Indian Movement), Dennis Banks, took refuge there. He was sought by South Dakota authorities because of his participation in a 1973 incident at Wounded Knee (see "Chippewa" and "Sioux").

First, Banks had fled to California, where the governor at the time, Jerry Brown, was sympathetic to his cause. When Brown lost the election, Banks had decided to move to New York, where Governor Mario Cuomo was also sympathetic. The Onondagas offered him sanctuary. While Dennis Banks lived among them, he helped organize the Great Jim Thorpe Longest Run in honor of the great Indian athlete (see "Sac"). In 1984, Indian runners from many different tribes carried medicine bundles in relay fashion from Onondaga through 14 states, all the way to Los Angeles, California, where the Jim Thorpe Memorial Pow-Wow and Games were held the same summer as the Los Angeles Olympics. Later that same year, however, Dennis Banks, tired of the life of a fugitive, left Onondaga to surrender to South Dakota officials. He was sentenced to three years in jail.

Many Onondagas, who are considered the most traditional of the Iroquois, participate in the Longhouse Religion founded by Handsome Lake in 1799 (see "Seneca").

Osage

The Osages, who spoke the Siouan language, lived along the Ohio River Valley, then later migrated onto the eastern Plains. The Osages were originally one people with the Kaws, Omahas, Poncas, and

Quapaws (see entries for those tribes). The group that became the Osages settled along the Osage River tributary of the Missouri in what is now the state of Missouri. They also claimed territory as far south as the Arkansas River in what is now northern Arkansas, southeastern Kansas, and northeastern Oklahoma.

The Osages called themselves *Ni-U-Ko'n-Ska*, meaning "children of the middle waters." The name *Osage*, pronounced *O-saje*, is the French version of *Wazhazhe*, the largest Osage band. There were two main early bands of Osages: the Great Osages on the Osage River, and the Little Osages on the Missouri River. Another band broke off in the early 1800s from the Great Osages and migrated to the Arkansas River, becoming the Arkansas Osages.

Scholars classify the Osages among the Prairie division of the Plains Indians (see "Prairie Indians" and "Plains Indians"). That is to say, they were seminomadic. Most of the year, they lived in villages along wooded river valleys and farmed the rich soil. While at home, they stayed in oval or rectangular pole-frame houses covered with woven mats or hides. But they also depended on the buffalo for food. They went on several buffalo hunts every year during which time they lived in tepees. Before acquiring horses, they often killed the large animals by waving fur robes to stampede the herd and lighting prairie fires to direct the animals toward the edge of a cliff.

Each Osage village had two chiefs, a peace chief and a war chief. One clan, the Sky People, under the peace chief, lived to the north; another clan, the Earth People, under the war chief, lived to the south. A council of elderly men, called the Little Old Men, made tribal laws and settled tribal disputes.

The French explorers Jacques Marquette and Louis Jolliet visited the Osages along the Osage River in 1673. The tribe became allies of the French. During the 1700s, the Indians conducted much trade with them, bartering furs for guns and other European goods. They called all whites *I'n-Shta-Heh*, meaning "heavy eyebrows," because the Europeans seemed hairy to them. The Osages supported the French in the latter part of the French and Indian Wars (1689-1763) against the English. After England and Spain gained control of France's holdings in 1763, Osage trade decreased. Yet with time, more and more English traders began arriving in their territory.

In 1801, France regained control of the huge Louisiana Territory, which then included the Mississippi and Missouri river valleys. Two years later, President Thomas Jefferson bought the land from Napolean Bonaparte of France for $15 million. After the Lewis and Clark Expedition of 1803-06, American traders and settlers began arriving in great numbers on Osage lands.

At first, the Osages were hostile to the new intruders. But in 1808, they agreed to a treaty giving up huge tracts of their territory. They agreed to other land

Osage bear claw necklace with otter fur

cessions in treaties of 1818, 1825, 1839, and 1865. The Osages served as scouts for the U.S. Army in Sheridan's Campaign of 1868-69 (see "Cheyenne"). Another treaty in 1870 established the Osage Reservation in the northeastern part of the Indian Territory (now near the town of Pawhuska in the state of Oklahoma), which had formerly been Osage hunting grounds.

In 1897, oil was discovered on the Osage Reservation, making some of the Osages the richest Indians in the United States. Others, however, were tricked into selling their valuable land by unscrupulous whites.

A famous Osage of recent times is the dancer Maria Tallchief, born in 1925. She was a prima ballerina who danced all over the world and gained respect for American ballet at a time when most great dancers came from other countries. Her younger sister Marjorie Tallchief, born in 1927, was also a well-known dancer.

Oto

According to tribal legend, the Otos, or Otoes (both pronounced *O-to*), who spoke the Siouan language, were formerly one people with the Winnebagos, Iowas, and Missouris, and lived in Winnebago country in the Great Lakes region. Then the ancestors of Otos, Iowas, and Missouris split off from the Winnebagos and migrated soutwestward. Another separation took place at the mouth of the Iowa River, on the Mississippi River. The group that stayed in this location became the Iowas. The group that pushed westward divided into two other tribes on the Missouri. This final split supposedly occurred because two chiefs quarreled when the son of one seduced the daughter of another. Those who stayed where they were, the band of the girl's father, became the Missouris. The band of the boy's father traveled northward, farther up the Missouri River. They became known as the Otos, meaning "lechers," in reference to the boy's behavior (see "Iowa"; "Missouri"; and "Winnebago").

The Otos eventually settled in territory that is now the state of Nebraska. They also roamed and had temporary villages in parts of neighboring states—Iowa, Kansas, and Missouri. The Otos retained some cultural traits of the eastern woodlands, including farming and permanent villages. Scholars sometimes describe them as Prairie people (see "Prairie Indians"). But they eventually adopted lifeways typical of Plains tribes, including hunting buffalo and using horses and tepees. As a result, the Otos are usually grouped in the Great Plains Culture Area (see "Plains Indians").

The Otos had contacts with early French explorers, such as Jacques Marquette and Louis Jolliet in 1673. The Lewis and Clark Expedition, organized by the United States in 1803, encountered them on the banks of the Missouri River near their main villages on the lower course of the Platte River.

With increased white settlement west of the Mississippi, starting in the 1830s, the Otos were pressured by white officials into giving up their lands. Along with the Missouris, who joined them permanently in 1829, the Otos signed away lands in Nebraska, Missouri, and Iowa in the 1830s. Then, in 1854, the Otos signed away all remaining lands in Nebraska except for a strip along the Big Blue River. When it was found out that there was no timber on this piece, they received instead a tract in Kansas. In 1876 and 1879, they sold off the western part of this reservation. In 1881, they sold the rest and moved to a reservation in the Indian Territory.

The Otos and Missouris are presently known as the combined Otoe-Missouria tribe. They presently hold trust lands together near Pawnee, Oklahoma.

Ottawa

With the Chippewa and the Potawatomi tribes, the Ottawas formed the Council of Three Tribes. All three Algonquian tribes supposedly migrated to the Great Lakes country from the north as one people, then separated. In the early 1600s, when French explorers and missionaries arrived in the area, the Ottawas controlled the northern reaches of Lake Huron—especially Manitoulin Island and the shores of Georgian Bay.

The Ottawas lived like other Great Lakes Algonquians—surviving through a combination of hunting in the forests, fishing in the lakes and rivers, gathering wild rice in the marshes, and, when conditions allowed, planting crops in cultivated fields (see "Algonquian" and "Northeast Indians"). They shared many typical Algonquian beliefs—for example, in Manitou, the Great Spirit—but they had their own unique legends and traditions too. Their creation myth tells the story of their descent from three different creatures—Michabou, the Great Hare; Namepich, the Carp (a kind of fish); and the Bear's Paw.

After the arrival of whites, the Ottawas became noted in two connections: first, as traders; then, as the tribe that produced one of the great Indian leaders, Pontiac. Their fame as traders came about while the French controlled much of North America, up until 1763. Their name, pronounced *AHT-uh-wuh*, means "to trade." The name was given to the river that runs through what was once their territory, and which now separates Quebec from Ontario in Canada, as well as to the capital city of Canada. The Ottawa River was a main trade route for Indians and Frenchmen alike. It probably had more canoes going up and down it than any other river in history.

The Ottawas were part of the Great Huron Trade Circle. They supplied furs to Huron middlemen, who took them to the French in Quebec and Montreal and then returned to pay off the Indians with European trade goods (see "Huron"). After 1649, when the tribes of the Iroquois League defeated the Hurons (see "Iroquois"), the Ottawas took over as middlemen. Now it was their turn to deal directly with the French, bartering furs for European-made knives, hatchets, tomahawks, pipes, cloth, beads, kettles, and paints.

Ottawa birchbark dish

But in 1660, the Iroquois defeated and dispersed the Ottawas too, breaking up their trade monopoly. The Ottawas took refuge in the west, fleeing in their boats to the islands off Green Bay. Some eventually went farther west to Keweenaw Bay in Lake Superior. Others passed overland as far as the Mississippi River, carrying their light birchbark canoes between streams. This group migrated again because of attacks by Sioux. They ended up on Chequamegon Bay in northern Wisconsin. Then, 10 years later in 1670, when the French promised to protect them from the Iroquois, many Ottawas returned to Manitoulin Island. Many also joined their old trading partners, the Hurons, who were now at Mackinac, Michigan.

Yet these were just some of many migrations for the Ottawas. In the years to follow, their lives and homelands were disrupted by more power struggles and warfare. And one of the most famous of all Indian leaders would rise to prominence. His name was Pontiac.

Pontiac's Rebellion

The French and Indian Wars, from 1689 to 1763, pitted for the most part French and Algonquians against English and Iroquois. In all of the four major wars of

that period (see "Abnaki"), Ottawa warriors fought alongside Frenchmen. But both Quebec and Montreal fell to British forces. And then French forces in Europe also lost important battles. By the time the French signed the Treaty of Paris, which officially gave their North American territory (called New France) to England, British troops had marched in and taken control of the French forts in the Great Lakes country.

In the spring, summer, and fall of 1763, an Ottawa chief by the name of Pontiac led an uprising of many Old Northwest tribes that came to be known as Pontiac's Rebellion. Pontiac, an energetic and dynamic man, resented having new landlords. He had a solid trade relationship with the French. In his experience, French fur traders treated Indians as equals whereas English settlers generally acted superior. Lord Jeffrey Amherst, the British commander in chief for America, was especially arrogant toward Indians. He was also stingy with supplies. Pontiac, who had previously fought with the French against the British, believed that if the Indians could unite, they could win French support and have enough forces to drive the English from the Great Lakes once and for all. Pontiac traveled among and sent messages to the tribes of the region to urge Indian unity.

An Indian named Delaware Prophet helped Pontiac in his cause (see "Delaware"). The Prophet, a spellbinding orator, like Pontiac, claimed that Manitou, or the Great Spirit, had communicated with him to bring about a united Indian country where Indians could practice traditional ways. But whereas Delaware Prophet preached against guns, Pontiac considered force necessary to defeat the British.

After much planning, Pontiac and his warriors began a siege of Fort Detroit. He also sent messages—wampum belts calling for war—to chiefs of other tribes. Fighting broke out all over the region. Many tribes participated, many more than the Indian chief King Philip had had under him in his united rebellion of 1675 (see "Wampanoag"). In addition to Pontiac's Ottawas, there were Chippewas, Kickapoos, Illinois, Miamis, Potawatomis, Senecas, and Shawnees who made attacks on outlying settlements as well as on forts. About 2,000 settlers died during the rebellion. Many British posts surrendered to the Indian forces: Fort Sandusky, Fort St. Joseph (now Niles, Michigan); Fort Miami (Fort Wayne, Indiana); Fort Ouiatenon (Lafayette, Indiana); Fort Michilimackinac (Mackinac, Michigan); Fort Edward Augustus (Green Bay, Wisconsin); Fort Venango (Franklin, Pennsylvania); Fort Le Boeuf (Waterford, Pennsylvania); and Fort Presqu' Isle (Erie, Pennsylvania).

The Indians also were victorious at Point Pelee on Lake Erie, stopping supply boats on their way to

Detroit and killing 56 whites; and at Bloody Run, just outside the fort, killing 54 British troops. The only major British victory was at Bushy Run, south of Lake Erie outside Fort Pitt (Pittsburgh, Pennsylvania). Nevertheless, despite these Indian victories, the British ultimately won the war.

Part of the reason Pontiac's Rebellion failed is that the two most important forts did not surrender: Fort Detroit and Fort Pitt. The defenders at Fort Pitt used an early form of biological warfare to hold out against the siege. At Amherst's suggestion, the defending garrison sent out smallpox-infected blankets and handkerchiefs, starting an epidemic among the Indians that summer. Meanwhile, at Detroit, the schooner *Huron* broke through Indian lines with fresh men and supplies.

To Pontiac's dismay, the Indians began to lose interest in the siege of Detroit. The French never delivered the help they had led the Indians to expect. And, with winter coming, the warriors became worried about providing food for their families. The warriors dispersed.

Pontiac clung to his cause for some time to come. He traveled farther west, where there were fewer forts and fewer settlers. He continued to preach Indian unity. Then in 1766, he negotiated a peace accord with Sir William Johnson and was pardoned by the English (see "Mohawk"). He returned to his village on the Maumee River. During a trip west to Illinois in 1769, he was killed by an Illinois Indian, who, it is thought, was in the pay of the British. Although Pontiac had been counseling peace to younger, hot-blooded members of his band, the British had continued to distrust him and to fear his great leadership abilities. But his former friends and allies had not forgotten him either. Because of his murder by one Illinois, the Ottawas, Chippewas, Potawatomis, Sacs, and Foxes united against the rest of the Illinois people and defeated them (see "Illinois").

Pontiac would also be remembered by many great Indian leaders to follow. Men such as Joseph Brant (see "Mohawk"), Little Turtle (see "Miami"), Tecumseh (see "Shawnee"), and Black Hawk (see "Sac") would also call for unity among the tribes of the Old Northwest, but not against the British. The new enemy would be the Americans.

After the United States came to control the southern Great Lakes country, some Ottawas were forced to move westward to Kansas and Oklahoma. Today, descendants live in both places but without reservation lands. Others live in their traditional homeland, the Great Lakes country of Michigan and Ontario, also without reservation lands.

Paiute

The Paiutes, or Piutes (pronounced *PIE-oot*), included many different bands, spread out over a vast region. They are usually organized into two groups for study: the Northern Paiutes and the Southern Paiutes. The northern branch occupied territory that is now northwestern Nevada, southeastern Oregon, southwestern Idaho, and northeastern California. The southern branch lived in territory now part of western Utah, southern Nevada, northwestern Arizona, and southeastern California.

Lifeways

The Northern and Southern Paiutes spoke varying dialects of the Uto-Aztecan language family, related to the Shoshone dialect (see "Shoshone"). The name Paiute is thought to mean "true Ute" or "Water Ute," also indicating an ancestral relationship with the Ute Indians of Utah (see "Ute").

The Paiutes as a whole are considered part of the Great Basin Culture Area (see "Great Basin Indians"). Nomadic Paiute bands wandered the rugged and arid Great Basin in search of whatever small game and wild plant life they could find, sometimes venturing into the highlands surrounding the desert lowlands—roughly the Rockies to the east, the Sierra Nevada to the west, the Columbia Plateau to the north, and the Colorado Plateau to the south.

For the Paiute bands, their activities and whereabouts in the course of a year were dictated by the availability of food. They traveled a great deal, constructing temporary huts of brush and reeds strewn over willow poles, known as wickiups, which were similar to Apache dwellings (see "Apache"). The first plant food available in the springtime was the cattail, growing in marsh ponds. The Indians ate the shoots raw. Other wild plant foods—roots and greens—soon followed. Spring was also a good time to hunt ducks in ponds on the birds' migration northward, and, in the

Paiute wickiup

highlands to the north of the Great Basin, to fish the rivers and streams during annual spawning runs.

In summertime, many more wild plant foods ripened, such as berries and rice grass. The Indians ground the seeds of the latter into meal. In the autumn, the primary food was pine nuts. The Indians collected them from piñon trees growing on the hills and plateaus rising above the Great Basin. In the late fall, the Indians returned to the desert lowlands to hunt game throughout the winter, especially rabbits. Year-round, Paiutes ate whatever else they could forage, such as lizards, grubs, and insects. The Paiutes, along with other Great Basin tribes, have been called Digger Indians by whites because they dug for many of their foods.

Wars of the Northern Paiutes

The Northern Paiutes are generally considered to have been more warlike than the Southern Paiutes, and they fought in a number of conflicts with the whites. At first, in contacts with fur trappers and traders, such as Jedediah Smith in 1825, Peter Skene Ogden in 1827, and Joseph Walker in 1833, the Northern Paiutes were friendly. But, after gold was discovered in California in 1848, and miners and migrants began streaming across Indian territory in great numbers, the Northern Paiutes turned hostile.

The Northern Paiutes played a prominent role in the Coeur d'Alene War of 1858-59 (see "Coeur d'Alene"). Then the following decade, during the Civil War, while federal troops were busy fighting in the East, the Northern Paiutes carried out numerous raids on miners and mining camps; stagecoaches and stage stations; wagon trains and freight caravans; and ranches and farms. Nevada and Oregon volunteers had little success in tracking down the hostile bands. In 1865, after the Civil War, army troops were assigned to forts in the region in an effort to bring peace to the area.

The conflict that followed during 1866-67 is usually called the Snake War. Two Northern Paiute bands, the Walpapis and the Yahuskins, were known collectively to whites as the Snake Indians. Two chiefs, Paulina and Old Weawea, led Snake warriors against troops in lightning-quick raids, after which the Indians would disappear into the highlands. But a wily white fighter named George Crook, who fought in many different campaigns, beat the Indians at their own game. He divided his troops into many small tracking patrols that kept constant pressure on the insurgents for a year and a half, forcing about 40 different skirmishes. In one of them, in January 1867, Chief Paulina was killed. Old Weawea eventually surrendered with 800 warriors. Most of them were settled on the Malheur Reservation in Oregon.

Some of these same warriors were caught up in the Bannock War of 1878. When the Bannock leader, Chief Buffalo Horn, was killed in that conflict, two Northern Paiutes took over the leadership of the rebels, Chief Egan and the medicine man Oytes (see "Bannock").

The Paiute War

Other Northern Paiute bands fought in an uprising referred to as the Paiute War (or the Pyramid Lake War). This conflict started just before the Civil War, in 1860, when traders at the Williams Station, a Central Overland Mail and Pony Express station on the California Trial just east of the present-day Nevada-California border, kidnapped and raped two Northern Paiute girls. Warriors attacked and burned the station, killed five whites, and rescued the girls.

Miners in the region organized a volunteer force under Major William Ormsby. But a Northern Paiute chief named Numaga outmaneuvered them at the Big Bend of the Truckee River by having his men hide in sagebrush along the pass and attack from both sides. After this defeat, control of the military operation was given to a former Texas Ranger, Colonel Jack Hays. He organized a force of 800 Nevada and California volunteers plus some army regulars and tracked the Indians to Pinnacle Mountain, where he defeated them. He then established Fort Churchill to guard the valley and keep the California Trail open.

The Ghost Dance Religion

The Southern Paiutes were indirectly involved in the last significant Indian violence to erupt in the West. In 1888, a Paiute from Nevada by the name of Wovoka (also known as Jack Wilson) founded a religion called the Ghost Dance. He was the son of another mystic, Tavibo, and was affected by his father's teachings. Wovoka experienced a vision during an eclipse of the sun and afterward began preaching that the earth would soon perish, then come alive again in a natural state with lush prairie grass and huge herds of buffalo. There would be no more whites. The Indians, as well as their dead ancestors, would inherit this new world.

Wovoka believed that in order to bring about this new existence, Indians had to purge themselves of the white man's ways, especially alcohol, and live together harmoniously. He also called for meditation, prayer, chanting, and, most of all, dancing. He claimed that Indians could catch a glimpse of this future paradise by performing the Ghost Dance.

The Ghost Dance religion spread to tribes all over the West, especially Arapahos, Shoshones, and Sioux (see entries for those tribes). Some of the Sioux medicine men called for violence against the whites, claiming that magical Ghost Dance Shirts could protect the Indians from the soldiers' bullets. This newfound faith and militancy led up to the massacre of Indians by whites at Wounded Knee in 1890.

Today, Northern and Southern Paiutes live on various reservations in Nevada, Oregon, Utah, Arizona, and California. Many others live off-reservation in those states. The Paiutes have a reputation among ranchers and farmers in the region as highly skilled and dedicated workers. A Paiute from Nevada by the name of Melvin Thom helped found the National Indian Youth Council in 1961, one of the most important of the modern intertribal activist groups (see "Ponca").

Palouse

The Appaloosa breed of horse, with its distinctive spotted coat and its renowned intelligence, speed, and stamina, takes its name from the Palouse Indians. Members of this tribe lived along the Palouse River in territory that now includes parts of eastern Washington State and northern Idaho. The horse, brought to North America by the Spanish, reached this part of North America by the early 1700s, after which the Palouses, Nez Perces, Cayuses, and other tribes of the region became famous as horse breeders and horse traders.

The Palouses, or Palus (both pronounced *puh-LOOS*), are thought to have once been one people with the Yakimas, another tribe who spoke the Penutian language. They also had close ties with the Nez Perces. It was among the Nez Perces that the Lewis and Clark Expedition first saw Appaloosa horses in 1805. These tribes and others on the Columbia Plateau depended heavily on fishing in the many rivers draining toward the Pacific Ocean, and they are considered part of the Plateau Culture Area (see "Plateau Indians").

The Palouses played an important part in the heavy fur trade among whites and the tribes of the American Northwest during the first half of the 1800s. But, with increased white settlement by the mid-1800s, the Palouses joined other tribes in their stand for native lands. Palouse warriors fought in both the Cayuse War of 1847-50 and the Coeur d'Alene War of 1858 (see "Cayuse" and "Coeur d'Alene").

The Palouses as a tribe declined to lead the reservation life forced on many tribes of the region. Some individuals did, however, join their Penutian kinsmen on reservations.

Papago

The name of the Papagos, pronounced *PAH-puh-go*, is derived from *Papahvio-otam*, for "bean people," given by the neighboring Pimas. Their name for themselves was *Toho'no-o-otam*, meaning "desert people." These Indians lived in the Sonoran Desert near the Gulf of California in territory now along the international border between southwest Arizona and northwest Sonora, a state of Mexico.

The Papagos spoke a dialect of the Uto-Aztecan language family, similar to that of the Pima tribe (see

"Pima"). Anthropologists consider both the Papagos and Pimas as part of the Southwest Culture Area (see "Southwest Indians"). They theorize that the two tribes were descended from the ancient Hohokam culture (see "Cliff Dwellers and Desert Farmers").

Lifeways

The peoples of the Hohokam culture irrigated their farmlands by channeling water from rivers. The Pimas also practiced desert irrigation and were able to live in permanent village sites year round. The Papagos, however, were seminomadic, with two different village locations. They passed the warm weather months—from spring until the fall harvest—in the desert, usually at the mouth of an arroyo where flash floods from rainstorms provided water for their fields of corn, beans, squash, tobacco, and cotton. The Indians called these sites their "field villages." They spent the winter in the sierra, near mountain springs. These were the "well villages." Here, they hunted deer and other game for food. In times of famine, Papago families sometimes moved to the Pima villages along the Gila River and worked under the supervision of the host tribe to earn their keep. While working with their kinsmen, the Papagos might sing the following corn song:

Here on the field, corn comes forth.
My child takes it and runs happy.
Here on the field, squash comes forth.
My wife takes it and runs singing.

Since Papago farming was so dependent on rainfall, which did not always come, the Indians made extensive use of wild plant foods as well. They ate the heart of the mescal plant, which took them at least 24 hours to cook in a pit-oven. They also collected the bean-like seeds of the mesquite tree. The sweet and fleshy fruit of the giant saguaro cactus was a delicacy for them. Women used a long pole called a *kuibit*, made from the ribs of the plant, to knock the fruit down. It was eaten fresh or dried. The fresh fruit was also boiled into jam or syrup; the dried fruit was ground into powder and mixed with water for a drink. The Papagos also made saguaro syrup into wine.

Other than their ways of getting food, the lifeways of the Papagos and Pimas were very similar. They both lived in houses covered with brush and mud. They also built open areas called ramadas for socializing. They both wore cotton and leather clothing and favored sandals over moccasins. Both peoples made beautiful coiled baskets out of a variety of materials,

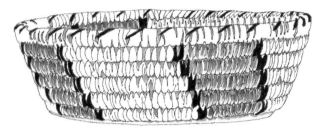

Papago coiled basket

including willow, devil's claw, bear grass, and yucca. They both had village chiefs (although the Papagos had no overall tribal chief as the Pimas did). Each village had a ceremonial leader called the Keeper of the Smoke. The villages of both tribes were divided into two clans or family groups. The names of the Papago clans were the Buzzard and the Coyote. Every four years, both the Papagos and the Pimas celebrated the Viikita, a ceremony with costumed and masked dancers and clowns in order to bring about tribal good fortune. Both tribes worshipped gods known as Earthmaker and Elder Brother.

The Papagos, unlike the Pimas, made annual pilgrimages over the hot desert sands to salt flats near the Gulf of California. They believed that rain spirits lived there, and prayed to them for more of the valuable water. They believed that the drinking of saguaro wine in great amounts would help bring rain.

The Papagos are also famous for their calendar sticks. These were sticks with carved markings to help villagers remember their history over a number of years. The Indians usually used dots and circles to record important ceremonies. Notches usually represented other events such as earthquakes or the building of waterworks or an attack by their longtime enemies, the Apaches (see "Apache").

Contacts with Whites

Although the Papagos might have met up with Spanish explorers in the 1500s, they did not have extensive outside contacts until the late 1600s. Father Eusebio Kino reached what the Spanish called Papagueria in 1687 and in the following years established missions among the Papagos.

Because of their extreme desert environment, the Papagos managed to avoid much of the forced labor and agricultural taxes the Pimas endured under the Spanish. However, some Papagos participated in the Pima Uprising of 1751. The Papago people came under Mexican rule in 1821, with Mexican independence from Spain. Then in 1853, with the Gadsden Purchase, the Papago territory was divided with most falling under United States domain. In the 1860s, for mutual protection from Apache raiders, the Papagos allied themselves with the Pima and Maricopa tribes and the Anglo-Americans. That did not stop the white ranchers from taking Papago water holes and grazing land for their cattle, resulting in some violence between Indians and ranchers.

The Papagos presently hold three reservations in Arizona: the Ak Chin Reservation, the San Xavier Reservation, and the largest of the three, the Papago Reservation. There are also Papagos living in Mexico. Indians of both countries come and go across the international boundary through a gap in the barbed-wire fence known as "The Gate." Tribal members earn some income from farming, cattle raising, and arts and crafts. Papago baskets are famous worldwide. Tribal

Papago awl of mesquite wood and pin (modern)

members also make pottery, wooden bowls, horsehair miniatures, and horsehair lariats.

There are deposits of copper and other minerals on Papago lands. Until recently, powerful Arizona mining concerns owned the rights to these resources. But this situation has been rectified and the Papagos now earn income from mining leases. But they do not have the money to start their own companies, which would give them a larger share of the profits from the mining of their lands.

Passamaquoddy

The Passamaquoddies, like the Penobscots, are often discussed under the more general heading of Abnaki Indians. These Algonquian-speaking people were part of the Abnaki Confederacy, along with other Algonquians. Their history, especially their participation in the Abnaki Wars (the New England phase of the French and Indian Wars), is similar to that of other Abnakis. Although the Passamaquoddies still exist today as a tribe by themselves, to understand them better see also the entries for "Northeast Indians," "Algonquian," and "Abnaki."

Their name (pronounced *pah-suh-muh-KWOD-ee*) means "those who pursue the pollack," which is appropriate. The pollack is a kind of fish. Although the

Passamaquoddy knife for basketmaking

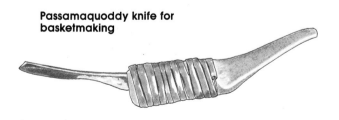

Passamaquoddies, like other New England Algonquians, were hunter-gatherers as well as farmers, they depended more on fishing than many other Woodland Indians, taking advantage of the numerous lakes, rivers, and bays in their territory. The Passamaquoddy Bay in Maine, a major source of their food, was named after them.

The two existing Passamaquoddy reservations —Pleasant Point and Indian Township—are near the town of Calais, Maine. This is the easternmost land in the United States held by Native Americans. As stated in the "Abnaki" entry, the name Abnaki means "those living at the sunrise" or "easterners."

In 1980, the Passamaquoddies and their Penobscot kinsmen won a judgment against the state of Maine in the Maine Indian Claims Settlement Act. The federal and state governments granted them $81 million as repayment for lands unfairly taken away from them by early settlers. The warrior ancestors of the Passamaquoddies would have been proud of them. In this case they applied their fighting spirit not to a physical battle but to a legal battle.

Here is a traditional Passamaquoddy war song:

I will arise with my tomahawk in my hand, and I must have revenge on that nation which has slain my poor people. I arise with warclub in my hand, and follow the bloody track of that nation which killed my people. I will sacrifice my own life and the lives of my warriors. I arise with club in my hand, and follow the track of my enemy. When I overtake him, I will take his scalp and string it on a long pole, and I will stick it in the ground, and my warriors will dance around it for many days. Then I will sing my song for the victory over my enemy.

Patwin

The name of the Patwins (pronounced *PAT-win*), as is the case with many other Indian tribes, means "person" or "people" in their native language. They spoke a dialect of the Penutian language family, similar to that of the Wintuns, a neighboring people. Both tribes had villages along the Sacramento River Valley north of San Francisco Bay into which the river flows. The Patwin homeland is now part of northern California.

Nevertheless, the Patwin Indians are discussed by scholars as a central California tribe along with the Maidus, Pomos, Miwoks, Yokuts, and the tribe of which they are considered a subgroup, the Wintuns (see entries for those tribes). All these Indians, along with peoples farther south, are classified within the California Culture Area (see "California Indians").

These California peoples ate varying foods, and used varying plant materials for their handiwork. Yet all lived in villages and were hunter-gatherers. For all of them, the acorn, prepared in a number of ways, was a staple in their diet. And for all of them, basketry was an important technology.

The Patwins usually lived in domed huts with a pole framework and earthen covering. But they built more simple brush shelters as well.

With regard to social organization, the Patwins had a system for passing from father to son such specialized skills as hunting, fishing, the making of ceremonial objects, bow and arrow making, pipe making, fire building, or salt making. In other words, a family had a monopoly on a certain activity and would perform this service for other members of the tribe in exchange for payment. This type of social organization was unusual among native peoples.

Concerning religion and mythology, the Patwins, like most other Central California peoples, participated in the Kuksu Cult. The Kuksus were a secret society. Members impersonated spirit beings in order to get closer to them and acquire some of their power. Kuksus wore long feather or grass headdresses that disguised them from fellow villagers. Kuksu was a principal god, shared by several tribes. Different tribes had different names for their gods, however. Moki was the most powerful god-figure to the Patwins. To disguise oneself as Moki was a major responsibility. The Patwins believed that to make a mistake in the ritual meant death. Other powerful spirits in the Patwin religion were Tuya the Big-Headed, and Chelitu the Unmasked.

The Kuksu Cult held its ceremonies in the cold months to bring about an abundance of wild plant foods and game the following spring and summer. The Patwin Kuksus called the first of their rituals *Hesi*. Hesi was a four-day dance, with one Kuksu acting out Moki, and others, in pairs, representing different versions of Tuya and Chelitu. While villagers looked on, drummers provided a beat for the dancers, usually by stomping on a foot drum, and singers chanted sacred Kuksu songs.

The arrival of a great number of whites in the Sacramento Valley, especially after the California Gold Rush of 1849, was hard on the Patwins. White diseases killed many of the tribe, as did isolated incidents of violence carried out by miners. The Patwins eventually lost their land and their traditional culture and, by the early 1900s, their tribal identity. The descendants of the Patwins use the Wintun tribal name, as do the Nomlakis and Wintus (see "Wintun").

Pawnee

The Pawnee name (pronounced *PAW-nee* or *paw-NEE*) probably comes from the Caddoan word *pariki*, meaning "horn," after the upright and curved scalplock hairstyle particular to the tribe. Or their name might be derived from the word *parisu*, meaning "hunter."

The Pawnees split off from other Caddoan-speaking peoples before whites came to North America. They migrated northward from what is now Texas, first to the Red River region of southern Oklahoma, and then to the Arkansas River region of northern Oklahoma and southern Kansas. They may have been the first Indians on the Great Plains since much earlier prehistoric peoples (see "Prehistoric Indians"). The Pawnees lived there when early Spanish explorers pushing northeastward out of Mexico—such as Francisco de Coronado in 1541, and Juan de Onate in 1601—encountered them.

By the early 1700s, the Pawnees had divided into four major bands: the Skidi; the Grand; the Republican; and the Tapage (or Noisy). The Grand, Republican, and Tapage bands spoke a similar dialect and came to be called the Southern Pawnees (or Black Pawnees). They stayed along the Arkansas River for much of their history. The Skidi Pawnees migrated farther north to the Platte River, the Loup River, and the Republican Fork of the Kansas River in what is now Nebraska. They are referred to as the Northern Pawnees.

During the 1700s, French traders made regular stops at Southern Pawnee villages to trade guns, tools, and other European trade items for buffalo robes and other animal pelts. Caddoan relatives of the Pawnees—the Caddos and Wichitas—were central to French trade west of the Mississippi River (see "Caddo" and "Wichita"). Other Caddoan relatives, the Arikaras, also had important trading villages on the upper Missouri (see "Arikara").

When France lost its holdings in North America in 1763 after the French and Indian Wars, the fur trade declined for the Missouri River Indians. In 1770, the Southern Pawnees migrated northward to join the Skidi Pawnees.

The opening of the American frontier after the Louisiana Purchase of 1803 brought more and more settlers to the lands of the Pawnees. From the very outset, the Pawnees were peaceful in their relations with the newcomers. In addition to trade advantages from this friendship, the Pawnees wanted allies against their traditional enemies—the Sioux, Cheyennes, Arapahos, Kiowas, and Comanches—who often raided Pawnee villages and vice versa. (One Sioux warrior bore the name "Pawnee Killer," because of his deeds in battle against the Pawnees.)

The fact that the Pawnees were allies and friends of the settlers did not stop whites from taking their lands. By the mid-1800s, tribal representatives had signed a number of treaties giving all their territory to the United States, except for a reservation along the banks of the Loup River near present-day Fullerton, Nebraska.

Even so, the Pawnees continued to support the whites against other Indians in the wars for the Plains. They became the most famous of all Indian scouts for the U.S. Army under Frank and Luther North, who organized a battalion of Pawnee scouts active from 1865 to 1885. Other Pawnees under Sky Chief worked as guards for railroad construction crews.

The Pawnees' assistance to whites angered other tribes. In 1873, a Sioux war party ambushed a Pawnee hunting party in southern Nebraska and killed 150, including Sky Chief, before an army detachment came to the rescue. The site of this incident became known as Massacre Canyon.

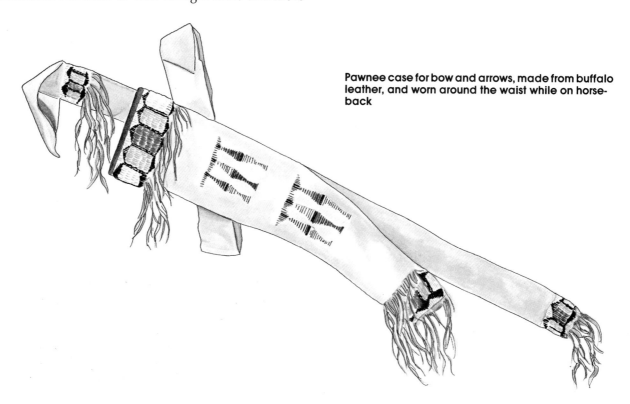

Pawnee case for bow and arrows, made from buffalo leather, and worn around the waist while on horseback

Pawnee skull representing the First Man

Despite their great contribution and sacrifice on behalf of the United States, the Pawnees were pressured into giving up their Nebraska reservation in 1876. They were relocated to the Indian Territory (Oklahoma), where their descendants live today near the city of Pawnee.

The Pawnees are an intriguing cultural mix. Since they lived in permanent villages much of the year and farmed, they are classified as part of the Prairie group of the Great Plains Culture Area (see "Prairie Indians" and "Plains Indians"). They were such skillful farmers that some varieties of their seeds are still used by modern farmers. In their villages, the Pawnees lived in earthlodges, unlike their kinsmen the Caddos and Wichitas, who lived in grass houses. While on the trail in pursuit of buffalo, however, the Pawnees lived in tepees. After they acquired horses, they roamed far from their homeland to hunting grounds in Wyoming and New Mexico. They shared many other customs of the Prairie and Plains tribes, such as several rituals surrounding the growing of corn and the buffalo hunt.

But the Pawnees also possessed cultural traits similar to the early Temple Mound culture of the Southeast and by extension to Mesoamerican cultures (see "Mound Builders" and "Aztec"). They even kept these traits longer than their relatives the Caddos, who lived nearer to the Southeast tribes.

Pawnee religion had a strict and complex structure. Their medicine men constituted a whole class of people, like a priesthood. These priests were responsible for many elaborate ceremonies. The ceremonies were made up of songs, poetry, and dances, all rich in symbolism concerning the heavenly bodies. Like the Aztecs and the Mound Builders, the Pawnees can be called sun-worshipers and moon-worshipers.

There was one Skidi Pawnee custom that was especially unusual for Indians north of Mexico in the historic period—the practice of human sacrifice. As late as the early 1800s, the Pawnees still performed this now-shocking deed. The ritual was called the Morning Star Ceremony. The Skidi Pawnees believed that the supreme god was Tirawa, the Sun. Tirawa and Mother Earth conceived Morning Star, the God of Vegetation.

Once a year, the Skidis would raid another tribe with the purpose of capturing a young girl about 13 years old. They would let this girl live among them for months, treating her with kindness and keeping secret from her their frightening plans. Early in the morning at the time of the summer solstice, the longest day of the year, the priests would paint half the maiden's body red, for day, and the other half black, for night. Then they would tie her to a rectangular frame in the fields outside the village. As the morning star rose, three priests would perform the horrible murder with a torch, an arrow, and a knife. Then every male who could handle a bow would shoot arrows into the body. The corpse was left behind to fertilize the earth. The tribe then held a festival of dancing and singing.

Not all Pawnees approved of this terrible act passed down among priests over the centuries. Finally, one Pawnee chief was brave enough to stop it. His name was Petalesharo ("Man-Chief"). In 1816, when he was only 19, he rescued a Comanche girl from the scaffold at the last minute and commanded the priests to stop their barbarism and cruelty. Other warriors backed him up despite the priests' threats of placing curses on them. Petalesharo became a hero of future generations of Pawnees for standing up to the powerful priesthood.

Of course, the Morning Star Ceremony is no longer a part of Pawnee religion. What remains from the past are beautiful songs, poetry, and dances. These can be enjoyed at the annual pageants of the Pawnees and Wichitas of Oklahoma.

Pawnee man

Pennacook

The Pennacooks inhabited the region of North America that has become New Hampshire. They also had hunting grounds in Maine and northeast Massachusetts. There were many different Algonquian-speaking bands, with different names, living in various parts of New Hampshire (see "Northeast Indians" and "Algonquian"). But these bands are grouped together under the general name of Pennacook, which was the name of a band and village at the site of present-day Concord, now the capital of the state. Pennacook, pronounced *PEN-uh-cook*, means "at the bottom of the hill." The various Pennacook bands are sometimes classified with the Abnaki Indians of Maine, with whom they were allied in a confederacy for part of their history (see "Abnaki").

If one travels through New Hampshire, and all New England, one notices many towns and geographical features bearing Algonquian names. Each place name has a story that can shed light on Indian history, legend, and custom. For example, there is a town of Penacook and a lake called Penacook (note the alternate spelling).

There are hundreds more Indian names across the granite and birch landscape of New Hampshire. A road through the Sandwich Range along the state's southern border, connecting Conway and Lincoln, is called the Kancamagus Highway. This name honors the last sachem, or chief, of the Pennacooks; one of the mountains in the Sandwich Range also bears his name. Other mountains nearby in the same range bear the name of Paugus and Passaconaway.

In 1675, at the time of King Philip's War, led by King Philip, chief of the Wampanoags (see "Wampanoag"), Kancamagus of the Pennacooks decided to keep the peace with the British colonists. His cousin Paugus, however, favored the path of war. Both men were grandsons of Passaconaway, the first Pennacook sachem to establish relations and trade with the British settlers.

The British, in order to set an example of toughness to all the Indians, tricked some of the peaceful bands into coming to a sporting meet at Dover. Then the whites attacked, killed, and captured many of their guests, and sold many into slavery. At that time, Kancamagus became an enemy of the British. Years later in 1689, at the beginning of the French and Indian Wars between England and France, Kancamagus found his revenge, with an attack on the settlement of Dover. His squaws tricked the settlers into leaving the gates of their stockade open. Many settlers died in the ensuing fight.

Now it was the British turn for revenge. They persuaded their allies, the Mohawks, to attack the Pennacooks. The Mohawks swept in from the west and destroyed many Pennacook villages. Kancamagus and his warriors took up positions behind log walls at Lake Winnisquam (an Algonquian name referring to the salmon there). The Mohawks attacked in great numbers. The Pennacooks repelled the attackers; then they snuck away at night. This place of battle today has an Indian name—Mohawk Point. Then Kancamagus led his people through the mountains, following much of the route the Kancamagus highway now takes, to the Connecticut Valley and on to Quebec, in Canada, where they joined up with Abnakis (Connecticut is also an Indian name, meaning "the long river").

Other place names speak to us of Indian legends. One such location is Squaw Cove in Big Squam Lake (meaning "big salmon lake"). A granite boulder that once stood along the shore resembled a crouching woman. Legend has it that an old Indian sachem wanted a young bride and chose a girl named Suneta. But Suneta loved a young brave by the name of Anonis. Anonis, far away at the time, could not make it back in time to prevent the wedding. After the wedding feast, the old sachem fell asleep. A storm arose on the lake. Suneta, alone in her wigwam, wept quietly. Anonis suddenly appeared out of the rain and darkness. He beckoned Suneta to flight. They would start a new life elsewhere. But, as they hurried off, the sachem awoke. He strung his bow and shot Anonis in the back. Suneta, heartbroken, ran to the shore, crouched down, and prayed to Manitou, the Great Spirit, asking to be saved from her fate. At daybreak, when the storm had passed, the figure of Suneta still crouched on the shore. But she had been turned to granite. The rock became known as Squaw Rock.

Still other place names tell of Indian customs. Those with animal or fish names, like Lake Winnisquam and Big Squam Lake, indicate that the Pennacooks once came there in search of salmon for food. Another example is the place called Indian Leap along the Lost River Highway near Franconia Notch. Over the centuries, a stream has worn large potholes in the granite boulders, forming deep pools and high ledges. It is reported that Indians brought young boys to this spot to test their courage. They would have to jump from boulder to boulder, along the jagged points jutting out over the dark, cold pools 20 feet below. A slip would mean death or injury. Supposedly, those who hesitated were not ready for warfare. But those who leaped fearlessly would one day be great warriors.

Few Indians are left in New Hampshire, and there are no reservation lands in the state. But Indian place names remind us of their once-great presence. And some of the Algonquian peoples of Canada can claim to be partly descended from the Pennacooks who came from the south to settle among their other ancestors.

Penobscot

In some books, the Penobscots are discussed, along with other Indians of Maine, as Abnakis. The Penobscots belonged to the Abnaki Confederacy and had a history, language, and culture in common with their fellow Algonquians (see "Northeast Indians"; "Algonquian"; and "Abnaki"). But their descendants still use their more specific tribal name, Penobscot (pronounced *puh-NOB-scot*), which means "the rocky place," and refers to rocky falls in the river where their ancestors lived and where they still live today. Like many towns and geographical features in the United States and Canada, the river bears an Indian name—their own name, Penobscot—as does the bay it feeds. The river's waters roll along the bordering rocks like Algonquian phrases once rolled upon Indian tongues.

To better understand the way of life of all the Algonquians who lived in northern New England, we can view a typical year in the life of Penobscot families.

Winter

Winter, of course, was the hardest time. Food was scarce. Families had to leave the central Penobscot village of square houses with pyramid roofs plus cone-shaped wigwams and follow the game animals into the snow-laden forests. Since no one area could support too many people, each family had its own hunting grounds. With everyone dressed warmly in furs and sometimes wearing foxskin hats, a father and mother would paddle their children and possessions in a birchbark canoe, then carry the canoe the rest of the way over land. Sometimes they even carried fire in a shell inside a deerskin bag since fires were so hard to start with only the friction method of rubbing sticks.

Once established in their camp, having constructed their temporary wigwams and lean-tos, the father set out to track or trap whatever game, large or small, he could. Boys who were old enough to take care of

themselves on the trail might accompany him, wearing snowshoes like their father's. Deer or elk was a favorite catch. Hunters wore deerskins, with the horns on their heads, in order to trick the swift animals. Sometimes a deadfall—a trap designed to drop a heavy weight on an animal—would prove more successful than an arrow or spear. The Penobscots did not shun dangerous game either, like bears. One method of catching the eastern brown bears was to throw a piece of wood at the animals when they reared up to attack. When the bears went to catch the wood with their deadly front claws, hunters could strike them on the head with a club. If the Indians were lucky enough to capture game too big to carry, they could drag it back to camp on toboggans.

Penobscot cradleboard

In the meantime, the women were working hard—keeping the fire going, cooking and storing food, curing leather, sewing furs, and making containers. Little girls had to learn these crafts at a young age. Survival depended on everyone doing his or her job. And when the game ran out in one area, the family had to move on, but not so far as to encroach on some other family's territory.

Spring and Summer

The various families returned to their permanent villages along the river in the spring and summer. After the cramped quarters of the winter camps, the larger village lodges and wigwams seemed roomy and comfortable. The villages were surrounded by upright log walls, or palisades, as protection from raiding enemies, such as the Mohawks to the west.

In early spring, the Penobscots harvested the sap from the maple trees and boiled it to make maple syrup. Then, when the ground thawed and early morning freezes stopped, they cultivated the rocky northern soil to plant their gardens. Corn was the staple crop. The first harvest càme as early as July. But even during the mild months, when plant foods were available, the Penobscot men left the village to hunt. And they fished the river, using harpoons and nets. In the difficult Penobscot existence, there was never too much food. Any excess could be preserved by various means—drying in the sun, or smoking, to help endure the long winter months. Now that the weather was milder, children had more time to play games and make toys. Quite often their games, such as throwing a spear at a hoop, served to develop later survival skills.

One of the favorite times of year was the summer trip down the Penobscot River to the Atlantic Ocean. Here, the Penobscots had a change of diet—clams, lobsters, crabs, and possibly even seals. And the children rode the surf as children today do on summer trips to the beach. There was time for socializing and for rituals—song and dance and communication with the spirits of nature that the Penobscots believed provided their food.

Fall

Work was continuous. In the fall, families, back in their villages, made final preparations for the winter journey—preserving food, making and repairing weapons, utensils, and clothing. This was also a good time for moose-hunting, because the animals began to travel farther in search of food.

When one wanders through the sometimes lush and sometimes bleak northern woods, along the swift-flowing rivers, and along the pounding surf, one can almost feel the Indian presence—patient hunters, diligent farmers and artisans, playful children. Probably every square foot of soil was crisscrossed by moccasin or snowshoe.

Fortunately, one can still see the Indian presence as well—at Indian Island, the beautiful Penobscot Reservation on the Penobscot River, next to Old Town, Maine. In 1980, the Penobscots and Passamaquoddies were granted a settlement of $81 million from the state and federal government because of lands unfairly taken from them by early settlers. The Penobscots have invested their money well and are building a good life for themselves.

Penobscot basket (modern)

Pequot

For early Indians southern New England was choice territory. First, this part of North America has good topsoil for growing corn, beans, and squash. The soil of the lower Connecticut River Valley and along Narragansett Bay is especially fertile. Second, the forests, with all kinds of hardwood and evergreen trees, are a good environment for all sorts of game. And third, unlike the east shore in northern New England that faces the Atlantic, the south shore is sheltered from the elements. Long Island, which extends eastward into the Atlantic Ocean, protects much of the coast from the heavy winds and large waves of the open ocean. Block

Island, Fishers Island, Martha's Vineyard, and Nantucket also break the path of storms, as do numerous smaller islands. As a result, in the southern part of all three states touching the south shore—Connecticut, Rhode Island, and Massachusetts—there are many quiet bays and inlets, with fish and shellfish for the taking.

Various groups of Algonquian-speaking peoples competed for this rich territory (see "Algonquian" and "Northeast Indians"). One of the most powerful and warlike tribes was the Pequots. Before the arrival of whites, they supposedly had migrated from the Hudson River Valley in New York State. They fought with other Algonquians, both the Narragansets and Niantics, for land (see "Narraganset"). Soon after the arrival of the Puritans and other English colonists in the early 1600s, the Pequots had gained control of most of the Connecticut coastal area from the Connecticut River to Rhode Island. They had even attacked and defeated many of the Montauk tribes on Long Island. No wonder they were known as the Pequots (pronounced *PEE-kwot*), meaning "Destroyers." Their name is sometimes spelled *Pequod*.

At the time of Pequot dominance, Sassacus was the grand sachem, or great chief. His village was situated on the Thames River. He had 26 subordinate chiefs under him, each with his own walled village of wigwams. One of these lesser chiefs, Uncas, was dissatisfied with Sassacus's rule and broke off to form his own tribe. This group came to be known as the Mohegans (see "Mohegan"). The Mohegans became allies of the colonists. But Sassacus and his Pequots resented the growing presence of the British settlers. There were disputes over land and trade goods. Tensions mounted.

The Pequot War

War finally broke out in 1636. The Pequot War was the first major conflict in New England. The death of a coastal trader, John Oldham, in July of that year caused the outbreak of violence. Another coastal trader, John Gallup, discovered Oldham's hijacked boat off Block Island, skirmished with the Pequots aboard, then reported the incident to colonial officials.

Massachusetts Bay Colony ordered out an expedition under John Endecott. His force attacked Indians on Block Island and burned their villages. But many of those killed were Narragansets and not Pequots. In their thirst for revenge, the soldiers did not bother to distinguish among the various Algonquian tribes.

Then Endecott's army sailed to the Connecticut mainland in search of Pequots. The settlers at Fort Saybrook tried to talk Endecott out of further attacks because they feared Indian reprisals. But Endecott was intent on revenge and burned several Pequot villages, killing one brave. The strict Puritans of the Massachusetts Bay Colony regarded the Pequots as agents of Satan and would stop at nothing to punish them.

Now it was Sassacus's turn for revenge. During the winter of 1636-37, his warriors laid siege on Fort Saybrook and raided isolated settlements. In the spring, they killed nine colonists at Wethersfield, up the Connecticut River.

The colonies mounted a large army under Captain John Mason and Captain John Underhill. The force sailed westward along the Connecticut coast, then circled back, overland, from Narragansett Bay. Despite the attack on their people on Block Island, Narragansets joined the colonial force against their enemies the Pequots, as did Mohegans and Niantics.

At dawn on May 25, 1637, the invading army attacked Sassacus's village. The Pequots fought bravely from behind their palisades (walls made by setting upright logs in the earth), repelling the first attack. But the colonists managed to set the Pequot wigwams on fire. Those who fled the flames were cut down in the surrounding countryside. Those who stayed behind, mostly women and children, burned to death. Perhaps 600 Pequots died that morning, or as many as 1,000. Sassacus and others escaped. His group was attacked in a swamp west of New Haven the following July, but he managed to escape again, seeking refuge in Mohawk territory. However, the Mohawks did not want war with the British. To prove that they had no part in the Pequot uprising, they beheaded the Pequot grand sachem.

Pequot captives were sold into slavery in the Caribbean, or given as slaves to the Mohegans, Narragansets, and Niantics as payment for their help in the war. The colonists no longer permitted the use of the Pequot tribal name or the use of Pequot place names. Some Pequots escaped to Long Island and Massachusetts, where they settled with other Algonquians. In 1655, the colonists freed Pequot slaves in New England and resettled them on the Mystic River.

Some Pequot descendants still live in Connecticut. They share three small reservations with their relatives the Mohegans in New London and Fairfield counties. Another Pequot group, the Schaghticokes, who settled along the Housatonic River after the Pequot War, hold a third reservation along with the Paugusset band of Wappingers in Litchfield County (see "Wappinger").

Pima

The Pima name (pronounced *PEE-mah*) is derived from the native phrase *pi-nyi-match*, which means "I don't know." It came to be applied to the tribe when the Indians used it in response to questions by early Spanish explorers. The Pimas originally called themselves *Ah-kee-mult-o-o-tam*, meaning "river people," to distinguish themselves from the *Toho'no-o-otam*, or "desert people," their kinsmen the Papagos. Both the Pimas and Papagos spoke dialects of the Uto-Aztecan language family (see "Papago").

The Pimas dwelt in lands now mapped as part of southern Arizona and northern Sonora, a state of Mexico. They were divided into two major groups—the Pima Alto, or Upper Pima, and the Pima Bajo, or Lower Pima. The Upper Pimas lived along the Gila and Salt rivers. The Lower Pimas, or Nevones, as they are called in Mexico, lived along the Yaqui and Sonora rivers much farther south. The Papagos lived to the immediate west of the Upper Pimas. Both Pimas and Papagos are categorized in the Southwest Culture Area by scholars (see "Southwest Indians").

It is thought that the ancient ancestors of the Pimas and Papagos were the people of the Hohokam Culture. *Hohokam* is a Pima word, meaning "vanished ones." The Hohokam peoples constructed advanced irrigation systems in the Gila and Salt river valleys (see "Cliff Dwellers and Desert Farmers").

Lifeways

The Pimas, villagers and farmers, irrigated their fields by diverting water from rivers. They grew corn, squash, pumpkins, kidney beans, tobacco, cotton, and, after the whites brought the seeds to them, wheat and alfalfa. The men were the farmers and the fishermen, as well as the hunters of small game, such as rabbits. The men also did all the building. Pima houses were small, round, flat-topped, pole-framed structures, covered with grass and mud. Their villages also contained a number of ramadas, rectangular structures similarly built but with no walls at all or just one wall as a windbreak. The ramadas were used as clubhouses. Small square huts were used for storage.

The women gathered wild plant foods, such as saguaro cactus fruits and mesquite seeds. Women made baskets from willow and other plants and

Pima house

shaped and polished red-and-black pottery. They also made clothing—cotton breechcloths for men and outfits of shredded bark for themselves, as well as hide sandals and cotton and rabbit-skin blankets for both sexes. Men wove cotton on a horizontal loom.

The Pimas had an overall tribal chief, elected from among the various village chiefs. He presided over councils. The responsibilities of the village chiefs under him included overseeing communal farm projects and defending against Apache raiders (see "Apache"). Each village had a ceremonial leader as well, known as the Keeper of the Smoke. Each village was organized into two clans—the Red Ant and White Ant clans—who opposed each other in games. Unlike some tribes, the Pimas allowed members from the same clan to marry. Every fourth harvest, the Pimas held a festival, called the Viikita, to celebrate continuing tribal well-being and ensure future good fortune. In the Pima religion, the most powerful gods were the Earthmaker and Elder Brother.

Contacts with Whites

Europeans first learned of the Pimas when the Spanish explorer Marcos de Niza visited them in 1589. Then Father Eusebio Kino entered their territory on several occasions from 1694 to 1698. He grouped the Indians in missions and introduced them to livestock and wheat. Another Spanish explorer, Father Francisco

Garces, traveled deeper into Pima country from 1768 to 1776.

Although the Pimas could be warlike—as the Apaches who mounted raids against them well knew—they were generally friendly toward the Spanish. During the 1600s, Spanish officials organized Pima territory into the district of Pimeria Alta, establishing missions, presidios (forts), ranches, and mines among them. And the Spanish began imposing taxes on the Indians, demanding a percentage of their crops as well as labor from them. In 1695, the Lower Pimas rebelled, carrying out some violence against missionaries as well as looting and burning of Spanish property. Spanish officials sent in soldiers, who quickly put down the rebellion. Some Pimas, however, escaped northward and joined the Upper Pimas on the Gila and Salt rivers.

Some of the descendants of the rebels revolted again in 1751. A Pima by the name of Luis Oacpicagigua, who served the Spanish as a captain-general against other Indians, began to resent Spanish treatment of his people. He saw that the Spanish ranching and mining frontier was expanding northward into Upper Pima country, and he knew that more and more forced

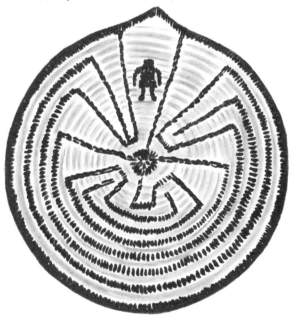

Pima basket with labyrinth design

labor would follow. He plotted a rebellion, sending word to neighboring tribes—Papagos, Apaches, and Sobaipuris—to join his cause.

On the night of November 20, the rebels struck. Luis and his war party attacked and killed 18 Spaniards at the settlement of Saric. A missionary managed to escape, however, and spread word of the uprising. Still, small groups of Pimas and Papagos plundered a number of other missions and rancherias. The

Apaches and Sobaipuris did not join the fight, however. And the majority of Pimas and Papagos, fearful of Spanish reprisals, refrained from violence.

Spanish officials ordered presidio captains and troops into the field. They quelled the revolt in several months, executing some of the rebels. Luis Oacpicagigua saved himself by agreeing to supervise the rebuilding of churches destroyed in the uprising.

After that, the Pimas were peaceful toward whites. During the California Gold Rush, starting in 1849, when many Anglo-Americans passed through their territory, they even provided food and supplies for weary travelers.

Pima territory came under United States authority with the Gadsden Purchase from Mexico in 1853. In the following years, many Anglo-American farmers began settling along the Gila River. The settlers, despite the friendly nature of the Pimas, took advantage of the Indians. They appropriated the best farmland. They diverted the Pimas' water supply for use on their own crops. A reservation on the Gila River was established in 1859. Nevertheless, many Gila River Pimas ended up resettling to the north on the Salt River, where a reservation was established in 1879.

Pimas Today

The Pimas share the Gila River and Salt River reservations with the Maricopas. The Maricopas, a Yuman-speaking people, originally migrated to Pima country from the west during the 1700s because of attacks on them by the warlike Yumas (see "Yuma"). There are also some Pima descendants living among the Papagos on the Ak Chin Reservation. A Pima Indian by the name of Ira Hayes, a marine in World War II, was one of six men who helped raise the flag on Iwo Jima, a famous event on the Pacific Front. He died in 1955.

The modern-day Pimas have a low standard of living. They lack funds to drill wells for farming and lease much of their land to white farmers. Moreover, a recent study has shown that the Pimas have the highest rate of diabetes in the world. It is theorized that their susceptibility to this disease results from the fact that the Pima ancestors were accustomed to life in the Sonoran Desert where they had very little food. Then, with the arrival of whites, their pattern of living changed. They were less active and ate more. Many of them became overweight, a major contributing factor to diabetes. In 1979, Indian Health Services began a project among the Pimas, using blood-sugar monitoring and changes in diet to try to solve this serious problem.

Plains Indians

Even those people who know little about Native Americans, their numerous tribes and many different ways of life, are familiar with the Plains Indians. They are the most famous of all the Indians. Their horsemanship, buffalo-hunting, tepees, and warbonnets are the most often represented symbols from Indian history.

Some people think that all Indians looked and lived like the Plains Indians. Some people even think that modern Indians still dress and act like the Plains Indians. As this book shows, there was and is a great variety to Native American culture, and it is difficult to generalize about the many different tribes. There are all kinds of lifestyles and professions among contemporary Indians. These contemporary Indians do not like to be stereotyped. They want their wide range of cultures, identities, and histories to be recognized and understood.

But why are the Plains Indians, of all the Native Americans, so famous? One reason is that many of the Plains tribes retained their original way of life longer than most other native peoples, through most of the 19th century. Most of the final wave of Indian wars involved the Plains tribes. This is a period of American history re-created time and again in books, movies, and television shows. The Indian fighters of that period captured the national imagination then, and they still do today, for their bravery, skill, and resourcefulness. Moreover, there is something especially romantic about the Plains way of life—freedom of movement and independence on the open range, plus colorful clothing and homes—that still strikes a chord in us.

Who exactly were the Plains Indians? What and where are the Plains? The phrase *Plains Indians* is one way to refer to the many tribes of the Great Plains Culture Area. A culture area is a category devised by scholars. It is a geographical region where different peoples shared cultural traits. The Great Plains Culture Area, as defined by experts on Indian culture, extends over a vast area: east to west, from the Mississippi River Valley to the Rocky Mountains; north to south, from territory in present-day Manitoba, Saskatchewan, and Alberta in Canada all the way to central Texas in the United States.

Most of the country in this region is treeless grassland. There are two types of grasslands: (1) that of the

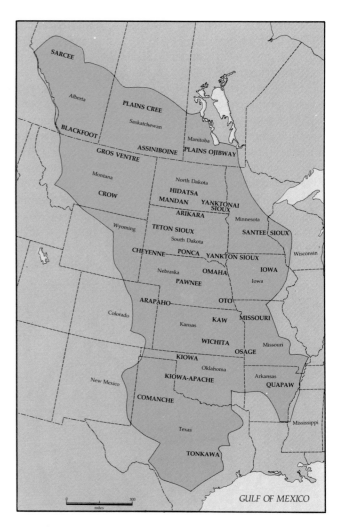

The Great Plains Culture Area, showing the approximate locations of Indian tribes listed in this book—circa 1820, after the acquisition of horses and migration onto the Plains, and before displacement by whites (with modern boundaries)

Mississippi Valley region, where there is plenty of rainfall—about 20 to 40 inches—and tall grass; sometimes called the Prairie Plains, or simply the prairies; (2) that of the west, where there is less rain—about 10 to 20 inches—and short grass; known as the high plains, or the Great Plains.

The flat or rolling grasslands are interrupted in places by stands of trees, especially willows and cottonwoods along the numerous rivers flowing eastward into the Missouri and the Mississippi. Moreover, in some locations, highlands rise up from the Plains: the Ozarks of Missouri and Arkansas; the Black Hills of South Dakota and Wyoming; and the Badlands of South Dakota. These mountains, hills, plateaus, and buttes are often dotted by pine trees. Yet what is remarkable about the Plains is the sameness—an enormous ocean of grass stretching over thousands of miles.

Many different kinds of animals, both large and small, lived on these grasslands, including antelope, deer, elk, bears, wolves, coyotes, and rabbits. The environment was especially suitable to one big grazing animal: the shaggy-maned, short-horned, fleshy-humped, hoofed creature known as the American bison, or the buffalo. The buffalo was central to the Plains Indian economy, providing meat for food, as well as hides, bones, and horns for shelter, clothing, and tools.

The Great Plains Culture Area is different from other Native American culture areas in that the typical Indian way of life evolved only after the arrival of whites. What made the nomadic buffalo-hunting life possible was the horse, which was first brought to North America by the Spanish in the 1500s. (Native North American horses had died out in prehistoric times; see "Prehistoric Indians.") Indians in the Southwest gained widespread use of horses by the late 1600s. And Plains tribes acquired use of the animal in the early to mid-1700s.

Because of horses, native peoples were no longer dependent on farming along the fertile river valleys to supply enough food for their people. They could now range over a wide area in search of the great buffalo herds, carrying all their possessions with them. Portable tepees of poles and buffalo hide proved practical for life on the trail. Not all tribes on the Plains completely abandoned their permanent villages of earth or grass lodges and their farming. But, with horses, the Indians tended to leave the villages for longer periods on wide-ranging hunting expeditions.

Many different peoples adopted the new nomadic way of life, migrating onto the Plains from different directions. Many of these peoples were being pushed from their ancestral homelands by white settlers or by eastern tribes armed with guns acquired from whites.

Once on the Plains, the Indians began sharing other customs besides horses, buffalo-hunting, and tepees. They passed on religious rituals and methods of warfare. In order to communicate with one another for purposes of council or trade, Plains Indians also devised a language of the hands. In this shared sign language, each tribe had its own gesture to identify it.

Plains Indians are sometimes described as belonging to a Composite Plains tribe because different ways of life merged into one.

Ancient Indians had once lived on the Plains. But it is thought they left the region, probably because of drought, in the 13th century. The earliest inhabitants on the Plains after that time may have been the early agricultural tribes of the Missouri River Valley: Caddoan-speaking Pawnee, Arikara, and Wichita; and Siouan-speaking Mandan and Hidatsa. It is thought that there were only two non-farming tribes on the Great Plains before 1500: the Algonquian-speaking Blackfoot and the Uto-Aztecan-speaking Comanche. But then, during the 1600s and 1700s, other tribes came to the region: the Algonquian-speaking Arapaho, Cheyenne, Gros Ventre, Plains Cree, and Plains Ojibway; the Kiowa-Tanoan-speaking Kiowa; the Athapascan-speaking Kiowa-Apache and Sarcee; the Tonkawan-speaking Tonkawa; and the Siouan-speaking Assiniboine, Crow, Iowa, Kaw, Missouri, Omaha, Osage, Oto, Ponca, Quapaw, and Sioux.

Plains tribes really consisted of bands of related families. Each band had a few hundred members. The bands lived apart most of the year, but gathered in the summer for communal buffalo hunts and religious rituals.

Some books make a distinction between the tribes of the tall-grass prairies, and those of the short-grass high plains, since many of the former had permanent villages and continued farming part of the year, while the more western peoples set up only temporary camps and gave up farming altogether. Nevertheless, the so-called Prairie tribes are depicted on the accompanying map as part of the Great Plains Culture Area along with the western Plains peoples. (See the entry under "Prairie Indians" to learn which tribes are sometimes classified differently.)

Each one of the tribes mentioned has its own particular history and lifeways. Be sure to see the entries under their tribal names to learn about the historical and cultural distinctions among the various Plains tribes. The following text will discuss some of the most important cultural traits shared by most Plains peoples in order to give an overview of the region.

The Horse

It has already been mentioned how the horse revolutionized the mode of transportation and the economy of many Indian peoples, and led to the typical way of life found in the Great Plains Culture Area. Some Plains tribes called the horse Sacred Dog, Spirit

Dog, or Medicine Dog. Imagine what Native Americans may have thought when they saw these magnificent creatures for the first time—first fear and then, perhaps, wonder. Imagine too their excitement on learning how to ride horses, hunt on them, and fight on them. Imagine how horses made life easier. Now the Indians could readily travel great distances. They could also carry heavy loads with them on the trail.

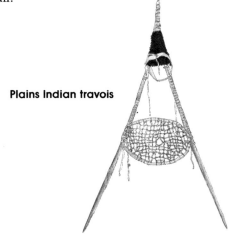

Plains Indian travois

Many of the Plains Indians had originally used dogs to carry possessions. The dogs pulled two poles tied together in the shape of a V; the closed end rested on their shoulders, and the open end on the ground, with hide stretched between the poles. These primitive sleds are called *travois*. Women sometimes also pulled travois. But, with the horse, Indians could utilize much larger travois and place many more supplies on them. Horse travois could even support the sick or elderly or children if need be. And the wooden framework doubled as tepee poles.

In addition to travois, Plains Indians crafted other gear for horses. They generally rode bareback, with only a rawhide thong noosed around the horse's lower jaw as a bridle. But some Indians used blankets or small hide saddles stuffed with buffalo hair or grass. Others used more elaborate wood saddles covered with deerskin and decorated with beadwork, plus decorated stirrups and bridles. Leather and beadwork ornaments were sometimes attached to bridles or draped over the horse's shoulders. Parfleches (leather bags) were also hung from saddles. And some Indians painted their war mounts with symbols, or trimmed and dyed their mounts' manes and tails, or placed eagle feathers or ribbons in their manes.

However they chose to ride, Plains Indians proved the best horsemen in the world. Their prowess on the hunt or in battle was legendary. With only ropes tied around their horses' neck, in which they hooked their elbows, some warriors could suspend themselves along the horses' flanks, using the animals as shields, and shoot arrows under their necks. Grasping their mount firmly with their legs, some warriors could also bend over far enough while moving to pick up wounded comrades.

Horses became a sign of wealth for Plains Indians. Some war chiefs were known to personally own 1,000 horses. A man commonly gave horses to the family of his wife-to-be. Indians acquired horses in the wild, and tamed them, but also carried out raids to take other tribes' horses. Plains Indians became skilled breeders as well as riders. They chose the fastest and most responsive stallions for breeding. Indian ponies consistently outperformed the larger U.S. Army mounts in battle during the Plains wars of the 1800s.

The Buffalo

Before they acquired horses, Indians used various means to hunt buffalo, such as sneaking up on them in an animal disguise or stampeding them over cliffs or into corrals. On horseback, they could ride with the galloping herds, picking off game with bows and arrows, lances, or rifles. The early muzzle-loading rifles brought to the Plains by European traders were less effective than traditional hunting weapons. They were difficult and slow to reload on horseback. The Indians readily took to the new breech-loading rifles in the mid-1800s, however.

Buffalo meat was the staple food of Plains Indians. It was eaten raw in small pieces or roasted. The flesh from the buffalo's hump was favored. Buffalo meat could also be prepared for use on the trail. Indians made jerky by drying meat in the sun, and pemmican by pounding meat with fat and berries. Indians also ate the tongue, liver, kidneys, bone marrow, and intestines of buffalo.

Buffalo provided Indians with materials for numerous other applications. At least 86 non-food uses have been counted. Some of them are: tepee coverings, shields, travois platforms, parfleches, blankets, and clothing from the skins, either in rawhide form or softened into leather; thread and rope for various purposes from sinews or buffalo hair; various tools from bones, including sled runners from ribs; rattles and other ceremonial objects from hooves, horns, and skulls; and buffalo chips as fuel.

Indian women mastered the art of preparing hides. They stretched the skins on frames or on pegs in the ground, then scraped away the flesh. They then worked the hide to an even thickness. If they stopped at this stage, they had rawhide. To soften the hide into leather, they worked a mixture of ashes, fat, brains, liver, and various plants into it, then soaked it in water. Sometimes the hair was left for warmth. In other instances, it too was scraped off.

Tepees

As few as six or as many as 28 buffalo skins were sewn together to make a tepee covering, depending on the size of the pelts and the size of the structure. Although men provided the materials for tepees, cutting the pine trees for poles as well as hunting the buffalos, women usually erected them.

According to tribal custom, either three or four poles were used as the basic framework. They were tied together near the top and raised with the bottoms at equal distances, forming a cone shape. Then other

Plains Indian tepee

poles were propped against them. The final pole set in place served to hoist the sewn buffalo skins. This covering was stretched around the framework and held in place around the bottom edge with wooden pegs or stones, and along the front seam with wooden lodge pins. Part of the front seam was left unfastened to serve as an entrance with closable flaps. An opening was also left at the top to serve as a smokehole.

Tepees were very practical. The various openings could be adjusted for ventilation. The bottom edge could also be rolled up to allow for increased air flow. On the other hand, when completely sealed, with extra pelts added to the walls for insulation and a fire inside, the tepees were warm in wintry weather. Furthermore, the Indians situated them in such a way as to reduce the wind factor. Because of prevailing

westerly winds on the wide-open plains, the entrance faced eastward. And the tepees leaned slightly to the east so air could more easily flow over the top, thus decreasing wind pressure on the structure.

Plains Indians thought of tepees as more than just homes. They considered them sacred places, with the floor symbolizing the earth and the walls the sky. Moreover, the base of the tepee was in the shape of a circle, a sacred symbol for the Plains Indian indicating how all aspects of existence were interconnected. Every tepee had a small altar of stone or earth where incense was burned during prayers. Both the outside walls and inner linings of the tepee were commonly painted with symbolic designs. Brightly colored figures and shapes referred to spirit beings, ancestors, family histories, and honors gained in battle.

Clothing

Similarly, the designs on Plains Indian clothing, such as honors insignia on robes, in some instances had specific meanings, but in other cases simply provided decoration. Dyed quillwork was originally used to decorate buffalo-skin or deerskin shirts, vests, leggings, dresses, boots, and moccasins. It was later replaced by beadwork. Fringes added another decorative element to clothing. Other articles of clothing commonly seen on the Plains included leather breechcloths in warm weather, and fur robes, caps, and headbands in cold weather. Indians also wore various types of headdresses.

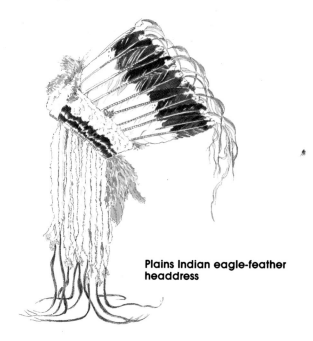

Plains Indian eagle-feather headdress

The eagle-feather headdress, more commonly known as a warbonnet, is the most recognizable of all Native American clothing. At modern-day festivals and powwows, one sees warbonnets on Indians of tribes from other parts of North America besides the Plains. But this particular type of headdress originated among the Plains tribes.

Only a few braves wore warbonnets, those who earned the privilege to do so in warfare. War chiefs usually had the longest warbonnets. The number of black-tipped tailfeathers of the male golden eagle represented the wearers' exploits. The feathers were attached to a skullcap of buffalo or deerskin, with a brow-band that was decorated with quillwork or beadwork and dangling strips of fur or ribbons. Additional downy feathers were tied to the base of the eagle feathers and tufts of dyed horsehair to their tips.

Counting Coup

In warfare on the Plains, bravery was not measured simply by the number of enemy killed or wounded. Plains Indians had a custom known as "counting coup" in which the object was simply to touch an enemy in battle without hurting him. A special coup stick was sometimes used for this purpose, although a warclub or lance or bow or even the hand itself would do. An eagle feather was awarded to the warrior for each coup. If after counting coup on an armed enemy, he managed to kill him, then scalp him, a brave received three coup feathers. Capturing an enemy's possessions, especially his eagle feathers, brought great honor to a Plains warrior.

Plains Indian coup stick

The Sacred Pipe

Another important possession of Plains Indians was the sacred pipe. Some pipes were owned by the entire tribe. These beautifully crafted pipes, with long wooden stems (sometimes as long as five feet) and stone bowls, are usually called peace pipes, although they were used in other ceremonies besides peace councils. Ash and sumac were the favorite woods for the stems because they were soft enough to easily be hollowed out. The chosen stone for carving the bowl was catlinite, also called pipestone. A pipestone quarry is located in Minnesota. Many different tribes came from far and wide to take the red-colored stone that was soft

enough to carve with a knife until it dried in the air. Another workable stone was steatite, or soapstone. Sacred pipes were decorated with feathers, quills (later beads), fur, and horsehair. The most common smoking substance was tobacco, although other plants were used too.

Medicine Bundles and Sacred Shields

Pipes were kept in medicine bundles with other sacred objects. Skin pouches or wrappings were generally used as medicine bundles. The objects inside were thought to have magical powers. In addition to pipes, medicine bundles contained such objects as a stone or arrow or part of an animal. Quite often these were objects seen in a dream or vision. Individuals kept their own personal medicine bundles for good fortune, but tribal chiefs or shamans kept bundles for the entire tribe. The talismans inside had special meanings with regard to tribal legends.

Plains Indian personal medicine bundle

We have seen how many Plains Indian possessions had special and sacred significance to them. Their shields also had religious meanings, intended to offer magical protection to the bearer. The paintings on Sacred Shields served as a link between the natural and spiritual worlds, pointing to mystical places.

Military Societies

Some of the paintings also identified the warrior as belonging to a particular military society or soldier society. Each society or club, some of them intertribal, had its own insignia, costumes, medicine bundles, songs, dances, and code of behavior. Some societies were age-graded and open. That is to say, a member automatically entered a society depending on his age. Others were exclusive and a warrior could join only when invited to, based on his deeds in battle. The most famous of the soldier societies were respected and feared all over the Plains.

The Vision Quest

Visions, both those in dreams and those experienced in a semi-wakeful state, played an important role in the religious and spiritual life of Indians all over North America. Visions were thought to have significance for individuals and for the entire tribe. Native peoples thought that, through visions, people could come in contact with the spirit world and receive power, or "medicine." The quest for visions usually occurred around some important event, such as passage from boyhood into manhood, or preparation for war. There were various ceremonies and means to induce visions. Some involved the use of hallucinogenic plants, such as peyote or jimsonweed. The striving for visions among Plains peoples is usually referred to as the Vision Quest.

In order to achieve visions, a Plains Indian normally first purified himself with a sweat bath in a sweat lodge, stripped himself naked, painted himself with white clay, went off to an isolated place, and fasted for days. If hunger, thirst, and exposure to the elements alone failed to bring on a trancelike experience and resulting visions, the individual sometimes further tortured himself by cutting off a finger, or by some other self-mutilation.

The vision usually came in the form of an animal. But it could be a plant, place, object, ancestor, or some natural phenomenon, such as a storm. After the experience, a medicine man would help the individual interpret the vision. What was seen in the vision would henceforth symbolize the individual's guardian spirit. The individual would prepare a medicine bundle with sacred objects somehow relating to his vision.

The Sun Dance

The quest for visions also played a part in the ceremony common to many Plains tribes and known to most people as the Sun Dance. The name Sun Dance comes from the Sioux tribe. Other tribes had different names. The Cheyennes called it the New Life Lodge. The Poncas called it the Mystery Dance. Moreover, different tribes had different rituals. But for all those tribes who held the ceremony, the overall purposes were the same: to come into contact with the spirit world; to renew nature, including the sun, the sky, and the earth; to keep buffalo plentiful, thereby assuring future prosperity; to bring victory in battle; to make marriages successful; to heal the sick; and to settle old quarrels.

Tribes held their annual Sun Dance in summertime. Summer was the season when the various bands of a tribe gathered for communal buffalo hunting. The bands set up their tepees in a great circle. Men and women of different bands socialized together and courted one another. They held horse races and other games. Tribal leaders smoked tobacco together and

Plains Indian sacred pipe

reestablished tribal unity. The Sun Dance, the most important of summer ceremonies, usually occurred during a full moon in the latter part of summer when berries were ripe. The entire ceremony lasted from eight to twelve days.

The various Sun Dance rituals were numerous and complex. Every act had a special significance. Many of the rituals involved drumming, singing, and dancing. In the course of the Sun Dance, the Indians found and erected a sacred tree trunk, usually a cottonwood, sometimes as much as 30 feet high, in the center of a sacred lodge of poles and branches. On top of the tree, they placed a figure, usually made of rawhide.

One particular ritual, coming near the end of the Sun Dance, has come to be associated with the entire ceremony above all others. Some braves had skewers implanted in their chests which were tied to the sacred pole with ropes. Blowing eagle-bone whistles and dancing to the drumbeat, they danced backwards until the skewers ripped through their flesh. Other braves dragged buffalo skulls about the camp, the skulls attached to their flesh with similar skewers. Their self-mutilation supposedly brought visions for their own well-being, and their self-sacrifice brought good fortune for the entire tribe.

There is much more to Plains Indian culture than what has been discussed here. It is of course impossible to describe all the fascinating Plains Indian lifeways and the related artifacts in such limited space. For a view of other customs as well as a view of particular tribal histories, see the entries for the tribes mentioned earlier in this section.

Plateau Indians

The designation *Plateau Indians* comes from the name of the Columbia Plateau. The Columbia Plateau is a region of highlands through which the Columbia River flows.

The Columbia River is one of the largest rivers in North America. It is 1,200 miles long, situated in both the United States and Canada. It starts in the southeastern part of British Columbia, then flows a meandering route to the Pacific Ocean, forming much of the border between Washington and Oregon. It has many tributaries, including the Snake, Thompson, Okanagan, Deschutes, Umatilla, Willamette, and Kootenai rivers.

The Columbia River and its tributaries receive water from three mountain ranges—the Rocky Mountains, the Cascade Mountains, and the Coast Range. Another large river, the Fraser River—also starting in the Rocky Mountains in British Columbia—is not part of the Columbia watershed.

What scholars define as the Plateau Culture Area is situated between the Cascades to the west and the Rockies to the east, the Fraser River to the north and the Great Basin to the south. It includes territory now mapped as southeastern British Columbia, eastern Washington, northeast and central Oregon, northern Idaho, western Montana, and a small part of northern California.

The mountains flanking the Plateau region—the Cascades and the Rockies—catch a great deal of rain and snowfall, making for the great number of rivers and streams. The mountains and river valleys have enough precipitation to support some of the tallest trees in the world. These are evergreen forests of needle-bearing conifers, including pine, hemlock, spruce, fir, and cedar. The giant forests are too dense and shady for much smaller vegetation to grow beneath them.

The Columbia Plateau lying between the mountain ranges has little rainfall, since the Cascades block the rain clouds blowing in from the ocean. The land consists mainly of flatlands and rolling hills. Grasses and sagebrush are the dominant vegetation in this part of the culture area.

The sparse ground vegetation of both mountain and plateau meant little game for the Indians. Some elk, deer, and bear could be found at the edge of the forest. Some antelope and jackrabbits lived out on the dry plains of the plateau. Yet the abundant rivers and

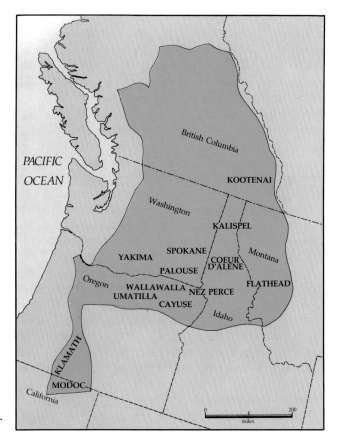

The Plateau Culture Area, showing the approximate locations of Indian tribes listed in this book—circa 1500, before displacement by whites (with modern boundaries)

streams offered up plentiful food, enough to support many people. Among the many different kinds of fish were the salmon that swam upriver from the ocean to lay their eggs. The river valleys also provided plentiful berries, including blackberries and huckleberries. On the grasslands of the plateau, the Indians found other wild plant foods—roots and bulbs, especially from the camas plant, a kind of lily; bitterroot; wild carrots; and wild onions.

The Plateau Indians were therefore mainly fishers and gatherers, then hunters. Perhaps a better name for them would be River Indians instead of Plateau Indians. They did not farm. In cold weather, most Plateau Indians lived along rivers in villages of semiunderground earth-covered pit houses, which provided natural insulation. In the warm weather, most lived in temporary lodges with basswood frames and bullrush-mat coverings, either along the rivers at salmon-spawning time, or on the open plains at camas-digging time. Plateau Indians also used the rivers as avenues of trade, with many contacts among different tribes.

Plateau Indians spoke dialects of two main language families: Penutian and Salishan. The Penutian-speaking Plateau tribes listed in this book are as follows: Cayuse, Klamath, Modoc, Nez Perce, Palouse, Umatilla, Wallawalla, and Yakima (see entries for those tribes). The Salishan tribes listed in this book are as follows: Coeur d'Alene, Flathead, Kalispel, and Spokane (see entries for those tribes). The Kootenai tribe, also listed in this book, is an exception. They spoke a unique language, probably related to Algonquian (see "Kootenai").

Plateau Indian (Colville) warclub

There were many other tribes in the Plateau Culture Area that are not listed here for lack of space. For those wishing to further pursue Indian studies concerning this part of North America, here are the tribal names of some: Lake, Lillooet, Nicola, Ntlakyapamuk (or Thompson), Okanagan, and Shuswap of British Columbia; the Chelan, Columbia, Colville, Klickitat, Methow, Sanpoil, Wanapam, and Wenatchee of Washington; and the Molala, Tenino, and Wishram of Oregon.

Pomo

In a part of North America where native basketry reached an exquisite level of development, territory known to whites as California, the Pomos are considered the foremost basketmakers of all. The Pomos created their beautiful baskets for functional purposes, but collectors now value them as works of fine art. In some Pomo baskets, the weaving is so tight that a microscope is needed to count the stitches.

The Pomos crafted many different kinds of objects with their basketmaking skills, such as cooking pots, containers, trays, cradles, hats, mats, ceremonial objects, games, fish traps, and boats. Unlike men of most other Indian tribes, the Pomo men participated in this craft. Moreover, the Pomos, using grasses, reeds, barks, and roots as basic materials, had two distinct methods of weaving baskets, twining and coiling. In twining, two or more horizontal strands (called wefts) are twined around each other as they are woven in and out of a set of vertical strands (called warps). In coiling, thin strips of plant matter are wrapped in a bundle and coiled into a continuous spiral. The Pomos had variations of these basic techniques and created designs and decorations with dyes, shells, and feathers.

The Pomos lived along the Pacific Coast and some distance inland, starting about 50 miles north of San Francisco Bay. Their small villages were located as far as Clear Lake, with a concentration of communities

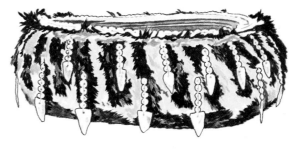

Pomo basket decorated with feathers and shells

around that lake and along the Russian River. Like many of the other tribes in the region, the Pomos spoke a dialect of the Hokan language family. Their name, pronounced *PO-mo*, is taken from the native sound *pomo* or *poma*, the meaning of which is unknown, but which was placed by them after village names.

The Pomos were hunter-gatherers like other California tribes, relying on acorns, small mammals, fowl, and fish (see "California Indians"). The coast Pomos, separated from the inland Pomos by a redwood forest, piled slabs of redwood bark against a center pole to make cone-shaped dwellings, large enough for only one family. The Clear Lake and Russian River Pomos built pole-framed and thatch-covered rectangular structures that housed several families. The men shared partially underground, earth-covered buildings called singing lodges for councils and ceremonies. Many of their rituals surrounded the secret Kuksu Cult (see "Patwin"). Smaller pit houses served as sweat lodges.

The Pomos were great traders. At times, they dealt in finished products, such as their baskets, but they also traded raw materials. The Clear Lake Pomos, for instance, had a salt deposit. They bartered the mineral for tools, weapons, shells, and furs. The Pomos also manufactured a kind of money. Many California tribes used tooth shells as a kind of currency. The Pomos, however, rejected this currency in favor of baked and polished magnesite, and strings of beads made from ground, rounded, and polished clamshells. They became accomplished mathematicians. They did not learn multiplication or division, but, by using units of strings, they added beads as high as the number 40,000.

Unlike all the other coastal California tribes to the south of them, the Pomos were never organized into missions by the Spanish. They did, however, fall under the Russian sphere of influence.

The Russians began developing the fur trade in North America along the Pacific Coast, starting after Vitus Bering's exploration of the Bering Strait in 1741 (see "Aleut" and "Tlingit"). The Russians worked their way southward from Alaska. By 1812, they had established a trading post, Fort Ross, on Bodega Bay in Pomo country. The heavily armed Russian traders forced the Pomos to hunt animals and clean hides for them. The Pomos resisted this oppression, carrying out acts of vandalism on Russian property. The Russians punished individuals with death or torture in order to set an example for other Indians. Murder, disease, and forced labor reduced the Pomo population, but they kept up their resistance.

By 1841, the Russians had abandoned the post. In the following years, especially after the California Gold Rush of 1849, the Pomos further suffered from whites entering their domain, this time Anglo-Americans. The Pomos managed to hold on to a number of parcels from their ancestral homeland, now organized as reservations. The largest of these is the Hopland Rancheria in Mendocino County.

Ponca

The Poncas (pronounced *PONG-kuh*), a Siouan people, spoke a dialect similar to those of the Kaws, Omahas, Osages, and Quapaws (see entries for those tribes). The ancestors of all these peoples lived long ago as one people, along the Ohio Valley, but eventually migrated westward across the Mississippi River onto the eastern Plains. The various groups then separated under different chiefs. The Poncas and Omahas lived together in southern Minnesota near Pipestone Quarry, a site famous for the catlinite stone used to make pipes. But they too eventually separated. The Omahas ended up settling on the Missouri River in what is now northeast Nebraska. But the Poncas built their villages farther to the northwest at the mouth of the Niobrara River, on both sides of what has become the boundary line between Nebraska and South Dakota.

The Poncas are part of the Great Plains Culture Area because they hunted buffalo on the Plains, especially after they gained use of the horse (see "Plains Indians"). But they also retained many of the traits of more eastern Indians, including permanent villages and agriculture (see "Prairie Indians").

In the 19th century, the Poncas were involved in an incident that had a positive, long-term effect on the rights of Native Americans. In 1876, Congress passed an act to relocate the Poncas from their homeland in Nebraska to the Indian Territory. The Poncas were forced to move the following year. They suffered greatly during the first years after removal. Their new land was difficult to farm. There was little grass to feed livestock. Winters were fierce. Hunger and disease took their toll, killing about a quarter of the tribe.

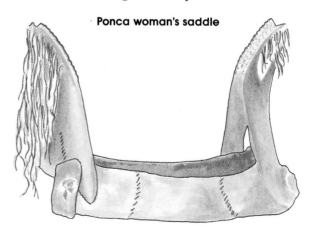

Ponca woman's saddle

One of those to die was the son of Chief Standing Bear. While dying, the youth made his father promise to bury him with his sister by the Swift Running Water of their homeland—along the Niobrara River in Nebraska. When the boy died, his father loaded the body in a box on a wagon drawn by two feeble horses, then headed north. Sixty-five members of Standing Bear's clan went with him on the long funeral procession.

Settlers living in Kansas and Nebraska were alarmed to see the Poncas crossing through lands that by now were supposed to be cleared of all Indians. They notified the army of a potential Indian uprising. Standing Bear and his people reached their earlier homeland but were soon arrested by a cavalry detachment and taken to Omaha as prisoners.

The Poncas had always been peaceful in their relations with whites. On learning of their real purpose in returning to Nebraska, some whites reacted with sympathy. General George Crook, who had led campaigns against many other tribes, expressed his support. Two lawyers, John Webster and Andrew Poppleton, offered their free services to the Poncas.

At the trial in 1879, Judge Elmer Dundy ruled in favor of the Indians, saying that they had inalienable rights under the law, like all men, and that the government could not forcibly restrain them from returning to their original homeland. After the trial, because of public sympathy for Standing Bear's band, the federal government granted them a reservation along the Niobrara.

A precedent was established. In this case, Indians were shown to be equal under the law. Nevertheless, it would take many more years for all Native Americans to be treated fairly by government officials. For example, other Poncas in the Indian Territory—Standing Bear's brother Big Snake was one of them—were not allowed to leave the Indian territory and join their relatives in the north for many years. But at least Judge Dundy's decision was a step in the right direction on the long road to equality for Native Americans.

Today, the Poncas live in both locations, in Oklahoma and in Nebraska. Lands in both states have been allotted to individual tribe members. Lands in Oklahoma are designated as a federal trust area.

Modern Poncas have worked peacefully for Indian rights, as Chief Standing Bear did during the last century. In 1961, Indian leaders from 67 tribes gathered in Chicago for the American Indian Chicago Conference (also called the American Indian Charter Convention). The leaders issued a Declaration of Indian Purpose, calling for greater Indian involvement in the decision-making process in all federal and state programs affecting Indians.

Yet some of the younger tribal delegates did not think their tribal elders had gone far enough in making a stand for Indian rights. Soon afterward, this group, led by a Ponca named Clyde Warrior and a Paiute named Melvin Thom, founded the National Indian Youth Council (NIYC) in Gallup, New Mexico. The NIYC has since been involved in many Native American causes. For example, in 1964, the NIYC sponsored a number of "fish-ins" along rivers in the state of Washington to make a case for Indian fishing rights. The NIYC also publishes an important newspaper called *ABC: Americans Before Columbus*, which covers issues concerning native peoples in both North and South America.

Potawatomi

The Potawatomis are also known as the Fire Nation because their name in Algonquian means "people of the place of fire" (see "Algonquian"). There are often several different acceptable spellings of an Indian tribe's name. Sometimes the different versions are preserved in place names as well as historical records. One might see Potawatami, Pottawatami, or Pottawatomie. But modern tribal members have designated the official spelling as Potawatomi, so this is the version most commonly used today. All the different versions are pronounced *pot-uh-WOT-uh-mee*.

The original homeland of the Potawatomis is usually given as the lower peninsula of Michigan (see "Northeast Indians"). It is reported that they lived between Lake Huron and Lake Michigan just before the arrival of French explorers. According to their tradition, they were originally one people with the Chippewas and Ottawas when they arrived in the country of the western Great Lakes. By 1670, when the Frenchman Nicholas Perrot explored the region, they were living west of Lake Michigan near Green Bay, Wisconsin, probably pushed westward by the Iroquois invasions from the east (see "Iroquois"). Then from there, over the years, they migrated south toward the Chicago area.

The Potawatomis were military allies and trading partners of the French until the French were defeated by the English in 1763 to end the French and Indian War (see "Abnaki"). The Potawatomis continued the fight against the English in Pontiac's Rebellion of 1763-64 (see "Ottawa"). In 1769, the Potawatomis joined an alliance of other Algonquians to fight the Illinois and push them southward (see "Illinois"). At that time, the Potawatomis expanded their territory around the southern end of Lake Michigan back toward their original homeland, almost a full circle.

While holding these lands, the Potawatomis joined their former enemies, the British, in the fight against the rebels in the American Revolution of 1775-83 (see "Iroquois"). Then in the late 1700s and early 1800s, the Potawatomis fought in a series of wars in a

Potawatomi doll, used as a totem of love

vain attempt to stop the American settlers from overrunning their lands—Little Turtle's War of 1790-94 (see "Miami"); Tecumseh's Rebellion of 1809-11 (see "Shawnee"); and the Black Hawk War of 1832 (see "Sac"). With each passing conflict, the situation became more hopeless for the Potawatomis and for the other tribes of the Old Northwest. Most of the Potawatomis were dispersed west of the Mississippi River by the white men.

Some Potawatomis moved from Illinois, Indiana, and Michigan to Missouri; then to Iowa; and from there to Kansas. Others went straight to Kansas from the Great Lakes region. Some of these Kansas Potawatomis then moved to Oklahoma. Some Potawatomis stayed in both Wisconsin and Michigan. Others managed to return there from the west. During the 1800s, other Potawatomis accompanied the Kickapoos to Mexico (see "Kickapoo"). Still others went to Canada.

The history of Potawatomi migration is very complex. Their many moves resulted from poverty and hardship. The Potawatomis struggled to find suitable lands and ways to earn a living after having been dislodged from their homeland and their way of life. The migration from Indiana that began in 1838 is called the Trail of Death because of the many lives lost to disease and hunger. It is not as famous as the Cherokee Trail of Tears (see "Cherokee"), but just as tragic.

Today, the Prairie Band of Potawatomis has a reservation in Kansas. The Citizen Band of Potawatomis holds trust lands in Oklahoma. Other bands of Potawatomis have two reservations in Michigan and one in Wisconsin. And the Caldwell Band has a reserve in Ontario. Like most Native Americans, the Potawatomis are for the most part not a wealthy people, but they have raised their standard of living recently through sound business investments. And they are reviving traditional crafts.

When speaking of traditional Potawatomi culture, one usually compares them to their kinsmen, the Chippewas and the Ottawas (see "Chippewa" and "Ottawa"). Like those tribes and other Algonquians of the Great Lakes, the Potawatomis hunted in the forests, fished and gathered wild rice on the lakes, and grew corn and other crops in the fields. One of their bands, the Mascoutens, also hunted buffalo on the prairies along the Mississippi Valley.

As for their religious customs, the Potawatomis were like other Great Lakes Algonquians in that they smoked tobacco in calumets (sacred pipes) and participated in the Midewiwin Society, also known as the Grand Medicine Society, an exclusive club with elaborate rituals and important in religious and tribal matters (see "Chippewa"). In the 1880s, long after their displacement by whites, the Potawatomis also helped develop the Dream Dance, which some Native Americans still practice today. This was not a war dance, but one of good will, even toward whites. In this ritual, Indians danced for hours to the beat of a sacred drum, working themselves into a revery. To seal the spirit of fellowship, gifts were exchanged.

Powhatan

Pocahontas

Pocahontas is probably the most famous of all Indian women. Her lovely name evokes the image of a beautiful Indian princess. She was a princess in fact, the daughter of Wahunsonacock, a powerful chief of about 30 different bands and 200 villages in the part of North America that is now Virginia. The alliance of bands under Wahunsonacock's rule was called the Powhatan Confederacy, after his particular band. Powhatan (pronounced *pow-uh-TAN* or *pow-HAT-un*) in Algonquian means "at the falls." The English colonists who established the colony of Jamestown in Virginia in 1607, the first permanent English settlement in North America, had trouble pronouncing and remembering Wahunsonacock's real name. So they started calling him by his tribe's name. He became known as Chief Powhatan.

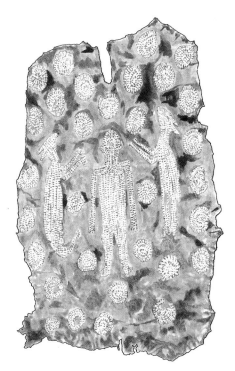

Hide decorated with shells, showing a man and two deer. It is thought to have belonged to Chief Powhatan and is known as Powhatan's Mantle.

According to legend, Pocahontas saved the life of Captain John Smith, the leader of the Jamestown colonists. Supposedly, she intervened just before her father was about to behead Smith, who was his prisoner. Whether or not her intercession actually led to Captain Smith's release is uncertain. But it is known for sure that the English angered Chief Powhatan because they took the best land for themselves. He retaliated by having his warriors take prisoners, Captain Smith among them. The English appeased him by crowning him a king in an English-style ceremony. Chief Powhatan released Smith unharmed.

Then in 1613, Pocahontas was captured by the English and held as a hostage to bargain with Chief Powhatan for the freedom of other prisoners. While at Jamestown, she was converted to Christianity and baptized. Then she was courted by a settler by the name of John Rolfe. After having gained her father's permission, she married the Englishman in 1613. Their marriage brought about a period of peace between Indians and whites.

Pocahontas sailed across the Atlantic to visit England with her husband. There, she was received as

royalty herself and met the king and queen. Yet, like so many Indians who came into contact with whites, she died from a European disease. This was 1617. Chief Powhatan died the following year.

Powhatan's earlier words of peace to Captain Smith were recorded for posterity: "Why will you take by force what you may quietly have by love? Why will you destroy us who provide you with food? . . . We are unarmed, and willing to give you what you ask, if you come in a friendly manner, and not with swords and guns, as if to make war upon an enemy."

Opechancanough's Wars

The peace that Chief Powhatan shaped lasted another five years. His brother, Opechancanough, was now the leader of the Powhatan Confederacy. He recognized a disturbing pattern in Indian-white relations.

Tobacco, now popular in Europe (see "Arawak"), was a lucrative cash crop. Boatload after boatload of settlers arrived along the ports of the Chesapeake Bay to cultivate it. Tobacco depleted the soil, necessitating new fields every several years. As a result, the English needed more and more land. But they usually ignored the rights of the native peoples, tricking them into signing away huge tracts. The settlers would then move in and carve the land into plantations, cutting down trees and killing or driving away the game. In the process, Indian hunting grounds were ruined. A centuries-old way of life was destroyed.

Opechancanough wanted to break this pattern. He plotted a strike against the settlers to drive them from Powhatan country. But he wavered in his purpose. He remembered the peace established by his brother and niece. He wondered if his warriors could really defeat the now-numerous colonists. The arrest and execution of a brave by the name of Nematanou for the alleged murder of a white trader made up his mind once and for all. Opechancanough ordered a surprise attack.

On the morning of March 22, 1622, hundreds of warriors swept out of the forest and through the colony's tobacco fields, killing every colonist in sight—all in all, 347 men, women, and children. In response, the English organized a militia. The troops began a campaign of regular patrols against the Indians, burning houses and crops and pushing the Indians farther inland. Opechancanough agreed to a peace council. But, when he and his warriors arrived, they were poisoned and attacked by the treacherous colonists. Opechancanough escaped, however.

Both sides continued their raids for 10 years. Finally in 1632, they agreed on a peace treaty. But Opechancanough never forgave the English. Twelve years later in 1644, when he was supposedly over 100 years old, he ordered another attack. This time, almost 500 colonists lost their lives. Again, the colonists responded with a stepped-up campaign against the Powhatans. In 1646, Governor William Berkeley of Virginia and his militiamen captured the wily but weary leader and carried him on his royal litter back to Jamestown. He was jeered at by an angry crowd and later shot by a vengeful guard.

While dying, Opechancanough reportedly said, "If it had been my fortune to take Sir William Berkeley prisoner, I would not have meanly exposed him as a show to my people."

His people received the same harsh treatment, forced out of Virginia or placed on small reservations where their numbers dwindled over the centuries. Some Powhatans remain in Virginia today, members of the Chickahominy, Mattaponi, Nansemond, Pamunkey, Potomac, and Rhappahanock bands. Of these, only the Mattaponis and Pamunkeys hold state reservation lands.

Lifeways

Much is known about the Powhatans from the writings of Captain John Smith and other Englishmen. The various Tidewater Algonquians, along with some Iroquoian-speaking peoples of the area, are usually classified as part of the Northeast Culture Area (see "Northeast Indians"). This is because they shared most cultural traits with other Atlantic Coast Algonquians farther north (see "Algonquian"). Other Virginia and North Carolina tribes farther inland, many of them Siouan-speaking, are classified in the Southeast Culture Area, however (see "Southeast Indians").

Yet in some ways the Powhatans were more like the Southeast tribes. For example, they had a more autocratic system of government than the northern tribes. That is to say, their leaders—men like Wahunsonacock and Opechancanough—had absolute authority, with power of life and death over their subjects. To the north, the Indian tribes were more democratic, with a council of leaders often making decisions.

It is the Powhatans' combination of hunting, fishing, gathering, and farming in and around Chesapeake Bay that determines the Northeast classification for the tribe. The writings of Captain Smith describe in great detail how the Powhatans collected and prepared food. He speaks of how they hunted deer, beaver, opossums, otters, squirrels, and turkeys with various weapons, including bows and arrows, spears, clubs, snares, and rings of fire; how they dried acorns plus other nuts and fruits to keep for winter; how they made a milky drink from ground walnuts; how they fished in giant dugout canoes as much as 40 and 50 feet long, using spears and nets; how they planted their crops, making holes four feet apart with a digging stick and placing four grains of

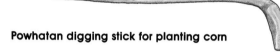

Powhatan digging stick for planting corn

corn and two of beans in each; and how they roasted or boiled green corn to eat on the spot, or soaked and pounded ripe corn to make cornmeal cakes.

Captain Smith also wrote about how the Powhatans usually located their villages along a river, near a spring of water. Their houses, anywhere from two to a hundred per village, would be in the middle of their fields of 20, 40, 100, or even 200 acres. The houses were made of saplings, bent and tied and covered with bark or woven mats. The structures had rounded roofs but were elongated, much like Iroquoian longhouses.

As with Indians all over the continent, there was a division of labor between men and women. For the most part, the men were the hunters, fishermen, gatherers, and warriors. They built the houses and boats and most of the tools and weapons. The women were the farmers and food-preparers, and made clothing, pottery, baskets, mats, and wooden vessels called mortars that were used for grinding foods.

The Powhatans lived in harmony with nature. Wildlife flourished and the tribe flourished in a delicate balance.

Prairie Indians

Indian cultural studies are especially difficult because of the great number of tribes and their many different ways of life. In order to have some basis for making distinctions and comparisons among the many tribes, scholars have invented different cultural groupings based on geography. That way, the lifeways of more than one tribe can be discussed together. These cultural and geographic categories are called Indian culture areas.

Yet scholars differ on the number of culture areas. This book summarizes the most common groupings, showing them on maps. For the area now comprising the United States and Canada, the most common breakdown is as follows: Arctic, California, Great Basin, Great Plains, Northeast, Northwest Coast, Plateau, Southeast, Southwest, and Subarctic. But some books break down these culture areas even further. For instance, they add a separate culture area for the prairies. This geographical area includes territory most scholars represent as the western part of the Northeast Culture Area and the eastern part of the Great Plains Culture Area.

The word *prairie* (or the phrase *Prairie Plains*) is applied to the grasslands flanking the Mississippi and Missouri rivers. The difference between the Great Plains and the Prairie Plains is the amount of rainfall and the resulting type of vegetation. The Great Plains are drier than the Prairie Plains. As a result, there are more ponds and swamps on the prairies. And, with the more frequent rains, the Prairie Plains' grasses grow taller than the Great Plains' grasses. The Great Plains are located to the west of the Prairie Plains. To the east, the Prairie Plains give way to woodlands.

The Prairie Plains are located in what is now the central part of the United States. Iowa and Illinois are mostly prairie country. North Dakota, South Dakota, Nebraska, Kansas, Oklahoma, and Texas all have prairies in their eastern parts. Minnesota has prairies in its southern and western parts. Missouri has prairies in its northern and western parts. Indiana has prairies in its northern part. Ohio has prairies in its western part. Some of these states, especially Illinois and Iowa, are referred to as Prairie States.

The Native Americans sometimes cited as Prairie Indians shared cultural traits with both the Northeast Indians and the Plains Indians. Many of them lived in semi-permanent villages along wooded river valleys. They lived for the most part in sizable earthlodges or in grass-covered dome-shaped houses. They had extensive cultivated fields where they grew corn, beans,

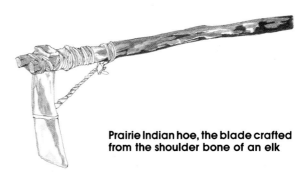

Prairie Indian hoe, the blade crafted from the shoulder bone of an elk

squash, tobacco, and other crops. They made use of pottery for cooking, carrying, and storage.

Yet many of the Prairie peoples left their homes to hunt part of the year. While on the trail, they lived in temporary lean-tos or portable tents and used unbreakable containers made of animal skins. Their chosen game was buffalo. Late in their history, after the arrival of Europeans, they acquired use of the horse for hunting and raiding. In addition to tepees and buffalo-hunting, the Prairie Indians shared other cultural traits with the more nomadic Plains Indians to the west.

The Prairie peoples east of the Mississippi are generally classified in the Northeast Culture Area (see "Northeast Indians"). These include the tribes of the western Great Lakes: Fox, Kickapoo, Menominee, Potawatomi, Sac, Winnebago, as well as tribes to their south, the Illinois, Miami, and Shawnee (see entries for those tribes).

The Prairie peoples west of the Mississippi are generally classified as part of the Great Plains Culture Area (see "Plains Indians"). Most of them occupied territory in the stretch of land from the Missouri to the Mississippi rivers. These include the following tribes: Mandan, Hidatsa, Arikara, Iowa, Oto, Missouri, Kaw, Omaha, Osage, Ponca, Quapaw, Pawnee, Wichita, and some of the eastern bands of Sioux (see entries for those tribes).

Prehistoric Indians

There are many Indian tribes listed in this book. Most of these tribes existed when Europeans first came into contact with Native North Americans. A few formed into tribal groups long after whites had come to North America. Some tribes have since become extinct. These various tribes are central to the study of Indian peoples.

Yet the study of Indian peoples also involves the story of the ancestors of these tribal Indians—Prehistoric Indians. The word *prehistoric* means whatever occurred before there were written

records. Another term, *precontact*, refers to the Indians who had no contact with whites. Another label applied is *pre-Columbian*, referring to Indians and cultures before the arrival of Christopher Columbus in the Americas in 1492.

Who were the early Indians? Did Indians always live in the Americas? If not, where did come from? How did they live? What kind of tools did they make?

Scholars have not always known the answers to these questions. Archaeologists, who search for and analyze ancient artifacts, and anthropologists, who study physical and cultural characteristics of mankind, have worked hard to piece together information concerning ancient inhabitants of the Americas. Other scientists have helped them decipher these clues: paleontologists, who study fossils and ancient life forms; geologists, who study rock formations; and chemists, who study the composition of matter.

Knowledge of ancient Indians, as well as that of prehistoric peoples in all parts of the world, remains to a large degree hypothetical. Most human remains have disappeared, other than scattered bones; most ancient artifacts have decayed, other than stone articles. Moreover, scientific techniques for dating ancient matter, such as the radiocarbon measuring process, are inexact and must allow for a margin of error.

As a result, the study of ancient Indians can be very confusing. One scholar might have a theory about the migrations of a people, with which other scholars disagree. Or he or she might use one term to label a period of prehistory or a cultural group or an artifact, while other scholars use other terms. Or he or she might apply a set of dates for the existence of an ancient people that are considerably different from dates applied by other scholars. Nevertheless, much information about early Indians is now held as conclusive. The following is a general consensus among the experts.

Paleo-Indians

In the geologic time scale devised by scholars, the Age of Mammals is called the Cenozoic Era. The period in the Cenozoic Era in which mankind came into existence is called the Pleistocene Epoch. During the Pleistocene Epoch, which is thought to be at least a million years long, the world experienced a series of four Ice Ages. In each of these Ice Ages, much of the world was covered with glaciers. Between the Ice Ages were periods of warmer weather and melting ice. During the last of the four Ice Ages, man first arrived in the Americas.

It is theorized that during the last Ice Age, so much of the earth's water was locked up in glaciers that the oceans were lower than today and more land was thus exposed. Where there is now water between Alaska and Siberia (eastern Russia)—known as the Bering Strait—there was once a wide strip of land. Scholars refer to this once-exposed land mass as the Bering Strait land bridge, or Beringia.

Animals could have migrated across this land bridge—now-extinct creatures such as mammoths,

mastodons, bighorn bison, and saber-toothed tigers. And the ancient ancestors of the Indians—the big-game hunters who depended on these animals for food—could have followed them out of Asia to North America.

The exact time that the first bands of hunters and their families arrived in North America is not known. Increasing archaeological evidence has pushed the estimated date as far back as about 50,000 B.C., but a new discovery might one day prove that humans arrived even earlier than that. Moreover, the migration of humans from Asia to North America did not happen all at once, but over many thousands of years in many waves of small bands along the same route. Then over the following thousands of years, their descendants worked their way southward, probably first following an ice-free passage during a temporary melt along the Rocky Mountains, before dispersing to every corner of the Americas. By about 20,000 B.C., early Indians lived in much of North America. By about 10,000 B.C., Indians had reached the southern end of South America.

The first Indians, the true discoverers of the Americas, had only wooden and stone tools and no metal. The period in human evolution before the invention of metal tools is known as the Stone Age, or the Paleolithic Age. As a result, the first Indians are called Paleo-Indians, or Lithic Indians.

The Paleo-Indians lived for the most part in caves, under overhangs, and in brushwood lean-tos. They wore hide and fur clothing. They used fire to keep warm, to cook, to protect themselves from animals while sleeping, and to hunt. By lighting fires on the grasslands, the hunters could drive herds of animals over cliffs and into swamps and bogs, where they could be killed. The early Indians had different methods for lighting fires: striking a spark with certain stones, such as flint, or by rubbing wood together. Fire drills, made from two sticks and a strip of rawhide, enabled the rapid spinning of wood against wood to create friction and generate heat.

In addition to wooly mammoths, mastodons, bighorn bison, and saber-toothed tigers, the Paleo-Indians hunted American lions, camels, short-faced bears, dire wolves, giant beavers, giant sloths, giant armadillos, curve-snouted tapirs, musk oxen, peccaries, native horses, plus smaller game. These species are of course now extinct. The first Indians were also gatherers of wild plant foods—greens, seeds, berries, roots, and bulbs.

The craftsmanship of the Paleo-Indians was essential to their big-game hunting way of life. The early Indians had techniques for making spearheads razor-sharp. The first Paleo-Indians did not have stone-pointed spears. They probably used fire to harden the tips of wooden spears, but this theory is unproven because the wooden spears decayed long ago. The earliest Indians did, however, have roughly shaped stone and bone tools for scraping and chopping. Later Paleo-Indians developed methods of shaping certain types of stone—especially flint, chert, and obsidian—into sharp points and edges. In percussion-flaking, they sharpened the point by striking it with a stone. In pressure-flaking, they pressed antler or bone against the point to sharpen it.

Scholars use the different types of points found at campsites, hunting sites, and quarry sites, to determine different technological phases, or cultures, among the Paleo-Indians. For example, the Sandia culture, named after a cave site in the Sandia Mountains of New Mexico, was characterized by stone points two to four inches long with rounded bases and a bulge on one side where they were attached to wooden shafts. The Sandia points were dated to at least 9500 B.C. The culture was located in the Southeast.

Sandia point

The Clovis culture is named after the Clovis site in New Mexico, but Clovis-style points have been found all over North America, usually with mammoth and mastodon bones. They were one and a half to five inches long, with fluting (lengthwise channels) along both sides of the base, where they were attached to wooden shafts. The Clovis points were dated to at least 9000 B.C.

Clovis point

The Folsom culture is named after the Folsom site in New Mexico. Evidence of Folsom hunters has been found mostly in the Southwest, but especially on the High Plains along with the remains of bighorn bison. The Folsom period lasted from about 8000 to about 7000 B.C. The Folsom points, three-quarters of an inch to three inches long, were unique in that they had flut-

ing on both sides running almost the entire length of the point. It is theorized that these long channels, which are very difficult to make in stone, served an additional purpose besides helping to attach the point to the spear shaft. Perhaps they increased the flow of blood from an animal or increased the spear's velocity when it was thrown.

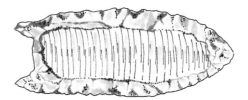

Folsom point

It was during the Folsom period that Indians first used spear-throwing devices called atlatls. These were wooden sticks about two feet long with animal-hide hoops to provide a firm grasp, a stone weight for balance, and a hook to hold the spear shaft. With an atlatl, a hunter had increased leverage that allowed him to fling his spear harder and faster. Bows and arrows were not invented until much later.

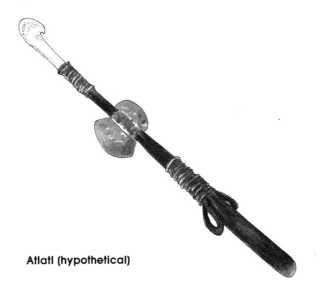

Atlatl (hypothetical)

The Plano, or Plainview, culture, named after the Plainview site in Texas, is also associated primarily with the Great Plains and the bighorn bison. Plano craftsmen did not flute their points, however. The Plano Indians also demonstrated a more varied culture than the Indians before them. For example, they built corrals to trap animals. They also developed a method of preserving meat by mixing it with animal fat and berries and packing it in hide or gut containers. This period in Indian evolution lasted from about 7500 to 4500 B.C.

The late Pleistocene Epoch was a time of great transition. During the years from about 10,000 to 8000 B.C., the climate warmed and the great glaciers retreated northward once and for all. The Ice Age became the Watershed Age. The melting ice created numerous lakes and swamplands, many of which would eventually evaporate. North America had gradually evolved to its present form by about 5000 B.C.

The changing climate probably contributed to the extinction of the big-game animals. The Paleo-Indians might also have played a part in this phenomenon. The Paleo-Indians became such skilled hunters —using, for example, the communal drives of huge herds and the atlatls—that they killed more game than they needed. Archaeologists hold this theory because they have found at kill sites the bones of many large animals with stone points in them. This killing of more animals than necessary is sometimes referred to as the Pleistocene Overkill.

Archaic Indians

The end of the Pleistocene Epoch marked the beginning of the current geologic period called the Holocene Epoch. The Paleo-Indian period also evolved into the Archaic Indian period at this time. The Paleo-Indian period lasted from about 50,000 to 8000 B.C. The transitional period (the Watershed Age) between the Paleo-Indian period and the Archaic Indian period lasted from about 8000 to 5000 B.C. The Archaic Indian period lasted from about 5000 to 1000 B.C. It should be kept in mind that these dates are not exact. The lifeways described for each period were the dominant ones. That is to say, while most Indians lived a certain way, there were other cultures in different parts of the Americas that were exceptions to the rule. For example, the Indians of the Plano culture, normally considered Paleo-Indians, continued their same way of life into the Archaic.

Archaic Indian point

What distinguished Archaic Indians from Paleo-Indians was a more varied diet. The big game were now extinct, and Archaic Indians hunted and trapped the species of mammals we know today. They fished in rivers and lakes. They gathered many different kinds of edible wild plants and planned their migrations around the ripening of berries as well as the movements of animal herds. Like the Paleo-Indians, they generally led a nomadic way of life, but it was more localized since they no longer tracked the huge herds such great distances. Archaic Indians are sometimes referred to as Foraging Indians.

In addition to a more varied diet, the Archaic Indians also had a wider variety of tools and utensils. Archaic craftsmen shaped spears, atlatls, bolas, harpoons, knives, axes, adzes, wedges, chisels, scrapers, celts, hammers, mauls, anvils, awls, drills,

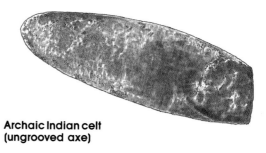

Archaic Indian celt (ungrooved axe)

fishhooks and lines, traps, mortars and pestles, and pipes. They used many different kinds of material, including stone, wood, bone, antler, shell, and ivory.

Archaic Indians made a number of key inventions. They learned to weave plant materials into clothing and baskets. They also learned new methods of food preparation and food preservation. For cooking, they placed heated stones into stone pots to boil water. They used their baskets and hide containers to store food. Archaic Indians constructed boats and domesticated the dog.

Archaic Indians also shaped materials into ornaments and ceremonial objects. They had elaborate ceremonies for burying their dead. Their religions were more highly ritualized than those of their predecessors.

Archaic Indian wooden animal effigy

Five cultures, each in a different region of North America, show the diversity of Archaic Indian life. The Old Cordilleran (or Cascade) culture, which actually began about 9000 B.C., during the Paleolithic period, existed in the Pacific Northwest along the Columbia River until 5000 B.C. or afterward. Cascade spear points, in the shape of willow leaves, were used to hunt small game.

Another culture that began early in the Paleo-Indian period but evolved to a more typically Archaic way of life was the Desert culture in the Great Basin region of what is now Utah, Nevada, and Arizona. It lasted from about 9000 to 1000 B.C. At Danger Cave in Utah, archaeologists have found woven containers, the first example of basketry in North America. They also have found grinding stones used to prepare seeds, and traps made of twine used to capture small game.

The Cochise culture in what is now Arizona and New Mexico evolved out of the Desert culture and lasted from about 7000 to 1000 B.C. Cochise Indians hunted many different kinds of small mammals, such as deer, antelope, and rabbits. They also foraged for snakes, lizards, insects, and edible wild plants. Archaeologists have found many Cochise millstones, called manos and metates (like mortars and pestles), that the Indians used to grind seeds, nuts, and grains. The abundance of these utensils shows the growing importance of plant foods in the Archaic Indians' diet.

Among Cochise remains have also been found the first evidence of farming north of Mexico. In Bat Cave, New Mexico, archaeologists discovered dried-up cobs of corn from a cultivated species of the plant, probably dating from about 3500 B.C.

Another Archaic culture is the Old Copper culture of the Great Lakes region, lasting from about 4000 to 1500 B.C. This grouping takes its name from the copper objects discovered among the culture's remains, the earliest use of metal known among Indians north of Mexico. Old Copper Indians used natural deposits of copper—sheets in rock fissures or nuggets in the soil—to make beautiful tools and ornaments. They shaped it by heating it then hammering it, again and again.

Still another eastern Archaic people were the Red Paint people of present-day New England and eastern Canada. The Red Paint culture takes its name from the use of ground-up red iron ore to line its graves. This culture lasted from about 3000 to 500 B.C.

Archaeologists have found objects of many other Archaic Indians in different parts of North America. Those mentioned above are the most famous. Far to the north, another remarkable development occurred during this period. Ancestors of the Eskimos and Aleuts migrated to North America across the Bering

Sea in small boats, from about 3000 to 1000 B.C. The Eskimos and Aleuts are therefore not descended from the Paleo-Indians that migrated across the Bering Strait land bridge, as are other Indians (see "Eskimo" and "Aleut").

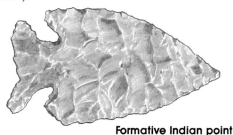

Formative Indian point

Formative Indians

As stated before, the end of the Archaic Indian period is given as 1000 B.C. The next period of prehistoric Indians is usually called the Formative period, which lasted right up until the time of Native American contact with Europeans, about A.D. 1500. Broadly speaking, the Formative period is defined by the following cultural traits: farming, domesticated animals, village life, houses, trade, pottery, weaving, basketry, the bow and arrow, refined craftsmanship,

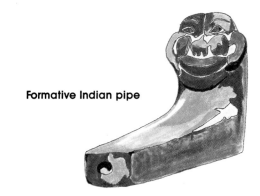

Formative Indian pipe

and elaborate religious ceremonies. Many of the cultural traits typical of Formative Indians were developed during the Archaic period or even before. For example, Indians in what is now Mexico cultivated plants as early as 7000 B.C.; Indians north of Mexico farmed as early as 3500 B.C.; but agriculture and other typical Formative lifeways became widespread among Native North Americans only after 1000 B.C.

After 1000 B.C., highly developed civilizations came into existence. Most of these were located in territory that is now Mexico. When speaking of this region with regard to Indians, the term Mesoamerica or Middle America is used. Civilizations in Mesoamerica occurred among the Olmecs, Mayas, Toltecs, and Aztecs. Because these Indians had such highly organized societies, with cities even, what is usually called the Formative period in North America is referred to as the Classic period in Middle America. (Before the Classic period was the Preclassic period; after the Classic was the Postclassic.) These civilizations are discussed separately in this book (see "Olmec"; "Maya"; "Toltec"; and "Aztec").

The Incas in the Andes Mountains of what is now Peru in South America also had a highly organized civilization with farming, cities, classes of society, highly refined architecture and art forms, and hieroglyphic writing systems. Yet, since this book deals only with North American Indians (with Mexico and the Caribbean area considered part of North America), the Incas are not included. The civilizations of both the Incas of South America and the Aztecs of Mesoamerica existed at the time of contact with whites, and their downfall was brought about by the Spanish, as recorded in written records from the time. Therefore, the Aztecs and Incas cannot really be thought of as prehistoric or precontact Indians as the others mentioned in this section are. Moreover, the Mayas' hieroglyphics are now being translated by scholars, giving us a recorded history of these people.

There were also highly developed farming civilizations north of Mexico. These civilizations were influenced by the cultures of Mesoamerica. They occurred in the Southwest and are known as the Anasazi

Mesoamerican ceramic toy deer with wheels

culture, the Hohokam culture, and the Mogollon culture (see "Cliff Dwellers and Desert Farmers"). Other highly advanced cultures occurred east of the Mississippi River and are known as the Adena culture, the Hopewell culture, and the Mississippian culture (see "Mound Builders").

Once again, the terms used by scholars—such as Prehistoric Indians, Paleo-Indians, Archaic Indians, Formative Indians, Classic Indians—are designed to help in Indian studies. They are not absolute. Exact dates cannot be applied to them. Knowledge about early Indians keeps growing with continuing archaeological excavations. And different terms are applied in different parts of the continent, depending on how Indians evolved in that particular area. Yet these general terms help give an overview of the intriguing ancestry of Native American peoples and tribes.

Pueblo Indians

Pueblo (pronounced *PWEB-lo*) means "village" in Spanish. The word has come to stand for a certain kind of Indian village with a certain type of architecture, as well as for the Indians themselves who lived there. As a result, the word sometimes appears without a capital first letter to denote a village or building, or with a capital to denote the people.

The name, when used for people, is a general term. There were many different Pueblo peoples in the American Southwest, which is referred to as the Southwest Culture Area by scholars. Some of these Indians lived on the Colorado Plateau. These were the Hopis and Zunis. The Hopis were the westernmost Pueblo peoples, living in what is now the state of Arizona. The Zunis lived to their east in what is now western New Mexico. They are discussed separately in this book (see "Hopi" and "Zuni").

Other Pueblo Indians lived along a 130-mile stretch of the Rio Grande, the long river flowing through

much of the Southwest all the way to the Gulf of Mexico. There were four tribal groups, speaking different languages: (1) Tiwa (or Tigua); (2) Tewa; (3) Towa (or Jemez); and (4) Keres. The first three spoke varying dialects of the Kiowa-Tanoan language family. The Keres spoke a different language called Keresan.

All four groups had different pueblos, or villages, often situated on the tops of mesas (small plateaus). The different pueblos had names. These names are sometimes used as distinct tribal names because each village was a separate unit with its own leaders and traditions.

The Pueblo Indians are thought to be descendants of Anasazi and Mogollon peoples of the early Southwest cultures. Blood descendants or not, they inherited many cultural traits from these peoples, including architecture, farming, pottery, and basketry (see "Cliff Dwellers and Desert Farmers").

Lifeways

Pueblo-style houses are unique among Indian dwellings because of their apartment-building design. They were built as high as five different levels. The flat roof of one level served as the floor and front yard of another. The different stories were interconnected by ladders. For much of history, the walls, especially on the ground level, had no doors or windows, making the villages easier to defend from attacks. The Indians entered their rooms through holes in the roofs.

Two different types of building material were used for the walls: the Hopis and Zunis used stones which were mortared and surfaced with plaster; the Rio Grande Indians used adobe bricks, made from sun-dried earth and straw. The Pueblo Indians stretched log beams across the roofs, covering them with poles, brush, and more plaster. Sometimes the beams projected beyond the walls and were used to hang food for drying.

The Pueblo Indians also dug pit houses as ceremonial chambers or clubhouses. The Hopis called these underground chambers kivas. They were usually located at a central place in the pueblo, such as the plaza.

The Pueblo Indians skillfully cultivated a variety of crops, including corn of many colors, squash, beans, sunflowers, cotton, and tobacco. They also kept tame turkeys. The domestication of animals, except the dog, was rare before the arrival of whites. Pueblo hunters also pursued wild deer, antelope, and rabbits.

Pueblo men wore kilts of cotton plus leather sandals. The women wore cotton dresses and sandals or high moccasin boots. They also used deerskin and rabbit-skin for clothing. The women made beautiful

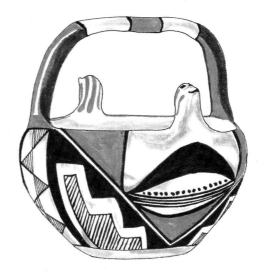

Pueblo Indian pottery from Acoma

pottery which they coiled, polished, and painted with exquisite designs. They also made baskets, both coiled and wicker types.

Pueblo men carved wooden masks to wear in elaborate ceremonies. Many of these were for the purpose of bringing rain, so essential to their farming. In the case of the Hopis and Zunis, these masks and the beings they were supposed to represent were called kachinas. The Indians also carved kachina dolls to teach their children about their religion.

Early Contacts with Whites

The early history of the Pueblo Indians after the coming of Europeans is interwoven with that of the Spanish. It was the Spanish who first claimed the region and gave it the name New Mexico. A Spanish

Pueblo Indian adobe architecture

explorer named Marcos de Niza reached Zuni country as early as 1539, only 18 years after the colony of New Spain was founded in North America. Then Francisco de Coronado followed in 1540. And Antonio de Espejo came in 1582.

Yet these expeditions did not alter the Pueblo way of life. In 1598, however, Juan de Onate arrived with 129 colonists—entire families—to establish the colony of New Mexico. He brought horses, goats, and sheep with him. In 1610, he founded the capital of this colony, Santa Fe. He also forced his will on the Indians through his soldiers. He made them pay taxes in cotton crops, cloth, and work. The Spanish taught the Indians to grow new crops, such as wheat, peppers, and peaches; to tend flocks; and to spin and weave wool. Missionaries also tried to eradicate native religions and spread Catholicism.

Juan de Onate was a cruel man. During his first year in New Mexico, he sent word to the various Indians that they were henceforth subjects of the Spanish monarch. When the Keres Indians of the Acoma Pueblo rose up and killed the soldiers who brought this command, he sent others to punish the Indians. The soldiers, after scaling the steep cliffs of the mesa and capturing the pueblo, massacred hundreds of inhabitants. Onate sentenced the survivors in a public trial. He ordered his soldiers to cut off one foot of all the males over 25. All females plus boys over 12 were to serve as slaves for 20 years. Children under 12 were to be placed in missions. Onate's action against the Acoma Indians made it easier for the Spanish to subjugate the other pueblos because the Indians now feared Spanish reprisals.

The Pueblo Rebellion

Nevertheless, the Indians finally did rise up again in a revolt called the Pueblo Rebellion. The year was 1680. The uprising was led by a Tewa Indian named Pope. He was a medicine man. The issue of religion was central to the Pueblo Rebellion. The generally peaceful Pueblo Indians had tolerated the Spanish for years. They were willing to do the bidding of the Spanish if allowed to practice their traditional religion in the kivas. But when Spanish officials consistently punished practitioners through floggings, the Indians took up arms.

Pope prepared for war by sending word to all the other villages from his pueblo at San Juan that the rebellion would soon come. His runners carried cords of maguey fibers indicating a certain number of days until the general uprising. On the given day, August 11, 1680, warriors from numerous pueblos, along the Rio Grande and to the west, moved against soldiers and priests stationed in the pueblos as well as ranchers living on outlying haciendas. They killed many.

In fact, the Pueblo Indians actually drove the Spanish out of New Mexico. The Spanish did put up a fight at Santa Fe, holding out for days against Pope's men by firing brass cannon from behind the palace walls. But when the Indians grew tired of the siege and withdrew to their pueblos, the Spanish headed south to El Paso.

The Pueblo Indians had regained control of their homeland. They were now free to practice their traditional culture and religion. Unfortunately, Pope's newfound power corrupted him and he became an exacting leader himself, not even permitting his people to use Spanish tools left behind. To Pope anything Spanish was evil.

Later History

Spanish troops marched north out of El Paso in 1689 and recaptured Santa Fe in 1692. The Pueblo Indians were again wards of the Spanish state. Yet one lasting cultural trait grew out of the Pueblo Rebellion and came to influence Indians far and wide. It was during the revolt that the Indians first acquired their own horses, left behind by the fleeing Spanish. The Pueblo Indians traded these with northern tribes or lost them in raids. The more northern Indians, such as the Utes, traded the horses with other Plains peoples (see "Ute"). By the mid-1700s, when the horse had spread to many tribes, a whole new way of life had emerged on the Plains (see "Plains Indians").

The Pueblo Indians remained under Spanish rule until 1821, the year of the Mexican Revolution. Then Mexico gained its independence from Spain. Mexican rule lasted until 1848 and the treaty of Guadalupe Hidalgo ending the Mexican War. At that time, when Mexico was forced to give this huge territory to the United States, the Pueblo Indians came under the authority of the American government.

The Pueblos remained consistently peaceful through this period. The one exception was during the Mexican War of 1845-48, when Tiwa braves of the Taos pueblo, angry because American troops stole their crops and livestock and even kidnapped their women, launched a series of raids against settlers. U.S. forces responded with a heavy artillery attack on the pueblo. The thick adobe walls repelled the shells, however. But the overwhelming firepower of the soldiers eventually routed the Indians.

Pueblo Indian black pottery from San Ildefonso (modern)

Pueblo Indians Today

When visiting the present-day pueblos, it is difficult to imagine any war occurring in their peaceful setting. The pueblos are the best place to visit Indians in the United States in order to get a sense of what traditional life was like for them. Much has changed, of course, with the addition of a certain amount of modern technology. Yet the Pueblo Indians still live in stone or adobe terraced buildings, still practice many of their ancient crafts, and still dance their masked dances. One potter, Maria Martinez, of the San Ildefonso Pueblo has gained an international reputation for her black-on-black pottery designs.

The following is a list of current pueblos in the upper Rio Grande region of New Mexico, near Santa Fe, with the tribal group in parentheses (Hopi and Zuni pueblos are discussed separately in this book; see "Hopi" and "Zuni"): Acoma (Keres); Cochiti (Keres); Isleta (Tiwa); Jemez (Towa); Laguna (Keres); Nambe (Tewa); Picuris (Tiwa); Pojoaque (Tewa); Sandia (Tiwa); San Felipe (Keres); San Ildefonso (Tewa); San Juan (Tewa); Santa Ana (Keres): Santa Clara (Tewa); Santo Domingo (Keres): Taos (Tiwa); Tesuque (Tewa); Zia (Keres).

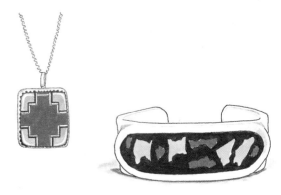

Pueblo Indian jewelry from Santo Domingo (modern)

Quapaw

The name *Quapaw* (pronounced *KWAW-paw*) comes from the Siouan word *Ugakhpa*, meaning "downstream people." This translation helps place the tribe geographically because the Quapaws lived most of their history along the west side of the lower Mississippi, south of most other Siouan-speaking Indians.

The Quapaws were also called the Arkansas by Algonquians and the French. It is from this latter version of their name that the name of the river and state is taken. The *ansas* part of the word is Siouan for "people of the south wind" (see "Kaw"). The *ark* part is taken from the French word *arc* for "bow." The territory of the Quapaws (and Osages) is famous for the wood of a kind of mulberry tree, called Osage Orange, which was prized for making bows. The name of the Ozark Mountains is an Americanization of the French phrase *aux arcs*, meaning "at the place of bows."

The Quapaws are thought to have once lived in the Ohio Valley with their Siouan kinsmen, the Kaws, Omahas, Osages, and Poncas (see entries for those tribes). But they eventually migrated westward, descending the Mississippi to the mouth of the Arkansas River, territory that is now in southeastern Arkansas. Their kinsmen settled to the north of them.

The Quapaws lived in palisaded villages of bark-covered, rectangular houses with domed roofs. (Palisades are walls made of upright logs.) The Quapaws also covered their houses with woven mats, hides, and grass. They were skillful farmers. They built mounds to hold both temples and graves. And they made exquisite pottery.

Sometimes Indians living along the Mississippi, and possessing cultural elements of tribes from both the woodlands to the east and the Great Plains to the west, are called Prairie people, after the tall grass prairies of the region (see "Prairie Indians"). The Quapaws are usually classified as part of the Great Plains Culture Area, however. The horse, brought to North America by the Spanish, reached them in the early 1700s. From that time on, the Quapaws lived much like other Plains people, hunting herds of buffalo on horseback (see "Plains Indians").

Such classifications are not absolute, of course, because each Indian tribe had its own unique culture.

The Quapaws lived just across the Mississippi River from tribes considered part of the Southeast Culture Area, such as the Chickasaws and Tunicas, with whom they traded and exchanged ideas (see "Southeast Indians").

The Quapaws had early contacts with French explorers, including Jacques Marquette in 1673, Rene Cavalier de la Salle in 1682, and Henri Tonti in 1686. They became allies of the French, who, in the 1700s, traveled up and down the Mississippi between Quebec and Louisiana in order to trade.

The Quapaws managed to stay in their homeland throughout the colonial period. They were a peaceable people and avoided taking up arms in most of the clashes among the three European powers in North America—France, England, and Spain—over the Mississippi region.

In 1818 and 1824, however, with the great influx of American settlers from the east, the Quapaws were pressured into signing away all their lands along the Arkansas River. In 1824, they agreed to live in Texas on the south side of the Red River, among the Caddos. But because the Red River often overflowed, destroying their crops, and because there was much illness among them, they were unhappy in their new homeland and drifted back to their ancestral territory.

In 1833, when white settlers complained about their presence in Arkansas, the federal government forced the Quapaws to relocate within the Indian Territory. Then in 1867, soon after the northern part of the Indian Territory became the state of Kansas, the Quapaws again had to sign away most of their lands. They were allowed to keep only a small portion in what is now the northeastern corner of Oklahoma, where they still hold lands in trust.

Fortunately, the tribe has been able to make the most of its limited land holdings. In 1905, lead and zinc deposits were discovered on parcels of Quapaw land, which have provided decent incomes for tribal members.

Sac (Sauk)

This tribe has two common versions of its name, Sac (pronounced *SACK*) and Sauk (pronounced *SAWK*). The name is derived from an Algonquian word meaning the "yellow earth people." For much of their history, the Sacs were allied with the Foxes, the "red earth people." The two tribes were also closely related to the Kickapoos. In their distant past, perhaps all three tribes were one (see "Fox" and "Kickapoo").

All three peoples are considered western Great Lakes Algonquians because of their locations and their languages (see "Algonquian"). They are also called Northeast Woodland Algonquians because they usually situated their villages in stands of trees along river valleys (see "Northeast Indians"). They are also referred to as Prairie Algonquians because they hunted buffalo in the tall grass prairies of the Mississippi Valley (see "Prairie Indians").

Still another classification of the Sacs is encountered in historical writings: the Indians of the Old Northwest. The Old Northwest phrase results from the fact that white settlers pushing westward from the Atlantic Seaboard once thought of the area around the Great Lakes as the Northwest. When this region became settled, the concept of the Northwest changed to mean a new frontier in the vicinity of the Pacific. So historians started calling the former wilderness area around the Great Lakes the "Old Northwest." Of course, to Canadians the Northwest means something else.

These various categories help us to identify certain aspects of tribes—their relationships with one another, their languages, their lifeways, and their histories—but the Indians did not use them. The categories were created by anthropologists, historians, and linguists to make Indian studies easier.

Lifeways

The lifeways of the Sacs, as with many other Northeast Indians, revolved around a farming and village existence in warm seasons, then a hunting and nomadic existence in cold seasons. In the villages, their houses were relatively large—bark-covered wigwams that were either rectangular or domed. When Sacs were out on the trail, the shelter had to be portable. Most favored the oval wigwam with a reed covering.

Like many of the tribes of the region, the Sacs migrated often, especially when the whites started coming in great numbers into their original territory.

It is thought that the Sacs once lived on Michigan's southern peninsula. Then they moved west of Lake Michigan to what is now Wisconsin sometime before the white explorers came in the 1600s. At that time the biggest Sac villages were on the Wisconsin River. But in 1769, they united with other tribes to defeat the Illinois Indians, after which most Sacs resettled southward in what used to be the Illinois's land (see "Illinois"). Many Fox Indians, who had been allies of the Sacs since 1734, lived near or among them (see "Fox"). The Rock River in Illinois became the summer homeland of many bands.

The Black Hawk War

It was the Rock River bands who played the biggest part in the Black Hawk War of 1832. The Black Hawk War was the last of the wars for the Old Northwest, and it is a powerful story, symbolizing the end of the Prairie Algonquian way of life. The central issue, as with the majority of Indian wars, was land.

In 1804, some Sac and Fox bands were tricked into signing away all their tribal lands in Illinois by William Henry Harrison, who later became president of the United States. But the Sacs and Foxes of the Rock River claimed that those who had signed the treaty at St. Louis did not represent all the Sacs. One such leader was Ma-ka-tai-me-she-kia-kiak, or Black Sparrow Hawk, or simply Black Hawk. He and his band from the village of Saukenuk (now Rock Island), at the junction of the Mississippi and Rock rivers, refused to depart from their homeland.

As Black Hawk later wrote in his biography, "My reason teaches me that land cannot be sold. The Great Spirit gave it to his children to live on. So long as they occupy it and cultivate it they have the right to the soil. Nothing can be sold but such things as can be taken away."

The forces of history proved otherwise. White settlers kept coming and white officials kept favoring their land claims over Indian claims. In 1818, Illinois Territory became the 21st state of the Union. In 1829, when Black Hawk and his band left the village for the winter hunt, white squatters moved onto their land. They even took over some of the Indian lodges. On returning the following spring, some of the Sacs and Foxes under a chief named Keokuk agreed to relocate across the Mississippi in Iowa. Yet Black Hawk and his followers stayed on in lodges that the squatters had not occupied. Despite some quarreling, the Indians and whites survived a planting season together. And Black Hawk vowed to return again the following spring.

Troops were called in to keep the Indians out of Saukenuk once and for all. There were some young men in this army who later became famous in American history, such as Abraham Lincoln, Zachary Taylor, and Jefferson Davis. Daniel Boone's son, Nat, was also among them. Despite warnings to stay away, Black Hawk's band of 300 warriors plus their families returned the next spring, in 1830. But, when the combined force of state militia and federal regulars reached the village, they found that the Indians had slipped back across the Mississippi during the night. War had been avoided for the time being.

The clash finally came in 1832. By then, Black Hawk's followers had grown in number. White Cloud, a Winnebago shaman (or medicine man) who was usually called by the name Winnebago Prophet, preached against the whites and rallied Winnebagos, Kickapoos, and Potawatomis to the Sac and Fox cause. His message of living in traditional Indian ways resembled the teachings of other prophets before him, such as Delaware Prophet (see "Delaware" and "Ottawa") and Shawnee Prophet (see "Shawnee").

The first fighting occurred in May. It broke out when jittery and inexperienced militiamen fired on an Indian party sent to parley under a white flag of truce. Black Hawk had been prepared to surrender, but now his warriors attacked and routed the enemy, who fled in panic. The Indian victory is named Stillman's Run after Major Isaiah Stillman, who had been in charge of the unit.

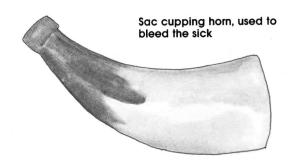

Sac cupping horn, used to bleed the sick

The renegade Indians headed north up the Rock River into Wisconsin. The army organized a pursuit. The next clash occurred in June along the Wisconsin River. Black Hawk had hoped to descend the Wisconsin to the Mississippi, from where his followers could reach the safety of Keokuk's village in Iowa. Many Indians died in this battle. The rest managed to escape across the river on makeshift rafts. Black Hawk decided to push on for the Bad Axe River, which also joined up with the Mississippi. By now, his people were exhausted and starving.

Troops caught up with them once more in July. Again Black Hawk tried to parley a surrender under a flag of truce. Again soldiers fired on his men. While the Indians were making rafts and canoes to cross the river, soldiers attacked them along the bank. Other soldiers fired on them from the steamship *Warrior*, which was outfitted with cannon. Many women and children were killed. Warriors trying desperately to swim across the swift waters were picked off by sharpshooters. As many as 300 died in the massacre.

This was a sad day in American history. And the symbolism was evident to those who cared about America's native peoples. The Mississippi River was the new boundary set up by the federal government to separate Indians from whites. But Indians were slaughtered as they were trying to cross it. And many more Indians would be killed west of it in years to come when that boundary, like all the others before it, was overrun by white settlers.

Black Hawk and Winnebago Prophet were among the few Indians to escape. They headed north into Winnebago country. But, weary of hiding out, they turned themselves in the following July. Black Hawk closed his surrender speech with these words: "Farewell my nation! Black Hawk tried to save you, and avenge your wrongs. He drank the blood of some of the whites. He has been taken prisoner, and his plans are stopped. He can do no more. He is near his end. His sun is setting, and he will rise no more. Farewell to Black Hawk."

He dictated his autobiography in 1833. He was eventually released under the condition he no longer act as a chief among his people. He met President Andrew Jackson, the man who had shaped the policy of relocating eastern Indians westward, in Washington, D.C., and toured other eastern cities. But, stripped of his homeland and his authority, Black Hawk died a bitter man in 1838. In a final insult to this great leader, grave robbers raided his tomb and displayed his head in a traveling carnival.

In 1842, the other Sac and Fox chief, Keokuk, was pressured into selling tribal lands in Iowa. The Sacs and Foxes moved to the Indian Territory in Kansas. Then in the 1850s, when whites were rapidly settling Kansas, some Sacs and Foxes relocated to the new, smaller Indian Territory which is now Oklahoma. Some later returned and bought back part of the Iowa land. The combined tribes now hold small reservations and trust lands in all three states. Yet they hold no land in their homelands of Wisconsin and Illinois.

Jim Thorpe

One of the most famous of all 20th-century Native Americans, and thought by some to be the greatest all-around athlete who ever lived, was a Sac—Jim Thorpe. He was born in Oklahoma in 1888, and his mother named him Bright Path. He attended the Carlisle Indian School in Pennsylvania. Founded by Richard Henry Pratt in 1879, the Carlisle school was the first Indian school off a reservation to be funded by the federal government. Jim Thorpe became its most famous alumnus. He was the halfback on the football team, which beat many big football powers.

Then in 1912, Jim Thorpe participated in the Stockholm Olympics in Sweden, where he won gold medals in two events, the pentathlon and the decathlon. The following year, when it was discovered that Bright Path had played a season of semi-professional baseball, which supposedly made him a professional athlete instead of an amateur, he was stripped of his awards. He did receive other recognition for his greatness, however. He played briefly for the New York Giants baseball team plus various professional football teams. And Jim Thorpe, Pennsylvania, is named after him. Thorpe's Olympic gold medals were reinstated in 1982, 30 years after his death.

Sarcee

The Sarcees, or Sarcis (both pronounced *SAR-see*), were the only northern Plains tribe to speak the Athapascan language. Most of the Athapascan tribes lived in the icy evergreen forests of the Subarctic, what is now northwestern Canada, leading a hunting-gathering existence (see "Athapascan"). From the 9th through the 11th centuries, long before whites came to North America, some bands of Athapascans migrated to what later became the American Southwest and the southern Plains; these tribes became the Apaches and Navajos (see "Athapascan"; "Apache"; and "Navajo").

The Sarcees stayed in the north, along the North Saskatchewan River in what is now the Canadian province of Alberta. But since their territory was part of the northern Plains, their lifeways came to differ from those of the Athapascans of the Subarctic. The

Sarcee knife with steel blade

use of the horse spread from the Spanish to the tribes of the West, starting in the 1600s. The Sarcees probably did not acquire horses until the early 1800s. Once they did, the Sarcees became a typical Plains tribe, depending on buffalo as their main food. They are therefore classified as part of the Great Plains Culture Area (see "Plains Indians").

The Sarcees were traditional enemies of the Plains Crees (see "Cree"), and they became part of the Blackfoot Confederacy (see "Blackfoot") for mutual protec-tion against the Crees. The biggest killer of the Sarcees, however, was disease, brought to their people through regular contacts with the white Hudson's Bay traders. Many Sarcees died in the smallpox epidemics of 1836 and 1870, and the scarlet fever epidemic of 1856.

In 1877, the Sarcees signed away most of their lands to the Canadian government. In 1880, they were placed on a reservation near what is now Calgary, Alberta, where their descendants live today.

Seminole

The word *Seminole* (pronounced *SEM-in-ole*) means "one who has camped out from the regular towns" or "runaway." The Seminole Indians of Florida have this name because their ancestors broke off from other Native Americans living to the north in Georgia and Alabama—mainly the Creeks—and migrated south during the 1700s (see "Creek").

The Seminole Wars

The Seminoles have a proud and exciting history. In the early 1800s, before the Civil War, they were friends of other runaways—escaped black slaves. They hid the slaves and welcomed them into their families. Many generals tried in vain to conquer the Seminoles.

A Seminole Indian in his dugout

General Andrew Jackson, who later became president, led an army against the Seminoles during the First Seminole War of 1817-18. The Indians called Jackson "Sharp Knife." His troops looted and burned Indian villages before returning north to Georgia. His invasion started a war with Spain which at the time claimed Florida as its own. Afterward, Florida became part of the United States.

When Andrew Jackson became president, he wanted to send the Seminoles to the Indian Territory west of the Mississippi River. About 3,000 Seminoles were forced to relocate during the Trail of Tears of the 1830s, along with Indians from other Southeastern tribes, namely the Cherokees, Creeks, Choctaws, and Chickasaws (see entries for those tribes).

The Indian families were herded westward like cattle by U.S. soldiers, the hated bluecoats. The Indians did not have enough food or blankets and many died of starvation and disease. Others were killed by bandits who preyed on them. Survivors were not even permitted to stop and bury their dead.

Yet some Seminoles refused to leave Florida and waged a guerilla war from their native swamps, successfully using hit-and-run tactics. This was the Second Seminole War of 1835-42. Osceola was the most important Seminole leader in this struggle. He was not a hereditary chief, but rose to prominence because of his militant stand against whites. When officials tried to make him sign a treaty agreeing to leave Florida, he slashed it with a knife. Then he led his men into the wilderness to resist the forced removal. He and his warriors won a great victory at the Withlacoochee River against a much larger force of soldiers under General Duncan Clinch.

Osceola was captured through deceit. General Thomas Jesup tricked him to coming to a peace council, then had his men seize the fighter. Osceola lasted only three months in captivity. He wasted away from malaria and a throat disease. The frontier painter George Catlin painted a famous portrait of the Seminole leader just before his death. Catlin reported that the proud Osceola was ready to die, bitter at the whites for their treachery.

The Second Seminole War had not ended. Other Seminoles continued to fight and, indeed, never surrendered. The war wound down after the federal government had lost 1,500 men and spent at least $30 million, making it the most costly Indian war ever. For every two Seminoles relocated, one soldier died.

The Third Seminole War took place in 1855-58. Billy Bowlegs' band attacked settlers, surveyors, trappers, and traders from their headquarters in the Florida Everglades. Once again, the army couldn't contain the Seminoles. Some tribal members agreed to move to the Indian Territory when relatives from the Indian Territory were brought in to meet with them. Yet the tribe never signed a treaty and many Seminoles stayed in Florida.

Lifeways

The Seminoles are considered part of the Southeast Culture Area (see "Southeast Indians"). They were farmers as well as hunter-gatherers. They build their villages near rivers in swamplands. Their houses, made from palmetto trees, had pole foundations, thatched roofs, raised platforms, and open walls. The houses, called chickees, were perfectly suited to the warm, wet climate: open to stay cool and high enough

Seminole chickee

to stay dry. A small attic was used for storage, as were outdoor poles from which utensils could be hung. The Seminoles also built cooking huts that were shared by different families.

By throwing embers from a fire onto logs and scraping out the charred wood with stone and bone scrapers, the Seminoles made sleek and graceful dugout canoes. Sometimes the hull walls were only an inch thick. These dugouts had platforms in the rear where a man could stand and use a long pole to push through swamps. Meanwhile, passengers could spear fish as well as large and deadly alligators.

The Seminoles still are famed for their handling of these fierce creatures. Tourists can watch alligator-wrestling at Indian festivals. Seminole braves approach the animals from behind, grab their jaws, and flip them onto their backs to pacify them.

Seminole children as young as four years old had to help with chores, such as gathering wood for fires, stirring soup, and kneading dough. Older boys went hunting and fishing with their fathers while the girls learned domestic skills such as cooking and sewing.

The Seminoles developed a unique style of clothing. Using patchwork and rickrack techniques, they pieced together shirts and dresses with bright, stunning colors.

Today, the Seminoles and their close relatives—the branch tribe known as the Miccosukees (pronounced *mick-o-SOO-kee*)—have five reservations in southern Florida. Many other Seminoles live in Oklahoma. The annual Miccosukee Art Festival in southern Florida draws Native American participants and tourists from all over North America.

Seminole palmetto doll with rickrack dress (modern)

Seneca

The Senecas were the westernmost tribe of the powerful Iroquois League. Their original homeland extended from Seneca Lake to the Allegheny River in western New York. Their name in its original form, before being altered to the familiar-sounding Latin name by whites (pronounced *SEN-uh-kuh*), means "great hill people." To the other members of the Iroquois Confederacy, the Senecas were the Keepers of the Western Door or simply Door-Keepers. The Iroquois thought of their combined territory as one large longhouse with the Senecas guarding the western entrance and the Mohawks guarding the eastern entrance.

The numerous Senecas have been called the most powerful of all the Iroquois, although the Mohawks were formidable too. At the annual Great Council, held in Onondaga territory, the Senecas sent eight sachems, or chiefs, as representatives.

The six tribes of the Iroquois League—the Mohawks, Oneidas, Onondagas, Cayugas, Tuscaroras and Senecas—had history and culture in common. For a more thorough understanding of the Seneca tribe, in addition to this section, see the entries "Iroquois" and "Northeast Indians."

There were many famous Seneca leaders. Two of them rose to prominence during and after the American Revolution: Cornplanter and Red Jacket. Both leaders sided with the British against the American rebels and led war parties against American settlers. Red Jacket received his English name from the British military redcoat he wore.

After the war, both men, unlike the Mohawk chief Joseph Brant and his followers who resettled in Canada (see "Mohawk"), recognized the sovereignty of the new American nation and negotiated for Seneca lands. Cornplanter became a trusted friend of the whites. Red Jacket, however, held out against white influences, urging his people to live in their traditional manner.

Both Cornplanter and Red Jacket were articulate. Some of Cornplanter's most famous words were addressed to President George Washington: "When your army entered the country of the Six Nations, we called you *Caunotaucarius*, the Town Destroyer; and to this day when that name is heard, our women look behind them and turn pale, and our children cling to the knees of their mothers . . . . When you gave us peace, we called you father, because you promised to secure us in possession of our lands."

Red Jacket, an eloquent man with an excellent memory for detail, is remembered for many different speeches and letters. When protesting Seneca land sales, he said, "We stand as a small island in the bosom of the great waters . . . . They rise, they press upon us and the waves will settle over us and we shall disappear forever. Who then lives to mourn us, white man? None."

When complaining about missionaries among the Senecas, Red Jacket said, "The black coats tell us to work and raise corn; they do nothing themselves and would starve to death if someone did not feed them. All they do is pray to the Great Spirit; but that will not make corn and potatoes grow; if it will why do they beg from us and from the white people. The red men knew nothing of trouble until it came from the white men; as soon as they crossed the great waters they wanted our country, and in return have always been ready to teach us to quarrel about their religion . . . . We are few and weak, but may for a long time be happy if we hold fast to our country, and the religion of our fathers."

Seneca ash-splint basket (modern)

Another famous Seneca was Cornplanter's half-brother, Handsome Lake, who founded the Long-house Religion in 1799 to help the Iroquois adapt to their new life after they had lost most of their lands and had been surrounded by American settlers. The Longhouse Religion combines elements of both Christianity and the Iroquois religion. Handsome Lake was raised traditionally, but later studied the Quaker religion. Like Quakerism, his Longhouse Religion, which is still practiced by many Iroquois, emphasizes good deeds and silent prayer. Followers worship one god, as Christians do, known to them as the Great Spirit. Their churches are longhouses.

In 1869, a Seneca by the name of Ely Samuel Parker (Donehogawa) became the first Native American commissioner of the Bureau of Indian Affairs, the branch of the federal government that deals with Native American matters. Parker had earlier fought

under General Ulysses S. Grant in the Civil War as an assistant adjutant general and had served as Grant's secretary. Then when Grant became president, he appointed Donehogawa commissioner. Donehogawa helped shape Grant's Peace Policy toward the Indians of the Great Plains and Far West, which included a new approach to solving the frequent outbreaks of violence there (see "Plains Indians").

The Senecas presently hold three state reservations in western New York near the city of Buffalo: the Allegany Reservation, the Cattaraugus Reservation, and the Tonawanda Reservation; plus an additional small parcel, the Oil Springs Reservation.

The Senecas have been in the news in recent years because of questions concerning their lands. In the 1950s, many tribal members opposed the flooding of lands on their Allegany Reservation for a dam. They lost their case, however, and the Army Corps of Engineers built the huge Kinzua Dam in 1958, flooding 10,500 acres. Some of these lands were sacred to tribal members. Cornplanter's grave was flooded.

More recently, in 1985, some Senecas tried to block construction of a part of Route 17, called the Southern Tier Expressway, crossing the Allegany Reservation. They claimed that tribal leaders had no right to sell the land to the state in 1976. But a New York State Supreme Court justice issued an order barring the group from further interference with construction, and the road was completed.

There is also the issue of the Salamanca lease. The city of Salamanca is built on Indian reservation land. In 1892, white citizens signed lease agreements lasting 99 years with the Seneca Nation. Some of the leases cost only $1.00 a year for a piece of property. But the leases are due to expire in 1991. The Senecas plan to receive fair payment for any new leases.

Shawnee

Shawnee (pronounced *shaw-NEE*) means "southerners" in the Algonquian language. This meaning helps a student of Indian history locate the Shawnees among all other Algonquian peoples, because for most of their history the Shawnees lived south of the other tribes of their Algonquian language family (see "Algonquian").

Yet the historical location of the tribe is still very complicated. The Shawnees split up into different groups and migrated often. It is difficult to pick one state to call their original homeland. Perhaps the best way to think of their territory is generally to the west of

the Cumberland Mountains of the Appalachian chain, with the Cumberland River at the center. At one time or another, the Shawnees had villages along many of the rivers of that region: the Cumberland, the Ohio, the Tennessee. This area now comprises parts of the states of Tennessee, Kentucky, Ohio, and West Virginia.

Nonetheless, when whites first crossed the Appalachians, they found very few Indian villages in Kentucky and West Virginia. We know the Indians spent time there because there is much archaeological evidence of Indians in those states: Farmers still plow up spear points and arrowheads, and both amateur and professional archaeologists have found grave sites. Scholars theorize that perhaps this territory of forested mountains, hills, and valleys, plus rolling bluegrass prairies, served not so much as a homeland for the Shawnees and other tribes of the region, like the Cherokees, but as sacred hunting grounds.

But the Shawnees also ranged far to the north, south, and east of this core area, on both sides of the great Appalachian Divide—especially as whites started entering the Indians' domain. In the course of their history, in addition to the states mentioned above, the Shawnees had temporary villages in northern parts of South Carolina, Georgia, and Alabama; western parts of Maryland, Virginia, Pennsylvania, and New York; and southern parts of Indiana and Illinois. And then in the 1800s, they were relocated by whites to the Indian Territory—first Kansas and Missouri, then Oklahoma. Some Shawnees also ended up in Texas.

As wanderers, the Shawnees had a unique place in Indian history and culture, introducing cultural traits of the northern tribes to the southern tribes and vice versa. They might be called intermediaries between different cultures. The Shawnees are generally classified as Northeast Indians, since they hunted, fished, gathered, and farmed in ways similar to the more northern Algonquians (see "Northeast Indians"). But they picked up Southeast lifeways too (see "Southeast Indians"). They are sometimes referred to as Prairie Indians because they ranged as far west as the prairies of the Mississippi River Valley (see "Prairie Indians").

The Shawnees not only shifted territory. They also shifted allegiances among different colonial powers. Like most other Algonquians, they usually sided with the French against the English during the many years of fighting from 1689 to 1763 known as the French and Indian Wars (see "Abnaki" and "Iroquois"). But some Shawnee bands considered English trade goods better than French goods. Pickawillany, in Shawnee territory in Ohio, became a major British trading post. Moreover, some Shawnee groups were conquered by the Iroquois and, as their subjects, fought with them and the English against the French.

Nevertheless, the majority of Shawnees rebelled against the English in Pontiac's Rebellion of 1763-64 (see "Ottawa"). Then in 1774, one year before the start of the American Revolution, the Shawnees fought Virginians in Lord Dunmore's War.

Lord Dunmore's War

The Shawnees rebelled when the governor of Virginia, the Earl of Dunmore, ignored the Proclamation of 1763, signed by the king of England, promising an Indian Country west of the Appalachians. Dunmore gave veterans of the French and Indian Wars who had fought under him land that belonged to the Shawnees. When the settlers came to stake their claims, the Shawnees, led by Chief Cornstalk, attacked them. Dunmore sent in a force of volunteers, but it was routed by a Shawnee ambush on the Kentucky River.

Next Dunmore organized a much larger army of 1,500 militiamen. Cornstalk asked the Iroquois for help. Most refused to fight their former allies, the British. But Logan, the Mingo chief, and some of his warriors joined the Shawnee cause (see "Cayuga").

The decisive battle occurred on October 6, 1774, at Point Pleasant, West Virginia. The Indians suffered many casualties in the bitter fighting. Cornstalk signed a peace treaty with Dunmore in which the Shawnees agreed to give up some lands.

The American Revolution and Little Turtle's War

Yet the peace did not last long. The American Revolution erupted the next year in 1775. Now the Shawnees sided with the British against the American rebels. It was after all the British government who had originally proclaimed an Indian Country; and it was the American settlers who had ignored the proclamation.

During the Revolution, the Shawnees fought the famous frontiersman Daniel Boone, the man who had cut a path through the Cumberland Gap. They even captured him in 1778 and held him prisoner at the village of Chillicothe in Ohio, but he managed to escape. Boone had learned the ways of the wilderness from the Shawnees and other Indians. Now he was using his skills against them.

The Americans of course won the War of Independence. Now they could turn their attention to clearing the path for white settlement. The Shawnees, many of whom were now living north of the Ohio River in the Old Northwest, joined other tribes of the region under Little Turtle to resist the incoming settlers. When army after army came at them, the Indians finally yielded in 1794. Another war was lost and more territory signed away (see "Miami").

Tecumseh's Rebellion

In the late 1700s and early 1800s, when the young United States was just beginning to flex its muscles and expand to its present shape, two Shawnees rose to prominence. They were twins, among the most remarkable set of twins in all of history. One was named Tenskwatawa, but called Shawnee Prophet by whites. He was a shaman, or medicine man. Like Delaware Prophet before him (see "Delaware" and "Ottawa"), he preached to Indians of many tribes, telling them to return to traditional ways and abandon all customs that came from whites, such as the Christian religion and liquor. He claimed to have special "magic" in the fight against whites.

His twin brother, Tecumseh, was a great orator and a man of energy and action. He was also a visionary. He dreamed of a great Indian country from Canada to the Gulf of Mexico where all the tribes would be united—sort of a United Tribes of America—as a neighbor to the United States of America. He believed that no single Indian or tribe had the right to give up lands to whites because the lands belonged to all Indians and all tribes. For that reason, he refused to sign the Treaty of Fort Greenville in 1795 after Little Turtle's War. Tecumseh considered himself an Indian first and a Shawnee second. To carry out his dream, he believed a united military stand would be necessary.

Tecumseh did not hate whites, even though they had killed his father and brother in previous wars. Tecumseh admired whites for their many accomplishments. He studied world history and literature in order to better understand them. He even supposedly had a romance with a white schoolteacher, Rebecca Galloway. And he believed that one should treat prisoners fairly, whatever their nature or nationality, without degradation and torture.

For his wisdom, compassion, and, as he later proved, his military genius, many consider him the greatest man of his age, a man who would have made the perfect leader for the Indian country that might have been, a man to rival in capabilities any president the United States has ever produced.

Tecumseh worked hard to accomplish his goal. He traveled from the Old Northwest to the Deep South to urge unity among the Indians. He spoke to many tribes. Some resisted the idea of allying with former enemies. But Tecumseh persisted. Unity was everything, he claimed. If the tribes didn't unite, they would go the way of the tribes of the Atlantic Seaboard who were now extinct or dispersed.

"Where today are the Pequots?" he asked his fellow Indians. "Where are the Narragansets, the Mohawks, the Pocanets, and many other once-powerful tribes of our people? They have vanished before the avarice and oppression of the white man, as snow before the summer sun . . . . Will we let ourselves be destroyed in our turn without making an effort worthy of our race?"

Tecumseh was such a persuasive speaker and a magnetic personality that even stubborn chiefs started to come around to his way of thinking. With trip after trip, speech after speech, council after council, Tecumseh's dream was becoming a reality.

Yet all his work became unraveled by bad luck and by his brother's misjudgment. While Tecumseh was in the South, William Henry Harrison, then the governor of Indiana Territory, ordered an attack on Tenskwatawa's village of Prophetstown on the Tippecanoe River. Harrison's excuse for the expedition was that Indians had stolen army horses. His real reason, however, was to achieve military glory and further his own career. Rather than avoid fighting at all costs and wait until the Indian military alliance was in place, Tenskwatawa followed the advice of some young, hot-blooded warriors and ordered an ambush. The Indians were repelled. Harrison's army marched on Prophetstown and burned the village to the ground. Most of the warriors escaped, however.

It was not a major victory in a military sense, although Harrison later claimed so in his presidential campaign. But it broke the momentum of Tecumseh's Rebellion. Tenskwatawa's magic had been proven ineffective. Many of the tribes decided to make raids prematurely in their own territories, rather than wait for a united stand under Tecumseh.

Then the War of 1812 broke out between the United States and Great Britain, at that time in firm control of Canada. Tecumseh, hoping for British help in organizing an Indian homeland, joined the fight against the Americans. The British recognized his leadership abilities and made him a brigadier general in their army. Because of his participation, some Indians joined the British cause. But others held off their support, waiting to see the outcome.

Tecumseh proved himself a great general. His skill often made up for the incompetency of the other British generals. He helped take Detroit. He slowed the victorious advance of an American force under William Henry Harrison. When most of the British fled in panic back to Canada, Tecumseh and his men covered the white force's retreat. Unlike other generals, he stayed on the front lines, urging his men on. But on October 5, 1813, at the Battle of Thames, Tecumseh took bullet after bullet from soldiers in the larger American force and finally fell dead.

Although a group of Kentuckians skinned a body they thought to be Tecumseh's for souvenirs, they never found his actual corpse. Fellow warriors must have hidden it from the enemy. Rumors persisted among the tribes that Tecumseh would one day return. But of course he never did. His twin brother lived about another 20 years and continued to preach to the tribes of the region. Other Indian rebellions would occur, such as in the Black Hawk War (see

A modern-day Shawnee Indian girl

"Sac"). But without Tecumseh's organizational abilities, there was no hope for an Indian rebellion on the huge scale he had worked for. And eventually most of the Indians of the Old Northwest and the Southeast were pushed west of the Mississippi.

Present day Shawnees living in Oklahoma on trust lands in Pottawatomi, Cleveland, and Ottawa counties have adjusted well to their situation, combining traditional with modern ways. It is thought that perhaps they have managed as well as they have under adverse conditions because they were a tribe that wandered a great deal and frequently had to adapt to new neighbors and cultures.

Perhaps too they are well-adjusted because they always had a good system of rearing children. Among Shawnee children, the best prize for good behavior was praise. And the worst punishment was to hear their bad behavior revealed to a friend or visitor. The children didn't mind pain. They could tolerate being hit. But they hated to hear criticism. And so they worked extra hard to hear words of praise being spoken by their parents and other elders.

Shoshone

Sacajawea (or Sacagawea, translated as "Bird-woman"), next to Pocahontas, is probably the most famous Indian woman in history. Pocahontas's renown came from her contact and mercy toward some of the first English settlers in North America along the Atlantic Coast. Sacajawea's fame arose because of her work as a guide to the most important voyage of exploration to the American West, the Lewis and Clark Expedition. Despite the different locations, there are similarities in the two women's stories. Pocahontas saved Captain John Smith's life from the hand of her angry father (see "Powhatan"). Sacajawea saved the lives of the members of the Lewis and Clark expedition on many different occasions because she not only showed them the way, but also acted as diplomat to the hostile Indians through whose land they passed. Sacajawea deserves as much credit for the expedition's success as anyone. This great woman was a Shoshone Indian.

The Shoshones, sometimes spelled Shoshonis (pronounced *sho-SHO-nee*), spoke a dialect of the Uto-Aztecan language and lived in the Great Basin. There were two distinct groups: (1) the Western Shoshones in central and northeastern Nevada, central and

western Idaho, and northwestern Utah; and (2) the Northern Shoshones of western Wyoming, eastern Idaho, northeastern Utah, and eastern California. The Snake River in Idaho can be thought of as the heart of Shoshone territory, in the center of the two groups.

Lifeways

It is difficult to place the Shoshone groups culturally. As a whole, the Shoshones are placed by scholars in the Great Basin Culture Area (see "Great Basin Indians"). The Great Basin is the vast, cupped desert area lying west of the Rocky Mountains and east of the Sierra Nevada, broken up by intermittent highlands. Indians who lived in this arid and barren environment were called Diggers by whites since they dug for the scarce food, such as roots, nuts, seeds, lizards, insects, squirrels, and rabbits.

This foraging way of life was especially true of the Western Shoshones, who lived in primitive brush shelters, open at one end. The Goshutes, or Gosiutes, a band of Shoshones living along the desolate shores of the Great Salt Lake in Utah, were typical of this group. Their name indicates the ancestral relationship among the Shoshones, Utes, and Paiutes (see "Ute" and "Paiute"). The Panamint (or Koso) Shoshone band in eastern California, which lived in one of the most extreme environments in all of North America—the Panamint Mountains and Death Valley—were also typical Diggers.

Yet the Northern Shoshones found more plentiful game on the forested slopes of the Grand Teton and Wind River mountains, part of the Rocky Mountain chain in present-day Wyoming. And, with the acquisition of the horse in the late 1600s, the Northern Shoshones gained greater mobility in their hunting. The pronghorn antelope was a favorite game for meat and hides, as was the buffalo. The Northern

Shoshones came to live in tepees like the Plains Indians east of the Rocky Mountains (see "Plains Indians"). The Wind River Shoshones were typical of this group. These were the horse-mounted warriors who frequently fought the Arapaho and Blackfoot tribes living east of them (see "Arapaho" and "Blackfoot").

Sacajawea

Although early Spanish explorers might have had previous contacts with the Shoshones, particularly the western group, it was the Lewis and Clark Expedition that made white America aware of them. This voyage

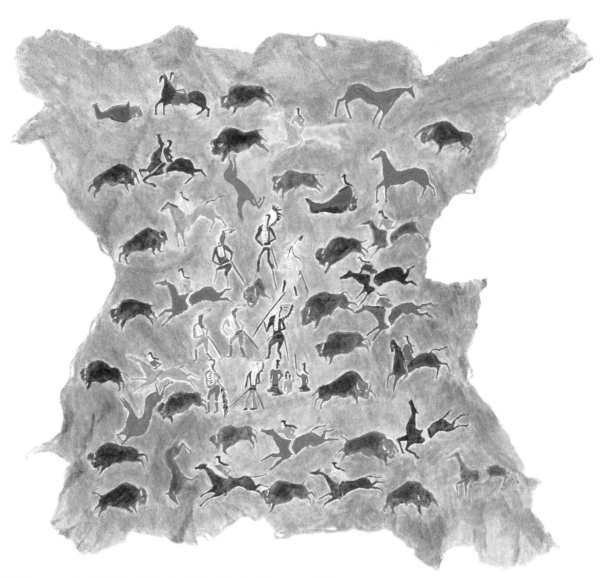

Shoshone painted buffalo hide, depicting the Sun Dance and the return of the buffalo

of exploration is mentioned in connection with many Indian peoples, since Lewis and Clark covered so much territory and encountered as many as 50 tribes. Thomas Jefferson, the president at the time, conceived of a scientific expedition west of the Mississippi River. The United States was a young country seeking out its boundaries. In 1803, Jefferson signed the Louisiana Purchase with France, which had recently been granted the land by Spain. A vast expanse of mostly wilderness territory, about 828,000 square miles, from the Gulf of Mexico to Canada, came under United States domain. Jefferson chose his private secretary, Captain Meriwether Lewis, to explore the northern part of this enormous tract. Lewis chose his friend, Captain William Clark, as his associate in command.

In the winter of 1803-04, Lewis and Clark organized a team of 29 additional men in Illinois, across the Missouri River from the settlement of St. Louis. One of these was a black man known simply as York in historical writings. He would generate much interest among the Indians, who had never seen such dark skin before. The explorers set out up the Missouri River in May 1804. They spent the next winter in Mandan Indian villages (see "Mandan"). It was during this period that a Montrealer named Toussaint Charbonneau and his Indian wife, Sacajawea, joined the expedition. Charbonneau had just purchased Sacajawea from the neighboring Hidatsa Indians. She had been brought to their villages by Gros Ventre Indians, who had captured her four years earlier in a raid on a Shoshone band.

This was a remarkably fortunate turn of events for the explorers. Sacajawea's presence reassured Indians whom they later encountered. She was able to communicate with the different tribes through sign language. She obtained horses for the expedition from her own tribe to cross the Great Divide. She showed the way through the Lemhi Pass in the Rockies that led from the Missouri to the Columbia River. With her help, the expedition successfully reached the Pacific Ocean and made its way back again, with only one man killed. Charbonneau and Sacajawea left the expedition where they had joined it, at the Mandan villages. Lewis and Clark returned triumphantly to St. Louis in 1806.

It is not known for certain when or where Sacajawea died. Some historians believe she passed away about 1812. But others have claimed that she died in Wyoming many years later, in 1855.

Later Contacts

In any case, after the opening of the American West by the Lewis and Clark Expedition, the Shoshone way of life would never be the same. Trappers and traders, the rugged Mountain Men, such as Jedediah Smith in 1825, crisscrossed their territory. In 1847, the Mormons founded their settlement on Great Salt Lake. During the California Gold Rush of 1849, prospectors and settlers also passed through Shoshone lands. Then in 1857, the discovery of the Comstock Lode, a rich strike of silver, led to mining settlements in Nevada.

Wars

The rights of the Indians were generally disregarded by the white newcomers. During the early 1860s, while federal troops were engaged in the Civil War in the East, Great Basin Indian bands resisted white expansion. They raided wagon trains and stagecoaches along the Central Overland Route to California; they waylaid Pony Express riders carrying mail along the route from Salt Lake City to California; they also attacked the crews stringing new telegraph lines and destroyed the wires.

To keep communication lines open, California officials sent the volunteer Third California Infantry eastward under Colonel Patrick Connor. In 1862, Connor founded Fort Douglas in the foothills of the Wasatch Mountains overlooking Salt Lake City.

Meanwhile, Chief Bear Hunter's band of Shoshones were raiding miners and Mormons alike. In January 1863, Connor led 300 troops out of Fort Douglas in the Bear River Campaign. In the bitter cold and over deep snowbanks, his men marched 140 miles north along the eastern side of the Great Salt Lake to Bear Hunter's village.

The Bear River Indians had time to prepare barricades of rocks and earth, further reinforcing their village, which was in a steep-walled ravine. But still they were no match for the superior firepower of the California volunteers, who poured round after round of ammunition into the village. With 224 of their people killed, the Indians retreated. Only 22 soldiers died. Bear Hunter's resistance had ended.

That same year, the United States government laid claim to much of the Great Basin. In the so-called treaty, the Indians received no payment. By 1865, practically all native resistance had ended. In 1869, the Union Pacific and Central Pacific railroads met at Promontory Point, Utah, in Shoshone country, completing the transcontinental railway and further encouraging white settlement in the West. In the 1860s and 1870s, all the Shoshone bands were assigned reservations.

In 1878, a band of Indians called the Sheepeaters, probably made up of both Bannocks and Shoshones, launched a shortlived uprising in the Salmon River Mountains of central Idaho (see "Bannock").

In the meantime, the Wind River Shoshones in Wyoming proved themselves valuable allies of the whites. Under their famous chief Washakie, they helped the army fight the Sioux in several battles, including the Battle of the Rosebud in 1876 (see "Sioux"). The tradition of friendly relations between these easternmost Shoshones and whites dated back to Sacajawea. Yet the Wind River band felt betrayed when white officials placed their traditional enemies, the Arapahos, on their reservation in 1878.

The Shoshones presently have one reservation in Utah, which they share with the Arapahos; two reservations in Utah, under the name of Goshute; one in Idaho, which they share with the Bannocks; 11 in Nevada, four of which they share with the Paiutes; and three in California, which they share with the Paiutes. Some of these reservations generate income from grazing or mining leases. Yet, because of the harsh environment and lack of capital, many of the modern-day Shoshones are poor. Because of the high rate of unemployment and the sense of alienation from modern American culture, the Wind River Reservation recently suffered an epidemic of suicides among its young tribesmen 14 to 25 years old. Nine people in all died. This is a tragic comment on the modern-day plight of Native Americans.

Sioux

Horse-mounted Indians, wearing long eagle-feathered warbonnets and fringed leather clothing with colorful beadwork, ride across the grasslands of the Great Plains. They hunt buffalo. They fight the cavalry. They sit in council inside painted tepees, wearing buffalo robes and smoking long-stemmed peace pipes. These images of Indians have been shown to us again and again, in books, movies and television shows about the West. These images, more likely than not, depict the Sioux.

Two of the most famous incidents in Indian and American history—Custer's Last Stand (also called the Battle of Little Bighorn) and Wounded Knee—involved the Sioux. The numerous Sioux fought many other battles against whites on the northern Plains. Some of the most famous Indian fighters in history, such as Red Cloud, Sitting Bull, and Crazy Horse, were Sioux. Also, one of the most famous incidents in recent Indian history occurred on a Sioux reservation, again at Wounded Knee.

Branches of Sioux

The Sioux (pronounced *SUE*) were really made up of different groups with varying lifeways and histories. In studying the Sioux, our first challenge is to learn the various names and locations of the different bands.

Siouan was a widespread Indian language family. Tribes in many parts of North America spoke Siouan

A Sioux war chief, a familiar image of the Plains Indian, as represented on a cigarette silk, distributed in metal tins of cigarettes in the early 1900s

dialects. The tribal name *Sioux* is applied only to the largest of these tribes, however. The name comes from the French version of a Chippewa word in the Algonquian language. The Chippewa tribe called their enemies *Nadouessioux* for "adders," a kind of snake. The Sioux are also known as the Dakota Indians, from which has come the names of two states, North and South Dakota. In the Siouan language, the name *Dakota* (or *Lakota* or *Nakota*) means "allies."

There were four branches of Sioux, with different bands in each. The first and largest branch was the Teton Sioux, with the following bands: (1) Oglala; (2) Brule (Sicangu); (3) Hunkpapa; (4) Miniconjou; (5) Oohenonpa; (6) Itazipco (Sans Arcs); and (7) Sihasapa.

A second branch was the Santee Sioux, with the following bands: (1) Sisseton; (2) Wahpeton; (3) Wahpekute; and (4) Mdewkanton.

A third branch was the Yankton Sioux, with only one band, the Yankton.

A fourth branch was the Yanktonai Sioux, with the following bands: (1) Yanktonai; (2) Hunkpatina; and (3) Assiniboine. The Assiniboine separated from their relatives and are discussed under their own entry (see "Assiniboine").

Of all four branches, the Tetons use the *Lakota* version of the tribal name; the Santees say *Dakota*; and the Yanktons and Yanktonais use *Nakota*.

The Sioux originally lived as Woodland Indians along the upper Mississippi River. It is known from early records of Jesuit explorers of the 1600s, that the Sioux once dominated territory which now comprises the southern two-thirds of Minnesota, as well as nearby parts of Wisconsin, Iowa, and North and South Dakota. By the mid-1700s, some Sioux were migrating westward toward and across the Missouri River. The reason: Their traditional enemies, the Chippewas, were now armed with French guns, making warfare with them much more dangerous (see "Chippewa"). Moreover, with the European demand for furs, game in the Sioux's prairie country was becoming scarcer.

The Teton Sioux migrated the farthest west, to the Black Hills region of what is now western South Dakota, eastern Wyoming, and eastern Montana. They are therefore sometimes called the Western Sioux. The Yankton Sioux settled along the Missouri River in what is now southeastern South Dakota, southwestern Minnesota, and southwestern Iowa. The Yanktonai Sioux settled to their north along the Missouri in what is now eastern North and South Dakota. The Yanktons and Yanktonais are sometimes referred to together as the Middle Sioux. The Santees stayed along the Minnesota River in what is now Minnesota. They are therefore known as the Eastern Sioux.

Sioux ceremonial buffalo skull with a design representing the sky, sun, and rain

Lifeways

Because of their different locations, the lifeways of the four branches were different. The Tetons acquired horses, followed the great buffalo herds, lived in tepees, and became the Indians so prevalent in the popular imagination.

The way of life of the Yanktons and Yanktonais became like that of other Missouri River tribes, such as the Mandans and Hidatsas, other Siouan-speaking peoples (see "Mandan" and "Hidatsa"). The Yanktons and Yanktonais began using horses in the 1700s and also hunted buffalo like the Tetons, but they lived most of the time in permanent villages of earthlodges. They also continued to cultivate crops. The Yanktons and Yanktonais can be described as Prairie Indians.

The Santees retained many of the cultural traits of the western Great Lakes Indians. Their culture was something like that of the Winnebagos, another Siouan-speaking people (see "Winnebago"). They lived in wooded river valleys and made bark-covered houses. They hunted buffalo in the tall grassland country of the Mississippi River. They eventually began to use the horse, but they did not keep as many mounts as their more westerly relatives did. The Santees can be thought of as a cross between Woodland and Prairie Indians.

Of all the culture areas defined by scholars in Indian studies, the Great Plains Culture Area is the most confusing. First, unlike the other culture areas, the typical way of life on the Great Plains did not evolve until long after contact with whites, when the Indians acquired the horse. Second, although most tribes on the Plains

Sioux wooden horse effigy with real horsehair

became equestrian nomads who lived in tepees year-round, not all the tribes gave up their villages, their farming, and their pottery after acquiring horses.

As we have already seen, the Teton Sioux are the typical Plains Indians. Their lifeways—their tepees, warbonnets, buffalo robes, medicine bundles, sacred shields, horsemanship, horse gear, military societies, buffalo-hunting, sign language, coup-counting, Sun Dances, and Vision Quests—are therefore summarized under the entry "Plains Indians." Yet see also "Prairie Indians" to help understand the way of life of the Yankton, Yanktonai, and Santee branches of the Sioux people.

The Sioux Wars

The Sioux, because of their stubborn resistance to white expansion, were the most famous of Plains warriors. The various conflicts involving the Sioux have been given names by historians (sometimes more than one name). Nevertheless, the conflicts did not always have distinct beginnings and endings, but were part of an ongoing pattern of raids and counterraids lasting from about 1850 to 1890 and collectively known as the Sioux Wars.

The different phases of the Sioux Wars are: (1) the Grattan Affair in 1854-55; (2) the Minnesota Uprising (or Little Crow's War) in 1862-64; (3) the War for the Bozeman Trail (or Red Cloud's War) in 1866-68; (4) the War for the Black Hills (or Sitting Bull's and Crazy Horse's War) in 1876-77; and (5) the Massacre at Wounded Knee in 1890.

The Grattan Affair

In 1851, white officials negotiated a treaty at Fort Laramie in Wyoming with the Sioux and their allies the Northern Cheyennes and Northern Arapahos, in order to assure safe passage for whites along the Oregon Trail, running from Missouri to Oregon (see "Cheyenne" and "Arapaho"). However, it only took three years after the signing of the treaty for violence to erupt.

A party of Mormons traveling west lost one of their cows, which wandered into a camp of the Brule band of Teton Sioux. The Mormons reported to troops at Fort Laramie that the Indians had stolen the cow. In the meantime, a Sioux named High Forehead killed the cow for food.

Although the Indians offered to pay for the cow, an over-eager lieutenant from the fort named John Grattan insisted on the arrest of High Forehead and rode to the Indian camp with a force of about 30 men. When the brave refused to turn himself in, Grattan ordered an attack. A Sioux chief named Conquering Bear was killed in the first volley. The Sioux counter-attacked and wiped out the detachment. The army sent in more troops to punish the Sioux. In 1855, at Blue Water in Nebraska, a force under General William Harney attacked another Brule camp and killed 85.

War had been brought to the Sioux. They would not forget this treatment at the hands of the whites. In fact, a young warrior of the Oglala band of Tetons—Crazy Horse—personally witnessed the killing of Conquering Bear. He would later become one of the most effective guerilla fighters in history.

The Minnesota Uprising

Another outbreak of violence involving the Sioux occurred far to the east, in Minnesota, among the

Sioux beads made from human finger and arm bones and traded as an early form of money

Santee bands. The central issue that caused the Minnesota Uprising (or Little Crow's War) was land, as more and more whites settled along the rich farmlands of the Minnesota River. Some of the young Santee braves wanted war against the people who were taking their lands. The Santee chief Little Crow argued for peace. But young militants forced the issue by killing five settlers. Little Crow then helped the other Santee chiefs organize a rebellion.

In August 1862, Santee war parties carried out surprise raids on white settlements and trading posts, killing as many as 400 people. Little Crow then led an assault on Fort Ridgely. The fort's cannon repelled the Indians, killing many. Another group of Santees stormed the village of New Ulm. The settlers drove the attackers away, but then evacuated the village.

General Henry Sibley led a large force into the field to combat the Indians. At Birch Coulee in September, the warriors attacked an army burial party, killing 23. But Sibley engaged the Santees at Wood Lake later that month and routed them with heavy artillery. Many warriors fled northwestward into the wilderness, Little Crow among them. Many others surrendered, claiming innocence in the slaying of the settlers.

Of those that stayed behind, 303 were sentenced to be hanged. President Abraham Lincoln took time out from his concerns with the Civil War to review the trial records, and he pardoned the large majority. Still, 33 braves, proclaiming their innocence to the end, were hanged the day after Christmas in 1862, the largest mass execution in American history.

Of those Santee Sioux that fled, many settled among Teton Sioux and Yanktonai Sioux in Dakota Territory (the part that was soon to become North Dakota). General Henry Sibley and General Alfred Sully engaged Sioux from various bands at Big Mound, Dead Buffalo Lake, and Stoney Lake in 1863; and at Whitestone Hill and Killdeer Mountain in 1864. The Santees and the other Sioux who helped them paid a high price in suffering for their Minnesota Uprising. Little Crow himself died in 1863 on a horse-stealing expedition out of Canada into Minnesota. Settlers shot him and turned in his scalp for the bounty.

The War for the Bozeman Trail

The War for the Bozeman Trail (or Red Cloud's War) began soon after the Minnesota Uprising ended. Land was again the central issue of this conflict, but it was the mining fever that brought increased traffic to the lands of the Western Sioux in what is now Montana and Wyoming.

In 1862, after having traveled to Montana's gold fields, the explorer John Bozeman followed a direct route through Teton lands back to the Oregon Trail in Wyoming rather than travel a longer way around to the east or west. Other migrants and miners followed along this new route. The various Teton bands—the Oglalas under Red Cloud; the Hunkpapas under Sitting Bull; and the Brules under Spotted Tail—resented the trespassing. So did their allies, the Northern Cheyennes under Dull Knife and the Northern Arapahos under Black Bear.

In 1865, the Indians began attacking military patrols and wagon trains as well as other travelers along both the Bozeman and the Oregon trails. General Patrick Connor sent in three different columns that year to punish the Indians. Their only success against the elusive warriors, who attacked swiftly, then disappeared into the wilderness, was the destruction of a camp of Northern Arapahos under Black Bear.

Sioux warclub

Some of the chiefs rode into Fort Laramie in 1866 to sign a treaty. Red Cloud insisted that no forts be built along the Bozeman, however. When the army refused to comply, the proud chief rode off with his warriors to make preparations for war.

Troops under Colonel Henry Carrington reinforced Fort Reno and built two new posts in northern Wyoming and southern Montana to keep the Bozeman Trail open. The Indian guerillas used hit-and-run tactics to harass the soldiers. Crazy Horse, a young Oglala warrior, began establishing his reputation as a fearless fighter and master strategist at this time. In 1866, he used a decoy tactic to trap an entire cavalry outfit: A few Indians attacked a woodcutting party, then fled; then Captain William Fetterman led an 80-man cavalry unit after them and to their death at the hands of 1,500 concealed warriors.

After the Fetterman Fight, the army sent in fresh troops with new breech-loading rifles. In two battles in 1866, the Hayfield Fight and the Wagon Box Fight, the Sioux lost many warriors to these modern weapons, but they succeeded in driving the whites back to their posts.

The Indians kept up their raids. The federal government, realizing the high cost of maintaining the Bozeman forts, yielded to Red Cloud's demands. In the Fort Laramie Treaty of 1868, the government agreed to abandon the posts if the Indians would cease their raids. When the army evacuated the region, the Indians celebrated by burning down the Bozeman forts. The Sioux had won this round of warfare on the Great Plains. But the whites would keep entering their domain. In the meantime, the southern and central Plains tribes—the Comanches, Kiowas, Southern Cheyennes, and Southern Arapahos—had forced concessions out of the whites in the Medicine Lodge Treaty of 1867 (see entries for those tribes).

The War for the Black Hills

The discovery of gold in the Black Hills of Wyoming and South Dakota in the year 1874 led to the next phase of the Sioux Wars: the War for the Black Hills (or Sitting Bull and Crazy Horse's War) of 1876-77. By now, the Sioux leaders Red Cloud and Spotted Tail had settled on reservations. Sitting Bull and Crazy Horse now led the allied hunting bands that refused to give up the traditional nomadic way of life. Opposing them were two generals who had become famous as Union commanders in the Civil War, General William Tecumseh Sherman, overall commander of the army, and General Philip Henry Sheridan, commander of the Division of the Missouri. In the field, the generals had various officers, including General George Crook, who had previously fought Apaches and Paiutes, and Lieutenant Colonel George Armstrong Custer, who had earlier campaigned against the Cheyennes.

War broke out when the military ordered the hunting bands onto the reservation. When the bands failed to report, the army went after them in the winter of 1876. During that year, some of the most famous battles on the Great Plains took place. The first three were great Indian victories. The final five were victories for the army and brought the resistance of the Sioux, Northern Cheyennes, and Northern Arapahos to a virtual close.

At Powder River in Montana in March 1876, Teton and Cheyenne warriors under Crazy Horse repelled a cavalry attack led by Colonel Joseph Reynolds. At Rosebud Creek in June, Crazy Horse's warriors routed General George Crook's huge force of soldiers and their Crow and Shoshone allies. Then, also in June, along the Little Bighorn River, Oglala warriors under Crazy Horse and Hunkpapa braves under Sitting Bull and Gall, plus their Cheyenne allies, wiped out Custer's Seventh Cavalry.

The Battle of Little Bighorn is the most famous battle in all the Indian wars. It is also called Custer's Last Stand or the Battle of Greasy Grass. George Armstrong Custer was a vain, ambitious, and impulsive young cavalry officer, called "Long Hair" by the Indians because of his long blond locks. He was trying to use the Indian wars as a means to further his own career. Although Custer had never won an impressive victory against the Indians, he still considered himself a great military strategist. His only victory to date had been against Black Kettle's peaceful band of Cheyennes in the Indian Territory in 1868. He brashly underestimated his opponents and considered himself superior.

When his scouts spotted the Indian camp along the Little Bighorn, rather than wait for reinforcements under General Alfred Terry and Colonel John Gibbon, Custer divided his men into four groups and ordered an attack. In a series of separate actions against the

Sioux painted hide shield, representing a dream in which a brave rides Thunder Horse in a contest with Turtle

Sioux Ghost Dance shirt

divided force, the Indians managed to kill at least 250 soldiers, including Custer's entire detachment and the Lieutenant Colonel himself.

This was the last great Indian victory on the Plains. The following battles proved disastrous for the Sioux and their allies. In July 1876, at War Bonnet Creek in Nebraska, a force under Colonel Wesley Merritt intercepted and defeated about 1,000 Cheyennes who were on their way to join up with Sitting Bull and Crazy Horse. In September 1876, at Slim Buttes in South Dakota, General Crook's advance guard captured American Horse's combined Oglala and Miniconjou band of Tetons. In November 1876, in the Battle of Dull Knife in Wyoming, Colonel Ranald Mackenzie's troops routed Dull Knife's band of Northern Cheyennes. In January 1877, at Wolf Mountain in Montana, General Nelson Miles's soldiers defeated Crazy Horse's warriors. Then in May 1877, in the Battle of Lame Deer, General Miles's men defeated Lame Deer's Miniconjou band.

Crazy Horse died in 1877, stabbed with a bayonet while trying to escape from prison. Although we have photographs of other great men from this period of history, we have none of Crazy Horse. He refused to pose for photographers, saying, "Why would you wish to shorten my life by taking my shadow from me." Sitting Bull and some of his followers hid out in

Canada until 1881, when he returned to the United States to surrender. He went on to play a role in events leading up to the famous Wounded Knee incident.

The power of the Northern Plains Indians had been broken. The southern and central Plains Indians—the Comanches, Kiowas, Southern Cheyennes, and Southern Arapahos—had previously yielded. Other Indian tribes to the west of the Rocky Mountains—such as the Apaches, Nez Perces, Utes, and Bannocks—would continue their resistance for some years, but the Indian wars were winding down (see entries for those tribes). The final Apache rebellion, under Geronimo, ended in 1886.

Wounded Knee

Yet the Indian wars of the previous four centuries were not quite over. One more incident shook the Plains as late as 1890. Because it was so unnecessary, the Massacre at Wounded Knee has come to symbolize the many massacres of Indians throughout American history.

The events of Wounded Knee sprung out of a new religion. In 1888, a Paiute Indian by the name of Wovoka started the Ghost Dance Religion. He claimed that the world would soon end, then come alive again.

All Indians, including the dead from past ages, would inherit the new earth, which would be filled with lush prairie grasses and huge herds of buffalo. To earn this new life, Indians had to live in harmony and avoid the ways of whites, especially alcohol. Rituals in the Ghost Dance Religion included meditation, prayers, chanting, and especially dancing. While dancing the Ghost Dance, participants could supposedly catch a glimpse of this world-to-be.

Many Indians of the Plains, Southwest, and Far West began practicing the Ghost Dance Religion. Its teachings offered hope to once free and proud peoples now living in poverty and depression on reservations in the midst of their conquerors. But Sioux medicine men—Kicking Bear and Short Bull of the Miniconjou band of Teton Sioux—gave the religion their own interpretation. They claimed that special Ghost Shirts could stop the white man's bullets.

White officials became alarmed at the size of Sioux gatherings and the renewed Indian militancy. As a result, they banned the Ghost Dance on Sioux reservations. But the Indians continued to hold the forbidden ceremonies. Troops rode into the Pine Ridge and Rosebud reservations in South Dakota to enforce the new rule. In defiance, Indians planned a huge gathering on a cliff in the northwest corner of the Pine Ridge Reservation known as the Stronghold. They even sent word to the great Hunkpapa chief Sitting Bull, now on the Standing Rock Reservation in North Dakota, to join them. The general in charge, Nelson Miles, who feared Sitting Bull's great leadership powers, ordered the chief's arrest. In the fight that resulted, Sitting Bull and seven of his warriors were slain, very similar to the way that Crazy Horse had lost his life 13 years before.

General Miles also ordered the arrest of a Miniconjou chief named Big Foot who had formerly advocated the Ghost Dance. But Big Foot, ill with pneumonia, only wanted peace now. He supported the once-great Oglala chief Red Cloud and other proponents of peace with the whites. He led his band of about 350—230 of them women and children—to Pine Ridge to join up with Red Cloud, not with the Ghost Dancers Kicking Bear and Short Bull. Nevertheless, a detachment of the army under Major S. M. Whitside intercepted Big Foot's band and ordered them to set up camp at Wounded Knee Creek. Then Colonel James Forsyth arrived to take command of the prisoners. He ordered his men to place four Hotchkiss cannon in position around the camp.

The next morning, Forsyth sent in troops to collect all Indian firearms. A medicine man named Yellow Bird called for resistance, saying that the Ghost Shirts would protect the warriors. Big Foot advocated peace.

When the soldiers tried to disarm a deaf Indian named Black Coyote, his rifle discharged in the air. The soldiers shot back in response. At first the fighting was at close quarters. But then the heavy artillery opened fire, cutting down men, women, and children alike.

At least 150—possibly as many as 300—Indians died unnecessarily at Wounded Knee, with others injured. Once again the spirit of the Sioux had been crushed. The Ghost Dancers soon gave up their dancing. Wounded Knee marked the end of the Indian wars. That same year, 1890, the Census Bureau of the federal government announced that there was no longer a line of frontier on the census maps. That is to say, other than scattered Indian reservations, no large Indian wilderness area remained free of white settlements.

Sioux in the 20th Century

Starting in 1927, the federal government sponsored the 14-year carving of some of the presidents' faces on Mount Rushmore in the Black Hills of South Dakota, which insulted the Sioux. To the Indians, the act was like carving up a church, since the hills were sacred in their religion.

During the 20th century, the Sioux have rebuilt their lives. Many are still poor, but they have a great power of spirit. Many important Native American philosophers and writers have been Sioux, such as Vine Deloria, Jr., who wrote *Custer Died for Your Sins* and many other books. A famous Sioux writer, educator, and physician by the name of Charles Eastman (Ohiyesa) helped found the Boy Scouts of America. Many Sioux Indians practice traditional ceremonies and traditional arts and crafts.

Some Sioux have devoted themselves to pan-Indian (intertribal) causes, joining organizations such as AIM, the American Indian Movement, formed in 1968. In honor of their ancestors and in protest of the treaties broken by the federal government and the lack of opportunity for Native Americans, members of AIM staged an occupation at Wounded Knee in 1973. The incident ended in violence, with two Indians, Frank Clearwater and Buddy Lamont, killed by federal agents.

Today, there are Sioux reservations in many different states: eight in South Dakota; two in North Dakota; four in Minnesota; one in Nebraska; and one in Montana (shared with Assiniboines). In Wyoming, some of which was also part of the vast Sioux homeland, no lands are held in trust for the tribe. There are also Sioux bands with reserve lands in Canada: five in Alberta (one shared with Crees); five in Saskatchewan (one shared with Assiniboines); and five in Manitoba.

Southeast Indians

The phrase *Southeast Indians* refers to the native peoples of the Southeast Culture Area. A culture area is a geographical region where tribes have similar cultural traits.

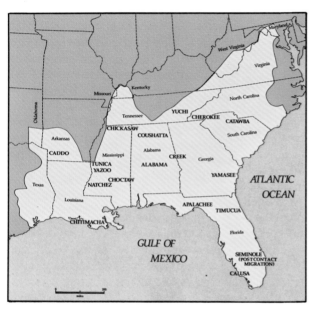

The Southeast Culture Area, showing the approximate locations of Indian tribes listed in this book—circa 1500, before displacement by whites (with modern boundaries)

The Southeast Culture Area, as defined by scholars, is bordered on the east by the Atlantic Ocean; on the south by the Gulf of Mexico; on the west by the Trinity, Arkansas, and Mississippi rivers (approximately); and on the north by the Tennessee and Potomac rivers (approximately). It includes all of the following states: Florida, Georgia, Alabama, Louisiana, and South Carolina; most of Mississippi, Tennessee, North Carolina, and Virginia; and parts of Texas, Oklahoma, Arkansas, Illinois, Kentucky, West Virginia, and Maryland.

This part of North America is mostly forested, much of it with yellow pine. As a result, the culture area is sometimes called the Southeast Woodland Culture Area. Yet there are many variations in terrain and vegetation in the Southeast. These include the coastal plains with saltwater marshes, grasses, and stands of cypress trees; the subtropical Everglades with jungle and swampland; the sandy soil of river valleys, plus the Mississippi floodplain; the fertile soil of the Black Belt; and the forested highlands of the Piedmont Plateau, Blue Ridge, Smoky Mountains, and Cumberland Mountains, all part of the southern Appalachian chain.

The Southeast is home to many species of fauna—mammal, bird, and fish. Southeast Indians hunted and fished for them, and they gathered wild plant foods. But they were also highly skilled farmers. Because they could grow enough food to support a sizable population, Southeast Indians for the most part lived in permanent villages, usually located in river valleys. The main type of architecture was wattle

Southeast Indian (Seminole) headdress in the Postcontact turban style

Postcontact Southeast Indian metal and leather quiver with shell beads, plus metal and bamboo harpoon

thatch, grass, bamboo stalks, palm fronds, bark, woven mats. And animal hides too were utilized.

Trying to organize the Southeast tribes by language families is difficult, since so many languages were spoken there. The largest language families were Muskogean, Iroquoian, Siouan, Caddoan, and Algonquian (the latter four were widespread in other culture areas besides the Southeast). But there were many other languages spoken in the Southeast, what scholars call language isolates because they were unique.

Tribes of the Muskogean language family included in this book are Creek, Choctaw, Chikasaw, Seminole, Alabama, Coushatta, Apalachee, and Yamasee (see entries for those tribes). The one Southeast Iroquoian tribe included in this book is Cherokee (see "Cherokee"). The only Southeast Siouan-speaking tribes listed in this book are Catawba and Yuchi (see "Catawba" and "Yuchi"). The one Southeast Caddoan tribe in this book is Caddo (see "Caddo"). Southeast tribes with unique languages included in this book are Calusa, Chitimacha, Natchez, Timucua, Tunica, and Yazoo (see entries for those tribes).

There are many other tribes of the Southeast Culture Area, which, because of limited space, do not have separate entries in this book. Many of them are now extinct. Here are the names of some of them for those students who wish to pursue further Indian studies concerning this part of North America: Atakapa, Bidai, Hasinai, Chawasha, Biloxi, Houma, Taensa, Ofo, Chakchiuma, Pensacola, Mobile, Chatot, Tohome, Napochi, Tuskegee, Tamathli, Chiaha, Hitchiti, Tekesta, Ais, Guale, Cusabo, Pedee, Waccamaw, Wateree, Cheraw, Woccon, Sugeree, Eno, Tutelo, Monacan, and Saponi.

and daub. Branches and vines were tied over pole frameworks, then covered with a mixture of mud plaster. But plant materials were also used to cover the both rectangular and circular structures, including

Southwest Indians

The phrase *Southwest Indians* applies to native peoples of the Southwest Culture Area. In some books, the Southwest Culture Area is defined as a geographical region in what is now the American Southwest, including most of Arizona and New Mexico, and small parts of California, Utah, Colorado, and Texas. In other books, the Southwest Culture Area is described as the American Southwest, plus much of northern Mexico as well.

The accompanying map shows both United States and Mexican territory. But most of the Southwest tribes listed in this book under separate entries lived in what became part of the United States.

The Southwest Culture Area has varied topography. There is the rugged high country of the Colorado Plateau in the northern part, with its tablelands of flat-topped mesas separated by steep-walled canyons. The enormous Grand Canyon, cut by the

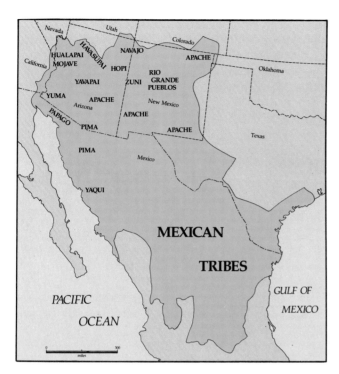

The Southwest Culture Area, showing the approximate locations of Indian tribes listed in this book—circa 1500, before displacement by whites (with modern boundaries)

is known as pueblo architecture. The pueblos, made from adobe brick or stone and with different apartment-like levels connected by ladders, were generally located on mesa tops. Some villages were located in the desert lowlands, however, or along rivers, where the Indians lived in other types of houses, small pole-framed huts covered with plant matter or earth. Those who did not farm, the nomadic hunters and gatherers, supplemented their diet by raiding the Pueblo Indians and other village peoples for their crops. The two main kinds of house among these people were wickiups (which were brush-covered) and hogans (which were earth-covered).

Southwest Indian (Hopi) kachina doll

long and winding Colorado River, is the most famous of all the world's canyons. There is mountain country as well, such as the Mogollon Mountains in New Mexico. Inland Mexico also has highlands of plateau and sierra. Much of the Southwest is desert. The Painted Desert lies along the Little Colorado River in Arizona. There are also desert lands along the Gulf of Mexico and Gulf of California.

All these different landscapes have one element in common—dryness. The average annual rainfall for the region ranges from less than four inches a year to less than 20. Most precipitation occurs within a six-week period of summer. Because of the extreme aridity, plants are sparse. There are three patterns of dominant tree growth in the Southwest, depending on altitude and rainfall: (1) western evergreen trees; (2) piñon and juniper trees; and (3) mesquite trees, plus varying species of cacti and desert shrubs. Animals are also scarce: mostly small mammals and reptiles, such as deer, rabbits, squirrels, mice, and lizards; and some large birds, such as eagles, hawks, and vultures.

Two main ways of life evolved among Southwest Indians—farming, and nomadic hunting and raiding. Those peoples who practiced agriculture were such skilled farmers that, even in the dry country, they could support sizable populations in permanent villages. Most Indian villages in the Southwest had what

The tribes of the region can be grouped as follows, according to their different lifeways: (1) the agricultural Pueblo peoples (see "Pueblo Indians"; "Hopi"; and "Zuni"); (2) the agricultural desert and river peoples (see "Papago"; "Pima"; "Mojave";

"Yuma"; "Havasupai"; "Hualapai"; "Yavapai"; and "Yaqui"); and (3) the nomadic hunting-and-raiding peoples (see "Apache" and "Navajo"). The ancestors of some of these peoples belonged to the Anasazi, Hohokam, and Mogollon cultures (see "Cliff Dwellers and Desert Farmers"). For those students who want to delve deeper into Indian studies concerning this part of North America, other Southwest peoples include the Karankawas, Coahuiltecs, Huichols, plus many other Mexican tribes.

Spokane

The Spokane, or Spokan Indians, lived along the Spokane River, a tributary of the Columbia River, in what is now the eastern part of the state of Washington as well as northern Idaho. Their name, pronounced *spo-KAN*, probably means "people of the sun." Along with other Salishan-speaking tribes of the inland region, the Spokanes are considered part of the Plateau Culture Area (see "Plateau Indians"). The Plateau tribes were among the foremost fishermen of North America, going especially after salmon during their freshwater spawning runs. Most Plateau tribes lived in cone-shaped dwellings placed over shallow pits and constructed out of pole frames and grass or woven-mat coverings.

Lewis and Clark had contact with the Spokanes in 1806, during their famous expedition to the American Northwest. Fur trade in the region was developed in the following years by the North West Company and the Hudson's Bay Company of Canada, as well as by John Jacob Astor's American Fur Company. Astor, through the fur trade with the Indians, became the richest man in America.

The Spokanes had peaceful relations with whites until the late 1850s. They witnessed the Cayuse War of 1847-50 and the Yakima War of 1855-56 (see "Cayuse" and "Yakima"). They saw the whites break the terms of the Walla Walla Council of 1855. When miners and settlers unfairly took their lands, they too revolted. They joined the Coeur d'Alenes, Yakimas, Palouses, and Paiutes in a general uprising in 1858. This conflict is usually referred to as the Coeur d'Alene War (see "Coeur d'Alene"). But it is also sometimes called the Spokane War.

After the war, the Spokanes settled on various reservations, including the Spokane Reservation near present-day Wellpinit, Washington, and the Colville Reservation near present-day Nespelem, Washington. Others joined the Flatheads, another Salishan-speaking people, on their reservation near present-day Dixon, Montana (see "Flathead"). The Spokanes hold an annual festival at the Wellpinit Fairgrounds on Labor Day weekend.

Subarctic Indians

The phrase *Subarctic Indians* refers to those native peoples living in the Subarctic Culture Area. Scholars have defined the Subarctic Culture Area as territory stretching across northern latitudes from the Pacific to the Atlantic Ocean. It covers a vast region, including most of Alaska's and Canada's interior.

What is termed the Northern Forest, filled mostly with evergreen trees—pine, spruce, and fir, with some birch, aspen, and willow as well—grows in the Subarctic. This kind of northern forest is called taiga. Since there is relatively little topsoil for deep root systems, the trees of the taiga are generally scraggy and

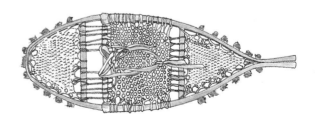

Subarctic Indian snowshoe

short. The northern edge of the taiga borders the treeless tundra of the Arctic (see "Arctic Peoples").

The Subarctic Culture Area, showing the approximate locations of Indian tribes listed in this book—circa 1500, before displacement by whites (modern boundaries)

The Northern Forest is broken up by a network of inland waterways. Some of the largest lakes are the Great Bear Lake, Great Slave Lake, and Lake Winnipeg. Some of the largest rivers are the Yukon, Mackenzie, Peace, Saskatchewan, Red River of the North, and La Grande. There are thousands of smaller lakes and rivers, plus many ponds, streams, and swamps. In the western part of the Subarctic, the rolling taiga and swamplands give way to highlands—the northern part of the Rocky Mountain chain, the Yukon Plateau, and the British Columbia Plateau.

The climate of the Subarctic is fierce. Winters are long and severe. During the seemingly endless stretch of cold weather, deep snow covers the woodlands, and thick ice covers the lakes. The summers are short. During warm weather, mosquitoes and black flies breed in the swamplands.

The Subarctic is home to abundant wildlife. Large mammals include caribou, moose, musk oxen, bear, and deer. Small mammals include beaver, mink, otter, porcupine, rabbits, and squirrels. Moreover, there are many species of birds, especially waterfowl, and fish.

Subarctic Indians were nomadic hunter-gatherers who traveled in small bands. The most common type of house was a small cone-shaped tent covered with animal hides. Lean-tos of brush and leaves were also fairly common, especially in the western part. Subarctic Indians did not farm.

There were two main groups of native peoples in the Subarctic Culture Area: the Athapascan-speaking peoples to the west and the Algonquian-speaking peoples to the east. The Churchill River, flowing northeastward into Hudson Bay, divided the peoples of these two different language families (see "Athapascan" and "Algonquian"). The particular Subarctic tribes of each language family discussed in detail in this book are the following: Among the Athapascans are the Carrier, Chipewyan, and Kutchin; among the Algonquians are the Cree, Montagnais, and Naskapi (see entries for those tribes). Some of the Algonquian-speaking Chippewa bands are considered as part of the Subarctic Culture Area; others are classified within the Northeast Culture Area (see "Chippewa"). The only tribe of the Subarctic Culture Area whose people did not speak either Athapascan or Algonquian dialects was the Beothuk tribe of Newfoundland. They spoke a unique language called Beothukan (see "Beothuk").

Susquehannock

The Susquehannocks lived along the river named after them, the Susquehanna River, flowing from the Cats-kill Mountains in New York, through central Pennsylvania, and emptying into the Chesapeake Bay in Maryland. Although the Susquehannocks ranged up and down the entire length of the river in the course of their history, they lived mostly within the present-day boundaries of Pennsylvania. Their name, pronounced *sus-kwuh-HAN-ock*, and meaning "roily river," also appears with the same spelling and pronunciation as the river—that is, Susquehanna. Or they are sometimes referred to as the Conestoga Indians.

The Susquehannocks spoke the Iroquoian language, but they separated from other Iroquoians long before Europeans arrived in North America. They lived like other Woodland Indians, combining hunting, fishing, and gathering with farming, and they shared many other cultural traits with fellow Iroquoians, such as the use of longhouses. But they are not referred to as Iroquois, a name applied to the tribes of the Iroquois League living to their north (see "Iroquois").

In fact, for much of their history, the Susquehannocks were bitter enemies of the Iroquois. During the 1600s, both tribes made frequent raids on each other. Small war parties, armed with bows and arrows, tomahawks, and scalping knives, would set out on foot through the virgin forests or in elm-bark canoes along the twisty Susquehanna River and travel into enemy territory for quick forays on stockaded villages. This was the period of Dutch activity in North America, and the colonists of New Netherland traded for furs with the Susquehannocks.

In 1675, a decade after the British had taken control of Dutch lands in North America, the Susquehannocks suffered a major defeat at the hands of their Iroquois enemies. It is thought that epidemics brought to the Susquehannocks by European traders helped weaken them prior to their defeat in battle. At this time, most Susquehannock bands left their original homelands.

Some of the Susquehannocks who resettled in Maryland were involved in the conflict known as Bacon's Rebellion that rocked Virginia and neighboring Maryland in 1676. Nathaniel Bacon was a younger cousin to the governor of Virginia, William Berkeley. Bacon and his followers—mainly farmers and frontiersmen—rebelled against colonial authority for several reasons, including high taxes, low prices for tobacco, special privileges granted to the Jamestown aristocracy, and the failure of colonial officials to defend the frontier against Indian attacks.

Bacon and his vigilante army did not distinguish one group of Indians from another. Fighting originally broke out because of a dispute between Nanticoke Indians and settlers over stolen hogs. But Bacon led attacks against other Indians in the region, including Susquehannocks. The Susquehannocks responded with frequent raids on settlers.

Bacon, before his death from disease, marched on Jamestown with his army and forced Berkeley and other colonial officials to grant much-needed farm reforms. But there was no justice for the Susquehannocks, who were reduced in numbers and dispersed from the area because of repeated attacks.

The Susquehannocks found themselves in the middle of a similar situation again almost a century later, in 1763. This was the time of Pontiac's Rebellion (see "Ottawa"). Colonists on the Pennsylvania frontier, angered because of attacks on their settlements by the rebelling tribes, sought revenge on all Indians. A mob out of Paxton, Pennsylvania, that came to be known as the Paxton Boys, descended upon the Christianized Indians of the Conestoga Moravian Mission and murdered three men, two women, and a boy, scalping all of them. The Paxton Boys used the excuse that an Indian had stolen and melted down a pewter spoon. Some sympathetic whites gave the surviving Conestogas refuge in the Lancaster jailhouse. But the Paxton Boys broke in and massacred 14 more men, women, and children.

The governor of Pennsylvania at the time was John Penn, a descendant of the Quaker William Penn who had founded the colony. Governor Penn issued a proclamation condemning the massacres. In response, the Paxton Boys marched on the capital of Philadelphia and threatened to kill all the Indians in the city. The city mobilized an army to defend itself, but Benjamin Franklin negotiated a treaty with the rebels. The Paxton Boys agreed not to attack peaceful Indians on the condition that the whites received bounties for scalps from the tribes participating in Pontiac's Rebellion.

It was already too late for the people known as Susquehannocks. They had suffered too much disease and warfare. Some survivors lived here and there among other Indian peoples, but the tribe ceased to exist.

Timucua

The Timucuas (pronounced *tim-uh-KOO-uh*), sometimes called the Utinas, lived in the part of the Southeast that is now northern Florida. Their territory extended from the Suwannee River to the St. Johns River. The Timucuas were really a confederacy of as many as 150 different villages with culture and language in common.

The Indians of the Southeast Culture Area spoke many different languages. Algonquian, Iroquoian, Siouan, Muskogean, and Caddoan are five important language families that were spoken in the Southeast. But there are other languages that scholars have been unable to classify, such as Natchez, Tunican, and the language of the Timucuas, called Timucuan (see "Southeast Indians").

The Timucuas had early contacts with the Spanish. Juan Ponce de Leon, who claimed Florida for Spain, encountered the Timucuas in 1513. Then other Spanish explorers passed through their territory: Panfilo de Narvaez in 1528 and Hernando de Soto in 1539.

The French lived among the Timucuas for a short time. Jean Ribault visited them in 1562. Then in 1564, the French under Rene de Laudonniere built Fort Caroline on the St. Johns River in the country of the Timucuas.

The Spanish drove the French out of Florida in 1565. Then they established missions among the Timucuas. The Timucuas suffered from several epidemics of European diseases in 1613-17, 1649-50, and 1672. In 1656, many of the Timucua villages, as well as Apalachee villages, joined forces to try to drive away the missionaries. Well-armed Spanish soldiers defeated the rebels, killing many.

During the French and Indian Wars of the 1700s, when the English fought the French and Spanish for control of North America, the Timucuas' population declined further. The English and their Indian allies, the Creeks, raided Timucua settlements in the vicinity of the Spanish fort at St. Augustine. The Spanish surrendered Florida to the English in 1763. They gained it back in 1783 and held it until 1819. By then, however, the Timucuas had died out or joined other tribes, making them extinct as a tribe.

Fortunately, much is known about the culture of the Timucuas. The Spanish missionaries recorded their language. And a Frenchman by the name of Jacques le Moyne who traveled among them in 1564 made many paintings with written commentaries depicting their lifeways. A Flemish artisan, Theodore de Bry, later converted Le Moyne's paintings into engravings for publication in 1591.

The Timucua villages were surrounded by walls of thick, upright logs about twice the height of a man. The log walls overlapped at one point to form a narrow entranceway with a gatehouse at each end, one just outside the palisades and one just inside. The village consisted of many round houses with pole frames and roofs of palmetto branches. The chief lived in the only rectangular building, at the center of all the other houses.

Each village had its own chief. But the chief of one particular village was the principal ruler and had king-like authority over all the other chiefs in the Timucua confederacy of villages. Each village had certain men, the notables, who participated in councils. At councils participants drank huge amounts of strong herbal tea.

The king chose the most beautiful girl among all the notable families as his queen. She was carried to the wedding ceremony on a litter covered with the fur of an animal. She was shielded from the sun by a canopy of boughs, as well as by two round screens on staffs carried by men walking next to her. Beautiful maidens, wearing skirts of moss and necklaces and bracelets of pearls, followed behind the litter bearers. Then came the bodyguards. The procession's arrival was signaled by trumpeters blowing on horns of bark. During the ceremony the king and queen-to-be sat on a raised platform of logs with the notables seated nearby. The king made a speech to the bride about why he had selected her. And she publicly expressed her thanks. Then the maidens performed. Holding hands, they formed a circle, chanted the praises of the king and queen, and, raising and lowering their hands in unison, danced.

The Timucuas planted and harvested crops twice a year, including corn, beans, pumpkins, and squash. To prepare the soil, men used hoes made from fish bones attached to wooden handles. Then one woman made holes with a digging stick and another followed behind to place the seeds. Timucuas also regularly harvested wild fruits. They made bread from a plant called arrowroot. Any excess food collected was placed in storage to be shared by all the villagers in hard times. This sharing impressed Le Moyne, who wrote: "Indeed, it would be good if among Christians there was as little greed to torment men's minds and hearts."

The Timucuas hunted many kinds of animals, including alligators, deer, brown bears, wildcats, lizards, and turkeys. They also fished for trout, flounders, turbots, and mullets, and collected clams, oysters, crayfish, and crabs. They used bows and arrows, clubs, spears, harpoons, traps, and underwater fences called weirs for hunting and fishing. They carved dugout canoes from single trees for travel on lakes, rivers, and the ocean. They traveled along the Atlantic coast of Florida to trade with other tribes, sometimes even crossing the open sea as far as Cuba. To catch alligators, the Timucuas rammed logs into the animals' open jaws, flipped them on their backs, then killed them with arrows and clubs. Extra meat and fish were preserved for the winter months by smoking on a log rack over an open fire.

The Timucuas prepared for war with special rituals. In one ceremony, the chief used a wooden platter to spill water on his warriors, saying: "As I have done with this water, so I pray that you may do with the blood of your enemies." Timucua warriors carried tea in gourds with them for energy on military expeditions.

Timucua weapons included bows and arrows and heavy clubs. The warriors filed their fingernails to sharp points, which they used in close combat to gouge their enemies' foreheads and blind them with their own blood. Tribesmen also tied their long hair into a knot to hold arrows. Archers shot arrows tipped with flaming moss to set fire to the houses of the enemy. If the warriors were successful on a raid, they

Timucua mask, used as a disguise while hunting

brought back trophies—severed arms, legs, and scalps—which they hung on poles at the victory celebrations. Timucuas made war for both personal glory and to protect their hunting territory from intruders.

The Timucuas tattooed their bodies with elaborate designs in black, red, and blue. The tattoos were a statement of individuality, status, and personal power. To make the designs, which in some instances covered their whole bodies, the Indians pricked their skin with needles dipped in soot or vegetable dyes made from plants such as cinnebar.

Tlingit

The Tlingits, or Tlinkits (both pronounced *TLING-kit*), are unique among Indian peoples in that they had much to do with ending the Russian colonial period in North America. The Russians called them *Kolush*. Their fierce, proud warriors proved a stubborn menace to the Russian fur-trading empire.

The Tlingits lived along the Pacific Coast and nearby islands in what is now southern Alaska and northern British Columbia, in Canada. To their north lived Eskimos and Aleuts, and to their south lived the Haidas and Tsimshians (see entries for those tribes). The Tlingits were really made up of various independent bands, the best-known of which were the Auk, Chilkat, Huna, Sitka, Stikine, Tongass, and Yakutat. The various bands divided the Tlingit territory into 13 different *kwans*. Many of the band names survive today as place names. The Tlingit bands spoke various related dialects of the Tlingit language, part of the Nadene language family and related to that of the Haidas. The Tlingits were probably also distant relatives of the Athapascan tribes living to their east (see "Athapascan").

Lifeways

The Tlingits, along with their closest neighbors, the Haidas and Tsimshians, are classified by anthropologists in the Northwest Coast Culture Area. The typical customs of the Pacific Northwest are salmon-fishing; sea-mammal as well as land-mammal hunting; large houses made from beams and planks of wood; totem poles; wooden ceremonial masks; dugout canoes; cedar chests and boxes; the potlatch (a ceremony for giving gifts) and other elaborate rituals; a society based on wealth and rank; powerful shamans (medicine men) and secret societies; the practice of keeping slaves; extensive trade contacts with other tribes (see "Northwest Coast Indians"). All are true of the Tlingits.

The Tlingits were master woodcarvers, like most Northwest Coast peoples. The Haidas were perhaps the most renowned of all the carvers of the region. But the Tlingits also made beautiful totem poles. Each delicately sculpted and brightly painted figure, representing both people and animals, had a special meaning to a clan's history. When the pole was erected, a speaker would relate stories about the clan's ancestors and about animal spirits.

Of the southern Northwest Coast tribes, the Chinooks were the most famous traders (see "Chinook"). But of the more northern tribes, the Tlingits had the most extensive trade contacts. They were middlemen among many different peoples: their coastal neighbors, the Athapascans of the interior, and the Eskimos. They dealt in all kinds of goods, some their own and some made by other tribes: boats, blankets, baskets, boxes, raw copper, copper plaques, cedar boards and bark, seal and fish oils, whale oil and bones, ivory, mountain goat and mountain sheep horns and hides, elk meat, caribou meat, sinews, lichens, beads made from tooth shells, abalone and other seashells, the mineral jadeite, slaves, and more.

The Tlingits' own most-sought-after product was the Chilkat blanket, named after one of the Tlingit bands but made by other Tlingit bands and Tsimshian Indians as well. Tlingit women made these beautiful blankets from cedar-bark fiber and mountain-goat or mountain-sheep wool. They worked on them as long as half a year. Some of the yarn spun from these materials was left white; the rest was dyed black, blue-green, or yellow. Then the women wove them with their fingers into intricate abstract designs and animal forms. The completed blankets had an unusual shape. They were about six feet long with a straight edge at the top. But the bottom edge was uneven—about two feet at the ends and three feet in the middle. There were long fringes on the sides and bottom but none along the top edge. The women also made Chilkat shirts. The designs had special meanings for families or clans. And the Indians said that, if one knew how to listen, the Chilkat blankets and shirts could actually talk.

The Tlingits were also famous for their armor. They placed wood slats over two or three layers of hide to repel enemy weapons. They also wore helmets of solid wood for protection, and masks to frighten their enemies. They used spears, bows and arrows, and dif-

Chilkat (Tlingit) blanket with designs that supposedly can talk

ferent-shaped clubs in their fighting. They also made daggers of stone with ivory handles. After Europeans came, the Tlingits used steel for the blades.

Tlingit iron, ivory, and leather knife

Wars Against the Russian Fur Traders

The Tlingits took up these various weapons against the Russians. During Vitus Bering's voyage of exploration in 1741, in which he claimed Alaska for Russia, the Tlingits killed several of his men. The *promyshlenniki* (the Russian word for fur traders) followed soon afterward to exploit the huge supply of fur-bearing mammals. But the story of their early years in North America centers on the Aleut Indians of the Aleutian Islands, where there were abundant sea otters to keep the traders busy for many years (see "Aleuts"). The Russian traders, led by Alexander Baranov, and their Aleut hunters, did not reach Tlingit territory until the 1790s.

After some early skirmishes with the Tlingits, the Russians built a fort at Sitka on Baranov Island in 1799. That same year, the Russian American Fur Company was founded. This huge monopoly competed with the British Hudson's Bay Company to supply the world with furs.

In 1802, the Tlingits attacked and destroyed the fort, killed many Russians and Aleuts, and stole thousands of pelts. They felt the furs belonged to them since they had been taken on Tlingit lands or in Tlingit waters. Two years later, Alexander Baranov returned with an armada. Russian ships bombarded the Tlingits with cannonfire. Then Russian soldiers stormed and recaptured the post.

The Tlingits kept up their attacks, however. In 1805, they moved on a post at Yakutat. The Russians dreaded the Tlingit raids and used whatever means they could to calm the Tlingits—violence and cruelty, or negotiations and gifts. But the Tlingits were not to be conquered or won over. They wanted to regain control of their ancestral homelands.

In the end, the Tlingits lost most of their lands, but not to the Russians. The Russians eventually gave up their foothold in North America, selling Alaska to the United States in 1867. The militant Tlingit presence helped influence their decision to abandon their posts in North America.

Tlingits in the Twentieth Century

For a time, the Tlingits were left alone by whites. Then the Klondike Gold Rush to the Yukon began in 1896, bringing many prospectors and settlers to the region (see "Kutchin"). With the loss of their lands, the Tlingits also lost much of their traditional way of life. Many of them ended up working in fish canneries.

The Tlingits struggled to preserve their identity. They also reached out to other Alaska natives. In 1912, they founded the Alaska Native Brotherhood, one of the earliest of the modern-day Indian organizations.

A land and cash settlement to Alaska's natives in 1971 has helped the Tlingits and other Native Americans there rebuild their lives. They have formed corporations to develop their natural resources. The Tlingits and Haidas are united in the Sealaska Corporation. Both peoples are considered some of the best Alaskan fishermen. More and more Tlingits practice traditional crafts too, such as the making of Chilkat blankets, which are highly prized the world over.

Toltec

The Toltecs (pronounced *TOLL-tec* or *TALL-tec*) migrated from the north into the Valley of Mexico about A.D. 900. There, over the following centuries to about A.D. 1200, they created one of the four great Mesoamerican civilizations. Mesoamerica is the name given by scholars to the culture area in what is now Mexico and parts of Central America, where Indians created highly organized societies with cities and farming.

When they first arrived in the Valley of Mexico, a broad valley on the Mexican Plateau, the Toltecs were one of the many nomadic hunting tribes called Chichimecs, meaning "sons of the dog." The local inhabitants feared them. After a prolonged power struggle, the Toltecs became the dominant tribe, under their leader Mixcoatl.

At that time in densely populated Mesoamerica, there were many different peoples and tribes. Some of them lived in great cities with magnificent stone architecture. Some developed hieroglyphic writing. The Olmecs had been the first great civilization in the

Preclassic period before A.D. 300 (see "Olmec"). The Mayas had followed in the so-called Classic period from about A.D. 300 to 900 (see "Maya"). Another great city during the Classic period was Teotihuacan. There were other centers of religion, learning, and commerce, many of these in the Valley of Mexico. Mixcoatl, the Toltec leader, encouraged his followers to learn from these other cultures. The Toltecs built their own city, calling it Tula.

The Toltecs and other cultures after them, such as the Aztecs, rose to power in a period labeled the Postclassic era, from about A.D. 900 to the arrival of Europeans in about 1500 (see "Aztec"). This label is applied because many of the cultural traits of the Postclassic civilizations were adopted from the earlier Classic peoples, who made great strides forward in knowledge.

The Toltecs reworked that earlier knowledge into new and wonderful forms. Mixcoatl's son Topiltzin came to power in 968. He was a great historical figure. He encouraged learning and art among his people. Much of what is known about the Toltecs comes from the later Aztecs. In Aztec legends, the Toltecs stood for what is civilized. Also, in Aztec mythology, both Mixcoatl and Topiltzin were considered gods—the father as a hunting god and the son as the Great Plumed Serpent, a deity among many different Mesoamerican peoples. The Aztecs might have regarded the Toltec leaders as such because Topiltzin took the name of the Plumed Serpent, or Quetzalcoatl.

Under Topiltzin-Quetzalcoatl, the Toltecs erected tall pyramids, beautiful palaces with columns and murals, ball-courts, and other elegant stone structures; they developed new kinds of corn, squash, and cotton; they crafted exquisite objects in gold and silver; they shaped new designs in pottery; they made beautiful clothing from textiles, decorated with feathers; and they used hieroglyphic writing. They also conquered other Indian peoples around them and influenced their architecture and art forms. At its

Toltec clay figurine made from a mold

peak, the Toltec Empire stretched from the Gulf of Mexico to the Pacific Ocean.

Yet Topiltzin-Quetzalcoatl fell from power. What led to his downfall is not known for certain. Aztec tradition says that the Plumed Serpent was overthrown when he tried to ban human sacrifice, which the Toltecs practiced on a large scale. Legend has it that the followers of the Plumed Serpent were defeated by the devotees of Tezcatlipoca, the deity of the night, and that they then fled from Tula.

Perhaps Topiltzin-Quetzalcoatl and his followers were the Toltecs who invaded the Yucatan Peninsula to the east, interbred with the Mayas, and brought about the Mayan Postclassic era. Whether the great king survived his downfall or not, the legend of Quetzalcoatl was so strong in the later Aztec culture that they awaited his return and thought that Cortes, the Spanish conquistador, might be he.

The Toltecs who overthrew Topiltzin-Quetzalcoatl and stayed in power in Tula and the Valley of Mexico gradually fell into a state of decline. They were plagued by a series of droughts, famines, fires, and invasions of tribes who, as they themselves once had, came from the north. Tula was destroyed in 1160. After a period of tribal rivalries and power struggles, the Aztecs, the founders of the last great Mesoamerican civilization, rose to dominance.

Tonkawa

The Tonkawas (pronounced *TAHN-kuh-wuh*) originally lived in territory that is now central Texas. They had a reputation as fierce raiders and skilled hunters who roamed the southern Plains throughout most of Texas and into eastern New Mexico and southern Oklahoma (see "Plains Indians").

Their language, called Tonkawan, is unique. As a result, their ancestry and place of origin are uncertain.

They might be distant relatives of people known as the Karankawas and the Coahuiltecs, who once inhabited southern Texas and northern Mexico.

The Tonkawas had early contacts with Spanish explorers, probably both Cabeza de Vaca in the 1530s and Francisco Vasquez de Coronado in the 1540s. Other than occasional expeditions and a few missions, Spain did little to establish its claim to Texas until

France gained a foothold along the lower Mississippi Valley in the years after Rene Cavalier de la Salle's expedition of 1682. But then Spain stepped up its activity and competed with the French for the support of Texas tribes until France lost its territory to England in 1763 after the French and Indian Wars. It was during the late 1600s and early 1700s that the Tonkawas acquired horses from the Spanish or from other Indians, which increased their effectiveness as warriors and buffalo hunters.

The Tonkawas were traditional enemies of the Apaches, who lived to their west in New Mexico and Arizona. The two peoples often launched raids against each other (see "Apache"). However, an Apache taken as a prisoner by the Tonkawas became a great chief among his new people. He was called by the Spanish name El Mocho, meaning "the cropped one," because he had lost his right ear while fighting the Osage Indians (see "Osage"). El Mocho's dream was to unite the Apaches and Tonkawas. In 1782, he organized a great council which was attended by more than 4,000 people of both tribes. He argued for a unified stand against the Spanish. But the two peoples were unable to put aside old grudges, and El Mocho's dream of alliance was never realized. The Spanish later captured and executed him.

In 1845, Texas became part of the United States. In 1855, the Tonkawas, along with other Texas tribes, were assigned two small reservations on the Brazos River. During that period, the Tonkawas served as scouts with the Texas Rangers against the Comanches (see "Comanche").

In 1859, because of increased settlement in the area by Anglo-Americans, the Tonkawas were relocated on the Washita River in the Indian Territory, now the state of Oklahoma. During the Civil War, some of the Tonkawas served as scouts for the Confederate Army. In 1862, other tribes used the Tonkawa involvement in the Civil War as an excuse to settle old scores. Caddo, Delaware, and Shawnee warriors raided the Tonkawa camps and killed many. The survivors fled to Texas, where they remained until 1884. At that time, government officials arranged a new home for them in the Indian Territory, farther north, near the Ponca tribe (see "Ponca"). Tonkawa descendants live there today in Kay County, Oklahoma.

Tsimshian

Tsimshian (pronounced *CHIM-shee-un* or *TSIM-shee-un*), sometimes spelled Chimmesyan, means "people of the Skeena River." The lower courses of the Skeena and Nass rivers flowing to the Pacific Ocean were the heart of Tsimshian territory. Yet most of their villages of roomy beam-and-plank houses were located along the ocean shore. The part of the Pacific Coast that was once Tsimshian homeland now lies in northern British Columbia and southern Alaska.

The Tsimshians were the northernmost tribe to speak the Penutian language. Most other tribes who spoke versions of the language lived to the south in Washington, Oregon, and California. Other Penutian tribes classified in the Northwest Coast Culture Area along with the Tsimshians are the Alseas, Coos, and Kalapuyas, who are not listed separately in this book (see "Northwest Coast Indians"). The dialect of the Chinooks, another Northwest Coast tribe, was probably Penutian too (see "Chinook").

The Tsimshians, like all northern Pacific peoples, depended on fishing for food. In the rivers, they caught salmon and candlefish, which left the ocean every spring to lay their eggs. Off the mainland and the Queen Charlotte Islands opposite their territory, the Tsimshians caught halibut, cod, flounder, and other fish from their long, sleek dugout canoes. Like modern fishermen, they used whatever means was best suited to the place and species: hooks and lines, harpoons, nets, traps, or enclosures called weirs. The

Tsimshian bow

Tsimshians also dug up shellfish and seaweed offshore. And they went after the sea mammals that offered plentiful food and materials for tools, clothing, and blankets: seals, sea lions, and sea otters. But they did not hunt whales, as certain other Northwest Coast tribes did.

The Tsimshians were also hunter-gatherers. They entered the tall, dense forests of the interior highlands, part of the Coast Range, to track deer, bear, and mountain goats. They used snares, corrals, spears, and bows and arrows to kill their prey. Seeking a varied diet, the Tsimshians foraged for edible wild plant foods as well—roots, berries, and greens.

Like most tribes of the Northwest Coast, the Tsimshians made exquisite woodwork and basketry. Also typically, they traded frequently for other tribes' products. The Tsimshians' spiritual culture—with powerful shamans, or medicine men, and secret

Tsimshian soul-catcher, supposedly containing the soul of a dead shaman. The charm was placed in a sick person's mouth from which point the soul would supposedly enter the body and expel the demon that caused the sickness.

societies—resembled that of other Northwest Coast tribes too. The potlatch ritual, where people gave away possessions, played a central part in Tsimshian society.

One of the most valuable gifts that could be given away in the potlatches were copper plaques. The Tsimshians hammered the ore into engraved metal sculptures. Copper tools were also highly valued.

The Tsimshians were famous for their Chilkat blankets. Their trading partners the Tlingits, who lived north of them, also made these blankets, named after one of the Tlingit bands (see "Tlingit"). The fringed blankets, and similar shirts, were woven from goat's hair and cedar bark into intricate animal and abstract designs. The mystical representations supposedly had the power to talk to people.

The history of the Tsimshians after the coming of the white man was more peaceful than that of the Tlingits, since the Tsimshians were not as close to Russian trading posts. Their experience paralleled that of the more southern peoples: (1) in the late 1700s, frequent sailing expeditions along the coast sponsored by the world's colonial powers, including the Spanish, English, French, and Russians; (2) fur-trading posts in the early 1800s, including the Hudson's Bay Company's Fort Simpson in 1831 and Fort Essington in 1835; (3) missionaries in the mid-1800s, including the Episcopalian William Duncan in 1857; and (4) in the late 1800s, with the completion of the Canadian Pacific Railway, white settlements.

Unlike some missionaries, who tried to take away the native peoples' traditional culture, William Duncan proved a valuable friend to the Tsimshians. When he came to live among them, the Tsimshian way of life had been corrupted by liquor brought in by white traders. Tsimshian bands carried out acts of murder, rape, and thievery. Some even practiced ritualistic cannibalism. Duncan studied their language and mythology and preached to them about the Bible in terms of their own legends. By 1862, after five years among them, he had converted four of the nine principal chiefs to Christian nonviolence. That same year, he built a mission at Metlakatla. In 1887, he moved with his followers to New Metlakatla on Annette Island. There, the Tsimshians learned carpentry, blacksmithing, spinning, soapmaking, as well as baseball and music. Duncan also helped the Indians develop a fishing and canning operation, plus a sawmill. Duncan stayed with the Tsimshians until he died in 1918, at the age of 85.

Today, those Tsimshians who moved to Annette Island are United States citizens, since the island is now part of Alaska. Fish processing and logging still provide ample incomes for the residents of the reservation. There are also seven Tsimshian bands in Canada, many of whom earn a living the same way.

Tunica

Various tribes living along the lower Mississippi River Valley spoke Tunican dialects. One of these tribes, the Tunicas (pronounced *TYOON-uh-cuh*) gave their name to the language. They lived in what is now the state of Mississippi near another Tunican people, the Yazoos (see "Yazoo"). Some Tunicas might have also located their villages on the opposite bank of the Mississippi

River, the west side, in territory that is now eastern Arkansas and eastern Louisiana.

The Tunicas were villagers who farmed the black, moist soil of the Mississippi floodplain, formed by the river overflowing its banks. The Tunicas grew corn, beans, squash, sunflowers, and melons. They hunted, fished, and gathered wild foods to supplement these staple foods. They built thatched houses and temples of worship. They carved dugout canoes. They made pottery. They made a cloth fabric from the mulberry plant. The Tunicas mined salt to trade with other tribes. Their leaders were more like kings than like chiefs. In their lifeways, the Tunicas had much in common with other tribes of the Southeast Culture Area (see "Southeast Indians").

The Spanish expedition of Hernando de Soto encountered Tunican-speaking peoples in 1541. Two centuries later, in the early 1700s, after Rene Cavelier de la Salle had claimed the region for France, a Jesuit missionary by the name of Father Davion lived among the Tunicas. From that time on, the Tunicas remained faithful allies of the French. In fact, some of their

warriors helped the French suppress the Natchez Revolt of 1729. Their kinsmen, the Yazoos, supported the Natchez, however. When the English gained control of the Tunicas' territory in 1763 at the end of the French and Indian Wars, the Tunicas began attacking their boats on the Mississippi River.

After the American Revolution, the Tunicas gradually departed from their homeland. Some resettled in Louisiana, where there are still Indians of mixed descent with Tunican blood. In 1981, the federal government granted recognition to the Tunica-Biloxi tribe (the Biloxis were a Siouan-speaking tribe living near the Tunicas). Other Tunicas joined the Choctaws, with whom they migrated to Oklahoma (see "Choctaw").

Tuscarora

The Tuscaroras (pronounced *tusk-uh-ROAR-uh*), who spoke the Iroquoian language, originally lived in the part of North America that was to become North Carolina. They made their homes especially along the Roanoke, Tar, Pamlico, and Neuse Rivers, near Cape Hatteras. While in this location near the Atlantic Ocean, they had lifeways similar to the other Iroquoian and Algonquian people of the coast, a region that is considered the southernmost part of the Northeast Culture Area (see "Iroquois," "Algonquian," and "Northeast Indians").

In the early 1700s, the Tuscaroras migrated to New York, among the northern Iroquoian-speaking tribes. There, in 1722, they were formally recognized as part of the Iroquois League, becoming the Sixth Nation. Then their culture became more typical of the other tribes of the League. For example, in their new location they could no longer supplement their diet with seafood. Another obvious difference was that they needed more clothes for the colder weather. Their Iroquoian dialect also changed.

The war that caused their departure from North Carolina is called the Tuscarora War. It was an especially unfortunate outbreak of violence between Indians and whites because previously the Tuscaroras had been friendly to Carolina colonists. They not only had provided them with valuable knowledge about wilderness survival and with food, but also had helped them fight other Indians. In return for their friendship and generosity, the Tuscaroras were taken advantage of by whites. Settlers took their best farmlands; traders cheated them; and slavers kidnapped them to ship them to the Caribbean or to Europe.

Tuscarora silver belt buckle (modern)

Because of the continuing abuses, Tuscarora warriors under Chief Hancock raided settlements between the Trent and Neuse rivers in 1711, killing perhaps as many as 200 men, women, and children. Angry settlers sought revenge. They managed to capture a brave, whom they roasted alive. Other local Indians, such as the Corees, joined the Tuscarora cause. The colonies of North and South Carolina raised a militia under Colonel John Barnwell. Many of his soldiers were Yamasee Indians (see "Yamasee"). They marched into Tuscarora territory and against Hancock's village of Cotechney. After a standoff, peace was made. But Barnwell violated it by seizing other Tuscaroras as slaves. The Indians started their raids again.

Another colonial army was organized under Colonel James Moore. Many Yamasees joined this force too. This army marched on the Tuscarora village of Neoheroka in 1713 and killed or captured almost 1,000 Tuscaroras. Captives were sold into slavery at 10 pounds sterling each to finance Moore's military campaign. It was at this time that many of the surviving Tuscaroras migrated to Iroquois country in New

York. Some members of those villages not part of the uprising were permitted to stay unmolested in North Carolina, but in years to come they too joined their relatives in the north. They felt especially welcome after 1722, when the Iroquois made the Tuscaroras official members of the League, as the Sixth Nation.

The Tuscaroras did not have direct votes at the League's Great Council every year. The Oneidas, among whom they originally settled, represented them. Otherwise, the Tuscarora were treated as equals.

In the American Revolution, most Tuscaroras and Oneidas sided with the Americans against the British. This caused a rift in the Iroquois League, since the other tribes supported the British. After the Revolution, the Tuscaroras were granted state reservation lands in the northwestern corner of New York, near Niagara Falls, where their descendants live today. Those Tuscaroras who had sided with the British settled at Oshweken on the Grand River in Ontario, Canada, as part of the Six Nations Reserve.

Umatilla

The Umatillas (pronounced *um-uh-TIL-uh*) spoke the Penutian language and were related to the Nez Perces, Modocs, Cayuses, Yakimas, Palouses, and Wallawallas (see entries for those tribes). They lived in what today is northern Oregon and southern Washington State, along the banks of the river named after them, as well as along the Columbia River, the largest river in the region.

The Umatillas are considered part of the Plateau Culture Area. They fished the rivers of the region, especially for salmon during the spawning season. They hunted small game. And they gathered wild plant foods, especially the bulbs of the camas plant (see "Plateau Indians").

After the Lewis and Clark Expedition in the first decade of the 1800s, the Umatillas and other Plateau tribes became important to the fur trade, developed in the region by both the North West Company and the Hudson's Bay Company, of Canada, and the American Fur Company. Their relations with whites were peaceful until the mid-1800s when they resisted white expansion in the Yakima War of 1855-56 (see "Yakima"). In the Bannock War two decades later, they aided the whites by alerting soldiers to the whereabouts of the rebels and by killing the Paiute chief Egan (see "Bannock").

The Umatilla Reservation was established in 1853. Umatillas share this tract of land near Pendleton, Oregon, with Cayuses and Wallawallas. There is a well-known annual rodeo called the Pendleton Roundup, featuring an Indian Happy Canyon pageant with dances and arts and crafts, as well as a tepee village. The tribes also sponsor an annual Indian Festival of Arts at La Grande, Oregon.

A Umatilla family in front of their rush-mat house on a reservation

Ute

The state of Utah takes its name from the Utes (pronounced *yoot*), meaning "high up" or the "land of the sun." The tribe is also associated historically with the state of Colorado. Their territory extended from the southern Rocky Mountains in present-day Colorado as far west as the Sevier River in present-day Utah. The Utes also ranged as far south as the upper San Juan River in northern New Mexico and as far north as southern Wyoming. At the peak of their power, there were seven main Ute bands.

Ute basket

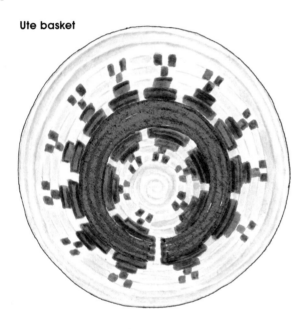

Lifeways

The Utes are classified as part of the Great Basin Culture Area, with lifeways similar to their neighbors the Paiutes and the Shoshones, who spoke related dialects of the Uto-Aztecan language family (see "Great Basin Indians"; "Paiute"; and "Shoshone"). Indians of the Great Basin, the huge cupped desert area between the Rocky Mountains and the Sierra Nevada, were nomadic hunter-gatherers. They are sometimes called Digger Indians because they had to dig for foods such as roots, seeds, rodents, lizards, and insects in this arid environment where little vegetation grew and where big game was scarce.

But the Utes, especially the bands to the east, can be thought of as mountain-dwellers as much as desert peoples. The forested slopes of the Rockies offered much more wildlife than the Basin floor and the Basin uplands. And the rivers flowing westward from the Great Divide provided plentiful fish for food.

The typical shelter for the Utes before whites came was a cone-shaped pole framework covered with brush, reeds, and grasses. The Utes were loosely knit into small bands that sometimes spent the winter together or joined one another for communal rabbit drives. Arrow and spearhead makers held a special place of honor in their society, along with the band leaders and shamans, or medicine men.

The Utes, who had frequent contacts with the Pueblo peoples in northern New Mexico, acquired horses from them in the late 1600s (see "Pueblo Indians"). The Ute homeland had enough pasture to graze horses. Henceforth, the Ute way of life became somewhat similar to the Indians east of the Rocky Mountains on the Great Plains (see "Plains Indians"). With increased mobility, the Utes became wide-ranging raiders and traders. Yet they rarely hunted buffalo, and their hide-covered tepees remained small, like their brush shelters. They painted these tepees with bright colors.

Contacts with Whites and the Ute War

The Utes had a reputation as a warlike tribe. The first writings about them come from the journal of Fray Francisco de Escalante, a Franciscan priest who explored the Great Basin with Francisco Dominguez in 1776. By that time, mounted on horses, the Utes carried out regular raids on Indians and Spanish alike. They captured slaves to trade with other tribes for horses and other goods. They also warred intermittently with the Arapaho Indians living on the other side of the Rocky Mountain Great Divide (see "Arapaho").

Nonetheless, because the Utes lived west of the Rockies in a rugged environment where few whites other than the Mountain Men traveled, they avoided early clashes with the Anglo-Americans who came from the east. Isolated early incidents of violence did happen when whites entered the Utes' domain. For example, Ute warriors killed the famous Mountain Man William Sherley Williams, nicknamed Old Bill Williams, who had previously acted as John Fremont's guide during one of Fremont's voyages of western exploration.

With the growth of mining in western Colorado and eastern Utah beginning in the mid-1800s, the Utes were pressured by whites into signing away most of their land. When Colorado achieved statehood in 1876, mining companies tried to expel the Utes from a remaining tract along the White River. The phrase "The Utes must go" became a political slogan, even though Utes had bravely served as guides and fighters for the federal regulars and state militiamen in campaigns against other Indians, such as the Navajos in the 1860s (see "Navajo").

An important Ute leader at this time was Chief Ouray. He spoke English and Spanish in addition to several different Indian languages. He was wise and patient and understood U.S. law. He had for many years protected the rights of his people through complex negotiations with the whites. Kit Carson considered him one of the greatest men he knew.

Yet even such a respected statesman and peacemaker as Ouray could not prevent violence. Unrest was growing among his people, who felt betrayed by land-grabbing whites. Moreover, some of the Utes resented their treatment by the uncompromising Indian agent Nathan Meeker, who forced a new way of life on them at White River. He taught the White River Indians agriculture and the Christian religion. But most of the Indians preferred their ancient ways. When the Indians refused to farm, Meeker wanted federal troops to help him impose his will. The federal government ignored his requests until a fight broke out. A medicine man named Canella (also known as Johnson) grew angry at having to plow lands that had always been Ute grazing land for horses. He physically attacked Meeker in September 1879. On learning of this incident through correspondence from Meeker, federal officials sent in a detachment of 150 troops under Major Thomas Thornburgh.

Warriors under Chief Nicaagat (Jack) and Chief Quinkent (Douglas) threw their support behind Canella. Warriors rode out to block the army column at Milk Creek. Before a parley could be arranged, shots were fired. A bullet struck down Major Thornburgh. Captain J. Scott Payne organized a defense behind wagons on the opposite side of Milk Creek from the Indians. The Utes lay siege for a week. On the third day, a regiment of black cavalrymen rode in as reinforcements. An even larger relief force arrived on the seventh day. The Indians withdrew, but they left behind 13 whites dead and 48 wounded.

The army advanced the rest of the way to the agency. On arriving there, they found the bodies of Meeker and nine other whites. Meeker's wife and daughter, plus another woman and two children, had been taken hostage. The ex-Civil War generals Philip Henry Sheridan and William Tecumseh Sherman wanted to launch major offensives against the Utes. But Secretary of the Interior Carl Schurz sent in a peace mission under Charles Adams.

Adams met with the one man who he knew could defuse the situation—Chief Ouray. Demonstrating his skill at diplomacy, Ouray negotiated the release of the hostages and guaranteed the freedom of the rebellious Indians. The following year, however, the same year that Ouray died at the age of 46, the White River Utes were forced to move.

Ute children and cradleboard

The Utes presently hold three reservations in Colorado and Utah. The Southern Ute Reservation near Ignacio, Colorado, includes the Mouache and Capote bands. The Ute Mountain Reservation near Towaoc, Colorado, with adjoining parcels of land in Colorado, Utah, and New Mexico, is the home of the Wimnuche band. The Uintah and Ouray Reservation near Fort Duchesne, Utah, is the home of mainly White River descendants. Income from these various bands comes from oil, gas, and mineral leases, as well as from farming and raising livestock. The bands hold annual Bear Dances and Sun Dances in the summer.

Wallawalla

The Wallawallas lived along the lower Wallawalla River and along the junction of the Snake and Columbia rivers in territory that is now part of northern Oregon and southern Washington State. Their name, pronounced *WOL-uh-WOL-uh*, means "little river" in their dialect of the Penutian language family. Sometimes their name is written as two words: Walla Walla. The tribe shared cultural traits with other Penutian peoples as well as Salishan-speaking peoples of the Columbia Plateau (see "Plateau Indians").

The Wallawallas became known to whites after the Lewis and Clark Expedition in the early 1800s. Afterward, white fur traders had many contacts with them. Like other tribes of the region, they were peaceful toward whites until the 1850s, when several wars erupted. The Wallawallas participated in the Yakima War of 1855-56 (see "Yakima"). An important chief of the Wallawallas during this period was Peo-peo-mox-mox. Colonel James Kelly, who led a volunteer force into Indian country, called a parley with the chief. When he came, he was murdered by Kelly's men. Then they displayed his scalp and ears to the white settlers to show that they had taken revenge for earlier Indian attacks. Peo-peo-mox-mox's murder rallied other tribes to rebellion and led to continued violence through 1858 (see "Coeur d'Alene).

The Wallawallas were settled on the Umatilla Reservation in Oregon with the Umatillas and the Cayuses, where their descendants still live today and participate in a number of annual festivals (see "Umatilla").

Wampanoag

The Wampanoags (pronounced *wam-puh-NO-ag*) have a unique place in colonial history as the foremost friends of the New England colonists in the early 1600s and the worst enemies of these colonists in the late 1600s. How did this reversal come about? Why did these peaceful Algonquians of New England's south shore—territory that now includes parts of eastern Rhode Island and southern Massachusetts (see "Algonquian" and "Northeast Indians")—turn hostile?

Squanto

The story starts with a Wampanoag brave named Tisquantum, or Squanto for short. He was of the Pawtuxet band of Wampanoags, one of some 30 Wampanoag bands and villages. In 1615, he was kidnapped by Captain Thomas Hunt, an English trader, and taken to Spain and sold into slavery. But a sympathetic Englishman ransomed him and took him to England. Squanto longed for his homeland and finally accomplished the ocean crossing under Captain Thomas Dermer in 1619.

Rather than hate the English who had once tried to enslave him, Squanto showed himself to be a forgiving and loyal friend. When the Pilgrims arrived in North America and founded Plymouth in 1620, Squanto used his knowledge of English to instruct them in the ways of wilderness living, particularly planting corn and fishing. Without his help, the Pilgrims probably would have perished during their first winter. Squanto, more than any other individual, is responsible for the holiday of Thanksgiving, proclaimed by the Plymouth governor, William Bradford, after a successful harvest. Squanto died in 1622 from "Indian fever," which was really smallpox brought by whites from Europe.

Samoset

Another Wampanoag, a local sachem by the name of Samoset, also helped the Pilgrims, using his knowledge of English picked up from traders to communicate with them. Again, it is remarkable that a Wampanoag offered his assistance so willingly. After all, it was traders who had brought the first great smallpox epidemic that had decimated the Wampanoags and other tribes in the years just prior to the Pilgrims' arrival. Samoset also introduced Captain Miles Standish of the Pilgrims to Massasoit, the grand sachem, or great chief, of the Wampanoags.

Massasoit

Massasoit became a trusted ally of the colonists for 40 years until his death in 1662. His friendship helped keep the Wampanoags neutral in the Pequot War of 1636 (see "Pequot"). It also enabled the Pilgrims and other colonists to maintain their foothold in the New World. If the Wampanoags had been hostile in these early years, they certainly could have slowed the pace of European expansion in North America.

However, the peace was shaky, as the colonists abused their friendship with the Indians time and again. They wanted land for farming and tried to trick the Indians into signing it away for little payment or no payment at all. One method they used was to get the Indians drunk before negotiating with them. Another was to bribe one Indian and make him an honorary chief, then have him sign away land that belonged not to him but to the whole tribe.

King Philip's War

Massasoit had two sons, named Metacom and Wamsutta. The colonists came to call them Philip and Alexander, after Philip of Macedon and Alexander the Great from ancient history. The boys grew up while the number of settlers was rising dramatically—along with the number of abuses against Indians. Unlike their father, Massasoit, they became militant, believing it was necessary to make a stand to protect the Indian way of life.

The new generation of Wampanoag militants resented the fact that when an Indian committed a crime

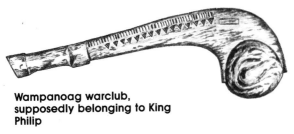

Wampanoag warclub, supposedly belonging to King Philip

under English law, he was taken before a colonial court to be tried rather than before his own people. After one such incident, Alexander, who had succeeded Massasoit as sachem, died during the trip home. Now it was Philip's turn to be sachem. He believed that the colonial officials had poisoned his brother. He wanted revenge. He wanted the Wampanoags to achieve their former greatness.

Yet Philip did not rush foolishly to battle. He bided his time, sending runners to other tribes to ask their help. His goal was to organize an alliance of tribes that would be strong enough to oust the British settlers

from New England. He was the first great Indian leader to envision such an alliance of tribes.

Colonial officials sensed the growing militancy and tried to harass Philip, calling him before a court and ordering the Wampanoags to turn in their flintlocks. Philip yielded to their demands in order to buy more time, relinquishing some but not all of the Wampanoag guns.

Even so, fighting came prematurely. In June 1675, the colonists arrested and hanged three Wampanoags accused of killing a Christian Indian. In the increased state of tension, fighting broke out near the Wampanoag village of Mount Hope. A settler fired at and wounded a brave in an argument over cattle. The Wampanoags retaliated, killing 11 colonists. King Philip's War had begun.

After these first hostilities, the Indians began a campaign of violence against the settlers. The Narraganset and Nipmuc tribes joined the Wampanoag cause. Small bands of warriors attacked outlying settlements all over New England, from the Connecticut River all the way to the Atlantic Coast.

The New England Confederation of Colonies, including Massachusetts Bay, Plymouth, Rhode Island, and Connecticut, mustered armies. They engaged the Indians in several major battles. The first occurred in July at Pocasset Swamp, in Wampanoag territory. The next two occurred the following autumn along the northern Connecticut River Valley in Nipmuc country—at Bloody Brook and Hopewell Swamp. Then the deciding battle took place in Narraganset territory. This was the Great Swamp Fight of December 1675 (see "Narraganset").

After these colonial victories, it was only a matter of time before the remaining rebels were tracked down. There were two more major encounters, one near Deerfield, Massachusetts, and the other near Plymouth. In the latter, known as the Bridgewater Swamp Fight, Philip was betrayed by an Indian informer and killed. His killers cut up his body and kept the parts as trophies.

King Philip was dead and, except for a few militants still hiding out, King Philip's War was over. In the aftermath, Philip's wife and son were shipped to the Caribbean to be sold as slaves for 30 shillings apiece. The colonists took their revenge on peaceful tribes as well, seizing more and more Indian territory.

But some Wampanoags did manage to keep their lands, in particular, those on the islands of Martha's Vineyard and Nantucket, who stayed out of the conflict. White diseases continued to take their toll over the years, further reducing the Wampanoags' numbers. Today, however, the group on Martha's Vineyard is a thriving community.

Wappinger

The Wappingers (pronounced *WOP-in-jer*) lived along the Hudson River between Manhattan Island and Poughkeepsie, especially on the east bank, now the southern part of New York State. Some of the Wappingers' territory also extended into Connecticut (see "Northeast Indians"). An Algonquian people, they were a confederacy of many different bands (see "Algonquian"). They were flanked by the Mahicans to the north and the Delawares to the west and south (see "Mahican" and "Delaware"). In fact, there is some confusion among scholars as to which bands belonged to which tribe.

For example, some scholars consider the Manhattans of Manhattan Island, the island now at the center of New York City, to have been a Delaware tribe. Others write about them as Wappingers. This example points up the difficulty historians and anthropologists have in classifying Indian tribes. To the Indians, of course, the local or band classification was usually the most important. In other words, the Manhattans considered themselves a separate group even if they had a military alliance with other bands plus a similar language and similar lifeways. This book covers the major groupings, calling them tribes, and refers to their subdivisions as bands. But students of Indian history should keep in mind that the distinction between a tribe and a band is sometimes hazy.

In any case, the bands of all three major tribal groups along the Hudson River—Wappinger, Delaware, and Mahican—were all Algonquians and had typical Algonquian technologies and beliefs. Moreover, the histories of the various Hudson River Indians were similar, since they were all affected by the arrival of Dutch traders and settlers.

Henry Hudson, who was an Englishman sailing under a Dutch flag, explored the territory along the river that bears his name and claimed it for the Netherlands in 1609-10. In the following years, many Dutch trading ships plied the waters of the Hudson River, exchanging European trade goods for furs. The Algonquian Indians called the Dutch *swanneken*.

Then in 1621, the Dutch West India Company received the charter to develop New Netherland. Dutch settlers started arriving in great numbers for the purposes of both fur trading and farming. They bartered with the Indians for land. The Manhattans sold Manhattan Island for 60 guilders' (24 dollars) worth of trade goods. The Mahicans sold property near the northern end of the Hudson River. Soon both New Amsterdam (now New York) and Fort Orange (now Albany) were thriving Dutch communities. And, with the expanding Dutch presence, there was a need for additional land on both sides of the Hudson River.

Pressures on the Indians along the Hudson River mounted. Finally, in the 1640s, there was violence. The first incident involved the Raritan Indians on Staten Island, generally considered a subtribe of the Delawares. They rebelled in 1641 when Dutch livestock destroyed their crops (see "Delaware").

The second incident, in 1643, called the Pavonia Massacre, or the Slaughter of Innocents, involved Wappinger bands from farther up the Hudson. The governor-general of New Netherland at that time was Willem Kieft. He believed in a policy of harassment and extermination of Hudson River Indians to make room for Dutch settlers. He paid the Mohawks, who were members of the Iroquois League and traditional enemies of the Hudson River Algonquians, to attack them. The Wappingers fled to the Dutch settlement at Pavonia for protection. That was a mistake. Dutch soldiers attacked the unsuspecting Indians while they slept, killing and beheading 80, many of them women and children, and taking 30 more as prisoners. The soldiers brought the 80 heads back to New Amsterdam, where they played kickball with them. They also publicly tortured many of the Indian prisoners. Governor-General Kieft is said to have "laughed right heartily" at the sight.

Algonquian Indians from the Delaware Bay to the Connecticut River Valley began raiding Dutch settlements in retaliation for the massacre. It was during this period that the Dutch built a defensive wall in lower Manhattan, where Wall Street is today. Dutch and English soldiers raided and burned Indian villages. By 1644, the Indian uprising had been crushed.

Still another outbreak of violence, usually called the Peach Wars, occurred in the 1650s. A Dutch farmer killed a Delaware woman for stealing peaches from his orchard, which sparked another Indian rebellion of Delawares and Wappingers. Peter Stuyvesant, the new governor-general, was also harsh in his treatment of Indians. He finally squelched this uprising in 1664 by taking Indian women and children hostages and threatening to harm them in order to make the men negotiate.

That same year, British troops invaded New Netherland and took control of the region, which became New York. But it was too late for the Wappingers. Their once-great power had been broken. In the years to follow, Wappinger survivors joined the Delawares and Nanticokes to the south, or the Mahicans and Pequots to the north and east. The Wappingers who share the Schaghticoke Reservation in Litchfield County with the Pequots are known as the Paugusset band (see "Pequot").

Wichita

The Wichitas, who spoke a dialect of the Caddoan language family, were related to the Caddos, Pawnees, and Arikaras (see entries for those tribes). The Wichitas (pronounced *WITCH-i-taw*) were also sometimes called Picts, from the French word *pique*, meaning "punctured" or "pricked," because they tattooed their faces and bodies, using sharp implements to make the elaborate designs. Other Caddoan-speaking tribes not covered separately in this book—the Kichais, Tawakonis, and Wacos—merged with the Wichitas in the 1800s.

The Wichitas occupied territory that became parts of Kansas, Oklahoma, and Texas. They probably migrated onto the Plains from the south early in their history, after breaking off from other Caddoan people. They are classified as part of the Great Plains Culture Area. They acquired horses about 1700, which they used to pursue buffalo. Like other Plains people, they lived in tepees while on the trail (see "Plains Indians").

Yet the Wichitas had a mixed economy of hunting and farming and are sometimes referred to as Prairie people (see "Prairie Indians"). Much of the year they lived in permanent villages and grew corn and other crops. Their village homes were conical grass houses which looked something like large haystacks.

To construct this type of dwelling, the Wichitas erected long poles in a circle, with the tops meeting in a dome shape. The framework was tied together with many wattles (slender branches or reeds), then covered with thatch. The name of the tribe might be derived from the Muskogean word *wia-chitch*, meaning "big arbor," because of these houses. To the Wichitas themselves, however, their name meant "man."

The Wichitas were among those tribes met by the early Spanish expedition of Francisco Vasquez de Coronado. That was in 1541. At that time, the Wichitas lived along the Arkansas River, in what is now central Kansas. Coronado sought but never found great riches in Wichita country, which he called the Kingdom of Quivira. A Franciscan missionary named Juan de Padilla stayed behind with the Indians to try to convert them to Catholicism. But the Wichitas killed him three years later when he began working with another tribe as well.

Over a century later in 1662, the Spaniard Diego Dionisio de Penalosa led an army against the Wichitas and defeated them in battle. Soon afterward, the tribe migrated south to the Canadian River, in what is now Oklahoma. The French explorer, Bernard de la Harpe, encountered them there in 1719 and established trade relations with them.

Wichita grass house

Wichita traders, along with Caddo traders, were called Taovayas by the French fur traders, or the *coureurs de bois* ("runners of the woods"). The Taovayas established a profitable business as middlemen between the French and the more westerly Plains tribes, who brought buffalo robes and other furs to trade for crops and French tools. The French traders, many of whom had Indian families, carried the furs on pack trains of horses from the Indian villages to river landings. From there, flatboats and canoe-like boats called pirogues carried the pelts downriver to the Mississippi and on to New Orleans. Then seaworthy ships transported the goods to Europe.

Osage war parties attacking from the north drove the Wichitas farther south during the mid-1700s. They then settled on the upper Red River in what is now southern Oklahoma and northern Texas. There, the Taovayas and French traders kept up their trade out of San Bernardo and San Teodoro (called the Twin Villages), and out of Natchitoches. An alliance with the powerful Comanches helped protect the Taovayas from Apaches, Osages, and the Spanish.

In 1763, at the end of the French and Indian Wars, France lost its North American possessions to England and Spain. In the years to follow, Spanish traders managed to drive most of the French out of business, and the Taovayas no longer had a trade monopoly. In 1801, France regained the Louisiana Territory from Spain, but sold it to the United States two years later.

American exploration and settlement west of the Mississippi followed.

In 1835, the Wichitas signed their first treaty with the United States. By 1850, the Wichitas had moved again into the Wichita Mountains near Fort Sill of the Indian Territory (now Oklahoma). The Wichitas and Caddos were assigned a reservation north of the Washita River in 1859. At the time of the Civil War in the 1860s, the Wichitas returned to Kansas to a site that became the city of Wichita. They returned to the Indian Territory after the Civil War. In 1872, they officially gave up all their other lands to the United States.

The Wichitas, Caddos, and Delawares now jointly hold a trust area in the Caddo, Canadian, and Gray counties of Oklahoma. The Wichitas are also in close contact with their Pawnee relatives. The two tribes entertain each other every year at a powwow. One year, the celebration is held at the Wichita center near Anadarko. The next year, the event is held at Pawnee, Oklahoma.

Winnebago

The Winnebagos, unlike all the other Indians of the western Great Lakes, spoke a Siouan language, not an Algonquian one. Their dialect is close to the Siouan languages spoken by the Iowa, Oto, and Missouri tribes who split off from them and resettled farther west (see "Iowa"; "Oto"; and "Missouri"). But the name of the Winnebagos is Algonquian, supposedly given to them by the Sac and Fox tribes. It means "people of the filthy water." As a result, early Frenchmen among them sometimes called them *Puants*. And some Englishmen used the translation of the French, "Stinkards." The Indians' own proud name for themselves was *Hotcangara*, for "people of the big speech." But even this was misrepresented. Some outsiders thought it meant "fish-eaters." It is the name Winnebago, pronounced *win-uh-BAY-go*, that has stuck, however. And, with their proud history, modern-day Winnebago Indians bear it happily despite its early meanings.

The Winnebagos lived along the Door Peninsula, the eastern arm of Green Bay, on Lake Michigan in what is now Wisconsin, when the French explorer Jean Nicolet encountered them in 1634. A large lake nearby in Wisconsin, feeding the Fox River which drains into Lake Michigan, is named after the tribe—Winnebago Lake.

Many other tribes also lived in the country just to the west of Lake Michigan along the Fox and Wisconsin

rivers, and they all eventually came to be allies of the Winnebagos. The Menominees on the opposite side of Green Bay were early trading partners of the Winnebagos; in later years, the Sacs, Foxes, and Kickapoos also became their allies (see entries for those tribes). They considered the Winnebagos reliable friends.

But the Winnebagos could also make dangerous enemies. Some of them fought against the British in the French and Indian Wars of 1689-1763 (see "Abnaki" and "Iroquois"). Then they sided with the British against the rebels in the American Revolution of 1775-83 (see "Iroquois") and in Tecumseh's Rebellion of 1809-11 (see "Shawnee").

The Winnebagos mounted further resistance to American settlers in 1826-27. The trouble began when the Winnebagos started to take part in the lead mining that whites were developing around Galena, near the Wisconsin-Illinois border. Whites wanted all the profits for themselves, so government officials forbade Indian mining. As a result, the Winnebagos raided some settlements. Then an incident occurred when two Mississippi keelboats stopped at a Winnebago village north of Prairie du Chien. The boatmen, who had been drinking, kidnapped some Winnebago women. Warriors followed the boat down river, attacked it, managed to kill some of the whites, and liberated their women.

The Winnebagos also took part in the Black Hawk War, which occurred soon afterward, in 1832 (see "Sac"). White Cloud, also known as Winnebago Prophet, fostered support among various tribes of the area for Black Hawk's fighters. Like Delaware Prophet and Shawnee Prophet before him (see "Delaware"; "Ottawa"; and "Shawnee"), Winnebago Prophet preached against white culture and called for a return to traditional Indian ways.

Winnebago bone tube, used to suck disease from the sick

The Winnebago traditional way meant living in villages in rectangular bark lodges. It meant farming corn, beans, squash, and tobacco. It meant cooking corn in a deep pit by piling up layers of husks, fresh corn, more husks, and a layer of dirt on top of heated stones, then pouring water on top to trickle down and make steam. It meant tracking and trapping small game in the dense virgin forests. It meant living in tents and lean-tos on the trail. It meant buffalo hunting on the prairies of tall, coarse grass along the Mississippi Valley. It meant paddling across Green Bay in birchbark canoes to trade buffalo robes with the Menominees for wild rice. It meant spearing fish on Lake Michigan or on the Fox and Wisconsin rivers. It meant shaping beautiful artistic work with dyed porcupine quills, bright feathers, and supple leather. It meant carving sophisticated hickory calendar sticks that accurately marked lunar and solar years.

The traditional Winnebago way also meant social organization into two groups, or moieties—the Air (or Sky) and the Earth. Each moiety was further divided into clans with animal names symbolizing the air or earth, such as the Thunderbird and the Bear. It also meant that one could only marry someone in the opposite moiety. It meant that children would belong to the clan of one's father, not one's mother (patrilineal, not matrilineal). It meant participation in the secret Midewiwin, or Grand Medicine Society (see "Chippewa"). It meant belief in mythological beings or culture heroes such as Trickster, who supposedly played practical jokes on the Winnebagos. It also meant reverence for nature. As a Winnebago saying goes, "Holy Mother Earth, the trees and all nature, are witnesses of your thoughts and deeds."

After the Black Hawk War, the Winnebagos were forced to relocate west of the Mississippi, first to Iowa; then to Minnesota; then to South Dakota; and finally, to Nebraska, where today they share a reservation with the Omahas (see "Omaha"). Other Winnebagos managed to stay in or return to Wisconsin, where they were finally granted reservation lands. Some tribal members also live in Minnesota.

Wintun

The Wintuns lived on the west side of the Sacramento River, from the valley to the Coast Range, in territory now part of the state of California. Their name, pronounced *WIN-tun*, means "people" in their native language, a dialect of the Penutian language family.

The Wintun Indians consisted of three subgroups: the Patwin (Southern), the Nomlaki (Central), and the Wintu (Northern). The Penutian-speaking tribes, along with some Hokan-speaking peoples nearby, are sometimes called central California Indians to distinguish them from tribes to the north, which drew some elements from Northwest Coast tribes, and tribes to the south, which became heavily missionized by the Spanish. The central California Indians make up one broad category of the California Culture Area (see "California Indians").

The Wintuns, like their neighbors, were organized into tribelets, made up of a main permanent village

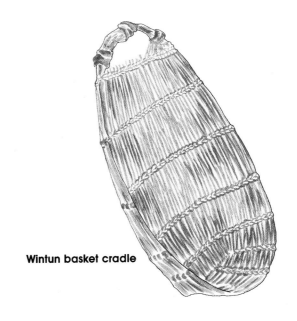

Wintun basket cradle

and several temporary satellite villages. They were hunter-gatherers who did not farm. Their staple foods included deer, rabbits, grubs, grasshoppers, fish, acorns, seeds, nuts, and greens. They wore little clothing, mainly breechcloths, aprons, blankets, and robes. They lived in a variety of simple types of shelters—brush, grass, rush and bark-covered houses, sometimes partly underground. They made beautiful baskets for cooking, storing, and carrying. Tribal members participated in the Kuksu Cult.

The central California tribes managed to endure the first stages of white expansion: the period of exploration, when Spanish, Portuguese, and English navigators sailed the coast, starting in the 1500s; the Spanish mission period, from 1769 to 1834; and the Mexican occupation from 1821 to 1848. But, with the United States takeover of California in 1848, the Gold Rush of 1849, and California statehood in 1850, pressures on the Indians increased and led to their rapid decline.

Few Indians of pure Wintun blood remain. The tribe occupies four small rancherias: Grindstone Creek in Glenn County; Cortina and Colusa in Colusa County; and Rumsey in Yolo County. The Wintuns also share the Round Valley Reservation in Mendocino County with many other tribes.

Yahi

For students of Native Americans, the Yahi Indians (pronounced *YAH-hee*) will always be thought of as Ishi's tribe. He was the last Yahi Indian, a people of the California Culture Area (see "California Indians"). He was also the last Indian in the United States to be pure of all white influences.

In August of 1911, a gaunt and weary man walked out of the foothills of Mount Lassen in Northern California to a town called Oroville, about 70 miles northeast of Sacramento. Townspeople found him leaning in exhaustion against a fence. He wore little clothing, only a tattered poncho. He had apparently closely cropped his hair by singeing it with fire. His eyes showed his great fear. When questioned, his words were unintelligible. He was recognized as an Indian. But the sheriff who took him into custody had never seen an Indian with such light skin in the area. And none of the Indians brought to talk with him recognized his dialect.

Word spread about the mystery Indian. Two anthropologists in San Francisco, Alfred Kroeber and Thomas Waterman, read about him in a newspaper. They knew that the Yana Indians once lived in the Oroville region. They also knew that a neighboring, related band of Indians, who spoke a different dialect of the Hokan language family, had once lived to the south of the Yanas. These were the Yahis. It occurred to them that the Indian at Oroville just might be a member of this supposedly extinct tribe. They hurriedly made arrangements to meet with him.

In the man's cell, Waterman tried using a dictionary of the Yana language to communicate with him. The withdrawn, still frightened Indian, who had refused all food out of fear of being poisoned, did not recognize any of the words. Finally, the anthropologist read the Yana word for wood while pointing to the frame of a cot, *siwini*. The Indian became excited, smiling broadly. A word in common! He asked the scholar if he were of the same tribe, the Yahis. To gain his trust, Waterman replied that he was. With the Indian's help, he also learned how to modify the Yana language enough to fit the sounds of the related Yahi dialect.

The Anthropological Museum of the University of California took full responsibility for the Indian. Kroeber and Waterman gave him the name Ishi, which was the word for "man" in the Yahi language. Ishi eventually managed to communicate his story to them.

Ishi was born about 1862. During his youth, he witnessed the period in American history when California was growing at a rapid pace. In 1849 alone, the start of the California Gold Rush, about 80,000 prospectors came to California to seek their fortune. Then during the 1850s and 1860s, whites continued to enter the Yana and Yahi domain, following Indian trails in search of goldfields and farmlands. They took the best lands for themselves and forced Indians to the rugged, parched highlands. When the Indians resisted, miners and ranchers acted with swift violence against them. A pattern developed of small Indian raids, then white retaliation, culminating in an attack on the Yahi village on Mill Creek in 1865 in which whites massacred men, women, and children. Then, in the ensuing years, whites launched further attacks on the Yahis in an effort to exterminate them. They thought they had accomplished this by 1868, when they killed 38 Yahis at a cave on Milk Creek.

Yet a dozen or so Yahis had escaped into the wilderness, including a boy about six years old. Over the next decades, the remaining Yahis hid out from whites and lived off the land, occasionally pilfering from white camps. There were some reports of sightings of mysterious Indians. But the Yahis were careful to camouflage their shelters, leave no footprints, make no noise, and light only small campfires. They assumed, even after so much time had passed since the conflict between Yahis and whites, that if they were discovered, they would be killed.

By 1908, only four Yahis remained—Ishi himself, now 40 years old; his sister; an old man; and an old woman. They lived at *wowunupo mu tetnu*, or "the grizzly bear's hiding place," a narrow ledge about 500 feet above Mill Creek. In that year, a party of whites discovered their hiding place. The Yahis fled, all except the old woman who was too sick to travel. She died soon after her discovery. The old man and Ishi's sister drowned while in flight.

Ishi lived in the wilderness for three more years, hunting small game and gathering wild foods. He burned his hair off in mourning for his lost friends and relatives. But the game ran out. Hungry and desperate, he opted for a quick death at the hands of whites rather than the slow death of starvation. He made the walk to Oroville.

As it turned out, Ishi was treated well. The whites gave him work at the museum, which he performed with dedication. He demonstrated to museum visitors how his people used to make arrowheads and spearheads. He also helped clean the grounds. Ishi learned about 600 English words and became accustomed to white ways—clothes, table manners, urban transportation—but he never got used to crowds. He had spent his life with only a few people and was continually amazed at the great number of whites. When he went to a movie for the first time, he watched the audience instead of the film. When he visited the shore for the first time, he was in awe of the people on the beach rather than the water itself.

The gentle and kind-hearted Ishi met with many people who were interested in native ways. He proved an invaluable source of information concerning native culture. Kroeber and Waterman accompanied Ishi on a camping trip to his former home on Milk Creek, where he shared his earlier experiences and his wilderness skills with them.

Yahi glass arrowhead made by Ishi

Ishi demonstrated how to make arrow and spear points out of obsidian, and bows out of juniper wood for hunting; how to make two-pronged bone harpoons and how to weave nets out of milkweed fibers or animal sinew for catching salmon and other fish; and how to make a brush hut. He demonstrated how to start a fire with a wooden drill and softwood kindling; how to move noiselessly through the underbrush; how to swing on ropes over canyon cliffs; how to snare a deer or lure it into arrow-range by wearing the stuffed head of a buck; how to make animal and bird calls to attract game. Ishi also identified about 200 plants and their uses as food or medicine. He showed how to make acorn meal. He sang many songs and narrated many stories about his ancestors, about the spirit world, about wildlife, and about love and other emotions. He also demonstrated to the whites around him the qualities of bravery, stoicism, patience, kindness, enthusiasm, and humor. And all this from a man who had lost everything—his friends and family, his homeland, and his heritage.

Ishi became ill with tuberculosis in 1915 and died the following year. Those who knew him, and those who empathized with the plight of all native peoples in the Americas, mourned his passing. The last of the Yahis, the final holdout for an earlier way of life, had, through his knowledge and character, made an enduring impression on the culture that displaced him.

Yakima

The Yakimas lived along the river named after them, a tributary of the Columbia River, in territory now in southern Washington State. They spoke a dialect of the Penutian language family. Their name, pronounced *YAK-uh-muh*, means "runaway." They are considered a part of the Plateau Culture Area, living primarily on salmon, small game, roots, berries, and nuts (see "Plateau Indians").

The Yakimas participated in an uprising that erupted among the Columbia River tribes in the 1850s, known as the Yakima War. The first war to break out in the area was the Cayuse War of 1847-50 (see

"Cayuse"). In the following years, what was known as Oregon Country was organized into the Oregon and Washington territories, and new military posts were built. More and more white settlers and miners migrated westward along the Oregon Trail to this land of opportunity. The growing number of whites aggravated tensions with the Indians.

In 1855, the governor of Washington Territory, Isaac Stevens, organized the Walla Walla Council, where he encouraged Indians of the region—the Yakimas, Cayuses, Umatillas, Wallawallas, and Nez Perces—to give up most of their land for reservations, homes, schools, horses, cattle, and regular payments. He also promised the Indians a period of two to three years to relocate. Most tribal representatives signed. Others distrusted whites because of earlier broken promises.

Yakima cornhusk bag

Those with distrust were proven right. Twelve days after the signing, rather than the promised two years, Governor Stevens declared Indian lands open to white settlement. Kamiakin, a Yakima chief, called for an alliance of tribes to resist white intrusions but not before they were ready to face the more numerous white soldiers. His nephew, Qualchin, forced events, however. He and five other young Yakimas attacked and killed five prospectors. When an Indian agent tried to investigate the incident, he too was killed by angry young warriors.

A reconnaissance force rode out of Fort Dalles to learn the extent of the uprising. Five hundred warriors

routed them and drove them back to the fort. Other expeditions also failed against the Indian rebels. Volunteers under Colonel James Kelly tricked a chief of the Wallawallas, Peo-peo-mox-mox, into coming to a parley, where they killed him. This rash act caused Wallawalla, Cayuse, and Umatilla warriors to join the Yakima cause and to attack white settlements (see entries for those tribes).

A deadly pattern of raid and retaliation followed. The army built new forts. A few indecisive battles were fought, such as the engagement at Grande Ronde Valley in July of 1856. But when troops were sent out to fight, the hostile warriors usually hid among tribes to the east. In some instances, the army had to protect innocent Indians from revenge-seeking whites.

Other Indian tribes to the west along the Northwest Coast carried out raids on white settlers. Indians attacked the town of Seattle on Puget Sound, but were driven off by a naval force in the harbor. Moreover, two tribes in what is now southern Oregon near the California border—the Penutian-speaking Takelmas and the Athapascan-speaking Tututnis—rose up against settlers in their midst. The Takelma and Tututni Indians were known to the whites as Rogue Indians because they frequently attacked travelers along the Siskiyou Trail. The river in their territory was also called the Rogue. And their conflict, although related to the Yakima War, is usually referred to by its own name, the Rogue River War.

The three most important Rogue River chiefs at the time were Old John, Limpy, and George. Because of a massacre of 23 of their people—men, women, and children—these chiefs led their warriors in raids on a white settlement, killing 27 whites. In May 1856, at Big Meadows, a force of regular soldiers routed the rebels, who soon surrendered.

Meanwhile, the Yakima War to the east of the Cascade Mountains was in a brief period of inactivity. Another outbreak of violence involving more tribes, known as the Coeur d'Alene War, occurred in 1858. Since Kamiakin, Qualchin, and other Yakimas played a part in this conflict as well, the Coeur d'Alene War can be thought of as the second phase of the Yakima War (see "Coeur d'Alene").

In 1859, after the Coeur d'Alene War, the Yakimas agreed to settle on a reservation. Their descendants live there today along with Paiutes and other Native Americans. Many Yakima Indians still fish the Columbia River as their ancestors did. The Yakima tribal headquarters is located in Toppenish, Washington. The reservation sponsors an all-Indian rodeo every summer.

Yamasee

As discussed in the entry "Creek," there were many tribes of the Southeast who spoke the Muskogean language, as did the Creeks, and who had lifeways similar to the Creeks, but who are now extinct (see "Southeast Indians" and "Creek"). One of these extinct Muskogean tribes is the Yamasee (pronounced *YAM-uh-see*).

When Europeans first settled among them—Spanish missionaries in the late 1500s and the 1600s—the Yamasees lived in territory that was to become the southern part of Georgia and the northern part of Florida. In 1687, the Yamasees became discontented with Spanish regulations and headed northward to British territory in the colony of South Carolina.

In South Carolina the Yamasees became valuable allies of the British. They traded with them and worked for them. They even fought alongside them against the Tuscaroras in the Tuscarora War of 1711-13 (see "Tuscarora"). Yet, as it turned out, the British mistreated them just as the Spanish had done.

The British settlers insulted them. They also cheated them by taking land and never paying for it. And traders forced the Yamasees at gunpoint to help carry trade goods through the wilderness. Yet the most horrible deeds against them were carried out by British slavers. First, they gave the Indians all the rum they wanted plus trade goods. Then they demanded immediate payment from the Indians. The Indians could not pay off their huge debts and asked for more time. To settle the debts, the slavers then seized Yamasee wives and children for the slave market.

The Yamasees organized a surprise attack for revenge. They asked the help of some neighboring tribes, including Catawbas, Apalachees, Creeks, Choctaws, and Cherokees, who were also angry with the colonists' methods of trickery (see entries for those tribes). On Good Friday, April 15, 1715, the Indians raided many outlying settlements, killing more than 100 whites. Other settlers fled to the port city of Charleston.

The governor of South Carolina, Charles Craven, organized a militia that, during a summer campaign and then a second fall campaign, attacked Yamasee villages and tracked bands of warriors through the wilderness. Surviving Yamasees fled back southward to Georgia and Florida. One group settled near St. Augustine in Florida, becoming allies of the Spanish once again. Their village was destroyed by the British in 1727. Other Yamasees settled with the Apalachees, Creeks, and Seminoles, among whom they lost their tribal identity.

Yaqui

The name of the Yaquis, pronounced *YAH-kee*, is taken from the river on which these people originally lived, the Rio Yaqui, and probably translates as "chief river" in a dialect of the Uto-Aztecan language family. The Rio Yaqui flows from the highlands of Sonora, a state in Mexico, to the Gulf of California.

The Yaquis farmed, hunted, fished, and foraged to support themselves. They lived much like other Indians to the north, who are classified with them in the Southwest Culture Area (see "Southwest Indians"). They made two plantings a year in the fertile soil along the river and its tributaries, which overflowed regularly. They cultivated corn and cotton, using the latter to make clothing. They lived in rectangular structures of poles, reeds, grass, and mud (or sometimes adobe bricks), with flat or gently sloping roofs. They cooked and performed other chores in connected shelters.

The Yaquis remained fiercely independent throughout Spanish and Mexican rule. Spaniards first had contact with them as early as 1533 when an expedition under Nuno de Guzman entered their domain. In 1609-10, a force of 50 mounted soldiers and 4,000 Indian allies launched three successive attacks on the Yaquis, only to be repelled each time. Nevertheless, in 1610, the Yaquis signed a peace treaty with Spain. Before long, the Jesuits established missions among them. Although they pretended to convert to Catholicism, the Yaquis never abandoned their tribal customs and they considered themselves independent of Spanish authority.

When Spanish settlers tried to take the Yaquis' lands, the Yaquis revolted. This rebellion occurred in the year 1740. Another revolt followed in 1764. But the tenuous peace held for the remaining period of Spanish rule.

After gaining independence from Spain in 1821, the Mexican government declared the Indians full citizens and began charging them taxes. Once again, the Yaquis resisted interference in their affairs. They staged many guerilla uprisings over the next century. In their rugged homeland, they proved unbeatable in battle, even for large Mexican armies.

Starting in the 1880s, the Mexican government began to deport Yaquis to work on plantations in the Yucatan, over 2,000 miles away. But the Yaqui spirit remained unbroken. Some managed to escape and make the difficult return trek to their homeland. In the Mexican Revolution of 1910-11, some Yaquis joined the forces of the bandit-general Pancho Villa. Then, in 1927, another Yaqui uprising flared up. A lasting peace was finally achieved and the Yaquis were granted permanent landholdings along the Yaqui River. Descendants of these Yaquis currently live much as their ancestors did, still farming the rich soil along their ancestral river.

Yet, during this entire period, from the 1880s to the 1920s, many Yaquis fled from Mexican oppression across the international border to the state of Arizona. Their descendants, the American Yaquis, now occupy six communities in southern Arizona, located at Eloy, Marana, Pascua, Scottsdale, Tempe, and Tucson. Because of their history, they do not have the same special status with the federal government as other Native Americans do, receiving no services from the

Yaqui Pascola mask

Bureau of Indian Affairs. Most American Yaquis earn a living as farm or construction workers. So far, because of a lack of opportunities, few American Yaquis have managed to attend college.

The Mexican and American Yaquis maintain strong cultural ties. They often celebrate together the week-long Pascola ceremony at Eastertime, a blending of Catholic and native rituals. Musicians play drums, rattles, and rasping sticks while dancers in masks and deer costumes perform before a doll representing the Infant Jesus.

Yavapai

The Yavapais, the "people of the sun," occupied territory now located in western Arizona, from the Pinal and Mazatzal mountains in the east to the neighborhood of the Colorado River in the west, and from the Williams and Santa Maria rivers in the north to the Gila River in the south.

The Yavapais spoke a dialect of the Yuman language family. Linguistically, they were closely related to the Upland Yumans, such as the Havasupais and Hualapais, who lived to their north; as well as the River Yumans, such as the Mojaves and Yumas, who lived to their west (see entries for those tribes). Nevertheless, culturally and historically, the Yavapais

were more closely related to the Tonto band of Apaches living to their east, with whom they sometimes intermarried (see "Apache"). In fact, at times the Yavapais have been referred to as Mojave Apaches and Yuma Apaches.

The Yavapais (pronounced *yah-vuh-PIE*) consisted of three major divisions: the Kawevikopaya, or Southeastern, Yavapai; the Yawepe, or Northeastern, Yavapai; and the Tolkepaya, or Western, Yavapai.

The Yavapais were a nomadic people, traveling in families or in small bands. Their movements corresponded to the ripening of wild plant crops, such as mescal and saguaro cactus fruit. Some of the

Yavapais, particularly those living near the Mojaves and Yumas, grew corn, sunflowers, tobacco, and other crops in small plots. The Yavapais hunted deer, antelope, rabbits, and other game. They lived in either caves or dome-shaped huts framed with poles and covered with brush or thatch, much like Apache wickiups. Their crafts included pottery and basketry. Shamans, or medicine men, presided over healing rituals.

The Yavapais first had contact with whites in 1582, when a Spanish expedition under Antonio de Espejo visited them. Other explorers from out of Mexico reached their domain. Juan de Onate met with them in 1604. Father Francisco Garces lived among them in 1776, after which contacts with white traders and trappers became common.

The Yavapais were ruggedly independent, resisting white missionary work and settlement. Some bands, especially of the Southeastern group, joined with the Apaches in raids on whites and on other Indians. With the Mexican Cession in 1848 and the United States takeover of the Southwest, the territory of the Yavapais came to be increasingly traveled and mined by white prospectors, causing sporadic violence by Yavapai bands.

Their resistance reached a climax in 1872 during General George Crook's Tonto Basin Campaign against Tonto Apaches and Yavapais. Crook's scouts located a war party in Salt River Canyon of the Mazatzal Mountains. In the ensuing Battle of Skull Cave, his soldiers pumped bullets into a cave high on the canyon wall. Some fired from below on the canyon floor; others from above on the rim of the canyon. Bullets ricocheted inside the cave, striking many of the Yavapai warriors. Some managed to escape from the cave and fight back from behind rocks. But soldiers on the escarpment rolled boulders down on top of them. About 75 braves lost their lives at Skull Cave.

White officials settled the Yavapais with Apaches on the Camp Verde Reservation and the San Carlos Reservation. By 1900, most of the Yavapais had left San Carlos to join their kinsmen at Camp Verde and at Camp McDowell, which became the Fort McDowell Reservation, shared by Mojaves, Apaches, and Yavapais. In 1935, a separate Yavapai reservation was created north of Prescott. The present Yavapai economy consists of raising stock, subsistence farming, and wage work. Some Yavapais generate additional income by selling beautiful coiled baskets.

Yazoo

The Yazoos lived along the lower Yazoo River, a tributary of the Mississippi River. Their main villages were located on the south side of the river near present-day Vicksburg, Mississippi. The Yazoo River parallels the Mississippi for about 175 miles before it joins the larger river, separated from it by natural levees, or dikes. So the name *Yazoo* (pronounced *YAH-zoo*) is applied to any river that belatedly joins another. The Yazoo Indians also have a county and city in Mississippi named after them. Their name probably means "waters of the dead."

The Yazoos spoke a dialect of the Tunican language family. They were villagers and farmers with lifeways in common with the Tunicas living near them (see "Tunica"). Yet it is known they were a group distinct from the Tunicas because, unlike them, they used an *r* sound when speaking. Both tribes are part of the Southeast Culture Area (see "Southeast Indians").

It is possible that the Spanish expedition of Hernando de Soto that traveled throughout much of the Southeast had contact with the Yazoos in the 1540s. Yet most of what we know about the Yazoos has

come from French records of the late 1600s and early 1700s.

Rene Cavalier de la Salle, who claimed the Mississippi Valley for France in 1682, mentioned the Yazoos. Then in 1718, the French established a military and trading post on the Yazoo River within the tribe's territory. And in 1729, a Jesuit missionary, Father Seul, settled among them.

That very year, however, the Yazoos joined the Natchez, who lived to their south on the Mississippi, in the Natchez's revolt (see "Natchez"). The Yazoos killed Father Seul and routed the French soldiers. Then a Yazoo warrior, dressed in the clothes of the missionary, traveled to the Natchez to offer them the Yazoos' support driving the French from the area.

Yet, with the defeat and dispersal of the Natchez, the Yazoos also departed from their ancestral homelands and joined other tribes in the area—probably the Chickasaws and Choctaws—among whom they eventually lost their tribal identity.

Yokuts

The name of the Yokuts, pronounced *YO-kuts*, is generally written with an "s" whether singular or plural. It means "person" or "people" in the various dialects of the Penutian language family spoken by different Yokuts groups. The Yokuts Indians lived in a wide expanse of territory that is now located in central California along the San Joaquin River Valley and the foothills of the Sierra Nevada.

The Yokuts are classified in the California Culture Area (see "California Indians"). They were hunter-gatherers, depending on small mammals, fowl, fish, and wild plant foods, especially acorns, for their food. They constructed enclosures called blinds where they could hide to trap pigeons. They also hunted eagles. The following is a Yokuts prayer that was recited before killing an eagle:

> *Do not think that I will hurt you.*
> *You will have a new body.*
> *Now turn your head northward and lie flat.*

The Yokuts made exquisite baskets, coiling thin bundles of grass stems upward in a spiral and binding them with marsh grass. They also drew elaborate picture messages, called pictographs, on rocks.

The Yokuts did not make up a unified tribe. Scholars sometimes use the word *tribelet* to describe the political or territorial organization of the Yokuts and other California Indians, a category between a tribe and a village. The Yokuts had about 50 tribelets. A tribelet contained a main permanent village and several smaller satellite villages that were moved from time to time. Each tribelet had a chief and a shaman, or medicine man. A chief's messenger carried his commands to other villages. A village crier made announcements within his main village. These various positions were hereditary offices, passed to a younger brother or to a son. Each tribelet had a distinct name to differentiate it from other tribelets, and a distinct language dialect. Sometimes, among the Yokuts, the different tribelets had disputes that led to violence.

The Yokuts, unlike most Indians, practiced cremation at death. When someone died, his or her possessions were burned along with the body, even the entire house in some cases.

The Yokuts fought in one of the few wars involving California Indians, the Mariposa Indian War. This conflict began in 1850 during the California Gold Rush when the number of whites radically increased. The Yokuts and neighboring Miwoks attacked miners and trading posts. The Mariposa Volunteer Battalion quelled the outbreak in 1851 (see "Miwok").

The Yokuts, who presently hold the Santa Rosa Rancheria and the Tule River Reservation, have strong tribal ties and meet to celebrate traditional ways.

Yokuts tule (cattail) raft

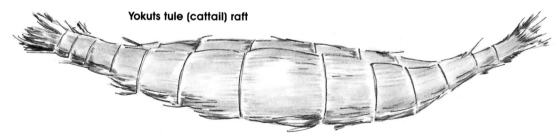

Yuchi

The Yuchis (pronounced *YOO-chee*) spoke a unique dialect, usually referred to simply as Yuchi. When scholars cannot find sounds or words in a native language resembling elements in other languages, they have a difficult time tracing the ancestry and ancient history of a tribe. Until recently, this was the case with the Yuchis. Now it is thought that the Yuchi dialect has some elements in common with dialects of the Siouan language family. Therefore, the Yuchis probably long ago split off from other Siouan-speaking peoples and settled in the Southeast. They lived near the Catawba Indians, another eastern Siouan people (see "Catawba").

The earliest known location of the Yuchis was in what is now eastern Tennessee. But, after that early period, the Yuchis came to live in territory now part of many different states, including Georgia, Florida, and South Carolina. Scholars classify the Yuchis within the Southeast Culture Area (see "Southeast Indians"). That is to say, they were Woodland Indians who built villages and planted crops along river valleys. They lived by farming, hunting, fishing, and collecting wild plant foods.

The known history of the Yuchis begins with Hernando de Soto's expedition of 1539-43 that explored much of the Southeast and encountered many Indian peoples. Other Spaniards mention various bands of Yuchis under different names in their historical accounts. A Spaniard by the name of Boyano under the explorer Juan Pardo claimed to have battled and killed many Yuchis on two different occasions in the mountains of either North Carolina or Tennessee. Because the explorers' maps were inexact, it is difficult to pinpoint the locations.

In the 1630s, various Yuchi bands swept south out of the Appalachian highlands to raid Spanish settlements and missions in Florida. Some of these Yuchis settled in what was then called West Florida, in Apalachee country (see "Apalachee").

Yuchi Feather Dance wand

In the 1670s, various Englishmen, exploring southwestward out of Virginia and the Carolinas, made contact with Yuchis still in Tennessee and North Carolina. In the following years, many Yuchi bands, probably because of pressure from hostile Shawnees, migrated from the high country, following the Savannah River toward the coastal country in Georgia. The Yuchis who had previously gone to Florida also migrated to Georgia. Both groups of Yuchis became allies of the English colonists and helped them in slave raids on mission Indians of Spanish Florida, including the Apalachees, Calusas, and Timucuas (see those tribes).

By the mid-1700s, the Spanish military and mission systems in Florida were weakened. From that period into the 1800s, many Yuchis migrated southward and settled on lands formerly held by other tribes.

The Yuchis eventually lost their tribal identity. Those who stayed in Tennessee and North Carolina merged with the Cherokees; those who settled in Georgia joined the Creeks; and those who migrated to Florida united with the Seminoles (see entries for those tribes).

Yuma

The Yumas gave their name to the Yuman language family spoken by many tribes in the region of western Arizona and southeastern California. The name, pronounced *YOO-muh*, probably means "people of the river." The various Yuman-speaking peoples are generally categorized as the Upland Yumans and the River Yumans. Upland Yumans include the Havasupais, Hualapais, and Yavapais among others (see entries for those tribes). River Yumans include the Mojaves and the Yumas proper in addition to other tribes not covered in this book (see "Mojave"). The Yuman-speaking peoples are classified by scholars as part of the Southwest Culture Area, although they border the California Culture Area (see "Southwest Indians").

The Yumas proper lived on both sides of the Colorado River, near the mouth of the Gila River, not far from the present-day Mexican border. This is desert country, extremely hot and arid. Temperatures often reach as high as 105 to 120 degrees Fahrenheit. In order to survive this harsh environment, the Yumas placed their villages along the bottomlands of rivers. They lived in rectangular, open-sided structures; in rectangular, earth-covered pit houses; or in domed brush huts (wickiups). In the mosquito season, they burned dung at the doorway to keep the insects away. They fished the river and farmed the fertile soil of the riverbanks that flooded every year. They grew corn, beans, pumpkins, gourds, and tobacco. Both men and women tended the crops. The men also hunted small game, especially rabbits.

The Yumas wore minimal clothing. Men usually wore only rawhide sandals and sometimes a breechcloth. Women wore sandals and an apron made from willow-bark. In cool weather, both used blankets of rabbit-skin or woven bark. Both men and women painted and tattooed themselves. The various Yumans were tall and powerfully built. A Spanish explorer described Yuman people as "the tallest and the most robust that I have seen in all the provinces, and their nakedness the most complete."

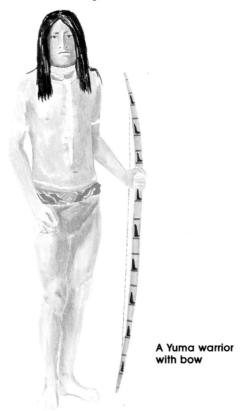

A Yuma warrior
with bow

The River Yumans were generally more warlike than their Upland kinsmen. Warriors carried five-foot bows and long arrows, mallet-headed war clubs, or lances.

The Spanish were the first Europeans to visit the Yumas. Hernando de Alarcon reached Yuma territory as early as 1540. The Jesuit Father Eusebio Francisco Kino visited them in 1698. The Franciscan Padre Francisco Garces established missions among them in 1775. But the Yumas resisted being missionized, rebelling in 1781. They continued their traditional way of life, unlike many neighboring tribes in California who settled on or next to the missions (see "Mission Indians").

In the mid-1800s, the Yumas sometimes fought travelers along the Southern Overland Trail (which later came to be called the Butterfield Southern Route). They attacked wagon trains and stole supplies. The travelers for their part stole Yuman crops. The numbers of migrants rose drastically with the start of the California Gold Rush of 1849. The Yumas controlled the Yuma Crossing, a natural passage of the Colorado River near the mouth of the Gila River. For a time, the Yumas provided a ferry service on rafts across the river. When a group of whites established their own ferry service in competition with that of the Indians, the Yumas became incensed and blocked passage.

In 1850, to keep the crossing open, the army built Fort Yuma on the California side of the Colorado. The Yumas launched attacks on the fort and cut off its supplies. The soldiers had to abandon the post for a year. On returning, however, the soldiers were better equipped for Indian fighting. A one-armed Irishman by the name of Thomas Sweeney, nicknamed "Fighting Tom," led expeditions against the Indians. On one raid into California with only 25 men, he managed to take 150 prisoners. Before long, the rest of the Yumas ceased their hostilities.

The federal government created the Fort Yuma Reservation in California and Arizona for the Yumas in 1883. The tribe formally signed away most of its land in 1886. The Fort Yuma Indians use the band name Quechan. The Cocopah Reservation near Somerton, Arizona, formed in 1917, bears the name of another Yuman-speaking tribe, the Cocopahs, and once included members of that tribe and the Maricopa tribe as well as the Yumas. But many of the Cocopahs and Maricopas quit the alliance of three tribes. As a result, the reservation has many descendants of the Yumas proper.

The Indians of the Cocopah Reservation recently signed an agreement with a development company for the construction of a 234-acre recreational-vehicle park on tribal land bordering the Colorado River. The park will have many modern facilities and will hopefully attract many visitors to help provide income for tribal members.

Yurok

The Yuroks (pronounced YOUR-ock) were neighbors of the Karoks (pronounced KAH-rock), both peoples living along the Klamath River in territory now mapped as part of northern California. The Karoks, whose name translates as "upstream," lived farther inland, up the river. The Yuroks, whose name means

Yurok headdress of sea lion's teeth

"downstream" in the Karok language, lived near the mouth of the river, along the Pacific Coast.

It is interesting to note that even though these two peoples had similar cultures and that the Karoks even gave the Yuroks the tribal name that has lasted to modern times, they spoke different languages. The Karoks spoke a dialect of the Hokan language family. The Yuroks, on the other hand, spoke what scholars consider to be a dialect of Algonquian. That would make the Yuroks the westernmost Algonquian-speaking people (see "Algonquian").

The Yuroks, the Karoks, and the Hoopas, another tribe who had a similar culture, are all grouped by scholars in the California Culture Area (see "California Indians" and "Hoopa"). The northern California tribes were hunter-gatherers, who depended heavily on acorns. They lived in villages in the winter and wandered in bands in the summer, like other California Indians. And, like the tribes to their south, they crafted beautiful, tightly woven baskets. But they also were influenced by the Northwest Coast tribes to their north (see "Northwest Coast Indians"). For example, they fished the Klamath River for the staple food of the Northwest tribes—salmon. They built rectangular

houses with slanted roofs out of cedar planks. And they determined social status by an individual's wealth.

The Yuroks practiced the annual World Renewal ceremonies, as did the Karoks and Hoopas, one more cultural trait used to distinguish northern California Indians from other California peoples. The purpose of the rituals was to renew the world, or "firm the earth," as the Indians described it, provide food, and perpetuate tribal well-being.

There is one cultural element, however, that the Yuroks did not share with their neighbors, or with any other Indians in North America for that matter. For Native Americans, land was considered a source of life shared by the entire tribe. There was no such thing as private land. The Yuroks, however, individually owned land, measured wealth by it, and even sold it to one another.

But whites came to Yurok territory—first British and American trappers starting in 1826-27, and a rush of settlers after the California Gold Rush of 1849-50, leading to permanent settlement—and the Yuroks eventually lost most of their land once and for all. The tribe presently holds several small reservations, or rancherias, in Humboldt County. The largest of these is called the Hoopa Extension Reservation. The Yuroks still live mainly by hunting, fishing, and gathering, as their ancestors did. Some Karoks, who have no reservation lands under their tribal name, live among them.

In 1983, the Yuroks, along with the Karoks and Tolowas, another California tribe, won a 10-year battle over a sacred site in the mountainous Six Rivers National Forest of northern California, just south of the Oregon border. Members of the three tribes climb into the unspoiled high country in order to be closer to the spirit world in which they believe.

Zuni

Zuni (pronounced *ZOO-nee* or *ZOON-yee*) is the name of both a people and a pueblo, or village. The Zunis originally called themselves *Ashiwi*, meaning "the flesh." They originally lived in seven pueblos along the north bank of the upper Zuni River, flowing out of the highlands of the Colorado Plateau. Zuni territory has since become a part of the state of New Mexico, and lies in the state's western region near the Arizona border.

The Zunis spoke a language unlike that of any other Pueblo Indians. Some scholars now place this distinctive dialect of Zunian in the Penutian language family. Archaeological evidence indicates that two diverse cultural groups—one from the north and the other from the west or southwest—merged in prehistoric times to become the ancestors of the Zunis. Some of their ancestors might have been of the Mogollon culture (see "Cliff Dwellers and Desert Farmers"). Much later, Indians from Mexico who served as bearers for the conquistadors, especially the Tlacalans, deserted the Spanish to settle among the Zunis.

The Zunis, like other Pueblo Indians, lived in multi-storied houses interconnected by ladders. (The houses, like the Indians and the villages, are called

Zuni buffalo-head altar carving

pueblos.) The Zuni pueblos were built of stones and covered with plaster, unlike the Rio Grande pueblos to the east of the Zunis, which were built with adobe bricks (see "Pueblo Indians").

Farming provided the primary source of food for the Zunis. They also hunted, fished, and foraged for wild plants. As in the case of the Hopis, another western Pueblo people living on the Colorado Plateau, the kachinas, benevolent guardian spirits, played an important part in Zuni mythology (see "Hopi"). The Zunis, the Hopis, and the Rio Grande Pueblo Indians are classified as part of the Southwest Culture Area (see "Southwest Indians").

The Spanish originally called the Zuni villages the Seven Cities of Cibola (the Spanish word for "buffalo" and consequently for any buffalo-hunting Indians). Rumors of native cities filled with great riches in this Kingdom of Cibola reached the ears of the conquistadors in the 1500s soon after the Spanish conquest of Mexico.

Fray Marcos de Niza, a Franciscan monk, set out with a contingent of soldiers and Indian bearers in 1539 to look for Cibola. He also took with him a black man from Barbary named Estevanico, sometimes

called Estevan the Moor. Estevan had had earlier experience dealing with Indians. He had participated in Cabeza de Vaca's expedition of 1528-36, which had met up with many native peoples along the Gulf of Mexico from Texas to northern Mexico. Some of the Indians thought the tall, dark-skinned Estevan was a god. He wore ribbons, badges, feathers, rattles, and bells to call attention to himself. Niza sent him ahead with a scouting party to offer presents to any Indians he met and to win them over.

The Zuni Indians, however, were angered by Estevan's arrogance and attacked and killed him. A messenger reported the incident to Niza. The monk decided to continue on to see for himself whether these Indian cities were truly the Kingdom of Cibola. He advanced far enough to see Hawikuh, one of the Zuni pueblos. From a distance, the reddish-brown adobe buildings must have glistened in the sunlight like gold, because Niza returned to Mexico claiming he had found Cibola.

The following year, a Spaniard named Francisco de Coronado organized an expedition to conquer Cibola and claim its vast riches. To Coronado's disappointment, the Seven Cities of Cibola turned out to be ordinary Indian pueblos without streets of gold and without abundant jewels. After defeating the Zunis in battle, Coronado pushed northeastward, still in search of wealth. On hearing rumors of the Kingdom of Quivira, Coronado explored as far north as Kansas. During his travels, he encountered many tribes, such as the Wichitas, and recorded information about them (see "Wichita"). He never made his fortune, however, and died in obscurity in Mexico City.

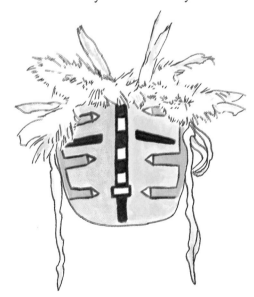

Zuni kachina mask of painted leather, showing earth and sky beings

Other Spanish explorers visited the Zunis: Francisco Chamuscado in 1580; Antonio de Espejo in 1583; and Juan de Onate, the colonizer of New Mexico, in 1598. The Spanish established their first mission in Zuni territory at Hawikuh in 1629. In 1632, the Zunis attacked and killed the missionaries. In 1672, the Apaches raided Hawikuh and forced the abandonment of the mission.

In 1680, the Zunis participated in the Pueblo Rebellion that started among the Rio Grande pueblos. At that time, the Zunis lived in only three pueblos of their original seven—Halona, Matsaki, and Kiakima. Villagers from three pueblos fled to a stronghold on the mesa of Towayalane (Corn Mountain) to defend themselves from the Spanish troops approaching under Don Diego de Vargas. The Spanish negotiated with them to return to their village at Halona. Although a new church was built there in 1699, it was abandoned by the missionaries in the 1800s. The Zunis favored their traditional religion over Christianity despite the presence of priests among them.

The ancient site of Halona is the site of modern-day Zuni, located in McKinley and Valencia counties near the Arizona border. Since their days of conflict with the Spanish, the Zunis have lived at this site peacefully through the Mexican period, from 1821 to 1848, and the subsequent American period.

The Zunis farm and raise livestock for a living. Some among them spend their summers in the neighboring farming villages of Pescado, Nutria, and Ojo. Zuni craftsmen have gained international reputations for their silver and turquoise jewelry. Almost a thousand Zunis participate in silversmithing and stonecutting. Traditional pottery, weaving, and basketry are also still practiced. Zuni men have also earned fame as expert firefighters. The Forest Service frequently flies them to help battle the nation's worst forest fires.

Zuni silver and turquoise pin (modern)

Tourists can visit the Zuni Pueblo to watch the Shalako festival in late November or early December. Part of the ceremonies include giant, bird-like kachina figures dancing in and around new homes to bless them. The tribe also holds an annual fair in late August or early September. Among other sights, one can observe Zuni women baking bread in outdoor adobe ovens.

Glossary

activism Political involvement, sometimes militant. Used in reference to modern Indian organizations with political and social goals.

adobe A kind of brick made from mud and straw that is sun-dried. (Or a type of mud used as a mortar to hold stones together.) Used by Southwest Indians to make pueblos.

adz A woodworking tool with an arched axlike blade at right angles to the handle.

allotment A policy of the U.S. federal government, starting with the General Allotment Act of 1887 and lasting until 1934. Under the policy, Indian lands held by tribes were broken up and distributed to individual Indians. A large portion of lands held by Indians in Oklahoma was allotted.

appliqué A technique in decorating articles of clothing or other objects in which pieces of one material are applied to another. (See also "ribbonwork.")

archaeology The recovery and study of objects remaining from early cultures.

artifact An object made by humans, especially a tool, weapon, ornament, or piece of pottery.

assimilation A policy practiced by whites, especially in the late 1800s and early 1900s, in an effort to absorb Indians into white culture. Also called "acculturation."

atlatl A prehistoric spear-thrower that increased the leverage of the human arm and let hunters throw spears harder and straighter. It was made from a stick about two feet long, with hide hoops to provide a firm grasp, a stone weight for balance, and a hook and groove to hold the spear shaft.

awl A pointed tool for making holes in wood or hide.

babiche Rawhide strips, used in toboggans, snowshoes, and other objects, for binding and support.

ball-court An ancient playing field, sometimes sunken and sometimes paved, common in Mesoamerica, where violent games were played with a rubber ball.

band A subdivision or subtribe of an Indian tribe, often made up of an extended family.

bannerstone A polished stone artifact, often in a winged, birdlike shape, used as a weight on an atlatl or on a staff as a symbol of authority. Sometimes called a "birdstone." (See also "atlatl.")

beadwork Decorative work in beads, stitched on clothing, bags, and other items. Beadwork commonly replaced quillwork among Indians after Europeans brought glass beads to the Americas. (See also "quillwork.")

bison   A hoofed mammal with a dark-brown coat, shaggy mane, and short curved horns, more commonly called "buffalo." Bison were essential to the Plains Indians for food, clothing, shelter, tools, and ceremonial objects.

Black Drink   A tea made by Southeast Indians, from *Ilex vomitoria*, tobacco, and other ingredients, for ceremonial purposes. The drink induced vomiting and was thought to purify the body.

bola   A hunting weapon made from two or more stone weights tied on thongs that are attached to a longer line. When thrown, it entangles the legs of mammals or the wings of birds.

breechcloth   A cloth, usually made from deerskin, used to cover the loins. Also called "breechclout" or "loincloth."

buffalo   See "bison."

bullboat   A circular, cup-shaped boat made from hide stretched over a wooden frame. Used by Indians of the upper Missouri River.

Bureau of Indian Affairs (BIA)   An agency of the U.S. federal government which handles Indian issues; part of the Department of the Interior. It was formed in 1824.

calendar stick   A wooden stick with cuts and notches representing events in tribal history. Typical of the Papago tribe.

calumet   See "sacred pipe."

camp circle   Plains Indians frequently placed their tepees in a circle around a central fire.

canoe   A sleek boat with pointed ends, propelled by paddles. Some canoes were made of wood frames with bark coverings; others were dugouts, carved from a single log.

cassava   See "manioc."

caste system   Social and political organization in which classes of society are separated by hereditary rank or profession. Common among Southeast Indians and Mesoamerican Indians.

catlinite   See "pipestone."

celt   An ungrooved ax, used mainly without a handle, for woodworking.

ceremonial object   Any object used in religious rituals or with a sacred tribal meaning.

chert   A kind of rock, similar to flint, which can be shaped into tools or spear and arrow points. (See also "flaking.")

chickee   A kind of house, raised on stilts and open on four sides, with a wood platform and thatched roof. The Seminoles lived in chickees.

chiefdom   A tribe in which a chief has absolute power over other tribal members. Used in reference to some Southeast tribes.

chinampas   An artificial island made by piling silt and plant matter on wickerwork baskets. The Aztecs used this technique to create additional land for their city of Tenochtitlan on Lake Texcoco.

city-state   A city that has its own government independent from other cities. Used in reference to Mesoamerican Indians.

clan   A social group within a tribe, made up of several families who trace descent from a common ancestor.

coiling   A technique of making pottery in which ropelike coils of clay are built up from the bottom of the pot, then smoothed over to form the inner and outer walls. Also used to describe a similar technique of weaving baskets.

Composite Tribe   A change of culture within a tribe, resulting in a new way of life shared with other tribes. Used in reference to Plains tribes whose diverse customs merged into a single way of life, hunting buffalo on horseback and living in temporary camps of tepees.

confederacy   A political union of several tribes.

conquistador   The Spanish word for "conqueror." Used in reference to Spanish explorers and soldiers who subjugated Indian peoples.

Contact   A term used to describe the first meetings between Indian peoples and Europeans, with subsequent cultural changes among the Indians.

"Precontact" refers to the period before Indians met whites (see also "Pre-Columbian"). "Postcontact" refers to the period after Indians established communication and trade with whites. "Contact" for one tribe might have come at a different time than for another.

corral   An enclosure made of stones, wood, or brush for trapping and confining animals.

council   A gathering of tribal leaders for discussion of plans.

coup   Touching an enemy in battle with the hand or an object to prove one's bravery. Plains Indians used "coup sticks" in some instances, rather than true weapons, and they "counted coup."

coureur de bois   Literally, French for "runner of the woods." A fur trader of French descent who worked independently of the large trading companies and who lived most of the time with Indians. (See also "voyageurs.")

cradleboard   A carrier for babies, usually made of wood and leather, worn on the back.

creation myth   A tribal legend, recounting the supernatural origin of the tribe. Also called "emergence myth."

culture area   A geographical region where different Indian tribes had similar ways of life. A classification used to organize tribes.

culture hero   A legendary figure, thought to have supernatural powers and usually considered a tribal ancestor.

deadfall   A trap in which a heavy object, such as a log or a stone, is set up to fall on the prey.

dialect   A variation of a language, different from other dialects of the same language in vocabulary, grammar, or pronunciation.

digging stick   A simple wooden tool used to cultivate soil for farming.

dugout   A type of boat made by hollowing out a log. (See "canoe.")

earthlodge   A large dwelling, usually dome-shaped, with a log frame covered with smaller branches or other plant matter, then packed with mud or sod.

earthwork   See "mound."

emergence myth   See "creation myth."

fire drill   A device for making fire in which one stick is twirled rapidly in a hole of another piece of wood, creating enough friction to ignite wood powder or shredded grass.

firing   The process of baking pottery to make it hard.

flaking   To remove chips of stone, usually from chunks of flint, chert, or obsidian, in order to shape tools or spear and arrow points. In percussion-flaking, the chips are removed by striking with a tool of stone, bone, or wood. In pressure-flaking, the chips are removed by applying pressure with a tool of bone or antler.

flint   A kind of rock, a variety of quartz that can be worked into tools and points through flaking. (See also "flaking.")

fluting   Grooves or channels in points. (See also "point.")

Ghost Dance   An Indian religion of the late 19th century founded by the Paiute mystic Wovoka and popular for a number of years among many Plains tribes. The main ritual was a dance to bring about the restoration of traditional tribal ways.

glyph writing   See "hieroglyphics."

gorget   An ornament or piece of armor, usually made of shell or copper, worn over the throat.

Grand Medicine Society   See "Midewiwin."

hieroglyphics   A system of writing using pictures instead of letters. Also called "glyph writing."

hogan   A dwelling with a log and stick frame covered with mud or sod (or occasionally made from stone). It can be cone-shaped, six-sided, or eight-sided. It traditionally faces east. The Navajos lived in hogans.

holism   A philosophy in which all aspects of reality and nature are viewed as a unified whole. Indians in general were a "holistic" people.

hunting-gathering Obtaining food through hunting, fishing, and foraging for wild plant foods, without farming.

igloo A dome-shaped dwelling made from blocks of ice. Also called a "snow house." The Eskimos (Inuits) lived in igloos.

incising A technique of decorating pottery by cutting a design in the still-wet clay with a sharp tool.

Indian Territory A tract west of the Mississippi set aside as a permanent homeland for Indians in the 1830s, then diminished over the following years until it became the state of Oklahoma in 1907.

isolate See "language isolate."

jade A kind of rock, usually pale green in color, used to make sculptures and jewelry.

jerky Sun-dried strips of meat.

jimsonweed A tall poisonous plant of the nightshade family, with large trumpet-shaped flowers and prickly fruit. Indians of California, the Southwest, and Mesoamerica made a tea from leaves, stems, and roots for ritualistic and medicinal purposes.

kachina (or katchina) A supernatural being in the religion of the Hopis, Zunis, and other Pueblo Indians. Kachina masks are worn in tribal ceremonies. Kachina dolls are carved icons of the deities.

kayak A one- or two-man boat with an enclosed cockpit, made by stretching hide over a wooden frame. Typical of the Eskimos.

kill site An archaeological site where remains of many animals have been found along with human artifacts.

kinnikinnik A mixture of tobacco and other plant matter, such as willow bark, for smoking. An Algonquian word.

kiva An underground ceremonial chamber or clubhouse. Typical of Southwest Indians.

labret An ornamental plug of shell, bone, or stone, worn in the lower lip (or sometimes in the chin).

lacrosse A game invented and played by eastern Indians, using long-handled rackets and a small ball. Lacrosse is now played all over the world.

land cession Land given up by Indians to whites through a treaty. Most land cessions were forced upon the Indians against their will. (See also "treaty.")

language family A term used in linguistics (the study of languages) to describe languages spoken by different tribes but with elements in common.

language isolate A unique language with few or no elements in common with other languages.

lean-to A temporary, open brush shelter, generally consisting of a single-pitched sloping roof. Some western Subarctic Indians constructed double lean-tos with two roofs meeting in a peak.

leister A three-pronged harpoon used for fishing by Arctic peoples.

lifeways Cultural traits or customs of a people.

Lithic Indians See "Paleo-Indians."

longhouse A long dwelling, with a pointed or rounded roof and doors at both ends, made with a pole frame and usually covered with elm bark. The Iroquois lived in longhouses, several families to each one.

loom A device used to weave thread or yarn to make cloth.

maize Indian corn.

mammoth A large extinct mammal, similar to the elephant, once common in North America and hunted by prehistoric peoples. The wooly mammoth was one variety. (See also "mastodon.")

manioc A tropical plant with a large starchy root, important in the diet of Caribbean Indians. Used to make tapioca. Also called "cassava."

Manitou A supernatural being or force of nature in the religion of Algonquians. Known by other names in other Indian religions. Sometimes translated as "Great Spirit." (See also "Orenda" and "Wakenda.")

mano and metate   A set of millstones, with an upper and lower part, used to grind corn and other grains. (See also "mortar and pestle.")

mastodon   A large extinct mammal, similar to an elephant. (See also "mammoth.")

matrilineal   A term used to describe a social organization in which descent is traced down through the female members, as is ownership of property. (See also "patrilineal.")

medicine bundle   A collection of various materials, often in a pouch or wrapped in leather or cloth, to which spiritual powers are assigned.

medicine man   See "shaman."

mesa   A tableland, or flat-topped elevation with steep sides. Found in the American Southwest.

Mesoamerica   The name of a culture area that is now part of Mexico and Central America. Some Indians in this part of the Americas lived in cities and had highly organized societies.

mesquite   A spiny tree or shrub with sugar-rich pods, growing in the American Southwest.

metis   Literally, French for "mixed-blood." Many Canadian fur traders, especially French Canadian but also Scottish, lived among and intermarried with the Indians. They came to constitute a special class of people, like an Indian tribe but with a combined Indian-white culture. The word is capitalized when it identifies this special group. (See also "voyageur.")

Midewiwin   A secret society whose members supposedly have a link to the spirit world and strive to assure the well-being of the tribe. Typical of western Great Lakes tribes. Also called "the Grand Medicine Society."

military society   A club with special rituals and clothing, made up of warriors. Typical of Plains Indians. Also called "soldier society" or "warrior society."

Mission Indians   A phrase used to denote those Indians who gave up their tribal way of life and came to live at missions. Used especially in reference to California Indians missionized by the Spanish.

moccasin   A soft leather shoe. Originally an Algonquian word, but now used in reference to footware of many different Indian peoples.

moiety   A social group within a tribe. The word means "half." Some tribes with clans divided their clans into halves. The two halves were responsible for different chores and played against each other in games. (See also "clan.")

mortar and pestle   A two-part milling tool, with a bowl-shaped stone, plus a club-shaped stone (or wooden bowl and wooden club), used for pulverizing plant or animal matter. (See also "mano and metate.")

mosaic   A picture or design made from small, colorful pieces of stone, shell, or other material cemented together to form a design.

mound   A large earthwork made by ancient Indians for burials, to represent animals or to contain or support temples or houses. The Indians who made these earthworks are known as "Mound Builders."

mukluk   A soft and supple Eskimo (Inuit) boot, usually made from sealskin.

nomadic   A way of life in which people frequently moved from one location to another in search of food. "Seminomadic" people had permanent villages, but left them in certain seasons to hunt, fish, or gather wild plant foods. (See also "hunting-gathering.")

obsidian   Volcanic glass that is generally black and was prized by Indians because it could be readily flaked to a sharp point or edge. (See also "flaking.")

Orenda   The supernatural force or "Great Spirit" in the religion of the Iroquois. (See also "Manitou" and "Wakanda.")

paddling   A technique of decorating pottery by pressing a flat or curved wood paddle against the wet clay before firing. The paddle had a design carved in it or cords wrapped around it.

Paleo-Indians   The Paleolithic (Stone Age), prehistoric ancestors of modern Indians. The Paleo-Indians were known as makers of stone tools and hunters of now-extinct big game. Also called "Lithic Indians."

paleontology The study of ancient life forms and fossil remains.

palisade A fence, usually made of upright logs and placed around a village, for purposes of defense.

pan-Indian Having to do with all Indians and not just isolated tribes. Used in reference to cultural activities, common goals, and organizations relevant to all Indian peoples.

papoose The Algonquian word for "baby."

parfleche A storage bag used to hold clothing, ceremonial objects, or meat, and made from rawhide with the hair removed.

patrilineal A type of social organization in which descent and property are passed along through the male line. (See also "matrilineal.")

peace pipe See "sacred pipe."

pemmican A concentrated food made by pounding together meat, fat, and berries and used especially on the trail.

percussion-flaking See "flaking."

permafrost Permanently frozen subsoil, typical of the Arctic tundra. (See also "tundra.")

peyote A type of cactus eaten by some Indian peoples for its trance-like effect. Considered a sacrament by the Native American church.

piñon A small pine tree producing edible nuts, growing in the American West and Southwest.

pipestone A type of clay, usually red in color, used to make pipes. Also called "catlinite" after the frontier painter George Catlin, who wrote about the Pipestone Quarry in Minnesota.

pit house A dwelling, placed over a hole, usually made with a log frame and walls and roof of saplings, reeds, and mud.

plaiting A technique used in weaving baskets and cloth in which two different elements cross each other to create a checkerboard effect.

plank house A dwelling, made of hand-split planks over a log frame. Northwest Coast Indians built plank houses.

point A stone spearhead or arrowhead.

potlatch A tribal ceremony of feasting, speechmaking, and dancing during which possessions are given away to demonstrate wealth and rank. Typical of Northwest Coast Indians.

powwow A council or festival among Indians for socializing, trading, and dancing. Originally an Algonquian word.

pre-Columbian The period of history in the Americas before Christopher Columbus's voyage of exploration.

prehistory A general term applied to the cultural stage of a people before written records.

pressure-flaking See "flaking."

pueblo Originally, the Spanish word for an Indian village. Used for a particular type of architecture common among Southwest Indians—apartment-like, up to five stories high, interconnected by ladders, made from stone or adobe bricks. Also, with a capital "P," when in reference to the people living in pueblos.

pyramid A massive stone monument with a rectangular base and four sides extending upward to a point. Found in Mesoamerica, where they were used to support temples.

quarry site A location where Indians went for workable stone, such as flint, and made stone tools. (See also "flaking.")

quillwork Decorative work on clothing, bags, and other items, made from porcupine quills dyed with vegetable colors. (See also "beadwork.")

radiocarbon dating A technique for dating ancient materials by measuring the amount of carbon 14 (a radioactive isotope) present. Also called "carbon 14 dating."

relocation A term used to describe the forced removal of a tribe from one location to another. A common U.S. governmental practice in the 1800s. From the early 1950s into the 1960s, the federal government adopted a modern relocation policy, pressuring Indians to move from reservations to urban areas. (See also "removal.")

removal A term used to describe a 19th-century policy of the U.S. federal government in which eastern tribes were taken from their ancestral homelands and forced to live elsewhere, especially west of the Mississippi River in the Indian Territory. (See also "Indian Territory" and "relocation.")

reservation A tract of land set aside historically by the federal government or state governments for Indians. Reservations originally served as a kind of prison for Indians, who were not permitted to leave them. Nowadays, reservations are tribally held lands, protected by the government, where Indians are free to come and go as they choose. Commonly called "reserves" in Canada.

restoration A term used to describe cultural renewal, or a return to traditional ways and values. Often appearing as "tribal restoration," indicating a rediscovery of tribal identity and the establishment of tribal economic goals. Tribal restoration became widespread in the 1930s, when the U.S. federal government under President Roosevelt launched a "New Deal" for Indians.

ribbonwork A kind of patchwork or appliqué in which ribbons or cutout designs of silk are sewn in strips on garments. Typical of the Seminoles. (See also "appliqué.")

roach A construction of animal hair or fur worn on the top of the head as a hairstyle. Also, the featherwork part of a headdress. "Roach spreaders," usually carved of antler, held the featherwork erect.

saber-toothed tiger A now-extinct mammal of the cat family with long upper teeth, hunted by early Indians.

sachem The chief of a tribe. Originally an Algonquian word, but also used in reference to Iroquois chiefs. A "grand sachem" is the leader of a confederacy of tribes. (See also "sagamore.")

sacred pipe A pipe with a special meaning for a tribe; used in ceremonies. Usually with an intricately carved pipestone bowl and a long wooden stem and decorated with quills, beads, or feathers. Also called "calumet" or "peace pipe."

Sacred Shield The paintings on shields had religious meanings to the Indians, supposedly serving as a link to the spiritual world and offering magical protection to the bearers.

sagamore A subordinate chief of the Algonquian Indians, below a sachem in rank. (See also "sachem.")

saguaro A giant cactus, growing in the American Southwest. Used by the Pimas and Papagos for its edible fruit.

sand painting A design made by trickling colored sand onto plain sand for ceremonial purposes. An art practiced by the Navajos.

scalplock A lock of hair on an otherwise shaved head.

sedentary A way of life in which people live in permanent villages. Most sedentary tribes practiced agriculture.

seine A large net for fishing that hangs vertically in the water, with floats on top and weights on the bottom.

self-determination A tribal and governmental policy calling for Indian self-government and cultural renewal.

seminomadic See "nomadic."

shaman A member of a tribe who keeps tribal lore and rituals, and interprets and attempts to control the supernatural. He applies his powers to evoke visions, to cure the sick, and to bring success in food gathering and warfare. Also called "medicine man."

sign language A method of intertribal communication using hand signs. Typical of Plains Indians.

slash-and-burn agriculture A type of farming in which the ground is cleared by cutting down and then burning trees and undergrowth. The resulting ashes help enrich the soil. Common in Mesoamerica.

slave-killer A weapon used to kill slaves in potlatch ceremonies. (See also "potlatch.")

sled A vehicle used for carrying people and possessions over snow and ice. A sled has runners and a raised platform. (See also "toboggan.")

slip   A thin mixture of fine clay and water applied to the surface of pottery before firing.

snare   A device to trap game, mostly birds and small mammals, usually with a rope or leather noose.

snow-pit   A hole in the snow in which a hunter can hide to surprise game.

snowshoe   A device for walking on top of deep snow, made from a racket-shaped wooden frame with leather webbing, and with thongs to attach it to the foot.

soapstone   A kind of stone with a soapy texture; a variety of talc; used to make pots and sculptures. Also called "steatite."

sodality   A club, often with closed membership and secret rites.

soldier society   See "military society."

soul-catcher   A ceremonial object used by a shaman to hold the patient's soul in curing ceremonies.

staple   A basic food essential to survival. Corn, buffalo meat, deer meat, salmon, and acorns are examples of dietary staples for various Indian peoples.

steatite   See "soapstone."

stone-boiling   A method of cooking in which pre-heated stones are placed inside containers of water.

Sun Dance   The most famous of all the Indian festivals, an annual renewal rite, taking place in the summer and centered around the sun. There were many rituals in the Sun Dance, the most dramatic of which involved self-torture by warriors. Typical of most Plains tribes.

sweathouse   A structure used for sweating, a ritual purification through exposure to heat. Heat could be generated with a fire in an open fire pit or by pouring water onto hot stones and making steam. Sweathouses were generally dome-shaped. Large sweathouses are sometimes called "sweatlodges" and often doubled as clubhouses.

syllabary   A list of language symbols, each one representing a syllable. Sequoyah, a Cherokee, invented a syllabary for his people so that their language could be written.

taiga   The evergreen forests and swamplands of the Subarctic region to the south of the treeless tundra.

temple   A shrine or place of worship.

tepee (or tipi)   A conical tent with a pole frame and usually covered with buffalo hides. Typical of the Plains Indians.

Termination   A policy of the federal government practiced in the 1950s which sought to end the special protective relationship between the government and Indian tribes.

toboggan   A vehicle for transporting people or possessions over snow or ice. Toboggans, unlike sleds, have no runners. Their platforms sit directly on the snow. (See also "sled.")

tomahawk   A type of warclub. "Tomahawk" is an Algonquian word. Unlike the more general word warclub, often applied to stone or wooden clubs, the word tomahawk is generally used to describe an axlike weapon with a metal head (which sometimes doubled as a pipe). Tomahawks were often made by Europeans for trade with Indians.

totem   An animal or plant, or some other natural object or phenomenon, serving as the symbol or emblem of a family or clan. (See also "clan.")

totem pole   A post carved and painted with a series of figures and symbols, of special meaning with regard to tribal legends and history. Typical of Northwest Coast Indians.

travois   A device used for transporting people and possessions behind dogs ("dog travois") or horses ("horse travois"). It consists of a wooden frame shaped like a V, with the closed end over the animal's shoulders, and the open end dragging on the ground, with a plank or webbing in the middle.

treaty   A formal agreement, pact, or contract negotiated between the federal government (or state government, or territorial government) and Indian tribes.

tribal government   The leadership of a tribe,

sometimes hereditary and sometimes elected. May consist of a chief and/or tribal council.

tribal headquarters The location where a tribal government meets, or simply the post office address of a tribe. It is a modern term commonly appearing with reservation names.

tribe A general term applied to a number of different kinds of Indian social organization. Tribes usually have descent, territory, culture, and history in common, and are comprised of a number of bands or villages. (See also "band.")

tribelet A grouping of Indians with a main, permanent village and a number of temporary satellite villages. Applied to California Indians.

trust lands Indian lands that are protected by the U.S. federal government and state governments, but that are not true reservations. Applied especially to the allotted lands of Oklahoma tribes. (See also "allotment" and "reservation.")

tule A bulrush or reed growing in California, the Southwest, and Mexico and used to make rafts, sandals, mats, and other items.

tundra The treeless area of the Arctic, with a permanently frozen subsoil and low-growing vegetation, such as moss and lichens. (See also "permafrost.")

umiak A large, open, flat-bottomed boat made by stretching hide (usually walrus hide) over a wooden frame. Typical of the Eskimos (Inuits).

Vision Quest Seeking visions or dreams through self-deprivation, exposure to the elements, or hallucinogenic drugs, usually for a rite of passage, such as from childhood to adulthood. Typical of the Plains Indians.

voyageur Literally, French for "traveler." A fur trader who traveled the rivers and backwoods for the large fur companies, such as the North West Company and Hudson's Bay Company. Many of the voyageurs were of mixed descent, especially French Canadian and Cree Indian. (See also "coureur de bois" and "metis.")

Wakanda The supernatural force or Great Spirit in the religion of the Sioux. Also spelled "Wakenda" and "Wakonda." (See also "Manitou" and "Orenda.")

wampum An Algonquian word, originally referring to strings or belts of small beads made from shells, especially purple and white quahog clam shells. Indians used "wampum belts" as tribal records and to communicate messages of peace or war to other tribes. After Europeans came to the Americas, the Indians began making wampum out of glass beads. The Europeans also made wampum for trade with the Indians. Wampum then became a form of money.

warbonnet A headdress with different feathers representing feats in battle. Typical of the Plains Indians.

warrior society See "military society."

wattle and daub A type of construction using a pole framework intertwined with branches and vines and covered with mud and plaster. Found especially in the Southeast.

weir A fenced-in enclosure placed in water for trapping or keeping fish.

wickiup A conical or domed dwelling with a pole frame covered with brush, grass, or reeds. Typical of the Apaches.

wigwam A domed or conical dwelling with a pole frame overlaid with bark, animal skin, or woven mats. Typical of Algonquian tribes.

wild rice A tall plant of the grass family, with an edible grain (not a true rice), growing especially along the western Great Lakes and gathered by Algonquian peoples.

For Further Reading

The following is a list of books about Native Americans, organized into general categories. Those included are especially helpful in giving an overview of Native American history and culture. They are of varying difficulty, ranging from anthropological classics to works for young readers. For those students who wish to study a particular tribe in great depth—or a particular person, historical event, or cultural trait—there are many more specialized titles about Indians to be found in public and school libraries, in bookstores, or through publishers' catalogues. Further entering the Indian reality and world-view—past or present—is well worth the undertaking.

Some Reference Classics in Indian Studies

Bancroft, Hubert Howe   *The Native Races*
Driver, Harold E.   *Indians of North America*
Hodge, Frederick, W.   *Handbook of American Indians North of Mexico*
Jenness, Diamond   *The Indians Of Canada*
Kroeber, A.L.   *Cultural and Natural Areas of Native North America*
Morgan, Lewis H.   *League of the Ho-de-no-sau-nee or Iroquois*
Parkman, Francis   *France and England in North America*
Prescott, William Hickling   *The Rise and Decline of the Spanish Empire*
Royce, Charles C.   *Indian Land Cessions in the United States*
Schoolcraft, Henry R.   *Thirty Years with the Indian Tribes*
Sturtevant, William (ed.)   *Handbook of North American Indians* (different volumes for different culture areas)
Swanton, John R.   *The Indian Tribes of North America*

Some Other Books Providing a Broad View of Indian Tribes and Peoples

Brandon, William   *Indians*
Collier, John   *Indians of the Americas*
Debo, Angie   *A History of the Indians of the United States*
Embree, Edwin R.   *Indians of the Americas*
Farb, Peter   *Man's Rise to Civilization as Shown by the Indians of North America*
Garbarino, Merwyn S.   *Native American Heritage*
Georgakas, Dan   *Red Shadows*
Gibson, Arrell Morgan   *The American Indian*
Highwater, Jamake   *Native Land: Sagas of the Indian Americas*
Jones, Charles (ed.)   *Look to the Mountain Top*
Josephy, Alvin, Jr.   *The Indian Heritage of America*
Klein, Barry T. (ed.)   *Reference Encyclopedia of the American Indian*
La Farge, Oliver   *A Pictorial History of the American Indian*
Lurie, Nancy O.   *North American Indian Lives*
Marriott, Alice and Carol Rachlin   *American Epic: The Story of the American Indian*
Maxwell, James (ed.)   *America's Fascinating Indian Heritage*
McKenney, Thomas L. and James Hall   *History of the Indian Tribes of North America*
Roe, Frank G.   *The Indian and the Horse*
Spencer, Robert and Jesse Jennings   *The Native Americans*
Spicer, Edward H.   *The American Indians*
Turner, Geoffrey   *Indians of North America*
Underhill, Ruth M.   *Red Man's America*
Waldman, Carl   *Atlas of the North American Indian*
White, Jon Manchip   *Everyday Life of the North American Indian*
Wissler, Clark   *Indians of the United States*
Yenne, Bill and Susan Garrett   *Pictorial History of the North American Indian*

Prehistoric Indians

Baity, Elizabeth Chesley   *Americans Before Columbus*
Brennan, Louis A.   *American Dawn*
Bushnell, G.H.S.   *The First Americans: The Pre-Columbian Civilizations*
Ceram, C.W.   *The First American*
Coe, Michael D.   *Mexico: Ancient Peoples and Places*
Jennings, Jesse   *Prehistory of North America*
Martin, Paul (et al)   *Indians Before Columbus*
Perceval, Don   *From Ice Mountain: Indian Settlement of the Americas*
Snow, Dean R.   *The Archaeology of North America*
Willey, Gordon R.   *Introduction to American Archaeology*
Willey, Gordon R. (ed.)   *Prehistoric Settlement Patterns in the New World*

Explorers, Frontier Painters, and Early Photographers

Bakeless, John   *The Eyes of Discovery*
Catlin, George   *Drawings of the North American Indian*
Current, Karen and William   *Photography of the Old West*
Curtis, Edward S.   *The North American Indian*
Goetzman, William (et al)   *Karl Bodmer's America*
Homer, Rachel J. (ed.)   *In a Sacred Manner We Live: Photographs of the North American Indian by Edward S. Curtis*
Horan, James D.   *The McKenney-Hall Portrait Gallery of American Indians*
Morison, Samuel Eliot   *The European Discovery of America*
Scherer, J.C. and J.B. Walker   *Indians: Great Photographs that Reveal North American Indian Life*
Thomas, Davis and Karin Ronnefeldt (eds.)   *People of the First Man*
Trimble, Stephen (ed.)   *Our Voices, Our Land*
University of Nebraska (eds.)   *Atlas of the Lewis and Clark Expedition*
University of Nebraska (eds.)   *Journals of the Lewis and Clark Expedition*

Indian Wars

Beal, Merrill D.   *I Will Fight No More Forever: Chief Joseph and the Nez Perce War*
Brady, Cyrus   *Indian Fights and Fighters*
Brown, Dee   *Bury My Heart at Wounded Knee*
Debo, Angie   *Geronimo: The Man, His Time, His Place*
Dillon, Richard H.   *North American Indian Wars*

Glassley, Ray   *Indian Wars of the Pacific Northwest*
Haley, James L.   *The Buffalo War*
Hunt, George T.   *The Wars of the Iroquois*
Josephy, Alvin, Jr.   *The Patriot Chiefs: A Chronicle of American Indian Resistance*
Leckie, William H.   *The Buffalo Soldiers: A Narrative of the Negro Cavalry in the West*
Nye, Wilbur S.   *Plains Indian Raiders: The Final Phases of Warfare from the Arkansas to the Red River*
Selby, John   *The Conquest of the American West*
Tebbel, John   *The Compact History of the Indian Wars*
Tebbel, John and Keith Jennison   *The American Indian Wars*
Utley, Robert   *Frontier Regulars*
Utley, Robert   *Indian, Soldier, Settler*
Utley, Robert and Wilcomb Washburn   *The Indian Wars*

Indian Land Cessions, Federal Indian Policy, and Sociology

Barnett, Louise K.   *The Ignoble Savage: American Literary Racism*
Barsh, Russell and James Henderson   *The Road: Indian Tribes and Political Liberty*
Deloria, Vine, Jr.   *Behind the Trail of Broken Treaties: An Indian Declaration of Independence*
Deloria, Vine, Jr.   *Custer Died for Your Sins*
Deloria, Vine, Jr.   *Nations Within: The Past and Future of American Indian Sovereignty*
Fey, Harold and D'Arcy McNickle   *Indians and Other Americans: Two Ways of Life Meet*
Foreman, Grant   *Indian Removal: The Emigration of the Five Civilized Tribes of Indians*
Getty, I.A.L. and Antoine Lussier   *As Long as the Sun Shines and Water Flows: A Reader in Canadian Native Studies*
Giago, Tim   *Notes from Indian Country*
Hagan, William T.   *American Indians*
Jacobs, Wilbur R.   *Dispossessing the American Indian*
Josephy, Alvin, Jr.   *Now that the Buffalo's Gone: A Study of Today's American Indians*
Josephy, Alvin, Jr.   *Red Power: The American Indian's Fight for Freedom*
Matthiessen, Peter   *Indian Country*
Matthiessen, Peter   *In the Spirit of Crazy Horse*
Prucha, Francis Paul   *The Indians in American Society: From the Revolutionary War to the Present*
Rosentiel, Annette   *Red and White: Indian Views of the White Man, 1492-1982*
Stedman, Raymond W.   *Shadows of the Indian: Stereotypes in American Culture*
Steiner, Stan   *The New Indians*

Talbot, Steve   *Roots of Oppression: The American Indian Question*

Taylor, Theodore W.   *The Bureau of Indian Affairs*

Tyler, S. Lyman   *A History of Indian Policy*

U.S. Department of Commerce   *Federal and State Indian Reservations and Indian Trust Areas*

U.S. Indian Claims Commission   *Final Report*

Van Every, Dale   *Disinherited: The Lost Birthright of the American Indian*

Wax, Murray L.   *Indian Americans: Unity and Diversity*

Indian Art and Artifacts

Appleton, Le Roy   *American Indian Design and Decoration*

Coe, Ralph T.   *Lost and Found Traditions: Native American Art, 1965-1985*

Coe, Ralph T.   *Sacred Circles: Two Thousand Years of North American Indian Art*

Dockstader, Frederick J.   *Indian Art of the Americas*

Feest, Christian F.   *Native Arts of North America*

Furst, Peter and Jill   *North American Indian Art*

Highwater, Jamake   *Arts of the Indian Americas*

Highwater, Jamake   *Song from the Earth: American Indian Painting*

Hothem, Lar   *North American Indian Artifacts*

La Farge, Oliver (et al)   *Introduction to American Indian Art*

Mallery, Garrick   *Picture Writing of the American Indians*

Mathews, Zena and Aldona Jonaitis   *Native North American Art History*

Miles, Charles   *Indian and Eskimo Artifacts of North America*

Naylor, Maria   *Authentic Indian Designs*

Roosevelt, Anna and James Smith   *The Ancestors: Native Artisans of the Americas*

Wade, Edwin L. (ed.)   *The Arts of the North American Indian*

Whiteford, Andrew Hunter   *North American Indian Arts*

Indian Religion, Mythology, Music, Songs, and Dances

Beck, Peggy and Anna Waters   *The Sacred: Ways of Knowledge, Sources of Life*

Bierhorst, John   *The Mythology of North America*

Bierhorst, John   *The Sacred Path: Spells, Prayers, and Power Songs of the American Indians*

Brown, Vinson   *Voices of Earth and Sky: Vision Search of the Native Americans*

Burland, Cottie and Marion Wood   *North American Indian Mythology*

Deloria, Vine, Jr.   *God Is Red*

Highwater, Jamake   *Ritual of the Wind: North American Ceremonies, Music, and Dance*

Hofmann, Charles   *Frances Densmore and American Indian Music*

Hultkrantz, Ake   *The Religions of the American Indians*

Krickeberg, Walter (et al)   *Pre-Columbian American Religions*

Laubin, Reginald and Gladys   *Indian Dances of North America: Their Importance to Indian Life*

Underhill, Ruth M.   *Red Man's Religion*

Wood, Marion   *Spirits, Heroes, and Hunters from North American Indian Mythology*

Philosophy, Fiction, Poetry, and Indian Voices

Bartlett, Mary (ed.)   *The New Native American Novel: Works in Progress*

Cooper, James Fenimore   *The Last of the Mohicans* (and the other *Leatherstocking Tales*)

Curtis, Natalie   *The Indians' Book*

Day, A. Grove   *The Sky Clears: Poetry of the American Indians*

Eastman, Charles (Ohiyesa)   *From the Deep Wood to Civilization*

Eastman, Charles (Ohiyesa)   *Indian Boyhood*

Green, Rayna (ed.)   *That's What She Said: Contemporary Poetry and Fiction by Native American Women*

Hamilton, Charles (ed.)   *Cry of the Thunderbird: The American Indian's Own Story*

Highwater, Jamake   *Anpao: An American Indian Odyssey*

Highwater, Jamake   *The Primal Mind: Vision and Reality in Indian America*

Highwater, Jamake   *The Sun, He Dies*

Hill, Ruth Beebe   *Hanta Yo*

Hillerman, Tony   *Dance Hall of the Dead* (and his other mysteries)

Kroeber, Theodora   *Ishi in Two Worlds*

Krupat, Arnold   *For Those Who Come After: A Study of Native American Autobiography*

La Farge, Oliver   *Laughing Boy*

La Farge, Oliver   *The Enemy Gods*

Lesley, Craig   *Winterkill*

Lincoln, Kenneth   *Native American Renaissance*

McLuhan, T.C. (ed.)   *Touch the Earth: A Self-Portrait of Indian Existence*

Mohawk, John   *Basic Call to Consciousness*

Momaday, N. Scott   *House Made of Dawn*

Momaday, N. Scott   *The Way to Rainy Mountain*

Neihardt, John G. *Black Elk Speaks*
Ortiz, Simon J. *Earth Power Coming: Short Fiction in Native American Literature*
Petrone, Penny (ed.) *First People, First Voices*
Rothenberg, Jerome (ed.) *Shaking the Pumpkin: Traditional Poetry of the Indian North Americas*
Standing Bear, Luther *Land of the Spotted Eagle*
Turner, Frederick W. (ed.) *Indian Oratory: A Collection of Famous Speeches by Noted Indian Chieftains*
Velie, Alan R. (ed.) *American Indian Literature: An Anthology*
Waldo, Anna Lee *Sacajawea*
Zitkala-Sa *American Indian Stories*

Travel to Indian Reservations, Festivals, and Archaeological Sites

Ferris, Robert G. (ed.) *Explorers and Settlers: Historic Places Commemorating the Early Exploration and Settlement of the United States*
Ferris, Robert G. *Soldier and Brave: Historic Places Associated with Indian Affairs and Indian Wars in the Trans-Mississippi West*
Highwater, Jamake *Indian America*
Lister, Robert H. and Florence *Those Who Came Before: Southwest Archaeology in the National Park System*
Marquis, Arnold *A Guide to America's Indians: Ceremonials, Reservations, and Museums*
Noble, David Grant *Ancient Ruins of the Southwest*
Wilson, Josleen *The Passionate Amateur's Guide to Archaeology in the United States*
Wright, Muriel H. *A Guide to the Indian Tribes of Oklahoma*
Yeager, C.G. *Arrowheads and Stone Artifacts: A Practical Guide for the Surface Collector and Amateur Archaeologist*

Children's Books (Easier Reading but Informative for Adults, Too)

Bemister, Margaret *Indian Legends*
Berry, William D. *Buffalo Land*
Campbell, Maria (ed.) *Achimoona*
Cody, Iron Eyes *Indian Talk: Hand Signals of the North American Indian*
Cody, Iron Eyes and Birdie Parker *Indian Legends*
Common, Dianne L. *Little Loon and the Sun Dance*
Common, Dianne L. *Little Wild Onion of the Lillooet*
Common, Dianne L. *Marie of the Metis*
Culleton, Beatrice *April Raintree*

Culleton, Beatrice *Spirit of the White Bison*
Daly, Richard *Native Peoples of North America*
Dressman, John *On the Cliffs of Acoma*
Eastman, Charles (Ohiyesa) *Indian Scout Craft and Lore*
Fichter, George S. *American Indian Music and Musical Instruments*
Fichter, George S. *How the Plains Indians Lived*
Franklin, Paula *Indians of North America*
Grinnell, George Bird *When Buffalo Ran*
Hartman, Jane E. *Cougar Woman*
Hillerman, Tony *The Boy Who Made Dragonfly: A Zuni Myth*
Holling, Holling C. *The Book of Indians*
Holling, Holling C. *Paddle-To-The-Sea*
Kennedy, Paul *North American Indian Design Coloring Book*
Kleitsh, Christel and Paul Stephens *Dancing Feathers*
Kleitsh, Christel and Paul Stephens *A Time to be Brave*
Levinson, David and David Sherwood *The Tribal Living Book: 150 Things to Do and Make from Traditional Cultures around the World*
Longfellow, Henry Wadsworth *Hiawatha*
Macfarlan, Allan and Paulette *Handbook of American Indian Games*
Manfred, Frederick *Conquering Horse*
Manfred, Frederick *Scarlet Plume*
McKeown, M.F. *Come to Our Salmon Feast*
McNichols, Charles L. *Crazy Weather*
Metayer, Maurice *Tales from the Igloo*
Mitchell, Emerson Blackhorse and T.D. Allen *Miracle Hill: The Story of a Navajo Boy*
Nault, William H. (ed.) *The Indian Book*
Ney, Marian Wallace *Indian America: A Geography of North American Indians*
O'Dell, Scott *Island of the Blue Dolphins*
Parker, Arthur C. *The Indian How Book*
Payne, Elizabeth *Meet the North American Indians*
Sauer, Carl *Man in Nature*
Searcy, Margaret Z. *Charm of the Bear Claw Necklace: A Story of Stone Age Southeastern Indians*
Searcy, Margaret Z. *Wolf Dog of the Woodland Indians*
Simon, Nancy and Evelyn Wolfson *American Indian Habitats: How to Make Dwellings and Shelters with Natural Materials*
Wilson, Eleanore Hubbard *The Magical Jumping Beans*
Wolfson, Evelyn *American Indian Tools and Ornaments: How to Make Implements and Jewelry with Bone and Shell*
Wolfson, Evelyn *American Indian Utensils: How to Make Baskets, Pottery, and Woodenware with Natural Materials*

Index